Scott Foresman

CALIFORNIA MATHEMATICS

Authors and Advisors

Jennie Bennett
Charles Calhoun
Mary Cavanagh
Lucille Croom
Stephen Krulik
Robert A. Laing
Donna J. Long
Stuart J. Murphy
Jesse A Rudnick
Clementine Sherman
Marian Small
William Tate

Randall I. Charles
Alma B. Ramirez
Jeanne F. Ramos

Editorial Offices: Glenview, Illinois • Parsippany, New Jersey • New York, New York
Sales Offices: Reading, Massachusetts • Duluth, Georgia • Glenview, Illinois
Carrollton, Texas • Ontario, California

ISBN: 0-328-00469-3

5 6 7 8 9 10-VH-07 06 05 04 03 02

Mathematician Content Reviewers

Roger Howe *Grades K–2*
Professor of Mathematics
Yale University
New Haven, Connecticut

Edward Barbeau *Grades 3–4*
Professor of Mathematics
University of Toronto
Toronto, Ontario, Canada

Gary Lippman *Grades 3–6*
Professor of Mathematics and Computer Science
California State University Hayward
Hayward, California

David M. Bressoud *Grades 5–6*
DeWitt Wallace Professor of Mathematics
Macalester College
Saint Paul, Minnesota

California Content Standard Reviewers

Damien Jacotin *Kindergarten*
Los Angeles, California

Jennifer Lozo *Kindergarten*
Lodi, California

Sharon Frost *Grade 1*
Burbank, California

Beth Gould-Golland *Grade 1*
Encinitas, California

Linda Newland *Grade 2*
Santa Clarita, California

Wendy York *Grade 2*
Merced, California

Shakeh Balmanoukian *Grade 3*
Glendale, California

Donna M. Kopenski *Grade 3*
Poway, California

Armine Aghajani *Grade 4*
Tujunga, California

Floyd Flack *Grade 4*
Westminster, California

Donna Crist *Grade 5*
Turlock, California

Jimmy C. Jordan *Grade 5*
La Crescenta, California

Felicia Clark *Grade 6*
Compton, California

Vahe Tcharkhoutian *Grade 6*
Pasadena, California

Contents

Chapter 1 Understanding Place Value

Adding and Subtracting Whole Numbers and Decimals

Using Data and Statistics

Multiplying Whole Numbers

Dividing Whole Numbers

Multiplying and Dividing Decimals

Fraction Concepts

Fraction Computation

Integers, Equations, and Graphs

Geometry

Measurement

Ratio, Percent, and Probability

California Mathematics Content Standards
Grade 5

By the end of grade five, students increase their facility with the four basic arithmetic operations applied to fractions, decimals, and positive and negative numbers. They know and use common measuring units to determine length and area and use formulas to determine the volume of simple geometric figures. Students know the concept of angle measurement and use a protractor and compass to solve problems. They use grids, tables, graphs, and charts to record and analyze data.

Number Sense

1.0 Students compute with very large and very small numbers, positive integers, decimals, and fractions and understand the relationship between decimals, fractions, and percents. They understand the relative magnitudes of numbers:

1.1 Estimate, round, and manipulate very large (e.g., millions) and very small (e.g., thousandths) numbers.

1.2 (🔑) Interpret percents as a part of a hundred; find decimal and percent equivalents for common fractions and explain why they represent the same value; compute a given percent of a whole number.

1.3 Understand and compute positive integer powers of nonnegative integers; compute examples as repeated multiplication.

1.4 (🔑) Determine the prime factors of all numbers through 50 and write the numbers as the product of their prime factors by using exponents to show multiples of a factor (e.g., $24 = 2 \times 2 \times 2 \times 3 = 2^3 \times 3$).

1.5 (🔑) Identify and represent on a number line decimals, fractions, mixed numbers, and positive and negative integers.

2.0 Students perform calculations and solve problems involving addition, subtraction, and simple multiplication and division of fractions and decimals:

2.1 (🔑) Add, subtract, multiply, and divide with decimals; add with negative integers; subtract positive integers from negative integers; and verify the reasonableness of the results.

2.2 (🔑) Demonstrate proficiency with division, including division with positive decimals and long division with multidigit divisors.

2.3 (🔑) Solve simple problems, including ones arising in concrete situations, involving the addition and subtraction of fractions and mixed numbers (like and unlike denominators of 20 or less), and express answers in the simplest form.

2.4 Understand the concept of multiplication and division of fractions.

2.5 Compute and perform simple multiplication and division of fractions and apply these procedures to solving problems.

Algebra and Functions

1.0 Students use variables in simple expressions, compute the value of the expression for specific values of the variable, and plot and interpret the results:

1.1 Use information taken from a graph or equation to answer questions about a problem situation.

1.2 (🔑) Use a letter to represent an unknown number; write and evaluate simple algebraic expressions in one variable by substitution.

1.3 Know and use the distributive property in equations and expressions with variables.

1.4 (🔑) Identify and graph ordered pairs in the four quadrants of the coordinate plane.

1.5 (🔑) Solve problems involving linear functions with integer values; write the equation; and graph the resulting ordered pairs of integers on a grid.

Measurement and Geometry

1.0 Students understand and compute the volumes and areas of simple objects:

1.1 (🔑) Derive and use the formula for the area of a triangle and of a parallelogram by comparing it with the formula for the area of a rectangle (i.e., two of the same triangles make a parallelogram with twice the area; a parallelogram is compared with a rectangle of the same area by pasting and cutting a right triangle on the parallelogram).

1.2 (🔑) Construct a cube and rectangular box from two-dimensional patterns and use these patterns to compute the surface area for these objects.

1.3 (🔑) Understand the concept of volume and use the appropriate units in common measuring systems (i.e., cubic centimeter [cm^3], cubic meter [m^3], cubic inch [$in.^3$], cubic yard [$yd.^3$]) to compute the volume of rectangular solids.

1.4 Differentiate between, and use appropriate units of measures for, two- and three-dimensional objects (i.e., find the perimeter, area, volume).

2.0 Students identify, describe, and classify the properties of, and the relationships between, plane and solid geometric figures:

2.1 (🔑) Measure, identify, and draw angles, perpendicular and parallel lines, rectangles, and triangles by using appropriate tools (e.g., straightedge, ruler, compass, protractor, drawing software).

Reproduced from the Mathematics Content Standards for California Public Schools. The symbol (🔑) indicates a key standard as designated by a green oval in the Mathematics Framework for California Public Schools.

2.2 (🔑) Know that the sum of the angles of any triangle is 180° and the sum of the angles of any quadrilateral is 360° and use this information to solve problems.

2.3 Visualize and draw two-dimensional views of three-dimensional objects made from rectangular solids.

Statistics, Data Analysis, and Probability

1.0 Students display, analyze, compare, and interpret different data sets, including data sets of different sizes:

1.1 Know the concepts of mean, median, and mode; compute and compare simple examples to show that they may differ.

1.2 Organize and display single-variable data in appropriate graphs and representations (e.g., histogram, circle graphs) and explain which types of graphs are appropriate for various data sets.

1.3 Use fractions and percentages to compare data sets of different sizes.

1.4 (🔑) Identify ordered pairs of data from a graph and interpret the meaning of the data in terms of the situation depicted by the graph.

1.5 (🔑) Know how to write ordered pairs correctly; for example, (x, y).

Mathematical Reasoning

1.0 Students make decisions about how to approach problems:

1.1 Analyze problems by identifying relationships, distinguishing relevant from irrelevant information, sequencing and prioritizing information, and observing patterns.

1.2 Determine when and how to break a problem into simpler parts.

2.0 Students use strategies, skills, and concepts in finding solutions:

2.1 Use estimation to verify the reasonableness of calculated results.

2.2 Apply strategies and results from simpler problems to more complex problems.

2.3 Use a variety of methods, such as words, numbers, symbols, charts, graphs, tables, diagrams, and models, to explain mathematical reasoning.

2.4 Express the solution clearly and logically by using the appropriate mathematical notation and terms and clear language; support solutions with evidence in both verbal and symbolic work.

2.5 Indicate the relative advantages of exact and approximate solutions to problems and give answers to a specified degree of accuracy.

2.6 Make precise calculations and check the validity of the results from the context of the problem.

3.0 Students move beyond a particular problem by generalizing to other situations:

3.1 Evaluate the reasonableness of the solution in the context of the original situation.

3.2 Note the method of deriving the solution and demonstrate a conceptual understanding of the derivation by solving similar problems.

3.3 Develop generalizations of the results obtained and apply them in other circumstances.

Understanding Place Value

- **1-1** Place Value Through Billions
- **1-2** Problem-Solving Skill: Exact and Estimated Data
- **1-3** Place Value Through Thousandths
- **1-4** Comparing and Ordering Whole Numbers and Decimals
- **1-5** Problem-Solving Strategy: Draw a Diagram
- **1-6** Rounding Whole Numbers and Decimals
- **1-7** Variables and Tables
- **1-8** Problem-Solving Application: Using Data from Tables and Graphs

Diagnosing Readiness

In Chapter 1, you will use these skills:

A Whole Number Place Value

(Grade 4)

Tell what place each underlined digit is in.

1. 298 **2.** 46,212

3. 9,021 **4.** 70,295

5. 4,268,941 **6.** 635,621

B Reading and Writing Whole Numbers

(Grade 4)

Write each number in standard form.

7. four hundred twenty-five

8. seventy-six thousand, seventy-nine

9. eighty thousand, thirty-two

10. five million, two hundred twenty-two thousand, sixty

11. A large wheat-growing company had 928,312 acres to plant. Write this number in word form.

C Decimal Place Value

(Grade 4)

Tell what place each underlined digit is in.

12. 6,924.0<u>7</u> **13.** 10.<u>3</u>7

14. 77<u>9</u>.46 **15.** 4<u>2</u>5.1

Write each number in standard form.

16. Five and two tenths

17. 924 and 27 hundredths

18. 93 and 55 hundredths

D Rounding Numbers

(Grade 4)

Round each number to the underlined place.

19. 227,<u>9</u>31

20. <u>7</u>,984,503

21. 67<u>9</u>.49

22. 293.<u>7</u>6

23. The Ruiz family bought a new car. It cost them $17,924. Round this amount to the nearest thousand dollars.

E Comparing and Ordering Whole Numbers

(Grade 4)

Compare. Write >, <, or = for each ●.

24. 2,597 ● 6,216

25. 659 ● 651

Write the numbers in order from least to greatest.

26. 2,721 2,496 2,671

F Comparing and Ordering Decimals

(Grade 4)

Compare. Write >, <, or = for each ●.

27. 7.16 ● 7.92 **28.** 6.5 ● 6.50

Write the numbers in order from least to greatest.

29. 6.04 6.72 6.51

30. Three students had money for snacks. Sam had $1.25, Al had $1.60, and Joli had $1.45. Who had the most money?

To the Family and Student

Looking Back	Chapter 1	Looking Ahead
In Grade 4, students learned how to read, write, and compare whole numbers through the millions place, and decimal numbers through the hundredths place. In 9.06, the 6 is in the hundredths place	**Understanding Place Value** In this chapter, students will learn how to round, compare, and order whole numbers through the hundred billions place, and decimal numbers through the thousandths place. $2{,}921.428 > 2{,}921.112$	In Grade 6, students will learn to use place value to compare positive and negative decimals. $4.072 > 4.012$ $^{-}3.159 < {}^{-}3.059$ $0.012 > {}^{-}0.45$

Math and Everyday Living

Opportunities to apply the concepts of Chapter 1 abound in everyday situations. During the chapter, think about how understanding place value can be used to solve a variety of real-world problems. The following examples suggest just a few of the many situations that could launch a discussion about the value assigned to numbers.

Math at the Grocery Store Your father needs to buy the largest turkey he can for a special dinner he is preparing. At the grocery store, he sees that the 3 largest turkeys weigh 16.651 lb, 15.015 lb, and 14.975 lb. Which one should he buy?

Math and Money Meagan's mother needed to round her income to the nearest dollar for her tax form. Her income was $56,723.26. What is the number she should put on her tax form?

Math and Astronomy The planet Saturn is about 1,400,000,000 km from the sun. Neptune is about 4,500,000,000 km from the sun. Which planet is closer to the sun?

Math at the Library Books are arranged according to their call numbers. Four books with the following numbers need to be reshelved. Place them in order from least to greatest.

701.56, 797.3, 204.929, 240.1

Math and Transportation The car's odometer read 58,211.7 miles. About how many miles had the car been driven (to the nearest thousand)?

Math and the Weather Use the data in the table below. Which month had the most rainfall? Which month had the least?

Month	Rainfall
May	13.7 cm
June	7.9 cm
July	11.9 cm
August	6.5 cm

Math and Journalism As a reporter for a local television station, one of your stories is on the lack of rainfall in Southern California. Bakersfield receives only 0.145 inches of rain per year. How would you read this number in your story?

 California Content Standards in Chapter 1 Lessons*

	Teach and Practice	Practice
Number Sense		
1.0 Students . . . understand the relative magnitudes of numbers.	1-4	
1.1 Estimate, round, and manipulate very large (e.g., millions) and very small (e.g., thousandths) numbers.	1-1, 1-3, 1-6	1-2, 1-4
1.5 (🔑) Identify and represent on a number line decimals	1-4	
Algebra and Functions		
1.2 (🔑) Use a letter to represent an unknown number	1-7	1-4, 1-8
1.5 (🔑) Solve problems involving linear functions with integer values;	1-7	

	Teach and Practice	Practice
Mathematical Reasoning		
1.1 Analyze problems by identifying relationships	1-2	1-3
2.3 Use a variety of methods, such as words, numbers, symbols, charts, graphs, tables, diagrams, and models, to explain mathematical reasoning.	1-5, 1-8	
2.5 Indicate . . . approximate solutions to problems and give answers to a specified degree of accuracy.		1-6
3.2 Note the method of deriving the solution and demonstrate a conceptual understanding of the derivation by solving similar problems.		1-5

* The symbol (🔑) indicates a key standard as designated in Mathematics Framework for California Public Schools. Full statements of the California Content Standards are found at the beginning of this book following the Table of Contents.

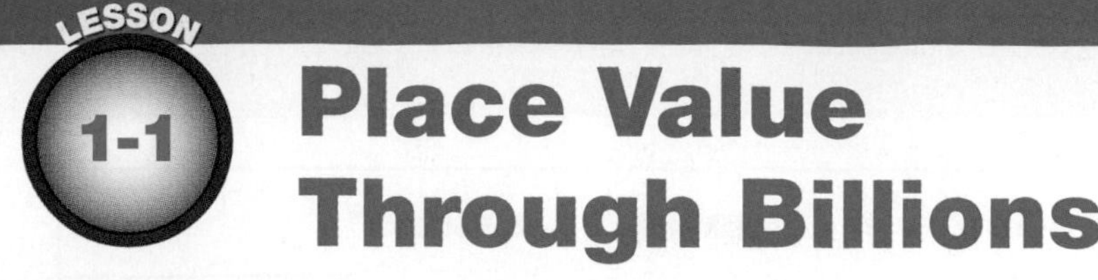

LESSON 1-1

Place Value Through Billions

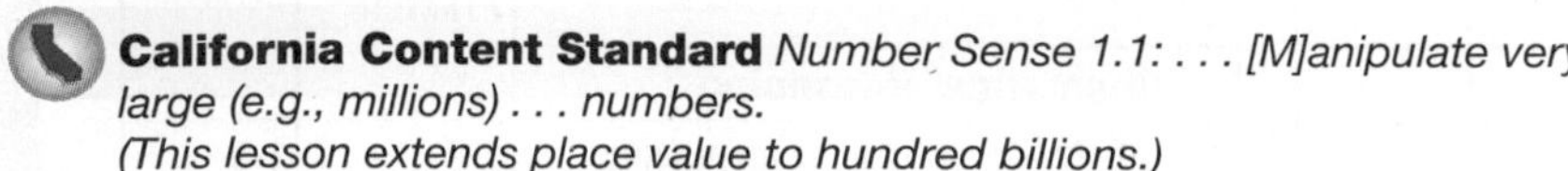

California Content Standard *Number Sense 1.1: . . . [M]anipulate very large (e.g., millions) . . . numbers.*
(This lesson extends place value to hundred billions.)

Warm-Up Review

1. 6 × 10 **2.** 4 × 1,000

Tell what place each underlined digit is in.

3. 7,2$\underline{9}$5 **4.** 10$\underline{3}$,000

5. $\underline{8}$56

6. $\underline{4}$2,657

7. Ed is 9 years old. Al is 17 and Meg is 8. How much older is Al than Meg?

Math Link You know how to work with numbers in the millions. Now you will learn about larger numbers.

The **place-value chart** shows the **standard form** of the number that is read *465 billion, 923 million, 180 thousand.* You can use a place-value chart to find the value of a digit in a number.

Word Bank

place-value chart
standard form
expanded form

period	BILLIONS			MILLIONS			THOUSANDS			ONES		
place value	hundred billions	ten billions	billions	hundred millions	ten millions	millions	hundred thousands	ten thousands	thousands	hundreds	tens	ones
	4	6	5,	9	2	3,	1	8	0,	0	0	0

Example 1

Find the value of the underlined digit in 4$\underline{6}$5,923,180,000.

The 6 is in the ten billions place.

6 × 10 billion = 60 billion ⟵ **short word form**

The value of the 6 in 465,923,180,000 is 60 billion, which is written as 60,000,000,000 in standard form.

Example 2

Write 465,923,180,000 in **expanded form**.

Find the value of each digit according to its place. Then express 465,923,180,000 as the sum of the values of its digits.

The expanded form of 465,923,180,000 is:

400,000,000,000 + 60,000,000,000 + 5,000,000,000 + 900,000,000 + 20,000,000 + 3,000,000 + 100,000 + 80,000

Guided Practice *For another example, see Set A on p. 28.*

Write the value of each underlined digit using short word form.

1. 452,307,831 **2.** 821,553,479,000 **3.** 195,246,053,827

4. Saturn, the sixth planet from the sun, travels about 5,553,580,000 miles in its orbit. Write this number in expanded form.

Independent Practice *For more practice, see Set A on p. 30.*

Write the value of each underlined digit using short word form.

5. 784,294,523 **6.** 6,452,809,756 **7.** 432,148,675

The nine planets of the Solar System are closer to each other at some times than at other times. The table at the right gives the greatest and the least distance from Earth for each of the other planets.

8. Find the greatest distance that Saturn is from Earth. What digit is in the ten millions place in this number?

9. Find the greatest distance that Pluto is from Earth. Write this number in expanded form.

Distance of Planets from Earth

Planet	Greatest Distance (miles)	Least Distance (miles)
Mercury	136,000,000	50,000,000
Venus	161,000,000	25,000,000
Mars	248,000,000	35,000,000
Jupiter	600,000,000	368,000,000
Saturn	1,031,000,000	745,000,000
Uranus	1,953,000,000	1,606,000,000
Neptune	2,915,000,000	2,667,000,000
Pluto	4,644,000,000	2,663,000,000

Mixed Review

10. Mental Math Find 5 × 15.

11. Algebra Find n if $5 + n = 22$.

12. Pam bought 9 tickets of equal value for $27. How much did each one cost?

13. 8,706 − 568 **14.** 53 + 863 **15.** 72 ÷ 8 **16.** 9,000 − 827

Test Prep **Choose the correct letter for each answer.**

17. 300 − 127 =
(Gr. 4)

A 173 **D** 427
B 183 **E** NH
C 227

18. 582 + 208 =
(Gr. 4)

F 700 **J** 800
G 780 **K** NH
H 790

Problem-Solving Skill:

Exact and Estimated Data

Warm-Up Review

1. 16 + 98
2. 124 − 87
3. 141 + 17
4. 235 − 113
5. 7 × 9
6. 8 × 6
7. 72 ÷ 9
8. 56 ÷ 7
9. Juan had $30. He spent $14 on a CD and $12 on a book. How much money did he have left?

California Content Standard *Mathematical Reasoning 1.1: Analyze problems by identifying relationships . . ..*

Read for Understanding

There are 88 different constellations, or groupings of stars in the sky. We do not know the exact number of stars in each constellation. The picture at the right shows how one artist pictures the constellation Orion, using 24 of its stars. In the picture, you can count the number of stars on Orion's belt, the number on his shield, and so on. Scientists estimate that one star in Orion is about 320 light-years away from earth.

1. How many constellations are there in the sky?
2. How many stars make up this picture of Orion?
3. About how far from Earth is one of Orion's stars?

Think and Discuss

Exact and Estimated Data

Exact data represents an amount that can be counted. Estimated data represents an amount that has been rounded or that cannot be counted or measured.

Reread the paragraph at the top of the page.

4. List the words that tell you a number is an estimate.
5. Is the distance from Earth to Orion exact? Explain.
6. Not including the stars that make up the belt and shield, how many stars make up Orion in the picture above? Did you use exact or estimated data?
7. Give an example from everyday life of an amount that can be counted.

Additional Standard: Number Sense 1.1 *(See p. 3.)*

Guided Practice

The Big Dipper, often thought of as a constellation, is really part of a constellation called Ursa Major, or Big Bear. Ursa Major was first observed thousands of years ago by peoples of the ancient world. Dubhe, one star in Ursa Major, is about 75 light-years from Earth. You can count the 20 major stars shown as part of Ursa Major in the picture at the right. You can also count the 7 stars in the Big Dipper.

1. Which phrase best describes the distance of Dubhe from Earth?
   - **a.** exactly 75 light-years from Earth
   - **b.** about 75 light-years from Earth
   - **c.** much more than 75 light-years from Earth

2. Which numbers are estimates?
   - **a.** 7 stars in the Big Dipper
   - **b.** 75 light-years and thousands of years ago
   - **c.** both of the above

3. Which phrase best describes the difference in the number of major stars pictured on Ursa Major and the number that make up the Big Dipper?
   - **a.** exactly 13 stars
   - **b.** about 13 stars
   - **c.** less than 13 stars

Independent Practice

Ulugh Beg was an astronomer born in Persia in 1393. He used a curved object more than 130 feet long to study stars. In 1437 he produced a book that gave the positions of 992 stars. With data from his observatory, he computed the length of the year as 365 days 5 hours 49 minutes 15 seconds, an accurate value for the 1400s.

4. Which phrase best describes the length of the curved object that Beg used to study the stars?
   - **a.** exactly 130 feet
   - **b.** more than 130 feet
   - **c.** less than 130 feet

5. **Math Reasoning** List all of the numbers used in the paragraph above that are estimates. Then list all the numbers that are exact. Tell how you know.

Use Homework Workbook 1-2.

Place Value Through Thousandths

Warm-Up Review

For Exercises 1–6, tell what digit is in each place in the number 1,753.42.

1. ones
2. tens
3. hundreds
4. thousands
5. tenths
6. hundredths
7. A pen costs $0.89 and a notebook costs $1.29. What is the total cost?

California Content Standard *Number Sense 1.1: . . . [M]anipulate . . . very small (e.g., thousandths) numbers.*

Math Link You know about place value in whole numbers and some decimals. Now you will learn how to work with smaller numbers.

The picture at the right shows the locations of three cities with the greatest average annual rainfall in the United States. The place-value chart below shows the standard form of each of the numbers used in the picture.

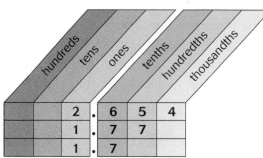

Astoria, OR 1.77 m
Quillayute, WA 2.654 m
United States
Blue Canyon, CA 1.7 m

hundreds	tens	ones	.	tenths	hundredths	thousandths
		2	.	6	5	4
		1	.	7	7	
		1	.	7		

Example 1

Find the value of the 4 in 2.654.

Look at the place-value chart.
The digit 4 is in the thousandths place.
Its value is 0.004, which is read "four thousandths."

Example 2

Write each of the numbers from the chart using words.

Standard Form	Word Form	Short Word Form
2.654	two and six hundred fifty-four thousandths	2 and 654 thousandths
1.77	one and seventy-seven hundredths	1 and 77 hundredths
1.7	one and seven tenths	1 and 7 tenths

When you read or write a decimal number, remember to use the word *and* for the decimal point.

 Additional Standard: Mathematical Reasoning 1.1 *(See p. 3.)*

Guided Practice *For another example, see Set B on p. 28.*

Write the value of each underlined digit in short word form.

1. 324.09$\underline{5}$ **2.** 48.0$\underline{9}$6 **3.** 0.$\underline{7}$89 **4.** 973.40$\underline{5}$ **5.** $\underline{8}$42.965

6. Rain forests in Colombia have recorded annual rainfall as great as 6.743 meters each year. Write this number in word form.

Independent Practice *For more practice, see Set B on p. 30.*

Write the value of each underlined digit in short word form.

7. 48.5$\underline{2}$3 **8.** 0.78$\underline{5}$ **9.** 809.$\underline{7}$56 **10.** 800.39$\underline{6}$ **11.** $\underline{7}$48.143

Write each number in standard form.

12. 85 and 17 hundredths **13.** 999 thousandths **14.** 314 and 8 thousandths

Make a place-value chart. Show each decimal on the chart. Then write the word name for each decimal.

15. 0.06 **16.** 0.891 **17.** 51.7 **18.** 322.406 **19.** 12.009

20. Math Reasoning How are 0.44 and 0.044 alike? How are they different? Write each number in short word form.

Mixed Review

Algebra **Find each missing number.**

21. 8 + ■ = 12 **22.** ■ − 7 = 9 **23.** ■ ÷ 7 = 0 **24.** 5 ÷ ■ = 1

25. Mental Math How many seconds are in 8 minutes?

Write the value of each underlined digit in standard form.

26. 5,$\underline{3}$84,000,000 **27.** 1$\underline{7}$8,000,000,000 **28.** 427.36$\underline{5}$

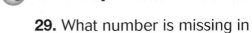

Test Prep **Choose the correct letter for each answer.**

29. (Gr. 4) What number is missing in the pattern?

3, 6, 9, ____, 15, 18

A 10 **B** 12 **C** 13 **D** 10 **E** NH

30. (Gr. 4) What is the standard form for three hundred forty-six thousand?

F 346,000,000 **G** 3,046 **H** 346,000 **J** 3,460 **K** NH

Comparing and Ordering Whole Numbers and Decimals

Warm-Up Review

For Exercises 1–3, write <, >, or = to compare the numbers.

1. 63 ● 84
2. 47 ● 38
3. 1,243 ● 1,086
4. Write 32 thousand in standard form.
5. Ben has $356 in the bank and $27 in his wallet. Kate has $450. Who has more?

California Content Standard *Number Sense 1.0: Students . . . understand the relative magnitudes of numbers. Also Number Sense 1.5* *(See p. 3)*

Math Link You have learned about place value for very large and very small numbers. Now you will learn to compare and order these same kinds of numbers.

The table at the right lists the average distance of each planet from the sun.

Planet	Distance from Sun (in kilometers)
Earth	149,600,000
Jupiter	777,000,000
Mars	228,000,000
Mercury	57,900,000
Neptune	4,500,000,000
Pluto	5,900,000,000
Saturn	1,400,000,000
Uranus	2,900,000,000
Venus	107,800,000

Example 1

Compare the distance of Earth from the sun with that of Venus. Which is farther?

Compare 149,600,000 and 107,800,000. First line up the two numbers on the right. Starting at the left, compare digits in the same place.

Step 1
Compare the digits in the hundred millions place. They are the same.

149,600,000
107,800,000

Step 2
Compare the digits in the ten millions place. 4 > 0, so 149,600,000 > 107,800,000

149,600,000
107,800,000

Example 2

The four closest planets to the sun are Earth, Mars, Mercury, and Venus. List their distances from the sun in order from least to greatest.

Step 1
Line up the digits in the ones place. Then start at the left and compare digits in the same place.

149,600,000
228,000,000
57,900,000
107,800,000

There are no hundred millions in 57,900,000, so 57,900,000 is the least number.

2 > 1, so 228,000,000 is the greatest.

0 < 4, so 107,800,000 < 149,600,000

Step 2
Write the numbers in order, starting with the least number.

Mercury	57,900,000 km
Venus	107,800,000 km
Earth	149,600,000 km
Mars	228,000,000 km

Additional Standards: Number Sense 1.1, Algebra and Functions 1.2 *(See p. 3.)*

You can see groups of ***equal decimals*** on the number lines.

0.6 = 0.60 = 0.600   0.68 = 0.680   0.7 = 0.70 = 0.700   0.72 = 0.720

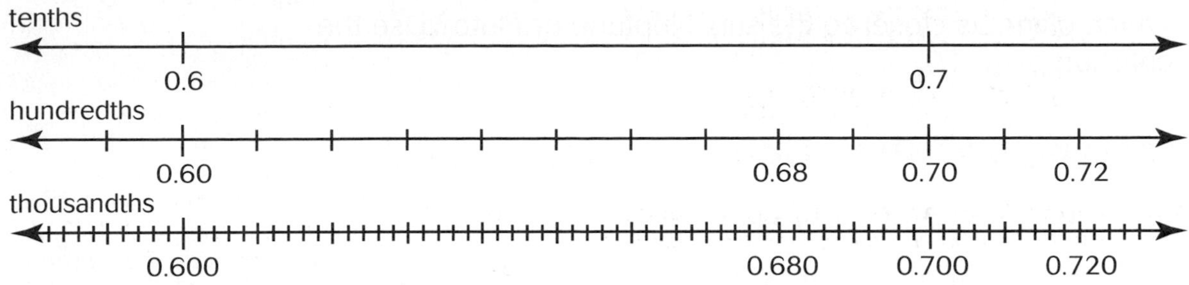

When you compare and order decimals, it is helpful to write them with the same number of digits after the decimal point. You can do this by writing zeros to the right of the other digits in any decimal.

Example 3

Compare 0.385 and 0.38

0.385 ● 0.38 The ones are the same. The tenths are the same. The hundredths are the same.

0.385 ● 0.380 Think: 0.38 = 0.380 Compare the thousandths.

0.385 > 0.38 5 thousandths is greater than 0 thousandths.

Example 4

List the decimals 0.71, 0.631, and 0.66 in order from least to greatest and represent them on the number line.

0.71   0.631   0.66
↓   ↓   ↓
0.710   0.631   0.660   Write all three decimals as thousandths.

0.631   0.660   0.710   Order as with whole numbers.
0.631   0.66   0.71

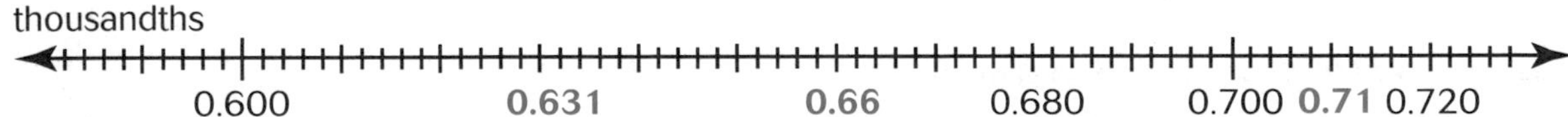

Guided Practice *For another example, see Set C on p. 29.*

Compare. Write >, <, or = for each ●.

1. 23,878 ● 26,799   **2.** 4.26 ● 4.88   **3.** 0.250 ● 0.25

Write the numbers in order from least to greatest.

4. 23,004 322,008 32,008

5. 0.2 0.510 0.07

6. Which planet is closer to the sun, Neptune or Pluto? Use the chart on page 10.

Independent Practice

For more practice, see Set C on p. 31.

Compare. Write $>$, $<$, or $=$ for each ●.

7. 10,198 ● 1,203

8. 1,444 ● 1,447

9. 35,271 ● 35,271

10. 0.331 ● 0.332

11. 6.200 ● 6.2

12. 1.989 ● 1.981

13. 0.16 ● 0.4

Write the numbers in order from least to greatest.

14. 33,881 33,188 33,818

15. 2,334,556 2,344,566 2,343,655

16. 0.45 0.458 0.5

17. 0.11 0.108 0.1

18. 1.399 1.37 1.43

19. Tell which point on the following number line represents each of the numbers in Exercise 16.

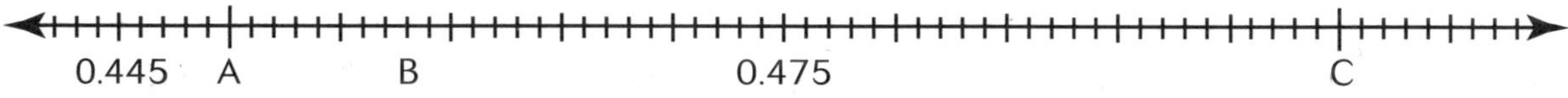

20. Algebra The numbers at the right are arranged from greatest to least. They follow a pattern. Write the number represented by x.

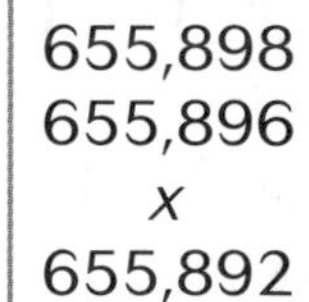
655,898
655,896
x
655,892

Mixed Review

21. Mental Math Joe drove 130 miles in the morning and 170 miles in the afternoon. How far did he drive in all?

Write each number in standard form.

22. 27 billion 386 million

23. 12 and 185 thousandths

24. 9 thousandths

Compare. Write $<$, $>$, or $=$ for each ●.

25. 2,456,000,000 ● 2,459,100,000

26. 27.986 ● 27.95

Test Prep **Choose the correct letter for each answer.**

27. Algebra If $6 + n = 15$, then $n =$
(Gr. 4)

A 9 **C** 19

B 21 **D** 90

28. Algebra If $n - 3 = 9$, then $n =$
(Gr. 4)

F 6 **H** 12

G 27 **J** 3

Use Homework Workbook 1-4.

Diagnostic Checkpoint

Write the value of each underlined digit using short word form.

1. 72$\underline{3}$,176 (1-1)

2. 2$\underline{5}$,355 (1-1)

3. 3$\underline{7}$,719,827 (1-1)

4. $\underline{5}$,255,366,177 (1-1)

5. 4$\underline{5}$1,728,013 (1-1)

6. 63,$\underline{5}$21,423 (1-1)

7. 12,6$\underline{8}$8,276 (1-1)

8. 1$\underline{6}$2,733,261 (1-1)

9. 923.12$\underline{7}$ (1-3)

10. 2.$\underline{3}$19 (1-3)

11. 2.0$\underline{8}$ (1-3)

12. 0.22$\underline{1}$ (1-3)

Write each number in expanded form.

13. 3,025 (1-1)

14. 64,037 (1-1)

15. 18,510,655 (1-1)

16. 198,073 (1-1)

Write each number in standard form.

17. 101 and 17 hundredths (1-3)

18. 9 thousandths (1-3)

19. 4 and 9 tenths (1-3)

Write the numbers in order from least to greatest.

20. 999,991 99,991 9,991 (1-4)

21. 7,022 7,020 7,002 (1-4)

22. 13,242 11,221 13,144 (1-4)

23. 109,817 109,871 109,877 (1-4)

24. 0.15 0.008 0.9 (1-4)

25. 0.8 0.002 0.01 (1-4)

26. 0.7 0.12 0.81 (1-4)

27. 0.912 0.921 0.9 (1-4)

28. (1-2) The cost for the vacation trip to Hawaii will be about $2,300. Is this an exact cost or an estimate? Which word in the problem helped you decide if it was an estimate or exact cost?

29. (1-4) Tina and her friends collect stamps. One collection has 11,082 stamps, another has 4,826 stamps, a third has 600 stamps, and a fourth has 7,132 stamps. Order the number of stamps in the collections from least to greatest.

30. (1-1) The greatest distance of Mars from Earth is 248,000,000 miles. Write this number in expanded form.

31. (1-3) The least distance of Neptune from Earth is 2,667,000,000 miles. Write this number in word form.

Problem-Solving Strategy:

Draw a Diagram

California Content Standard *Mathematical Reasoning 2.3: Use a variety of methods, such as words, numbers, symbols, charts, graphs, tables, diagrams, and models, to explain mathematical reasoning.*

Warm-Up Review

1. 18 + 9 + 6
2. 9 + 8 + 12
3. 16 + 7 + 4
4. 4 × 2 × 9
5. 3 × 5 × 2
6. Bus A has 27 passengers on board and Bus B has 18. If 12 passengers get off of each bus, how many passengers in all will still be on board?

Example

Pablo wants to build a simple telescope, using two tubes. Five inches of the small tube extend beyond the big tube and three inches fit inside the big tube. The tubes are the same length. How long is each tube?

Understand

What do you need to find?

You need to find the length of each tube.

Plan

How can you solve the problem?

Draw a diagram and label the lengths you know.
Use the diagram to help you find the length of each tube.

Solve

The diagram shows that the length of the small tube is 5 inches plus 3 inches, or 8 inches. The big tube is the same length.

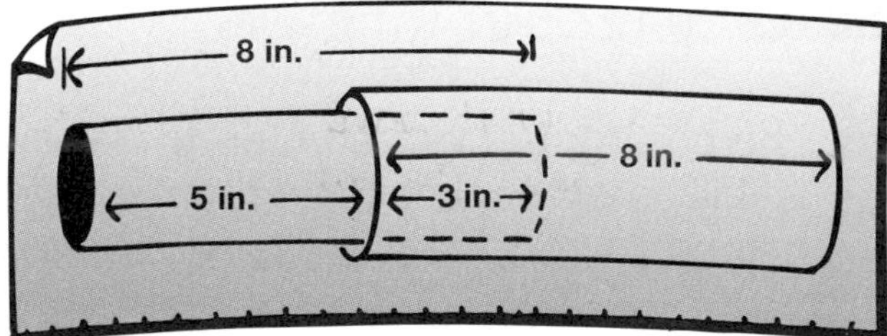

Look Back

Explain how to find the total length of the telescope.

Guided Practice

Draw a diagram to solve each problem.

1. Four girls are waiting in line. Beth is ahead of Kelly. Lisa is behind Kelly. Beth is behind Erika. What is the order of the girls in line from front to back?
2. Bob is older than Jeff. Amir is younger than Jeff. Glenn's age is between Amir's and Jeff's. What is the order of the boys by age from youngest to oldest?

Additional Standard: Mathematical Reasoning 3.2 (See p. 3.)

Independent Practice

Use the diagram on page 14 to solve Exercises 3 and 4. Draw diagrams to solve Exercises 5–7.

3. Suppose 4 inches of the small tube were pushed inside the big tube. What would the total length of the telescope be?

4. Suppose the small tube were pushed completely inside the big tube. How long would the telescope be?

5. A model car is built using two strips of cardboard. The short strip is 12 inches long and the long strip is 3 times as long. How long are the two strips when placed end to end?

6. Terry has pictures that are 2 inches wide and 4 inches long. She wants to put them in a photo album with pages that are 8 inches wide by 12 inches long. How many pictures can she fit on a page if she does not allow space between pictures?

7. Cal lives 12 blocks north of Bea. Sue lives 4 blocks south of Bea. Lee lives north of Sue, halfway between Cal and Sue. How far does Lee live from Bea?

Mixed Review

Try these or other strategies to solve each problem. Tell which strategy you used.

Problem-Solving Strategies

- *Work Backward*
- *Find a Pattern*
- *Make a Table*
- *Make a List*

Use the sign at the right to solve Problems 8 and 9.

8. A group arrives at the museum on Tuesday. They have time to see a 45-minute movie and to spend an hour and a half looking at exhibits before the museum closes. By what time do they arrive?

9. The museum is empty at 8:00 A.M. on Saturday. Three people enter the first hour, 4 enter in the second hour, 6 enter in the third hour, and 9 enter in the fourth hour. If the pattern continues, how many people will enter in the fifth hour? the last hour?

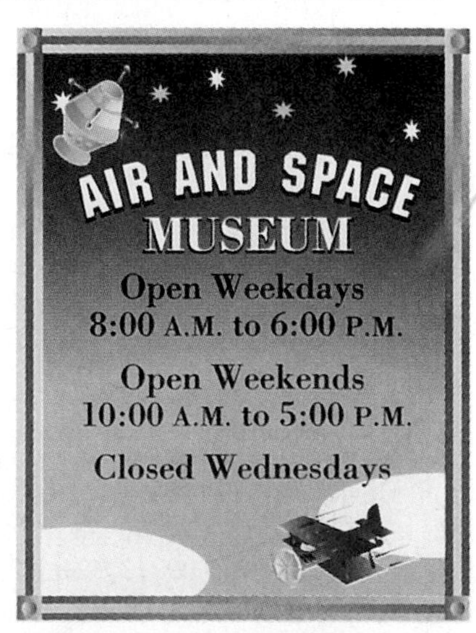

AIR AND SPACE
MUSEUM
Open Weekdays
8:00 A.M. to 6:00 P.M.
Open Weekends
10:00 A.M. to 5:00 P.M.
Closed Wednesdays

Use Homework Workbook 1-5.

Rounding Whole Numbers and Decimals

California Content Standard *Number Sense 1.1: Estimate, round, . . . very large (e.g., millions) and very small (e.g., thousandths) numbers.*

Math Link You have learned how to work with place value and with numbers on a number line. Now you will use those ideas to round whole numbers and decimals.

Warm-Up Review

For the number 23,568.471, tell what digit is in each given place.

1. tens **2.** tenths

3. hundreds **4.** hundredths

5. thousands **6.** thousandths

7. Karla's score on a video game was 45,357. Bo's score was 45,349. Whose score was higher?

Example 1

Every year, the fifth-grade class takes a trip to Washington, D.C. Included in the trip is a visit to a space museum. Look at the picture to find the cost for this year's trip. To the nearest hundred dollars, about how much will this year's class trip cost?

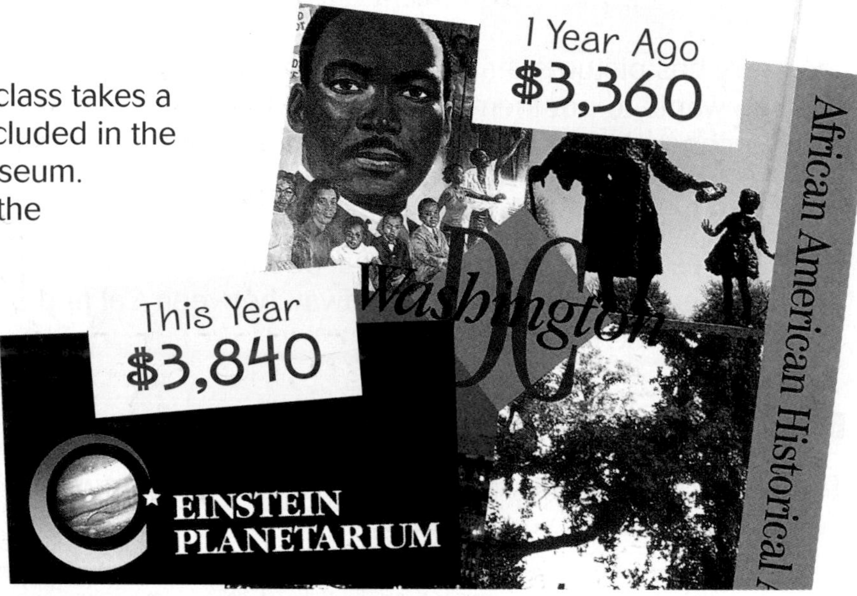

Round 3,840 to the nearest hundred.

Step 1 Find the hundreds place.	**Step 2** Look at the digit to the right.	**Step 3** If the digit to the right is less than 5, round down. If that digit is 5 or greater, round up.	
3,<u>8</u>40	3,<u>8</u>40	3,840 rounds to 3,800	Since 4 < 5, keep the digit in the hundreds place the same.

The fifth-grade class trip will cost about $3,800.

Here's WHY It Works

3,840 is between 3,800 and 3,900. Since 3,840 is less than the halfway number, it rounds to 3,800.

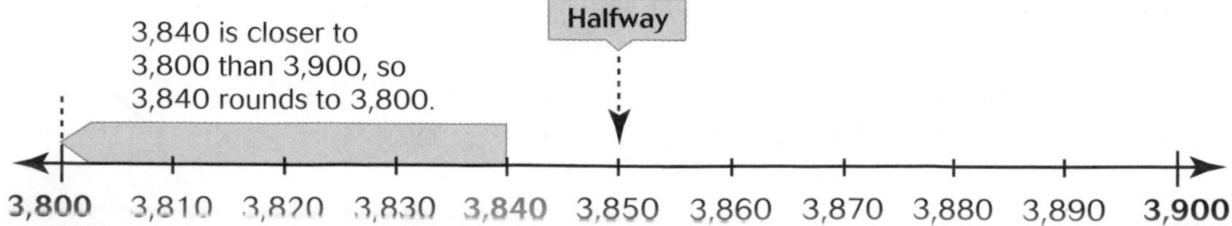

 Additional Standard: Mathematical Reasoning 2.5 (See p. 3.)

Example 2

At the space museum, students learn that America's space-shuttle launch system is about 56.08 meters tall. Round 56.08 to the nearest tenth.

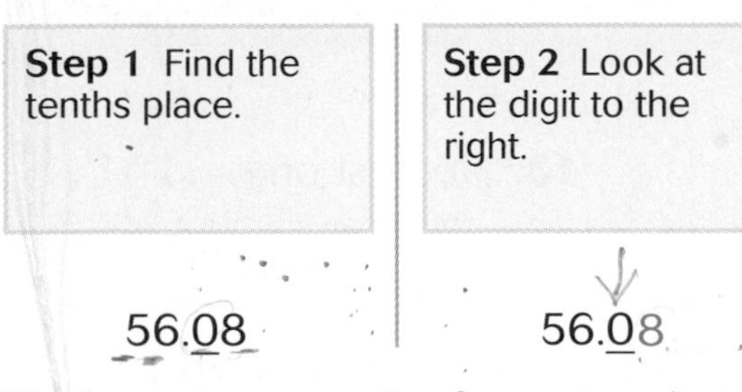

Step 1 Find the tenths place.	**Step 2** Look at the digit to the right.	**Step 3** If the digit to the right is less than 5, round down. If that digit is 5 or greater, round up.
56.<u>0</u>8	56.0<u>8</u>	56.08 rounds to 56.1

Since 8 > 5, increase the digit in the tenths place by one.

To the nearest tenth of a meter, America's space-shuttle launch system is about 56.1 meters tall.

Here's WHY It Works

56.08 is between 56.0 and 56.1. Since 56.08 is greater than the halfway number, it rounds to 56.1.

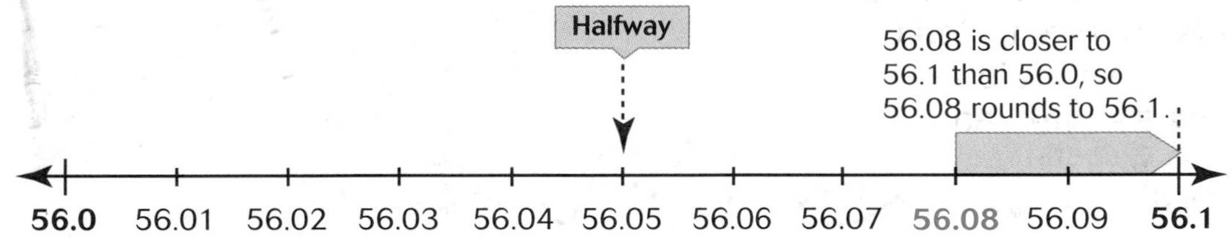

More Examples

A. Round 6.51 to the nearest one.

The digit to the right of the ones place is 5, so the digit in the ones place increases from 6 to 7.

To the nearest one, 6.51 is 7.

B. Round 2.964 to the nearest tenth.

Since the digit to the right of the tenths place is 6, the tenths place increases from 9 to 10. But 10 tenths equals 1. So the tenths digit becomes zero and the ones place increases from 2 to 3.

To the nearest tenth, 2.964 is 3.0.

Guided Practice *For another example, see Set D on p. 29.*

Round 2,716,934 to the given place.

1. Nearest hundred
2. Nearest thousand
3. Nearest hundred thousand

Round 38.952 to the given place.

4. Nearest hundredth
5. Nearest tenth
6. Nearest ten

7. Use the information on page 16 to find the cost of last year's trip to Washington. Round this number to the nearest hundred.

Independent Practice *For more practice, see Set D on p. 31.*

Round 32,567,480 to the given place.

8. Nearest ten million **9.** Nearest million **10.** Nearest ten thousand

Round 45.193 to the given place.

11. Nearest hundredth **12.** Nearest tenth **13.** Nearest one

Round each number to the underlined place.

14. $\underline{4}30$ **15.** $1,\underline{5}50$ **16.** $86\underline{4},932$ **17.** $\underline{1}21,200$

18. $0.\underline{8}3$ **19.** $0.6\underline{2}5$ **20.** $\underline{0}.555$ **21.** $0.6\underline{9}2$

For Exercises 22 and 23, use the information on page 16.

22. To the nearest thousand dollars, what was the cost of the trip to Washington for the fifth-grade class last year? this year?

23. Math Reasoning Tom said that the cost of the Washington trip increased by about $1,000 from last year to this year. Bill said it increased by about $400. Who is more accurate?

Mixed Review

Use the graph to answer Exercises 24–27.

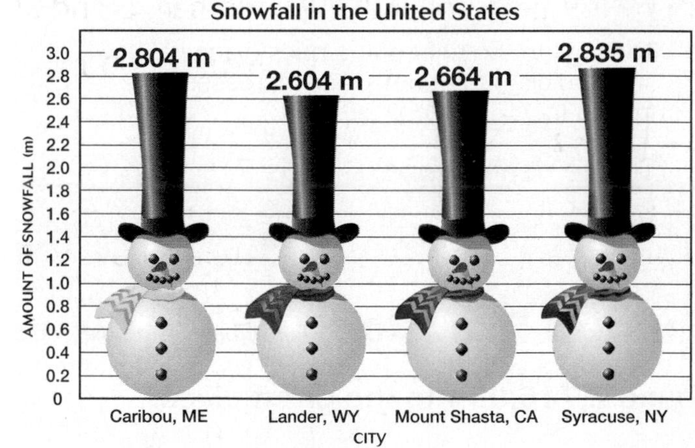

24. Which city had the most snow?

25. Which city had the least snow?

26. Order the amounts of snow from least to greatest.

27. Round each amount of snow to the nearest tenth of a meter.

Give the value of each underlined digit.

28. $2,\underline{3}56,900,000$ **29.** $0.47\underline{8}$ **30.** $932.\underline{4}5$ **31.** $450,000.9\underline{2}0$

Test Prep Choose the correct letter for each answer.

32. Algebra Find $16 + n$ if $n = 18$.
(Gr. 4)

A 14 **C** 240

B 34 **D** 2

33. Algebra Find n if $6 + 8 = 8 + n$.
(Gr. 4)

F 48 **H** 14

G 2 **J** 6

 Use Homework Workbook 1-6.

Variables and Tables

California Content Standard *Algebra and Functions 1.2(🔑): Use a letter to represent an unknown number . . .. Also Algebra and Functions 1.5 (🔑)* *(See p. 3.)*

Math Link You already know that variables such as *x, y,* and *z* represent numbers. Now you will use variables to describe number relationships shown in tables.

Warm-Up Review

1. 64 ÷ 8
2. 9 × 6
3. 16 − 7
4. 8 + 9
5. 63 ÷ 9
6. 7 × 7
7. 14 − 7
8. 9 + 9
9. The total rainfall for March was 6 inches. In April it rained twice as much. What was the total rainfall for April?

Example 1

In the table at the right, the same rule is used with each number in Column A and the corresponding result is given in Column B. So, each pair of numbers is related in the same way. Find a rule for this table.

A	B
2	12
5	30
8	48
9	54
12	72

Step 1

Look at the first pair of numbers, 2 and 12.
How are they related?
One way is by adding.

$$2 + 10 = 12$$

Check this method for the second pair, 5 and 30.

$$5 + 10 = 15, \text{ not } 30$$

Step 2

Go back to the first pair and try another way.
The numbers 2 and 12 are also related by multiplying.

$$6 \times 2 = 12$$

Try this relationship on the other pairs.

$$6 \times 5 = 30 \qquad 6 \times 9 = 54$$
$$6 \times 8 = 48 \qquad 6 \times 12 = 72$$

The relationship is the same for all of the pairs, so a rule is:

Multiply by 6.

When using a table like the one above, you can state each rule in words as we did in Example 1, or by using a **variable**. A variable can be any kind of symbol or a letter such as *n* or *x*. For the table above, we could let *n* represent any number in column A. Then the rule we found would be stated as **6 × *n*.**

Word Bank

variable

Example 2

Complete the table. Find a rule and write it using words and using a variable. Let the variable represent any number in Column A.

A	B
7	1
14	2
28	4
49	
63	
77	11

To get from 7 to 1 you could either subtract 6 or divide by 7. Try each method for the next pair.

$14 - 6 = 8$, not 2, but $14 \div 7 = 2$
Check the other pairs of numbers.
$28 \div 7 = 4$ and $77 \div 7 = 11$
In each pair, the number in Column A is divided by 7 to get the number in Column B.

Complete the table.
$49 \div 7 = 7$ and $63 \div 7 = 9$

A	B
7	1
14	2
28	4
49	7
63	9
77	11

The rule we found is: Divide by 7. If x represents any number in Column A, this rule could be stated as $x \div 7$.

Guided Practice

For another example, see Set E on p. 29.

Find a rule for each table. Give that rule using words and using a variable that represents any number in Column A.

1.

A	B
24	3
32	4
48	6
56	7
64	8
88	11

2.

A	B
5	12
10	17
15	22
20	27
25	32
30	37

3.

A	B
7	2
9	4
11	6
13	8
15	10
17	12

4.

A	B
0	0
1	5
3	15
6	30
8	40
10	50

Independent Practice

For more practice, see Set E on p. 31.

Find a rule for each table. Give that rule using words and using a variable that represents any number in Column A.

5.

A	B
9	3
15	5
24	8
30	10

6.

A	B
1	10
3	30
7	70
10	100

7.

A	B
0	0
8	1
24	3
56	7

8.

A	B
1	6
2	7
3	8
4	9
5	10

Write each rule using a variable.

9. Add 7 to a number. **10.** Divide a number by 10. **11.** Multiply a number by 1.

Write each rule using words.

12. $34 \times n$ **13.** $n \div 13$ **14.** $3 \times n$ **15.** $n - 4$ **16.** $n + 2$

Copy and complete each table. Find a rule and write it using words and using a variable that represents any number in Column A.

17.

A	B
4	20
5	
7	35
12	

18.

A	B
9	1
36	
72	8
90	

19.

A	B
27	20
15	
9	
7	0

20.

A	B
0	18
12	
18	
30	48

For Exercises 21 and 22, write a rule using words and using a variable.

21. Kim and her brother Jim have the same birthday, but Jim is five years older. What rule could be used to find Jim's age, using *k* to represent Kim's age at the time?

22. What rule could be used to find the number of days in *w* weeks?

Mixed Review

Use the given data for Exercises 23–26.

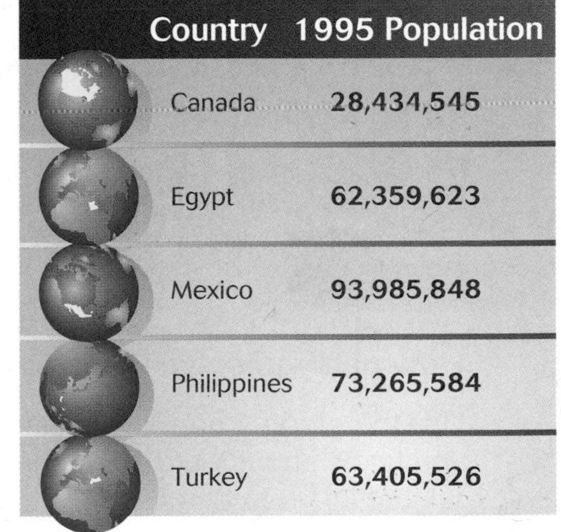

Country	1995 Population
Canada	28,434,545
Egypt	62,359,623
Mexico	93,985,848
Philippines	73,265,584
Turkey	63,405,526

23. Write the names of the five countries in order from least population to greatest.

24. Write the population of Turkey in expanded form.

Round each population to the given place.

25. Nearest million **26.** Nearest thousand

Algebra **Write each rule using the variable *n*.**

27. Multiply a number by 7.

28. Divide 12 by a number.

Test Prep **Choose the correct letter for each answer.**

29. (1-4) Which choice makes the statement true?

465,980 > ■

A 400,990
B 465,990
C 4,000,900
D 4,650,980

30. (1-4) What number is represented by each letter on the number line?

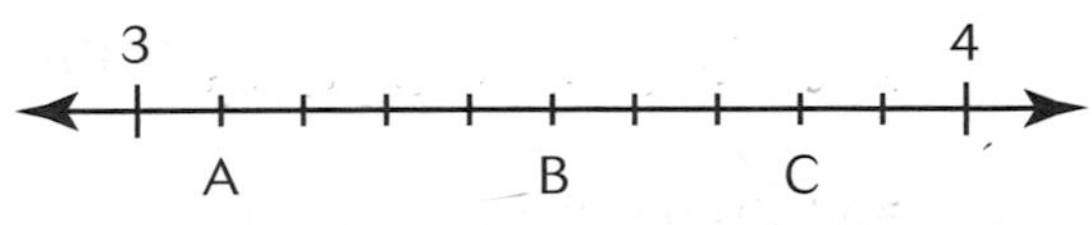

F *A*: 3.2, *B*: 3.5, *C*: 3.8
G *A*: 3.1, *B*: 3.4, *C*: 3.8
H *A*: 3.1, *B*: 3.5, *C*: 3.9
J *A*: 3.1, *B*: 3.5, *C*: 3.8

Problem-Solving Application:

Using Data from Tables and Graphs

Warm-Up Review

1. 22 + 16
2. 48 − 32
3. 12 × 4
4. 11 × 9
5. 81 ÷ 9
6. 64 ÷ 8
7. On Monday the high temperature was 83° and the low was 67°. On Tuesday the high temperature was 94°. How much warmer was Tuesday than Monday?

California Content Standard *Mathematical Reasoning 2.3: Use a variety of methods, such as words, numbers, symbols, charts, graphs, tables, diagrams, and models, to explain mathematical reasoning.*

Example

Ron made the graph and the table at the right to show how fast he can read a book when he is reading for his own enjoyment. How long will it take Ron to read 30 pages?

Ron's Reading for Enjoyment Rate

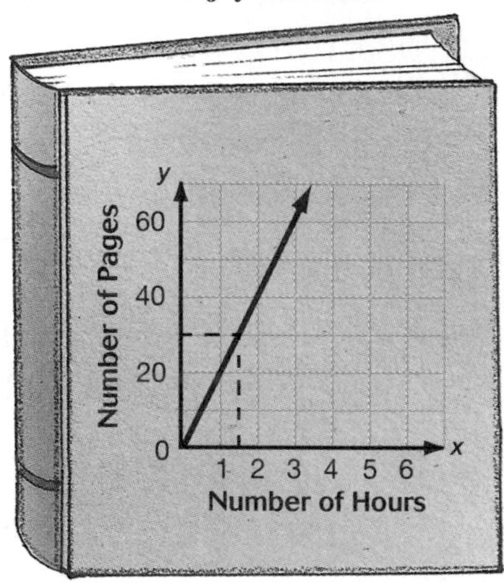

Understand

What do you need to find?

You need to find the length of time it takes Ron to read 30 pages.

Plan

How can you solve the problem?

Use the graph. You will also need to use what you know about the order of numbers.

Solve

You know that 30 comes between 20 and 40. On the graph, find the line between 20 and 40 on the vertical scale. Follow the dotted line to the right until it meets the red line. Follow the dotted line down from that point to the number of hours. The number of hours is halfway between 1 and 2. Ron can read 30 pages in $1\frac{1}{2}$ hours.

Number of Pages	Number of Hours
20	1
40	2
60	3
80	4
100	5

Look Back

Look at the table. The answer is correct because the table shows that Ron can read 20 pages per hour or 40 pages in 2 hours. 30 is halfway between 20 and 40 and $1\frac{1}{2}$ hours is halfway between 1 hour and 2 hours.

Additional Standard: Algebra and Functions 1.2 (key); (See p. 3.)

Guided Practice

Use the graph and table on page 22.

1. How long does it take Ron to read 50 pages?

2. How many pages can Ron read in $\frac{1}{2}$ hour?

Independent Practice

Use the graph and table on page 22 to solve Exercises 3 and 4.

3. How long does it take Ron to read 70 pages?

4. About how many pages can Ron read in $3\frac{1}{2}$ hours?

The graph and table at the right show Ron's reading rate when he is studying. Use them to solve Exercises 5–9.

Ron's Reading for Studying Rate

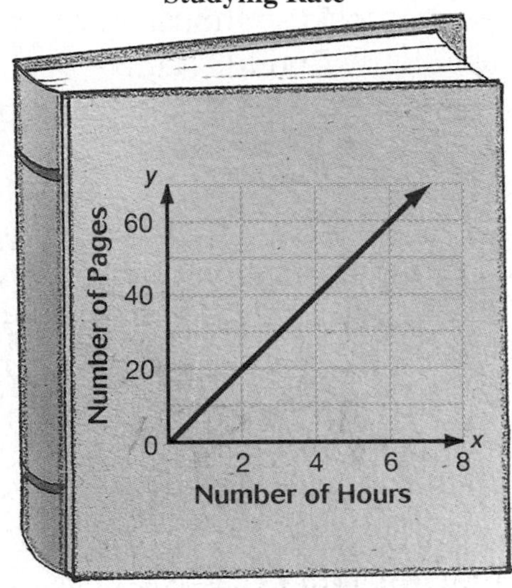

Number of Pages	Number of Hours
20	2
40	4
60	6

5. Ron is studying social studies from 7:00 to 8:00 tonight. How many pages will he be able to read?

6. How long would it take Ron to study 60 pages?

7. The science chapter Ron is reading is 30 pages long. How much time should he set aside to read it?

8. How many pages of his favorite novel could Ron read in the same amount of time he had set aside for studying 30 pages of science?

9. **Algebra** If Ron studies x pages for a test, how many pages would he be able to read for enjoyment in the same amount of time?

Mixed Review

Lee spent $0.75 for lemonade, $1.50 for pizza, $0.90 for fruit, and $0.50 for a pretzel. He paid with a $10 bill. Tax was $0.31.

10. How much did he spend in all?

11. How much change did he receive?

12. Lee's friend Sam bought a pretzel for $0.50 and a box lunch, which contained a slice of pizza, an apple, and lemonade. The box lunch cost $3.00. He paid $0.29 tax. Who spent more, Lee or Sam? How much more?

Use Homework Workbook 1-8.

Diagnostic Checkpoint

Write the missing words that complete each sentence.

Word Bank
variable
thousandths
standard form
expanded form

1. To write a number in ________________, you express it as the sum of the values of its digits. (1-1)

2. In the expression $x + 6$, x is a ________________. (1-7)

3. In 29.16<u>7</u>, the 7 is in the ________________ place. (1-3)

Round 59,512,939 to the given place.

4. nearest ten thousand (1-6)
5. nearest ten (1-6)
6. nearest million (1-6)

Round 63.2639 to the given place.

7. nearest one (1-6)
8. nearest tenth (1-6)
9. nearest thousandth (1-6)

Find a rule for each table. Give that rule using words and using a variable. Let the variable represent any number in Column A.

10. (1-7)

A	B
4	1
12	3
16	4
28	7

11. (1-7)

A	B
2	9
5	12
7	14
10	17

12. (1-7)

A	B
2	10
5	25
6	30
10	50

13. Four students are in line for lunch. Tom is in front of Michaela. James is behind Michaela. Tom is behind Daniella. Draw a diagram to find the order of the students in line from front to back. (1-5)

14. The table below gives the average speed of the Johnsons' car on a recent highway trip. Use the table to find how far the Johnsons might have traveled in $3\frac{1}{2}$ hours. (1-8)

Number of miles	60	120	180	240
Number of hours	1	2	3	4

Chapter 1 Test

Write each number in standard form.

1. 2,000 + 500 + 60 + 1

2. One hundred forty-five and sixty-five hundredths

Write the value for each underlined digit in short word form.

3. $\underline{1}$,009,020,023   4. 9.8$\underline{6}$1   5. 1.46$\underline{2}$

Compare. Write >, <, or = for each ●.

6. 88.020 ● 88.02   7. 12,366 ● 12,368   8. 54.081 ● 54.08

Order each set of numbers from least to greatest.

9. 554   286   560   10. 260   26.0   2.60   11. 32.08   99.14   2.45

Round each number to the underlined place.

12. 748,$\underline{3}$22   13. 2$\underline{2}$9,111   14. 0.1$\underline{8}$9   15. 0.$\underline{2}$24

Write each rule using a variable.

16. Subtract 3 from a number.   17. Divide a number by 12.

18. The table shows Mike's earnings for 1 to 5 hours of work. Use the table to find how much he would earn in $3\frac{1}{2}$ hours.

Hours	1	2	3	4	5
Dollars earned	3	6	9	12	15

Solve.

19. Draw a diagram to solve this problem. A tour bus travels 2 blocks north, 3 blocks east, 4 blocks south, 9 blocks west, and 2 blocks north. Where is the bus in relation to its starting point?

20. The constellation Ursa Major is about 75 light-years from Earth. What word tells you that this is an estimate?

TEST PREP

Multiple-Choice Chapter 1 Test

Choose the correct letter for each answer.

1. The standard form for twenty-six billion, nine thousand, eight is:

   A 260,900,008
   B 2,600,900,008
   C 26,000,009,008
   D 26,000,090,008

2. The standard form for 2,000,000 + 10,000 + 300 + 2 is:

   F 21,320
   G 210,302
   H 2,010,302
   J 2,100,032
   K NH

3. The standard form for 203 and 17 hundredths is:

   A 203,017
   B 203.17
   C 203.107
   D 203.017

4. Which number is NOT greater than 4,021.035?

   F 4,201.036
   G 4,121.021
   H 4,021.935
   J 4,010.010
   K NH

5. Which number is NOT less than 926.09?

   A 921.62
   B 926.19
   C 926.05
   D 920.09

6. Round 289,721 to the nearest thousand.

   F 280,000
   G 289,000
   H 289,700
   J 290,000

7. Round 62.053 to the nearest hundredth.

   A 62.0
   B 62.05
   C 62.06
   D 62.1

8. Amber wanted to arrange her scores in order from least to greatest. Which is the correct way to show that?

   F 95.5, 87.5, 92, 98
   G 87.5, 92, 95.5, 98
   H 92, 95.5, 87.5, 98
   J 87.5, 95.5, 92, 98

9. The boys needed to line up in order from tallest to shortest for their gym class. Paul was 145.25 cm tall. Steve was 152.75 cm tall. Tim was 151.0 cm tall. Mike was 159.50 cm tall. Who was first in line?

A Paul

B Steve

C Tim

D Mike

---

10. Choose the one that is clearly an estimate.

F 49,234,354.23 pounds

G Exactly 48 hours

H 529 people

J About 93 million miles

---

11. Study the numbers in the box. Then answer the question.

13,184
5,020
74,056

Choose the greatest number and round it to the nearest ten thousand.

A 74,000

B 70,000

C 14,000

D 10,000

12. Denise lives 6 blocks north of Sean. Cheryl lives 8 blocks south of Sean. Alex lives north of Cheryl halfway between Denise and Cheryl. How far does Alex live from Sean?

F 14 blocks

G 7 blocks

H 2 blocks

J 1 block

K NH

---

13. Choose the rule shown in the table. Let the variable represent any number in Column A.

A	B
2	5
5	8
8	11
11	14

A $y \times 3$

B $y - 3$

C $\frac{y}{3}$

D $y + 3$

---

14. The table shows the average speed of a runner. Use the table to find the distance she could run in 6 hours.

Hours	3	5	7
Miles	15	25	35

F 20 miles

G 30 miles

H 40 miles

J 45 miles

K NH

Reteaching

Set A *(pages 4–5)*

Find the value of the 3 in 430,921.

The 3 is in the ten thousands place.

3 × 10,000 = 30,000

The 3 in 430,921 has a value of 30 thousand.

Remember to think of the place-value chart (p. 4) to find the value of a digit in a number.

Write the value of each underlined digit using short word form.

1. 95,275,00 **2.** 28,912

3. 1,293,704 **4.** 7,214,576

5. 856,493 **6.** 79,700,000

7. 3,458,000,000 **8.** 54,824,527,863

9. 32,567,320 **10.** 562,298,000,000

Set B *(pages 8–9)*

Write 7 and 354 thousandths in standard form.

Use the place-value chart to help you.

7	3	5	4
ones	tenths	hundredths	thousandths

Standard form: 7.354

Remember to write the decimal point for the word ***and.***

Write each number in standard form.

1. 24 and 7 tenths

2. six and 5 hundredths

3. 10 and 379 thousandths

4. 9 and 9 hundredths

5. 13 and 56 thousandths

6. 352 and 1 hundredth

7. 59 and 25 hundredths

8. 12 and 103 thousandths

Set C (pages 10–12)

Compare 3,205,928 and 3,250,707.

Line up the numbers by place value.
3,205,928
3,250,707

Start at the left and compare digits in the same place.

The 5 in the ten thousands place is greater than the 0.
So, 3,250,707 $>$ 3,205,928.

Remember to line up the digits and compare from left to right.

Compare. Write $<$, $>$, or $=$ for each ●.

1. 3,250 ● 3,105

2. 36,895 ● 36,995

3. 45.04 ● 45.4

4. 62.98 ● 6.298

Set D (pages 16–18)

Round 5.932 to the nearest hundredth.

Find the hundredths place. $5.9\underline{3}2$

Look at the digit to the right of the hundredths place. If it is less than 5, the 3 stays the same. If it is 5 or greater, the 3 rounds up.

2 is less than 5.
So, 5.932 rounds to 5.93.

Remember, if the digit to the right is less than 5, round down. If that digit is 5 or greater, round up.

Round each number to the underlined place.

1. $28,\underline{9}42$

2. $7\underline{6}1,385$

3. $\underline{3}92,419$

4. $76\underline{1}.8$

Set E (pages 19–21)

Find a rule for the table. Give that rule using words and using a variable. Let the variable represent any number in Column A.

A	B
3	15
4	20
5	25

Multiply the number in A by 5 to get the number in B.
Multiply by 5.
$5 \times y$

Remember that each pair of numbers in the table must be related in the same way to find a rule.

Find a rule for each table. Give that rule using words and using a variable. Let the variable represent any number in Column A.

1.

A	B
2	8
4	10
9	15

2.

A	B
40	10
32	8
16	4

More Practice

Set A *(pages 4–5)*

Write each number in standard form and expanded form.

1. seven thousand, eight hundred ninety-two
2. four hundred thousand, seven hundred two
3. two million, three hundred sixty-six thousand
4. one hundred twenty-seven billion, twenty-nine million

Write the value of each underlined digit using short word form.

5. $8{,}\underline{3}48{,}000$
6. $\underline{2}6{,}918$
7. $4\underline{2}4{,}000{,}000$
8. $\underline{7}98{,}725$
9. $\underline{8}1{,}392{,}000{,}000$
10. $\underline{3}{,}461{,}000{,}000$
11. $\underline{6}{,}381{,}410$
12. $\underline{6}12{,}833{,}410$
13. Greenland is the largest island in the world. Its area is about 840 thousand square miles. Write the number of square miles in standard form.
14. The greatest distance that Mercury is from Earth is 136,000,000 miles. Write this number in expanded form.

Set B *(pages 8-9)*

Write the value of each underlined digit in short word form.

1. $8.9\underline{3}$
2. $2.\underline{5}04$
3. $56.\underline{1}79$
4. $69.73\underline{6}$
5. $4{,}43\underline{6}.27$
6. $9.\underline{3}81$
7. $24.0\underline{8}$
8. $\underline{1}41.501$
9. $25.76\underline{3}$
10. $517.4\underline{3}2$

Write each number in standard form.

11. 36 and 7 tenths
12. 582 and 321 thousandths
13. 53 thousandths
14. 16 and 27 hundredths
15. 3 and 3 tenths
16. 859 and 1 thousandth
17. A television weather reporter announced that the amount of rainfall for the week was two tenths of an inch. Write the number in standard form.

Set C *(pages 10–12)*

Compare. Write >, <, or = for each ●.

1. 395 ● 892
2. 632 ● 635
3. 9.81 ● 9.18

Write the numbers in order from least to greatest.

4. 580 750 612
5. 48,000 47,681 49,361
6. 30,800 30,080 30,008
7. 88,252 89,150 98,010
8. 25.1 25.01 25.07
9. 6.34 603.4 66.3
10. Sue planted five bushes. The heights of the bushes were 4.7 feet, 3.75 feet, 4.87 feet, 3.57 feet, and 4.07 feet. Order the bushes from tallest to shortest.

Set D *(pages 16–18)*

Round each number to the underlined place.

1. 3$\underline{5}$4
2. $\underline{6}$89
3. 8,1$\underline{2}$6
4. 5,$\underline{4}$72
5. 6,$\underline{8}$75,941
6. 42.$\underline{1}$7
7. 26.5$\underline{1}$1
8. 0.$\underline{2}$24
9. $\underline{0}$.993
10. \$$\underline{1}$.38
11. Luis bought items at the museum costing \$1.95, \$0.99, \$4.95, and \$6.25. To the nearest dollar, how much did he spend?

Set E *(pages 19–21)*

Find a rule for each table. Give that rule using words and using a variable that represents any number in Column A.

1.

A	B
49	7
35	5
21	3
41	2

2.

A	B
3	10
5	12
8	15
11	18

3.

A	B
21	14
19	12
15	8
8	1

4.

A	B
1	7
3	21
4	28
6	42

Write each rule using words.

5. $21 \times n$
6. $n - 5$
7. $\frac{n}{11}$
8. $n + 14$

TEST PREP

Problem Solving: Preparing for Tests

Choose the correct letter for each answer.

---

1. One toy car is 0.03 m long. Another is 0.13 m long. A third is 0.25 m long. Which number sentence can be used to show the combined length of the two shortest cars?

A $0.13 - 0.30 = \_\_\_\_\_$

B $0.13 + 0.25 = \_\_\_\_\_$

C $0.03 + 0.25 = \_\_\_\_\_$

D $0.03 + 0.13 = \_\_\_\_\_$

Tip

When reading a problem, decide what information is necessary to solve the problem.

---

2. On Monday the number of cards at a gift shop was 134 cards. Each day during the week 5 cards were sold. How many cards were left at the end of the fourth day?

F 20

G 109

H 114

J 129

K NH

Tip

Use one of these strategies to solve this problem.

- Find a pattern.
- Make a graph.
- Make a table.

---

3. Mark lives 22 miles from Sally along a straight road. Juan lives between them, and his house is 14 miles from Mark. How far does Sally live from Juan?

A 8 mi

B 12 mi

C 36 mi

D 44 mi

E NH

Tip

Using the *Draw a Diagram* strategy can help you solve this problem.

4. Sid is taller than Betty, but shorter than Walt. Pete is taller than Sid. Which of the following is a reasonable conclusion?

- **F** Sid is the tallest.
- **G** Walt is the tallest.
- **H** Walt is taller than Pete.
- **J** Betty is the shortest.

---

5. Jack had a board that was 8 feet long. He cut seven 10-inch pieces from the board. Which is the best estimate of the length of the board that was left?

- **A** less than 1 ft
- **B** about 2 ft
- **C** about 3 ft
- **D** more than 3 ft

---

6. Gil and two classmates divide 18 pens equally among them. How can you find the number of pens each person has?

- **F** Subtract 2 from 18.
- **G** Divide 18 by 2.
- **H** Multiply 18 by 3.
- **J** Divide 18 by 3.

---

7. For a science project, the fifth grade collected about 40 pictures of spiders, 28 pictures of bees, 12 pictures of wasps, and about 60 pictures of butterflies. Which best describes the total number of pictures?

- **A** exactly 140
- **B** about 100
- **C** about 140
- **D** more than 200

8. Lucy and Paul drove in separate cars to a campground. Lucy drove 74.1 miles in the morning and 31.5 miles in the afternoon. Paul drove 35.2 miles in the morning and twice that far in the afternoon. Which number sentence shows how far Paul drove in the afternoon?

- **F** $74.1 - 35.2 =$ _____
- **G** $35.1 + 35.2 =$ _____
- **H** $35.2 + (2 \times 35.2) =$ _____
- **J** $2 \times 35.2 =$ _____

---

9. The weights of four cartons, in pounds, are 32, 41, 18, and 29. Which is the best estimate for the total weight of the cartons?

- **A** 100 pounds
- **B** 120 pounds
- **C** 140 pounds
- **D** 150 pounds

---

10. This graph shows the number of teenage volunteers at a hospital.

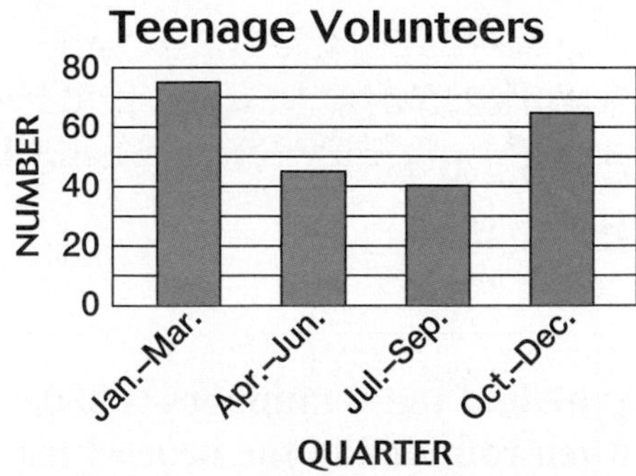

To the nearest ten, which is the number of volunteers from January through June?

- **F** 90
- **G** 120
- **H** 150
- **J** 200

Multiple-Choice Cumulative Review

Choose the correct letter for each answer.

Number Sense

1. Casey had 10 bushes to plant. Friday evening he planted 6 of the bushes. What fraction of the bushes did he plant?

   A $\frac{2}{5}$ C $\frac{1}{2}$
   B $\frac{4}{10}$ D $\frac{3}{5}$

2. Which fraction does NOT equal $\frac{1}{2}$?

   F $\frac{2}{5}$
   G $\frac{3}{6}$
   H $\frac{4}{8}$
   J $\frac{5}{10}$

3. Which number is NOT less than 4,234,912?

   A 4,233,567
   B 4,221,907
   C 4,230,455
   D 4,345,932

4. Which of these numbers is 250,000 when rounded to the nearest ten thousand AND 200,000 when rounded to the nearest hundred thousand?

   F 239,345
   G 244,879
   H 245,999
   J 251,462

Measurement and Geometry

5. Identify the quadrilateral.

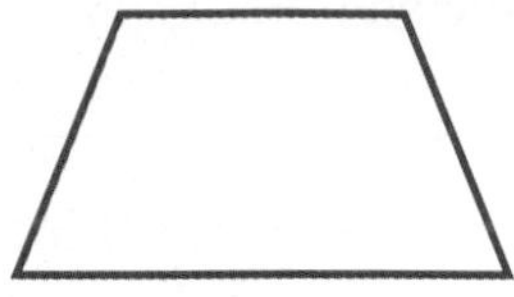

   A square
   B rectangle
   C trapezoid
   D rhombus

6. The perimeter of the rectangular vacant lot next to Cal's house is 340 feet. If the lot is 70 feet wide, how long is it?

   F 100 ft
   G 140 ft
   H 170 ft
   J 200 ft

7. An elephant named Rosie weighs 2.5 tons. How many pounds does Rosie weigh? (1 T = 2,000 lb)

   A 250 lb
   B 500 lb
   C 3,000 lb
   D 5,000 lb

8. The sports field at Heartland School is 330 feet long. How many *yards* is this?

   F 330 yd H 100 yd
   G 110 yd J 30 yd

Algebra and Functions

9. In the number sentence $7 \times (14 + 10)$, which operation should you do first?

A Subtract **C** Add

B Divide **D** Multiply

---

10. If $n \div 8 = 9$, then $n =$

F 17 **H** 72

G 64 **J** 74

---

11. Houses on the east side of State Street have consecutive even numbers. If n represents the number of the first house, which expression represents the number of the fourth house?

A $n + 4$ **C** $4 \times n$

B $n + 2$ **D** $n + 6$

---

12. Which point represents the ordered pair (3, 5)?

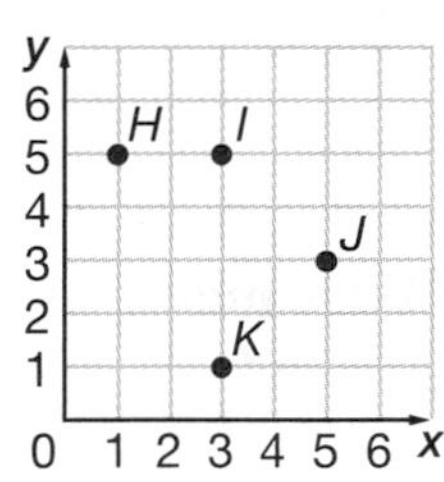

F H **H** J

G I **J** K

Statistics, Data Analysis, and Probability

13. Which is the best description for this event?

All of the members of the basketball team are the same height.

A Impossible **C** Very likely

B Not likely **D** Certain

Use the graph below for Questions 14–16.

Books Read This Year

Sara	
Colin	
Josh	
Maria	

= 4 books

14. Who read 12 more books than Maria read?

F Sara

G Colin

H Josh

J Maria

---

15. How many books were read altogether?

A 16 **C** 40

B 20 **D** 80

---

16. Who did NOT read fewer than 25 books?

F Sara **H** Josh

G Colin **J** Maria

Adding and Subtracting Whole Numbers and Decimals

2-1 Addition Properties

2-2 Mental Math: Using Compatible Numbers and Compensation

2-3 Relating Addition and Subtraction

2-4 Solving Addition and Subtraction Equations

2-5 Problem-Solving Skill: Is an Estimate Enough?

2-6 Estimation Strategies

2-7 Using Expressions

2-8 Problem-Solving Strategy: Write an Equation

2-9 Adding and Subtracting Greater Whole Numbers

2-10 Adding and Subtracting Decimals

2-11 Problem-Solving Application: Using Money

Diagnosing Readiness

In Chapter 2, you will use these skills:

Ⓐ Place Value Through Thousandths

(pages 8–9)

Write the value of each underlined digit in short word form.

1. $7.8\underline{3}5$ **2.** $12.06\underline{9}$

3. $268.\underline{7}5$ **4.** $29.0\underline{4}3$

5. Write thirty-six and twenty-four thousandths in standard form.

6. The mass of Uranus is 14.54 times the mass of Earth. Write the value of the five in this number in short word form.

Ⓑ Rounding Whole Numbers

(pages 16–18)

Round 745,264 to the given place.

7. Nearest thousand

8. Nearest ten-thousand

9. Nearest hundred

10. Nearest hundred-thousand

11. California has an area of 158,869 square miles. Round this number to the nearest ten-thousand.

C Adding Three- and Four-Digit Numbers

(Grade 4)

12. $\begin{array}{r} 3{,}435 \\ +8{,}357 \\ \hline \end{array}$

13. $\begin{array}{r} 657 \\ 90 \\ +323 \\ \hline \end{array}$

14. $\begin{array}{r} 6{,}243 \\ +2{,}928 \\ \hline \end{array}$

15. $\begin{array}{r} 5{,}642 \\ +\quad 974 \\ \hline \end{array}$

16. One month Stewart School collected 2,526 pounds of paper to recycle. The next month, the school collected 2,475 pounds. How much did the school collect in the two months?

D Subtracting Three- and Four-Digit Numbers

(Grade 4)

17. $\begin{array}{r} 873 \\ -269 \\ \hline \end{array}$

18. $\begin{array}{r} 1{,}208 \\ -\quad 249 \\ \hline \end{array}$

19. $\begin{array}{r} 2{,}548 \\ -2{,}156 \\ \hline \end{array}$

20. $\begin{array}{r} 6{,}296 \\ -1{,}821 \\ \hline \end{array}$

21. Sandy's penny collection is worth $71.00. Sue's is worth $26.79. How much more is Sandy's penny collection worth than Sue's?

E Expressions

(Grade 4)

Evaluate each expression for $\blacksquare = 48$.

22. $\blacksquare + 9$

23. $15 + \blacksquare$

24. $\blacksquare - 18$

25. $\blacksquare - 39$

26. $60 - \blacksquare$

27. $72 - \blacksquare$

28. Sandi has saved $26. The expression $26 + \blacksquare$ gives how much she will have if she saves $\blacksquare$ more dollars. Evaluate the expression when $\blacksquare = 8$ and when $\blacksquare = 15$.

F Equations

(Grade 4)

Solve each equation.

29. $\blacksquare + 5 = 9$

30. $\blacksquare + 11 = 25$

31. $\blacksquare - 8 = 12$

32. $\blacksquare - 28 = 34$

33. What can you do to solve $\blacksquare - 6 = 25$?

To the Family and Student

Looking Back	Chapter 2	Looking Ahead
In Grade 4, students learned how to add and subtract four-digit numbers. They also learned about expressions and equations with addition and subtraction. Solve ■ + 6 = 7.	**Adding and Subtracting Whole Numbers and Decimals** In this chapter, students will learn how to add and subtract five-digit whole numbers and decimals. They also learn to evaluate expressions and to solve equations. Solve $x - 8 = 15$.	In Grade 6, students will learn how to write and evaluate expressions and write and solve equations with addition and subtraction of decimals. Solve $x - 2.4 = 4.56$.

Math and Everyday Living

Opportunities to apply the concepts of Chapter 2 abound in everyday situations. During the chapter, think about how addition and subtraction of whole numbers and decimals can be used to solve a variety of real-world problems. The following examples suggest just a few of the many situations that could launch a discussion about addition and subtraction.

Math in Your Town A new sign has just been put up outside your town. The old sign gave the population ten years ago as 129,482. How much has the town grown since then?

Millville
A great place to live!
Population 274,583
Elevation 3,648 ft

Math and Travel The expression $\frac{d}{55}$ gives the time it takes to drive d miles at 55 miles per hour. Use the expression to find how long it would take to drive 165 miles.

Math and Nutrition Corn flakes have 2.4 grams of sodium in a serving. Another cereal has 2.75 grams in a serving. How many more grams of sodium does the other cereal have than corn flakes?

Math in the Neighborhood You earn $8 for walking the neighbors' dog, $17 for mowing their lawn, and $12 for cleaning their car. How can you find your total earnings using mental math?

Math and the Mall You see the sign at the mall.

You have $65. Do you need an exact total cost or an estimate to decide whether or not you have enough to buy 2 videos and a CD?

Math and Fitness You ran 1.8 miles Monday, 0.75 miles on Wednesday, and 1.3 miles on Friday. How far did you run in all?

California Content Standards in Chapter 2 Lessons*

	Teach and Practice	Practice
Number Sense		
1.1 Estimate, round, and manipulate very large (e.g., millions) and very small (e.g., thousandths) numbers.	2-6	
2.1 (key) Add, subtract, . . . with decimals; . . . and verify the reasonableness of the results.	2-10, 2-11	
3.1 (Gr. 4) (key) Demonstrate an understanding of, and ability to use, standard algorithms for the addition and subtraction of multidigit numbers.	2-9	
Algebra and Functions		
1.1 (Gr. 6) (key) Write and solve one-step linear equations in one variable.	2-4, 2-8	
1.2 (Gr. 4) (key) Interpret and evaluate mathematical expressions that now use parentheses.	2-1	
1.2 (key) Use a letter to represent an unknown number; write and evaluate simple algebraic expressions in one variable by substitution.	2-3, 2-7	2-6, 2-9
2.0 (Gr. 4) (key) Students know how to manipulate equations.		2-8

	Teach and Practice	Practice
Mathematical Reasoning		
1.0 Students make decisions about how to approach problems.	2-2	
2.0 Students use strategies, skills, and concepts in finding solutions.	2-9	2-8
2.4 Express the solution clearly and logically by using the appropriate mathematical notation and terms and clear language; support solutions with evidence in both verbal and symbolic work.		2-1
2.5 Indicate the relative advantages of exact and approximate solutions to problems	2-5	
2.6 Make precise calculations and check the validity of the results from the context of the problem.		2-11
3.2 Note the method of deriving the solution and demonstrate a conceptual understanding of the derivation by solving similar problems.		2-8

* The symbol (key) indicates a key standard as designated in the Mathematics Framework for California Public Schools. Full statements of the California Content Standards are found at the beginning of this book following the Table of Contents.

Lesson 2-1 Addition Properties

California Content Standard *Algebra and Functions 1.2 (Grade 4) (Key): Interpret and evaluate mathematical expressions that now use parentheses.*

Warm-Up Review

1. 29 + 71
2. 23 + 77
3. 65 + 0
4. 0 + 74
5. 198 + 27
6. 27 + 198
7. 15 + (2 + 13)
8. (15 + 2) + 13
9. Josie bowled scores of 135, 150, and 165 on Tuesday. Last Friday she bowled 210 in her first game. What was her total score on Tuesday?

Math Link You already know that sums such as 5 + 7 and 7 + 5 are equal. This illustrates one of the important properties of addition. You'll learn more about these properties in this lesson.

Word Bank

associative property
commutative property
identity property

Properties	Examples
Associative Property The way in which addends are grouped does not change the sum. **(When computing sums, do the work in parentheses first.)**	$(2 + 3) + 4 = 2 + (3 + 4)$ $(n + 5) + 6 = n + (5 + 6)$ $(a + b) + c = a + (b + c)$
Commutative Property The order in which numbers are added does not change the sum.	$18 + 9 = 9 + 18$ $n + 7 = 7 + n$ $a + b = b + a$
Identity Property When 0 is added to any number, the sum is that number.	$16 + 0 = 16$ $n + 0 = n$

More Examples

A. Name the property used.

$(3 + 5) + 8 = 3 + (5 + 8)$

The associative property is used.

B. Show that $(42 + 24) + 36 = 42 + (24 + 36)$ is true.

$$(42 + 24) + 36 = 42 + (24 + 36)$$
$$66 + 36 = 42 + 60$$
$$102 = 102$$

C. If $27 + 33 = n + 27$, find n. Name the property used.

$$27 + 33 = n + 27$$
$$33 + 27 = n + 27$$
$$33 = n$$

The commutative property is used.

D. If $n + (15 - 15) = 34$, find n. Name the property used.

$$n + (15 - 15) = 34$$
$$n + 0 = 34$$
$$n = 34$$

The identity property is used.

Additional Standard: Mathematical Reasoning 2.4 (See p. 39.)

Guided Practice *For another example, see Set A on p. 72.*

Name the property used.

1. $76 + 0 = 76$ **2.** $76 + 17 = 17 + 76$ **3.** $(6 + 4) + 8 = 6 + (4 + 8)$

Find each *n*. Name the property used.

4. $36 + n = 52 + 36$

5. $84 + (86 + n) = (84 + 86) + 57$

6. $n + 0 = 673$

7. $52 + 362 + 190 = 52 + 190 + n$

8. Show that $75 + (25 + 92) = (75 + 25) + 92$.

Independent Practice *For more practice, see Set A on p. 74.*

Name the property used.

9. $47 + 0 = 47$ **10.** $29 + 7 = 7 + 29$ **11.** $(1 + 9) + 2 = 1 + (9 + 2)$

12. $6 + (3 - 3) = 6$ **13.** $4 + 3 + 7 = 4 + 7 + 3$ **14.** $5 + (4 + 6) = (5 + 4) + 6$

Find each *n*. Name the property used.

15. $84 + n = 41 + 84$

16. $14 + (61 + n) = (14 + 61) + 99$

17. $n + 0 = 875$

18. $13 + 112 + 290 = 13 + 290 + n$

19. Show that $27 + (30 + 19) = (27 + 30) + 19$.

20. Mental Math Ed, Luisa, and Ann are building a model of a pool. Ed brings 45 tiles; Luisa, 20 tiles; and Ann, 30, tiles. How many tiles do they have for the model?

Mixed Review

21. Use words to state the rule for the table at the right.

A	B
3	15
4	20
5	25
6	30

22. Write 218 thousandths in standard form.

23. Round 3.146 to the nearest tenth.

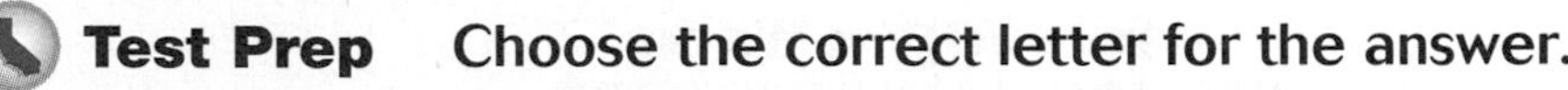

Test Prep **Choose the correct letter for the answer.**

24. (1–5) Sue has photos that are 3 inches wide by 4 inches long. She wants to put them on pages of an album that is 9 inches wide by 12 inches long. How many photos can she put on a page?

A 7 Photos **B** 8 photos **C** 9 photos **D** 12 photos

Use Homework Workbook 2-1.

Mental Math: Using Compatible Numbers and Compensation

California Content Standard *Mathematical Reasoning 1.0: Students make decisions about how to approach problems.*

Math Link In the previous lesson you learned about addition properties used to find sums. Looking for compatible numbers and using compensation will also help you find sums more quickly.

Compatible numbers are numbers that are easy to compute mentally.

Warm-Up Review

1. 13 + 9
2. 29 + 12
3. 39 + 11
4. 18 + 32
5. 45 + 30
6. (17 + 3) + 5
7. 70 + 48
8. 50 + 57
9. 57 − 30
10. 76 − 40
11. Thea saved $55 last week and $45 this week. She wants to save $279 for a new stereo. How much more does she need?

Word Bank

compatible numbers

compensation

Example 1

Find 19 + 25 + 11.

Look for compatible numbers. Add these numbers first.

19 + 25 + **11** = **30** + 25
= 55

Here's WHY It Works

19 + 25 + 11	**= 19 + 11 + 25**	Commutative Property
	= (19 + 11) + 25	Associative Property
	= 30 + 25	
	= 55	

Another useful technique is **compensation**. Deciding which number to adjust makes it easier to add or subtract. Compensate by changing the other number.

Example 2

47 + 16

47: Add 3. → 50

16: Subtract 3 to adjust. → 13

50 + 13 = 63

Here's WHY It Works

47 + 16 = 47 + 16 + 0
= 47 + 16 − 3 + 3
= (47 + 3) + (16 − 3)
= 50 + 13
= 63

Example 3

73 − 38

73: Add 2 to adjust. → 75

38: Add 2. → 40

75 − 40 = 35

Here's WHY It Works

73 − 38 = 73 − 38 + 0
= 73 − 38 − 2 + 2
= 73 + 2 − 38 − 2
= (73 + 2) − (38 + 2)
= 75 − 40
= 35

Guided Practice *For another example, see Set B on p. 72.*

Use mental math to find each sum or difference.

1. 9 + 1 + 25 **2.** 7 + 13 + 19 **3.** 80 + 36 + 20 **4.** 52 + 362 + 48

5. 29 + 37 **6.** 48 + 29 **7.** 67 + 14 **8.** 38 − 19 **9.** 89 − 37 **10.** 54 − 28

11. Sue earned $27, $36, and $14 on three days. Use mental math to find how much she earned in all.

Independent Practice *For more practice, see Set B on p. 74.*

Use mental math to find each sum or difference.

12. 8 + 2 + 45 **13.** 17 + 23 + 14 **14.** 70 + 66 + 30 **15.** 31 + 136 + 69

16. 34 + 49 **17.** 47 + 38 **18.** 35 + 28 **19.** 56 − 49 **20.** 63 − 34 **21.** 53 − 37

22. In 3 basketball games a player scored 16 points, 11 points, and 14 points. Use mental math to find how many points he scored in all.

23. Last month Ally saved $38 toward the cost of the coat shown in the advertisement at the right. Last week she earned $12 more. How much more money does she need to buy the coat?

24. Math Reasoning Explain how you could find the sum of 103 + 14 + 29 + 17 + 6 mentally.

Mixed Review

25. List 0.7, 0.89, and 0.685 in order from least to greatest.

26. Which addition property justifies that 1 + (9 + 3) = (1 + 9) + 3?

Write each rule using a variable.

27. 6 more than a number

28. Multiply a number by 3.

 **Test Prep** **Choose the correct letter for each answer.**

29. Round 7.894 to the nearest tenth. (1–6)

A 7 **C** 7.9
B 7.8 **D** 8

30. What is the value of 9 in 789,123? (1–3)

F 9 **H** 900
G 90 **J** 9,000

Relating Addition and Subtraction

Algebra

California Content Standard *Algebra and Functions 1.2 (🔑): Use a letter to represent an unknown number . . .*

Warm-Up Review

1. 619 + 100
2. 87 − 10
3. 49 + 10
4. 999 + 100
5. 2,986 − 100
6. Horace bought 3 movie tickets for $6 apiece. He paid with a $20 bill. How much change did he receive?

Math Link Sometimes one activity "undoes" another. Turning off the light undoes the result of turning on the light. Likewise, subtraction undoes addition.

Addition and subtraction are called **inverse operations.**

Word Bank

inverse operations

3 + 9 means 9 is added to 3. Subtraction can undo addition. 3 + 9 − 9 = 3	10 − 2 means 2 is subtracted from 10. Addition can undo subtraction. 10 − 2 + 2 = 10

You can also use the idea of inverse operations with algebraic expressions.

$n + 3$ means 3 is added to n. Subtracting 3 gets n alone. $n + 3 - 3 = n$	$n - 7$ means 7 is subtracted from n. Adding 7 gets n alone. $n - 7 + 7 = n$

Example 1

Tell what you would do to get the variable alone.

a. $x - 20$

Add 20.

b. $z + 100$

Subtract 100.

c. $47 + n$

Subtract 47.

Example 2

For each table, tell what you would do to find *n*. Then find *n*.

a.

Rule: Subtract 16.	
48	32
103	87
n	150

To find n, add 16 to 150.

$n = 166$

b.

Rule: Add 25.	
20	45
n	80
75	100

To find n, subtract 25 from 80.

$n = 55$

c.

Rule: Subtract 50.	
n	100
200	150
500	450

To find n, add 50 to 100.

$n = 150$

Guided Practice *For another example, see Set C on p. 72.*

Tell what you would do to get the variable alone.

1. $m + 50$ **2.** $a - 39$ **3.** $435 + z$ **4.** $360 + x$

For each table, tell what you would do to find *n*. Then find *n*.

5.

Rule: Add 26.	
31	57
100	126
n	310

6.

Rule: Subtract 80.	
100	20
n	70
339	250

7.

Rule: Add 1,000.	
n	2,000
1,500	2,500
2,000	3,000

Independent Practice *For more practice, see Set C on p. 74.*

Tell what you would do to get the variable alone.

8. $x - 45$ **9.** $n + 234$ **10.** $127 + z$ **11.** $x - 342$

For each table, tell what you would do to find *n*. Then find *n*.

12.

Rule: Subtract 26.	
83	57
200	174
n	357

13.

Rule: Add 80.	
100	180
n	316
420	500

14.

Rule: Subtract 500.	
n	500
800	300
1,385	885

15. Make a table that has the rule "Add 50." Complete the table when the values in the first column are 25, 50, and *n*.

16. Juan said, "I am thinking of a number. I get 17 if I subtract 77 from it." What is Juan's number?

Mixed Review

17. What is the value of 4 in 12.345?

18. Which addition property tells you that $3 + 9 = 9 + 3$?

19. Mental Math Use mental math to find $54 + 39$.

Test Prep Choose the correct letter.

20. (1–5) Carl lives 14 blocks north of Bernie. Sarah lives 6 blocks south of Bernie. Lars lives north of Sarah halfway between Carl and Sarah. How far does Lars live from Bernie?

A 4 blocks **B** 6 blocks **C** 10 blocks **D** 14 blocks

Use Homework Workbook 2-3.

Solving Addition and Subtraction Equations

Algebra

Warm-Up Review

1. 19 + 9 2. 30 + 129
3. 88 − 39 4. 50 − 23
5. 129 + 387
6. 766 − 124
7. 200 − 46
8. 500 + 347
9. June earned $5 an hour for working 30 hours. She also received an extra bonus of $25. How much did she receive in all?

California Content Standard *Algebra and Functions 1.1, (Grade 6) (🔑): Write and solve one-step linear equations in one variable.*

Math Link In the previous lesson you learned that using inverse operations will get a variable by itself. This idea and the properties of equality are used in solving equations.

Properties of Equality

You can add the same number to both sides of an equation.
You can subtract the same number from both sides of an equation.

Example 1

$$4 + 1 = 5$$
$$4 + 1 + 3 = 5 + 3$$
$$8 = 8$$

If you add 3 to both sides, the quantities on each side of the equal sign are still equal.

Example 2

$$7 + 5 = 12$$
$$7 + 5 - 3 = 12 - 3$$
$$9 = 9$$

If you subtract 3 from both sides, the quantities on each side of the equal sign are still equal.

Example 3

Solve $x + 6 = 17$.

$$x + 6 = 17$$
$$x + 6 - 6 = 17 - 6$$
$$x = 11$$

Check: $x + 6 = 17$
$$11 + 6 = 17$$
$$17 = 17$$

To get x by itself, subtract 6. But to keep the sides equal, subtract 6 from both sides of the equation.

Example 4

Solve $n - 189 = 200$.

$$n - 189 = 200$$
$$n - 189 + 189 = 200 + 189$$
$$n = 389$$

Check: $n - 189 = 200$
$$389 - 189 = 200$$
$$200 = 200$$

To get n by itself, add 189. But to keep the sides equal, add 189 to both sides.

Guided Practice *For another example, see Set D on p. 72.*

Solve each equation.

1. $x + 9 = 15$
2. $a - 3 = 10$
3. $50 = m + 12$
4. $50 = c - 48$
5. $y + 124 = 789$
6. $x - 429 = 654$

7. Todd wants to attend baseball camp. So far he has saved \$75 toward the total cost of \$300. Which equation below could you use to find n, the amount he needs to save?

$n - 75 = 300$ $n + 75 = 300$ $75 + 300 = n$

Independent Practice *For more practice, see Set D on p. 74.*

Solve each equation.

8. $x + 8 = 30$
9. $y - 5 = 40$
10. $m - 19 = 70$
11. $n + 65 = 255$
12. $x + 255 = 467$
13. $n - 351 = 584$
14. $365 = y + 211$
15. $s - 64 = 128$
16. $867 = x - 236$
17. Becky wants to buy a CD player costing \$129. She has saved \$175. Let x be the amount she will have left over. Which equation below could you use to find x?

$175 + 129 = x$ $175 - 129 = x$ $x - 175 = 129$

18. **Mental Math** If $599 + x - 599 = 7{,}869$, find x.

Mixed Review

19. Chris is taking a group of friends to a play to celebrate his birthday. Student tickets sell for \$3 and adult tickets sell for \$6. The total group will include 8 students and 2 adults. The group will also have to pay a total of \$15 for bus tickets. What is the total cost of the play tickets and the bus tickets?
20. Use a variable to write a rule for "Multiply a number by 2."
21. If $37 + n = 48 + 37$, find n. Name the property used.

Tell what you would do to get the variable alone.

22. $x - 320$
23. $n + 25$

Use mental math to find each sum or difference.

24. $24 + 6 + 18$
25. $60 + 29 + 40$
26. $86 - 49$

 **Test Prep** **Choose the correct letter for each answer.**

27. Which number is least? (1–4)

A 0.9 C 0.09
B 0.99 D 0.009

28. Round 1,325,000 to nearest million. (1–1)

F 1,000,000 H 1,400,000
G 1,300,000 J 2,000,000

Problem-Solving Skill:

Is an Estimate Enough?

Warm-Up Review

1. 3.5 ÷ 1
2. 3.5 × 3
3. 9.6 ÷ 3
4. 4.6 + 3.9
5. 7 + 4.5
6. 7.5 × 1
7. A train leaves the station every 20 minutes starting at 6:00 A.M. How many trains will have left before 10:00 A.M.?

California Content Standard *Mathematical Reasoning 2.5: Indicate the relative advantages of exact and approximate solutions to problems . . .*

Read for Understanding

Mandy, Zach, Linda, and Keith are starting out on the hiking trail at 8:00 A.M., as shown in the picture at the right. The trail is circular, ending where it begins. Mandy and Linda must be back at 1:00 P.M. to catch a bus to a movie. Zach and Keith need to be back for lunch between 11:30 A.M. and 1:30 P.M. Steve arrived late and started out on the trail half an hour after the others.

1. How long is the trail?
2. What time must Mandy and Linda be back?
3. What time did Steve start hiking?

Think and Discuss

Is an Estimate Enough?

Whether or not an estimate or an exact answer is needed depends on the situation.

Reread the paragraph at the top of the page.

4. Do Zach and Keith have to know exactly how much time they have to hike, or can they use an estimate?
5. Since Mandy and Linda have to be back at an exact time, how many miles per hour do they need to hike?
6. Give two examples from everyday life—one when an estimate is enough and one when an exact answer is needed.

Read the paragraph below to answer Exercises 1–6.

Refer to the sign at the right. Two groups of girls are hiking to a picnic site. The younger girls take the Blue Trail. They hike at an average speed of 3 miles per hour. The older girls take the Red Trail and hike at an average speed of 1 mile per hour.

Guided Practice

1. Which of the following is needed to calculate about how long it will take to hike the Red Trail?
   - **a.** an estimate of the trail length and the exact hiking speed
   - **b.** an estimate of the hiking speed and the exact trail length
   - **c.** the exact trail length and the exact hiking speed
   - **d.** an estimate of the trail length and an estimate of the hiking speed

Independent Practice

2. Which of the following describes how long it will take the girls to hike the Red Trail?
   - **a.** $5 + 1 = 6$
   - **b.** $5.3 \div 1 = 5.3$
   - **c.** $7.5 \div 3 = 2.5$
   - **d.** $5.3 \times 3 = 15.9$

3. Which best describes how long it will take to hike the Blue Trail?
   - **a.** Multiply the length of the trail by the hiking speed.
   - **b.** Divide the length of the trail by the hiking speed.
   - **c.** Add the length of the Red Trail and the Blue Trail.

4. Which number sentence best describes how long it will take to hike the Blue Trail?
   - **a.** $3 + 7.1 = 10.1$
   - **b.** $7.5 \div 3 = 2.5$
   - **c.** $5.3 + 7.1 = 12.4$

5. If the older girls start hiking on the Red Trail at 6 A.M., about what time will they arrive at the picnic area? Decide if an estimate or an exact answer is necessary. Explain how you found your answer.

6. **Math Reasoning** The groups decide to meet at the picnic area for lunch at 12:00 noon. What information do you need to find the time at which each group should start hiking so that they will reach the picnic area at exactly the same time? Explain.

Use Homework Workbook 2-5.

Diagnostic Checkpoint

Find each *n*. Name the property used.

1. (2-1) $17 + 0 = n$

2. (2-1) $55 + 8 = n + 55$

3. (2-1) $8 + (2 + 3) = (n + 2) + 3$

Use mental math to find each sum or difference.

4. (2-2) $8 + 15 + 22$

5. (2-2) $6 + 9 + 14$

6. (2-2) $24 + 19 + 111$

7. (2-2) $15 + 327 + 3$

8. (2-2) $68 - 17$

9. (2-2) $74 - 29$

10. (2-2) $46 - 24$

11. (2-2) $96 - 41$

Tell what you would do to get the variable alone.

12. (2-3) $x - 8$

13. (2-3) $x - 23$

14. (2-3) $x + 37$

Solve each equation.

15. (2-4) $x + 4 = 17$

16. (2-4) $b - 6 = 15$

17. (2-4) $35 = a + 23$

18. (2-4) $40 = y - 111$

19. (2-4) $z + 214 = 656$

20. (2-4) $m - 366 = 723$

21. (2-5) Taylor is going to the mall to buy some school supplies. She needs to buy some markers and at least two folders. Does Taylor have to know exactly how much money to take to the mall or can she use an estimate? Explain your answer.

22. (2-5) Osma needs to be home by 4:30 P.M. to get ready for soccer practice. She leaves a friend's house at 4:00 P.M. by bike. It is 2 miles from the friend's house to Osma's house. Osma estimates she will arrive at home on time if she rides 4 miles per hour or faster. Is she correct? Is an estimate enough in this situation?

23. (2-2) Last week Kyle earned \$28 raking leaves. This week he earned \$33. Use mental math to find out how much he earned altogether.

24. (2-4) Amanda wants to buy a pair of in-line skates. She has saved \$53 so far, and she needs \$75 to buy them. Which equation below could you use to find *n*, the amount she needs to save?

$n - 53 = 75$ $\quad$ $n + 53 = 75$ $\quad$ $53 + 75 = n$

Multiple-Choice Cumulative Review

Choose the correct letter for each answer.

1. It costs $9.95 for adults and $7.25 for children to go on a fishing trip. How much will it cost for Mr. Barnes and his eight-year-old son, Brian, to go?

A $14.50
B $16.20
C $17.20
D $24.45
E NH

2. Round 14.356 to the nearest tenth.

F 14.3
G 14.35
H 14.36
J 14.4
K NH

3. What is the *perimeter* of the figure shown below?

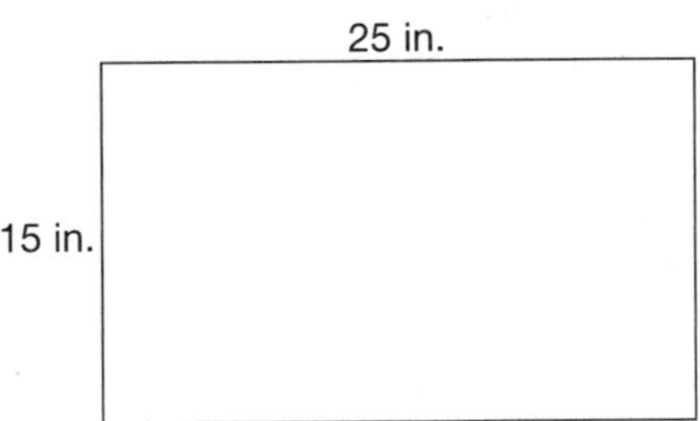

A 40 inches
B 65 inches
C 80 inches
D 125 inches

4. What can you do to get n alone in $n - 17$?

F Add 17.
G Subtract 17.
H Multiply by 17.
J Divide by 17.

5. Find a rule for the table. Let n represent any number in Column A.

A	B
4	28
10	34
12	36
15	39
18	42

A $n - 24$
B $24 \times n$
C $n \div 24$
D $n + 24$

6. Which is NOT correct?

F $0.25 > 0.24$
G $0.59 = 0.590$
H $0.453 < 0.45$
J $1.64 > 1.46$

7. Solve $n - 9 = 14$.

A $n = 5$
B $n = 15$
C $n = 23$
D $n = 126$

8. How might you find 24 + 42 + 36 by using compatible numbers?

F Add 6 + 4 + 2 first.
G Add 24 and 42 first.
H Add 42 and 36 first.
J Add 24 and 36 first.

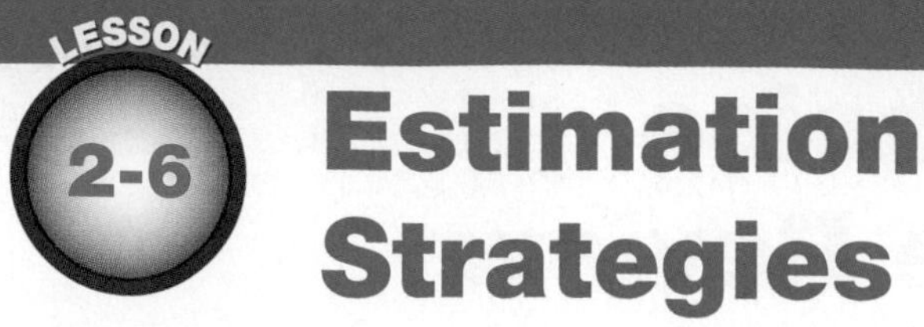

Estimation Strategies

California Content Standard *Number Sense 1.1: Estimate, round, and manipulate very large (e.g. millions) and very small (e.g., thousandths) numbers.*

Warm-Up Review

1. 40 + 70
2. 700 − 300
3. 4,000 + 7,000
4. 5 × 30
5. 7 × 20
6. Sue bought three items costing $17, $22, and $34. She also used a discount coupon for $10. She gave the clerk four $20 bills. How much change did she receive?

Word Bank

front-end estimation

clustering

Math Link You know that some situations do not require an exact solution. In this lesson you will learn some helpful estimation strategies.

One useful estimation strategy is to round each number to the largest place value involved in the numbers being used. Then use the rounded numbers to find an estimate.

Example 1

The school play was staged on three different days. Use the data at the right to estimate the total attendance.

Attendance	
Thursday	189
Friday	228
Saturday	312

Use **rounding.** Round each number to hundreds.

189 + 228 + 312

(rounds to) (rounds to) (rounds to)

200 + 200 + 300 = 700

The total attendance was about 700 people.

Another useful strategy is to estimate by using **front-end estimation.** First use the **front digits** to estimate. Then adjust the estimate to account for the remaining digits.

Example 2

Estimate 561 + 261 using front-end estimation.

Add the front digits in each number. 500 + 200 = 700

Adjust to account for the remaining digits. 61 + 61 is about 120.

700 + 120 = 820

561 + 261 is about 820.

 Additional Standard: Algebra and Functions 1.2 (🔑) *(See p. 39.)*

Clustering is another useful estimation strategy for certain addition problems. Clustering works when all the numbers are near the same number.

Example 3

Find 25 + 23 + 26 + 27.

Since the numbers all cluster around 25, the sum is about 4×25, or 100.

More Examples

A. Estimate 3,868 − 2,795 using rounding.

Round each to the nearest thousand.

$$\begin{array}{r} 3{,}868 \\ -\ 2{,}795 \\ \hline \end{array}$$

4,000 − 3,000 = 1,000

3,868 − 2,795 is about 1,000.

B. Estimate 939 − 582 using front-end estimation. Then adjust.

$$\begin{array}{r} 939 \\ -\ 582 \\ \hline \end{array}$$

900 − 500 = 400

Since 39 < 82, the difference is less than 400.

C. Estimate 789 − 356 using front-end estimation. Then adjust.

$$\begin{array}{r} 789 \\ -\ 356 \\ \hline \end{array}$$

700 − 300 = 400

Since 89 > 56, the difference is greater than 400.

Guided Practice *For another example, see Set E on p. 73.*

Estimate each sum or difference by rounding.

1. $\begin{array}{r} 78 \\ +\ 36 \\ \hline \end{array}$ **2.** $\begin{array}{r} 349 \\ +\ 254 \\ \hline \end{array}$ **3.** $\begin{array}{r} 648 \\ -\ 191 \\ \hline \end{array}$ **4.** $\begin{array}{r} 2{,}098 \\ +\ 7{,}198 \\ \hline \end{array}$

Estimate each sum or difference by using front-end estimation. Then adjust to find a closer estimate.

5. $\begin{array}{r} 137 \\ +\ 753 \\ \hline \end{array}$ **6.** $\begin{array}{r} 342 \\ +\ 287 \\ \hline \end{array}$ **7.** $\begin{array}{r} 289 \\ -\ 158 \\ \hline \end{array}$ **8.** $\begin{array}{r} 5{,}640 \\ -\ 4{,}522 \\ \hline \end{array}$

Estimate each sum by using clustering.

9. 29 + 31 + 32 **10.** 49 + 52 + 51 + 48 **11.** 24 + 23 + 26 + 27 + 24

12. 18 + 21 + 21 + 19 + 20 + 19 **13.** 49 + 51 + 48 + 49 + 52 + 51 + 50

14. One week a waiter made $78, $92, and $61 in tips. Estimate his total tips for the week.

Independent Practice *For more practice, see Set E on p. 75.*

Estimate each sum or difference by rounding.

15. $\begin{array}{r} 23 \\ +\ 87 \\ \hline \end{array}$ **16.** $\begin{array}{r} 167 \\ +\ 580 \\ \hline \end{array}$ **17.** $\begin{array}{r} 419 \\ -\ 283 \\ \hline \end{array}$ **18.** $\begin{array}{r} 4{,}308 \\ +\ 2{,}621 \\ \hline \end{array}$

19. 43 + 71 + 89 **20.** 867 + 129 **21.** 712 − 199 **22.** 4,308 − 1,321

Estimate each sum or difference by using front-end estimation. Then adjust to find a closer estimate.

23. $\begin{array}{r} 237 \\ +\ 237 \\ \hline \end{array}$ **24.** $\begin{array}{r} 138 \\ +\ 615 \\ \hline \end{array}$ **25.** $\begin{array}{r} 419 \\ -\ 322 \\ \hline \end{array}$ **26.** $\begin{array}{r} 8{,}324 \\ -\ 3{,}169 \\ \hline \end{array}$

27. 597 − 278 **28.** 648 + 321 **29.** 11,211 − 7,902 **30.** 276 + 538

Estimate each sum by using clustering.

31. 49 + 52 + 51 **32.** 39 + 41 + 42 + 38 **33.** 29 + 31 + 28 + 32 + 31

34. 61 + 59 + 60 + 62 + 61 + 59 **35.** 99 + 102 + 101 + 98 + 97 + 100

36. At a yard sale Geneva collected $321, $212, and $498 on three different days. Estimate the total amount she collected.

37. Algebra Estimate the value of $x + y$ if x = $487 and y = $784.

38. Mental Math If the maximum amount Cheri can spend is $100, how does she know that she cannot buy two items costing $54 and $59?

Mixed Review

39. Bill scored 27 points, 13 points, and 38 points in three different games. Use mental math to find his total score for the three games.

Solve each equation.

40. $x + 30 = 70$ **41.** $x - 25 = 100$ **42.** $267 = x + 138$

 **Test Prep** **Choose the correct letter for each answer.**

43. Which digit in 3,457,128 is in the ten thousands place? (1–1)

A 3 **C** 5

B 4 **D** 7

44. Round 2.73 to the nearest one. (1–6)

F 2 **H** 2.8

G 2.7 **J** 3

 Use Homework Workbook 2-6.

Using Expressions

Algebra

Warm-Up Review

1. 7×100 **2.** 4×145

3. $45 \div 9$ **4.** $79 + 400$

5. $98 \div 7$ **6.** $56 \div 8$

7. $1{,}000 - 139$

8. $278 + 778$

9. A board is 78 inches long. It must be trimmed to a length of 6 feet. How many inches must be cut from the board?

California Content Standard *Algebra and Functions 1.2 (🔑): Use a letter to represent an unknown number; write and evaluate simple algebraic expressions in one variable by substitution.*

Math Link You have already used variables in previous lessons. In this lesson you will learn to write expressions using variables. You will also evaluate expressions with variables.

Word Bank

expression
evaluate an expression

A mathematical phrase made up of a variable or combination of variables and/or numbers and operations is called an **expression.**

To **evaluate an expression** with variables, substitute values for each variable and simplify.

Example 1

Evaluate $6n$ when $n = 3$, $n = 100$, and $n = 345$.

When $n = 3$,
$6n = 6 \times 3$
$= 18$

When $n = 100$,
$6n = 6 \times 100$
$= 600$

When $n = 345$,
$6n = 6 \times 345$
$= 2{,}070$

Sometimes you need to translate words into an expression.

Example 2

Write an expression for each word phrase.

Word Phrase	Expression
the product of a number and 100	$100 \times n$ or $100n$
the quotient of a number divided by 10	$\frac{n}{10}$ or $n \div 10$
7 less than a number	$n - 7$
12 increased by a number	$12 + n$

Sometimes different word phrases can be translated into the same expression. For example, both "the sum of a number and 50" and "a number increased by 50" can be written as $x + 50$.

Guided Practice *For another example, see Set F on p. 73.*

Evaluate each expression for $x = 18$, $x = 45$, and $x = 99$.

1. $x - 7$ **2.** $10x$ **3.** $\frac{x}{3}$ **4.** $x + 500$

Write an expression.

5. 50 more than a number

6. 10 subtracted from a number

7. the product of 100 and a number

8. 50 divided by a number

9. Paul translated "10 increased by a number" as $10 + x$, while Lee Ann translated it as $x + 10$. What property tells you that both are correct?

Independent Practice *For more practice, see Set F on p. 75.*

Evaluate each expression for $x = 9$, $x = 45$, and $x = 108$.

10. $x + 19$ **11.** $100x$ **12.** $\frac{x}{9}$

13. $101 + x$ **14.** $12x$ **15.** $200 - x$

16. $x + 198$ **17.** $x + x$ **18.** $1{,}000 - x$

Write each word phrase as an expression.

19. a number increased by 90

20. 48 subtracted from a number

21. a number multiplied by 75

22. a number divided by 10

23. Write an expression for $25 off the sticker price p.

24. Juan translated "a number divided by 5" as $\frac{5}{n}$. Was he correct? Explain.

25. Ellie is 12 years old. Write an expression that tells her age n years ago.

26. Barry is n years old. His sister is 5 years older. Write an expression for his sister's age.

Math Reasoning **Write an expression for each of the following phrases.**

27. the number of inches in x feet

28. the number of ounces in y pounds

Mixed Review

29. Ally bought a skirt, a sweater, a pair of slacks, and a jacket. Refer to the sale prices shown. Use clustering to estimate the total cost of the four items.

skirts $23

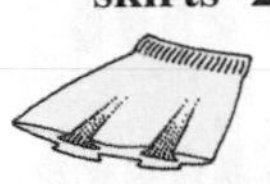

jackets $26

slacks $24

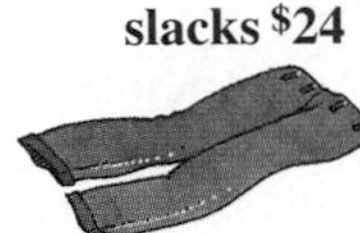

sweaters $27

Find the value of each underlined digit.

30. $\underline{7}$,897,125,000 **31.** 2,3$\underline{6}$0,000,000 **32.** 13.1$\underline{7}$6

Find each *n*. Name the property used.

33. $15 + 38 + 125 = 15 + 125 + n$ **34.** $n + 0 = 139$

Solve each equation.

35. $x + 42 = 89$ **36.** $x - 155 = 200$ **37.** $x + 259 = 985$

Estimate each sum or difference by rounding.

38. $57 + 62 + 89$ **39.** $7{,}891 + 1{,}781$ **40.** $787 - 213$

Test Prep **Choose the correct letter for each answer.**

41. (2-4) Jeremy is planning to buy a new television costing $399. He already has saved $250. If *n* is the amount he still needs to save, which equation could you use to represent the problem situation?

A $n - 250 = 399$

B $n + 250 = 399$

C $n = 250 + 399$

D $250n = 399$

42. (1-8) Refer to the table and the graph at the right to find how many miles the car would travel in $3\frac{1}{2}$ hours.

F 100 miles

G 150 miles

H 175 miles

J 200 miles

Number of hours	Number of miles
1	50
2	100
3	150
4	200

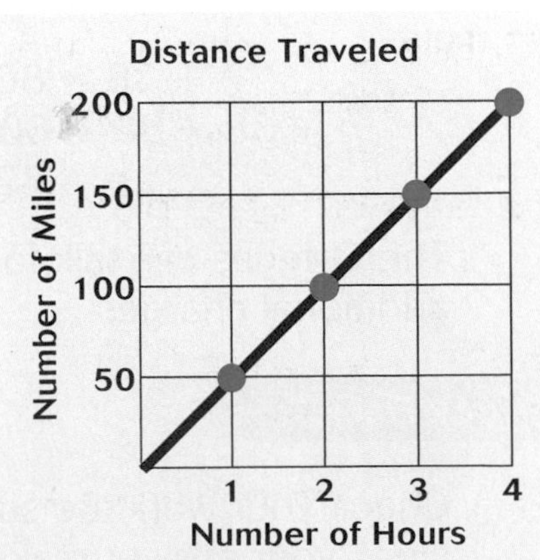

LESSON 2-8

Understand
Plan
Solve
Look Back

Problem-Solving Strategy:
Write an Equation

 **California Content Standard** *Algebra and Functions 1.1 (Grade 6) (key): Write and solve one-step linear equations in one variable.*

Warm-Up Review

1. 90 − 41 2. 97 − 49
3. 3,000 − 358
4. 100 − 28
5. 350 − 49 6. 934 − 500
7. A crate holds 8 boxes of flashlights. Each flashlight sells for $5. How many boxes of flashlights are in 12 crates?

Example 1

So far this month the Ortegas have used their cellular phone for 38 minutes. How many more minutes can they use the phone before they have to pay additional charges? Refer to the information at the right.

60 minutes free usage per month
Each additional minute: $0.25

Understand

What do you need to find?

You need to find how many more minutes the Ortegas can use their phone this month without paying additional charges.

Plan

How can you solve the problem?

You can write an equation. Remember that an equation is a number sentence with a variable, such as n.

Solve

Let n be the number of remaining minutes the Ortegas can talk without paying an additional charge. Write an equation using n. Then solve for n.

number of remaining minutes they can talk without additional charges

$$n + 38 = 60$$
$$n + 38 - 38 = 60 - 38 \leftarrow$$
$$n = 22$$

Property of Equality: Subtract 38 from each side.

The Ortegas can talk for 22 more minutes without paying additional charges.

Look Back

Check your work. Be sure the equation describes the problem. Does your answer make sense?

Additional Standards: Algebra and Functions 2.0 (Grade 4); Mathematical Reasoning 2.0, 3.2 (See p. 39.)

Guided Practice

Write an equation to solve each exercise. Then solve the equation. Refer to the information on page 58 for problems 1 and 2.

1. Peggy uses the same phone plan as the Ortegas. So far this month she has used up 49 minutes. How many more minutes can she talk without paying additional charges?

2. The Yager family used 77 minutes this month. For how many additional minutes will they be charged this month?

Independent Practice

3. One long distance phone plan allows 100 minutes of free usage per month before users pay an additional charge. The Pipers have used 64 long distance minutes this month. How many more long distance minutes can they use before paying an additional charge?

4. A football stadium holds 5,000 people. At a football game, 4,125 seats were occupied. Game tickets sell for $12 apiece. How many seats were empty?

5. A family is saving money to take a vacation. They plan to save $2,000. If they have saved $1,348 so far, how much more do they need to save?

Mixed Review

Try these or other strategies to solve each exercise. Tell which strategy you used.

Problem-Solving Strategies

- *Draw a Diagram*
- *Work Backward*
- *Make a List*
- *Solve a Simpler Problem*

6. Heather is buying a new blouse and a skirt. The blouse comes in white, blue, or yellow. The skirt comes in tan, black, or gray. List all possible choices she can make.

7. The total price for a plane ticket is $450, including taxes of $18 and a travel agent's fee of $10. What was the cost of the ticket before the taxes and the travel agent's fee?

Use Homework Workbook 2-8.

Adding and Subtracting Greater Whole Numbers

Warm-Up Review

1. 78 − 59
2. 38 + 89
3. 123 + 547
4. 761 − 184
5. 150 − 46
6. 900 − 64
7. 78 + 67 + 34
8. Mr. Piper bought four items costing \$55, \$23, \$78, and \$149. He had three \$100 bills in his wallet. Did he have enough to pay for all the items? If not, how much more did he need?

California Content Standard *Number Sense 3.1 (Grade 4) (🔑): Demonstrate an understanding of, and the ability to use, standard algorithms for the addition and subtraction of multidigit numbers. Also, Mathematical Reasoning 2.0 (See p. 39.)*

Math Link You already know how to add and subtract using one- and two-digit numbers. In this lesson you will learn how to add and subtract greater numbers involving 3 or more digits.

Example 1

Six of the seven largest national parks in the United States are in Alaska. Their areas are given in the table at the right. Use the table to find the areas of the two largest parks. What is the total area of these two parks?

Find 13,018 + 11,756.

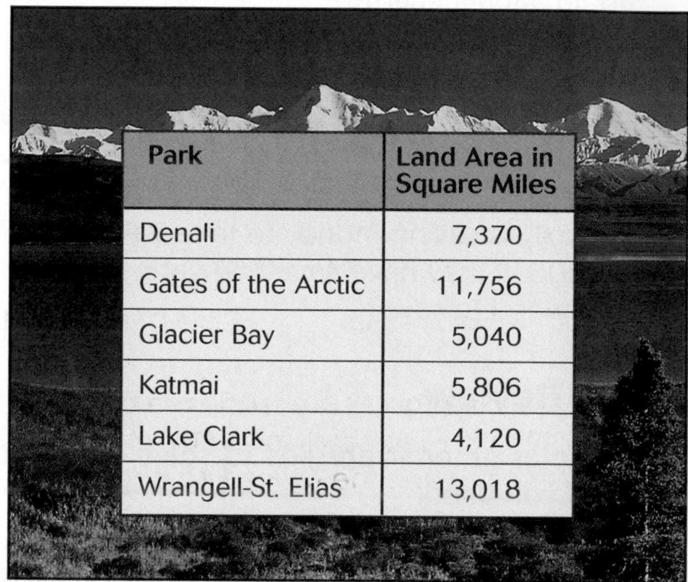

Park	Land Area in Square Miles
Denali	7,370
Gates of the Arctic	11,756
Glacier Bay	5,040
Katmai	5,806
Lake Clark	4,120
Wrangell-St. Elias	13,018

Step 1 Add the ones. Regroup if you can. 14 ones = 1 ten 4 ones

$$\begin{array}{r} \overset{1}{} \\ 13{,}018 \\ +\ 11{,}756 \\ \hline 4 \end{array}$$

Step 2 Add the tens. Regroup if you can.

$$\begin{array}{r} 13{,}0\overset{1}{1}8 \\ +\ 11{,}756 \\ \hline \end{array}$$

Step 3 Add the hundreds. Regroup if you can.

$$\begin{array}{r} 13{,}0\overset{1}{1}8 \\ +\ 11{,}756 \\ \hline \end{array}$$

Step 4 Continue to add.

$$\begin{array}{r} 13{,}0\overset{1}{1}8 \\ +\ 11{,}756 \\ \hline \end{array}$$

Check by estimating. (Round to the nearest thousand.)
13,000 + 12,000 = 25,000. The answer is reasonable because 24,774 is close to 25,000.

Additional Standard: Algebra and Functions 1.2 (See p. 39.)

Example 2

Find 762 − 395.

Step 1 Subtract the ones. Decide if you need to regroup.	**Step 2** Subtract the tens. Decide if you need to regroup.	**Step 3** Subtract the hundreds.
762 − 395 = 7	762 − 395 = 67	762 − 395 = 367

Add to check your answer: 367 + 395 = 762.

More Examples

A. 6,578 + 135 + 5,902 = 12,615

B. 3,622 − 1,487 = 2,135

C. $40,742 − $18,633 = $22,109

$22,109 + $18,633 = $40,742 Add to check the answer.

Guided Practice *For another example, see Set G on p. 73.*

1. 3,525 + 1,927

2. 75,050 + 7,850

3. 2,127 − 429

4. 2,632 + 867 + 803

5. 418 + 10,251 +4,136

6. 83,588 − 47,564

7. How much larger is the land area of Wrangell-St. Elias National Park than the land area of Gates of the Arctic National Park? Use the table on the preceding page.

Independent Practice *For more practice, see Set G on p. 75*

8. 9,092 + 4,160

9. 7,577 − 642

10. 63,835 − 43,632

11. $1,070 + 2,678

12. 36,489 − 516

13. 5,457 + 380

14. 640 + 187 +389

15. 3,476 + 275 + 652

16. 4,723 + 3,982 + 728

17. 4,261 − 302

18. 2,118 − 364

19. 44,426 − 43,386

20. 26,391 + 37,298

21. 40,280 + 6,321

22. 86,040 − 56,972

23. Algebra Find the value of n if $n + 295 = 5{,}000$.

24. Mental Math Diane has saved $1,294 toward her goal of $2,000. How much more does she need to save in order to reach 1,300? Then how much more does she need to save in order to reach $2,000? How much more does she need to save in all?

25. Use the data given in the table at the right. The United States has 12,380 miles of coastline. How much longer is the total coastline of Canada than that of the United States?

26. How much longer is the coastline of Canada than the total of the next three countries shown in the table?

Country	Total Miles of Coastline
Canada	151,485 mi
Indonesia	33,999 mi
Russia	23,396 mi
Philippines	22,559 mi

Mixed Review

27. Marge bought some plants to put in her garden. She planted half of them before it started to rain. Then she gave 5 plants to her neighbor. She still has 7 plants left. How many plants did she buy?

Use mental math to find each sum or difference.

28. $19 + 1 + 66$ **29.** $89 + 63$ **30.** $86 - 38$

31. For the table, tell what you would do to find n. Then find n.

Rule: Add 75.	
25	100
50	125
75	150
n	200

Estimate each sum or difference by using front-end estimation. Then adjust to find a closer estimate.

32. $261 + 489$ **33.** $8{,}892 - 7{,}612$ **34.** $715 - 393$

Evaluate each expression for $x = 31$, $x = 48$, and $x = 212$.

35. $x - 20$ **36.** $50x$ **37.** $500 - x$

Test Prep **Choose the correct letter for each answer.**

38. (2-7) Which expression represents "25 subtracted from a number"?

A $n - 25$ **C** $25n$
B $25 - n$ **D** $25 + n$

39. (1-6) Round 2,345,678 to the nearest thousand.

F 2,300,000 **H** 2,345,000
G 2,400,000 **J** 2,346,000

Use Homework Workbook 2-9.

Adding and Subtracting Decimals

California Content Standard *Number Sense 2.1 (🔑): Add, subtract, . . . with decimals; . . . and verify the reasonableness of the results.*

Math Link In earlier lessons you have been adding and subtracting whole numbers. In this lesson, you will add and subtract decimals.

Warm-Up Review

Write each number in expanded form.

1. 5,458 **2.** 13,125

Give the value of each underlined digit.

3. 3.7<u>8</u>5 **4.** 65.<u>2</u>6

5. Alice wants to buy a printer costing $179 and a printer stand costing $49. She has saved $90. How much more money does she need?

Example 1

Find 4.73 + 3.54.

Step 1 Line up the decimal points.

$$\begin{array}{r} 4.73 \\ +\ 3.54 \\ \hline \end{array}$$

Step 2 Add the hundredths. Regroup if you can.

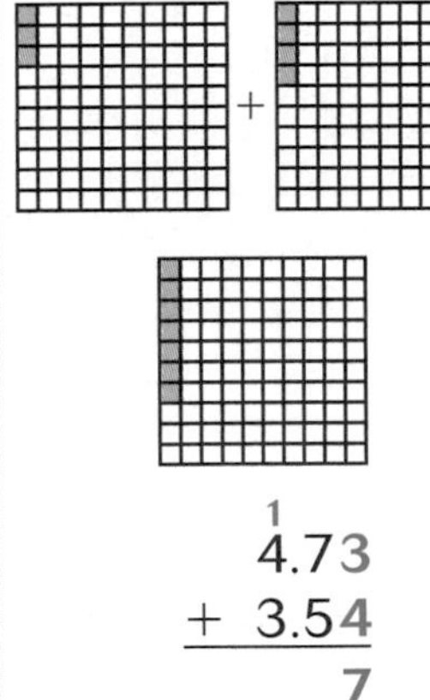

$$\begin{array}{r} \overset{1}{4}.73 \\ +\ 3.54 \\ \hline 7 \end{array}$$

Step 3 Add the tenths. Regroup if you can. 12 tenths = 1 one 2 tenths

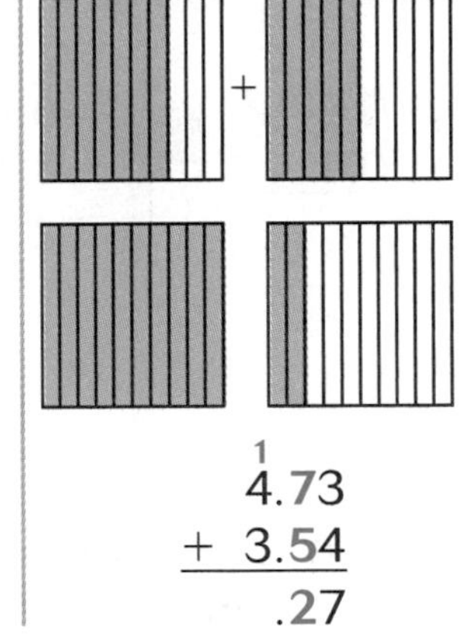

$$\begin{array}{r} \overset{1}{4}.73 \\ +\ 3.54 \\ \hline .27 \end{array}$$

Step 4 Add the ones. Place the decimal point in your answer.

$$\begin{array}{r} \overset{1}{4}.73 \\ +\ 3.54 \\ \hline 8.27 \end{array}$$

Check by estimating to the nearest whole number. 4.73 rounds up to 5 and 3.54 rounds up to 4. So, 5 + 4 = 9. The answer is reasonable because 8.27 is less than 9. The answer should be less than 9 since both addends were rounded up.

Here's WHY It Works

4.73 = 4 + 0.7 + 0.03
+ 3.54 = 3 + 0.5 + 0.04

Decimals can be written in expanded form.

= 7 + 1 + 0.2 + 0.07
= (7 + 1) + (0.2 + 0.07)
= 8 + 0.27
= 8.27

0.7 + 0.5 = 1.2 and 1.2 = 1 + 0.2.
Use the associative property.
0.2 = 0.20 and 0.20 + 0.07 = 0.27.

Example 2

Find 53.261 − 53.214.

Step 1 Line up the decimal points.	Step 2 Subtract the thousandths. Decide if you need to regroup.	Step 3 Subtract the hundredths and tenths. Decide if you need to regroup.	Step 4 Subtract the whole numbers. Place a decimal point in the answer.
53.261 − 53.214	5 11 53.261 − 53.214 7	5 11 53.261 − 53.214 047	5 11 53.261 − 53.214 0.047

Check by estimating. 53 − 53 = 0. The answer is reasonable because 0.047 is close to the estimate.

Example 3

Find 5.2 + 3.18.

$$\begin{array}{r} 5.2 \\ +\ 3.18 \\ \hline \end{array} \Rightarrow \begin{array}{r} 5.20 \\ 3.18 \\ \hline 8.38 \end{array}$$

You can use zeros as placeholders to help keep the place values lined up.

Example 4

Find 0.675 + 0.4.

$$\begin{array}{r} 0.675 \\ +\ 0.4 \\ \hline \end{array} \Rightarrow \begin{array}{r} 0.675 \\ 0.400 \\ \hline 1.075 \end{array}$$

More Examples

A. (regrouping: 15; 7 5 17)

$$\begin{array}{r} 86.7 \\ -\ 29.8 \\ \hline 56.9 \end{array}$$

B. (regrouping: 9; 3 10 10)

$$\begin{array}{r} 3.400 \\ -\ 1.327 \\ \hline 2.073 \end{array}$$

Guided Practice *For another example, see Set H on p. 73.*

1. $\begin{array}{r} 3.58 \\ +\ 7.41 \\ \hline \end{array}$ **2.** $\begin{array}{r} 39.67 \\ +\ 21.46 \\ \hline \end{array}$ **3.** $\begin{array}{r} 73.45 \\ -\ 53.52 \\ \hline \end{array}$ **4.** $\begin{array}{r} 344.75 \\ -\ 0.12 \\ \hline \end{array}$

5. 10.4 − 5.28 **6.** 19.87 − 13.017 **7.** 19.3 + 3.85

8. Deena has saved $5.00, $3.50, $3.00, and $4.75 from baby-sitting. She wants to buy a CD for $18.99, tax included. How much more money does she need to buy the CD?

Independent Practice

For more practice, see Set H on p. 75.

9. 772.09 + 48.78
10. 957.47 + 70.62
11. 28.39 + 52.66
12. 125.2 + 97.98
13. 0.984 + 0.179
14. 83.5 − 3.2
15. 72.69 − 66.40
16. 75.77 − 8.42
17. 1.79 − 0.09
18. 9.14 − 3.724
19. 8.02 + 83.48
20. 12.17 + 0.01 + 0.64
21. 202.7 + 6.43
22. 64.0 − 53.2
23. 426.1 − 30.2
24. 211.8 − 3.64
25. 7.21 − 4.9
26. 1.98 − 0.899
27. 321.80 − 24.90
28. Refer to the table at the right. What is the difference in weight between the record bass and the record whitefish?
29. What is the difference in weight between the record catfish and the record salmon?
30. **Algebra** If $n + 23.5 = 100$, find n.
31. **Mental Math** Find the sum of $0.05, $0.95, $0.75, $0.25, and $2.23.

Some World-Record Weights

Fish	Weight
Bass	10.09 kg
Catfish	43.99 kg
Perch	2.15 kg
Salmon	42.18 kg
Trout	19.10 kg
Whitefish	5.92 kg

Mixed Review

32. A scientist weighed three samples and found the weights to be 0.098 gram, 0.79 gram, and 0.005 gram. Which sample weighed the most?

Write each word phrase as an expression.

33. a number decreased by 28
34. the product of a number and 60
35. 7,376 + 1,459
36. 6,129 − 896

Test Prep Choose the correct letter for each answer.

37. (2-6) Which is the best estimate for 789 + 124 if you use rounding?
    - A 700
    - B 800
    - C 900
    - D 1000
38. (2-7) Evaluate $200 - x$ for $x = 55$.
    - F 145
    - G 155
    - H 245
    - J 255
    - K NH

Problem-Solving Application:

Using Money

 **California Content Standard** *Number Sense 2.1 (🔑): Add, subtract, . . . with decimals; . . . and verify the reasonableness of the results.*

Warm-Up Review

1. \$17.95 + \$ 34.50
2. \$ 195.50 − \$ 43.75
3. \$10,000 − \$499.50
4. \$2,189.45 + \$438.50
5. Joe bought a book for \$14.95 and a CD for \$8.95. He gave the clerk \$50. How much change did he get.

Example

Use the data at the right. The prices include sales tax.
Sam hopes to join the cross-country track team at school. He plans to use the \$48.00 he earned raking leaves to buy a sweat shirt, sweat pants, and a pair of sneakers at The Runner's Place. Does Sam have enough money to buy all of these items?

SALE
Sweat pants
Sweat shirts
\$9.50 each

FAMOUS
BRAND
SNEAKERS
\$27.90

Understand

What do you know?

You know the price of each item Sam wants to buy.

Plan

How can you solve the problem?

Add the costs of all the items to find the total cost.

Solve

$$\begin{array}{r} \$\ 9.50 \\ 9.50 \\ +\ 27.90 \\ \hline \$\ 46.90 \end{array}$$

It will cost Sam \$46.90 to buy the items he wants, so he has enough money.

Look Back

How can you use estimation to be sure your total is reasonable?

Additional Standard: Mathematical Reasoning 2.6 (See p. 39.)

Guided Practice

Use the information at the right and on page 66 to solve Exercises 1–4. All prices include sales tax.

SALE
Jogging Suits
$42.50
T-SHIRTS
$8.00
or
3 for $20.00

1. How much would it cost to buy a jogging suit and a pair of sneakers?

2. Nick plans to buy three T-shirts, a pair of sweat pants, and two pairs of sneakers. How much will he spend?

Independent Practice

3. Bonnie is thinking of buying either a jogging suit or sweat pants and a sweat shirt. How much would she save if she buys the sweat pants and the sweat shirt instead of the jogging suit?

4. Mrs. Perez plans to buy two T-shirts and a sweat shirt. How much would she save by buying three T-shirts instead?

5. The Runner's Place had total sales of $19,369.65 last week. Their goal was $20,000. By how much did they miss their goal?

6. On Monday Mr. Brandstadt had a balance of $1,234.89 in his checking account. Then he wrote checks for $79.81, $215.46, and $654.20. On Tuesday he made a deposit of $150. How much was in his checking account after the deposit?

7. **Math Reasoning** Sara wants to buy a pair of track shoes that cost $49.95, a stopwatch that costs $24.99, and two packages of socks at $4.99 each. She has $70 and a $10-off coupon. Does she have enough money to buy these items?

Mixed Review

8. Jill is covering a table top with square tiles that are 6 inches on a side. The table is 24 inches long by 18 inches wide. How many tiles does she need?

9. In one month there were only 4 days with rainfall. The measurements were 0.7 inch, 0.65 inch, 1.3 inches, and 0.09 inch. Which amount was greatest? Which amount was the least? What was the total rainfall?

(Use Homework Workbook 2-11.)

Diagnostic Checkpoint

Complete. For Exercises 1–3, use the words from the Word Bank.

Word Bank

associative property
commutative property
identity property
compatible numbers
compensation
inverse operations
expression

1. (2-2) ____________ are numbers that can be used to find sums and differences mentally.

2. (2-7) A mathematical phrase made up of a variable or combination of variables and/or numbers and operations is called an ____________.

3. (2-1) The ____________ says that the order in which numbers are added does not change the sum.

Estimate each sum or difference by rounding.

4. (2-6) 562 + 156 **5.** (2-6) 3,748 + 5,246 **6.** (2-6) 8,469 − 3,271

Estimate each sum or difference by using front-end estimation. Then adjust to find a closer estimate.

7. (2-6) 7,422 + 3,458 **8.** (2-6) 792 − 431 **9.** (2-6) 3,567 − 2,382

10. (2-7) Write an expression for two less than a number.

11. (2-7) Evaluate $20x$ for $x = 8$, $x = 12$, and $x = 56$.

12. (2-9) 75,249 + 8,695 **13.** (2-9) 6,134 − 2, 318 **14.** (2-9) 27,406 − 15,838

15. (2-10) 14.85 + 2.3 **16.** (2-10) 23.9 − 13.47 **17.** (2-10) 346.12 − 125.8

18. (2-8) Alex sold her skateboard for $63 and her kneepads for $12. She has $91. How much money did she have before she sold them? Write an equation to solve the problem. Then solve the equation.

19. (2-11) Mark has $2.00 to buy fruit bars. He wants to buy two bars for $0.79 each and one bar for $0.53. How much money does he need to buy the bars? Does he have enough money?

20. (2-11) Suzanne bought 3 shirts for $7.95 each and a pair of shorts for $12.99. She paid $2.58 in sales tax. She gave the sales clerk $40. How much change did she receive?

Chapter 2 Test

Find each n. Name the property used.

1. $26 + (432 + n) = (26 + 432) + 1{,}001$
2. $78 + 2{,}173 = n + 78$

Use mental math to find each sum or difference.

3. $8 + 15 + 22$
4. $78 + 24$
5. $92 - 67$

6. Tell what you would do to get the letter alone in $y - 85$.

Solve each equation.

7. $a - 9 = 23$
8. $t + 7 = 22$

9. Estimate 4,825 − 2,364 by rounding.

10. Estimate 3,481 + 5,216 by using front-end estimation. Then adjust to find a closer estimate.

11. Evaluate $187 - x$ when $x = 9$, $x = 48$, and $x = 117$.

12. $\begin{array}{r} 3{,}726 \\ +8{,}091 \\ \hline \end{array}$
13. $\begin{array}{r} 34{,}226 \\ -12{,}713 \\ \hline \end{array}$
14. $\begin{array}{r} 52{,}129 \\ +27{,}341 \\ \hline \end{array}$

15. $23.904 - 8.593$
16. $0.202 + 4.84$
17. $11.2 - 0.38$

18. Mia has $20 to spend at the mall. She wants to spend $3.95 for a magazine and $13.95 for a book, tax included. To determine if she has enough money, does she need to find an exact total or is an estimate enough? Explain.

19. Last year the Boonton Animal Shelter found homes for 796 cats and dogs. They found 385 homes for cats. How many homes did they find for dogs? Write an equation to solve the problem. Then solve the equation.

20. Rosa wants to buy a small tape player for $25.95 plus $1.50 tax. If Rose has $28.00, does she have enough money?

Multiple-Choice Chapter 2 Test

Choose the correct letter for each answer.

1. Which property could you use to find n?

$$0 + n = 249$$

- **A** Associative Property
- **B** Commutative Property
- **C** Identity Property
- **D** None of these

2. If you use compensation to find 38 + 43, which method is correct?

- **F** Add 2 to 38. Then subtract 2 from 43 to adjust.
- **G** Add 2 to 38. Then add 2 to 43 to adjust.
- **H** Subtract 2 from 38. Then subtract 2 from 43 to adjust.
- **J** Subtract 3 from 38. Then subtract 3 from 43 to adjust.

3. What would you do to get the n alone in $15 + n$?

- **A** Add 15.
- **B** Subtract 15.
- **C** Multiply by 15.
- **D** Divide by 15.

4. Solve $35 + x = 103$.

- **F** $x = 3$
- **G** $x = 68$
- **H** $x = 72$
- **J** $x = 138$

5. Evaluate $162 + x$ when $x = 17$.

- **A** 17
- **B** 145
- **C** 179
- **D** 324

6. Find 64,186 − 32,673.

- **F** 31,000
- **G** 31,513
- **H** 32,093
- **J** 96,859

7. Kate wants to buy a skirt that costs \$16.99 and a blouse that costs \$14.50. Tax is included. To find how much change she would get from \$50, which should she do?

- **A** Estimate the sum of \$16.99 and \$14.50.
- **B** Estimate the difference between \$16.99 and \$14.50.
- **C** Find the sum of \$16.99 and \$14.50. Then subtract the sum from \$50.
- **D** Add \$16.99, \$14.50, and \$50.

8. How might you find 29 + 31 + 32 + 28 by clustering?

- **F** Add 20 + 30 + 30 + 20.
- **G** Add 20 + 20 + 20 + 20.
- **H** Multiply 4×30.
- **J** Multiply 3×30.

9. Which expression represents the product of nine and a number?

- **A** $n + 9$
- **B** $9n$
- **C** $\frac{n}{9}$
- **D** $n - 9$

10. **A T-shirt costs $8, so n T-shirts cost $8n$. Use the expression to find the cost of 4 T-shirts.**

F $2

G $4

H $14

J $32

---

11. **Steven wants to run 14 miles this week to train for baseball season. He has run 9 miles so far. Which equation could be used to find how many miles he needs to run to meet his goal?**

A $m - 9 = 14$

B $m + 9 = 14$

C $9m = 14$

D $m + 14 = 9$

---

12. **Before a family left on a trip, they found that their odometer read 33,897 miles. After the trip it read 35,065 miles. How many miles did they travel?**

F 1,168 miles

G 2,278 miles

H 68,852 miles

J 68,962 miles

---

13. **Find 12,490 + 423,314.**

A 410,824

B 411,184

C 435,704

D 435,804

E NH

---

14. **On her camping trip, Lily drove 36.3 miles, bicycled 8.7 miles, and hiked 3.4 miles. How many miles did she travel altogether?**

F 39.7 miles

G 45.0 miles

H 48.4 miles

J 51.8 miles

---

15. **Find 9.91 − 0.802.**

A 0.189

B 0.9108

C 1.89

D 9.108

---

16. **Mary and Karen are saving money for a trip to an amusement park. An all-day ticket for one person costs $39.50. Mary has saved $19.50. Karen has saved $23.75. If they combine their money, how much more do they need?**

F $15.75

G $35.75

H $55.25

J They have enough money.

---

17. **Solve $n - 8 = 25$.**

A $n = 17$

B $n = 30$

C $n = 33$

D $n = 200$

---

18. **Find 6.32 + 0.181.**

F 6.139

G 6.4

H 6.5

J 6.501

Reteaching

Set A (pages 40–41)

If $(n + 4) + 11 = (4 + 15) + 11$, find *n*. Name the property used.

$(n + 4) + 11 = (4 + 15) + 11$

$(4 + n) + 11 = (4 + 15) + 11$

$n = 15$

The Commutative Property is used.

Remember you can use the Associative, Commutative, and Identity Properties to make addition easier.

Find each *n*. Name the property used.

1. $n + (4 - 4) = 5$

2. $(1 + 6) + 2 = 1 + (n + 2)$

Set B (pages 42–43)

Find 46 − 17 by using compensation.

46 − 17

Add 3 to adjust. | Add 3.

49 − 20 = 29

So, 46 − 17 = 29.

Remember you can change one number to make it easier to add or subtract, but you need to *compensate* by adjusting the other number.

Use compensation to find each sum or difference.

1. 72 − 29 **2.** 64 − 47

Set C (pages 44–45)

Tell what you would do to get the variable alone in $n + 8$.

$n + 8$ means 8 is added to *n*.
Subtracting 8 gets *n* alone.
$n + 8 - 8 = n$

Remember that addition and subtraction are inverse operations.

Tell what you would do to get the variable alone.

1. $x - 18$ **2.** $z + 29$

3. $169 + a$ **4.** $m - 278$

Set D (pages 46–47)

Solve $x - 45 = 32$.

$x - 45 + 45 = 32 + 45$ Add 45 to both sides.

$x = 77$

Remember you can add the same number to both sides of an equation or subtract the same number from both sides.

Solve each equation.

1. $n - 9 = 15$ **2.** $x + 8 = 34$

3. $y + 16 = 47$ **4.** $m - 31 = 56$

Set E (pages 52–54)

Estimate 429 + 282.

Add the front digits in each number.

400 + 200 = 600

Adjust to account for the remaining digits.

29 + 82 is about 110.

600 + 110 = 710

So, 429 + 282 is about 710.

Remember you can estimate sums and differences by using rounding or by using front-end estimation and then adjusting for the remaining digits.

Estimate each sum or difference by using front-end estimation. Then adjust to find a closer estimate.

1. $\begin{array}{r} 243 \\ +526 \\ \hline \end{array}$ **2.** $\begin{array}{r} 5{,}243 \\ -2{,}126 \\ \hline \end{array}$ **3.** $\begin{array}{r} 6{,}472 \\ +1{,}819 \\ \hline \end{array}$

Set F (pages 55–57)

Evaluate $n - 9$ when $n = 26$.

$n - 9 = 26 - 9$

$= 17$

Remember you can substitute values for each variable and simplify to evaluate an expression.

Evaluate each expression for $x = 10$, $x = 29$, and $x = 204$.

1. $5x$ **2.** $x + 32$ **3.** $300 - x$

Set G (pages 60–62)

Find 26,438 + 5,364.

$$\begin{array}{r} {}^{1}\ \ {}^{1}{}^{1}\ \ \\ 26{,}438 \\ +\ \ 5{,}364 \\ \hline 31{,}802 \end{array}$$

Remember to regroup whenever you can.

1. 18,501 + 2,659 **2.** 8,365 − 2,905

3. 23,850 − 2,433 **4.** 27,019 + 15,984

5. 13,988 + 10,752 + 3,462 + 1,641

Set H (pages 63–65)

Find 6.28 − 3.7.

You can use a zero as a placeholder.

$$\begin{array}{r} {}^{5}\ {}^{12}\ \\ \not{6}.\not{2}8 \\ -3.70 \\ \hline 2.58 \end{array}$$

Remember to line up the decimal points before you add or subtract.

1. 1.45 + 3.76 **2.** 17.2 − 3.5

3. 13.26 − 12.3 **4.** 6.8 + 3.92

5. 14.7 + 8.43 **6.** 32.9 − 14.85

More Practice

Set A (pages 40–41)

Find each n. Name the property used.

1. $17 + 0 = n$
2. $55 + 8 = n + 55$
3. $8 + (2 + 3) = (n + 2) + 3$
4. Name the property used: $x + (28 - 28) = x$
5. To find the sum of 18, 16, and 4, Josie wrote $18 + (16 + 4) = 18 + 20 = 38$. Sam wrote $(18 + 16) + 4 = 34 + 4 = 38$. Which property tells you that either method is correct?

Set B (pages 42–43)

Use mental math to find each sum or difference.

1. $1 + 52 + 99$
2. $56 - 44$
3. $3 + 97 + 19$
4. $91 + 17 + 83$
5. $95 - 28$
6. $69 + 31 + 11$
7. A wall map was made from three widths of cardboard placed side by side. The widths were 17 inches, 25 inches, and 13 inches. How wide was the wall map?

Set C (pages 44–45)

Tell what you would do to get the variable alone.

1. $n + 64$
2. $m - 35$
3. $x + 129$
4. $y + 594$
5. $z - 641$
6. $a - 306$
7. Tina said, "I am thinking of a number. I get 52 if I add 14 to it." What is Tina's number?

Set D (pages 46–47)

Solve each equation.

1. $x - 8 = 12$
2. $x + 37 = 49$
3. $13 + j = 35$
4. Mrs. Drum bought tires for $252, a car vacuum cleaner for $24, and some antifreeze. Altogether she spent $300. How much did she spend for the antifreeze?

Set E (pages 52–54)

Estimate each sum or difference by rounding.

1. 520 + 433
2. 6,308 − 3,200
3. 836 − 221
4. 1,306 + 891

Estimate each sum or difference by using front-end estimation. Then adjust to find a closer estimate.

5. 832 − 315
6. 1,397 + 2,492
7. $229 + $313
8. $534 − $218
9. In 1994 about 8,628,170 people visited Great Smoky Mountain National Park, 4,364,320 visited the Grand Canyon, and 3,962,120 visited Yosemite. About how many people visited these parks that year?

Set F (pages 55–57)

Evaluate each expression for $x = 7$, $x = 56$, and $x = 147$.

1. $x + 35$
2. $250 - x$
3. $9x$
4. $\frac{x}{7}$

Write an expression for each word phrase.

5. ten less than a number
6. a number increased by six
7. Let t be the number of telephone calls Marian made last week. Marian made five more telephone calls this week than she made last week. Write an expression for the number of telephone calls Marian made this week.

Set G (pages 60–62)

1. 2,129 + 7,341
2. 7,423 − 7,349
3. 55,482 + 2,628
4. Hector played a video game three times. His scores were 28,321, 16,274, and 25,016 points. How much greater was his highest score than his lowest score?

Set H (pages 63–65)

1. 205.64 + 34.02
2. 10.91 − 8.44
3. 65.18 + 12
4. If Winona's family walked 2.5 miles on Friday, 3.75 miles on Saturday, and 4.25 miles on Sunday, how many miles did they walk in all?

TEST PREP

Problem-Solving: Preparing for Tests

Choose the correct letter for each answer.

1. Cathy is arranging four pictures on a shelf. She puts the boat between the airplane and the dog. Then she puts the cat in the leftmost position. Which picture is third from the left?

A Airplane
B Boat
C Cat
D Dog

Tip
Use one of the strategies to solve this problem.
- *Draw a Diagram*
- *Use Logical Reasoning*

2. On a trip to the zoo, Terry spent $32. Mike spent $4 less than Terry. Which number sentence could you use to find the total, *t*, that both people spent?

F $t = 32 + (32 + 4)$
G $t = 32 + (32 - 4)$
H $t = 32 - (32 + 4)$
J $t = 32 - (32 - 4)$
K NH

Tip
To check your answer, do the computation and see if your answer choice makes sense.

3. Sam is putting a braid border around a rectangular rug with a 24-ft *perimeter*. Which of these is most reasonable for the longer dimension of the rug?

A 2 feet
B 4 feet
C 8 feet
D 24 feet

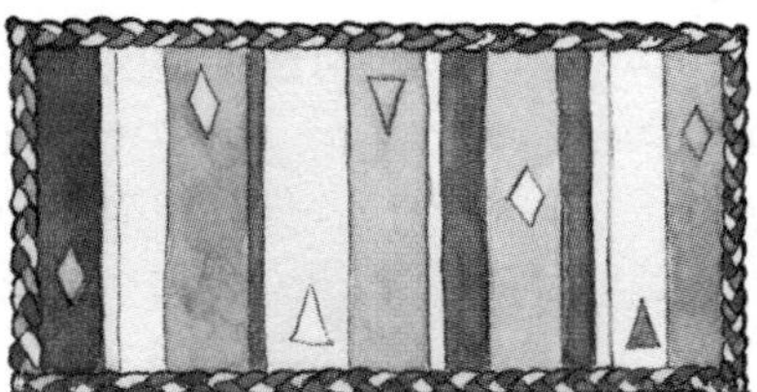

Tip
Make a Diagram to help you solve this problem. Draw several rectangles that have perimeters of 24 feet.

4. **The pictograph shows the numbers of different kinds of trees planted.**

Trees Planted in Our Town

Maple	
Spruce	
Elm	
Pine	
Other	

Key: = 20 trees

How many more pine trees than spruce trees were planted?

F 15 **J** 30

G 20 **K** NH

H 25

---

5. **The house numbers on Lyle's side of the street are 420, 422, 424, and 426. Which set would most likely be the numbers of the houses across the street?**

A 410, 412, 414, 416

B 421, 423, 425, 427

C 429, 430, 431, 432

D 428, 430, 434, 436

---

6. **Harriet has $72.00 in her savings account. She plans to save about $5 a week for 20 weeks. Which is a reasonable amount for Harriet to have in her account after 3 weeks?**

F About $170

G About $150

H About $90

J About $70

K NH

---

7. **Art has $20.00. He pays $6.50 admission to an amusement park and another $4.75 on lunch. He plans to spend the rest of his money on rides, which cost $2.45 each. Which is the best estimate for the number of ride tickets Art can buy?**

A 7

B 5

C 3

D 2

---

8. **A carton of books weighed 8.54 kg. John put a book weighing 1.6 kg into the carton and removed 3 books weighing 1.2 kg each. Which number sentence could be used to find the final weight of the carton?**

F $8.54 + 1.6 + 3.6 = ■$

G $8.54 + 1.6 - (3 \times 1.2) = ■$

H $(8.54 + 1.6) \times 3 - 1.2 = ■$

J $8.54 - 1.6 + (3 \times 1.2) = ■$

---

9. **In a dart game, Doris scored 132, 186, and 214 points. To the nearest hundred, what is the best estimate of her point total for the three games?**

A 300 **C** 500

B 400 **D** 600

---

10. **Fran had 24 tomatoes and 15 cucumbers from her garden. She gave half the tomatoes and about half of the cucumbers to her neighbor. How many tomatoes did she have left?**

F About 12

G Exactly 12

H About 20

J Exactly 20

Multiple-Choice Cumulative Review

Choose the correct letter for each answer.

Number Sense

1. Which figure has the *greatest* fractional part shaded?

A 

B

C

D

2. Which number sentence is true?

F $14.40 > 14.04$

G $3.11 < 0.311$

H $0.082 = 0.820$

J $55.12 < 55.021$

3. Which fraction is equivalent to $\frac{1}{2}$?

A $\frac{3}{8}$

B $\frac{2}{5}$

C $\frac{6}{12}$

D $\frac{5}{7}$

4. What is 77.54 rounded to the nearest tenth?

F 77.4

G 77.5

H 77.6

J 80

K NH

5. Tad earned $6.00 pulling weeds and $4.50 washing windows. Then he received $10.00 as a gift. He wants to buy a computer game that costs $24.99. How much more money does he need to buy the game?

A $4.99

B $4.54

C $4.49

D $4.39

6. Chen went shopping last Saturday. He drove 0.25 miles to the bookstore and 1.25 miles to the mall. If he returned home on the same route, how far did he drive altogether?

F 1.5 miles

G 2 miles

H 2.25 miles

J 3 miles

7. Which of the following is the product of 230 and 14?

A 3,220

B 2,220

C 322

D 244

E NH

8. $34.09 - 5.7 =$

F 39.73

G 29.02

H 28.39

J 2.839

K NH

Algebra and Functions

9. **Solve $8 + n = 19$.**

A $n = 8$ **C** $n = 21$

B $n = 11$ **D** $n = 27$

10. **Which property is used?**
$6 + (17 + 39) = (6 + 17) + 39$

F Associative Property

G Commutative Property

H Identity Property

J None of these

11. **Which expression represents a number divided by 2?**

A $n - 2$

B $2n$

C $\frac{2}{n}$

D $\frac{n}{2}$

12. **Find the value of $n + 17$ when $n = 24$.**

F 7 **H** 31

G 17 **J** 41

13. **Amanda's bedroom is 9 feet by 11 feet. One wall is 8 feet high and 11 feet long. How many square feet of wallpaper are needed to cover that wall?**
(Area = length × height)

A 88 square feet

B 78 square feet

C 38 square feet

D 19 square feet

Measurement and Geometry

14. **Mario's garden is 12 yards in length. What is the length in feet?**

F 144 ft

G 120 ft

H 36 ft

J 15 ft

15. **Which figure appears to be congruent to Figure *WXYZ*?**

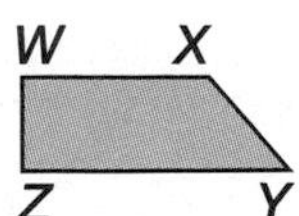

A

B

C

D

16. **An aquarium holds 30 liters of water. How many milliliters is this?**
(1L = 1,000 mL)

F 300 mL

G 3,000 mL

H 30,000 mL

J 300,000 mL

17. **Max was born May 1, 1985. How many *weeks* old was he on May 1, 1997? (1 year = 52 weeks)**

A 624 weeks **C** 572 weeks

B 612 weeks **D** 520 weeks

CHAPTER 3

Using Data and Statistics

3-1 Organizing and Displaying Data
3-2 Double Bar Graphs
3-3 Coordinate Graphing
3-4 Problem-Solving Skill: Understanding Line Graphs
3-5 Reading and Making Line Graphs
3-6 Problem-Solving Strategy: Make a Graph
3-7 Mean, Median, and Mode
3-8 Problem-Solving Application: Using Other Graphs

Diagnosing Readiness

In Chapter 3, you will use these skills:

A Adding or Subtracting Mentally

(pages 42–43)

Find each sum or difference mentally.

1. 66 + 860 + 34
2. 920 − 20 − 180
3. 750 − 25 − 125
4. On a field trip Bart collected 23 leaves, Nadia collected 67 leaves, Mary collected 29 leaves, and Hank collected 51 leaves. How many leaves were collected in all?

B Ordering

(pages 6–7)

Write the numbers in each set from least to greatest.

5. 62, 27, 57, 91
6. 3.82, 3, 3.2, 3.5
7. Five students in Mr. Greer's art class measure 44 inches, 51 inches, 51.5 inches, 44.9 inches, and 50 inches tall. Arrange the heights in order from shortest to tallest.

C Comparing

(pages 6–7)

Write >, <, or = for each ●.

8. $8 + 3$ ● $12 - 6$

9. $388 - 161$ ● $60 + 60$

10. $620 + 400$ ● $945 - 50$

11. $43 + 78$ ● $65 + 51$

12. Kara has a dog that weighs 68 pounds, a cat that weighs 18 pounds, and a pot belly pig that weighs 87 pounds. Does the pig weigh more or less than the dog and cat combined?

D Division by 5 or by 10

(Grade 4)

13. $120 \div 5$

14. $1,640 \div 10$

15. $680 \div 10$

16. $1,095 \div 5$

17. $65 \div 5$

18. $2,100 \div 10$

19. Ten teachers handed out a total of 890 homework assignments. How many assignments did each teacher hand out if each handed out the same amount?

E Locating Points on a Number Line

(Grade 4)

Create a number line for each exercise, using only multiples of 5. Plot each set of points.

20. 400, 408, 418, 403

21. 2,811, 2,814, 2,809, 2,821

22. 35, 27, 38, 29, 33

F Adding Whole Numbers and Decimals

(pages 60–65)

Find the sum.

23. $2 + 33 + 15 + 7 + 8.8$

24. $1.2 + 2.3 + 1.8 + 2.1$

25. $125 + 132 + 127 + 133 + 136 + 130 + 138 + 136$

26. Daniel donated 18 shirts, 6 jeans, 4 jackets, 7 pairs of dress pants, and 6 hats to a local charity. How many articles of clothing did he donate?

To the Family and Student

Looking Back	Chapter 3	Looking Ahead
In Grade 4, students learned how to collect data and evaluate data.	**Using Data and Statistics** In this chapter, students will learn how to organize and display data and determine measures of central tendency.	In Grade 6, students will learn how to interpret data and analyze statistical results.

Math and Everyday Living

Opportunities to apply the concepts of Chapter 3 abound in everyday situations. During the chapter, think about how data and statistics can be used to solve a variety of real-world problems. The following examples suggest just a few of the many situations that could launch a discussion about data and statistics.

Math in the Budget Last year's total utility expense for your home was approximately $2,100. Predict a monthly utility budget for the upcoming year.

Math in the Neighborhood In your neighborhood you notice the following colors of cars parked on the street:

white, blue, white, red, blue, tan, silver, silver, black, white, black, tan, green, green, white

What is the mode of the data? Explain what the mode represents.

Math and the Census On the U.S. Census form you must list every person in your household by name and age. The ages of people living in your friend's home are 2 years, 5 years, 9 years, 35 years, 41 years, and 76 years. What is the range of ages of people living in your friend's home?

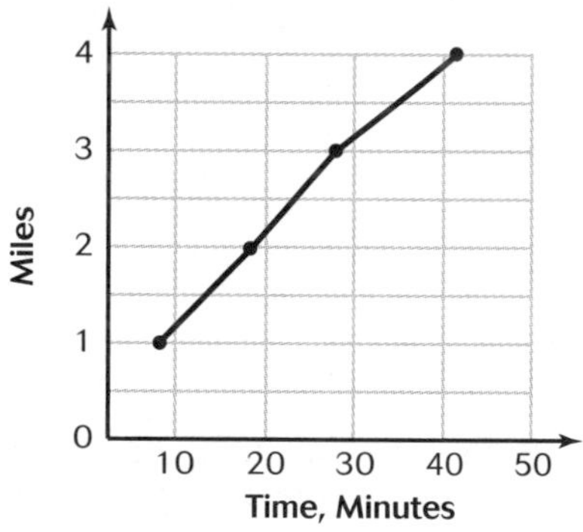

Math and Fitness To help you train for an upcoming 4-mile race, you ran 4 miles and recorded the time at each mile marker. You then graphed the results as shown above. Your goal is to complete the race in 37 minutes. Use the graph to pinpoint the place where you need to increase your pace to obtain your goal.

Math and Conserving Water Your family wants to reduce its monthly water bill. You collected the following data regarding shower usage.

Shower Usage

Person	Shower Times per Week	
You	A.M.	70 min
	P.M.	20 min
Mom	A.M.	100 min
	P.M.	40 min
Dad	A.M.	60 min
	P.M.	15 min
Brother	A.M.	100 min
	P.M.	100 min

Display the data in a double bar graph and use it to recommend a way to conserve water.

 California Content Standards in Chapter 3 Lessons*

	Teach and Practice	Practice
Algebra and Functions		
1.1 Use information taken from a graph . . . to answer questions about a problem situation.		3-3, 3-4, 3-5, 3-6
1.2 (🔑) Use a letter to represent an unknown number; write and evaluate simple algebraic expressions in one variable by substitution.		3-3, 3-5
Statistics, Data Analysis, and Probability		
1.1 Know the concepts of mean, median, and mode; compute and compare simple examples to show that they may differ.	3-7	
1.2 Organize and display single-variable data in appropriate graphs and representations (e.g., histogram, circle graphs) and explain which types of graphs are appropriate for various data sets.	3-1, 3-2, 3-5, 3-6, 3-8	
1.4 (🔑) Identify ordered pairs of data from a graph and interpret the meaning of the data in terms of the situation depicted by the graph.	3-3, 3-4, 3-5	
1.5 (🔑) Know how to write ordered pairs correctly; for example, (*x*, *y*).	3-3	

	Teach and Practice	Practice
Mathematical Reasoning		
2.3 Use a variety of methods such as words, numbers, symbols, charts, graphs, tables, diagrams, and models to explain mathematical reasoning.	3-4, 3-6, 3-8	3-1, 3-2, 3-5
3.2 Note the method of deriving the solution and demonstrate a conceptual understanding of the derivation by solving similar problems.		3-6, 3-7

* The symbol (🔑) indicates a key standard as designated in the Mathematics Framework for California Public Schools. Full statements of the California Content Standards are found at the beginning of this book following the Table of Contents.

LESSON 3-1

Organizing and Displaying Data

California Content Standard *Statistics, Data Analysis, and Probability 1.2: Organize and display single-variable data in appropriate graphs and representations and explain which types of graphs are appropriate for various data sets.*

Math Link You have seen different kinds of graphs in books and newspapers. Now you will learn more about these graphs and how to use them.

Warm-Up Review

Write the numbers in order from least to greatest.

1. 3,856 3,843 3,645
2. 14,865 14,799 14,709
3. 47.86 47.835 47.9
4. Of 100 people surveyed, 79 answered *yes* to the question. How many did not answer *yes?*

Example 1

Surveys are used to collect all kinds of information. For a school project, John asked some friends a survey question. His question, answer choices, and tallied responses are shown at the right.

What Color is Your Toothbrush?

Red	||||
Blue	|||
Purple	~~||||~~
Other	||

John organized the data he collected as shown below.

Toothbrush Colors

Response	Number
Purple	5
Red	4
Blue	3
Other	2

A **frequency table** shows the total responses for each choice as a number.

Toothbrush Colors

X			
X	X		
X	X	X	
X	X	X	X
X	X	X	X
Purple	**Red**	**Blue**	**Other**

A **line plot** shows each response by marking *X*s on a line above the choice.

Example 2

Jeans are sometimes sold by the waist size, measured in inches. The sizes in stock at one store are listed at the right.

31, 32, 41, 44,
33, 21, 22, 32,
36, 37, 42, 29

A **stem-and-leaf plot** is one way to organize numerical data.

Step 1
List the numbers in order from least to greatest.
21, 22, 29, 31, 32, 32, 33, 36, 37, 41, 42, 44

Step 2
List the tens digits in order (20, 30, 40) to the left of the vertical line.

Stem	Leaves
2	1 2 9
3	1 2 2 3 6 7
4	1 2 4

Step 3
For each tens digit, record the ones digits, in order, to the right of the vertical line.

Additional Standards: Mathematical Reasoning 2.3 (See p. 83.)

Sometimes, data is best displayed in a graph. Different kinds of data require different kinds of graphs. Data that expresses a count or a measure or a frequency is often displayed in a **pictograph** or a **bar graph**. Comparing the number of symbols or the lengths of the bars allows us to compare the data.

Word Bank

- survey
- frequency table
- line plot
- stem-and-leaf plot
- pictograph
- bar graph
- scale

Example 3

For six months, Jeremy kept track of how many library books he read. Choose a graph to display this data.

Books Read

Jan.		8
Feb.		11
Mar.		5
Apr.		2
May		6
June		1

A pictograph is easy to use when some of the data involves multiples of the same number. In this case, the numbers are small and some of them are even, so each whole symbol represents 2 books. Odd numbers are represented by using a half symbol following the whole symbols.

Record of Books Read

Month	Books
Jan.	
Feb.	
Mar.	
Apr.	
May	
June	

= 2 books

Example 4

Choose a graph to display the data below.

Students Who Read for Fun Every Day

Country	Number of Students per 100
Taiwan	17
Ireland	40
France	39
United States	29
Israel	43
Canada	36
Korea	11

The numbers in this data are not as easily represented by symbols and half symbols. In a bar graph, the **scale** can be made to accommodate the numbers.

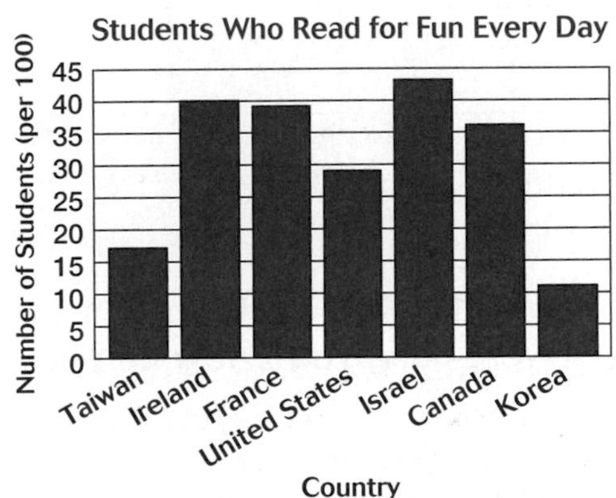

Guided Practice

For another example, see Set A on p. 114.

Use the line plot and the frequency table on page 84 for Exercises 1 and 2.

1. How many people were surveyed?

2. How many more people have purple toothbrushes than blue toothbrushes?

Use the stem-and-leaf plot on page 84 for Exercises 3 and 4.

3. **Mental Math** How many pairs of jeans are in stock? How can you tell?

4. How does the stem-and-leaf plot show that there is more than one pair of jeans in stock with a waist size of 32 inches?

5. List the following data in order from least to greatest: 11, 24, 39, 37, 18, 19, 10, 22, 47, 49, 18, 22, 34

6. Make a stem-and-leaf plot for the data in Exercise 5.

Use the pictograph and the bar graph on page 85 for Exercises 7 and 8.

7. In the pictograph, what does each book symbol represent? What does each half-book symbol represent? How can you tell how many books Jeremy read in February?

8. In the bar graph, what does the longest bar represent? What does the shortest bar represent?

Independent Practice *For more practice, see Set A on p. 116.*

Use the line plot and frequency table below for Exercises 9–11.

Toothbrushing Habits

```
          X
          X         X
          X         X
 X        X         X
 X        X         X
 X        X         X
---------------------------
Once     Twice    More than
a day    a day    twice a day
```

Toothbrushing Habits	
Response	**Number**
Once a day	3
Twice a day	6
More than twice a day	5

9. **Mental Math** How many people were surveyed? How can you tell?

10. **Mental Math** How many more people brushed twice a day than once a day?

11. **Math Reasoning** How are the line plot and the frequency table the same? How are they different?

Use the data at the right for Exercises 12 and 13.

12. Make a stem-and-leaf plot for the data. For one-digit numbers, use a zero in the tens place.

13. How does the stem-and-leaf plot show that two or more students wore jeans the same number of times?

Number of Times Each Student Wore Jeans in One Month

28, 20, 11, 9, 6, 21, 28, 15, 16, 17, 11, 11, 5, 21, 2, 9, 22, 15, 6, 12, 15, 17, 20, 21

Use the following tables of data for Exercises 14–19.

Favorite Things to Do on Saturdays	
Activity	**Students**
Soccer	9
Library	8
Board games	4
Museum	2
Movies	12

Number of School Days in a Year	
Country	**Days**
Germany	240
Haiti	175
Korea	251
Mexico	200
United States	180
Zimbabwe	225

Suppose you were assigned to make one pictograph and one bar graph using the data above.

14. Which set of data would you choose for the pictograph? Why?

15. In the pictograph you make, what would each symbol represent?

16. In your pictograph, would you use half of a symbol? Why or why not?

17. In your bar graph, what would the longest bar represent?

18. In your bar graph, what would the shortest bar represent?

19. Math Reasoning Which set of data would be just as easy to represent in either a bar graph or a pictograph? Explain.

Mixed Review

20. Use the ad at the right to decide how much Carmen would save by buying the 3-piece matched outfit instead of the individual pieces.

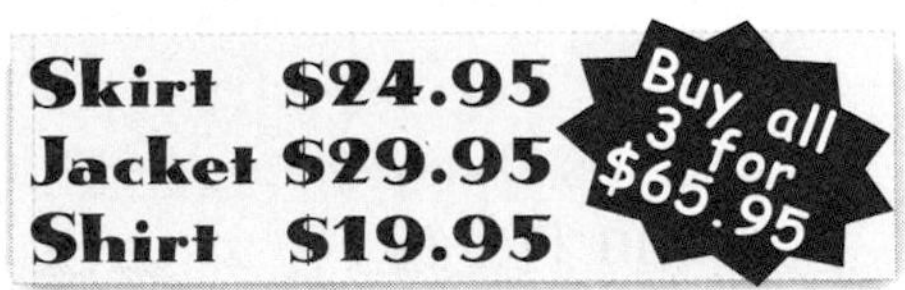

21. 5,356 + 83,245 **22.** 67,000 − 8,915 **23.** 32.45 − 21.23 **24.** 5.67 + 3.89

25. Algebra Evaluate $n - 27$ for $n = 45$. **26. Algebra** Evaluate $n + 132$ for $n = 98$.

Test Prep Choose the correct letter for each answer.

27. Algebra Solve $x - 18 = 25$
(2-4)

A $x = 7$ **C** $x = 17$

B $x = 43$ **D** $x = 33$

28. Algebra *Solve* $n + 43 = 57$.
(2-4)

F $n = 14$ **H** $n = 4$

G $n = 100$ **J** $n = 90$

Double Bar Graphs

California Content Standard *Statistics, Data Analysis, and Probability 1.2: Organize and display single-variable data in appropriate graphs and representations and explain which types of graphs are appropriate for various data sets.*

Warm-Up Review

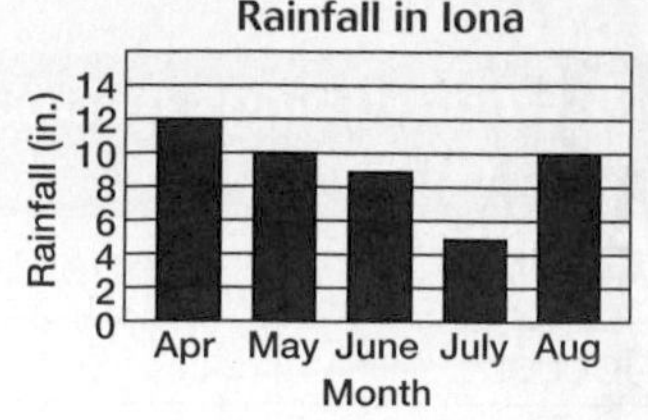

Tell which month had the rainfall described.

1. 12 inches **2.** 9 inches

3. The most **4.** The least

5. Same amount as May

Math Link You have used bar graphs to display data. Now you will learn to use double bar graphs to display two related data sets.

A **double bar graph** uses two different shaded or colored bars to display related data in pairs. It is then easy to compare the data from the two sets by comparing the bars.

The graph below gives information about the costs of three different bicycles during two different years. The key shows which colored bar represents which year. The **axes** represent the brand and the cost.

Word Bank

double bar graph
axis (pl., axes)

Example 1

Did the bicycles cost more or less in 1990 than in 1994?

For Bicycle B, the bar for 1990 is taller than the bar for 1994. For Bicycles D and S, the bar for 1990 is shorter than the bar for 1994.

- Bicycle B cost more in 1990 than in 1994.
- Bicycles D and S cost less in 1990 than in 1994.

Bicycle Costs

1990
1994
COST
$500
$400
$300
$200
$100
$0
Bicycle B
Bicycle D
Bicycle S
BICYCLE BRAND

Example 2

In both years, which bicycle was the most expensive and which was the least expensive?

For Bicycle B, both bars are taller than the bars for the other bicycles. For Bicycle D, both bars are shorter than the bars for the other bicycles.

- Bicycle B was the most expensive bike in both years.
- Bicycle D was the least expensive bike in both years.

Additional Standard: Mathematical Reasoning 2.3 (See p. 83.)

Example 3

The table at the right shows the bicycle equipment donated by two grades when Elm School held an equipment drive. Make a double bar graph using the data in the table.

Equipment Donated		
Equipment	**Grade 5**	**Grade 6**
Helmets	15	12
Water bottles	16	16
Air pumps	4	3
Reflector strips	30	24

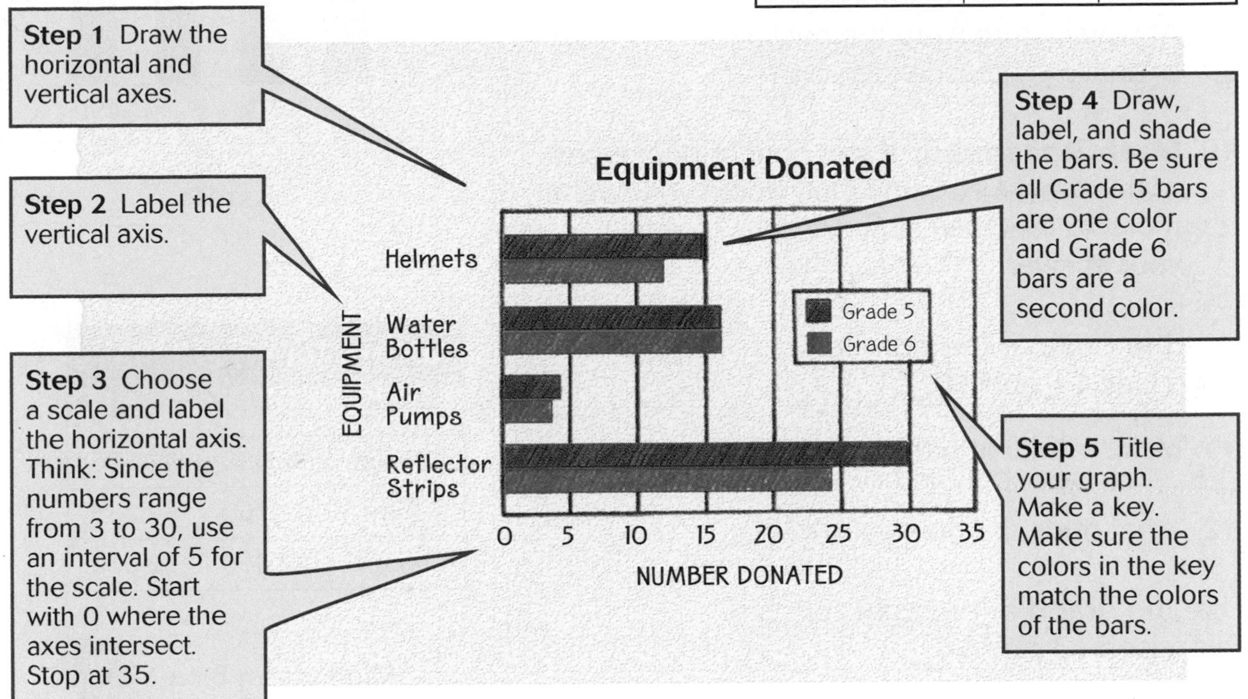

Step 1 Draw the horizontal and vertical axes.
Step 2 Label the vertical axis.
Step 3 Choose a scale and label the horizontal axis. Think: Since the numbers range from 3 to 30, use an interval of 5 for the scale. Start with 0 where the axes intersect. Stop at 35.
Equipment Donated
EQUIPMENT
Helmets
Water Bottles
Air Pumps
Reflector Strips
Grade 5
Grade 6
0 5 10 15 20 25 30 35
NUMBER DONATED
Step 4 Draw, label, and shade the bars. Be sure all Grade 5 bars are one color and Grade 6 bars are a second color.
Step 5 Title your graph. Make a key. Make sure the colors in the key match the colors of the bars.

Guided Practice *For another example, see Set B on p. 114.*

Use the graph in Example 3 above for Exercises 1–3.

1. What does each pair of bars represent?

2. For which item was there the greatest difference between the number of donations for the two grades?

3. For which item were the most donations made?

Use the table at the right for Exercises 4–6.

4. Make a double bar graph from the data.

5. What interval did you use for the scale?

6. What does the graph show?

Hours of Bicycle Repairs					
Kind of Bike	**Mon.**	**Tues.**	**Wed.**	**Thurs.**	**Fri.**
Racing	5	7	3	7	4
Mountain	7	10	5	2	11

Independent Practice *For more practice, see Set B on p. 116.*

Use the graph at the right for Exercises 7–10.

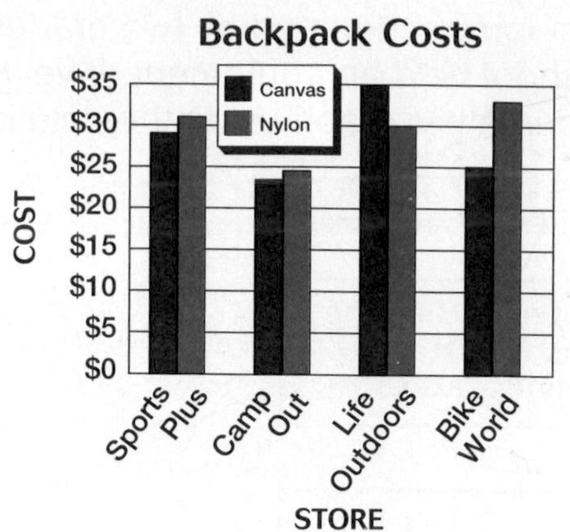

7. What does each pair of bars represent?

8. In which store is the difference in cost between the backpacks the greatest?

9. At which store were the backpacks the most expensive? Least expensive?

10. Math Reasoning If you bought both types of backpacks at Camp Out, would you spend more or less than at Sports Plus? Explain your answer.

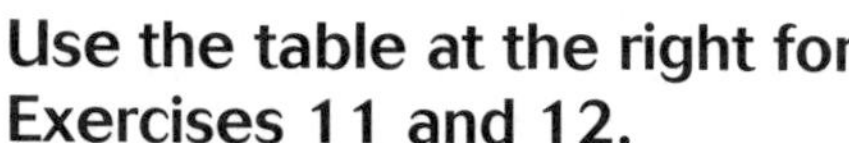

Use the table at the right for Exercises 11 and 12.

All-Terrain Wheelchairs

Model	Brand X	Brand Y
A-Frame	$2,395	$2,500
T-Tube	$2,250	$2,235
Chrome	$2,050	$2,055

11. Make a double bar graph from the data.

12. What does the graph show?

Use the graph at the right for Exercises 13 and 14.

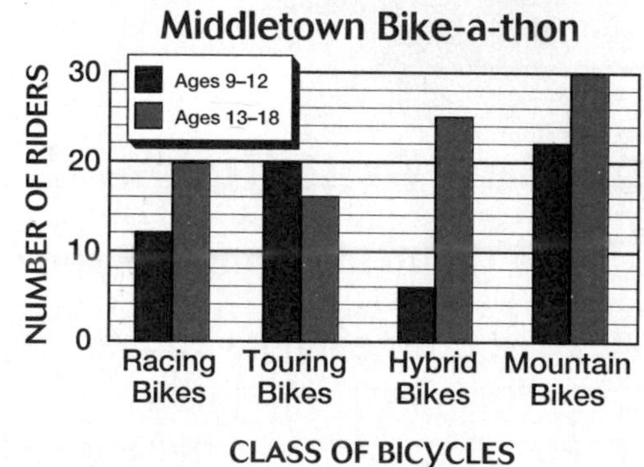

13. Mental Math What was the total number of riders in the 13–18 age group?

14. Math Reasoning In which class of bicycles was there the greatest difference between the number of riders in the two age groups? Explain.

Mixed Review

15. From the bar graph on page 85, what can you tell about France and Ireland?

16. $9.4 - 6.72$ **17.** $16.5 + 28.95$ **18. Algebra** Evaluate $n - 16$ for $n = 92$.

Test Prep Choose the correct letter for the answer.

19. (2-11) Cal bought a CD for $14.95, a book for $12.95, and a game for $8.95. Sales tax was $3.22. How much change did he get back from $50?

A $16.37 **B** $13.15 **C** $9.93 **D** $91.07 **E** NH

Coordinate Graphing

California Content Standard *Statistics, Data Analysis, and Probability 1.4 (🔑): Identify ordered pairs of data from a graph and interpret the meaning of the data in terms of the situation depicted by the graph. Also Statistics, Data Analysis, and Probability 1.5 (🔑) (See p. 83.)*

Math Link You know that graphs represent data. Now you will see how ordered pairs of numbers can represent, or locate, points on a grid.

Warm-Up Review

Use the double bar graph at the top of page 90. For 1–6, tell which store had the given price for the backpack named.

Canvas:
1. \$25 **2.** \$23 **3.** \$35

Nylon:
4. \$24 **5.** \$30 **6.** \$31

7. At which store did one backpack cost exactly \$5 more than the other?

Example 1

Fifth graders at West School placed a grid over a map of the United States and marked lettered points in the states where some inventions originated.

A coordinate grid is formed by two axes. The horizontal axis is labeled x and the vertical axis is labeled y. An **ordered pair** of numbers is used to locate a point on a grid. The first number in the pair tells how far to move to the right from zero. The second tells how far to move up from zero.

Word Bank

ordered pair
coordinates

Find the state and the invention located at (1, 4).

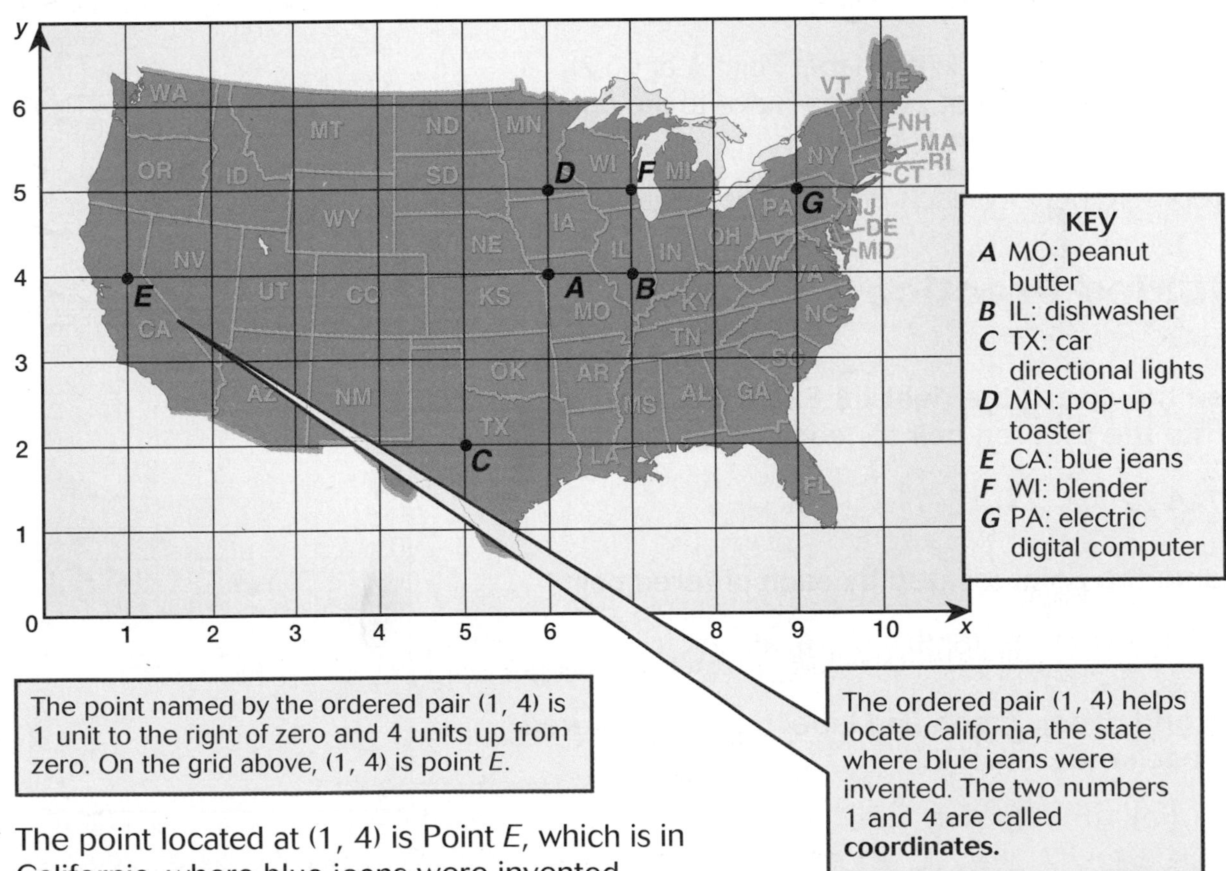

The point named by the ordered pair (1, 4) is 1 unit to the right of zero and 4 units up from zero. On the grid above, (1, 4) is point *E*.

The ordered pair (1, 4) helps locate California, the state where blue jeans were invented. The two numbers 1 and 4 are called **coordinates.**

The point located at (1, 4) is Point *E*, which is in California, where blue jeans were invented.

Additional Standards: Algebra and Functions 1.1, 1.2 (🔑) (See p. 83.)

Example 2

Write the ordered pair for Point *H* on the map at the right. It shows the state in which the crossword puzzle was invented.

- Start at 0
- Count to the right to the grid line for Point *H*. It is 7 spaces to the right of zero.
- Count up to Point *H*. It is 13 spaces above zero.
- Write the ordered pair (7, 13).

The ordered pair for Point *H* is (7, 13).

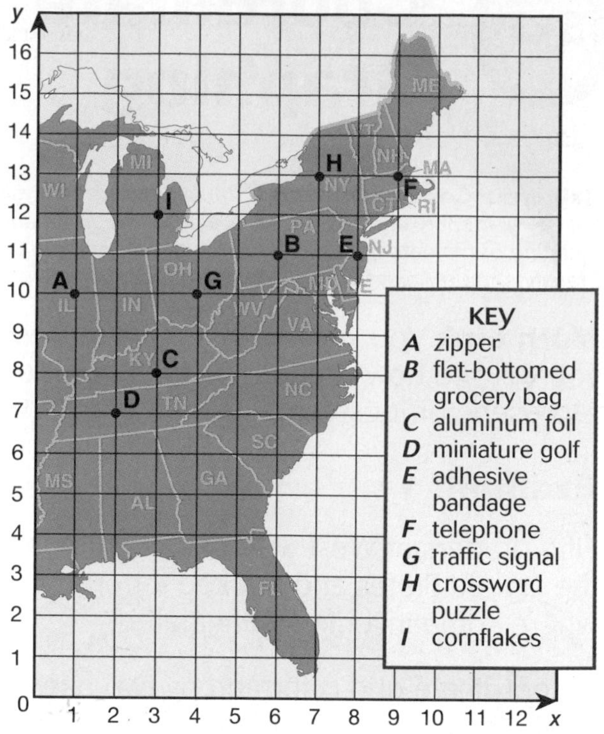

KEY
A zipper
B flat-bottomed grocery bag
C aluminum foil
D miniature golf
E adhesive bandage
F telephone
G traffic signal
H crossword puzzle
I cornflakes

Example 3

Graph these points on a coordinate grid.

Point *A* (1, 2), Point *B* (2, 4), Point *C* (3, 6)
Point *D* (4, 8) Point *E* (5, 10)

Step 1 Draw a horizontal axis and a vertical axis on grid paper. Number each axis from 0 to 10 as shown on the grid at the right.

Step 2 Locate, mark, and label Point *A* at (1, 2). Remember to start at zero and move to the right 1 space first, then up 2 spaces.

Step 3 Repeat for each of the other points.

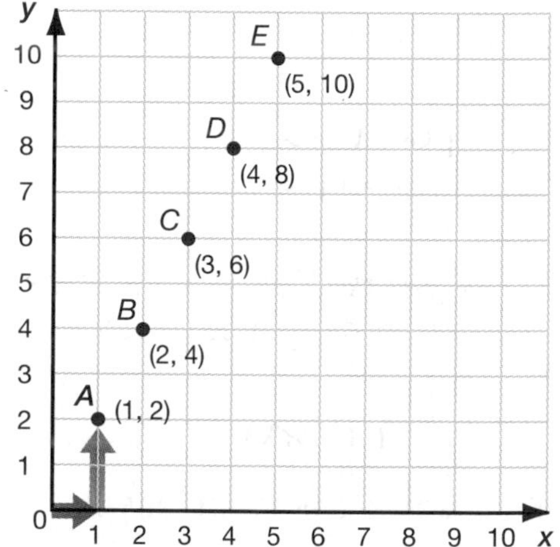

Guided Practice

For another example, see Set C on p. 115.

Use the grid at the right for Exercises 1–6. Write the ordered pair for each point.

1. *A* **2.** *B* **3.** *C*

Name the point located by each ordered pair.

4. (11, 1) **5.** (6, 5) **6.** (5, 2)

On grid paper, graph and label the point located by each ordered pair.

7. *A* (3, 4) **8.** *B* (0, 4) **9.** *C* (4, 0)

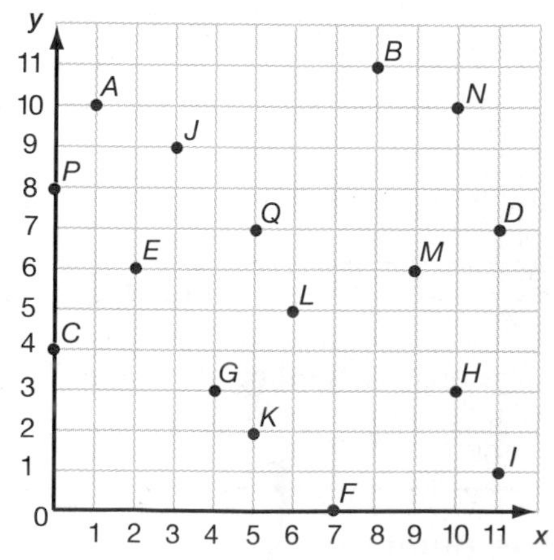

Independent Practice For more practice, see Set C on p. 117.

Use the grid at the bottom of page 92 for Exercises 10–17. Write the ordered pair for each point.

10. *E* **11.** *F* **12.** *G* **13.** *H*

Name the point located by each ordered pair.

14. (10, 10) **15.** (3, 9) **16.** (9, 6) **17.** (0, 8)

For Exercises 18–21, use grid paper. Graph and label the point located by each ordered pair.

18. *A* (3, 2) **19.** *B* (2, 3) **20.** *C* (8, 4) **21.** *D* (5, 0)

Use the map on page 92 for Exercises 22–29. Write the ordered pair for the state where each item was invented.

22. Zipper **23.** Miniature golf **24.** Traffic signal **25.** Telephone

Name the invention from the state located by each ordered pair.

26. (6, 11) **27.** (3, 8) **28.** (8, 11) **29.** (3, 12)

30. Math Reasoning Is it important which coordinate is written first in an ordered pair? Explain.

31. Algebra If the coordinates at (x, y) are (3, 2), what are the coordinates at $(x + 1, y + 1)$?

Mixed Review

14, 32, 45, 28, 28, 29, 43, 18, 24, 37, 39, 45, 32, 19, 22

32. Make a stem-and-leaf plot for the data at the right.

33. According to the double bar graph in Example 1 on page 88, in which year did all three bikes cost more than $300?

Mental Math **Use mental math to find each sum.**

34. 16 + 24 + 12 **35.** 21 + 48 + 9 **36.** 18 + 45 + 102

Test Prep **Choose the correct letter for each answer.**

37. Which decimal is equal to 0.9? (1-4)

A 0.90 **C** 0.09
B 0.009 **D** 0.090

38. Round 8.37 to the nearest tenth. (1-6)

A 8.0 **C** 9.0
B 8.3 **D** 8.4

Problem-Solving Skill:

Understanding Line Graphs

Warm-Up Review

Find the number halfway between the given numbers.

1. 50 and 250
2. 400 and 800
3. 3,000 and 4,000
4. Joel left on his trip at 9:30 A.M. and traveled 3.5 hours. What time was it then?

California Content Standard *Mathematical Reasoning 2.3: Use a variety of methods, such as words, numbers, symbols, charts, graphs, tables, diagrams, and models, to explain mathematical reasoning. Also Statistics, Data Analysis, and Probability 1.4 (key) (See p. 83.)*

Read for Understanding

Cars have changed a lot over time. One thing, though, has not changed. Nearly everyone loves to travel! The **line graph** at the right tells a story about a car trip.

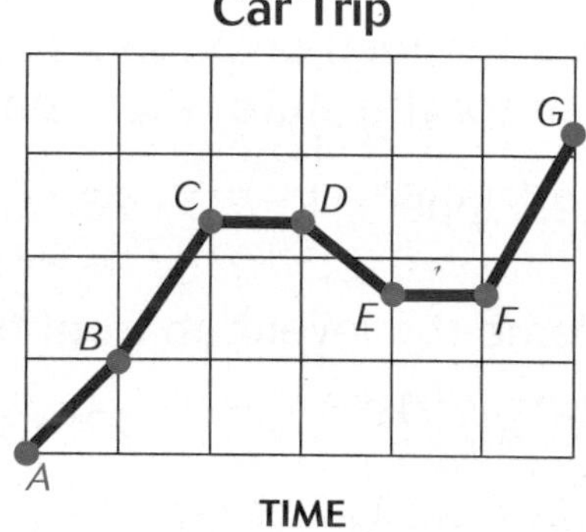

1. What does the line on the graph represent?
2. At what point is the car farthest from the starting point?

Think and Discuss

Understanding Line Graphs

A line graph shows how data changes over time. The direction of the line, up or down, and its steepness are visual clues to interpreting the graph.

Word Bank

line graph

3. Between Points *A* and *B*, the line rises. Is the car moving away from or nearer to the starting point?
4. Between Points *C* and *D*, the line does not rise or fall. Has time passed? Is the car moving?
5. Between Points *D* and *E*, the line falls. Is the car moving farther away from or closer to the starting point?
6. Do you think it is always necessary to have numbers on a graph to learn something from the graph? Why or why not?

Additional Standard: Algebra and Functions 1.1 (See p. 83.)

Miguel's mother belongs to a car pool. When she drives, she takes Miguel and some of his classmates from their homes to their school. The graph below shows one of these trips. Use it for Exercises 1–7.

Guided Practice

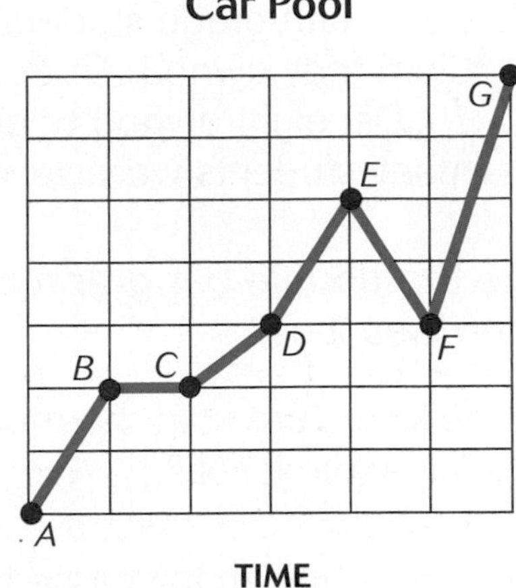

1. Which point represents Miguel at home?
   a. Point *A*
   b. Point *D*
   c. Point *E*

2. Which of the following best describes what happened between Points *F* and *G*?
   a. The car stopped.
   b. The car continued moving until it reached the school.
   c. The car went back home.

Independent Practice

3. Which point represents Miguel at school?
   a. Point *B*
   b. Point *F*
   c. Point *G*

4. Which is true about Miguel's distance from home at Points *B* and *C*?
   a. At *B* he is farther from home.
   b. At *C* he is farther from home.
   c. Equal distance from home at *B* and *C*.

5. Which of the following might be the reason for what happened between Points *B* and *C*?
   a. The car waited for a passenger.
   b. Miguel's mother stopped for gas.
   c. Either of the above.

6. Which of the following best describes what happened between Points *E* and *F*?
   a. The car stopped.
   b. The car moved closer to home.
   c. Both of the above.

7. **Math Reasoning** Explain what might have been the reason for the car's action between Points *D* and *F*.

8. Use the graph at the right. Tell what might have happened between each pair of points from point *A* to point *F*.

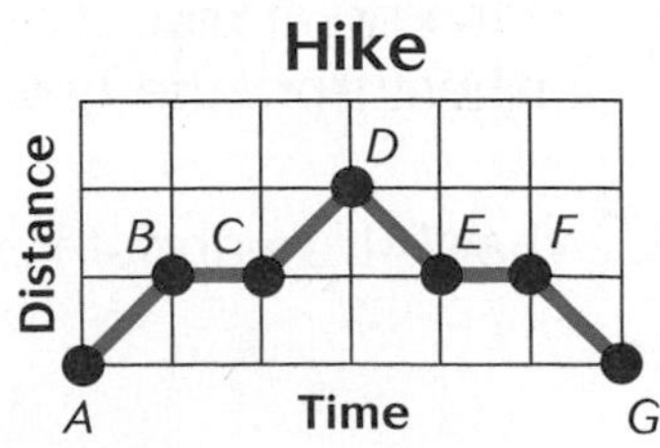

Diagnostic Checkpoint

Make a line plot using the data in Exercise 1. Then answer the question.

1. (3-1) Some fifth-grade students were asked how many compact discs they owned. Three students owned 4 CDs; six owned 5 CDs; eight owned 6; and five students owned 7 CDs. How many students were surveyed?

Use the double bar graph at the right for Exercises 2–4.

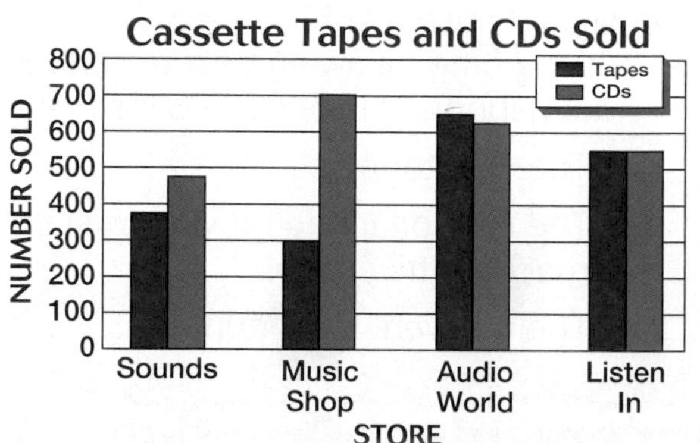

2. (3-2) Which store sold the most CDs? How many did it sell?

3. (3-2) About how many cassette tapes did Audio World sell?

4. (3-2) Which store sold the same number of CDs and cassette tapes? How do you know?

Use the grid at the right for Exercises 5–16. Name the point or write the ordered pair for each location.

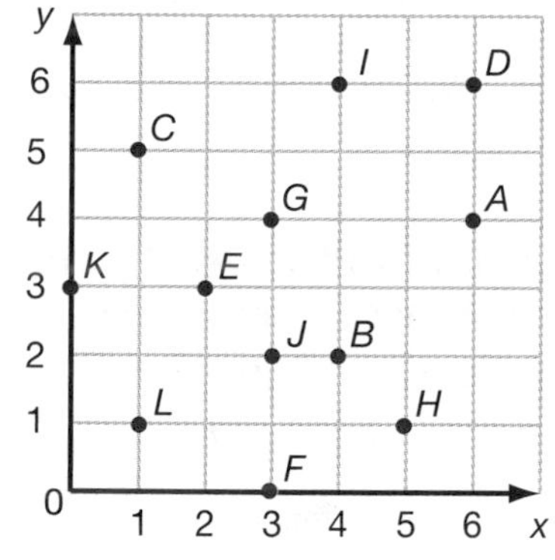

5. (3-3) (2, 3) **6.** (3-3) (6, 4) **7.** (3-3) *D*

8. (3-3) *C* **9.** (3-3) *G* **10.** (3-3) (3, 0)

11. (3-3) (4, 6) **12.** (3-3) *B* **13.** (3-3) *H*

14. (3-3) *K* **15.** (3-3) (3, 2) **16.** (3-3) *L*

For Exercises 17 and 18, use the line graph showing the route of a grocery store delivery truck.

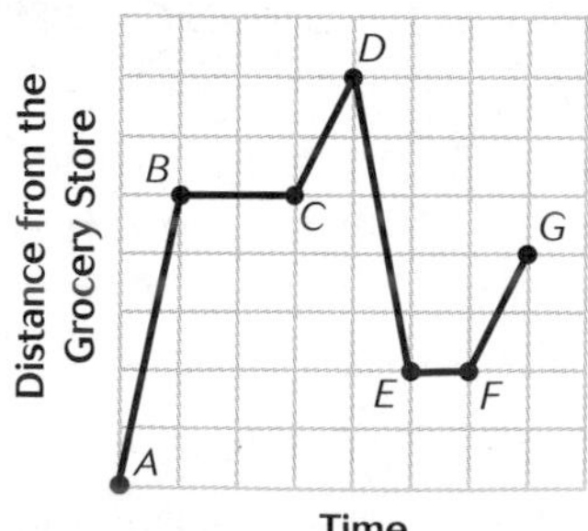

17. (3-4) Which point represents the delivery farthest from the grocery store?

18. (3-4) What is true about Points *E* and *F*?

Multiple-Choice Cumulative Review

Choose the correct letter for each answer.

1. Eve spends $625 per month on rent and $240 for food. Her gas bill for September was $97.34. Her electric bill for the same month was $49.46. Which is the best estimate for Eve's monthly rent and food expenses?

A Less than $650
B $650
C $750
D More than $800

2. The cost of a CD, including tax, is $18.01. A cassette tape costs $9.53 including tax. If you bought one of each, how much change should you receive from $30.00?

F $2.46 **H** $11.99
G $2.54 **J** $27.54

3. On the basis of the information in the graph, who volunteered more hours in November? How many more hours did he work?

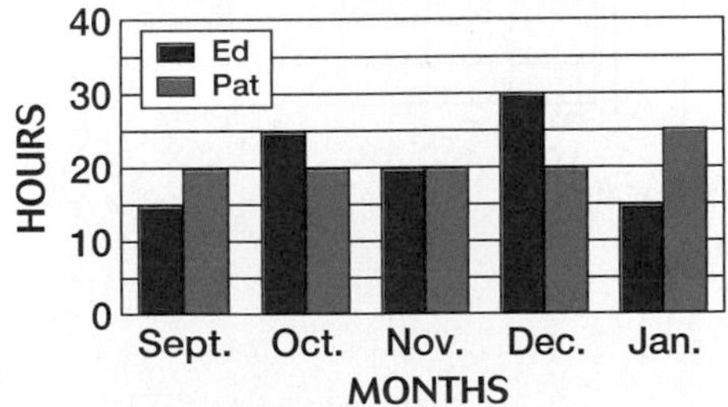

A Ed; 20 more hours
B Pat; 20 more hours
C Ed; 10 more hours
D They volunteered the same number of hours.

Use the price list for Questions 4 and 5.

Price List	
T-shirt	$14.99
Pennant	$2.95
Baseball hat	$13.99
Pom-pom	$0.75

4. Which lists the items in order, from least expensive to most expensive?

F Pennant, hat, pom-pom, T-shirt
G T-shirt, hat, pennant, pom-pom
H Pom-pom, T-shirt, hat, pennant
J Pom-pom, pennant, hat, T-shirt

5. Gale bought a T-shirt and a baseball hat. How much did Gale spend?

A More than $30.00
B $28.98
C $17.94
D $14.74

6. Which represents the number 202,685 rounded to the nearest thousand?

F 200,000
G 202,700
H 203,000
J 210,000

Reading and Making Line Graphs

California Content Standard *Statistics, Data Analysis, and Probability 1.2: Organize and display single-variable data in appropriate graphs and representations and explain which types of graphs are appropriate for various data sets. Also Statistics, Data Analysis, and Probability 1.4 (🔑) (See p. 83.)*

Warm-Up Review

Add or subtract mentally.

1. 400 − 250
2. 230 − 150
3. 2,675 + 100
4. 93 + 20
5. 245 − 50
6. 300 − 10
7. 310 + 90
8. 560 + 50
9. Carl had $55. He spent $37. Then he earned $17. He spent $5.50 to see a movie. How much did he have left?

Word Bank

trend

Math Link You have learned to interpret line graphs using visual clues. Now you will read and make line graphs using specific data.

A line graph may be used to show trends over a period of time. One common use of line graphs is to show changes in population data.

The line graph below shows the change in the population density of the United States between 1940 and 1990. Population density is the number of people per square mile. You can use the graph to find the population density in a particular year, or to see **trends** in the data over the 50-year period. Analyzing trends can help you make predictions about data.

Example 1

What was the population density in 1960?

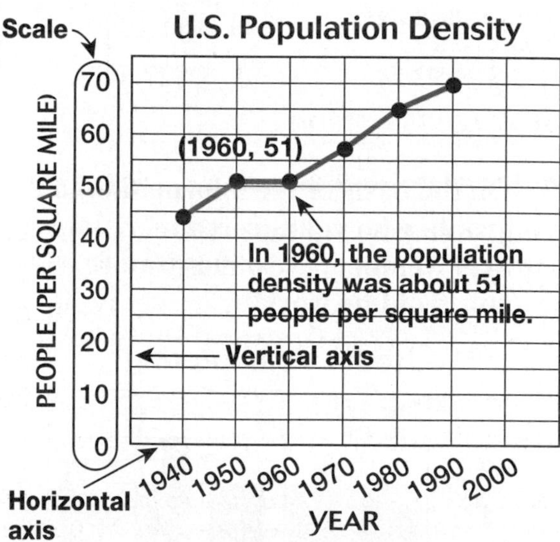

On the horizontal axis, find 1960. Follow that grid line up to the point on the graph. The point has coordinates (1960, 51) because it is on the grid line for 1960 and slightly above the grid line for 50.

The population density in 1960 was 51.

Example 2

In what year were there about 44 people per square mile in the United States?

44 is almost halfway between 40 and 50. On the vertical axis, find 40 and 50. Look to the right. The point that is about halfway between them is on the grid line for 1940.

In 1940 there were about 44 people per square mile in the United States.

Additional Standards: Algebra and Functions 1.1, 1.2 (🔑); Mathematical Reasoning 2.3 (See p. 83.)

Example 3

Use the graph at the right. During which 7-day period in September does the average daily high temperature drop the most?

The steepest section is from September 21 to September 28, as the temperature drops 4 degrees. During the first 7-day period, the temperature drops 1 degree; during the second 7-day period, 3 degrees.

The average daily high temperature for September drops the most during the 7-day period from the 21st to the 28th.

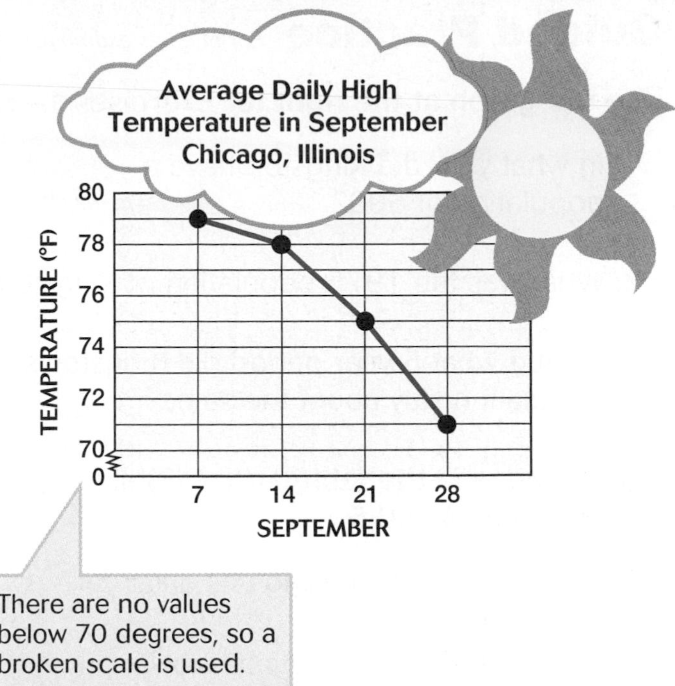

Example 4

Make a line graph to show the data in the table below. Then use the graph to estimate the number of people who ride the subway at 2:00 P.M.

New York City Subway Riders					
Hour	9 A.M.	11 A.M.	1 P.M.	3 P.M.	5 P.M.
Number of Riders (thousands)	203	114	118	207	300

First, make the graph.

- On grid paper, draw the axes and title the graph.
- Choose a scale and write the numbers of people on the vertical axis. Write the times of day on the horizontal axis.
- Place a point on the graph for each ordered pair. Use line segments to connect the points.

Second, use the graph you made to estimate the number of subway riders at 2:00 P.M.

- Find a point on the horizontal axis halfway between 1 P.M. and 3 P.M. Use a straightedge to find the point on the graph directly above that point.
- Then use the straightedge to find the number on the vertical axis directly to the left of this point on the graph.

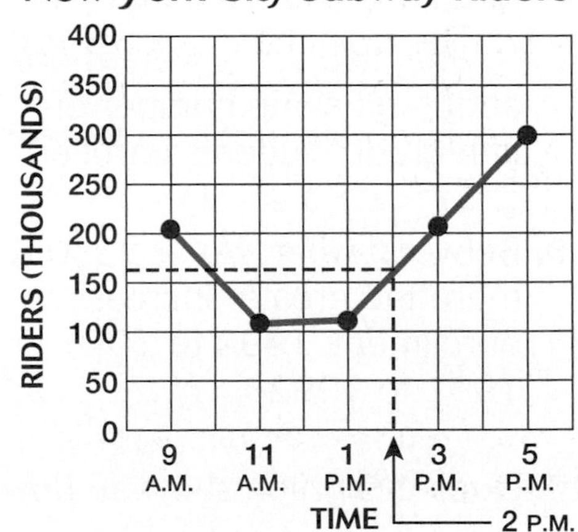

Approximately 160 thousand people ride the New York subway at 2:00 P.M.

Guided Practice *For another example, see Set D on p. 115.*

Use the graph at the right for Exercises 1–3.

Population of Kingston

POPULATION: 0, 400, 450, 500, 550, 600, 650

YEAR: 1970, 1975, 1980, 1985, 1990, 1995

1. In what year did Kingston have a population of 500?

2. What was the 1975 population of Kingston?

3. During what 5-year period did Kingston's population stay about the same?

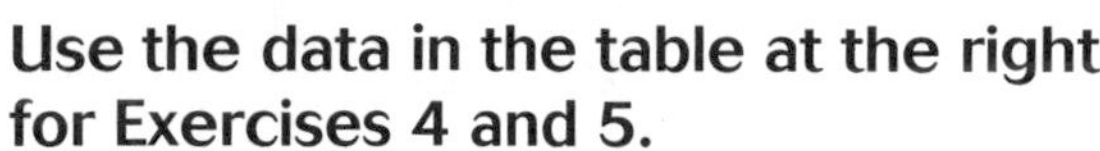

Use the data in the table at the right for Exercises 4 and 5.

4. Make a line graph using this data.

5. Use your graph to estimate how many riders there would be at 10 P.M.

New York City Subway Riders

Hour	Number of Riders (thousands)
7 P.M.	132
9 P.M.	60
11 P.M.	37

Independent Practice *For more practice, see Set D on p. 117.*

Use the graph at the right for Exercises 6–9.

6. In what year were there about 3,250,000 fifth-grade students enrolled in school?

7. About how many fifth-grade students were enrolled in 1995?

8. In what two years were there about the same number of fifth-grade students enrolled?

9. Between what two years was there the greater increase in enrollment, 1990 to 1991 or 1991 to 1992?

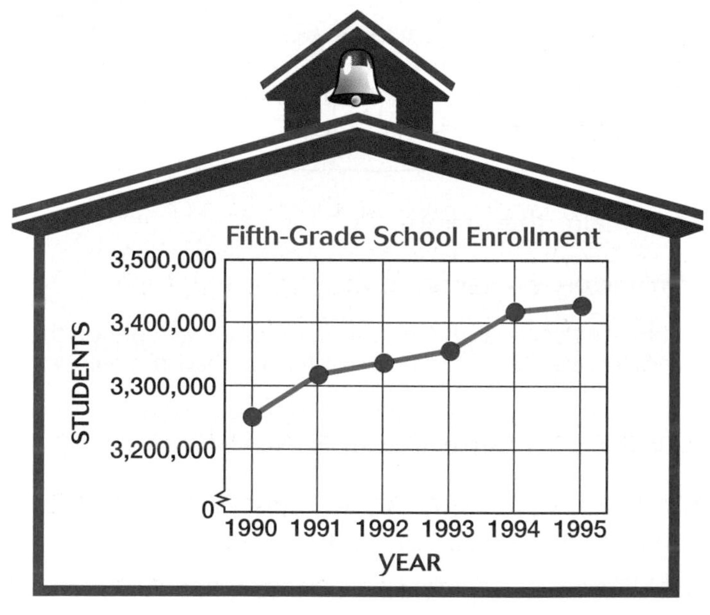

10. Does this graph show an upward trend or a downward trend?

11. **Math Reasoning** Explain how looking at the trend shown by a graph could help you predict values that do not show on the graph.

Use the table at the right for Exercises 12–16.

Time	Temperature (°F)
6:00 A.M.	48
9:00 A.M.	57
12:00 P.M.	70
3:00 P.M.	66
6:00 P.M.	60
9:00 P.M.	55
12:00 A.M.	51
3:00 A.M.	49

12. Make a line graph using this data.

13. Use the graph you made to estimate the temperature at 1:30 P.M.

14. What is the warmest temperature recorded on the graph? What is the coolest temperature?

15. Math Reasoning Explain why it might be a good idea to use a broken scale on this graph.

16. Algebra If (x, y) represents the ordered pair for the 3 P.M. temperature, what does $(x + 3, y - 6)$ represent?

Mixed Review

Use the graph at the right for Exercises 17 and 18.

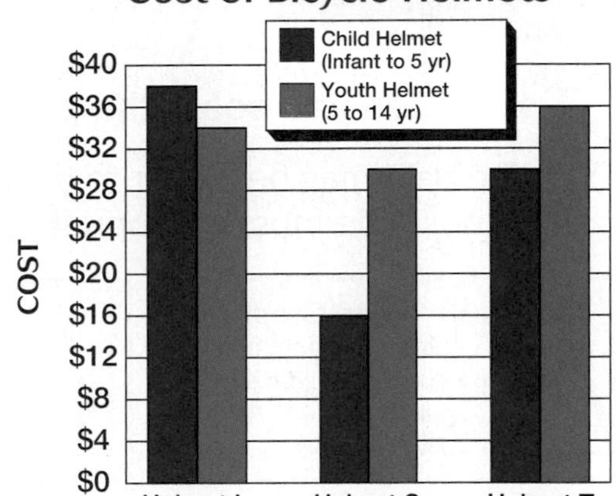

17. How much would it cost to buy 3 child helmets, Brand S, and 2 youth helmets, Brand T?

18. For which brand is the difference in the cost of a child helmet and the cost of a youth helmet the greatest?

19. On a coordinate grid, Carol drew a path starting at (6, 2). She moved 3 spaces up and 2 spaces to the right. What is the ordered pair for the point where she stopped?

Round each number to the underlined place.

20. 321,942 **21.** 5,463,427 **22.** 27,542,346 **23.** 72,976

Test Prep **Choose the correct letter for each answer.**

24. (2-11) Harold wants to buy a book that costs $14.95. He has a coupon for a $2.25 discount. How much will the book cost if he uses the coupon?

A $12.25 **C** $12.70
B $12.60 **D** $17.20

25. (2-10) Al increased the length of a fence that was originally 6.9 meters long. He made it 2.19 meters longer. How long is the fence now?

F 4.71 m **H** 9.19 m
G 9.09 m **J** 9.99 m

Use Homework Workbook 3-5.

Understand
Plan
Solve
Look Back

Problem-Solving Strategy:
Make a Graph

California Content Standard *Mathematical Reasoning 2.3: Use a variety of methods, such as words, numbers, symbols, charts, graphs, tables, diagrams, and models, to explain mathematical reasoning. Also Statistics, Data Analysis, and Probability 1.2 (See p. 83.)*

Warm-Up Review

Tell whether each is true for a pictograph, bar graph, and/or line graph.

1. Compares data
2. Shows how data changes over time.
3. Uses symbols to represent multiples

One hundred adults and one hundred students were surveyed about inventors. The results are shown in the table at the right. Which group could identify the most inventors?

Who Invented It

Invention	Number of Correct Answers	
	Adults	Students
Telephone	88	88
Propeller airplane	87	59
Rocket engine	85	51
Compact disc	62	81

Understand

What do you need to find?

You need to find which group could identify the most inventors.

Plan

How can you solve the problem?

The data may be easier to interpret if you **make a graph.** Choose the most appropriate graph for the problem.

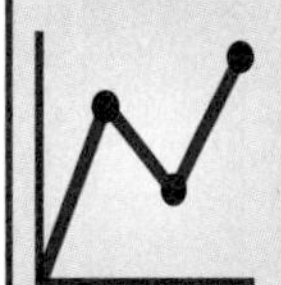

Line Graph
Since the data is not changing over time, a line graph is not a good choice.

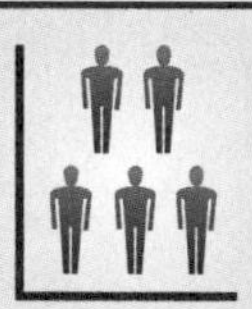

Pictograph
The data is not easily represented by symbols, so a pictograph is not a good choice.

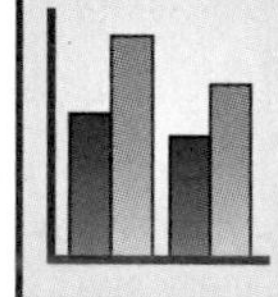

Bar Graph
A double bar graph makes it easy to compare the two groups.

Solve

Make a double bar graph and compare. In two cases, more adults gave correct answers. In one case, the numbers were equal. In only one case, the students had more correct answers. The graph shows that the adults identified more inventors.

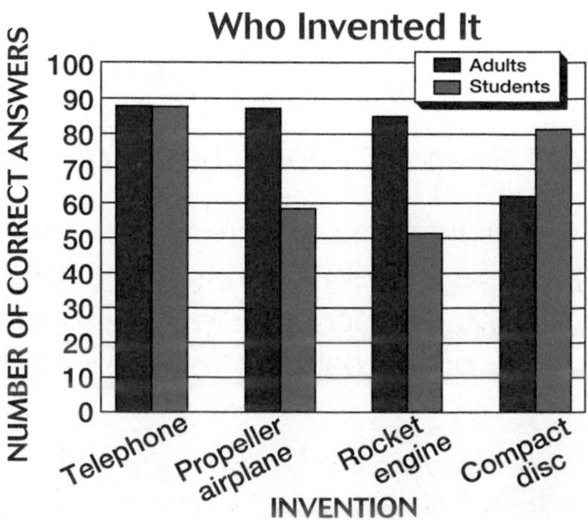

Look Back

Why does a double bar graph make it easy to compare the two groups?

Additional Standards: Algebra and Functions 1.1; Mathematical Reasoning 3.2 (See p. 83.)

Guided Practice

Make an appropriate graph to represent the data shown at the right. Then use your graph for Exercises 1 and 2.

Computer Boxes Packed	
Time	Cumulative Total
9:00	0
10:00	20
11:00	60
12:00	83
1:00	88
2:00	120

1. In which interval of 1 hour were the greatest number of computer boxes packed?

2. In which interval of 1 hour were the fewest computer boxes packed? Why might this be?

Independent Practice

Make an appropriate graph to represent the data shown at the right. Then use your graph to answer Questions 3–6.

CDs Purchases		
Type	Ages 9–10	Ages 13–17
Rock	37	38
Country	8	28
Classical	9	10
Jazz	12	30
Reggae	32	9

3. Which type of music was purchased most in both age groups?

4. In which age group was jazz the second-most purchased type of music?

5. Which age group purchased more CDs overall?

6. **Math Reasoning** Would you say that the two age groups prefer the same types of music? Explain.

Mixed Review

Try these or other strategies to solve each problem. Tell which strategy you used.

Problem-Solving Strategies

- *Draw a Diagram*
- *Write an Equation*
- *Find a Pattern*
- *Work Backward*

7. A tour bus has just traveled 2 blocks north, 3 blocks east, 4 blocks south, 9 blocks west, and 2 blocks north. Where is the bus now in relation to its starting point?

8. José is saving to buy a pair of in-line skates. He has saved $70.00. The skates cost $150.00. How much more does José have to save?

Use Homework Workbook 3-6.

Mean, Median, and Mode

Warm-Up Review

1. 35 + 43 + 98 + 102
2. 156 + 84 + 163 + 197
3. 72 ÷ 9 4. 56 ÷ 8
5. 540 ÷ 9 6. 630 ÷ 7
7. Sam bought 4 books. The prices were $7.50, $5.00, $9.50, $10.00. How much did the books cost in all?

California Content Standard *Statistics, Data Analysis, and Probability 1.1: Know the concepts of mean, median, and mode; compute and compare simple examples to show that they may differ.*

Math Link You have used different types of graphs to display all the values in a data set. Now you will use a single number to represent a set of data.

Statistics is the science of working with data. Statisticians often use statistical measures to represent and compare sets of numerical data. One of these statistical measures is the **mean,** which we often call the **average.**

Example 1

Jake's tips for 5 days are shown at the right.

Mon.	Tues.	Wed.	Thurs.	Fri.
$4.50	$7.00	$6.00	$5.50	$7.00

Find the mean value of Jake's tips.

First, add the amounts for the 5 days.

$4.50 + $7.00 + $6.00 + $5.50 + $7.00 = $30.00

Then, divide by the number of days.

$30 ÷ 5 = $6

The mean is $6.00.

Word Bank

mean
average
median
mode
range
outlier

Other statistical measures can more easily be found when the data is arranged in order from least to greatest. The **median** is the middle number when the numbers are arranged in order. The **mode** is the number that occurs most often. The **range** is the difference between the greatest and the least numbers. The line plot below uses the data about Jake's tips.

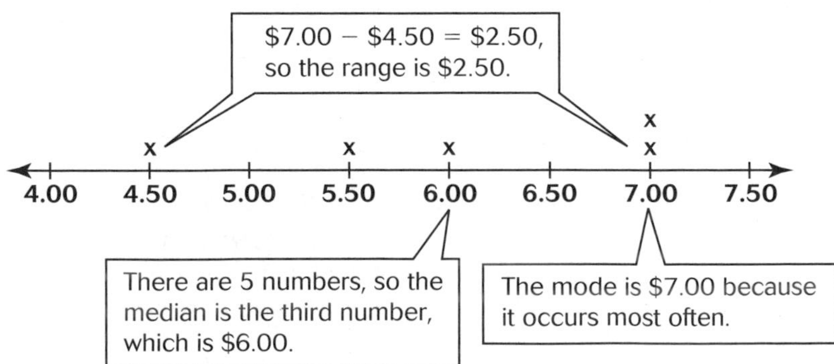

$7.00 − $4.50 = $2.50, so the range is $2.50.
4.00
4.50
5.00
5.50
6.00
6.50
7.00
7.50
There are 5 numbers, so the median is the third number, which is $6.00.
The mode is $7.00 because it occurs most often.

 Additional Standard: Mathematical Reasoning 3.2 (See p. 83.)

Example 2

During the same week, Jake worked on Saturday and received $18 in tips. Find the median amount in tips for the week.

Mon.	Tues.	Wed.	Thurs.	Fri.	Sat.
$4.50	$7.00	$6.00	$5.50	$7.00	$18.00

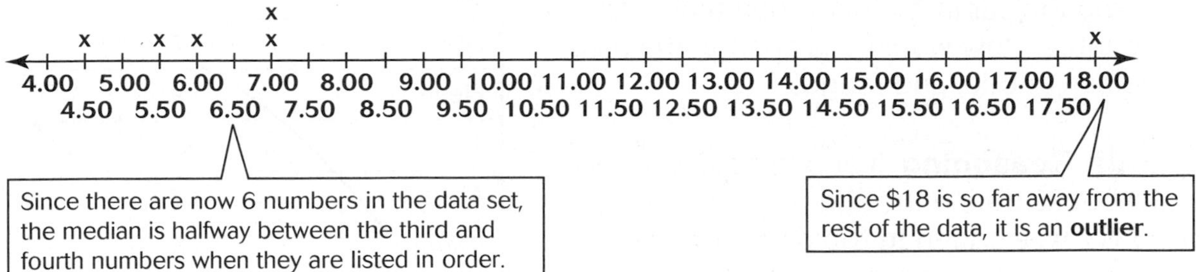
4.00 5.00 6.00 7.00 8.00 9.00 10.00 11.00 12.00 13.00 14.00 15.00 16.00 17.00 18.00
4.50 5.50 6.50 7.50 8.50 9.50 10.50 11.50 12.50 13.50 14.50 15.50 16.50 17.50
Since there are now 6 numbers in the data set, the median is halfway between the third and fourth numbers when they are listed in order.
Since $18 is so far away from the rest of the data, it is an **outlier**.

Guided Practice *For another example, see Set E on p. 115.*

Find the mean, median, and mode, for each set of data.

1. 8, 5, 4, 5, 5, 12, 10 **2.** 5, 8, 1, 2, 1, 1 **3.** 96, 83, 88, 88, 95

Independent Practice *For more practice, see Set E on p. 117.*

Find the mean, median, and mode for each set of data.

4. 66, 77, 68, 62, 77 **5.** 2, 1, 7, 9, 7, 5, 4 **6.** 53, 54, 40, 53

The table at the right shows the final medal standings for the top ten countries in the 1998 winter Olympics. Find each statistical measure described.

7. Mean: number of gold medals.

8. Median: number of gold medals.

9. Median: number of silver medals.

10. Mode: number of bronze medals.

11. Mean: total number of medals won.

12. Median: total number of medals won.

13. Mode: total number of medals won.

14. Range: total number of medals won.

Country	Gold	Silver	Bronze	Total
Germany	12	9	8	29
Norway	10	10	5	25
Russia	9	6	3	18
Austria	3	5	9	17
Canada	6	5	4	15
U.S.A.	6	3	4	13
Finland	2	4	6	12
Netherlands	5	4	2	11
Japan	5	1	4	10
Italy	2	6	2	10

15. In the set of data for the gold medals, what are the modes?

Use the table at the right for Exercises 16–18.

Books Read During Summer	
Students	**Number of Books Read**
Jorge	9
Bill	5
Lee	7
Elena	9
Joyce	9
Aisha	12
Darryl	5

16. Find the mean, median, mode, and range for the data in the table.

17. Mental Math Suppose you read 8 books during the summer and added that data to the table. How would this change the mean, median, mode, and range?

18. Math Reasoning If another student read 40 books during the summer and this outlier was added to the data, would the new mean, median, mode, and range still represent the data accurately? Explain.

19. Math Reasoning For each statistical measure (mean, median, mode, and range) tell whether that number is always, sometimes, or never, one of the numbers in the data set.

Mixed Review

Use the table at the right for Exercises 20 and 21.

Clock Preferences		
	Digital	**Analog**
Grade 1	13	14
Grade 2	15	13
Grade 3	20	11
Grade 4	25	6
Grade 5	12	20
Grade 6	21	11

20. How many more students preferred a digital clock than an analog clock?

21. Make an appropriate graph for the data.

22. Look at the line graph at the top of page 100. In what year did Kingston have a population of 400?

Write the numbers in order from least to greatest.

23. 15,276, 15,347, 15,263 **24.** 0.24, 0.243, 0.254 **25.** 1.927, 1.919, 1.79

Test Prep Choose the correct letter for the answer.

26. (3-4) The cost of home computers has been decreasing over the years. Which of these line graphs could represent this?

A

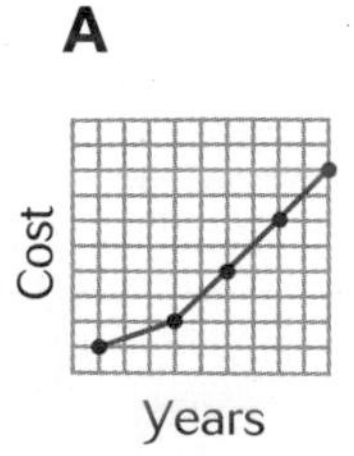

B

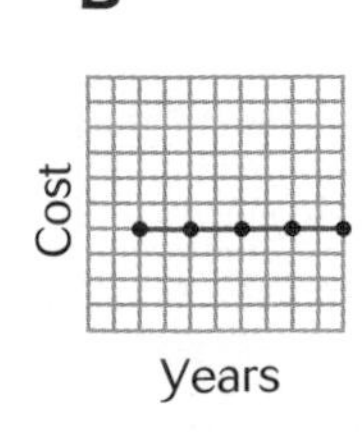

C

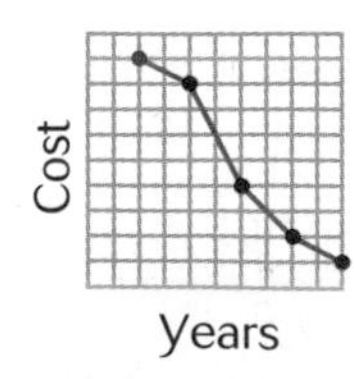

D

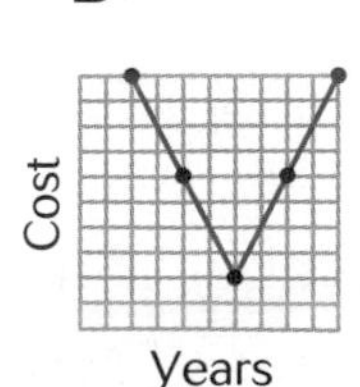

Problem-Solving Application:

Using Other Graphs

Warm-Up Review

Use the stem-and-leaf plot on page 84. Tell how many pairs of jeans are in stock in each waist-size range.

1. 20–29 inches
2. 30–39 inches
3. 40–49 inches

California Content Standard *Mathematical Reasoning 2.3: Use a variety of methods, such as words, numbers, symbols, charts, graphs, tables, diagrams, and models, to explain mathematical reasoning. Also Statistics, Data Analysis, and Probability 1.2 (See p. 83.)*

Example 1

A radio station surveyed 100 people in each of five different age groups to find out how many enjoyed rap music. The frequency table shows the results. Based on this survey, how does the popularity of rap music vary between age groups?

Age Group	Frequency
50–59	5
40–49	9
30–39	18
20–29	40
10–19	28

Understand

What do you need to find?

You need to find how the popularity of rap music varies between age groups.

Plan

How can you solve the problem?

You can display this data in a type of bar graph called a **histogram.** In a histogram, there is no space between the bars, and equal intervals are shown on the horizontal axis.

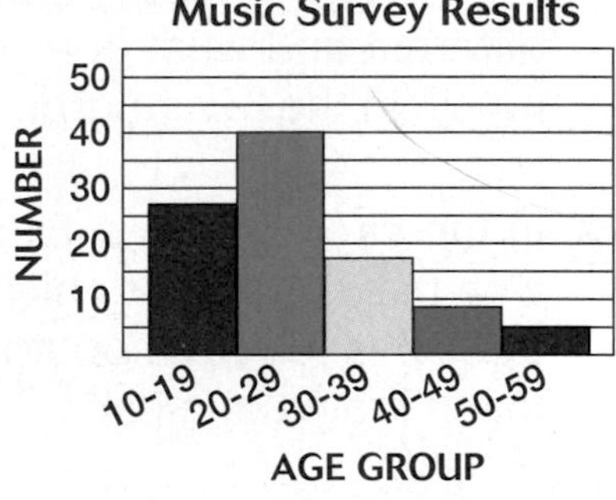

Solve

The histogram gives a clear picture of the survey results. It is easy to see that, among those surveyed, rap music is most popular in the second age group, from 20–29. It is a little less popular among the younger age group, 10–19, and popularity steadily declines after age 29.

Look Back

Did the histogram give a clearer picture of the data than the frequency table? Why or why not?

Example 2

A restaurant offers four main course choices on their dinner menu. This **circle graph** represents the main course ordered by the first twenty dinner customers one evening. Which main course was ordered by more customers than any other?

Circle graphs are used to represent data as parts of a whole. The parts can be easily compared.

Compare the sizes of the sections in the circle graph to find the main course that was ordered by more customers than any other. The largest section of the circle represents the most customers.

Main Course Orders

Turkey 3
Beef 5
Ham 2
Chicken 10
One fourth of the customers ordered beef.
Half of the customers ordered chicken.
Chicken was ordered by more customers than any other main course.

The main course that was ordered by more customers than any other is chicken.

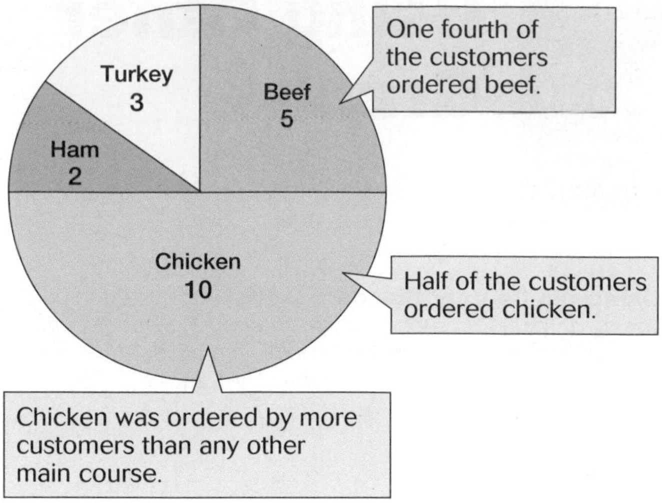

Word Bank
histogram
circle graph

Guided Practice

1. In the histogram in Example 1, compare the bars for the 20–29 age group and the 30–39 age group. How are the bars different and what does this tell you about the popularity of rap music in these age groups?

2. In the circle graph in Example 2, compare the section for beef with the section for chicken. What do you notice and what does this tell you about the number of customers choosing these main courses?

Independent Practice

3. In the histogram in Example 1, compare the bars for the 30–39 age group and the 40–49 age group. How are the bars different and what does this tell you about the popularity of rap music in these age groups?

4. In the circle graph in Example 2, compare the section for beef with the section for ham. What do you notice and what does this tell you about the number of customers choosing these main courses?

Use the table at the right for Exercises 5–7.

Median U.S. Weekly Earnings, 1998				
Age Group	25–34	35–44	45–54	55–64
Earnings ($)	839	991	1,118	876

5. Make a histogram showing the information in the table.

6. Using your graph, describe how weekly income varies between age groups.

7. Between which two consecutive age intervals is there the greatest difference in the median weekly income?

Use the table and the circle graph at the right for Exercises 8–10.

Students in Mr. Alaveda's class are writing reports about inventors and their inventions since 1900. Each student picked from the list shown.

Inventors and Their Inventions			
Year	**Invention**	**Inventor**	**Reports**
1903	Airplane	Wright Brothers	||||
1938	Ballpoint pen	Ladislas Biro	||
1939	Helicopter	Igor Sikorski	𝍸 |||
1960	Laser	Theodore H. Maiman	𝍸 |||
1971	Cellular phone	Henry T. Sampson	𝍸 𝍸

8. What does the circle graph tell you about the inventions represented by sections B and C?

Inventions Picked by Class

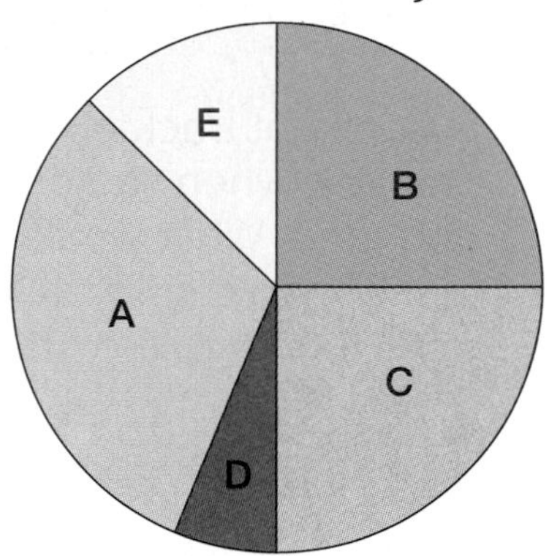

9. Copy the circle graph and write the name of the appropriate invention in each section, according to the number of students who chose it.

10. Tell how you knew which invention was represented by each section.

Mixed Review

11. The tour director at a factory gives souvenirs to visiting students. There are 540 souvenirs left for the last week of the school year. Three schools are scheduled to bring 145, 194, and 186 students. Is an estimate enough to decide if more souvenirs are needed?

12. Kelly has $50 saved. She is buying a jacket that costs $35.99. The sales tax will be $3.06. How much money will Kelly have left?

13. Write and solve an equation to find the original price of a sweater reduced by $5.25 to a sale price of $29.75.

Use Homework Workbook 3-8.

Diagnostic Checkpoint

Complete. For Exercises 1–3, use words from the Word Bank.

Word Bank
line graph
median
mode
ordered pair
trend

1. The ____________ is the number that occurs most often in a data set.
(3-7)

2. A ____________ shows how data changes over time.
(3-4)

3. The middle number in a set of ordered data is called the ____________.
(3-7)

Use the line graph for Exercises 4–6.

CD Sales at Audio World

NUMBER SOLD TO DATE (thousands)

800
700
600
500
400
300
200
100
0

1996 1997 1998 1999 2000

YEAR

4. By 2000, about how many CDs had been sold?
(3-5)

5. Between which two years did sales increase the least?
(3-5)

6. About how many CDs were sold between 1998 and 1999?
(3-5)

7. Susan kept track of the weight of her dog, Smokey, when she began feeding it a new dog food. What would be the best type of graph to display this data? Why? Use the table to create the graph.
(3-6)

Smokey's Weight

Week	Pounds
1	9
2	12
3	15
4	20

Find the range, mean, median, and mode for each data set.

8. 13, 25, 48, 25, 39
(3-7)

9. 13, 5, 1, 5
(3-7)

Use the circle graph at the right to answer each question.

Inventions Picked by Class

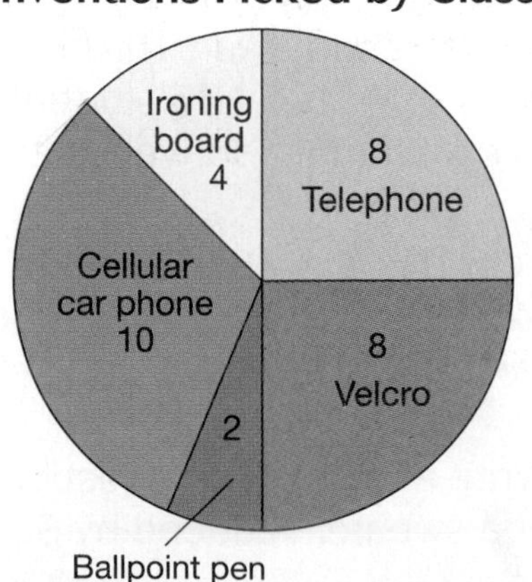

10. How many students are in the class?
(3-8)

11. Which invention was picked by the most students?
(3-8)

12. Which two inventions were picked by the same number of students?
(3-8)

Chapter 3 Test

Blue-jean Lengths Available
32, 50, 48, 37, 38, 55, 42, 58, 48, 31

1. Make a stem-and-leaf plot for the data at the right.

Use the graph for Questions 2–4.

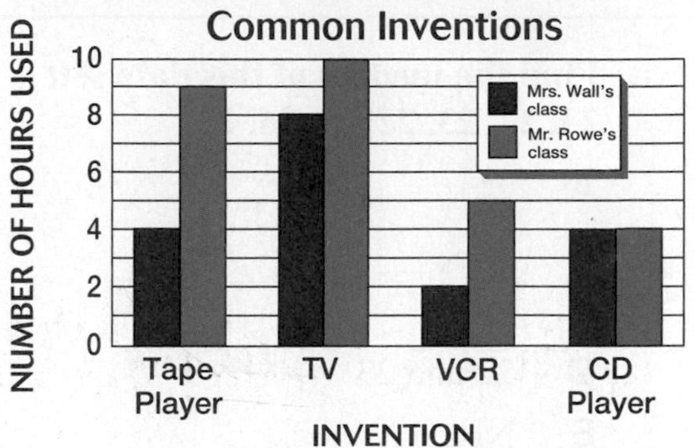

2. How many classes were polled?
3. How many hours did students watch a VCR in Mrs. Wall's class? in Mr. Rowe's class?
4. How many more hours did Mr. Rowe's class listen to a tape player than Mrs. Wall's class?

Name the point or the ordered pair.

5. (3, 2)
6. (5, 3)
7. E
8. D

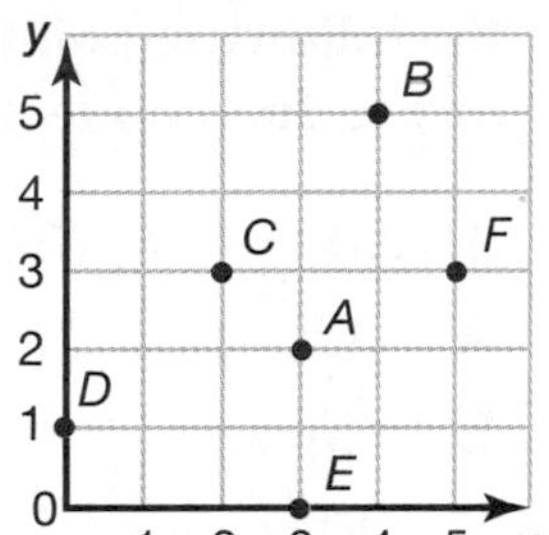

Use the circle graph for Questions 9 and 10.

9. How many students were surveyed?
10. Which eye color is the most common?

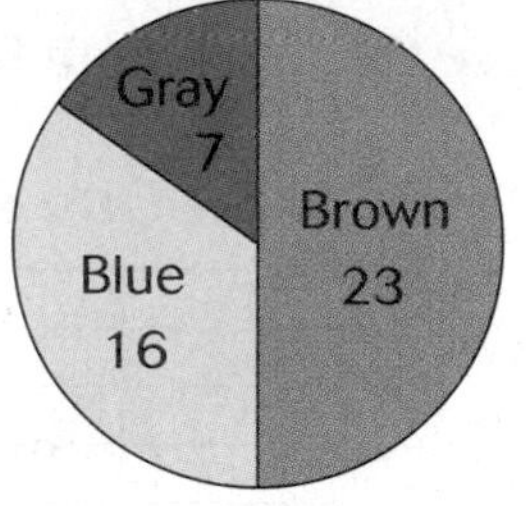

Use the graph for Questions 11 and 12.

11. How much did the bean plant grow between May and June?
12. Between which two months was there very little growth?

Bean Plant Growth

HEIGHT (INCHES): 0, 5, 10, 15, 20, 25, 30, 35, 40

MONTH: May, June, July, Aug., Sept.

Sam is inventing a machine to pick up paper clips. He tried four different magnets.

13. Make an appropriate graph to display the data.
14. What is the median of the data?
15. What is the mode of the data?

Paper Clips Picked Up	
Magnet	**Number**
1	36
2	40
3	36
4	28

Multiple-Choice Chapter 3 Test

Choose the correct letter for each answer.

1. **Find the median of this data set: 23, 22, 23, 22, 21, 26, 22.**

   A 21
   B 22
   C 23
   D 22 and 23
   E NH

Sharice invented a new shape of greenhouse. She tracked the growth of one particular plant in the greenhouse for 4 weeks.
Use the line graph for Questions 2 and 3.

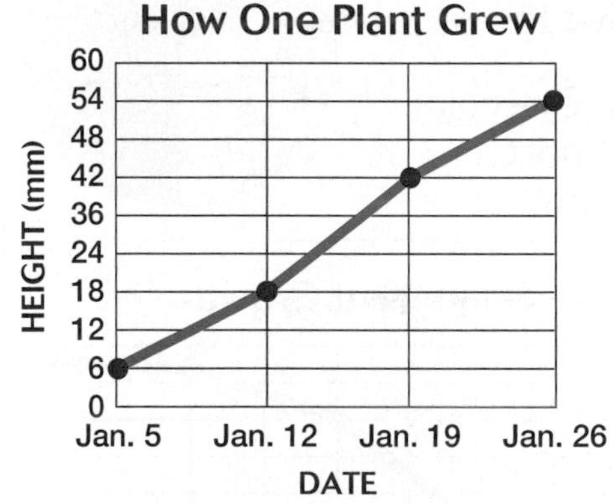

2. **During which week did the plant show the most growth?**

   F Jan. 5–Jan. 12
   G Jan. 12–Jan. 19
   H Jan. 19–Jan. 26
   J Growth was equal.

3. **About how much did the plant grow from Jan. 5 to Jan. 26?**

   A 54 mm
   B 42 mm
   C 18 mm
   D 48 mm

4. **Albert is graphing weekly in-line skate sales at stores in his town. What type of graph would be the best if Albert wants to study the sales trend?**

   F Line graph
   G Pictograph
   H Line plot
   J Stem and leaf

5. **What shape is formed if you graph the following points, connect them in order, and connect *D* to *A*?**

   ***A*(1, 3) *B*(6, 3) *C*(6, 6) *D*(1, 6)**

   A Triangle
   B Square
   C Rectangle
   D Circle

Use the line plot for Question 6.

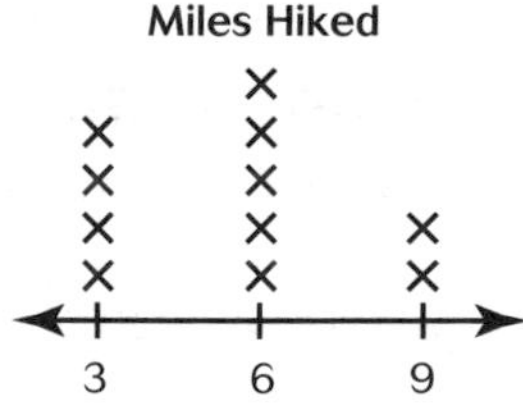

6. **How many more people hiked 6 miles than 3 miles?**

   F 1
   G 2
   H 3
   J 4

Use the graph for Questions 7 and 8.

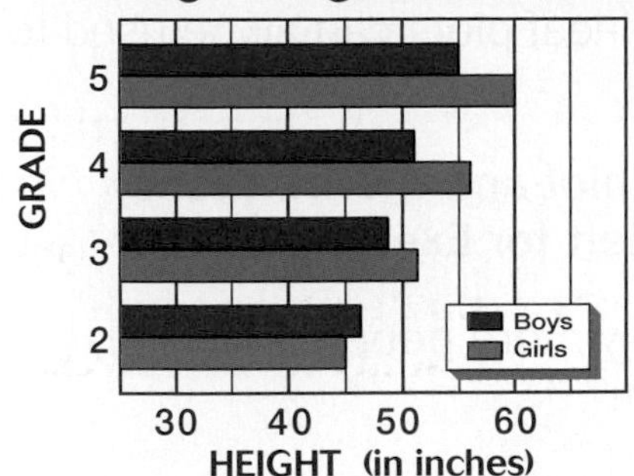

7. **In what grade did the girls begin to be taller than the boys?**

A 2 C 4
B 3 D 5

---

8. **How much did the girls' average height change from Grade 2 to Grade 5?**

F 15 inches H 8 inches
G 12 inches J 5 inches

---

9. **Which best represents how to graph the ordered pair (3, 5)?**

A 3 up, 5 down C 3 across, 5 up
B 3 up, 5 up D 3 up, 5 across

---

10. **These are the heights of five plants grown in the greenhouse for 5 weeks.**

5.8 cm, 0 cm, 6.4 cm, 4.5 cm, 6.4 cm

Another plant 4.5 cm tall is added to this group. What is the mode of the data set now?

A 6.4 cm and 5.8 cm
B 4.5 cm
C 4.5 cm and 6.4 cm
D 0 cm
E NH

Use the graph for Questions 11 and 12.

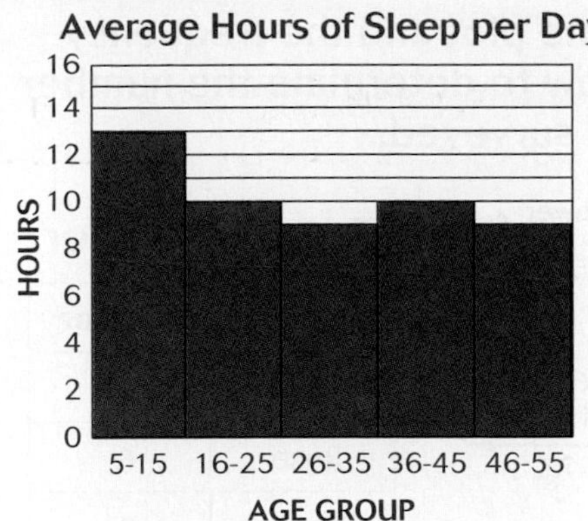

11. **What type of graph is displayed above?**

A Bar graph
B Double bar graph
C Histogram
D Line graph

---

12. **What age group sleeps the most?**

F 5–15 H 25–35
G 16–25 J 46–55

Use the graph for Question 13.

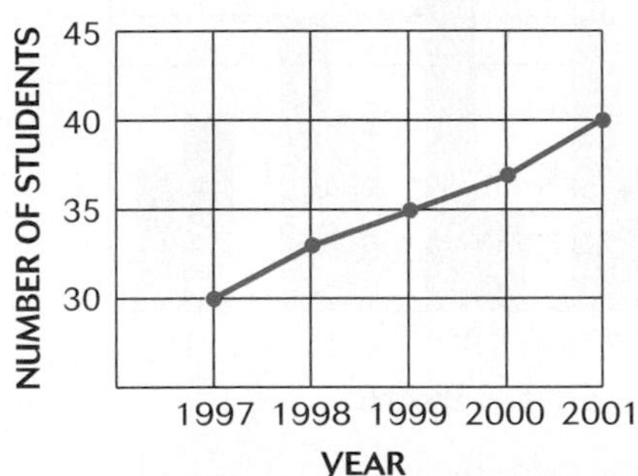

13. **Estimate how many students will be enrolled in the year 2002.**

F 40 H 43
G 37 J 52

Reteaching

Set A (pages 84–87)

Use the line plot and the frequency table below to determine the number of people surveyed.

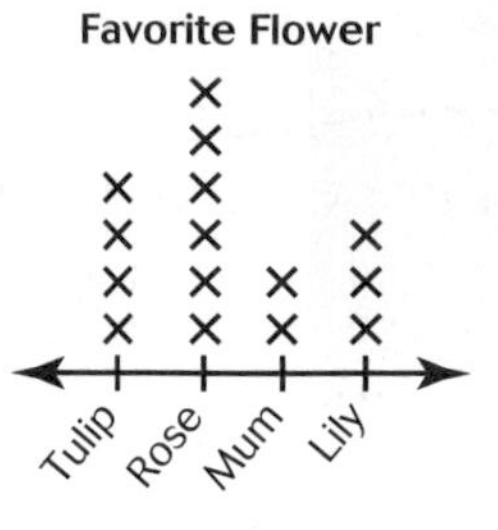

Favorite Flower

Response	Number
Tulip	4
Rose	6
Mum	2
Lily	3

To find the total surveyed, add the numbers in the frequency table.

$4 + 6 + 2 + 3 = 15$

Count the *X*s in the line plot to check.

Remember, frequency tables, line plots, and stem-and-leaf plots can all be used to organize data.

Use the line plot and the frequency table at the left for Exercises 1–3.

1. How many more people chose lily than mum?
2. How many people chose a flower other than the rose?
3. If six more people were surveyed and 4 chose tulip and 2 chose mum, which flower would then be the least popular?

Set B (pages 89–90)

Use the graph below. What does each bar represent?

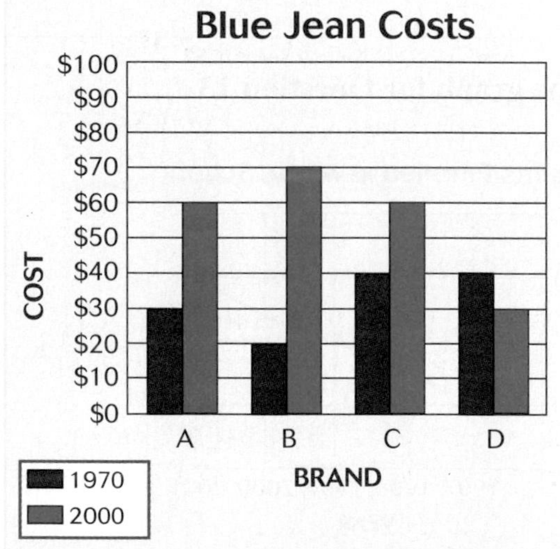

To find what each bar represents, look at the key of the bar graph. The key shows the purple bar is the cost of blue jeans in 1970 and the green bar is the cost of blue jeans in 2000.

Remember, a double bar graph uses two different shaded or colored bars to compare two sets of data.

Use the graph at the left for Exercises 1–4.

1. What brand increased in price the most?
2. What brand went down in price from 1970 to 2000?
3. For what brand is the cost increase from 1970 to 2000 the least?
4. How much did Brand A blue jeans cost in 1970?

Set C (pages 91–93)

Use the grid below to name the point located by the ordered pair (5, 3).

From zero, move 5 units to the right and 3 units up. The point is Point *B*.

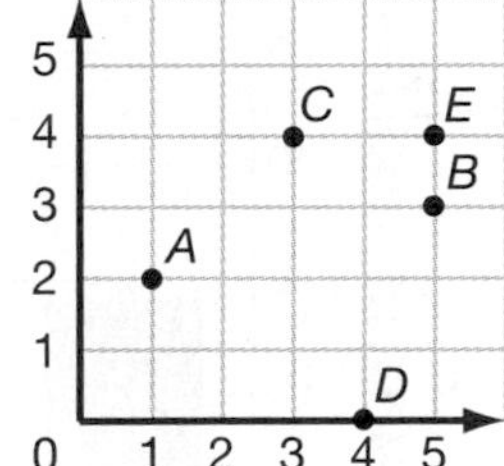

Remember, the first number in an ordered pair tells how far to move to the right from zero. The second number tells how far to move up from zero.

Use the grid at the left for Exercises 1–4. Write the ordered pair or name the point.

1. *A*

2. (3, 4)

3. *E*

4. (4, 0)

Set D (pages 98–101)

Use the graph below to find how deep the snow was on Day 2.

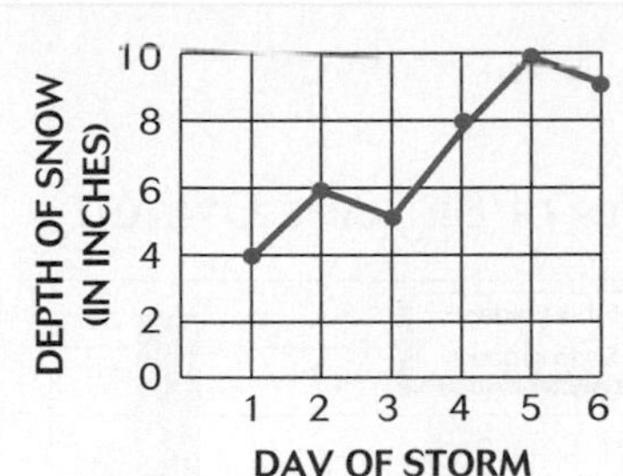

Locate Day 2 on the horizontal axis. Move up to the point on the line and read the corresponding depth. The snow was 6 inches deep on Day 2.

Remember, a line graph may be used to show how data changes over time.

Use the graph for Exercises 1–3.

1. Between what two days did the snow increase the most?

2. How much snow fell from Day 4 to Day 5?

3. On which day was the snow the deepest?

Set E (pages 104–106)

Find the mean, median, and mode for the following set of data.

23, 27, 24, 23, 28

To find the mean, first add the numbers.

23 + 27 + 24 + 23 + 28 = 125

Then divide the sum by 5, because there are 5 numbers in the set.

125 ÷ 5 = 25 ← The mean is 25.

Write the 5 numbers in order.
The mode is the number used most often.
The median is the middle number.

23, 23, **24**, 27, 28

The mode is 23. The median is 24.

Remember, a set of data might have no mode, one mode, or more than one mode.

Find the mean, median, and mode for each set of data.

1. 200, 200, 220, 235, 200

2. 12, 9, 7, 6, 9, 7, 13, 7, 9, 11

3. 2, 8, 7, 1, 3, 6, 1

More Practice

Set A (pages 84–87)

Use the graph at the right for Exercises 1–3.

1. What do the bars represent?
2. Which item do the most students have in their homes?
3. How else could you display the data?

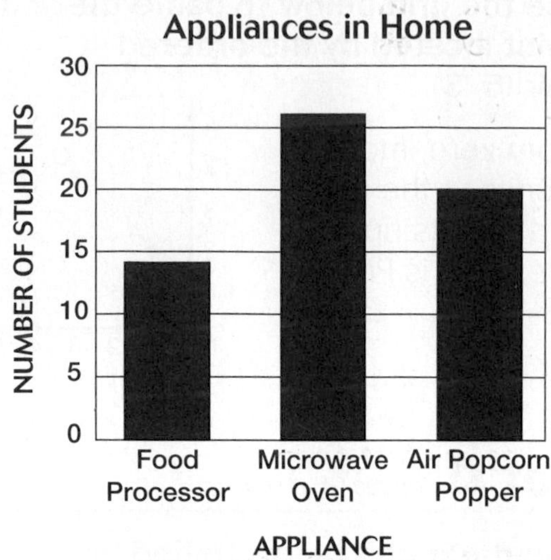

Set B (pages 89–90)

Use the graph at the right for Exercises 1–4.

1. What is the label on the horizontal axis? the vertical axis?
2. How many fifth graders own a blue bicycle? How many sixth graders own a blue bicycle?
3. Which color bicycle is owned by the same number of fifth and sixth graders? How many in each grade own one?
4. How many sixth graders have a bicycle of a color other than red, blue, or white? Is this more or less than the number of fifth graders?

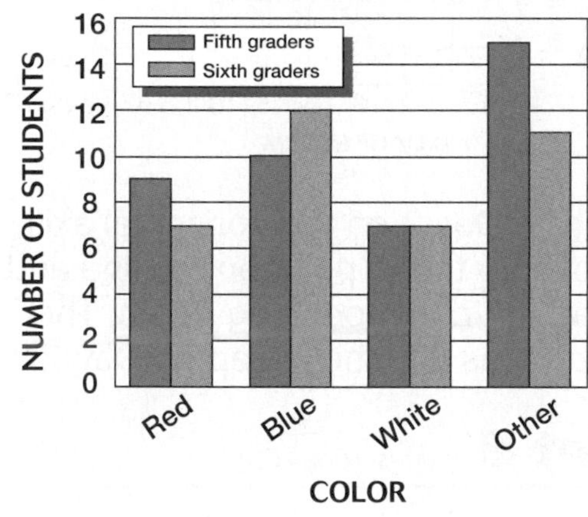

Use the table for Exercises 5 and 6.

5. Use the table to make a double bar graph.
6. What interval did you use for the number of hours? Explain your choice.

Bike Riding Times

Day of the Week	Paul	Karyn
Monday	2 hours	$1\frac{1}{2}$ hours
Wednesday	1 hour	3 hours
Friday	$2\frac{1}{2}$ hours	$2\frac{1}{2}$ hours

Set C (pages 91–93)

Use the grid to name the point at each location or to write the ordered pair for each point.

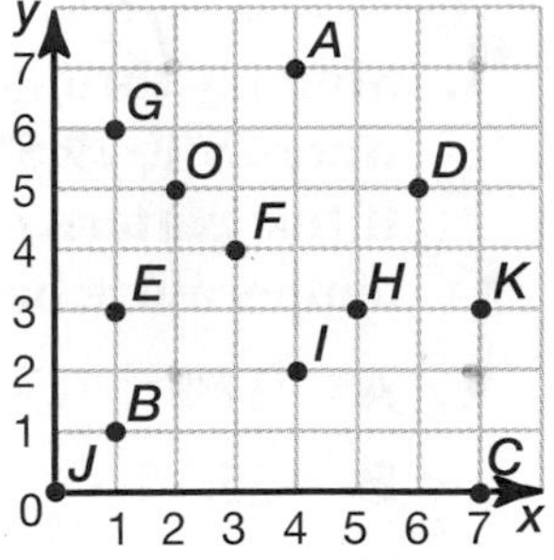

1. (1, 3)
2. (6, 5)
3. (7, 0)
4. (1, 6)
5. *B*
6. *O*
7. *A*
8. *F*
9. *J*
10. (4, 2)
11. *K*
12. (5, 3)
13. What shape is formed by connecting points at (2, 2), (7, 2), (7, 7), and (2, 7) in order, and by connecting the first point to the last point?

Set D (pages 98–101)

Use the graph at the right for Exercises 1–3.

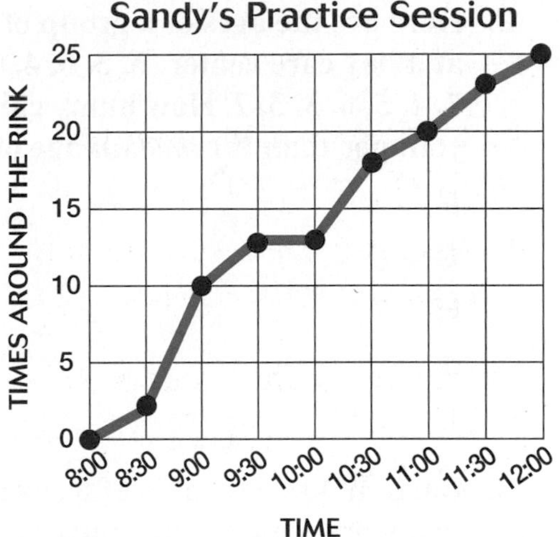

1. How many times around the rink did Sandy skate between 8:00 and 12:00?
2. During which half-hour interval did Sandy skate around the rink the greatest number of times?
3. What do you notice about the line between 9:30 and 10:00? Explain what this means.

Set E (pages 104–106)

Find the mean, median, mode, and range for the data in Exercises 1–6.

1. 12, 12, 15, 9, 17
2. 98, 96, 98, 100, 88
3. 2, 4, 7, 7, 8, 8, 6
4. 26, 30, 19, 20, 21, 12, 12
5. 25, 48, 28, 28, 28, 23
6. 21, 16, 16, 15, 17
7. Marcie's newest invention is a high-bouncing ball. In five bounces, the ball reached heights of 2 ft, 5 ft, 5 ft, 7 ft, and 9 ft. What is the range of heights the ball bounced?

Problem Solving: Preparing for Tests

Choose the correct letter for each answer.

1. Monday through Friday the low temperatures were 28°F, 29.5°F, 31°F, 32.5°F, and 34°F. If this pattern continues, what will the low temperature be next Tuesday?

A 37°F

B 35.5°F

C 40°F

D 41.5°F

Tip

Use *Find a Pattern* to help you solve this problem.

2. Here are the ages of a group of children at a day care center: 5, 3, 6, 4, 6, 5, 4, 6, 3, 2, 7, 4, 5, 6, 5, 3, 2. How many children are younger than the *median* age of the group?

F 5

G 6

H 7

J 8

Tip

The median is the middle number when the numbers are arranged in order.

3. Barb makes a display of 6 rows of videos in a store window. She puts 12 boxes in the bottom row, 10 boxes in the next row, 8 boxes in the next, and so on. There are 2 videos on top. How many videos does Barb use for this display?

A 32

B 36

C 42

D 43

Tip

Use one of these strategies to solve this problem.

- *Draw a Diagram*
- *Find a Pattern*

4. On his weekend job, Troy made \$97.50 on Saturday. At the end of the day on Sunday, he had a total of \$204.50 for the two days. Which is the best estimate for the amount Troy made on Sunday?

F Less than \$75

G About \$85

H About \$100

J More than \$150

---

5. The average of the ages of four brothers is 16. The youngest brother is 8 years old, and the oldest is 22. Which could be the ages of the other two brothers?

A 10 and 16

B 12 and 18

C 15 and 19

D 18 and 20

---

6. Jill is 4 years older than Pat. Bob is 2 years older than Pat. If you know that Pat is 12 years old, which number sentence can you use to find the sum, *s*, of the three ages?

F $s = 2 + 4 + 12$

G $s = (12 - 4) + (12 - 2) + 12$

H $s = (12 + 4) + (12 - 2) + 12$

J $s = (12 + 4) + (12 + 2) + 12$

---

7. Suki bought a book for \$7.95 and 2 notebooks. She gave the clerk \$20 and received \$9 change. Which is the best estimate for the price of each notebook?

A Less than \$1.00

B \$1.50

C \$2.00

D \$2.50

8. The students washed cars to raise money for charity. They made more than \$400 the first day, \$250 the second day, and less than \$200 the third day. Which is a reasonable amount for how much more they made the first day than the second day?

F Exactly \$150

G Less than \$150

H More than \$150

J More than \$650

Use the graph for Problem 9.

The graph shows the distance Greg and his brother drove to a campground.

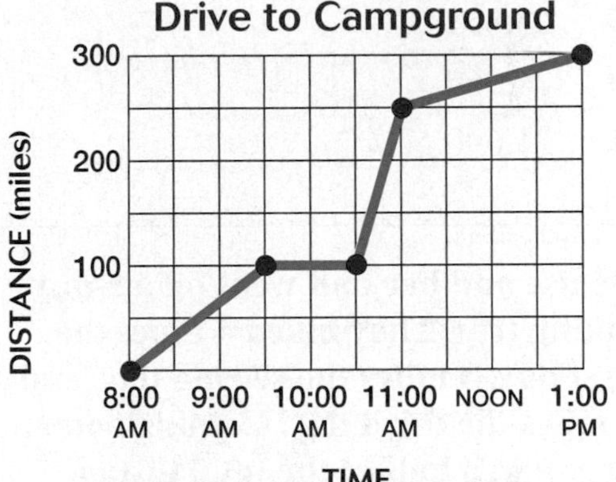

9. Choose the best interpretation of the graph.

A They drove to the campground without stopping.

B The campground is 300 miles from their starting point.

C They drove to the campground and stayed for 3 days.

D They stopped twice on their way to the campground.

TEST PREP

Multiple-Choice Cumulative Review

Choose the correct letter for each answer.

Number Sense

1. Alan scored 3 times as many goals as Lee scored. If Alan scored 27 goals, how many did Lee score?

A 3
B 9
C 30
D 81

2. Which is the sum of 1.08, 0.76, and 23.012?

F 23.196
G 24.852
H 24.960
J 31.690

3. Denise and her dad went on a 5-day hiking trip. They hiked 4 miles the first day, 3 miles the second day, and 5 miles the third day. Coming home, they hiked half of the total distance each day. How far did they hike each day of the return trip?

A 4 miles
B 5 miles
C 6 miles
D 12 miles

4. Ben wanted to make 34 copies of a 13-page booklet. The copies cost $0.03 per page. How much did the copies cost?

F $4.42
G $10.25
H $12.26
J $13.26

Algebra and Functions

5. Which of the following makes this number sentence true?

$$3 \times (2 + n) = 24$$

A $n = 6$
B $n = 8$
C $n = 10$
D $n = 12$

6. Which equation demonstrates the associative property of addition?

F $1 + 3 = 3 + 1$
G $3 + 0 = 3$
H $3 + (2 + 1) = (3 + 2) + 1$
J $3 + (2 + 1) = (2 + 1) + 3$

7. Which number sentence best represents this problem?

Tara bought 3 plants for $1.29 each and 3 clay pots for $2.29 each.

A (\$1.29 + \$2.29) + 3 = *n*
B (3 + \$1.29) × (3 + \$2.29) = *n*
C (3 × \$1.29) + (3 × \$2.29) = *n*
D 3 × (\$1.29 × \$2.29) = *n*

8. Which expression has the same value as $4 \times (3 + 2)$?

F $4 + 5$
G $7 + 6$
H $(4 \times 3) + (4 \times 2)$
J $(4 + 3) \times (4 + 2)$

Statistics, Data Analysis, and Probability

9. In a total of 80 spins, on which shape is it likely that the spinner will land most often?

A ♥

B ▲

C ●

D ★

Use the bar graph below to answer Questions 10 and 11.

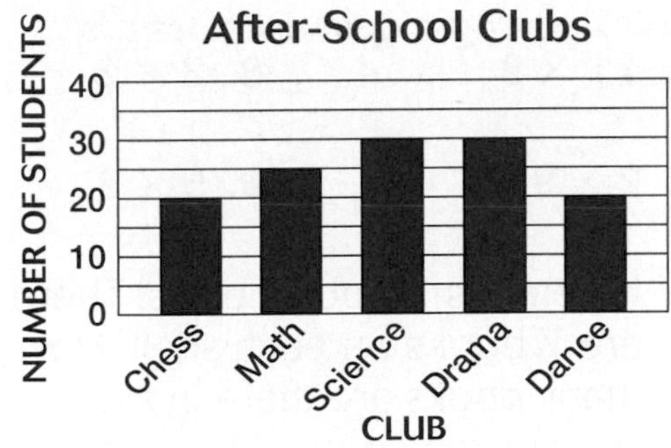

10. Which two after-school clubs have an equal number of students?

F Dance and Chess

G Math and Drama

H Chess and Drama

J Science and Dance

11. About how many students are involved in all of the after-school clubs?

A 125

B 120

C 100

D 90

Use the double bar graph below to answer Questions 12–14.

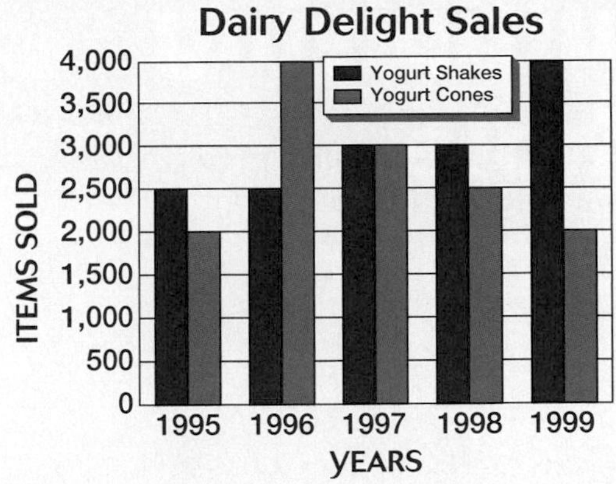

12. In which year did Dairy Delight sell more yogurt cones than shakes?

F 1995 **H** 1997

G 1996 **J** 1998

13. About how many more yogurt shakes than cones did Dairy Delight sell in 1999?

A 1,000 **C** 2,000

B 1,500 **D** 2,500

14. About how many yogurt cones were sold over the 5 years?

F 28,500 **H** 13,500

G 15,500 **J** 12,500

15. Stasia has a 93 average in English. She has already taken four tests. If she scores a 98 on her last test, what will her final average be?

A 93 **C** 95

B 94 **D** 96

Multiplying Whole Numbers

4-1 **Multiplication Properties**

4-2 **Order of Operations**

4-3 **Evaluating Expressions with Whole Numbers**

4-4 **Problem-Solving Skill: Choose the Operation**

4-5 **Mental Math: Multiplication Patterns Using 10, 100, and 1,000**

4-6 **Estimating Products**

4-7 **Multiplying by One-Digit and Two-Digit Numbers**

4-8 **Problem-Solving Strategy: Solve a Simpler Problem**

4-9 **Multiplying Greater Numbers**

4-10 **Exponents**

4-11 **Problem-Solving Application: Using Money**

Diagnosing Readiness

In Chapter 4, you will use these skills:

Ⓐ Multiplication Facts

(Grade 4)

1. 7 × 4 **2.** 4 × 8

3. 1 × 6 **4.** 6 × 9

5. 3 × 5 **6.** 7 × 4

7. 11 × 8 **8.** 3 × 3

9. 2 × 9 **10.** 5 × 9

11. Karen has 5 bookshelves. There are 7 books on each shelf. How many books are there in all?

Ⓑ Rounding

(pages 16–18)

Round each number to the underlined place.

12. 29,$\underline{7}$92 **13.** $\underline{1}$46,273

14. $\underline{6}$8,159 **15.** $\underline{4}$,411

16. $\underline{2}$7 **17.** $\underline{9}$6

18. 2$\underline{3}$7 **19.** $\underline{7}$89

20. 1,$\underline{1}$85 **21.** $\underline{5}$,188

C Adding Whole Numbers

(pages 60–62)

22. $\begin{array}{r} 427 \\ +\ 643 \\ \hline \end{array}$

23. $\begin{array}{r} 2{,}755 \\ +\ 8{,}757 \\ \hline \end{array}$

24. $\begin{array}{r} 92 \\ +\ 19 \\ \hline \end{array}$

25. $\begin{array}{r} 75 \\ +\ 67 \\ \hline \end{array}$

26. $\begin{array}{r} 8{,}401 \\ +2{,}637 \\ \hline \end{array}$

27. $\begin{array}{r} 5{,}442 \\ +\ 647 \\ \hline \end{array}$

28. $\begin{array}{r} 96 \\ +67 \\ \hline \end{array}$

29. $\begin{array}{r} 151 \\ +\ 99 \\ \hline \end{array}$

30. $\begin{array}{r} 5{,}620 \\ 44{,}687 \\ +64{,}040 \\ \hline \end{array}$

31. $\begin{array}{r} 89 \\ 643 \\ +8{,}650 \\ \hline \end{array}$

32. $\begin{array}{r} 2{,}148 \\ 23{,}620 \\ +62{,}500 \\ \hline \end{array}$

33. $\begin{array}{r} 768 \\ 1{,}950 \\ +27{,}200 \\ \hline \end{array}$

D Multiplying by 10

(Grade 4)

Copy and complete each table.

34.

	×10
7	70
4	
2	

35.

	×10
5	
8	
3	30

36. Jack bought 9 packages of pencils. There are 10 pencils in each package. How many pencils did he buy?

E Evaluating Expressions

(pages 55–57)

Evaluate each expression for $n = 4$, $n = 10$, and $n = 12$.

37. $n - 3$

38. $n + 27$

39. $5n$

40. $\frac{n}{2}$

41. $18 - n$

42. $\frac{60}{n}$

To the Family and Student

Looking Back	Chapter 4	Looking Ahead
In Grade 4, students learned multiplication facts.	**Multiplying Whole Numbers** In this chapter, students will learn to multiply whole numbers by one-digit, two-digit, and three-digit numbers.	In Chapters 6 and 8, students will learn how to multiply decimals and fractions.

Math and Everyday Living

Opportunities to apply the concepts of Chapter 4 abound in everyday situations. During the chapter, think about how multiplying whole numbers can be used to solve a variety of real-world problems. The following examples suggest just several of the many situations that could launch a discussion about multiplying whole numbers.

Math and Transportation To transport the band members to an amusement park for a parade, the band uses a combination of buses, cars, and vans. There are 3 buses with 56 members in each bus, 7 cars with 5 members in each car, and 4 vans with 7 members in each van. Write an expression for the total number of band members going to the parade. Then find the total.

Math and Shopping You leave your house with $40 and go to the craft store. You need to purchase the following materials to make a gift for your aunt's wedding. Estimate to see if you have enough money to buy everything you need.

Material	Cost
Paint	$3.75
Yarn	$5.89
Needles	$3.32
Glue	$0.68
Felt	$12.37
Ivy	$7.34

Math and the Zoo On a recent trip to the zoo you made a chart to keep track of the numbers of different animals that you saw.

Type of Animal	Number
Monkey	36
Zebra	18
Giraffe	10
Bald Eagle	3
Polar Bear	2
White Tiger	4

What operation would you use if you wanted to find the total number of animals that you saw at the zoo?

Math and Recreation A group of students plan to take a 22-mile white-water rafting trip down the New West River. Each raft can hold 8 people. Your group will need to rent 22 rafts. Each raft will be completely filled with students from your group. How many students will be going on the trip?

Math and the Environment The recycling club in your neighborhood collected 568 pounds of newspapers in a one-month period of time. At this rate, how many pounds of newspapers can they collect and recycle in one year?

Math and Money You make $20 every Saturday working at the indoor soccer concession stand. You plan on putting half of what you make into your savings account. How much money will you save in a one-year period?

Math and the Market The cost of six boxes of oatmeal, with a coupon for $1.50 off, can be represented by the expression $6x - 1.50$, where x represents the price of each box of oatmeal. Evaluate the expression if the price of each box of oatmeal is $3.

California Content Standards in Chapter 4 Lessons*

	Teach and Practice	Practice
Number Sense		
1.0 Students compute with . . . positive integers . . .and . . . understand the relative magnitude of numbers.	4-5, 4-7, 4-9	4-1, 4-4
1.1 Estimate [and] round . . .	4-6	
1.3 Understand and compute positive integer powers of nonnegative integers; compute examples as repeated multiplication.	4-10	
Algebra and Functions		
1.2 (🔑) Use a letter to represent an unknown number; write and evaluate simple algebraic expressions in one variable by substitution.	4-3	4-1, 4-2
1.3 Know and use the distributive property in equations and expressions with variables.	4-1	
1.3 (Gr. 6) (🔑) Apply algebraic order of operations and the commutative, associative, and distributive properties to evaluate expressions . . .	4-1, 4-2	4-3

	Teach and Practice	Practice
Mathematical Reasoning		
1.0 Students make decisions about how to approach problems.	4-4	
1.1 Analyze problems by identifying relationships . . . and observing patterns.	4-5	4-1, 4-3, 4-7, 4-8, 4-9
1.2 Determine when and how to break a problem into simpler parts.	4-11	
2.1 Use estimation to verify the reasonableness of calculated results.	4-7, 4-9	
2.2 Apply strategies and results from simpler problems to more complex problems.	4-8	
2.3 Use a variety of methods, such as words, numbers, symbols, charts, graphs, tables, diagrams, and models, to explain mathematical reasoning.		4-8
2.6 Make precise calculations and check the validity of the results from the context of the problem.	4-11	4-4
3.2 Note the method of deriving the solution and demonstrate a conceptual understanding of the derivation by solving similar problems.	4-8	

* The symbol (🔑) indicates a key standard as designated in the Mathematics Framework for California Public Schools. Full statements of the California Content Standards are found at the beginning of this book following the Table of Contents.

LESSON 4-1

Multiplication Properties

California Content Standard *Algebra and Functions 1.3: Know and use the distributive property in equations and expressions with variables; Also Algebra and Functions 1.3 (Grade 6) (See p. 125.)*

Warm-Up Review

1. 2.68 + 3.12
2. 43 + 98
3. 350 − 230
4. 20 + 18
5. \$25.00 − \$15.00
6. (3 × 10) + (3 × 7)
7. Louis has 6 boxes of markers. Margo has 5 more boxes than Louis. How many boxes does Margo have?

Word Bank

commutative property of multiplication
associative property of multiplication
identity property
zero property
distributive property

Math Link You learned in Chapter 2 about the properties of addition. In this lesson, you will learn about some important properties of multiplication.

Properties	Examples
Commutative Property The order of the factors does not change the product.	factors ↙ ↘ product ↓ 3 × 5 = 15 5 × 3 = 15
Associative Property The way the factors are grouped does not change the product. (When computing products, do the work in parentheses first.)	3 × (4 × 2) = 3 × 8 = 24 (3 × 4) × 2 = 12 × 2 = 24
Identity Property When 1 is one of two factors, the product is the other factor.	16 × 1 = 16 1 × 16 = 16
Zero Property When 0 is a factor, the product is 0.	0 × 7 = 0 7 × 0 = 0

The distributive property combines multiplication and addition.

Distributive Property	
Think of one factor as the sum of two addends. Then multiply each addend by the other factor and add the products.	3 × 14 = 3 × (10 + 4) = (3 × 10) + (3 × 4) = 30 + 12 = 42

More Examples

A. Find *n* if 6 × 78 × 0 × 399 = *n*. Name the property used.

n = 0

The zero property is used.

B. Find *n* if *n* × (10 + 8) = (7 × 10) + (7 × 8).

By the distributive property,
7 × (10 + 8) = (7 × 10) + (7 × 8).

So, *n* = 7.

Additional Standards: Algebra and Functions 1.2 (key); Number Sense 1.0; Mathematical Reasoning 1.1 (See p. 125.)

Guided Practice *For another example, see Set A on p. 156.*

Find each n. Name the property that you used.

1. $6 \times (4 \times 3) = (6 \times 4) \times n$ **2.** $5 \times 9 = n \times 5$ **3.** $6 \times n = 6$

4. $45 \times (n \times 6) = (45 \times 12) \times 6$ **5.** $4 \times (10 + 3) = n$ **6.** $0 \times 238 = n$

7. If Juan walks his dog for 15 minutes twice a day, how much time is needed to walk his dog in one week?

Independent Practice *For more practice, see Set A on p. 158.*

Find each n. Name the property that you used.

8. $17 \times n = 17$ **9.** $6 \times 20 = n \times 6$ **10.** $(3 \times 2) \times 7 = 3 \times (2 \times n)$

11. $(17 \times n) \times 4 = 0$ **12.** $n = 87 \times 1$ **13.** $n \times (10 + 3) = (6 \times 10) + (6 \times 3)$

Compare. Write $>$, $<$, or $=$ for each ●.

14. 3×19 ● $(3 \times 10) + (3 \times 9)$ **15.** $34 \times 0 \times 100$ ● $34 \times 1 \times 100$

16. $3 \times 8 \times 5$ ● $8 \times 3 \times 2$ **17.** $417 \times 3 \times 2$ ● $16 \times 0 \times 417$

18. Math Reasoning Lori has five packages of 48 beads. Carole has 48 packages of 5 beads. Who has more beads? How do you know without actually multiplying?

Mixed Review

19. 27,463 + 43,621 **20.** 3.08 + 4.23 **21.** 36,489 − 516

Algebra Solve for n.

22. $18 + n = 21$ **23.** $n - 29 = 36$ **24.** $88 + n = 108$

25. Mental Math Use compensation to find 47 + 16.

26. Find the mean of the following set: 27, 32, 20, 27, 34.

Test Prep **Choose the correct letter for the answer.**

27. Refer to the graph at the right. On which day was the high temperature about 45°?
(3-5)

A Monday **C** Thursday

B Tuesday **D** Friday

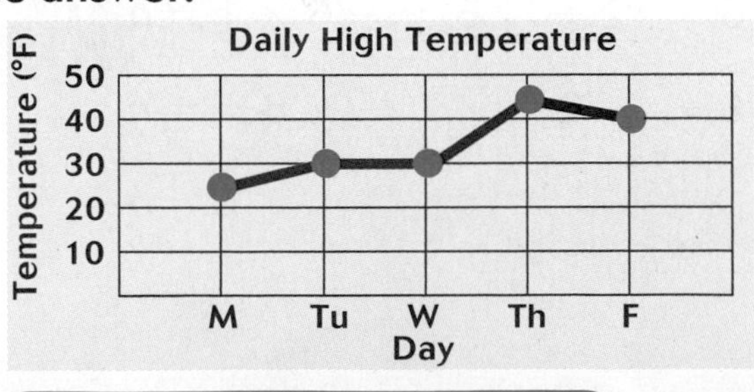

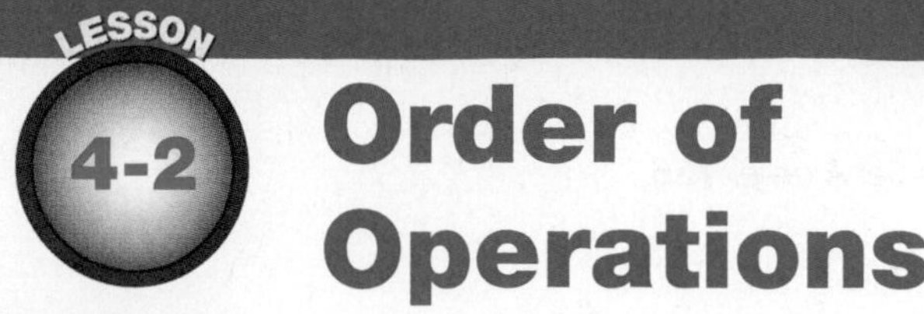

Order of Operations

California Content Standard *Algebra and Functions 1.3 (Grade 6): Apply algebraic order of operations . . . to evaluate expressions . . .*

Warm-Up Review

1. $4 \times (3 + 2)$
2. $(3 \times 4) + 5$
3. $23 + 78 + 77$
4. $7.3 + 4.2$
5. $4.72 - 2.84$
6. $3 \times (11 + 4)$
7. Kim has \$50.00 to spend. Does she have enough to buy a CD for \$18.95 and a sweater for \$32.99?

Math Link You have learned how the properties of addition and multiplication are useful in evaluating expressions. Sometimes you need to evaluate expressions involving two or more operations.

Example 1

Two different people were asked to evaluate $12 + 6 \div 3$.

One person did the division first.

$$12 + 6 \div 3 = 12 + 2$$
$$= 14$$

The other did the addition first.

$$12 + 6 \div 3 = 18 \div 3$$
$$= 6$$

As you can see, two different answers are possible in evaluating $12 + 6 \div 3$. To avoid having two different answers, mathematicians have agreed upon the following **order of operations.**

Word Bank

order of operations

Order of Operations

- First, do all the operations inside parentheses.
- Next, do all multiplication and division from left to right.
- Last, do all addition and subtraction from left to right.

Therefore, by applying the order of operations, the correct answer for the example above is 14.

Example 2

Find n if $6 + 12 \div (2 \times 3) - 6 \times 1 = n$.

$$6 + 12 \div \underbrace{(2 \times 3)} - 6 \times 1 = n$$
First, do operations inside parentheses.

$$6 + \underbrace{12 \div 6} - \underbrace{6 \times 1} = n$$
Next, do **multiplication** and **division** from left to right.

$$6 + 2 - 6 = n$$
$$2 = n$$
Last, do all **addition** and **subtraction** from left to right.

Additional Standard: Algebra and Functions 1.2 (🔑) *(See p. 125.)*

Guided Practice *For another example, see Set B on p. 156.*

Tell which operation should be done first. Then find each *n*.

1. $3 \times 5 + 12 = n$

2. $27 \div (18 - 9) = n$

3. $14 - 8 \div 4 + 6 = n$

4. Explain how the number sentence shown below represents this problem: *Find the total cost of twelve $8 train tickets and ten $3 subway tokens.*

$$(12 \times \$8) + (10 \times \$3) = n$$

Independent Practice *For more practice, see Set B on p. 158.*

Tell which operation should be done first. Then find each *n*.

5. $7 + 5 \times 8 = n$

6. $40 \div (12 + 8) = n$

7. $14 - 28 \div 7 \times 2 = n$

Choose a value from the box at the right to make each sentence true.

10	4	21
8	12	0
14	38	45
68	44	13
16	13	9

8. $8 - 6 \div 3 + 4 = n$

9. $10 \div 5 \times 4 - 8 = n$

10. $6 \times (8 + 4) - 2 \times 2 = n$

11. $(9 + 1) \div 2 \times 3 \times 3 = n$

12. $8 + 2 \div 2 - 1 = n$

13. $16 + 3 - 2 \times 3 = n$

14. $6 \times 6 + (5 - 3) = n$

15. $(7 + 7) \div 7 \times 7 = n$

16. $16 \div 8 + 5 \times 2 = n$

17. $n \times (3 + 4) = 63$

18. There are four cars with five people in each car and two vans with eight people in each van. Write a number sentence that tells the total number of travelers. Then find the answer.

Mixed Review

19. Sean wants to buy a small tape player for $25.95, plus $1.50 tax. If Sean has $28.00, does he have enough money?

20. Algebra If $6 \times 0 = n$, find n.

21. Mental Math $33 + 15 + 5$

Test Prep **Choose the correct letter for each answer.**

22. (3-7) Find the median of the following set of data: 2, 1, 7, 9, 7, 5, 4.

A 5 **C** 8

B 7 **D** 4

23. (2-6) Which is the best estimate for $36 + 48$ if you use rounding?

F 70 **H** 90

G 80 **J** 100

LESSON 4-3

Evaluating Expressions with Whole Numbers

Algebra

Warm-Up Review

1. $3.68 + 5.21$ 2. $68 - 49$
3. $2 + 4 \times 5$
4. $2{,}389 - 1{,}667$
5. $2{,}000 - 238$ 6. $54 \div 9$
7. A box of pencils costs $5.36. Each box contains 50 pencils. How many pencils are in 7 boxes?

California Content Standard *Algebra and Functions 1.2 (key): Use a letter to represent an unknown number; write and evaluate simple expressions in one variable by substitution.*

Math Link You know how to evaluate expressions such as $12 + n$ or $50n$. These expressions involve only one operation. In this lesson you will evaluate expressions that involve two operations.

If an expression contains more than one operation, you need to follow the order of operations when you evaluate the expression.

Example 1

Evaluate $4 + 2w$ when $w = 6$, $w = 2$, and $w = 8$.

Remember that $2w$ means $2 \times w$.

When $w = 6$.

$4 + 2w = 4 + 2 \times 6$ Replace w with 6.

$= 4 + 12$ Use the order of operations and multiply first.

$= 16$ Then add.

When $w = 2$,

$4 + 2w = 4 + 2 \times 2$

$= 4 + 4$

$= 8$

When $w = 8$

$4 + 2w = 4 + 2 \times 8$

$= 4 + 16$

$= 20$

Example 2

Evaluate $\frac{p}{2} + 5$ when $p = 4$, $p = 8$, and $p = 2$.

Remember that $\frac{p}{2}$ means $p \div 2$.

When $p = 4$,

$\frac{p}{2} + 5 = \frac{4}{2} + 5$

$= 2 + 5$

$= 7$

When $p = 8$,

$\frac{p}{2} + 5 = \frac{8}{2} + 5$

$= 4 + 5$

$= 9$

When $p = 2$,

$\frac{p}{2} + 5 = \frac{2}{2} + 5$

$= 1 + 5$

$= 6$

Additional Standards: Algebra and Functions 1.3 (Gr. 6) (key); Mathematical Reasoning 1.1 *(See p. 125.)*

Guided Practice *For another example, see Set C on p. 156.*

Evaluate each expression for $x = 3$ and $x = 6$.

1. $2x$ **2.** $x - 2$ **3.** $\frac{x}{3}$ **4.** $2x + 2$

5. $16 + 2x$ **6.** $\frac{12}{x} - 2$ **7.** $27 - 2x$ **8.** $6 + 3x$

9. The cost of 4 CDs, together with a coupon for $5.00 off, can be represented by the expression $4p - 5$, where p represents the price of each CD. Evaluate the expression if the price of each CD is $10.00.

Independent Practice *For more practice, see Set C on p. 158.*

Evaluate each expression for $b = 5$ and $b = 10$.

10. $3b$ **11.** $\frac{50}{b}$ **12.** $b - 3$ **13.** $5 + b$

14. $2b + 3$ **15.** $\frac{10}{b} + 3$ **16.** $7 + 3b$ **17.** $6b - 7$

18. Math Reasoning If you evaluate $2 + 3w$ for $w = 5$, would you get the same result as if you evaluated $(2 + 3)w$ for $w = 5$? Explain.

Mixed Review

19. Evaluate $3 + 5 \times 7 - 2$ using the order of operations.

20. Round 7.984 to the nearest hundredth.

21. Make a stem-and-leaf plot for the data in the table at the right.

22. Find the mode for the data in the table at the right.

Number of Tickets			
23	24	31	35
18	15	22	30
20	10	41	43
17	15	38	29

23. Which property of multiplication tells you that $5 \times 7 = 7 \times 5$?

24. Find z if $5 \times (z + 4) = (5 \times 10) + (5 \times 4)$. Name the property used.

Test Prep Choose the correct letter for each answer.

25. Which decimal is equal to 0.4?
(1-4)

A 0.40 **C** 0.04

B 0.004 **D** 0.040

26. Algebra Solve $n + 25 = 48$.
(2-4)

F $n = 3$ **H** $n = 23$

G $n = 13$ **J** $n = 73$

Use Homework Workbook 4-3.

Problem-Solving Skill:
Choose the Operation

Warm-Up Review

1. $2 + 3 \times 4 - 5$
2. $2 \times 3 \times 0$
3. $3.54 - 2.60$
4. $2,345 + 23,667$
5. Evaluate when x is 5: $x - 5$
6. $(3 \times 2) + 4 \times 5$
7. Four cars held 4 people each and 5 vans held 8 people each. How many people were there in all?

California Content Standard *Mathematical Reasoning 1.0: Students make decisions about how to approach problems.*

Read for Understanding

Thomas has been doing research on how fast birds fly. Some of his notes are shown on the notebook at the right.

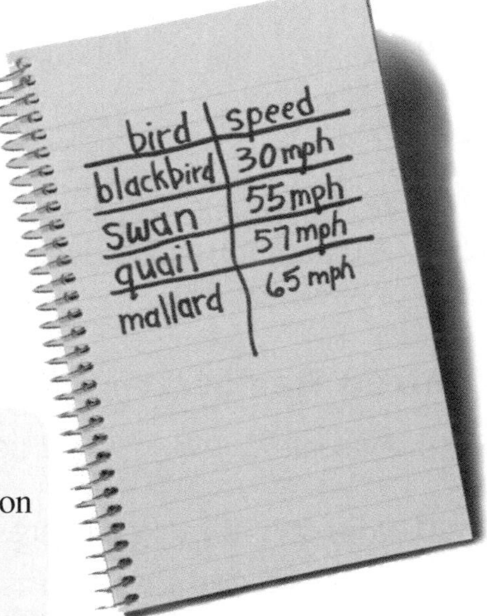

bird | speed
blackbird | 30 mph
swan | 55 mph
quail | 57 mph
mallard | 65 mph

1. How fast does a blackbird fly?
2. How fast does a mallard fly?
3. How fast does a swan fly?
4. How fast does a quail fly?

Think and Discuss

Choose the Operation

Clues in a problem help you decide which operation to use. You add to combine groups, subtract to compare groups, multiply to combine equal groups, and divide to separate into equal groups.

Reread the paragraph and the information in the notebook at the top of the page.

5. Which operation would you use to find the number of miles a swan can fly in 5 hours? Tell how you decided.
6. Which operation would you use to find how much faster a mallard can fly than a blackbird? Tell how you decided.
7. A swan flies for 3 hours, stops for 1 hour, and flies for 2 more hours. How many miles does the swan fly? Tell how you found your answer.
8. What can help you decide which operation to use?

Additional Standards: Number Sense 1.0; Mathematical Reasoning 2.6 *(See p. 125.)*

Guided Practice

Sea Animal	Weight
Giant octopus	125 lb
Giant clam	600 lb
Dolphin	400 lb

Sarah is interested in how much sea animals weigh. She recorded her data in a table like the one at the right.

1. How would you find the combined weights of the giant octopus and the giant clam?
   a. Multiply the weights.
   b. Add the weights.
   c. Subtract the weight of the giant octopus from the weight of the giant clam.

2. How would you find how much heavier the giant clam is than the dolphin?
   a. Multiply the giant clam's weight by the dolphin's weight.
   b. Add the weights of the dolphin and the giant clam.
   c. Subtract the weight of the dolphin from the weight of the giant clam.

3. Which number sentence would you use to find how much heavier the giant clam is than the dolphin?
   a. $600 \times 400 = h$
   b. $600 + 400 = h$
   c. $600 - 400 = h$

Independent Practice

4. How would you find the weight of four giant octopuses?
   a. Multiply the weight of the giant octopus by 3.
   b. Multiply the weight of the giant octopus by 4.
   c. Divide the weight of the giant octopus by 4.

5. Which number sentence would you use to find the weight of four giant octopuses?
   a. $170 \times 4 = x$
   b. $170 - 125 = x$
   c. $125 \times 4 = x$

6. A sea turtle's average weight is twice that of the giant octopus. Write and solve a number sentence that represents the weight of a sea turtle.

7. The total weight of five thresher sharks was 5,500 pounds. What was the average weight? Which operation did you use?

Use Homework Workbook 4-4.

Mental Math: Multiplication Patterns Using 10, 100, and 1,000

Warm-Up Review

1. 5×8
2. 4×8
3. 7×9
4. 7×6
5. 4 tens $\times$ 3
6. 5 hundreds $\times$ 7
7. Brendan received the following scores on his first five math quizzes: 88, 79, 95, 85, and 93. Find the mean score.

California Content Standard *Number Sense 1.0 Students compute with . . . positive integers . . . and understand the relative magnitude of numbers. Also Mathematical Reasoning 1.1* *(See p. 125.)*

Math Link You know the basic facts for multiplication. You can apply these basic facts and patterns with zeros to multiply mentally.

Example 1

A canvasback duck can fly about 100 kilometers per hour when it is migrating. How far can a canvasback duck travel if it flies for three hours at that speed?

$$3 \times 100 = n$$

number of hours — speed — distance traveled

Basic facts and patterns of zeros can help you multiply by 10, 100, and 1,000.

$3 \times 1 = 3$ } **Basic Fact**
$3 \times 10 = 30$
$3 \times 100 = 300$
$3 \times 1{,}000 = 3{,}000$ } **Patterns of Zeros**

The basic fact $3 \times 1 = 3$ and the pattern of zeros make it easy to see that the product of 3×100 is 300.

A canvasback duck can fly 300 kilometers in three hours.

More Examples

A. $8 \times 1 = 8$
$8 \times 10 = 80$
$8 \times 100 = 800$
$8 \times 1{,}000 = 8{,}000$

B. $1 \times 15 = 15$
$10 \times 15 = 150$
$100 \times 15 = 1{,}500$
$1{,}000 \times 15 = 15{,}000$

C. $60 \times 1 = 60$
$60 \times 10 = 600$
$60 \times 100 = 6{,}000$
$60 \times 1{,}000 = 60{,}000$

Patterns and basic facts can also help you multiply when a factor is a multiple of 10, 100, or 1,000.

Example 2

If a dolphin swims at a speed of 40 kilometers per hour, how far can it swim in two hours?

$2 \times 40 = n$ Think: $2 \times 4 = 8$.

Since there is one zero in the factors 2 and 40, place a zero at the end of the product of 2×4.

A dolphin can swim 80 kilometers in 2 hours.

More Examples

D. $9 \times 3 = 27$
$9 \times 30 = 270$
$9 \times 300 = 2{,}700$
$9 \times 3{,}000 = 27{,}000$

E. $5 \times 6 = 30$
$5 \times 60 = 300$
$5 \times 600 = 3{,}000$
$5 \times 6{,}000 = 30{,}000$

If the product of a basic fact has a zero, be sure to include that zero when you multiply by a multiple of 10, 100, or 1,000.

Guided Practice *For another example, see Set D on p. 156.*

Find each product. Use patterns to help you.

1. 50×3 **2.** 90×5 **3.** $1{,}000 \times 8$ **4.** 100×7

5. 60×100 **6.** 490×10 **7.** $1{,}000 \times 400$ **8.** 100×90

9. How can you tell that 6×400 equals 60×40 without multiplying?

Independent Practice *For more practice, see Set D on p. 158.*

Find each product. Use patterns to help you.

10. 200×70 **11.** 900×40 **12.** 500×7 **13.** $6{,}000 \times 30$

14. 820×100 **15.** 100×38 **16.** 760×100 **17.** $4{,}450 \times 100$

18. 10×5 **19.** 10×54 **20.** 43×100 **21.** 10×788

22. 4×50 **23.** 200×9 **24.** 70×8 **25.** 7×80

26. Look at Exercises 24 and 25. What do you notice about their products? Why does this happen?

Complete each table

27.

Rule: Multiply by 10.	
8	
17	
324	

28.

Rule: Multiply by 40.	
4	
70	
300	

29.

Rule: Multiply by 700.	
9	
80	
500	

30. A family hopes to save $100 a week. At the end of 1 year, how much money will they have saved?

31. If a car travels at an average speed of 60 miles an hour, how far will the car have traveled at the end of 8 hours?

32. Dry dog food comes in bags of different sizes. An animal shelter uses half a pound of dry dog food each day for every small dog. How much dry dog food does the shelter need to feed 20 small dogs for 4 weeks?

Mixed Review

Use the table at the right for Exercises 33–34.

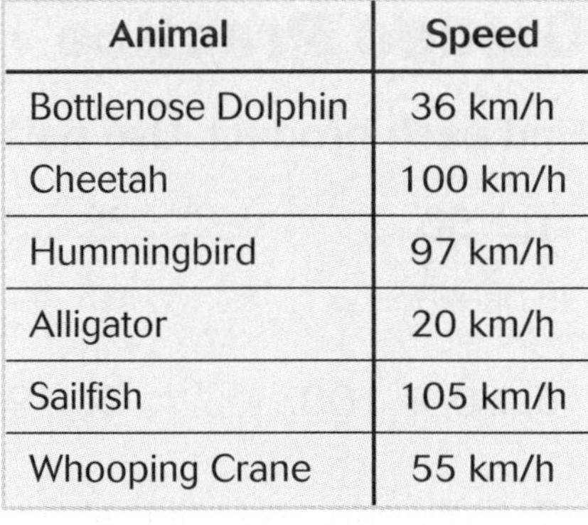

Animal	Speed
Bottlenose Dolphin	36 km/h
Cheetah	100 km/h
Hummingbird	97 km/h
Alligator	20 km/h
Sailfish	105 km/h
Whooping Crane	55 km/h

33. What is the difference of the speed of an alligator and a whooping crane?

34. Estimate the difference in the speed of a sailfish and a bottlenose dolphin.

35. $2 + 3 \times 4 - 5$

36. $6 \times 4 \times 0 \times 8$

37. Refer to the line graph at the right. During which 5-year period did the population of Swanville stay about the same?

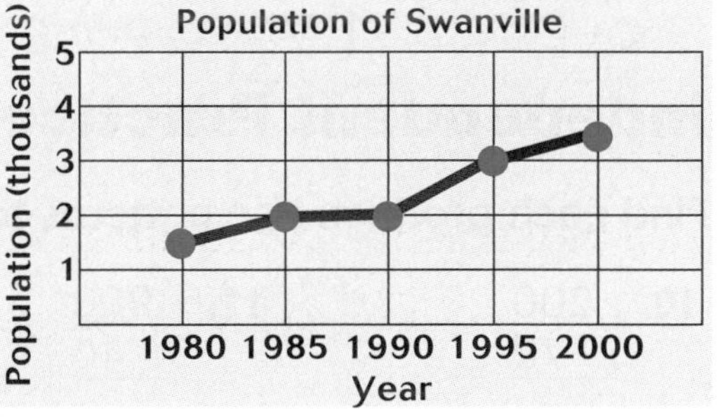

Test Prep Choose the correct letter for each answer.

38. Algebra Evaluate $2x - 3$ when $x = 4$. (4-3)

A 3
B 5
C 11
D 21
E NH

39. Algebra Which expression represents the following phrase? (2-7)

a number increased by 90

F $n + 90$
G $n - 90$
H $90n$
J $\frac{n}{90}$

Diagnostic Checkpoint

Find each n. Name the property that you used.

1. (4-1) $n \times (8 + 5) = (3 \times 8) + (3 \times 5)$

2. (4-1) $(2 \times 3) \times n = 2 \times (3 \times 10)$

3. (4-1) $7 \times 14 \times n = 0$

4. (4-1) $18 \times n = 0$

5. (4-1) $n \times 11 = 11$

6. (4-1) $94 \times 1 = n$

7. (4-1) $8 \times 6 = n \times 8$

8. (4-1) $9 \times (8 + n) = (9 \times 8) + (9 \times 4)$

Tell which operation should be done first. Then find each n.

9. (4-2) $8 \times 2 \div 8 + 6 \times 3$

10. (4-2) $(8 + 10) - 3 - 6 \div 2$

11. (4-2) $(8 + 6) \div 7 - 2$

12. (4-2) $11 + 3 \div 3 + 5 \times 5$

13. (4-2) $2 \times (8 \times 6 - 1) + 2$

14. (4-2) $2 + 6 + 9 + 1 - 9$

Evaluate each expression for $x = 12$ and $x = 4$.

15. (4-3) $6x - 20$

16. (4-3) $(x \div 4) - 1$

17. (4-3) $2x + 6$

18. (4-3) $3x \div 3$

Evaluate each expression for $c = 5$ and $c = 7$.

19. (4-3) $60c - 100$

20. (4-3) $5c + 12$

21. (4-3) $35 \div c - 2$

22. (4-3) $8 + 2c$

Find each product. Use patterns to help you.

23. (4-5) 200×5

24. (4-5) 80×20

25. (4-5) $54 \times 1{,}000$

26. (4-5) 900×40

27. (4-5) 80×50

Use the table for Questions 28–30.

28. (4-4) Which operation would you use to find how much faster a giraffe is than an elephant?

29. (4-4) Write and solve a number sentence to find how much slower a bat is than a dolphin.

30. (4-4) A wren's flying speed is half the speed at which a kangaroo moves. Write and solve a number sentence that represents the flying speed of a wren.

Maximum Speeds of Various Animals

Animal	Miles per hour
Kangaroo	45
Dolphin	38
Giraffe	31.5
Bat	30.8
Elephant	24
Butterfly	20.6

Lesson 4-6 Estimating Products

California Content Standard *Number Sense 1.1: Estimate [and] round . . . numbers.*

Warm-Up Review

1. 8×7
2. 400×7
3. $3.68 - 1.07$
4. $2 + 3 \times 4$
5. $2 \times (4 \times 1) \times 0$
6. Andy scores 18 points in the basketball game Friday. He scores five more points on Saturday than he did on Friday. How many points did he score on Saturday?

Math Link You already know how to round numbers. Now you will use this skill in estimating products.

Example 1

Maria makes a car payment of $187 each month. She has 18 payments left to make. Estimate the total amount she still owes for her car.

Estimate $187 × 18.

Round each number to the greatest place so that you can multiply mentally. Round 187 to the nearest hundred, and round 18 to the nearest ten.

$187 × 18
(rounds to) (rounds to)
$200 × 20 = $4,000

Maria still owes about $4,000 for her car.

More Examples

A. Estimate 147 × 353.

Round each number to the nearest hundred.

147 × 353
(rounds to) (rounds to)
100 × 400 = 40,000

B. Estimate $27.54 × 47.

Round each number to the greatest place.

$27.54 × 47
(rounds to) (rounds to)
$30 × 50 = $1,500

Guided Practice

For another example, see Set E on p. 157.

Estimate each product. Round to the greatest place.

1. 77×29
2. 87×23
3. 566×23
4. $\$1.28 \times 3$

Estimate each product. Round to the nearest 10.

5. $\begin{array}{r} 54 \\ \times\ 19 \\ \hline \end{array}$ **6.** $\begin{array}{r} 69 \\ \times\ 32 \\ \hline \end{array}$ **7.** 88×42 **8.** 67×91

9. Mrs. Warren needed 14 blocks for each of her 118 students. About how many blocks did she need in all?

Independent Practice *For more practice, see Set E on p. 159.*

Estimate each product. Round to the greatest place.

10. 66×59 **11.** 92×86 **12.** 276×88 **13.** 721×562

14. $\begin{array}{r} 159 \\ \times\ 25 \\ \hline \end{array}$ **15.** $\begin{array}{r} 146 \\ \times\ 13 \\ \hline \end{array}$ **16.** $\begin{array}{r} 208 \\ \times\ 263 \\ \hline \end{array}$ **17.** $\begin{array}{r} \$4.12 \\ \times\ 83 \\ \hline \end{array}$

Estimate each product. Round to the nearest 10.

18. $\begin{array}{r} 79 \\ \times\ 21 \\ \hline \end{array}$ **19.** $\begin{array}{r} 62 \\ \times\ 78 \\ \hline \end{array}$ **20.** 48×32 **21.** 98×89

Use the table at the right for Exercises 22–23.

Item	Cost
T-shirt	\$9.40
Souvenir Button	\$2.75
Sweatshirt	\$19.25

22. If Mark has \$20, will he have enough to buy 5 T-shirts?

23. Carly wants to buy 12 souvenir buttons and 5 sweatshirts. About how much money does she need?

Mixed Review

24. Joe had the following scores on his first four spelling tests: 78, 82, 94, and 86. Find the mean of his scores.

25. Algebra Evaluate $\frac{x}{4} - 3$ when x is 32.

26. $2 \times 5 - 3 + 4 \div 2$ **27.** 80×90 **28.** 88×1

 **Test Prep** Choose the correct letter.

29. Which line graph shows a downward trend?
(3-5)

A 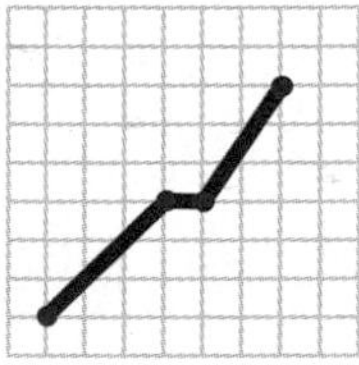 **B** 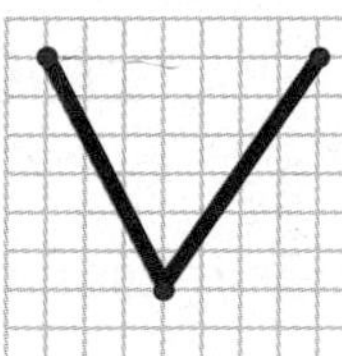 **C** 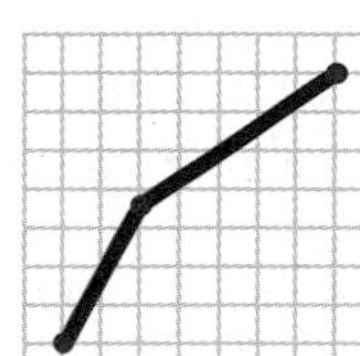 **D** 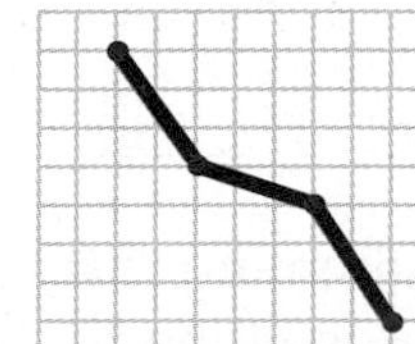

Multiplying by One-Digit and Two-Digit Numbers

California Content Standard *Number Sense 1.0 Students compute with . . . positive intergers . . .. Also Mathematical Reasoning 2.1* *(See p. 125.)*

Warm-Up Review

1. 38 + 12 + 26
2. 1,345 + 456
3. 30 × 9
4. $5.00 + $12.00
5. Round 26,934 to the nearest thousand.
6. Find the mode of the following scores: 99, 88, 84, 88, 77, and 95.

Math Link You already know your multiplication facts. Now you will use them to multiply larger numbers by one- and two-digit numbers.

Example 1

Find 28 × 12.

First use an array to show 28 × 12. Then break the problem into two parts that you already know how to do.

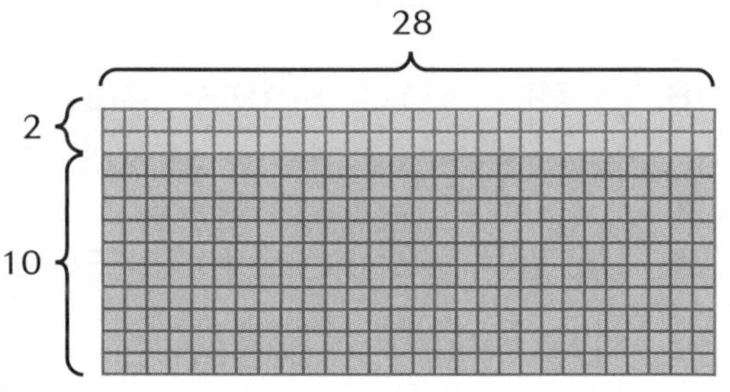

Part A	Part B
28 × 2	28 × 10
56	280

Add the two parts. 56 + 280 = 336.

So, 28 × 12 = 336.

Here's WHY It Works

$$\begin{aligned} 28 \times 12 &= 28 \times (10 + 2) \\ &= (28 \times 10) + (28 \times 2) \\ &= 280 + 56 \\ &= 336 \end{aligned}$$

Here's a way to record your work.

Step 1 Multiply by the ones. Regroup if necessary.	**Step 2** Place a zero in the ones place. Multiply by the tens. Regroup if necessary.	**Step 3** Add the products.
$\begin{array}{r} \overset{1}{2}8 \\ \times\ 12 \\ \hline 56 \end{array}$ ← 2 × 28 Part A	$\begin{array}{r} \overset{1}{2}8 \\ \times\ 12 \\ \hline 56 \\ \underline{280} \end{array}$ ← 10 × 28 Part B	$\begin{array}{r} \overset{1}{2}8 \\ \times\ 12 \\ \hline 56 \\ +\ 280 \\ \hline 336 \end{array}$

Check by estimating. 30 × 10 = 300. The answer is reasonable because 336 is close to 300.

 Additional Standard: Mathematical Reasoning 1.1 *(See p. 125.)*

Example 2

Find 354 × 23.

Step 1 Multiply by the ones. Regroup if necessary.

```
  1 1
  354
×  23
 1062
```

Step 2 Place a zero in the ones place. Multiply by the tens.

```
  1 1
  354
×  23
 1062
 7080
```

Step 3 Add the products.

```
   1
  1 1
  354
×  23
 1062
+7080
8,142
```

Example 3

Find 874 × 59.

```
  3 2        3 2
  6 3        6 3
  874        874
×  59      ×  59
 7866       7866
43700      4370
51,566     51,566
```

Many people do not write the extra zeros in the partial product. Instead, they use a blank space as a placeholder.

Move over one place because you are multiplying by 10.

More Examples

A. Find 5,603 × 6.

```
 3  1
 5,603
×    6
33,618
```

B. Find $27.57 × 14.

```
  3 2 2
 $27.57
×    14
  11028  ← 4 ones × 2757 = 11,028
  2757   ← 1 ten × 2757 = 27,570
$385.98
```

Remember to show dollars and cents in the product.

Guided Practice *For another example, see Set F on p. 157.*

1. 42 × 39 **2.** 64 × 14 **3.** 57 × 30 **4.** 91 × 36

5. 3,111 × 87 **6.** 97 × $1.02 **7.** 914 × 5 **8.** 451 × 7

9. Pedro wanted to buy 12 video games. Each game cost $27.95. How much did he have to pay?

Independent Practice *For more practice, see Set F on p. 159.*

10. $\begin{array}{r} 27 \\ \times\ 13 \\ \hline \end{array}$ **11.** $\begin{array}{r} 57 \\ \times\ 8 \\ \hline \end{array}$ **12.** $\begin{array}{r} 19 \\ \times\ 7 \\ \hline \end{array}$ **13.** $\begin{array}{r} 65 \\ \times\ 38 \\ \hline \end{array}$

14. 589×5 **15.** 67×896 **16.** $\$14.06 \times 23$ **17.** $\$1{,}302 \times 82$

18. 342×52 **19.** 28×379 **20.** $6{,}293 \times 67$ **21.** $1{,}024 \times 92$

22. Which property of multiplication says that the products 23×546 and 546×23 are equal?

23. Tiles are sold for $0.88 each. A new floor will need 126 tiles. Don budgeted $150.00 for the floor. Can he afford the tiles?

24. Mental Math Explain how you can use mental math to find the product of 15×99.

Use the menu at the right for Exercises 25–26.

25. Oscar wants to buy 3 sandwiches and 2 milks. He has $10.00. Does he have enough money?

26. Mrs. Emmory buys a sandwich and cole slaw for each of her 12 students. How much money does she need?

Menu	
Sandwiches	$1.75
Milk	$1.29
Cole Slaw	$0.95

Mixed Review

27. Michael spent $275 in May, $306 in June, and $188 in July. How much more did he spend in May than in July?

28. Estimate 718×36. **29.** $2 + 3 \times 4 - 2 \times 4$ **30.** 20×32

31. Round 2,756,872 to the nearest million.

32. Algebra Evaluate $2x - 3$ when $x = 4$.

Test Prep **Choose the correct letter for the answer.**

33. Which property tells you that $7 \times 1 = 7$?
(4-1)

A The Associative Property of Multiplication

B The Identity Property of Multiplication

C The Commutative Property of Addition

D The Zero Property

Multiple-Choice Cumulative Review

Choose the correct letter for each answer.

1. In order to take pets on a train or plane, you need to have a pet carrier. If a carrier for a medium-sized dog costs $44.95, how much would it cost to buy carriers for three medium-sized dogs?

A $131.50
B $134.65
C $134.85
D $143.56

2. What is the mode of the set of data?

7, 3, 0, 2, 0, 3, 0, 8, 7, 2

F 0
G 2
H 3
J 7

3. A shop sells picture frames in these sizes; 2 inches by 3 inches, 4 inches by 6 inches, 6 inches by 9 inches, and 8 inches by 12 inches. What would be the next largest frame if the pattern continues?

A 8 inches by 14 inches
B 9 inches by 12 inches
C 9 inches by 15 inches
D 10 inches by 15 inches

4. Shipping cost sometimes depends on the total cost of the order. Orders between $25.00 and $50.00 cost $5.00 for shipping. If the total is between $50.01 and $75.00, shipping is $6.00. If the order is $71.00, what is the total cost, including shipping?

F $73.00
G $74.00
H $75.00
J $77.00

5. After a class trip to a natural animal habitat, class members can order photographs of the day. Fifteen students out of a class of 26 order two prints each. The rest of the class orders three prints each. If the prints cost $0.43 each, how much does the class owe?

A $11.18
B $22.36
C $25.81
D $27.09

6. In which set are the numbers ordered from least to greatest?

F 0.07, 0.03, 0.14, 0.09
G 0.9, 1.4, 1.8, 9.2
H 7.3, 7.4, 7.1, 7.09
J 0.01, 0.001, 0.003, 0.06

7. Ken's family is building a dog run. They will put a post at each corner of the square run. There will be a total of four posts on each side of the run. How many posts does Ken's family need to buy?

A 4
B 8
C 12
D 16

8. Which value of x makes the equation true?

$$x - 4 = 12.2$$

F $x = 2.2$
G $x = 8.2$
H $x = 16.2$
J $x = 18$

Problem-Solving Strategy:

Solve a Simpler Problem

California Content Standard *Mathematical Reasoning 2.2: Apply strategies and results from simpler problems to more complex problems. Also Mathematical Reasoning 3.2* *(See p. 125.)*

Warm-Up Review

1. 197 + 28
2. 46 + 44
3. 236 × 2
4. 547 × 24
5. 3 × 3 + 4 − 5
6. Joanie bought 7 ribbons for $2 apiece. She paid with a $20 bill. How much change did she receive?

Example

Marc has a greeting card company. Suppose Marc and 7 of his artist co-workers have a meeting. As they arrive, each one hands a sample card to each of the other artists. How many greeting cards will be passed around?

Understand

What information do you have? What do you need to find?

You know there are 8 people passing cards around. You need to find the number of greeting cards passed around.

Plan

How can you solve the problem?

You can **solve a simpler problem.** Then you can find the number of cards passed around.

Solve

Start with 2 artists.
2 cards would be passed.

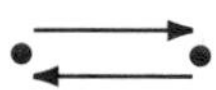

Continue with 3 artists.
6 cards would be passed.

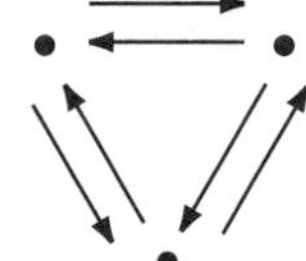

Use a table to organize the data. Find a pattern and complete the table.

Artists	2	3	4	5	6	7	8
Cards	2	6	12	20	30	42	56
Pattern	2 × 1	3 × 2	4 × 3	5 × 4	6 × 5	7 × 6	8 × 7

Look Back

What other strategy did you use to discover the pattern?

Additional Standards: Mathematical Reasoning 1.1, 2.3, 3.2 (See p. 125.)

Guided Practice

For questions 1–3, refer to the table on the preceding page.

1. Draw a diagram to show how many cards are passed around for 4 artists.

2. Why is it easier to use the table than to continue drawing diagrams?

3. Extend the table to determine how many cards would be passed around for 9 artists.

Independent Practice

4. If 8 artists are assigned to work in pairs, how many different pairs of artists are possible?

5. Mr. Perez teaches his 30 students a new skill in art class. He will teach it to 2 students. Then each of them will teach 2 others and so on. It takes 10 minutes to learn the skill. No one will teach it more than once. How long will it take for all 30 students to learn the skill?

6. When a quilt is completed, each row will contain 6 of these designs. There will be a total of 9 rows. How many pieces of each size rectangle will be used?

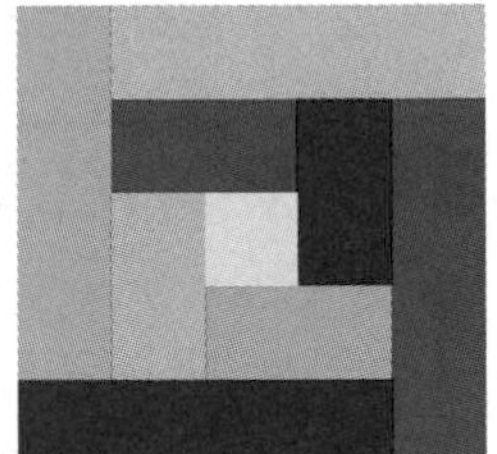

Mixed Review

Try these or other strategies to solve each problem. Tell which strategy you used.

Problem-Solving Strategies

- *Write an Equation*
- *Work Backward*
- *Draw a Diagram*
- *Solve a Simpler Problem*

7. What choices could you make from the menu at the right so that you had a sandwich, a drink, and a snack and spent exactly $5.00?

8. How much money would you need to buy any one choice of a sandwich, a drink, and a snack from the menu?

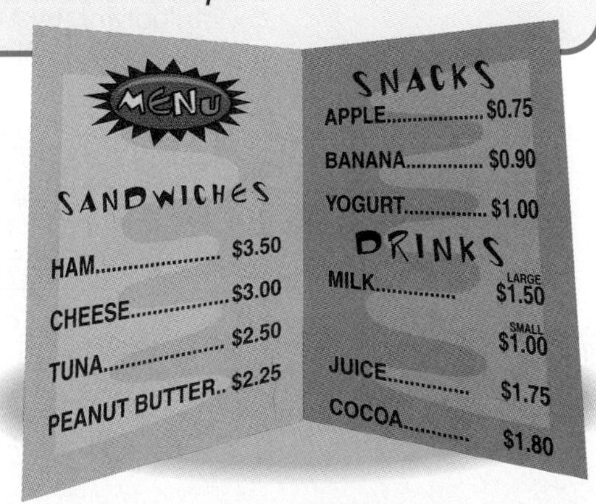

MENU
SANDWICHES
HAM $3.50
CHEESE $3.00
TUNA $2.50
PEANUT BUTTER $2.25
SNACKS
APPLE $0.75
BANANA $0.90
YOGURT $1.00
DRINKS
MILK LARGE $1.50
SMALL $1.00
JUICE $1.75
COCOA $1.80

Multiplying Greater Numbers

Warm-Up Review

1. 2,789 + 348
2. 354 × 7
3. 149 × 9
4. Estimate 906 × 387 by rounding to the nearest hundred.
5. Miguel received the following scores: 86, 77, 97, 88, and 95. Find the median of Miguel's scores.

California Content Standard *Number Sense 1.0: Students compete with . . . positive integers . . .. Also Mathematical Reasoning 2.1 (See p. 125.)*

Math Link You already know how to multiply by one- and two-digit numbers. In this lesson, you will learn to multiply greater numbers.

Example 1

Find 365 × 112.

Step 1 Multiply by the ones.	Step 2 Multiply by the tens. Move to the left one place or use one zero as a placeholder.	Step 3 Multiply by the hundreds. Move to the left two places or use two zeros as placeholders.	Step 4 Add the partial products.
1 1 365 × 112 730	1 1 365 × 112 730 3650	1 1 365 × 112 730 3650 36500	1 1 365 × 112 730 3650 + 36500 40,880

Check by estimating. 400 × 100 = 40,000. The answer is reasonable because 40,880 is close to 40,000.

Example 2

To find 287 × 104, you can show your work in any of the following ways.

Show a row of zeros as placeholders.	Move the partial product over 2 places since you are multiplying by 100. Then use two zeros as placeholders.	Move the partial product over 2 places, but leave off the two zeros.
287 × 104 1148 0000 28700 29,848	287 × 104 1148 28700 29,848	287 × 104 1148 287 29,848

 Additional Standard: Mathematical Reasoning 1.1 (See p. 125.)

Guided Practice *For another example, see Set G on p. 157.*

1. $\begin{array}{r} 501 \\ \times\ 143 \\ \hline \end{array}$
2. $\begin{array}{r} 558 \\ \times\ 295 \\ \hline \end{array}$
3. 89 × 32
4. 147 × 78

5. If one ticket costs $3.95, how much will 124 tickets cost?

Independent Practice *For more practice, see Set G on p. 159.*

6. $\begin{array}{r} 227 \\ \times\ 161 \\ \hline \end{array}$
7. $\begin{array}{r} 413 \\ \times\ 287 \\ \hline \end{array}$
8. $\begin{array}{r} 303 \\ \times\ 709 \\ \hline \end{array}$
9. 896 × 111

10. 651 × 782
11. 306 × 451
12. 210 × 402
13. 202 × $5.72

14. $4.09 × 786
15. $4.88 × 523
16. 412 × $8.90
17. 1,437 × 180

18. The Booster Club members washed 123 cars on Saturday. If they charged $1.25 per car, how much money did they make?

19. **Math Reasoning** Why are the two products, 234 × 564 and 564 × 234 the same?

20. Theo ordered 15 boxes of 144 pencils. How many pencils did he order in all?

Mixed Review

Use the line graph at right for Exercises 21–23.

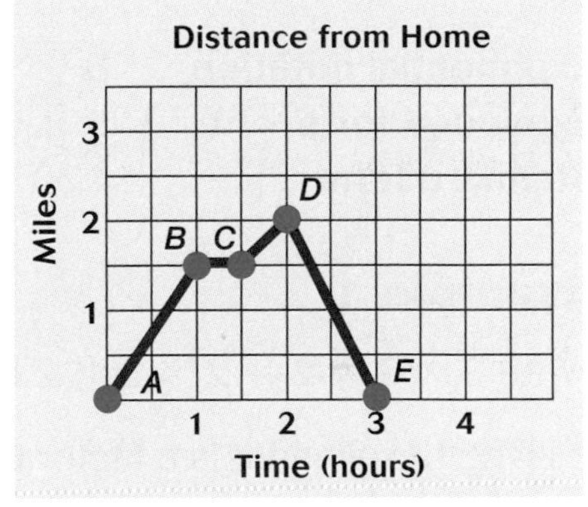

21. **Math Reasoning** What is happening on the bike trip between points B and C?

22. After two hours, how far from home is the rider?

23. How long did it take the rider to get 1.5 miles from home?

24. 234 × 322
25. 107 × 38
26. 23,567 − 3,789
27. 4 × 47 × 0

28. **Algebra** Evaluate $\frac{w}{2} - 3$ for $w = 18$.
29. **Mental Math** 70 + 43 + 30

Test Prep **Choose the correct letter for each answer.**

30. Which digit in 0.346 is in the hundredths place? (1-3)

A 0
B 3
C 4
D 6

31. Round 23,998 to the nearest thousand. (1-6)

F 20,000
G 24,000
H 23,000
J 30,000

Exponents

California Content Standard *Number Sense 1.3: Understand and compute positive integer powers of nonnegative integers; compute examples as repeated multiplication.*

Math Link You have learned to write large numbers and perform operations with large numbers. In this lesson, you will learn a way to write large numbers.

Warm-Up Review

1. $2 \times 2 \times 2$
2. $24 + 36 + 5$
3. $5 + 5 \times 4$
4. $2.562 - 1.23$
5. $2{,}000 \times 5$
6. $72 \div 8$
7. Marco worked 3 hours on Monday, 5 hours on Tuesday, 6 hours on Wednesday, 7 hours on Thursday, and 4 hours on Friday. What was the mean number of hours he worked?

When you multiply numbers, each of them is a **factor** of the product. So 2, 3, and 4 are factors of 24.

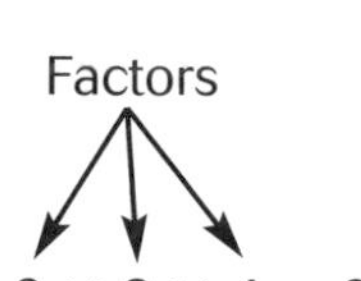

You can represent repeated multiplication of the *same* number by using exponential notation. The **base** is the number to be multiplied. The **exponent** is the number that tells how many times the base is used as a factor.

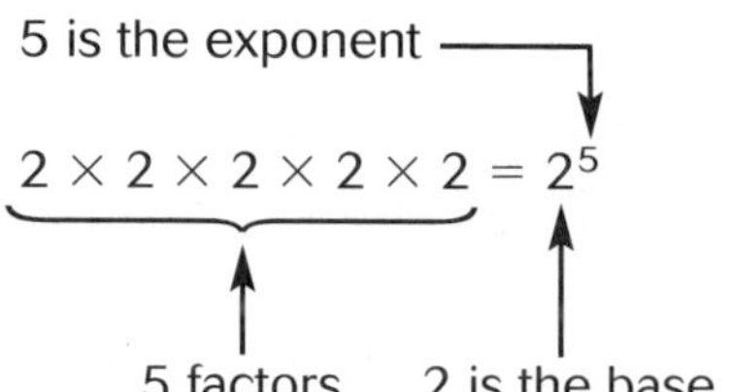

Numbers involving exponents can be written in 3 different forms.

Exponential notation	5^3
Expanded form	$5 \times 5 \times 5$
Standard form	125

Word Bank

factor
base
exponent
exponential form
expanded form
standard form
squared
cubed

Example 1

Write $2 \times 2 \times 2 \times 2 \times 2 \times 2$ in exponential notation.

2 is the base, and it is a factor 6 times.
So, 2^6 is the exponential notation.

Example 2

Write 3^4 in expanded form.
$3^4 = 3 \times 3 \times 3 \times 3$

Example 3

Write 10^5 in standard form.
$10 \times 10 \times 10 \times 10 \times 10 = 100{,}000$

An exponent is also called a power. Read 5^4 as "5 raised to the fourth power," or "5 to the fourth power." The second and third powers have special names. Read 3^2 as "3 to the second power," or 3 **squared.** Read 6^3 as "6 to the third power," or 6 **cubed.**

Guided Practice *For another example, see Set H on p. 157.*

Write using exponents.

1. 5 × 5 × 5 × 5 **2.** 9 × 9 × 9 × 9 × 9 **3.** 24 × 24 × 24 **4.** 79 × 79

Write in expanded form.

5. 4^3 **6.** 25 squared **7.** 13^5 **8.** 10^6

Write in standard form.

9. 5^2 **10.** 10^4 **11.** 1^{10} **12.** 4 cubed

13. Is 3^7 the same as 7^3? Explain.

Independent Practice *For more practice, see Set H on p. 159.*

Write using exponents.

14. 6 × 6 × 6 × 6 **15.** 11 × 11 × 11 × 11 **16.** 123 × 123 **17.** 7 × 7 × 7

Write each in expanded form and standard form.

18. 3^3 **19.** 2^4 **20.** 5^4 **21.** 1^9

Find each number.

22. The number that equals 100 when it is squared.

23. The number that equals 27 when it is cubed.

Mixed Review

24. The recycling club collected 106 pounds of paper in one week. How many pounds would they collect in 36 weeks?

25. 74×34 **26.** $2{,}047 - 1{,}839$ **27.** $3.86 + 5.25$ **28.** $\$125 \times 32$

29. Mental Math 19 + 25 + 11 **30. Algebra** Solve for *w*. $w + 243 = 478$

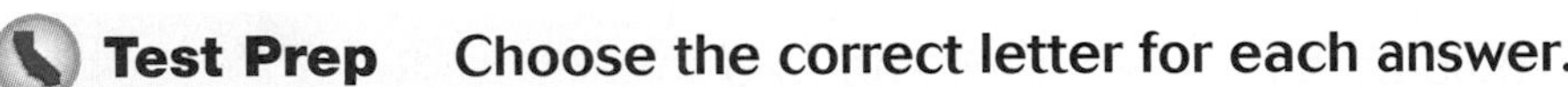

Test Prep **Choose the correct letter for each answer.**

31. (1-1) Which digit in 234,871,056 is in the millions place?

A 4 **C** 2

B 3 **D** 8

32. (1-7) Which means the same as "Multiply a number by 8"?

F $n - 8$ **H** $8n$

G $\frac{n}{8}$ **J** $n + 8$

Use Homework Workbook 4-10.

Problem-Solving Application:

Using Money

California Content Standard *Mathematical Reasoning 1.2 Determine when and how to break a problem into simpler parts. Also Mathematical Reasoning 2.6* *(See p. 125.)*

Warm-Up Review

1. 3.75 + 5.98
2. 42 + 6 + 28
3. Solve $x - 26 = 76$.
4. Estimate 2,768 + 3,042.
5. There are 42 seats on a bus. Each seat holds 3 students. How many students can sit on the bus?

The Anderson family and some friends spent a day at the zoo. The group needed one senior citizen ticket, two adult tickets, and four student tickets. How much did admission to the zoo cost this group?

Zoo Admission

Children under 4	Free
Students 4–18 years	$4.25
Adults	$7.50
Senior Citizens (65 and over)	$5.75

Understand

What do you need to know?

You need to find the total cost for the group.

Plan

How can you solve the problem?

Break the problem into simpler parts. First, find the cost for each age group. Then add to find the total cost.

Solve

Step 1	Step 2	Step 3
Students 4–18 years $4.25 × 4 $17.00	Adults $7.50 × 2 $15.00	Everyone Students $17.00 Adults $15.00 Senior Citizens $ 5.75 $37.75

The cost of admission to the zoo is $37.75 for this group.

Look Back

Does the answer seem reasonable?

The 4 student tickets would cost between $16 and $20. The 2 adult tickets would cost between $14 and $16. The 1 senior citizen ticket costs between $5 and $6.

$16 + $14 + $5 = $35 and $20 + $16 + $6 = $42

The answer is reasonable because $37.75 is between $35 and $42.

Guided Practice

Use the information on page 150 to solve Exercises 1–3.

1. What would the admission cost be for six student tickets, four adult tickets, and two senior citizen tickets?

2. If the admission for an adult were $8.00, what would the cost be for the Anderson family and their friends?

3. Mrs. Werner wanted to take a class of 24 students to the zoo. Besides Mrs. Werner, three parents agreed to go with the class. None were senior citizens. The zoo gave the group a discount of $20.00. What was the cost for the entire group?

Independent Practice

Use the table at the right for Exercises 4–6.

Video Village Price List	
Video games	$3.50
New release movies	$4.25
Movies	$3.75
Children's movies	$2.50

4. Drew wants to rent 3 video games and 2 movies. He has $25.00. How much change will he get?

5. Maria wants to rent 2 children's movies and 3 new release movies. How much will she have to pay?

6. Leon has $15.00. How many new release movies can he rent?

7. Maya opens a savings account with $25.00 her parents gave her for her birthday. She then saves $10.75 per month for 8 months. How much money does she have in her account at the end of 8 months?

8. Sherrie charges $3.00 an hour to baby-sit and $2.00 an hour to walk dogs. Last week she baby-sat for 5 hours and walked dogs for 6 hours. How much money did she make?

Mixed Review

9. An art school buys 8 jars of paint per carton. What is the least number of cartons they could buy to have 66 jars of paint?

10. Ryan has a gift certificate for $25.00. If he applies this to his purchase of $159.56, write and solve an equation to find how much money Ryan will actually need.

11. Edward bought a salad for $3.95 and a large ice tea for $1.50. He had a $10.00 bill. Did he have enough money? If so, how much change should he get?

Use Homework Workbook 4-11.

Diagnostic Checkpoint

Complete. For Exercises 1–3, choose a word from the Word Bank.

Word Bank
associative property of multiplication
commutative property of multiplication
distributive property
identity property
zero property

1. (4-1) The ______________ states that when 0 is a factor, the product is 0.

2. (4-1) $3 \times 6 = 6 \times 3$ is an example of the ______________.

3. (4-1) The ______________ states that the way the factors are grouped does not change the product.

Estimate each product.

4. (4-6) 55×7 **5.** (4-6) 79×68 **6.** (4-6) 129×36 **7.** (4-6) 298×185

Multiply.

8. (4-7) 8×92 **9.** (4-7) 3×927 **10.** (4-7) 890×7 **11.** (4-7) 609×5

12. (4-7) 51×81 **13.** (4-7) 85×27 **14.** (4-7) 49×58 **15.** (4-7) 99×56

16. (4-9) 643×188 **17.** (4-9) 591×109 **18.** (4-9) 178×774 **19.** (4-9) 421×603

Write using exponents.

20. (4-10) $2 \times 2 \times 2$ **21.** (4-10) $9 \times 9 \times 9 \times 9 \times 9$ **22.** (4-10) 62×62 **23.** (4-10) $4 \times 4 \times 4 \times 4$

Write each in expanded form and standard form.

24. (4-10) 2^6 **25.** (4-10) 8^2 **26.** (4-10) 6^4 **27.** (4-10) 4^6 **28.** (4-10) 1^8

29. (4-8) A rugby coach has to notify his 30 athletes that practice has been canceled. The coach will call 2 athletes, and then each of them will call 2 others and so on. Each pair of calls will take 2 minutes, and no one will be called more than once. How long will it take for all 30 athletes to be notified?

30. (4-11) Bikes sell for \$70, and helmets sell for \$15 at Marino's sporting goods store. In December the store sold 65 bikes and 73 helmets. How much money did the store make?

Chapter 4 Test

Find each *n*. Name the property you used.

1. $n \times 15 = 15 \times 21$

2. $(10 \times 6) \times n = 10 \times (6 \times 13)$

Tell which operation should be done first. Then find each *n*.

3. $48 \div (3 + 3) - 6 + 2 \times 4 = n$

4. $11 \times 10 - 5 \div 5 + 2 + 8 = n$

Evaluate each expression for $w = 4$ and $w = 10$.

5. $5w - 15$

6. $2w \div 4$

7. $50 - 3w$

Use patterns to find each product.

8. 8×400

9. $54 \times 1{,}000$

Estimate each product.

10. 887×129

11. 65×31

Multiply.

12. 136×21

13. 67×689

14. 688×757

15. 24×23

16. 119×4

17. 298×721

18. 451×118

19. 17×38

Write each in expanded form and standard form.

20. 3^7

21. 6^5

22. Lola buys 6 pounds of chicken, 4 pounds of turkey, and a gallon of juice. The chicken cost \$3 per pound, the turkey cost \$4 per pound, and a gallon of juice cost \$3. How much did Lola spend?

23. What operation would you use to find how much farther Joe has to drive than Brian? Write a number sentence to solve. Use the table at the right.

Driving Distance to Work	
Joe	26 miles
Brian	18 miles

24. It takes Adam's grandfather 27 hours to carve one wooden bird. How many hours would it take him to carve 112 birds?

25. Katie gets together with three of her friends to share vacation photos. Each girl hands a copy of her favorite photo to each friend. How many photos are there in total?

Multiple-Choice Chapter 4 Test

Choose the correct letter for each answer.

1. Which operation should be done first to solve for n?

$$64 - 4 \div 2 \times (3 + 5)$$

A Addition
B Subtraction
C Multiplication
D Division

2. Which of the following is an estimate of the product of 83 × 68?

F 2,400
G 3,700
H 4,800
J 5,600

3. Evaluate the expression $16b - 25$ when $b = 4$.

A 25
B 36
C 39
D 64
E NH

4. Which of the following pair of factors is equal to 8 × 300?

F 2×400
G 24×100
H 60×30
J 80×40

5. Which multiplication property can you use to solve for n?

$$(2 \times 13) \times 14 = 2 \times (13 \times n)$$

A Associative property
B Commutative property
C Distributive property
D Identity property

6. Which of the following shows 7^4 in standard form?

F 49
G 343
H 2,200
J 2,401

7. Which of the following number sentences is NOT true?

A $104 \times 25 > 13 \times 16$
B $247 \times 248 < 219 \times 355$
C $17 \times 4 < 11 \times 10$
D $310 \times 35 > 99 \times 198$

8. Frankie sells muffins for $5 a dozen and biscuits for $1 a piece. At the school bake sale, Frankie sells 12 dozen muffins and 39 biscuits. How much money did Frankie make at the bake sale?

F $60
G $71
H $99
J $105

9. **Each side of a square rabbit hutch requires 124 centimeters of wire. How many centimeters of wire will be needed for the four sides of the hutch?**

- **A** 496 centimeters
- **B** 500 centimeters
- **C** 724 centimeters
- **D** 2,976 centimeters

---

10. **Felix has to drive 150 miles to visit his grandmother. Felicia only has to drive half the distance that Felix does to visit her grandmother. How would you find how many miles Felicia has to drive?**

- **F** Add 150 and 2
- **G** Subtract 2 from 150
- **H** Multiply 150 by 2
- **J** Divide 150 by 2

---

11. **A wildlife park needs 34 pounds of fruit a day to feed its monkeys. At this rate, how many pounds of fruit will the park need to buy in a year? (Use 365 days in a year.)**

- **A** 10,510 pounds
- **B** 10,820 pounds
- **C** 12,410 pounds
- **D** 14,605 pounds

---

12. **Solve for *n*.**

$$n \times (8 \times 2) = (0 \times 8) \times 2$$

- **F** 0
- **G** 2
- **H** 8
- **J** 10
- **K** NH

---

13. **As eight people arrive for a business meeting, each one hands a business card to each of the other participants. How many business cards will be passed around?**

- **A** 20
- **B** 32
- **C** 42
- **D** 56

---

14. **Companies often sell their goods to distributors who see that the products get to stores near you. If a company sells a bird cage to a distributor for $14.99, and if the distributor adds $1.29 to the cost, about how much will the customer pay for 5 bird cages?**

- **F** $70
- **G** $80
- **H** $90
- **J** $100

---

15. **Which of the following is true?**

- **A** $700 \times 40 = 2{,}800$
- **B** $25 \times 300 = 7{,}500$
- **C** $1{,}000 \times 50 = 10{,}000$
- **D** $620 \times 10 = 62{,}000$
- **E** NH

---

16. **Scientists may sometimes collect crocodile eggs to protect them until they hatch. A crocodile can lay about 50 eggs. About how many eggs would 7 crocodiles lay?**

- **F** 35
- **G** 120
- **H** 350
- **J** 550

Reteaching

Set A (pages 126–127)

Find n if
$2 \times (3 \times n) = (2 \times 3) \times 8$.
Name the property used.

By the associative property of multiplication, $2 \times (3 \times 8) = (2 \times 3) \times 8$.

So, $n = 8$.

Remember the properties of multiplication are similar to the properties of addition.

Find each n. Name the property used.

1. $3 \times 4 \times n = 0$
2. $2 \times (n + 6) = (2 \times 12) + (2 \times 6)$
3. $101 \times n = 3 \times 101$

Set B (pages 128–129)

Find n if $8 + (2 + 3) \times 7 = n$.

First, do operations inside parentheses.

$8 + 5 \times 7 = n$

Next do all multiplication and division.

$8 + 35 = n$

Last, do all addition and subtraction.

$43 = n$

Remember multiplication and division are done from left to right. Then, addition and subtraction are done from left to right.

Tell which operation should be done first. Then find each n.

1. $6 - 3 \div 3 \times 2 = n$
2. $(2 + 3) + 20 \div 4 - 1 = n$

Set C (pages 130–131)

Evaluate $6q - 8$ when $q = 2$ and $q = 10$.

When $q = 2$,
$6q - 8 = 6(2) - 8$
$= 12 - 8$
$= 4$

When $q = 10$,
$6q - 8 = 6(10) - 8$
$= 60 - 8$
$= 52$

Remember to follow the order of operations when necessary.

Evaluate each expression for $s = 6$ and $s = 8$.

1. $2s - 1$
2. $\frac{24}{s}(2 - 1)$
3. $3 + 6s$
4. $100 - 4s$

Set D (pages 134–136)

Use a pattern to find $7 \times 4{,}000$.

$7 \times 4 = 28$
$7 \times 40 = 280$
$7 \times 400 = 2{,}800$
$7 \times 4{,}000 = 28{,}000$

The product is 28,000.

Remember basic facts and patterns of zeros can help you multiply.

Use patterns to find each product.

1. 600×200
2. $7{,}000 \times 4$
3. 10×98
4. $100 \times 2{,}320$

Set E (pages 138–139)

Estimate 63 × 88.

63 × 88

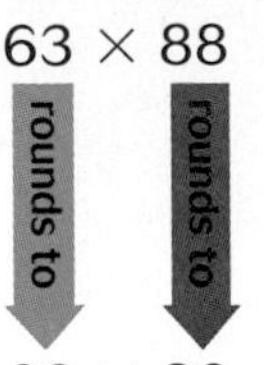

Round each number to the greatest place.

60 × 90 = 5,400

Remember, when estimating products, round each number to the greatest place so that you can multiply mentally.

Estimate each product. Round to the greatest place.

1. 33 × 76
2. 381 × 21
3. 982 × 104
4. 44 × 67

Set F (pages 140–142)

Find 6,412 × 13.

```
  6,412
×    13
  19236  ← Multiply by the ones.
  64120  ← Multiply by the tens.
 83,356  ← Add the products.
```

Remember you can write zeros or use blank spaces as placeholders.

Find each product.

1. 81 × 7
2. 31 × 25
3. 711 × 14
4. 17 × 84
5. 19 × 26
6. 813 × 6

Set G (pages 146–147)

Find 708 × 209.

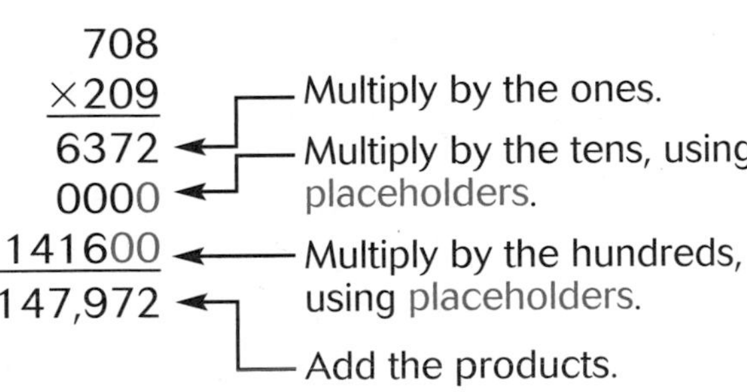

708
×209
6372
0000
141600
147,972
Multiply by the ones.
Multiply by the tens, using placeholders.
Multiply by the hundreds, using placeholders.
Add the products.

Remember there are several different ways you can show your work.

Find each product.

1. 215 × 317
2. 603 × 101
3. 806 × 132
4. 100 × 722
5. 812 × 643
6. 716 × 327

Set H (pages 148–149)

Write 6^4 in expanded form and standard form.

The base is 6. The exponent is 4.

Expanded form: 6 × 6 × 6 × 6
Standard form: 1,296

Remember the exponent tells how many times the base is used as a factor.

Write each in expanded form and standard form.

1. 17^3
2. 23^2
3. 10^6
4. 2^6

More Practice

Set A (pages 126–127)

Find each n. Name the property used.

1. $3 \times n = 3$
2. $4 \times 3 = 3 \times n$
3. $(2 \times 5) \times 4 = 2 \times (5 \times n)$
4. $4 \times (n \times 5) = 0$
5. $17 \times 1 = n$
6. $n \times (10 + 7) = (8 \times 10) + (8 \times 7)$
7. Arthur has 8 cans containing 6 ounces of tomato paste each. Ben has 6 cans containing 8 ounces of tomato paste each. Who has more tomato paste? How do you know without multiplying?

Set B (pages 128–129)

Tell which operation should be done first. Then find each n.

1. $12 \div 3 + 5 = n$
2. $7 + 10 \div 2 = n$
3. $15 - 10 \div 5 = n$
4. $10 \div (3 + 2) = n$
5. $16 - (5 + 5 \times 2) = n$
6. $5 \times (9 + 1) - 3 \times 3 = n$
7. Write an expression that has the same value as $(0 \div 9) + 2 \times 3 - 12 \div 3$.

Set C (pages 130–131)

Evaluate each expression for $w = 10$ and $w = 3$.

1. $8w - 6$
2. $16 - w$
3. $32 - 3w$
4. $15 + \frac{30}{w}$
5. $4w$
6. $11 + 2w$
7. $\frac{90}{w} - 2$
8. $2w + 60 \div w$
9. The total cost of 6 plants plus 6 plant holders can be represented by the expression $6p + 24$, where p represents the price of each plant. Evaluate the expression if the price of each plant is $15.

Set D (pages 134–136)

Find each product. Use patterns to help you.

1. 40×60
2. 30×70
3. 35×100
4. 90×200
5. 170×10
6. How can you tell that $200 \times 4 = 20 \times 40$ without multiplying?

Set E *(pages 138–139)*

Estimate each product.

1. 62×41 **2.** 37×19 **3.** 22×36 **4.** 81×22 **5.** 95×13

6. 28×84 **7.** 55×55 **8.** 16×89 **9.** 31×77 **10.** 56×31

11. A purple martin can eat 123 mosquitoes in a day. About how many mosquitoes can it eat in a week?

Set F *(pages 140–142)*

1. 86×7 **2.** 35×9 **3.** 72×5 **4.** 84×4 **5.** 12×3

6. 66×9 **7.** 6×29 **8.** 51×4 **9.** 5×81 **10.** 121×9

11. At a local pet store an iguana costs $14. How much would a dozen cost?

Set G *(pages 146–147)*

Find each product.

1. 296×321 **2.** 784×916 **3.** 401×123 **4.** 406×398 **5.** 592×174

6. Sheila's horse Champion exercises from 1 to 2 hours a day. Champion eats 105 pounds of hay each week. How much hay will Champion eat in 52 weeks?

Set H *(pages 148–149)*

Write using exponents.

1. $20 \times 20 \times 20$ **2.** 202×202 **3.** $7 \times 7 \times 7 \times 7$

4. $1 \times 1 \times 1 \times 1 \times 1 \times 1$ **5.** $56 \times 56 \times 56$ **6.** $6 \times 6 \times 6 \times 6 \times 6$

Write each in expanded form and standard form.

7. 6^2 **8.** 4^4 **9.** 1^8 **10.** 13^3 **11.** 10^3 **12.** 2^3

13. Find a number that equals 64 when it is cubed.

Problem Solving: Preparing for Tests

Choose the correct letter for each answer.

---

1. Bob is older than Joe, but younger than Susan. Susan is older than Al. Which is a reasonable conclusion?

A Bob is older than Al.

B Joe is older than Al.

C Bob is the oldest.

D Susan is older than Joe.

> **Tip**
> Using the *Make a List* strategy can help you solve this problem.

---

2. Leon has 20 coins. Some are dimes and some are quarters. The total amount is $3.05. How many dimes and how many quarters does Leon have?

F 11 dimes, 9 quarters

G 12 dimes, 8 quarters

H 13 dimes, 7 quarters

J 14 dimes, 6 quarters

> **Tip**
> Use one of the following strategies to solve this problem.
> - *Draw a Diagram*
> - *Make a Table*

---

3. Rosa is having a fence built around an 18-foot by 24-foot yard. The 24-foot side of the yard against the house doesn't need fencing. How much fencing does Rosa need?

A 42 feet

B 60 feet

C 66 feet

D 84 feet

> **Tip**
> *Make a Diagram* to help you solve this problem. Sketch the lawn and mark the sides that need fencing.

4. Harry bought 2 sweaters at $38.89 each and a pair of shoes for $43.90. Which is the best estimate of how much he spent before taxes?

F About $70 **H** About $115

G About $80 **J** About $120

5. The regular ticket price for a concert is $8.50. Senior citizens pay $5.00, and children under 6 are free. A senior citizen takes four children, ages 4, 6, 8, and 9, to the concert. Which is the best estimate for the cost of their tickets?

A Less than $20.00

B About $25.00

C About $30.00

D More than $35.00

6. Eve is twice as tall as her little sister Sue. Eve's father is 3 times as tall as Sue. Sue is *s* inches tall. Which number sentence shows that the difference between the father's height and Eve's height is 18 inches?

F $2 \times 3 \times s = 18$

G $3 \times s - 2 = 18$

H $(3 \times s) - (2 \times s) = 18$

J $(3 + s) + (2 + s) = 18$

7. Boxes of light bulbs are on sale at 3 boxes for $8.97. Which of these is reasonable for the cost of 2 boxes?

A About $2.00

B About $3.00

C About $4.50

D About $6.00

8. This graph shows how many students prefer seeing a movie at home or in a theater.

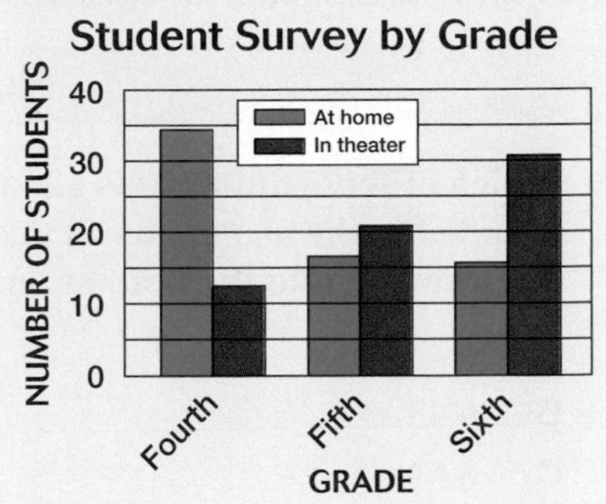

About how many students would rather watch movies at home?

F 55 **H** 65

G 60 **J** 70

9. Zelda and 3 friends went out to lunch. The bill was $46.85, and they decided to share the cost equally. How could you find each person's share of the bill?

A Multiply $46.85 by 3.

B Multiply $46.85 by 4.

C Divide $46.85 by 3.

D Divide $46.85 by 4.

10. For the recycling drive, each of 27 students is trying to collect 85 pounds of paper. Which of the following is needed to find about how many pounds the students hope to collect in all?

F An estimate of the sum

G The exact sum

H An estimate of the product

J The exact product

TEST PREP

Multiple-Choice Cumulative Review

Choose the correct letter for each answer.

Number Sense

1. Which of these numbers is 6.5 when rounded to the nearest tenth and 6 when rounded to the nearest one?

A 6.28
B 6.48
C 6.52
D 6.54

2. Three young gymnasts had very close scores. Which set of numbers could represent their scores ordered from least to greatest?

F 4.033, 4.03, 4.066
G 4.03, 4.033, 4.066
H 4.03, 4.066, 4.033
J 4.033, 4.066, 4.03

3. Which number sentence is true?

A $0.125 < 0.1$
B $0.375 > 0.5$
C $0.25 < 0.2$
D $0.5 > 0.25$

4. Which of these fractions is NOT equivalent to $\frac{1}{4}$?

F $\frac{2}{8}$
G $\frac{3}{12}$
H $\frac{6}{8}$
J $\frac{4}{16}$

5. It takes Mrs. Cortez 120 hours to make a small quilt. It takes her 14 hours longer to make a large quilt. She has orders for 13 large quilts. If each large quilt takes her the same amount of time to make, how long will it take her to complete the orders?

A 147 hours
B 402 hours
C 536 hours
D 1,742 hours

6. An airline charges $120 round trip to transport dogs in medium carriers and $180 to transport dogs in large carriers. How much will it cost to transport 3 dogs in medium carriers and 2 in large carriers?

F $360
G $720
H $1,260
J $2,400

7. What is the product of 515 and 55?

A 27,225
B 27,325
C 28,225
D 28,325

8. Two cats eat about 4 pounds of dry cat food every 14 days. About how many pounds of cat food would they eat in 12 weeks?

F 4 pounds
G 8 pounds
H 24 pounds
J 48 pounds

Geometry and Measurement

9. Which figure is NOT a polygon?

A

C

B

D

---

10. Which best describes congruent figures?

F Same shape

G Same size and same shape

H Same shape, different size

J Same size

---

11. Which dotted line is a line of symmetry?

A

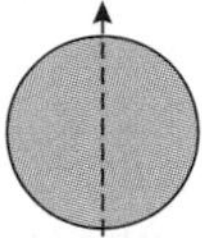

C

B

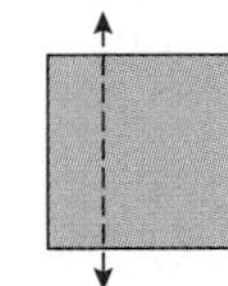

D

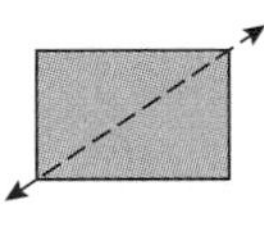

---

12. Which figure has fewer than four sides?

F Triangle

G Square

H Pentagon

J Rectangle

Statistics, Data Analysis, and Probability

Use the bar graph for Questions 13–15.

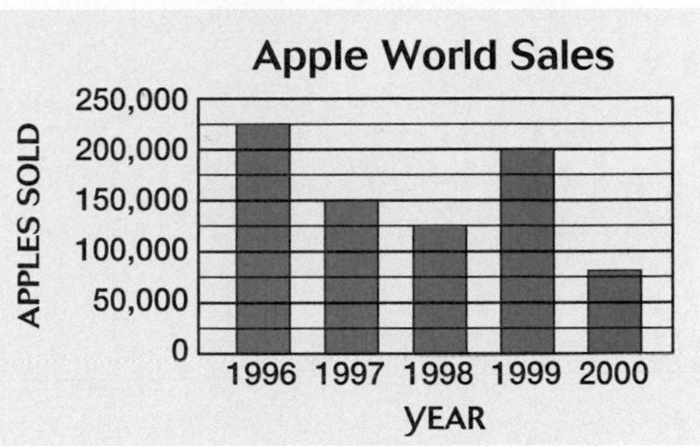

13. In which year were fewer than 100,000 apples sold?

A 1997 C 1999

B 1998 D 2000

---

14. Which of the following best describes the difference between the greatest and the least number of apples sold in 1 year?

F About 75,000

G About 95,000

H About 100,000

J About 150,000

---

15. Which is the best estimate of the average number of apples sold per year?

A 155,000 C 275,000

B 200,000 D 875,000

---

16. Which number is the median for the following set of data?

16 7 18 9 5

F 16 H 9

G 11 J 13

Dividing Whole Numbers

Diagnosing Readiness

In Chapter 5, you will use these skills:

A Multiplication and Division Facts

(Grade 4)

1. 10×4

2. 7×8

3. 11×6

4. $16 \div 2$

5. $72 \div 8$

6. $32 \div 4$

7. 7×4

8. 6×6

9. $24 \div 8$

10. $54 \div 9$

B Ordering

(pages 10–12)

Write the numbers in each set in order from least to greatest.

11. 92, 9, 9.7, 9.2

12. 0.82, 0.3, 0.13, 0.27

13. 88,000, 8,800, 80,000

14. 6,913, 6,899, 6,684

15. The ages of Stella's relatives are 15, 77, 53, 45, 68, 25, 29, 33, 4, 12, and 9. List the ages from oldest to youngest.

C Comparing Whole Numbers

(pages 10–12)

Write <, >, or = for each ●.

16. 9 + 3 ● 18 − 6

17. 81 ÷ 9 ● 7 × 7

18. 5 × 8 ● 6 × 12

19. Ben and Salvador each made 4 dozen wooden whistles. Ben sold 30 of his whistles and Salvador sold 3 dozen of his. Who has the most whistles remaining?

D Adding and Subtracting Whole Numbers

(Grade 4)

Find the sum or difference.

20. $\begin{array}{r} 817 \\ \underline{+223} \end{array}$

21. $\begin{array}{r} 3{,}001 \\ \underline{-\quad 87} \end{array}$

22. Caleb sold 22 paintings in August, 15 paintings in September, and 18 paintings in October. How many paintings did Caleb sell in three months?

E Using Inverse Operations

(pages 44–45)

State what to do to find *n*.

23. $64 + n$

24. $n - 440$

25. $1.6 + n$

26. $n - 15.99$

27. Jenna said if she added 117 to her weight the answer is 216. What is Jenna's weight?

F Solving Equations Involving Addition and Subtraction

(pages 46–47)

Solve for *x*.

28. $212 + x = 800$

29. $657 + x = 1{,}000$

30. $x - 24 = 36$

31. $x - 22 = 45$

32. $15 + x = 60$

33. $x - 50 = 125$

To the Family and Student

Looking Back

In Chapter 4, students learned how to multiply whole numbers.

Chapter 5

Dividing Whole Numbers

In this chapter, students will learn to divide whole numbers.

Looking Ahead

In Chapters 6 and 8, students will learn how to divide decimals and fractions.

Math and Everyday Living

Opportunities to apply the concepts of Chapter 5 abound in everyday situations. During the chapter, think about how dividing whole numbers can be used to solve a variety of real-world problems. The following examples suggest just a few of the many situations that could launch a discussion about dividing whole numbers.

Math and Hobbies You and your family collect miniature race cars. In your records you notice that you have spent over $600 for 25 cars. What is the approximate cost of each car?

Math and Music Your uncle likes to listen to many different types of music. You decide to make a table, listing how many CDs he has for each type of music.

Type of Music	Number of CDs
Jazz	14
Rock	18
Blues	10
Country	18
Big Band	17
Classical	19

Find the average number of CDs for all the types of music.

Math and Recreation A group of your relatives plans to take a 10-mile canoe trip. Each canoe can hold 4 people. You and 18 of your relatives plan on canoeing. How many canoes should you rent for the trip?

Math and the Environment For a community service project, your family decided to pick up the litter on a 3-mile stretch of highway. In a six-month period, your family collected 78 garbage bags full of trash. For the community newspaper you decide to make people aware of the littering problem. For your report, calculate how many bags of trash, per mile, your family collected in the six months.

Math in a Band The band at the wedding reception you attended with your family played for four hours. You noticed that the band took frequent 6-minute breaks. Out of the 4 hours, the actual playing time was only 168 minutes. How many breaks did the band take?

Math and Money You cleaned up the yard for 6 hours last Saturday. You were paid a total of $24. Find out how much you were paid for each hour of work.

California Content Standards in Chapter 5 Lessons*

	Teach and Practice	Practice
Number Sense		
1.0 Students compute with . . . positive integers . . .	5-1, 5-2	5-11
1.1 Estimate, round, and manipulate very large (e.g., millions) and very small (e.g., thousandths) numbers.	5-2	5-12
2.2 (🔑) Demonstrate proficiency with division, including . . . long division with multidigit divisors.	5-3, 5-5, 5-6, 5-7	5-2, 5-4, 5-9, 5-10, 5-11, 5-12
Algebra and Functions		
1.1 (🔑) (Grade 6) Write and solve one-step linear equations in one variable.	5-12	
1.2 (🔑) Use a letter to represent an unknown number; . . .	5-11	5-1, 5-5, 5-12
Statistics, Data Analysis, and Probability		
1.1 Know the concepts of mean, median, and mode; compute and compare simple examples to show that they may differ.	5-9, 5-10	

	Teach and Practice	Practice
Mathematical Reasoning		
1.0 Students make decisions about how to approach problems.		5-7
2.0 Students use strategies, skills, and concepts in finding solutions.		5-9, 5-10
2.1 Use estimation to verify the reasonableness of calculated results.		5-3, 5-7
2.3 Use a variety of methods, such as words, . . . symbols, . . . tables, diagrams, and models, to explain mathematical reasoning.	5-8	
2.4 Express the solution clearly and logically by using the appropriate mathematical notation and terms and clear language; support solutions with evidence in both verbal and symbolic work.	5-4	5-1, 5-6
3.1 Evaluate the reasonableness of the solution in the context of the original situation.		5-9
3.2 Note the method of deriving the solution and demonstrate a conceptual understanding of the derivation by solving similar problems.		5-8
3.3 Develop generalizations of the results obtained and apply them in other circumstances.		5-5

* The symbol (🔑) indicates a key standard as designated in the Mathematics Framework for California Public Schools. Full statements of the California Content Standards are found at the beginning of this book following the Table of Contents.

Mental Math: Patterns in Division

California Content Standard *Number Sense 1.0: Students compute with . . . positive integers . . . .*

Warm-Up Review

1. $56 \div 8$
2. $48 \div 8$
3. $32 \div 4$
4. $40 \div 8$
5. $42 \div 7$
6. $81 \div 9$
7. $24 \div 6$
8. $27 \div 3$
9. Jon worked 2 days babysitting. He earned $32 for 8 hours of work. How much did Jon earn per hour?

Math Link You already know division basic facts like $12 \div 3 = 4$ and $54 \div 6 = 9$. Now you will use basic facts and patterns with zeros to help you divide.

When the **dividend** or the **divisor** is a multiple of ten, use what you already know about basic facts and patterns with zeros to help you find the **quotient.**

Word Bank

dividend
divisor
quotient

Example

Find n. $160 \div 8 = n$

$160 \div 8 = n$	The dividend is 160. The divisor is 8.
$160 \div 8 = 20$	Think: $16 \div 8 = 2$
$n = 20$	The quotient is 20.

Here's WHY It Works

160 = 16 tens
16 tens ÷ 8 = 2 tens, or 20

More Examples

A.
$30 \div 5 = 6$
$300 \div 5 = 60$
$3{,}000 \div 5 = 600$

Use the basic fact $30 \div 5 = 6$. Look for patterns of zeros.

B.
$60 \div 30 = 2$
$600 \div 30 = 20$
$6{,}000 \div 30 = 200$

Use the basic fact $6 \div 3 = 2$. Look for patterns of zeros.

C. Find n. $720 \div n = 9$
Think: $72 \div 8 = 9$
So, $720 \div 80 = 9$

D. Find n. $n \div 5 = 300$
Think: $15 \div 5 = 3$
So, $1500 \div 5 = 300$

Guided Practice *For another example, see Set A on p. 202.*

For Exercises 1–3, find each *n*.

1.
$32 \div 4 = n$
$320 \div 4 = n$
$3{,}200 \div 4 = n$

2.
$48 \div 6 = n$
$480 \div n = 80$
$n \div 6 = 800$

3.
$210 \div 30 = n$
$2{,}100 \div 30 = n$
$21{,}000 \div 30 = n$

4. A cyclist completed a 2,000-mile bicycle race in 20 days, and pedaled the same distance each day. How many miles did the cyclist pedal each day?

Additional Standard: Algebra and Functions 1.2 (key), Mathematical Reasoning 2.4 (See p. 167.)

Independent Practice *For more practice, see Set A on p. 204.*

For Exercises 5–7, find each *n*.

5. $35 \div 5 = n$
$n \div 5 = 700$
$3{,}500 \div n = 70$

6. $54 \div n = 9$
$540 \div 6 = n$
$n \div 6 = 900$

7. $n \div 8 = 6$
$n \div 8 = 60$
$4{,}800 \div n = 600$

8. $140 \div 2$ **9.** $2{,}400 \div 6$ **10.** $4{,}200 \div 7$ **11.** $32{,}000 \div 8$

12. $450 \div 9$ **13.** $5{,}600 \div 7$ **14.** $4{,}000 \div 8$ **15.** $1{,}600 \div 40$

16. $490 \div 70$ **17.** $2{,}400 \div 80$ **18.** $8{,}100 \div 90$ **19.** $54{,}000 \div 900$

20. At the right is part of the map of the RAGBRAI®—Register's Annual Great Bicycle Ride Across Iowa. If Jennie traveled from Cresco to Guttenberg in 10 hours, find her average speed.

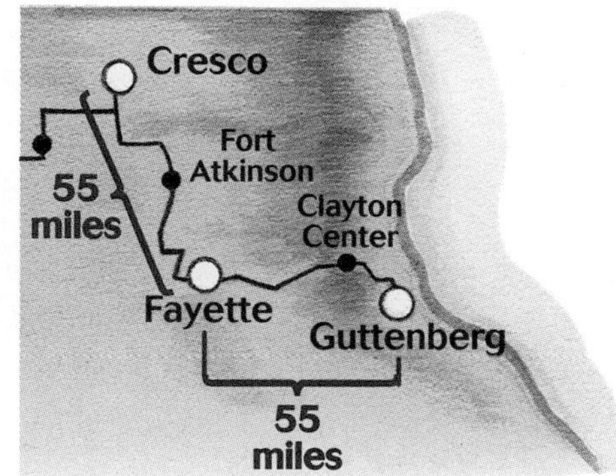

21. Algebra Evaluate $20{,}000 \div x$, for $x = 400$.

22. Math Reasoning How is the number of zeros in the quotient in $160 \div 8 = 20$ related to the number of zeros in the dividend?

23. Math Reasoning How is the number of zeros in the quotient in $30{,}000 \div 6 = 5{,}000$ related to the number of zeros in the dividend?

Mixed Review

24. Math Reasoning Explain how to find 20×500 mentally.

25. 3^3 **26.** 8^2 **27.** 345×206 **28.** $18 \times \$937$

29. Which is greater, 5.2 or 5.09? **30.** Which is less, 4,302 or 4,320?

Test Prep **Choose the correct letter for each answer.**

31. (2-8) **Algebra** On a bike hike, Josie rode for 4 hours and rested for 2 hours. Which equation can be used to find the total amount of time for the hike?

A $4 - t = 2$ **B** $t \times 2 = 4$ **C** $4 + 2 = t$ **D** $4 - 2 = t$

32. (3-7) Tell which number is the median of this set of data: 8, 5, 7, 9, 6, 12, 9

F 7 **G** 9 **H** 17 **J** 8 **K** NH

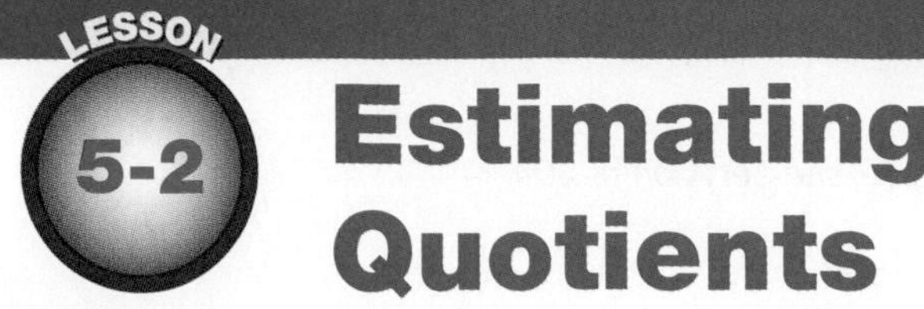

Estimating Quotients

California Content Standard *Number Sense 1.0: Students compute with . . . positive integers . . .. Also Number Sense 1.1* *(See p. 167.)*

Warm-Up Review

1. 500 ÷ 50
2. 2,700 ÷ 30
3. 180 ÷ 9
4. 560 ÷ 70
5. 36,000 ÷ 40
6. 360 ÷ 6
7. 7,200 ÷ 8
8. 4,000 ÷ 20
9. Amy made 2 kinds of muffins. She packaged 300 muffins in packages of 5 each. How many packages did she have?

Math Link You have used compatible numbers with adding and subtracting. Now you will use compatible numbers to estimate quotients.

Example

Suppose you could walk from one end of the Great Wall of China to the other. If you walked 7 kilometers an hour, about how many hours would it take to walk the entire length? Use the map above to help you solve the problem.

6,400	÷	**7**	=	***n***
length of wall		rate of walking		time to walk entire length

Word Bank

compatible numbers

To estimate the quotient, you can use **compatible numbers,** numbers that are easy to compute mentally. Change the dividend to a number that is compatible with the divisor.

$6{,}400 \div 7 \rightarrow 6{,}300 \div 7 = 900$

Here's WHY It Works

6,300 and 7 are compatible numbers, since 63 is divisible by 7.

It would take about 900 hours to walk the Great Wall.

More Examples

A. $4{,}128 \div 8 = m$
Think: $4{,}000 \div 8 = 500$, so $4{,}128 \div 8$ is about 500.

B. $152 \div 18 = b$
Think: $160 \div 20 = 8$, so $152 \div 18$ is about 8.

C. $8{,}175 \div 23 = q$
Think: $8{,}000 \div 20 = 400$, so $8{,}175 \div 23$ is about 400.

 Additional Standards: Number Sense 2.2 (🔑) *(See p. 167.)*

Guided Practice

For another example, see Set B on p. 202.

Estimate each quotient. Tell what compatible numbers you used.

1. $9\overline{)4,300}$ **2.** $5\overline{)293}$ **3.** $78\overline{)317}$ **4.** $89\overline{)938}$

5. $3,712 \div 6$ **6.** $912 \div 3$ **7.** $652 \div 83$ **8.** $572 \div 91$

9. Suppose it took 900 hours to walk the Great Wall. About how many 8-hour days of walking is this?

Independent Practice

For more practice, see Set B on p. 204.

Estimate each quotient.

10. $5\overline{)246}$ **11.** $4\overline{)3,401}$ **12.** $8\overline{)6,188}$ **13.** $7\overline{)1,398}$

14. $501 \div 8$ **15.** $1,196 \div 2$ **16.** $2,095 \div 3$ **17.** $1,694 \div 7$

18. $275 \div 29$ **19.** $621 \div 18$ **20.** $1,392 \div 68$ **21.** $20,963 \div 72$

22. Math Reasoning Give 3 different sets of compatible numbers you could use to estimate the quotient of $576 \div 87$.

23. Each day, Elena reads 18 pages of *The Secret Garden.* Use the table at the right. Estimate about how long it will take her to finish the book.

Book	Pages
The Secret Garden	298
Julie of the Wolves	170
The Cricket in Times Square	157

Mixed Review

24. Find the total number of pages in the books in the table above.

25. Write 4^3 in standard form.

26. Write 5×5 using an exponent.

27. Mental Math $3,200 \div 8$

28. Mental Math $4,500 \div 500$

Test Prep **Choose the correct letter for each answer.**

29. Which number is in the hundredths place in 507.832?
(1-3)

A 5 **B** 8 **C** 2 **D** 3 **E** NH

30. Which is the best estimate for 52×48?
(4-6)

F 2,000 **G** 2,400 **H** 2,500 **J** 3,000 **K** NH

Dividing by One-Digit Divisors

California Content Standard *Number Sense 2.2 (🔑); Demonstrate proficiency with division, . . . including long division with multidigit divisors.*

Warm-Up Review

1. 45 ÷ 9
2. 32 ÷ 8
3. 56 ÷ 7
4. 28 ÷ 4
5. 45 ÷ 5
6. 54 ÷ 6
7. 42 ÷ 7
8. 72 ÷ 9
9. Bob worked 6 hours Sunday and 2 hours Monday. His total pay was \$48. What was the rate per hour?

Math Link You already know the basic facts for division. Now you will use them to divide greater numbers.

Example 1

Find 96 ÷ 8. Estimate first: 80 ÷ 8 = 10.

Step 1 Think of 96 as 9 tens 6 ones. Divide the 9 tens into 8 equal groups.

```
   1     ← Divide: 9 tens ÷ 8 = 1 ten
 8)96
 − 8     ← Multiply: 1 ten × 8 = 8 tens
   1     ← Subtract: 9 tens − 8 tens = 1 ten
           Compare: 1 < 8
```

Step 2 Bring down the ones digit so you can continue dividing.

```
   1
 8)96
 − 8↓      Bring down the 6.
   16    ← There are 16 ones.
```

Step 3 Divide the 16 ones into 8 equal groups.

```
   12    ← Divide: 16 ÷ 8 = 2
 8)96
 − 8↓
   16
 − 16    ← Multiply: 2 × 8 = 16
    0    ← Subtract: 16 − 16 = 0
           Compare: 0 < 8
```

The answer is close to the estimate.

Step 4 Check by multiplying.

12 × 8 = 96

Here's WHY It Works

Divide 9 tens into 8 groups. There is 1 ten in each group. 1 ten and 6 ones are left.

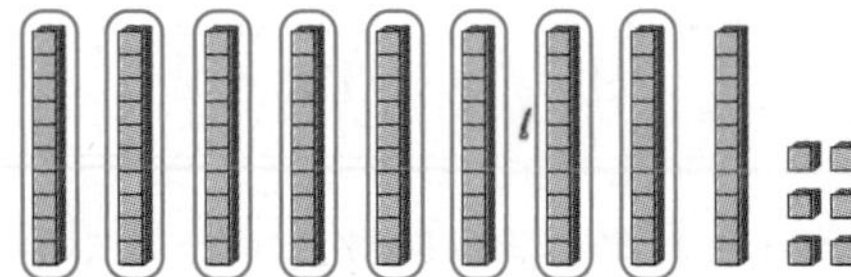

Regroup the 1 ten as 10 ones. Add the 6 ones to make 16 ones altogether.

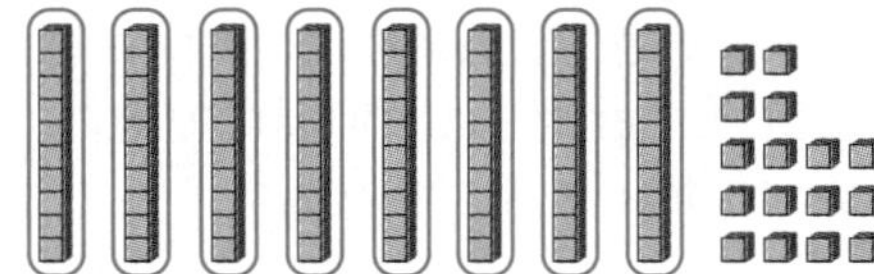

To divide the 16 ones equally among the 8 groups, put 2 ones in each group. Now there are 1 ten and 2 ones, or 12, in each group.

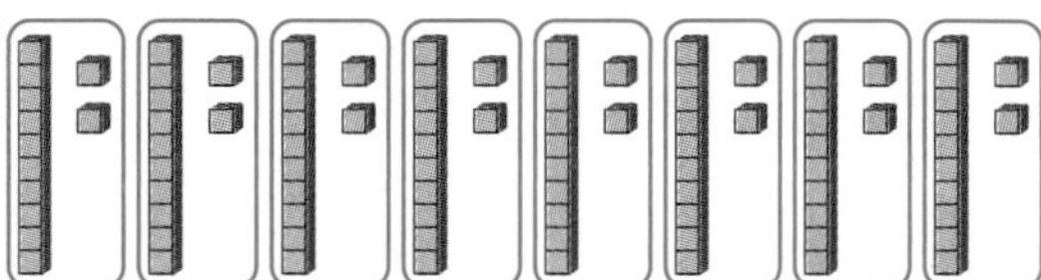

 *Additional Standard: Mathematical Reasoning 2.1**(See p. 167.)*

Example 2

Find 230 ÷ 8

Estimate: 240 ÷ 8 = 30. The estimate suggests that the quotient will be a two-digit number.

Step 1 Divide the tens.

```
   2
8)230
- 16
   7
```

- Divide. 23 ÷ 8
- Multiply. 2 × 8
- Subtract.
- Compare. 7 < 8

Step 2 Bring down the ones. Divide the ones. Write the remainder in the quotient.

```
  28 R6
8)230
- 16↓
   70
 - 64
    6
```

- Bring down the 0.
- Divide. 70 ÷ 8
- Multiply. 8 × 8
- Subtract.

Compare. 6 < 8

The remainder is 6.

Step 3 Multiply to check.

```
  28
×  8
 224
+  6
 230
```

- Multiply the quotient by the divisor.
- Add the remainder.
- The sum is the dividend.

Example 3

Find 1,810 ÷ 9.

Estimate: 1,800 ÷ 9 = 200. The quotient will be a three-digit number.

Step 1
Divide the hundreds.

```
    2
9)1,810
 - 18
    0
```

Step 2
Divide the tens.

```
    20
9)1,810
 - 18↓
    01
   - 0
     1
```

1 < 9 so place 0 in the quotient.

Step 3
Divide the ones.

```
    201 R1
9)1,810
 - 18
    01
   - 0↓
     10
    - 9
      1
```

Step 4
Multiply to check.

```
  201
×   9
 1809
+   1
1,810
```

More Examples

```
    10 R3
A. 6)63
   - 6
     3
   - 0
     3
```

```
    89 R1
B. 4)357
  - 32
    37
  - 36
     1
```

```
      207
C. 7)1,449
   - 14
       4
     - 0
      49
    - 49
       0
```

Guided Practice *For another example, see Set C on p. 202.*

1. $4\overline{)98}$ **2.** 175 ÷ 6 **3.** $5\overline{)508}$ **4.** 840 ÷ 6 **5.** 8,129 ÷ 8

6. Math Reasoning Ron said that he divided by 7 and got an answer of 15R7. Can this be correct? Why or why not?

Independent Practice *For more practice, see Set C on p. 204.*

7. $5\overline{)125}$ **8.** $3\overline{)95}$ **9.** $9\overline{)396}$ **10.** $8\overline{)911}$ **11.** $4\overline{)785}$

12. $5\overline{)4{,}015}$ **13.** $3\overline{)2{,}555}$ **14.** $8\overline{)4{,}638}$ **15.** $2\overline{)5{,}926}$ **16.** $7\overline{)6{,}917}$

17. 603 ÷ 9 **18.** 1,310 ÷ 4 **19.** 7,916 ÷ 9 **20.** 835 ÷ 8 **21.** 454 ÷ 5

22. 1,753 ÷ 7 **23.** 2,412 ÷ 2 **24.** $408 ÷ 4 **25.** $9,376 ÷ 4 **26.** $5,776 ÷ 8

For Exercises 27–30, use the data in the table at the right. Find the amount earned per day if the person worked a 5-day week.

27. For 1968 **28.** For 1978

29. For 1988 **30.** For 1998

Sample Weekly Earnings U.S. Production Workers

Year	Earnings
1968	$110
1978	$205
1988	$320
1998	$440

31. Math Reasoning When dividing a 3-digit number by a 1-digit number, how can you tell how many digits will be in the quotient?

Mixed Review

32. Mental Math The Art Guild received donations of $500, $300, $700, and $500, and will divide the total donations equally among four galleries. How much will each gallery receive?

33. Estimate 493 ÷ 78. **34.** Estimate 259 ÷ 53. **35. Mental Math** 540 ÷ 6

36. Algebra Solve $15 + x = 32$ for x. **37. Algebra** Find $50 - n$ if $n = 23$.

Test Prep **Choose the correct letter for each answer.**

38. Give the best estimate for 86 + 33.
(2-6)

A 110 **C** 120
B 130 **D** 140

39. Find 9.06 − 0.7.
(2-10)

F 2.06 **J** 8.99
G 9.09 **K** NH
H 8.36

Multiple-Choice Cumulative Review

Choose the correct letter for each answer.

1. **Tennis balls come in containers of three. A school orders 12 containers. Each week, two tennis balls are lost during gym class. After how many weeks will there be only two tennis balls left?**

A 6
B 14
C 17
D 18

2. **Which expression could be used to represent the following phrase?**

the product of 6 and a number

F $6n$
G $6 + n$
H $6 \div n$
J $6 - n$

3. **The third-, fourth-, and fifth-grade classes collected 568 pounds of newspapers. The sixth-grade class collected 195 pounds. Together the third and fourth grades collected 365 pounds. Which number sentence could be used to find the number of pounds, n, collected by the fifth grade?**

A $568 - 365 = n$
B $365 + 568 = n$
C $568 - 195 = n$
D $365 + 195 = n$

4. **An airplane is about 62 meters in length. If a luggage carrier is 9 meters long, about how many luggage carriers would have to line up end-to-end to match the length of the jet?**

F 4
G 6
H 7
J 10

5. **The first row of seats in a theater has 9 seats. The second row has 11 seats, the third row 14 seats, and the fourth row 18 seats. If the pattern continues, how many seats are in the eighth row?**

A 29
B 36
C 44
D 49

6. **Which number sentence is true?**

F $0.098 > 0.198$
G $7.007 < 7.002$
H $23.177 < 23.018$
J $100.431 > 100.429$

7. **What decimal is shown by the shaded part of the grid?**

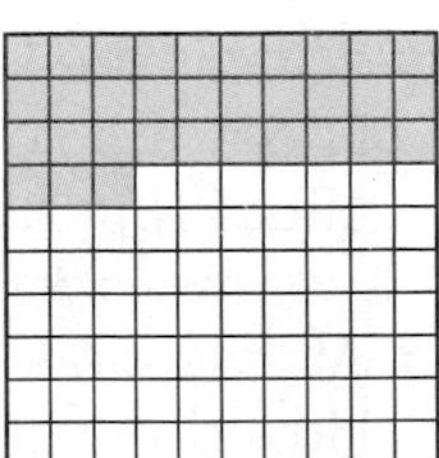

A 3.3
B 0.33
C 0.033
D 0.0033

Problem-Solving Skill:

Interpreting Remainders

Warm-Up Review

1. 20 ÷ 8
2. 45 ÷ 9
3. 27 ÷ 4
4. 32 ÷ 5
5. 55 ÷ 7
6. 34 ÷ 8
7. 56 ÷ 6
8. 75 ÷ 9
9. Gary biked 15 miles and then 13 miles more at a speed of 7 miles per hour. How long did he bike?

California Content Standard *Mathematical Reasoning 2.4: Express the solution clearly and logically by using the appropriate mathematical notation and terms and clear language; support solutions with evidence in both verbal and symbolic work.*

Read for Understanding

A campground rents motorboats, sailboats, and canoes. The number of campers signed up for Friday, Saturday, and Sunday sailing trips is given on the clipboard at the right. A sailboat can hold up to 4 people. No sailboat can go out with fewer than 2 people.

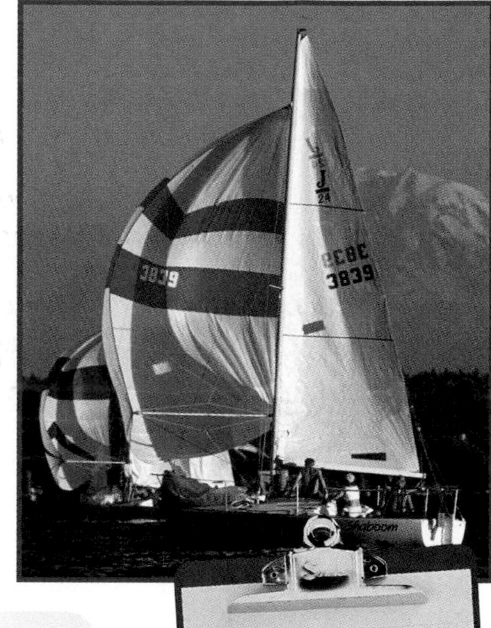

Weekend Sign up

Friday Trip	37
Saturday Trip	26
Sunday Trip	24

1. How many campers have signed up for the Friday trip?
2. What is the greatest number of campers that can go out in a sailboat? the least number?

Think and Discuss

Interpreting Remainders

When you divide, sometimes you need to interpret a remainder to find the solution. You may need to include the remainder, to drop it, or to increase the quotient to the next whole number.

Reread the paragraph at the top of the page.

3. What is the least number of boats that must be rented for the Friday trip so that everyone can go? How does the remainder affect your answer?
4. At least how many boats should be rented for the Sunday trip? How does the remainder affect your answer?
5. Name a situation in everyday life where interpreting the remainder correctly is important.

 Additional Standards: Number Sense 2.2 (See p. 167.)

Guided Practice

Rowboats rented by the campground must have exactly three people on board at all times. Boats are sent out every hour on the hour, and campers must wait at the dock for the next available boat. At 2:00 P.M., 20 people wanted to go out in rowboats.

1. Which number sentence could be used to find the number of rowboats that will go out at 2:00 P.M.?

a. $20 \div 6 = 3$ R2

b. $3 \times 20 = 60$

c. $20 \div 3 = 6$ R2

2. How many people have to wait until 3:00 P.M. for a rowboat?

a. 7 people

b. 6 people

c. 2 people

Independent Practice

On Saturday, 35 young campers went across the lake for a picnic, games, and swimming. The motorboat that transported them held a maximum of nine campers.

3. Which number sentence could be used to find the number of trips the motorboat made to transport all of the campers?

a. $9 \times 35 = 35$

b. $35 \div 9 = 3$ R8

c. $35 \div 3 = 11$ R2

4. How many trips did the boat need to make to transport all of the campers?

a. 1 trip

b. 3 trips

c. 4 trips

5. The 35 campers separated into teams of four for a game. Those left over were scorekeepers. Which part of $35 \div 4 = 8$ R3 gives the number of scorekeepers?

a. The remainder of 3

b. The quotient of 8

c. The divisor of 4

6. The campers separated into teams of five for a swimming race. How do you know that there will be no campers left over?

a. The quotient is 7.

b. There are 5 on each team.

c. The remainder is 0.

7. Math Reasoning Write a problem for which the answer is one more than the quotient. Then change the problem so that the answer is the quotient.

Use Homework Workbook 5-4.

Dividing by Two-Digit Divisors

California Content Standard *Number Sense 2.2 (🔑): Demonstrate proficiency with division, . . . including long division with multidigit divisors.*

Math Link You know how to divide whole numbers by one-digit divisors. Now you will learn to divide by two-digit divisors.

Warm-Up Review

1. 420 ÷ 70 **2.** 560 ÷ 80

3. 250 ÷ 50 **4.** 3,600 ÷ 40

5. Estimate 788 ÷ 23.

6. Estimate 5,302 ÷ 85.

7. The Anderson family is planning a 475-mile trip. At a speed of 60 miles per hour, estimate how long the trip will take.

Example 1

As part of an Earth Day celebration, students in the three schools shown in the table volunteered to plant seedlings. If each of the volunteers from Lincoln School is given the same number of seedlings to plant, how many will each student receive? How many seedlings will be left over?

Planting Seedlings

School	Number of Seedlings	Number of Students
Lincoln	179	26
Emerson	258	35
Taft	197	18

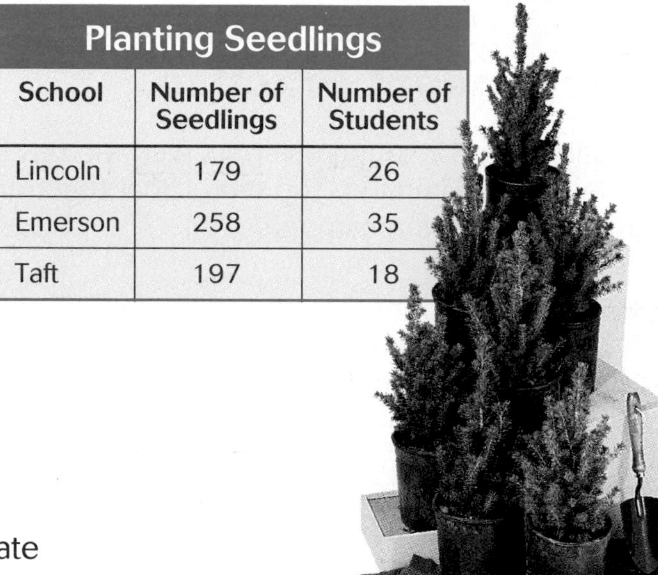

Find 179 ÷ 26.

Estimate first. 180 ÷ 30 = 6. The estimate helps you place the first digit correctly in the quotient.

Now divide to find the exact quotient.

Step 1 Divide using your estimate.

```
    6 R23
26)179
 - 156
    23
```

- Divide.
- Multiply.
- Subtract.
- Compare. $23 < 26$

Step 2 Check. Remember to add the remainder.

```
  26
×  6
 156
+ 23
 179
```

Each student will receive 6 seedlings. There will be 23 seedlings left over.

Additional Standards: Algebra and Functions 1.2 (🔑), Mathematical Reasoning 3.3 *(See p. 167.)*

Example 2

If each volunteer from Emerson School is given the same number of seedlings, how many seedlings will each person get? How many seedlings will be left over? Use the data in Example 1.

Find 258 ÷ 35.

Estimate: 240 ÷ 40 = 6.

Step 1 Divide using your estimate.

$$\begin{array}{r} 6 \\ 35\overline{)258} \\ -\ 210 \\ \hline 48 \end{array}$$

- Divide.
- Multiply.
- Subtract.
- Compare. $48 > 35$, so the estimate is too low.

Step 2 Adjust the quotient.

$$\begin{array}{r} 7\text{ R13} \\ 35\overline{)258} \\ -\ 245 \\ \hline 13 \end{array}$$

- Divide.
- Multiply.
- Subtract.
- Compare. $13 < 35$

Step 3 Check.

$$\begin{array}{r} 35 \\ \times\ 7 \\ \hline 245 \\ +\ 13 \\ \hline 258 \end{array}$$

Remember to add the remainder.

Each student will receive 7 seedlings. There will be 13 seedlings left over.

Example 3

Find 268 ÷ 32.

Estimate: 270 ÷ 30 = 9

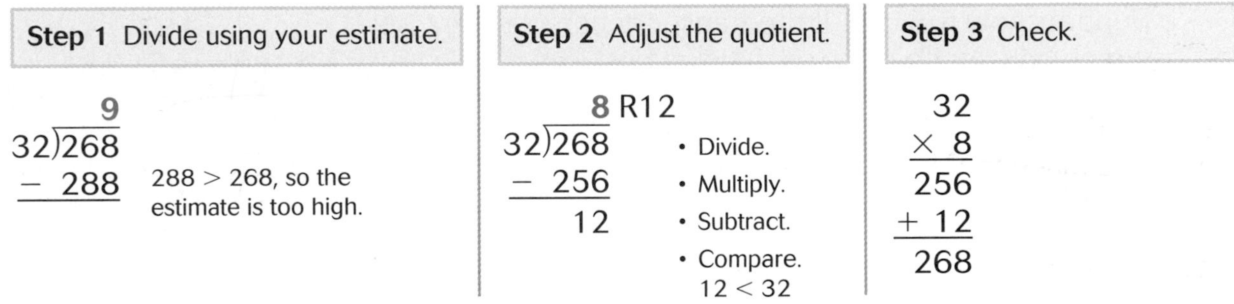

Step 1 Divide using your estimate.

$$\begin{array}{r} 9 \\ 32\overline{)268} \\ -\ 288 \\ \hline \end{array}$$

$288 > 268$, so the estimate is too high.

Step 2 Adjust the quotient.

$$\begin{array}{r} 8\text{ R12} \\ 32\overline{)268} \\ -\ 256 \\ \hline 12 \end{array}$$

- Divide.
- Multiply.
- Subtract.
- Compare. $12 < 32$

Step 3 Check.

$$\begin{array}{r} 32 \\ \times\ 8 \\ \hline 256 \\ +\ 12 \\ \hline 268 \end{array}$$

Guided Practice *For another example, see Set D on p. 202.*

1. $43\overline{)96}$ **2.** 339 ÷ 41 **3.** $56\overline{)504}$ **4.** 703 ÷ 82

5. Fifteen members of the photography club took 252 pictures. If they use film with 36 exposures per roll, how many rolls of film were used?

Independent Practice *For more practice, see Set D on p. 204.*

6. $26\overline{)84}$ **7.** $72\overline{)612}$ **8.** $33\overline{)231}$ **9.** $62\overline{)432}$

10. $94\overline{)500}$ **11.** $46\overline{)414}$ **12.** $31\overline{)85}$ **13.** $87\overline{)563}$

14. 274 ÷ 51 15. 88 ÷ 17 16. 117 ÷ 28 17. 342 ÷ 57

18. 96 ÷ 40 19. 328 ÷ 70 20. 299 ÷ 37 21. 56 ÷ 27

At the right is a table showing the sizes and prices of various grocery items. Find each price per ounce.

	Item	Weight in Ounces	Price in Cents	Price per Ounce
22.	Oatmeal	18	144	
23.	Oatmeal	42	336	
24.	Rice	16	48	
25.	Rice	32	64	
26.	Detergent	14	84	
27.	Detergent	22	110	
28.	Wheat Bread	16	80	
29.	Wheat Bread	24	168	

30. **Math Reasoning** Look at Example 2. What is the greatest remainder you can have when you divide by 35?

31. **Algebra** Find 160 ÷ n + 13 if n = 32.

32. The cost of tickets and transportation for 24 students going to a puppet show is $192. If the transportation costs $2 per student, how much does each ticket cost?

Mixed Review

33. Which number is the quotient in 350 ÷ 7 = 50?

34. Estimate 4,962 ÷ 8.

35. $8\overline{)561}$

36. **Algebra** Raul had $2,300 in his savings account before he withdrew $500. Write and solve an equation to tell how much he had left.

Test Prep **Choose the correct letter for each answer.**

37. Which number is greatest?
(1-4)

A 56.89

B 57.03

C 56.92

D 57.21

38. Write three hundred five thousand, twenty-nine in standard form.
(1-1)

F 35,029

G 305,290

H 3,529

J 305,029

Diagnostic Checkpoint

Find each *n*.

1. (5-1) $45 \div 5 = n$
$n \div 5 = 90$
$4{,}500 \div n = 900$

2. (5-1) $64 \div n = 8$
$640 \div 8 = n$
$6{,}400 \div 8 = n$

3. (5-1) $n \div 7 = 7$
$n \div 7 = 70$
$4{,}900 \div n = 700$

4. (5-1) $500 \div 5$

5. (5-1) $21{,}000 \div 300$

6. (5-1) $810 \div 90$

Estimate each quotient. Tell what compatible numbers you used.

7. (5-2) $756 \div 8$

8. (5-2) $273 \div 5$

9. (5-2) $310 \div 9$

10. (5-2) $134 \div 3$

11. (5-2) $500 \div 6$

12. (5-2) $299 \div 7$

Find each quotient.

13. (5-3) $5\overline{)63}$

14. (5-3) $7\overline{)85}$

15. (5-3) $3\overline{)19}$

16. (5-3) $253 \div 6$

17. (5-3) $586 \div 7$

18. (5-3) $3{,}549 \div 2$

19. (5-5) $26\overline{)128}$

20. (5-5) $25\overline{)160}$

21. (5-5) $41\overline{)376}$

22. (5-5) $37\overline{)280}$

23. (5-5) $92\overline{)736}$

24. (5-5) $68\overline{)\$544}$

25. (5-4) A train must have at least one conductor for every 3 cars. If the train is 26 cars long, how many conductors are needed? Explain your answer.

26. (5-5) The fifth grade has raised $1,500 for a class trip to a theater. It costs $30 per student. Do they have enough money for 48 students to go? Explain your thinking.

27. (5-4) A group of 53 students is taking a trip to the Henry Ford Museum. If 5 students can fit in a car, how many cars will they need?

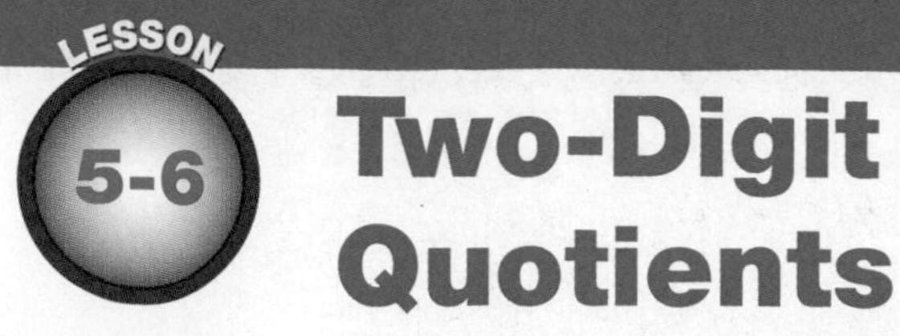

LESSON 5-6

Two-Digit Quotients

California Content Standard *Number Sense 2.2 (🔑): Demonstrate proficiency with division, . . . including . . . long division with multidigit divisors.*

Math Link You learned to divide with two-digit divisors and one-digit quotients. Now you will learn to divide with two-digit divisors and two-digit quotients.

Warm-Up Review

Estimate.

1. 963 ÷ 98
2. 561 ÷ 83
3. 815 ÷ 22
4. 463 ÷ 54
5. 384 ÷ 59
6. 733 ÷ 77
7. Serema stacks 24 cans of soup in each row on the store shelf. How many cans are in 13 rows?

Example 1

At a speed of 58 miles an hour, about how long would it take to drive from Phoenix to Flagstaff to Amarillo?

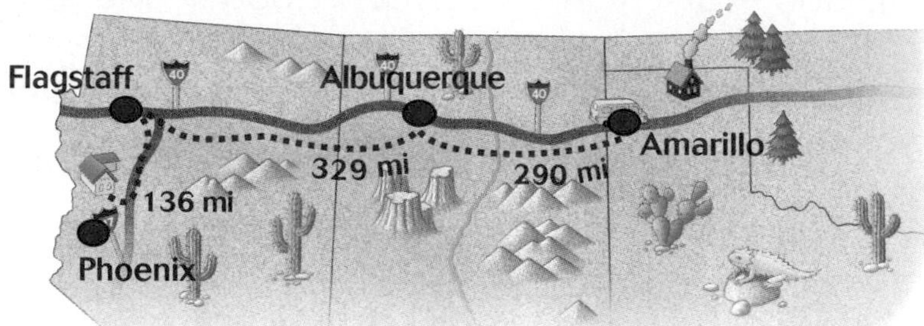

136 + 329 + 290 = 755 miles
Find 755 ÷ 58.

Estimate first: 600 ÷ 60 = 10.
The estimate tells you that the quotient is probably a two-digit number.

Step 1 Divide the tens.

```
     1
58)755
 − 58
   17
```

- Divide.
- Multiply.
- Subtract.
- Compare. 17 < 58

Step 2 Divide the ones.

```
    13 R1
58)755
 − 58↓
   175
 − 174
     1
```

- Bring down.
- Divide. 175 ÷ 58
- Multiply.
- Subtract.
- Compare. 1 < 58

Step 3 Check.

```
   13
 × 58
  104
+ 650
  754
+   1
  755
```

Remember to add the remainder.

The trip will take about 13 hours.

Example 2

Find 597 ÷ 33. Estimate first: 600 ÷ 30 = 20.

Step 1 Divide the tens.

```
     2
33)597
 − 66
```

66 > 59, so the estimate is too high.

Step 2 Adjust.

```
     1
33)597
 − 33
   26
```

- Divide.
- Multiply.
- Subtract.
- Compare. 26 < 33

Step 3 Divide the ones.

```
    18 R3
33)597
 − 33↓
   267
 − 264
     3
```

- Bring down.
- Divide.
- Multiply.
- Subtract.
- Compare. 3 < 33

Step 4 Check.

```
   33
 × 18
  264
  330
  594
    3
  597
```

 Additional Standard: Mathematical Reasoning 2.4 *(See p. 167.)*

Guided Practice *For another example, see Set E on p. 202.*

1. $21\overline{)483}$ **2.** $71\overline{)891}$ **3.** $840 \div 40$ **4.** $950 \div 57$

5. Use the map with Example 1. At a speed of 65 miles per hour, about how long would it take to drive from Flagstaff to Albuquerque?

Independent Practice *For more practice, see Set E on p. 205.*

6. $83\overline{)447}$ **7.** $17\overline{)586}$ **8.** $23\overline{)957}$ **9.** $75\overline{)900}$

10. $63\overline{)895}$ **11.** $15\overline{)403}$ **12.** $21\overline{)965}$ **13.** $47\overline{)987}$

14. $36\overline{)547}$ **15.** $14\overline{)439}$ **16.** $19\overline{)974}$ **17.** $26\overline{)864}$

18. $767 \div 32$ **19.** $924 \div 22$ **20.** $828 \div 59$ **21.** $673 \div 65$

22. Math Reasoning What is the least dividend possible for a divisor of 42 and a two-digit quotient? Explain.

23. Math Reasoning In Example 1, how do you know that the answer is closer to 13 hours than to 14 hours?

24. Use the map with Example 1. If a car gets 31 miles to a gallon of gasoline, about how many gallons will be used for a drive from Flagstaff to Amarillo?

Mixed Review

25. Mrs. Arnez is planning a 500-mile trip. Her car has a 16-gallon gas tank and averages 29 miles per gallon. Will 1 tankful of gas be enough?

26. $5.28 - 3.6$ **27.** $9\overline{)562}$ **28.** $26\overline{)272}$ **29.** $2{,}466 \div 8$ **30.** $602 \div 49$

Test Prep Choose the correct letter for each answer.

31. Algebra Find $72 - n \times 6 \div 3$ if $n = 12$.
(4-2)

A 120 **B** 0 **C** 48 **D** 15 **E** NH

32. A baseball team bought 22 new uniforms for $792.
(5-6) What was the cost of each uniform?

F $35 **G** $40 **H** $37 **J** $36 **K** NH

Dividing Greater Numbers

 **California Content Standard** *Number Sense 2.2 (🔑): Demonstrate proficiency with division, . . . including . . . long division with multidigit divisors.*

Warm-Up Review

1. 3,600 ÷ 40
2. 21,000 ÷ 30
3. 3,200 ÷ 800
4. 54,000 ÷ 900
5. 14,000 ÷ 70
6. 240,000 ÷ 600
7. A band rents space for rehearsals at $55 per hour. How much will it cost to rent the space for 15 three-hour rehearsals?

Math Link You learned to divide with two-digit divisors and one-digit or two-digit quotients. Now you will learn to divide with two-digit divisors and quotients with three or more digits.

Example 1

Several kinds of posters were sold at the annual music festival. The sale of posters showing the jazz band brought in $4,288. How many jazz-band posters were sold?

4,288	÷	16	=	p
total number of dollars		price per poster		number of posters sold

Estimate first: 4,000 ÷ 20 = 200

The estimate tells you that the quotient is probably a three-digit number.

Now divide to find the exact quotient.

Step 1 Divide the hundreds.

```
      2
16)4,288
 - 32
   10
```

- Divide.
- Multiply.
- Subtract.
- Compare. 10 < 16

Step 2 Divide the tens.

```
      26
16)4,288
 - 32↓
    108
  -  96
     12
```

- Bring down.
- Divide. 108 ÷ 16
- Multiply.
- Subtract.
- Compare. 12 < 16

Step 3 Divide the ones.

```
     268
16)4,288
 - 32  |
    108|
  -  96↓
     128
   - 128
       0
```

- Bring down.
- Divide. 128 ÷ 16
- Multiply.
- Subtract.
- Compare. 0 < 16

Step 4 Check by multiplying. 268 × 16 = 4,288

268 jazz-band posters were sold.

Example 2

Tickets for the concert cost $17. If ticket sales for the first day of the festival totaled $5,185, how many tickets had been sold?

$5,185	÷	17	=	t
total sales		cost per ticket		number of tickets sold

Estimate first: $6,000 ÷ $20 = 300.
The estimate tells you that the quotient is a three-digit number.

Then divide to find the exact quotient. Remember, sometimes you need to put a zero in the quotient when you divide.

Step 1 Divide the hundreds.

```
     3
17)5,185
 - 51
    0
```

Step 2 Divide the tens.

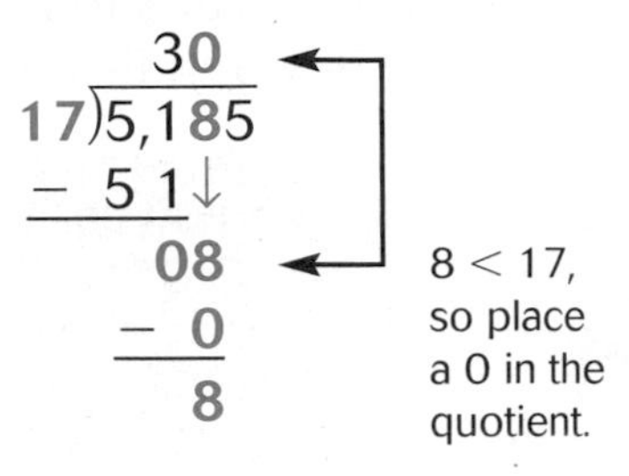

Step 3 Divide the ones.

```
     305
17)5,185
 - 51
    08
  -  0
    85
  - 85
     0
```

Step 4 Check by multiplying. $305 \times 17 = 5{,}185$

The first day, 305 tickets were sold.

More Examples

```
       223
A. 56)12,488
    - 112
       128
     - 112
       168
     - 168
         0
```

```
       470 R5
B. 38)17,865
    - 152
       266
     - 266
        05
      -  0
         5
```

```
       402 R4
C. 14)5,632
    - 56
      03
    -  0
      32
    - 28
       4
```

Guided Practice *For another example, see Set F on p. 203.*

1. $38\overline{)4{,}239}$ **2.** $9{,}041 \div 86$ **3.** $13\overline{)2{,}717}$ **4.** $28{,}636 \div 91$

5. Adult tickets for a chamber concert are $27 each, while youth tickets are $15 each. If adult ticket sales totaled $9,882, how many adult tickets were sold?

Independent Practice *For more practice, see Set F on p. 205.*

6. $15\overline{)3,159}$ **7.** $24\overline{)4,800}$ **8.** $58\overline{)7,275}$ **9.** $47\overline{)4,908}$

10. $54\overline{)11,670}$ **11.** $59\overline{)36,654}$ **12.** $87\overline{)40,951}$ **13.** $47\overline{)26,548}$

14. $6,985 \div 75$ **15.** $1,856 \div 83$ **16.** $5,369 \div 45$ **17.** $9,871 \div 64$

18. $25,925 \div 62$ **19.** $21,393 \div 56$ **20.** $56,400 \div 89$ **21.** $10,442 \div 18$

22. Math Reasoning Arrange the digits 1 through 7 in the boxes to get the least quotient. Use each digit exactly once. Describe how you decided where to place the digits. Then divide.

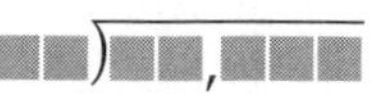

23. Tennis balls are packed 3 to a can and 24 cans to a carton. How many cartons are needed for 10,368 tennis balls?

24. Math Reasoning Is 47 R5 a reasonable answer for $17,865 \div 38$? Explain.

Mixed Review

25. A concert was attended by 762 students and 30 adults. If a bus seats 52 people, how many buses were needed to transport the students and the adults to the concert?

26. $88\overline{)528}$ **27.** $737 \div 82$ **28.** $21\overline{)391}$ **29.** $3,390 \div 72$

30. Find the range, the median, and the mode for this set of data: 12, 16, 17, 22, 9, 27, 23, 15, 18

31. Estimate 58×321. **32. Mental Math** $20,000 \div 500$

Test Prep **Choose the correct letter for each answer.**

33. Algebra Which value for n makes $n - 31 = 96$ true?
(2-4)

A $n = 2,976$ B $n = 65$ C $n = 127$ D $n = 136$

34. Algebra Which number sentence illustrates the distributive property?
(4-1)

F $5 + 6 = 6 + 5$

G $8 \times 9 = 9 \times 8$

H $9 + (8 + 4) = (9 + 8) + 4$

J $6 \times (5 + 9) = (6 \times 5) + (6 \times 9)$

Multiple-Choice Cumulative Review

Choose the correct letter for each answer.

1. This graph shows how many students signed up for recreational sports.

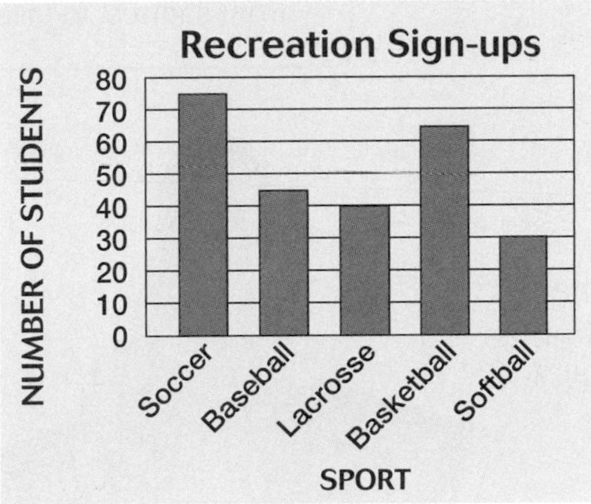

About how many students signed up for the most popular sport?

A 85 C 75

B 65 D 30

2. Which is the rule for the number sequence below?

13.1, 10.9, 8.7, 6.5, 4.3, . . .

F Add 2.

G Subtract 2.1.

H Subtract 2.2.

J Multiply by 0.5.

3. The shops on the east side of the street have consecutive even numbers. The first shop is number 302. Which number sentence would you use to find the number of the 15th shop?

A $302 + 14 = n$ C $302 + 28 = n$

B $302 + 15 = n$ D $302 \times 2 = n$

4. Which of these numbers is 2,750 when rounded to the nearest ten and 2,700 when rounded to the nearest hundred?

F 2,766

G 2,746

H 2,744

J 2,656

5. Estimate the product of 305 × 398.

A 1,200

B 12,000

C 90,000

D 120,000

6. Which value of *x* makes the number sentence true?

$$176.07 - x > 156.85$$

F 17.89

G 20.01

H 22.30

J 76.07

7. Bradley bought a magazine for \$3.99, a hat for \$16.99, some sunglasses, and sunscreen for \$7.99. Altogether he spent \$40.00. How much did he spend for the sunglasses?

A \$28.97

B \$20.00

C \$11.03

D \$6.99

Problem-Solving Strategy:

Logical Reasoning

Warm-Up Review

1. 4×6
2. 6^2
3. 4^2
4. 8×4
5. $12 \times \$0.06$
6. $17 \times \$0.05$
7. Jim is taller than Bob and Bob is shorter than Ned. Ned is not taller than Jim. List the boys in order from shortest to tallest.

California Content Standard *Mathematical Reasoning 2.3: Use a variety of methods, such as words, . . . symbols, . . . tables, diagrams, and models, to explain mathematical reasoning.*

Example

Rosa is hanging the pictures she is holding in a row. The green frame is to the left of the blue frame. The yellow frame is to the right of the blue frame. The red frame is between the green and blue frames. From left to right, what is the order of the frames?

Understand

What do you need to find?

You need to find the order, from left to right, in which Rosa is hanging the picture frames.

Plan

How can you solve the problem?

You can use **logical reasoning** to find the order of the frames on the wall.

Solve

green	blue			Green is to the left of blue.
green	blue	yellow		Yellow is to the right of blue.
green	red	blue	yellow	Red is between green and blue.

The order of the frames from left to right is green, red, blue, yellow.

Look Back

Check to be sure that the positions of the frames satisfy all the conditions.

Additional Standard: Mathematical Reasoning 3.2 (See p. 167.)

Guided Practice

1. Four friends each own a different pet, as shown in the table. Laura owns a dog. Maria does not own a cat. Jack's pet has four legs. Paul's pet does not walk. Copy and complete the table to help you find who owns each pet.

	Dog	Cat	Fish	Bird
Laura	Yes			
Maria	No	No		
Jack	No			
Paul	No			

Independent Practice

2. Al, Bob, Curt, and Don sit in the front four seats in their classroom. Al is not on either end. Bob is between Al and Curt. Don is not in the first seat. In what order are the four boys seated?

3. Four cousins each live in a different state. The states are Maine, Texas, Florida, and Hawaii. Allie's state is not in the Southeast. Tyrone and Stan do not live in a state that borders Canada. Betina's state is Texas. Tyrone's state has volcanoes. Where does each cousin live? Copy and complete the table.

	ME	TX	FL	HI
Allie				
Tyrone				
Stan				
Betina	No	Yes	No	No

4. Cathy, Daisy, Mike, and Tony each have a different favorite bagel. Use the clues at the right to determine which bagel is each person's favorite.

   a. Cathy's friend likes only sesame.
   b. Daisy likes either onion or plain.
   c. Mike and Cathy dislike plain.
   d. Tony likes only onion.
   e. One person likes raisin.

Mixed Review

Try these or other strategies to solve each problem. Tell which strategy you used.

Problem-Solving Strategies

- *Make a Table*
- *Draw a Diagram*
- *Find a Pattern*
- *Write an Equation*
- *Make a List*

5. Jenny cut out paper squares following this pattern for the areas of the squares: 1 square inch, 4 square inches, 9 square inches, 16 square inches, and so on. What was the area of the tenth square?

6. **Math Reasoning** Ty is buying stickers and stars to put on cards he is making. He puts 2 stickers and 5 stars on each card. The stickers cost $0.20 each, and the stars cost $0.04 each. Ty has $4.00. Is this enough money to buy stars and stickers for six cards? Explain.

Use Homework Workbook 5-8.

LESSON 5-9

Using Averages

California Content Standard *Statistics, Data Analysis, and Probability 1.1: Know the concept of mean, . . . ; compute . . . simple examples . . ..*

Warm-Up Review

1. 36 + 48 + 15 + 72 + 58
2. 85 ÷ 17 **3.** 124 ÷ 31
4. (24 + 36 + 12) ÷ 8
5. (55 + 25 + 75 + 45) ÷ 20
6. In 12 weeks, Tim scored a total of 200 points in basketball. If he played in 20 games, what was his average score per game?

Math Link You have learned to find the mean, the median, and the mode of a set of data. Now you will find the mean when the numbers in the set of data are larger.

Remember, to find the mean of a set of data, add to find the total. Then divide by the number of items in the data set. Also remember, the mean of a set of data is the same as the average.

Example

The bar graph at the right shows the number of students in each grade at Lines School. What is the average number of students per grade?

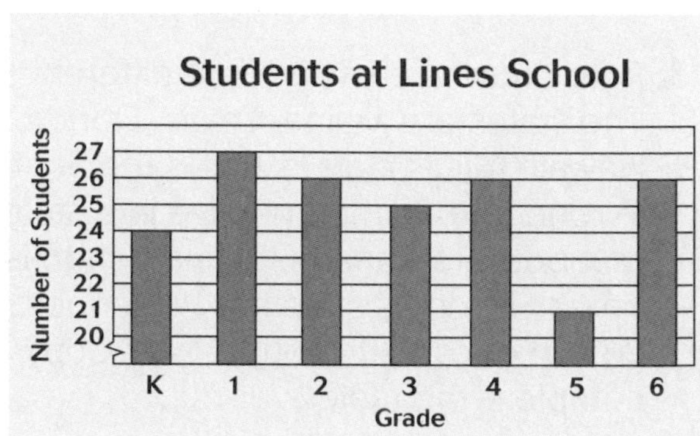

Add to find the total number of students.

24 + 27 + 26 + 25 + 26 + 21 + 26 = 175

Divide by the number of grades. 175 ÷ 7 = 25

The average number of students per grade is 25 students.

Guided Practice *For another example, see Set G on p. 203.*

Find the mean for each set of data.

1. $25, $16, $32, $39
2. 50 cm, 30 cm, 10 cm, 40 cm, 20 cm
3. 1,284 ft and 1,264 ft
4. 503 mi, 922 mi, 512 mi, 361 mi, 837 mi
5. These temperatures in degrees Celsius:
   21°, 9°, 7°, 15°, 13°, 11°, 9°, 14°, 13°, 8°, 12°
6. Michael's times for the 100-yard dash:
   13 sec, 12 sec, 16 sec, 11 sec, and 13 sec

Additional Standards: Number Sense 2.2 (key), Mathematical Reasoning 2.0, 3.1 (See p. 167.)

Independent Practice *For more practice, see Set G on p. 205.*

Find the mean for each set of data.

7. 158 ft, 164 ft, 185 ft

8. \$55, \$27, \$35, \$31

9. 76°F, 84°F, 90°F, 102°F

10. 183 days, 157 days, 170 days

11. \$2,476, \$2,295, \$1,904.

12. 600 km, 300 km, 400 km, 700 km

13. These distances in miles: 328, 480, 550, 372, 422, 520, 492

14. These baseball scores in runs: 2, 2, 1, 3, 4, 5, 2, 4, 4, 4, 5, 2, 3, 2, 2

15. These ages in years: 18, 15, 14, 14, 13, 13, 11, 10, 10, 8, 7, 6, 4

16. Math Reasoning The average number of students in each grade at Polk School is 28. Use the table at the right. How many sixth graders are in the school?

17. Math Reasoning Ronda hiked trails that were 2 miles, 5 miles, and 6 miles long. She thinks that her average hiking trail was 2 miles long. Without finding the mean, tell if this makes sense. Explain.

18. A fifth grade class of 28 students collected bottles to turn in for a \$0.05 deposit on each bottle. If the class received \$21.00, what is the average number of bottles each student collected?

Students at Polk School

Grade	Number of Students
K	32
1	25
2	27
3	31
4	26
5	28
6	?

Mixed Review

19. Find the mode of the ages in Exercise 15.

20. Find the median of the ages in Exercise 15.

21. $211 \div 48$

22. $23\overline{)474}$

23. $8{,}712 \div 72$

24. $49\overline{)9{,}960}$

Test Prep Choose the correct letter for each answer.

25. Algebra Find the value of $12 + 3 \times n - 4$ if $n = 4$.
(4-2)

A 56 **B** 20 **C** 28 **D** 0

26. Algebra Find n if $n - 12 = 24$.
(2-4)

F $n = 12$ **G** $n = 2$ **H** $n = 48$ **J** $n = 36$

Problem-Solving Application:

Analyzing Data

California Content Standard *Statistics, Data Analysis, and Probability 1.1: Know the concepts of mean, median, and mode; compute and compare simple examples to show that they may differ.*

Warm-Up Review

1. $(12 + 16 + 35 + 21) \div 14$

2. $(24 + 66 + 52 + 18) \div 32$

For Exercises 3 and 4, use this set of data: 55, 16, 23, 37, 49

3. Find the median.

4. Find the mode.

5. Jill had scores of 88, 88, 88 and 88 on four math tests. What was her average score?

Example

The picture below shows data that a bus company collected on the number of riders using Bus G. The company wanted to study the number of riders over the period of one week. What did the company find as the mode, the median, and the mean of the data?

Red Diamond
Bus Runs
Mon. 48
Tues. 43
Wed. 50
Thurs. 50
Fri. 54
Sat. 20
Sun. 15

Understand

What do you need to know?

You need to know the number of people riding Bus G each day.

Plan

How can you solve the problem?

You can use the numbers shown at the right to find the mode, median, and mean.

Solve

To analyze a set of numbers, it is helpful to first write the numbers in order.

Arrange the numbers from least to greatest:
15, 20, 43, 48, 50, 50, 54

- Mode = 50, the number that appears most often.
- Median = 48, the middle number
- Mean = 40, the sum of the numbers divided by the number of data items:
  $15 + 20 + 43 + 48 + 50 + 50 + 54 = 280$
  $280 \div 7 = 40$

Look Back

To find the mean, did you add 7 numbers? Did you divide by 7?

Additional Standards: Number Sense 2.2 (key), Mathematical Reasoning 2.0 *(See p. 167.)*

Guided Practice

Use the data on page 192, but remove the numbers for Saturday and Sunday. Find each of the following.

1. mode **2.** median **3.** mean

Independent Practice

Use the table at the right for Exercises 4–8.

Bus H					
Day	**Week 1**	**Week 2**	**Week 3**	**Week 4**	**Week 5**
Monday	45	47	50	17	46
Tuesday	55	68	36	63	68
Wednesday	45	58	41	65	51
Thursday	55	48	27	56	54
Friday	65	53	31	70	66
Saturday	45	55	55	60	55

4. Find the mean for the number of riders on Tuesday. Then find the median and mode for Tuesday. Write them in order from least to greatest.

5. Is the mean number of riders for Friday greater than or less than the median for Friday?

6. Math Reasoning The bus company used the mode to estimate the amount of money expected from Bus H on Saturday. Why was this done?

7. What if 15 more people rode the bus on Monday of Week 3? How would the mean, median, and mode for Monday change?

8. Find the mean number of riders for each day. Which day had the greatest average number of riders?

9. In 1662, Blaise Pascal, the mathematician, helped to introduce the first omnibus to Paris. It was horse-drawn and carried 8 passengers. Find the mean, median, and mode for the number of passengers on 7 trips if the omnibus were completely filled on all of the trips.

Mixed Review

10. Make a graph of the Week 1 data for Bus H.

11. Rectangular banquet tables can seat 4 people on each side and 1 person on each end. What is the greatest number of people that can be seated at 4 of these tables if the tables must share sides or ends and form a rectangle?

Use Homework Workbook 5-10.

Relating Multiplication and Division

Algebra

Warm-Up Review

Solve mentally.

1. $43 - 8 + 8$
2. $25 + 14 - 14$
3. $22 + 4 - 22$
4. $30 - 15 + 15$
5. Sam did 25 sit-ups in 5 minutes. In seconds, what is his average time per sit-up?

California Content Standard *Algebra and Functions 1.2 (key): Use a letter to represent an unknown number . . ..*

Math Link You learned in Chapter 2 that the operations of addition and subtraction undo each other. It is also true that multiplication and division undo each other. They are inverse operations.

13×7 means 7 is multiplied by 13. Division can undo multiplication. $(13 \times 7) \div 13 = 7$	$15 \div 3$, or $\frac{15}{3}$, means 15 is divided by 3. Multiplication can undo division. $\frac{15}{3} \times 3 = 15$

You can also use the idea of inverse operations with algebraic expressions.

$6 \times n$, or $6n$, means n is multiplied by 6. Dividing by 6 gets n alone. $6n \div 6 = n$	$\frac{n}{8}$ means n is divided by 8. Multiplying by 8 gets n alone. $\frac{n}{8} \times 8 = n$

Example 1

Tell what you would do to get each variable alone.

a. $\frac{x}{10}$

Multiply by 10.

b. $y \times 9$

Divide by 9.

c. $5a$

Divide by 5.

Example 2

For each table, tell what you would do to find *n*. Then find *n*.

a.

Rule: Multiply by 6.	
13	78
16	96
n	156

To find n, divide 156 by 6.

$n = 26$

b.

Rule: Divide by 25.	
50	2
n	4
150	6

To find n, multiply 4 by 25.

$n = 100$

c.

Rule: Multiply by 12.	
n	48
10	120
15	180

To find n, divide 48 by 12.

$n = 4$

 Additional Standards: Number Sense 1.0, 2.2 (key) (See p. 167.)

Guided Practice *For another example, see Set H on p. 203.*

Tell what you would do to get each variable alone.

1. $\frac{x}{15}$ **2.** $m \times 18$ **3.** $30c$ **4.** $\frac{a}{50}$

For each table, tell what you would do to find *n*. Then find *n*.

5.

Rule: Multiply by 16.	
3	48
5	80
n	112

6.

Rule: Divide by 8.	
104	13
n	15
200	25

7.

Rule: Divide by 10.	
n	7
130	13
240	24

Independent Practice *For more practice, see Set H on p. 205.*

Tell what you would do to get each variable alone.

8. $32n$ **9.** $\frac{x}{40}$ **10.** $\frac{x}{72}$ **11.** $36d$

For each table, tell what you would do to find *n*. Then find *n*.

12.

Rule: Multiply by 9.	
18	152
20	180
n	207

13.

Rule: Divide by 24.	
72	3
n	7
288	12

14.

Rule: Multiply by 20.	
n	160
10	200
15	300

15. Make a table which has the rule "Divide by 15." Complete the table when the values in the first column are 60, 90, and 150.

16. In a game of "Guess My Number," Suzie said, "If I divide my number by 32, the answer is 6." What is Suzie's number?

Mixed Review

17. Which property tells you that $15 \times 20 = 20 \times 15$?

18. Mental Math Find the average of 10, 30, 50, 20, and 40.

19. $23\overline{)9{,}250}$ **20.** $18{,}592 \div 56$ **21.** $459 \div 7$ **22.** $7{,}260 \div 9$

Test Prep **Choose the correct letter for the answer.**

23. Find the mode: 16, 24, 24, 8, 2, 4, 9, 24, 16, 38
(3-7)

A 16 **B** 24 **C** 26 **D** 165 **E** NH

Solving Multiplication and Division Equations

Warm-Up Review

Solve each equation.

1. $n - 12 = 17$
2. $x + 9 = 22$
3. $8 + y = 33$
4. $20 = a - 10$
5. $43 + a = 59$
6. $n - 37 = 6$
7. Beth worked 6 hours a day for 8 days. She was paid \$5.60 per hour. How many hours did she work?

California Content Standard *Algebra and Functions 1.1 (Grade 6) (🔑): Write and solve one-step linear equations in one variable.*

Math Link In the previous lesson, you learned to use inverse operations to get a variable by itself. In this lesson, you will use that idea and the properties of equality to solve multiplication and division equations.

Properties of Equality

You can multiply or divide both sides of an equation by the same nonzero number without changing the equality.

Example 1

$$2 \times 4 = 8$$
$$(2 \times 4) \div 2 = 8 \div 2$$
$$4 = 4$$

If you divide both sides by 2, the quantities on each side of the equal sign are still equal.

Example 2

$$30 \div 6 = 5$$
$$(30 \div 6) \times 6 = 5 \times 6$$
$$30 = 30$$

If you multiply both sides by 6, the quantities on each side of the equal sign are still equal.

Example 3

Solve $5x = 25$.

$$5x = 25$$
$$\frac{5x}{5} = \frac{25}{5}$$
$$x = 5$$

To get x by itself, divide by 5. But to keep the sides equal, divide both sides of the equation by 5.

Check: $5x = 25$

$$5 \times 5 = 25$$
$$25 = 25$$

Example 4

Solve $\frac{n}{4} = 7$.

$$\frac{n}{4} = 7$$
$$\frac{n}{4} \times 4 = 7 \times 4$$
$$n = 28$$

To get n by itself, multiply by 4. But to keep the sides equal, multiply both sides of the equation by 4.

Check: $\frac{n}{4} = 7$

$$\frac{28}{4} = 7$$
$$7 = 7$$

Guided Practice *For another example, see Set I on p. 203.*

Solve each equation.

1. $\frac{x}{8} = 6$
2. $9m = 72$
3. $54 = 18d$
4. $15 = \frac{x}{3}$

Additional Standards: Number Sense 1.1, 2.2, Algebra and Functions 1.2 (🔑) (See p. 167.)

5. Peter earned $90 for 15 hours of work. Which equation below could you use to find r, his hourly rate?

$\frac{15}{r} = 90$ $\frac{r}{90} = 15$ $15r = 90$

Independent Practice

For more practice, see Set I on p. 205.

Solve each equation.

6. $5j = 30$
7. $9k = 54$
8. $\frac{m}{4} = 9$
9. $\frac{d}{2} = 16$
10. $48 = 6n$
11. $5 = \frac{b}{8}$
12. $\frac{z}{9} = 18$
13. $16f = 32$
14. $10y = 80$
15. $\frac{x}{20} = 3$
16. $\frac{w}{7} = 14$
17. $30a = 600$
18. Dee shared some crackers equally among herself and 3 friends. Each person received 10 crackers. If x is the total number of crackers, which equation below can be used to find x?

$4x = 10$ $\frac{x}{4} = 10$ $10x = 4$

19. **Mental Math** If $203\left(\frac{x}{203}\right) = 72$, find x.

Mixed Review

20. Use a variable to write a rule for "Divide by 14."
21. Which operation is the inverse of division?
22. Find the average of 12, 17, 18, 15, 20, 11, and 19.

Test Prep **Choose the correct letter for each answer.**

Use the graph at the right.

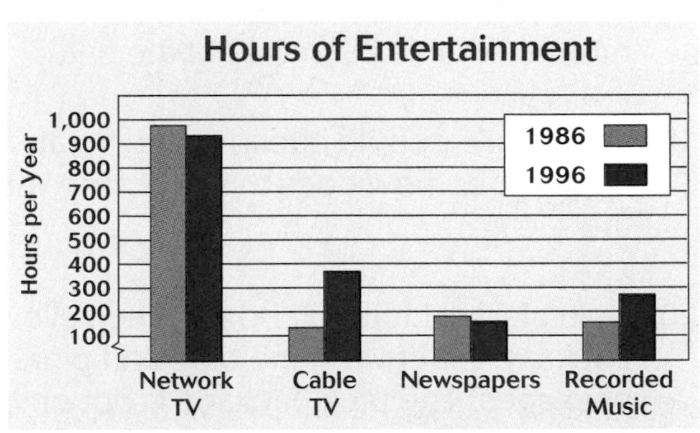

23. Which form of entertainment was most popular in 1986? (3-2)

A Network TV
B Cable TV
C Newspapers
D Recorded music

24. Which form of entertainment changed the most over the 10 years? (3-2)

A Network TV
B Cable TV
C Newspapers
D Recorded music

Diagnostic Checkpoint

Complete. For Exercises 1–3, use the words from the Word Bank.

Word Bank
compatible numbers
divisor
inverse operations
mean

1. (5-11) Multiplication and division are ________________.

2. (5-9) The ____________ is the average of a set of data.

3. (5-12) In $285 \div 5 = 57$, the ____________ is 5.

Find each quotient.

4. (5-6) $26\overline{)962}$ **5.** (5-6) $19\overline{)855}$ **6.** (5-7) $38\overline{)5,224}$ **7.** (5-7) $18\overline{)1,928}$

Find the mean of each set of data.

8. (5-9) 11, 14, 18, 16, 10, 15 **9.** (5-9) 200, 280, 180, 220

Tell what you would do to get each variable alone.

10. (5-11) $\frac{n}{4}$ **11.** (5-11) $7n$ **12.** (5-11) $\frac{n}{15}$ **13.** (5-11) $\frac{n}{30}$

Solve each equation.

14. (5-12) $\frac{n}{12} = 6$ **15.** (5-12) $4 \times n = 12$ **16.** (5-12) $n \times 7 = 14$ **17.** (5-12) $\frac{n}{5} = 45$

Use the chart for Exercises 18 and 19.

18. (5-10) The dinner theater uses the mode to predict the number of dinners to be served each month. What is the mode of the data?

19. (5-10) If 10 more people attended the theater in September, how does this affect the mode? the mean?

20. (5-8) Gale stacked four gift boxes. The yellow package is between the blue and pink packages. The pink package is not on top or bottom. The green package is not on top. What is the order of the packages from top to bottom?

Monthly Attendance at a Summer Dinner Theatre

Month	Attendance
May	300
June	311
July	290
August	311
September	278

Chapter 5 Test

Find each *n*

1. $900 \div 3 = n$
2. $2{,}400 \div 80 = n$

Estimate each quotient.

3. $7\overline{)495}$
4. $2\overline{)95}$
5. $38\overline{)1{,}625}$

Divide.

6. $6\overline{)4{,}332}$
7. $85\overline{)510}$
8. $41\overline{)861}$
9. $13\overline{)785}$
10. $7{,}625 \div 61$
11. $21{,}216 \div 52$

Find the mean of each set of data.

12. 110, 108, 98, 60, 139
13. \$15, \$18, \$26, \$21

Tell what you would do to get each letter alone.

14. $42n$
15. $\frac{n}{64}$

Solve each equation.

16. $\frac{x}{6} = 50$
17. $6n = 192$

Use the table at the right for Questions 18 and 19.

18. A bus can carry 43 students. How many buses will be needed to take all of the Central School students to a parade?

19. Find the mean, median, and mode for the number of students in each grade.

20. Put the furniture in order from left to right: The lamp is between the chair and the table. The chair is to the right of the desk. The desk is left of the lamp.

Central School

Grade	Number of Students
K	40
1	39
2	42
3	54
4	43
5	45
6	45

Multiple-Choice Chapter Test

Choose the correct letter for each answer.

1. You are reading a 342-page book. If you read 38 pages a day how long will it take you to finish the book?

A 6 days
B 9 days
C 10 days
D 15 days

2. The Rodriguez family was driving 270 miles from Miami to Tampa, Florida. After 5 hours of driving, they saw a sign that said Tampa: 45 miles. What was the average number of miles per hour they drove for the first 5 hours?

F 45 miles per hour
G 50 miles per hour
H 54 miles per hour
J 65 miles per hour

3. Which best describes how to solve for x?

$$3x = 102$$

A Multiply each side by 3.
B Divide each side by x.
C Subtract 102 from each side.
D Divide each side by 3.

4. Evaluate $x \div 12$ for $x = 144$.

F 1,728 **H** 132
G 156 **J** 12

5. The plant heights of five plants in Max's garden are 2 inches, 8 inches, 8 inches, 3 inches, and 6 inches. What happens to the mode if Max adds a 4-inch plant to his garden?

A It increases by 2.
B It remains the same
C It doubles.
D It decreases by 4.

6. $189 \div 10$

F 20
G 18 R9
H 10 R8
J 8 R10
K NH

7. Sam is older than Becky and Brenson. Brenson is older than Tray and younger than Becky. Who is the second oldest?

A Sam
B Tray
C Becky
D Brenson

8. In 26 days, the fifth grade planted 234 saplings. If they planted an equal number each day, how many trees did they plant each day?

F 20 **H** 9
G 11 **J** 6

9. **Sherman has 36 magazines that he plans to give away to his friends. He decides to give the same number to each friend. To how many friends can he give the magazines, and how many magazines will each friend get?**

A 9 magazines to 3 friends
B 4 magazines to 8 friends
C 6 magazines to 6 friends
D 10 magazines to 3 friends

---

10. **Which can be used as compatible numbers to solve 4,250 ÷ 83?**

F 4,200 ÷ 80
G 4,600 ÷ 85
H 4,250 ÷ 85
J 4,000 ÷ 80

---

11. **Which makes the statement true?**

750 ÷ 15 ● 8,190 ÷ 90

A >
B <
C =
D ≈
E NH

---

12. **Which value of *n* makes the equation true?**

$$\frac{n}{8} = 11$$

F 88
G $\frac{11}{8}$
H 3
J 19

Use the graph for Question 13.

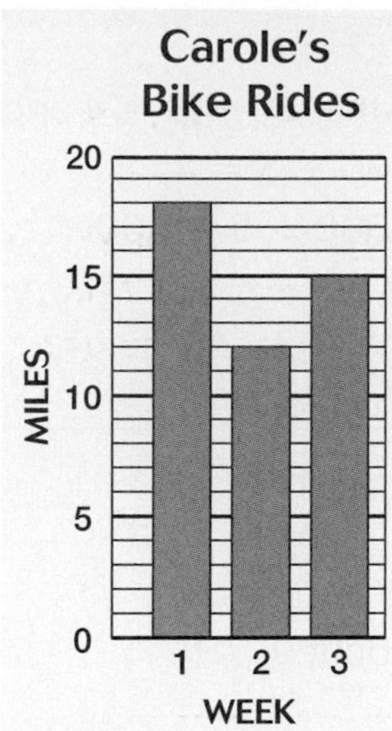

13. **What is the average number of miles Carole biked in a week?**

A 45 miles
B 18 miles
C 15 miles
D 12 miles

---

14. **Which statement about the following two division problems is true?**

① $7\overline{)200}$ ② $6\overline{)210}$

F The quotient of ① is greater than the quotient of ②.
G The quotients of ① and ② are equal.
H The remainder of ② is less than the remainder of ①.
J The remainder of ① is 7.

---

15. **Find *n* if 1,600 ÷ *n* = 40.**

A 4
B 40
C 400
D 6,400

Reteaching

Set A (pages 168–169)

Find *n*. 2,000 ÷ 5 = *n*

Use the basic fact that 20 ÷ 5 = 4 and patterns of zeros. 20 ÷ 5 = 4; 200 ÷ 5 = 40; 2,000 ÷ 5 = 400

Remember to use basic facts and patterns to help you divide.

1. 80 ÷ 4 **2.** 600 ÷ 30

3. 3,000 ÷ 50 **4.** 4,800 ÷ 600

Set B (pages 170–171)

Estimate the quotient.

534 ÷ 62

Think, 540 ÷ 60 = 9.

So, 534 ÷ 62 is about 9.

Remember to use compatible numbers to estimate quotients.

Estimate each quotient.

1. $9\overline{)486}$ **2.** $5\overline{)761}$

Set C (pages 172–174)

Find 661 ÷ 3.

Estimate:

600 ÷ 3 = 200

$$\begin{array}{r} 220 \text{ R1} \\ 3\overline{)661} \\ \underline{6} \\ 06 \\ \underline{6} \\ 01 \end{array}$$

Check:

3 × 220 + 1 = 661

Remember, when dividing, you can check the quotient by estimating or by multiplying the quotient by the divisor and adding the remainder.

1. 168 ÷ 8 **2.** 3,876 ÷ 7

3. 2,340 ÷ 4 **4.** 4,965 ÷ 6

Set D (pages 178–180)

Find 239 ÷ 53.

Estimate:

200 ÷ 50 = 4.

$$\begin{array}{r} 4 \text{ R27} \\ 53\overline{)239} \\ \underline{212} \\ 27 \end{array}$$

Check:

4 × 53 + 1 = 239

Remember, estimation helps you place the first digit in the quotient.

1. 183 ÷ 61 **2.** 301 ÷ 45

3. 115 ÷ 18 **4.** 127 ÷ 13

Set E (pages 182–183)

Divide 759 ÷ 28.

Estimate:

750 ÷ 25 = 30.

$$\begin{array}{r} 27 \text{ R3} \\ 28\overline{)759} \\ \underline{56} \\ 199 \\ \underline{-196} \\ 3 \end{array}$$

Remember, you can tell from your estimate if the quotient will be two digits.

1. $25\overline{)329}$ **2.** $16\overline{)425}$

3. $39\overline{)495}$ **4.** $25\overline{)9500}$

Set F (pages 184–186)

Divide 3,215 ÷ 12.

Estimate:

3,600 ÷ 12 = 300.

$$\begin{array}{r} 267\text{ R}11 \\ 12\overline{)3215} \\ \underline{24} \\ 81 \\ \underline{-72} \\ 95 \\ \underline{-84} \\ 11 \end{array}$$

Remember, sometimes you need to put a zero in the quotient when you divide.

1. $46\overline{)3,469}$
2. $12\overline{)9,543}$
3. $42\overline{)25,487}$
4. $23\overline{)15,129}$

Set G (pages 190–191)

Find the mean of the data.

70, 28, 64, 55, 38

$$\text{mean} = \frac{\text{sum of the data}}{\text{total number of data}}$$
$$= \frac{70 + 28 + 64 + 55 + 38}{5}$$
$$= \frac{255}{5}$$
$$= 51$$

Remember, the mean of a set of data is the same as the average.

Find the mean of each set of data.

1. 3, 8, 3, 2, 0, 1, 6, 1
2. 25, 20, 35, 15, 5

Set H (pages 194–195)

Tell what you would do to get *n* alone: 1,934*n*

1,934*n* means 1,934 × *n*.

Use division to undo multiplication.

So, divide by 1,934.

Remember, multiplication and division are inverse operations.

Tell what you would do to get *n* alone.

1. 15*n*
2. *n* ÷ 101

Set I (pages 196–197)

Solve the equation $\frac{x}{18} = 40$.

$\frac{x}{18} = 40$

$\frac{x}{18} \times 18 = 40 \times 18$ Multiply by 18.

$x = 720$

Remember, you can multiply or divide both sides of an equation by the same nonzero number without changing the equality.

Solve each equation.

1. $\frac{n}{101} = 3$
2. $2x = 1,204$

More Practice

Set A *(pages 168–169)*

Use basic facts and patterns of zeros. Find each quotient.

1. 210 ÷ 3
2. 350 ÷ 7
3. 8,100 ÷ 9
4. 4,800 ÷ 8
5. 540 ÷ 60
6. 630 ÷ 70
7. 1,800 ÷ 300
8. 2,400 ÷ 600
9. At the school carnival, a class earned $2,400 in 3 days. What was the average amount they earned per day?

Set B *(pages 170–171)*

Estimate each quotient.

1. 821 ÷ 9
2. 1,195 ÷ 6
3. 7,215 ÷ 8
4. 632 ÷ 89
5. Greenland is the largest island in the world. It is about 950 kilometers wide. If you walked 8 kilometers per day along a straight path, about how many days would it take you to walk across Greenland?

Set C *(pages 172–174)*

1. $6\overline{)93}$
2. $8\overline{)92}$
3. $7\overline{)95}$
4. $6\overline{)418}$
5. A train conductor takes 76 minutes to collect tickets from 4 cars. About how much time does it take him to collect tickets from one car?

Set D *(pages 178–180)*

1. $59\overline{)466}$
2. $89\overline{)827}$
3. $71\overline{)395}$
4. $91\overline{)737}$
5. A fifth-grade class wants to plant 125 flowers for Earth Day. If they plan to put 15 flowers in each row, how many complete rows can they plant? How many flowers will be left over?

Set E (pages 182–183)

1. $74\overline{)814}$ 2. $34\overline{)816}$ 3. $42\overline{)984}$ 4. $61\overline{)753}$

5. The Ellenberg family plans to travel 660 miles to spend Thanksgiving with their family. If they average 55 miles per hour, how long will it take them?

Set F (pages 184–186)

1. $16\overline{)13{,}184}$ 2. $95\overline{)26{,}423}$ 3. $26\overline{)16{,}205}$ 4. $44\overline{)16{,}016}$

5. The town art show attracted 3,220 people during 14 days. What was the average number of people that visited the show each day?

Set G (pages 190–191)

Find the mean of each set of data.

1. 46, 59, 80, 43
2. 3, 4, 8, 2, 9, 11, 15, 12
3. Jeremy spent $59, $129, $79, and $109 on plane tickets. What was the average amount that Jeremy spent on a plane ticket?

Set H (pages 194–195)

Tell what you would do to get each variable alone.

1. $12x$ 2. $\frac{n}{10}$ 3. $\frac{x}{12}$ 4. $17y$

5. In a game, George said, "I'm thinking of a number. If I divide the number by 9, the answer is 60." What number is George thinking of?

Set I (pages 196–197)

Solve each equation.

1. $x \div 7 = 40$ 2. $y \div 81 = 2$ 3. $12x = 36$

4. Abe rode his bike 30 miles in 2 hours. Write an equation to find Abe's pace in miles per hour.

Problem Solving: Preparing for Tests

Choose the correct letter for each answer.

---

1. Lonnie spent two and one half times as long as John did studying for a test. If you knew how long John spent studying, how could you find Lonnie's study time?

A Add Lonnie's time to John's time.

B Subtract Lonnie's time from John's time.

C Multiply John's time by 2.5.

D Divide John's time by 2.5.

Tip

Decide which operation to use by thinking about the action in the problem situation.

---

2. On Monday a warehouse had 1,053 boxes to ship. On Tuesday, 351 boxes were left to be shipped. On Wednesday, 117 boxes were left. If this pattern continues, how many boxes will be left on Friday?

F 3

G 13

H 17

J 39

Tip

Use the *Find a Pattern* strategy. Think about divisibility rules to find the pattern.

---

3. The numbers of people who used the library monthly from December through March were 2,675; 4,482; 3,781; and 1,083. Which is the best estimate of the total number who used the library *after* New Year's Day?

A 9,000 people

B 12,000 people

C 14,000 people

D 16,000 people

Tip

Be sure you use only the numbers you need to solve the problem.

4. Charlie pays $2.45 for a piece of fabric that is 4.5 meters long. Which number sentence could be used to find the number of 15-centimeter pieces, *n*, he can cut from the fabric? (1 m = 100 cm)

F $4.5 \times 100 \div 15 = n$

G $4.5 \div 100 \times 15 = n$

H $4.5 \times 15 \div 100 = n$

J $4.5 + 100 \times 15 = n$

---

5. Eight objects had these masses: 0.30 kg, 0.34 kg, 0.37 kg, 0.38 kg, 0.61 kg, 0.63 kg, 0.65 kg, 0.68 kg. Which two objects combine to equal exactly 1 kilogram?

A 0.38 kg and 0.61 kg

B 0.30 kg and 0.68 kg

C 0.34 kg and 0.65 kg

D 0.37 kg and 0.63 kg

---

6. This graph shows how membership in the science club changed over a 5-month period.

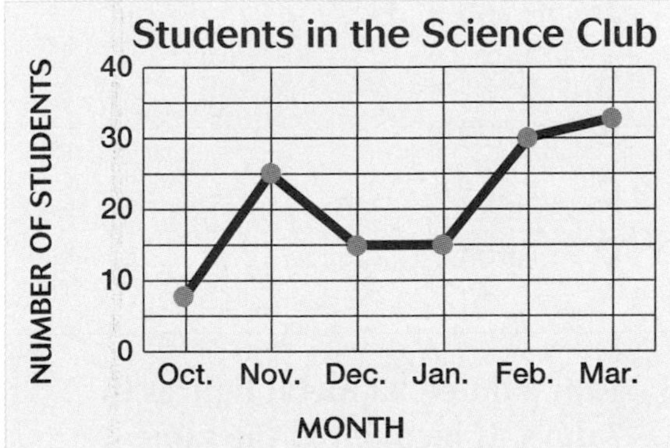

When did the membership increase the most?

F From Oct. to Nov.

G From Nov. to Dec.

H From Jan. to Feb.

J From Feb. to Mar.

7. Phyllis estimates that the average length of each step she takes is 3 feet. Which is a reasonable number of steps for her to take in half a mile? (1 mi = 5,280 ft)

A Fewer than 800 steps

B Between 800 and 1,000 steps

C Between 1,000 and 2,000 steps

D More than 1,200 steps

---

8. A vegetable garden is shaped like the letter *L*. The lengths of five of the sides are shown. What is the length of the sixth side?

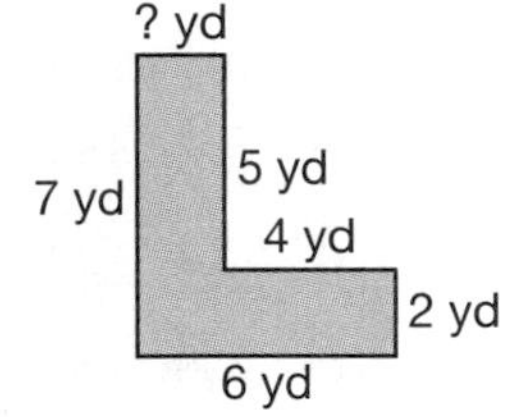

F 1 yard

G 2 yards

H 4 yards

J 6 yards

---

9. Alicia read 20 pages of a book in 60 minutes. Which is a reasonable amount of time for Alicia to take to read the rest of the 200-page book?

A 3 hours

B 9 hours

C 10 hours

D 20 hours

---

10. The numbers of minutes Rob spent driving to work during 1 week were 45, 38, 36, 44, and 39. Which is the best estimate for the average time he spent driving to work each day?

F Less than 30 minutes

G Between 30 and 35 minutes

H Between 40 and 45 minutes

J More than 45 minutes

TEST PREP

Multiple-Choice Cumulative Review

Choose the correct letter for each answer.

Number Sense

1. Which number sentence is true?

A $0.04 > 0.40$

B $1.0 < 0.1$

C $0.73 > 0.37$

D $2.75 > 2{,}750$

2. Which set of numbers is in order from *least* to *greatest*?

F 44,727 44,272 44,772

G 44,272 44,772 44,727

H 44,772 44,727 44,272

J 44,272 44,727 44,772

3. Which of these numbers is 4,750 when rounded to the nearest ten and 4,700 when rounded to the nearest hundred?

A 4,744

B 4,745

C 4,754

D 4,762

4. Which fraction is shown by the shaded part of the grid?

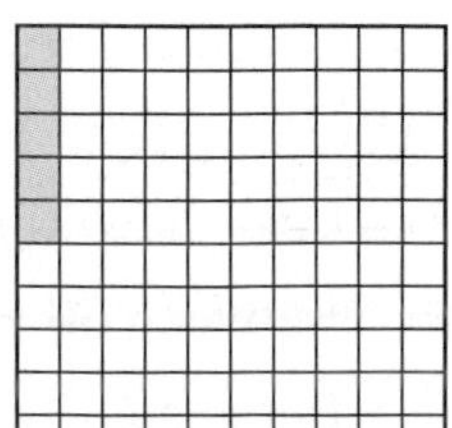

F $\frac{1}{50}$

G $\frac{5}{100}$

H $\frac{1}{5}$

J $\frac{5}{10}$

5. What is the difference between 781 and 377?

A 1,158

B 414

C 404

D 314

6. Six friends have season passes to the zoo. Three of the friends shared the cost of a season pass equally. If the pass cost $36, how much did each pay?

F $18

G $15

H $12

J $6

7. Which of these numbers is the sum of 252 + 768 + 345?

A 768

B 1,020

C 1,365

D 1,465

8. Sam painted 98 metal figures in 7 days. If he painted the same number each day, how many figures did he paint in 1 day?

F 7

G 14

H 98

J 105

Algebra and Functions

9. **Jack helped to arrange rows of chairs for a concert. The first row had 16 chairs, the second row 18 chairs, and the third, 20. If *n* represents the number of chairs in any row, which expression could be used to find the number in the next row?**

A $n - 2$ **C** $2n$

B $n + 2$ **D** $n \div 2$

10. **Which expression will always have the same value, no matter what number is substituted for *x*?**

A $x + 0$ **C** $0 - x$

B $x - 0$ **D** $0x$

11. **Which is the correct value of *n*?**

A	B
18	3
42	7
54	9
n	10

A 64 **C** 60

B 62 **D** 56

12. **Which number sentence represents this problem?**

A child's movie ticket costs $3 and an adult ticket costs $5. How much would it cost for 3 adults and 4 children to go to the movies?

F $(3 \times \$3) + (4 \times \$5) = n$

G $(3 + 4) + (\$3 + \$5) = n$

H $(\$3 + \$5) \times 7 = n$

J $(4 \times \$3) + (3 \times \$5) = n$

Measurement and Geometry

13. **What is the *volume* of the cube shown below?**

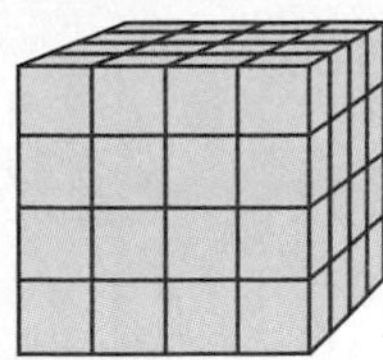

A 9 cubic units

B 14 cubic units

C 48 cubic units

D 64 cubic units

14. **The perimeter of a rectangular patio is 34 feet. The patio is made of 140 patio stones. If the width of the patio is 7 feet, what is the *length* of the patio?**

F 10 feet

G 14 feet

H 17 feet

J 20 feet

15. **Gavin has a snake that is 60 inches long. How many feet long is the snake? (1 ft = 12 in.)**

A 30 feet

B 20 feet

C 10 feet

D 5 feet

16. **A bucket holds 2.5 liters of water. How many milliliters of water does the bucket hold? (1 L = 1,000 mL)**

F 0.025 mL **H** 250 mL

G 25 mL **J** 2,500 mL

Multiplying and Dividing Decimals

Diagnosing Readiness

In Chapter 6, you will use these skills:

A Estimating Products of Whole Numbers

(pages 138–139)

Estimate each product.

1. $22 \times 4 \times 31$

2. 977×8 **3.** 101×26

4. $11{,}816 \times 11$

5. 72×18 **6.** $32{,}987 \times 96$

7. A children's horse ranch has 187 horses. Each horse is ridden 89 times a year for 2 hours at a time. Estimate how many hours are spent riding in a one year period.

B Multiplying Whole Numbers

(pages 146–147)

Find each product.

8. 29×92 **9.** 223×827

10. 91×3 **11.** 361×12

12. Kurt feeds an elephant 25 pounds of food every 12 hours. How much food does he give the elephant in 4 weeks?

C Comparing Numbers

(pages 10–12)

Write <, >, or = for each ●.

13. 19 × 3 ● 68

14. 673 × 866 ● 260 × 1,110

15. 620 × 2,400 ● 845 × 550

16. 12 × 9 ● 14 × 11

17. 71 × 22 ● 47 × 47

D Rounding Whole Numbers and Decimals

(pages 16–18)

Round each number to the underlined place.

18. $25.\underline{3}68$

19. $12{,}7\underline{5}6$

20. $1{,}00\underline{8}.32$

21. $0.11\underline{6}4$

22. $\underline{4}39$

23. $1\underline{1}6{,}789$

24. Bernice took 43,891 empty aluminum cans to the recycling center last year. Round this number to the nearest hundred.

E Multiplying and Dividing Whole Numbers by 10, 100, and 1,000

(pages 134–136, 168–169)

25. 75,000 ÷ 1,000

26. 57 × 1,000

27. 136 × 10

28. 722 ÷ 100

29. 15 × 100

F Dividing Whole Numbers

(pages 172–174, 178–180)

Find each quotient.

30. 175 ÷ 5

31. 1,041 ÷ 30

32. 5,488 ÷ 56

33. 50,084 ÷ 4

34. There are 156 phone lines in an area that contains 78 homes. If each home had the same number of phone lines, find the number of phone lines per home.

To the Family and Student

Looking Back	Chapter 6	Looking Ahead
In Chapters 4 and 5, students learned how to multiply and divide whole numbers.	**Multiplying and Dividing Decimals** In this chapter, students will learn to multiply and divide decimals.	In Chapter 8, students will learn how to multiply and divide fractions.

Math and Everyday Living

Opportunities to apply the concepts of Chapter 6 abound in everyday situations. During the chapter, think about how multiplying and dividing decimals can be used to solve a variety of real-world problems. The following examples suggest just a few of the many situations that could launch a discussion about multiplying and dividing decimals.

Math and Modeling You and your family build a 0.75-foot-long model airplane. The length of the actual airplane is 100 times as long as your model. What is the length of the actual plane?

Math and Sports The following table shows the sizes of the balls used in various recreational sports.

Ball Type	Diameter (in inches)
Volleyball	8.25
Tennis ball	2.6
Baseball	2.9
Softball	5.11
Table tennis ball	1.5
Golf ball	1.7

Which ball has a diameter that is about twice as large as the diameter of a table tennis ball?

Math on the Job

Type of Job	Miles Walked Each Day
Teacher	1.4
Computer Programmer	0.2
Waiter	4.1
Nurse	4.9
Receptionist	0.7
Attorney	1.1
Security Guard	2.3

If a teacher, a security guard, and an attorney each work 22 days in a month, how many miles does each one walk in a one-month period?

Math and Gift Giving You buy three of your friends picture frames for $4.75 each, your favorite teacher a book, and your six cousins bookmarks for $1.75 each. You spend $31.30. How much did the book cost?

Math in the Kitchen The following table shows the recipe for fruit salad and the price per pound of each fruit at Brock's Groceries.

Fruit Needed	Price per Pound
3 lb Oranges	$0.99
2 lb Pears	$1.21
1.5 lb Grapes	$1.75
4 lb Bananas	$0.49
0.5 lb Watermelon	$2.04
4 lb Peaches	$1.87
3 lb Strawberries	$2.05

How much money is needed to buy all of the ingredients for the fruit salad? Round to the nearest cent.

Math and Health The potato cheese soup you are preparing for dinner has 2.25 grams of fat for every half-cup serving. If you eat 3 cups of soup, how many fat grams will you have?

California Content Standards in Chapter 6 Lessons*

	Teach and Practice	Practice
Number Sense		
1.1 Estimate, round, and manipulate . . . numbers.		6-3
2.1 (key) . . . [M]ultiply and divide with decimals	6-1, 6-2, 6-3, 6-5, 6-6, 6-8, 6-9, 6-10	6-4, 6-11, 6-12
2.2 (key) Demonstrate proficiency with division, including division with positive decimals	6-8, 6-9	
Algebra and Functions		
1.2 (key) Use a letter to represent an unknown number; write and evaluate simple algebraic expressions in one variable by substitution.	6-11	6-1, 6-6

	Teach and Practice	Practice
Mathematical Reasoning		
1.0 Students make decisions about how to approach problems.	6-7	
1.1 Analyze problems by identifying relationships, distinguishing relevant from irrelevant information, sequencing and prioritizing information, and drawing patterns.	6-4	6-1, 6-2, 6-5, 6-6
2.1 Use estimation to verify the reasonableness of calculated results.		6-3, 6-10
2.3 Use a variety of methods, such as words, numbers, symbols, charts, graphs, tables, diagrams, and models, to explain mathematical reasoning.	6-7	
2.6 Make precise calculations and check the validity of the results from the context of the problem.	6-12	
3.2 Note the method of deriving the solution and demonstrate a conceptual understanding of the derivation by solving similar problems.		6-7
3.3 Develop generalizations of the results obtained and apply them in other circumstances.		6-1, 6-5, 6-11

* The symbol (key) indicates a key standard as designated in the Mathematics Framework for California Public Schools. Full statements of the California Content Standards are found at the beginning of this book following the Table of Contents.

Mental Math: Multiplying Decimals by 10, 100, or 1,000

California Content Standard *Number Sense 2.1 (🔑): . . . [M]ultiply . . . with decimals . . . .*

Warm-Up Review

1. 10 × 23
2. 100 × 65
3. 49 × 100
4. 17 × 10
5. 1,000 × 35
6. 78 × 1,000
7. A telephone marketer averaged 23 calls an hour and works 5 hours a day for 5 days. How many calls did the marketer make?

Math Link In an earlier chapter, you learned to multiply whole numbers by 10, 100, or 1,000. In this lesson, you will learn to multiply decimals by 10, 100, or 1,000.

Example

Samantha is saving money to buy special treats for sheltered dogs. If one dog bagel costs $0.25, how much will 100 dog bagels cost?

Find 0.25 × 100.

You can use the patterns in this table.

Multiply by	Example	Move the decimal point to the right
1	0.25 × 1 = 0.25	0 places
10	0.25 × 10 = 2.5	1 place
100	0.25 × 100 = 25.0	2 places
1,000	0.25 × 1,000 = 250.0	3 places

Since 0.25 × 100 = 25, 100 dog bagels cost $25.

More Examples

A. 2.38 × 1 = 2.38
2.38 × 10 = 23.8 = 23.8
2.38 × 100 = 238. = 238
2.38 × 1,000 = 2380. = 2,380

B. 0.78 × 1 = 0.78
0.78 × 10 = 07.8 = 7.8
0.78 × 100 = 078. = 78
0.78 × 1,000 = 0780. = 780

Guided Practice *For another example, see Set A on p. 246.*

1. 5.13 × 1 = ■
5.13 × 10 = ■
5.13 × 100 = ■
5.13 × 1,000 = ■

2. 0.0067 × 10 = ■
0.0067 × 100 = ■
0.0067 × 1 = ■
0.0067 × 1,000 = ■

3. 14.38 × 100 = ■
14.38 × 1 = ■
14.38 × 1,000 = ■
14.38 × 10 = ■

4. John wants to buy 100 rawhide bones at $1.29 each and 10 bags of dog food at $8.99 each. How much will he spend?

Additional Standards: Algebra and Functions 1.2 (🔑), Mathematical Reasoning 1.1, 3.3 (See p. 213.)

Independent Practice

For more practice, see Set A on p. 248.

Follow the rule to find each output.

	Rule: Multiply by 100.	
5.	0.83	
6.	4.7	
7.	39.5	

	Rule: Multiply by 10.	
8.	4.0	
9.	25.0	
10.	0.62	

	Rule: Multiply by 1,000.	
11.	2.6	
12.	0.156	
13.	426.5	

Algebra Find each n.

14. $6.59 \times n = 65.9$

15. $0.5 \times 1{,}000 = n$

16. $\$3.45 \times n = \$345.00$

17. $0.447 \times 10 = n$

18. $100 \times 0.0562 = n$

19. $\$16 \times 100 = n$

20. $1 \times 99.8 = n$

21. $n \times 0.216 = 21.6$

22. $0.00379 \times n = 3.79$

23. Math Reasoning Compare the process of multiplying by 10, 100, or 1,000 with the position of the decimal point in the product. Write a rule that relates the movement of the decimal point to the number of zeros in 10, 100, or 1,000.

24. Two hundred puppies were used in the filming of a movie. If two rawhide chews cost $0.75, how much would it cost to buy a chew for each puppy?

25. Algebra Find the value of $1{,}000x$ if $x = 3.25$.

Mixed Review

26. Samantha and John spent $25.80 on dog toys and $11.55 on dog brushes. How much change did they receive from $50?

Algebra Tell how to get n alone.

27. $12n$

28. $\frac{n}{7}$

Algebra Solve each equation for x.

29. $\frac{x}{4} = 16$

30. $5x = 60$

31. Find the range, the mode, and the median for this set of data: 33.5, 46.8, 44.9, 40.2, 38.7, 55.1, 52.6

Test Prep Choose the correct letter for each answer.

32. Algebra Solve $8 + x = 8$ for x.
(2-4)

A $x = 0$ **C** $x = 16$

B $x = 1$ **D** $x = 64$

33. Algebra Solve $n - 3 = 6$ for n.
(2-4)

F $n = 2$ **H** $n = 9$

G $n = 3$ **J** $n = 18$

Multiplying Decimals by Whole Numbers

Warm-Up Review

1. 6 × 59
2. 82 × 3
3. 9 × 235
4. 8 × 602
5. 15 × 26
6. 34 × 47
7. 60 × 31
8. 59 × 80
9. Nancy bought 10 packages of seeds at $0.89 and 10 packages at $1.29. How much did she spend on seeds?

California Content Standard *Number Sense 2.1 (🔑): . . . [M]ultiply . . . with decimals . . . .*

Math Link In an earlier chapter, you learned to multiply whole numbers with 2, 3, and 4 digits. In this lesson, you will learn to multiply decimals by whole numbers.

Example

Dean, Kerri, Ashvi, and Nathan are planning a community garden on a square lot. They plan to plant tomatoes, corn, carrots, lettuce, and sunflowers. If each package of seeds covers 0.12 of the lot, how much of the lot will 5 packages of seeds cover?

Find 5 × 0.12.

This is a model of the garden.

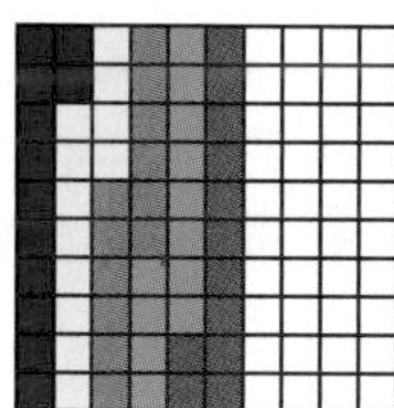

- tomatoes
- corn
- carrots
- lettuce
- sunflowers

1 square = 0.01 of the lot, so 12 squares are colored for each seed package. 60 squares, or 0.60, are colored in all.

To multiply 5 times 0.12, multiply as you do with whole numbers. Then place the decimal point to show 0.60.

```
  0.12
×    5
  0.60
```

5 × 12 hundredths = **60** hundredths

Notice that the product, 0.60, has the same number of decimal places as the total number of decimal places in the two factors.

```
  0.12  ← 2 decimal places
×    5  ← 0 decimal places
  0.60  ← 2 decimal places
```

Five packages of seeds will cover 0.60, or 0.6, of the lot.

More Examples

A.

```
   9.74  ← 2 decimal places
×     8  ← 0 decimal places
  77.92  ← 2 decimal places
```

B.

```
      219  ← 0 decimal places
×     7.2  ← 1 decimal place
      438
     1533
  1,576.8  ← 1 decimal place
```

 Additional Standard: Mathematical Reasoning 1.1 (See p. 213.)

Guided Practice *For another example, see Set B on p. 246.*

1. $\begin{array}{r} 36.5 \\ \times \quad 8 \\ \hline \end{array}$

2. $\begin{array}{r} \$0.79 \\ \times \quad 2 \\ \hline \end{array}$

3. $1{,}732 \times 0.24$

4. 12×0.019

5. The students mentioned in the first example want to plant an extra package of tomato seeds and an extra package of sunflower seeds. How much of the lot will be covered then?

Independent Practice *For more practice, see Set B on p. 248.*

6. $\begin{array}{r} 0.12 \\ \times \quad 4 \\ \hline \end{array}$

7. $\begin{array}{r} 1.365 \\ \times \quad 5 \\ \hline \end{array}$

8. $\begin{array}{r} \$0.37 \\ \times \quad 8 \\ \hline \end{array}$

9. $\begin{array}{r} 79 \\ \times 1.5 \\ \hline \end{array}$

10. $\begin{array}{r} 2.907 \\ \times \quad 4 \\ \hline \end{array}$

11. $\begin{array}{r} 0.004 \\ \times \ 39 \\ \hline \end{array}$

12. $\begin{array}{r} 3.025 \\ \times \quad 15 \\ \hline \end{array}$

13. $\begin{array}{r} 6{,}324 \\ \times \quad 2.2 \\ \hline \end{array}$

14. 0.14×5

15. $\$7.29 \times 31$

16. 3×0.824

17. 7.369×3

18. 6×6.8

19. 0.067×7

20. $\$36.25 \times 9$

21. 183×2.7

22. 12.6×35

23. 265.4×13

24. 7×6.325

25. 0.853×5

26. If seed packages cost $1.29 each, how much do 5 packages cost? 50 packages?

27. Mrs. Diaz bought 5 plants at $2.95 each, hand tools for $7.49, and 10 packages of seeds for $1.29 each. How much more did she spend on plants than on seeds?

Mixed Review

28. Jon has 88 CDs. If a CD case holds 12 CDs, how many cases will he need to store his CDs?

29. **Mental Math** $1{,}000 \times 3.07$

30. **Mental Math** 52.66×10

31. **Algebra** Solve $2n = 50$ for n.

32. **Algebra** Solve $\frac{x}{12} = 4$ for x.

 **Test Prep** **Choose the correct letter for each answer.**

Use the following set of data for Exercises 33 and 34:
12, 11, 10, 8, 16, 10, 17

33. Find the median for the data.
(3-7)

A 9
B 10
C 11
D 12

34. Find the mean for the data.
(5-9)

F 9
G 10
H 11
J 12

Estimating the Product of a Whole Number and a Decimal

Warm-Up Review

1. 80×0.6 **2.** 0.5×300

3. 8.4×3 **4.** 7×9.2

5. 87.1×4 **6.** 5×2.05

7. 1.1×56 **8.** 27×4.1

9. Estimate the total cost of 32 posters at $8 each.

California Content Standard *Number Sense 2.1 (🔑): . . . [M]ultiply . . . with decimals . . ..*

Math Link You know how to estimate products of whole numbers. Now you will round decimals to estimate products of whole numbers and decimals.

Example

José has sold 23 of the smaller posters pictured at the right to help raise money for the protection of endangered species. Estimate the amount of money José has raised.

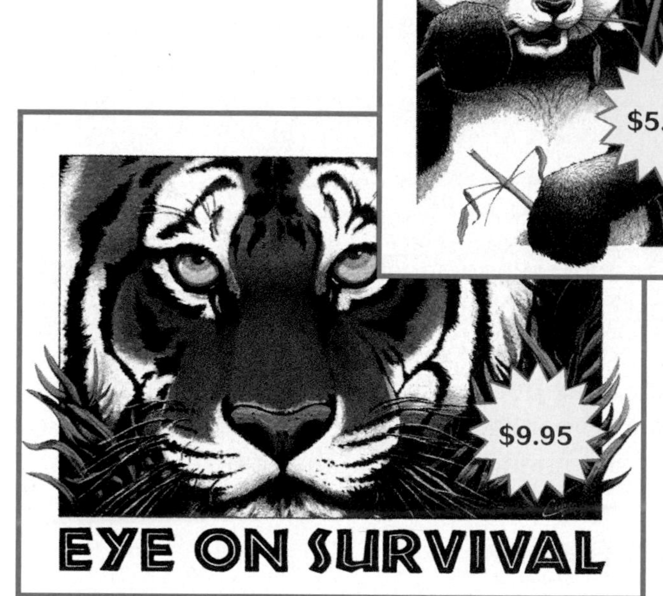

Estimate 23 × $5.75.

Estimate by rounding each number to the greatest place that has a nonzero digit.

23 × $5.75 rounds to **20 × $6**

20 × $6 = $120

José has raised about $120.

More Examples

A. Round to estimate.

938×0.17

$\downarrow \quad \downarrow$

$900 \times 0.2 = 180.0$

Remember to place the decimal point correctly.

B. Round to estimate.

8.79×5

$\downarrow \quad \downarrow$

$9 \times 5 = 45$

Remember that you do not have to round single-digit factors.

Additional Standards: Number Sense 1.1; Mathematical Reasoning 2.1 *(See p. 213.)*

Guided Practice *For another example, see Set C on p. 246.*

Estimate each product.

1. 5.9×8 **2.** 6×1.75 **3.** 0.32×20 **4.** 9×1.055 **5.** 0.059×8

6. Math Reasoning Will the actual product for Example B be less than or greater than the estimate? Explain your answer.

Independent Practice *For more practice, see Set C on p. 248.*

Estimate each product.

7. 2.43×7 **8.** 60×8.6 **9.** 8×0.328 **10.** 17.6×42 **11.** 0.045×39

12. 4.291×8 **13.** 21×0.058 **14.** 9×10.3 **15.** 10.1×99 **16.** 0.904×75

Estimate each product. Then predict if each product will be greater than or less than the estimate. Find the product and check by comparing it to your estimate and your prediction.

17. 12×4.21 **18.** 19.7×36 **19.** 86×0.049 **20.** 2.36×53 **21.** 94×0.12

22. Cindy sold 12 of the large posters pictured on page 218. About how much money did she raise?

23. Caleb is using yarn to make a lion's mane on an art project. He needs 21 loops of yarn. Each loop takes 7.5 in. of yarn.

a. About how much yarn will Caleb need?

b. If he has 180 inches of yarn, about how much will be left over?

Mixed Review

24. Refer to the first example in this lesson. Find the exact amount of money José raised by selling the 23 posters.

25. 352×0.7 **26. Mental Math** $1{,}000 \times 0.046$ **27.** $3{,}618 \div 67$

Test Prep **Choose the correct letter for each answer.**

28. (2-10) Find the sum of 2.35, 1.25, and 4.093.

A 44.53
B 76.93
C 7.693
D 7.593
E NH

29. (2-10) Find the difference: $9 - 0.03$.

F 0.027
G 8.97
H 9.03
J 8.097
K NH

Understand
Plan
Solve
Look Back

Problem-Solving Skill:

Multistep Problems

Warm-Up Review

1. $8 \times \$5.50$
2. $7 \times \$5.25$
3. $4 \times \$3.75$
4. $6 \times \$8.50$
5. $9 \times \$4.50$
6. $3 \times \$2.75$
7. $12 \times \$7.50$
8. A tour of Washington, D.C., costs \$10.50 for adults and \$7.50 for children. Find the cost of tours for 16 children.

California Content Standard *Mathematical Reasoning 1.1: Analyze problems by identifying relationships, distinguishing relevant from irrelevant information, sequencing and prioritizing information, and observing patterns.*

Read For Understanding

Sandi, two of her friends, and her two grandmothers are in Philadelphia. They want to visit historic sites, including those pictured. Sandi is 11 years old, and her friends are 10 and 14 years old.

1. How much do children's tickets cost?
2. How old are Sandi's two friends?

Think and Discuss

Multistep Problems

To solve some problems, you may need more than one step. Each step gives you some needed information.

Liberty Bell ▶

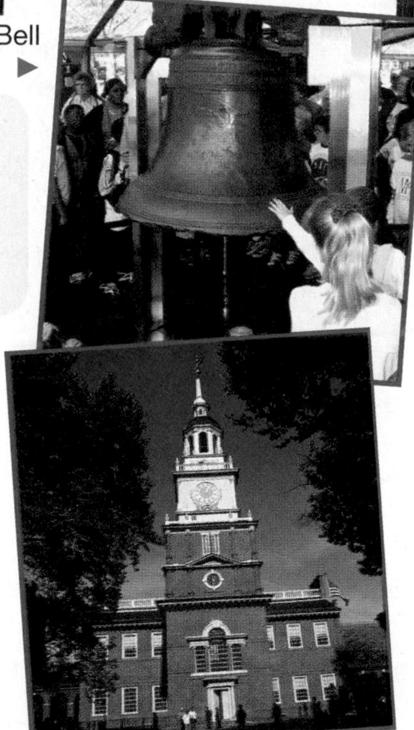

▲ Independence Hall

Reread the paragraph at the top of the page. Think about what you need to know to find out how much it will cost the group to take the historic tour.

3. How many adult tickets will the group buy? How many children's tickets?
4. How much will the adult tickets cost? the children's tickets?
5. How does knowing the cost of both kinds of tickets help you find how much it will cost for the whole group to take the historic tour?
6. How much will it cost Sandi, her two friends, and her grandmothers to take a tour of the city? List the steps needed to find the answer.

Additional Standard: Number Sense 2.1 (🔑) (See p. 213.)

Jim had $28.90. He bought 2 patches, 3 magnets, 1 cap, 2 flags, and 2 quill pens.

Guided Practice

1. What information is not needed to find the amount Jim had left after his purchases?
   - **a.** The amount of money Jim had
   - **b.** The cost of a cap
   - **c.** The difference between the cost of a cap and the cost of a pen

2. How can you find the amount Jim had left after his purchases?
   - **a.** Add the cost of the items Jim bought and divide by 2.
   - **b.** Add the cost of the items Jim bought and subtract that total from the amount of money he started with.
   - **c.** Add the cost of the items Jim bought and add that total to the amount of money he started with.

Independent Practice

3. Which number sentence tells you how much money Jim spent on flags and quill pens?
   - **a.** $9.75 + $1.50 = $11.25
   - **b.** (2 × $3.25) + (2 × $1.50) = $9.50
   - **c.** (2 × $3.25) − (2 × $1.50) + $1.50 = $5.00

4. Which number sentence tells you how much Jim spent for patches and magnets?
   - **a.** (2 × $3.25) + (3 × $2.00) = $12.50
   - **b.** (3 × $2.00) + (3 × $2.50) = $13.50
   - **c.** (2 × $2.50) + (3 × $2.00) = $11.00

5. How much did Jim have left after making his purchases? List the steps needed to find the answer.

LESSON 6-5

Multiplying Decimals

California Content Standard *Number Sense 2.1 (🔑): . . . [M]ultiply . . . with decimals . . ..*

Math Link You know how to multiply a whole number and a decimal. Now you will learn to multiply two decimals.

Warm-Up Review

1. 4.9 × 8
2. 2.5 × 17
3. 12 × 3.6
4. 5 × 9.24
5. Estimate 87.1 × 4.
6. Estimate 5 × 9.05.
7. Estimate 17 × 4.33.
8. Find the total cost of 4 boxes of crackers at $2.25 each and 3 packages of cheese at $2.09 per package.

Example

Mrs. Vance is buying snacks for an after-school group. Baked tortilla chips are among the low-fat snack foods she will buy. There are 1.5 grams of fat in a 1-ounce serving. How many grams of fat are in a 2.3-ounce serving?

Find 2.3 × 1.5.

The grid shows each of the factors broken into two parts. It also shows each of the partial products.

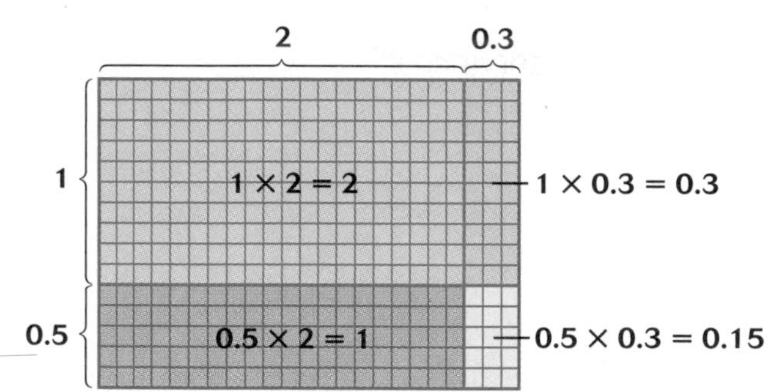

A 10-by-10 square is equal to 1.

Find the sum of the partial products.

2 + 0.3 + 1 + 0.15 = 3.45

Here is how you can record your work.

Step 1 Multiply as you would whole numbers.

```
   2.3
 × 1.5
   115
 + 230
   345
```

Step 2 Place the decimal point in the product.

```
   2.3   ← 1 decimal place
 × 1.5   ← 1 decimal place
   115
 + 230
  3.45   ← 2 decimal places
```

The number of decimal places in the product equals the total number of decimal places in the factors.

Check by estimating: 2.3 × 1.5
↓ ↓
2 × 2 = 4

There are 3.45 grams of fat in the 2.3-ounce serving. Since the estimate is 4, the answer is reasonable.

 Additional Standards: Mathematical Reasoning 1.1 and 3.3 (See p. 213.)

More Examples

A. $0.76 \times 0.9 = n$

Estimate: $0.8 \times 0.9 = 0.72$

$$\begin{array}{r} 0.76 \leftarrow \text{2 decimal places} \\ \times\ 0.9 \leftarrow \text{1 decimal place} \\ \hline 0.684 \leftarrow \text{3 decimal places} \end{array}$$

B. $2.67 \times 3.4 = n$

Estimate: $3 \times 3 = 9$

$$\begin{array}{r} 2.67 \leftarrow \text{2 decimal places} \\ \times\ 3.4 \leftarrow \text{1 decimal place} \\ \hline 1068 \\ +\ 8010 \\ \hline 9.078 \leftarrow \text{3 decimal places} \end{array}$$

Guided Practice *For another example, see Set D on p. 246.*

Find each product. Check by estimating.

1. 0.65×0.9 **2.** 2.5×0.6 **3.** 23.5×0.4 **4.** 0.052×0.7

Compare. Write >, <, or = for each ●.

5. 8.65 × 1.9 ● 8.65 **6.** 4.23 × 2.77 ● 14.23

7. Refer to page 222. How much fat is in a 0.5-ounce serving of the baked tortilla chips?

Independent Practice *For more practice, see Set D on p. 248.*

Find each product. Check by estimating.

8. 0.8×0.6 **9.** 0.91×0.8 **10.** 1.7×0.5 **11.** 7.36×0.4

12. 1.25×0.7 **13.** 0.28×3.7 **14.** 0.62×1.7 **15.** 4.7×6.3

16. 15.4×0.23 **17.** 3.14×6.2 **18.** 7.13×2.47 **19.** 6.73×36.8

20. 4.3 × 0.6 **21.** 8.5 × 0.7 **22.** 6 × 0.48 **23.** 54.1 × 0.5

24. 38 × 0.27 **25.** 0.32 × 4.6 **26.** 1.8 × 9.2 **27.** 18.6 × 4.03

Compare. Write >, <, or = for each ●.

28. 22 × 0.65 ● 0.75 × 15 **29.** 5.2 × 3.6 ● 0.36 × 52

30. 0.45 × 100 ● 5.4 × 10 **31.** 1.6 × 5.5 ● 5.4 × 1.5

32. **Math Reasoning** Will the product 3.1×0.2 be greater than or less than 3.1? Explain.

33. **Math Reasoning** Give a rule for placing the decimal point in the product of two decimals.

34. **Math Reasoning** If you made a mistake placing the decimal point in a product, how would estimating help you find that mistake and correct it?

35. A bean burrito contains 3.5 ounces of refried beans. One ounce of refried beans contains 0.56 gram of fat. How many grams of fat are in the beans of the burrito?

36. For lunch, you can choose chicken noodle soup (90 calories), crackers (75 calories), peanut butter (150 calories), fruit (100 calories), or milk (72 calories). You want to eat between 300 and 400 calories. What should you have for lunch? Explain your reasoning.

Mixed Review

37. What is the cost of two pounds of tomatoes at $1.29 a pound and two heads of lettuce at $1.59 a head?

38. Estimate 35.8×2.2.

39. Estimate 5.09×88.

40. 2.8×14

41. 38×0.045

42. $2{,}254 \div 98$

43. $3{,}348 \div 62$

44. **Algebra** Use the coordinate grid at the right. Write the coordinates for point *N*, point *V*, and point *C*. Then describe how you would graph point *M* at (3, 5).

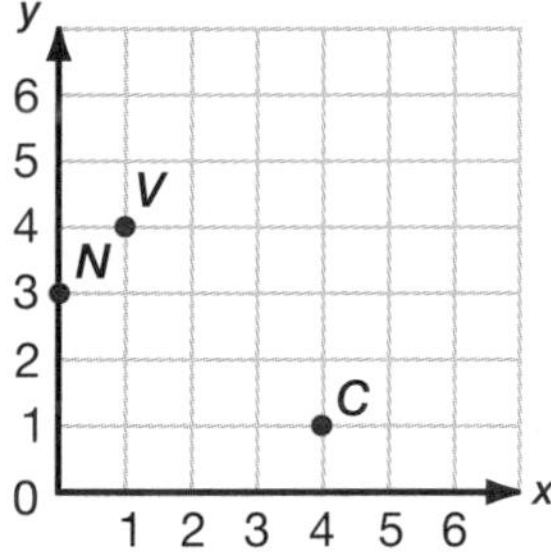

Test Prep **Choose the correct letter for each answer.**

45. Josh's test grades in history are 75 and 80. What grade must he get on his next test so that his average is 85?
(5-9)

A 80 **C** 95

B 90 **D** 100

46. A bag holds 5.8 lb of grass seed. How many pounds do 2.5 bags hold?
(6-5)

F 14.5 lb **H** 8.3 lb

G 13.8 lb **J** 3.3 lb

 Use Homework Workbook 6-5.

Diagnostic Checkpoint

Use patterns to find the products.

1. (6-1) $0.5 \times 10 = \blacksquare$
$0.5 \times 100 = \blacksquare$
$0.5 \times 1{,}000 = \blacksquare$

2. (6-1) $0.26 \times 100 = \blacksquare$
$0.26 \times 1{,}000 = \blacksquare$
$0.26 \times 10 = \blacksquare$

3. (6-1) $14.3 \times 1{,}000 = \blacksquare$
$14.3 \times 10 = \blacksquare$
$14.3 \times 100 = \blacksquare$

Find each *n*.

4. (6-1) $10 \times n = 4.5$

5. (6-1) $n \times 100 = 2.75$

6. (6-1) $0.109 \times 100 = n$

Multiply.

7. (6-2) 14.7×7

8. (6-2) $\$4.05 \times 6$

9. (6-2) 0.57×18

10. (6-2) $\$49.90 \times 30$

11. (6-2) 7.89×24

12. (6-2) 2×13.5

13. (6-2) 8.5×72

14. (6-2) 0.69×3

15. (6-2) 1.05×42

Estimate each product.

16. (6-3) 6.8×5

17. (6-3) 17.56×4

18. (6-3) 10×4.4

19. (6-3) 214×13.9

20. (6-3) 21×6.5

21. (6-3) $\$1.29 \times 32$

22. (6-3) 69×21.9

23. (6-3) 13×1.075

Find each product. Check by estimating.

24. (6-5) $\begin{array}{r} 6.75 \\ \times 0.03 \\ \hline \end{array}$

25. (6-5) $\begin{array}{r} \$42.60 \\ \times \quad 5 \\ \hline \end{array}$

26. (6-5) $\begin{array}{r} 0.65 \\ \times 2.6 \\ \hline \end{array}$

27. (6-5) $\begin{array}{r} \$11.33 \\ \times \quad 10 \\ \hline \end{array}$

28. (6-5) $\begin{array}{r} 1.08 \\ \times 0.19 \\ \hline \end{array}$

29. (6-5) $\begin{array}{r} \$21.90 \\ \times \quad 3 \\ \hline \end{array}$

30. (6-5) $\begin{array}{r} 12.5 \\ \times 0.38 \\ \hline \end{array}$

31. (6-5) $\begin{array}{r} 0.96 \\ \times 0.25 \\ \hline \end{array}$

32. (6-5) $\begin{array}{r} 15.50 \\ \times \quad 3.5 \\ \hline \end{array}$

33. (6-5) $\begin{array}{r} \$0.95 \\ \times \quad 15 \\ \hline \end{array}$

Solve.

34. (6-4) Mary Ann ordered 3 pens and a box of writing paper from a catalog. Each pen cost $2.98. The writing paper cost $4.95. How much did she spend?

35. (6-4) Kimberly wants to buy eight dog posters. A set of three posters sells for $10.00, and a single poster sells for $4.25. What is the least amount of money Kimberly will have to pay for the eight posters? Explain.

Multiplying with Zeros in the Product

Warm-Up Review

1. 8.7×0.6
2. 0.5×4.2
3. 6.3×2.5
4. 9.2×3.1
5. 85.6×0.4
6. 0.7×5.09
7. Find the cost of eight 100-watt light bulbs at $0.79 each.

 **California Content Standard** *Number Sense 2.1 (key): . . . [M]ultiply . . . with decimals . . . .*

Math Link You know how to find the product of two decimals. Now you will learn that you may need to place zeros in the product of two decimals.

Example

John's computer uses 0.16 kilowatt of electricity per hour. His bill, at the right, shows the cost per kilowatt hour (kWh). How much does the electricity cost for an hour of computer use?

Find $0.08 × 0.16.

Step 1 Multiply as you would whole numbers.

$$\begin{array}{r} 0.16 \\ \times\ 0.08 \\ \hline 128 \end{array}$$

Step 2 Place the decimal point in the product.

$$\begin{array}{rl} 0.16 & \leftarrow \text{2 decimal places} \\ \times\ 0.08 & \leftarrow \text{2 decimal places} \\ \hline \$0.0128 & \leftarrow \text{4 decimal places} \end{array}$$

Write a zero in the product to place the decimal point correctly.

Estimate to check: $0.1 \times 0.2 = 0.02$
The answer is reasonable.

Since $0.0128 rounds to $0.01, the electricity for an hour of computer use costs about 1 cent.

Other Examples

A. Find 7.2×0.009.

$$\begin{array}{rl} 7.2 & \leftarrow \text{1 decimal place} \\ \times\ 0.009 & \leftarrow \text{3 decimal places} \\ \hline 0.0648 & \leftarrow \text{4 decimal places} \end{array}$$

B. Find 0.07×0.8.

0.07	×	0.8	=	0.056
2 decimal places		1 decimal place		3 decimal places

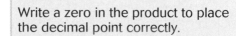

Additional Standards: Algebra and Functions 1.2 (key), Mathematical Reasoning 1.1 *(See p. 213.)*

Guided Practice

For another example, see Set E on p. 246.

1. 1.3×0.06 **2.** 0.03×0.2 **3.** 0.4×0.15 **4.** 3.1×0.09 **5.** 0.4×0.14

6. Math Reasoning In the first example on page 226, how did your estimate help you know it was correct to place a zero in front of the digits 128?

Independent Practice

For more practice, see Set E on p. 249.

7. 1.4×0.06 **8.** 0.05×0.9 **9.** 0.17×0.4 **10.** 0.013×7

11. 0.12×0.8 **12.** 5×0.008 **13.** 0.07×1.3 **14.** 3.2×0.03

Algebra Find each *n*.

15. $0.06 \times 0.5 = n$ **16.** $4.8 \times 0.06 = n$ **17.** $0.07 \times 0.2 = n$

18. $n \times 0.1 = 0.07$ **19.** $0.3 \times n = 0.009$ **20.** $0.34 \times n = 3.4$

21. Math Reasoning Is the product 0.03×0.03 the same as the product 0.3×0.003? Explain your answer.

22. Mental Math If one factor is 0.9 and the product is 0.072, what is the other factor?

Mixed Review

23. Cathy scored 90, 90, 92, 87, and 86 on five math tests. What was her average score?

24. Estimate 0.98×30.4. **25.** Estimate 4.23×79.

26. 0.38×5.2 **27.** 3.78×0.4 **28.** $607 \div 6$ **29.** $182 \div 9$

30. Algebra Find the value of $\frac{30}{x} - 2$ if $x = 3$.

Test Prep Choose the correct letter for each answer.

31. (4-7) In a 72-mile bike relay each rider will ride either 8 mi or 4 mi. The same number of riders will ride each distance. How many riders will ride each distance?

A 3 riders **C** 8 riders
B 6 riders **D** 32 riders

32. (5-8) At a square table, the tournament champion was on Mai's right. Jeffrey was across from Mai. Ann was on Jeffrey's right and across from Nicole. Who was champion?

F Mai **H** Ann
G Jeffrey **J** Nicole

Problem-Solving Strategy:

Choose a Strategy

Warm-Up Review

1. $50 − $35.79
2. $48.99 + $66.50
3. 0.3 × 5.98
4. 24 − (5 + 6)
5. 6 × (4 + 7)
6. Jean bought 3 puzzles at $4.95 each and 5 games. How much did the puzzles cost?

California Content Standard *Mathematical Reasoning 1.0: Students make decisions about how to approach problems. Also Mathematical Reasoning 2.3. (see p. 213.)*

Example

Eric bought two games, chess and checkers. He also bought some puzzles. He paid $46.48, including $2.00 tax. If the games together cost $12.48, how much did the puzzles cost?

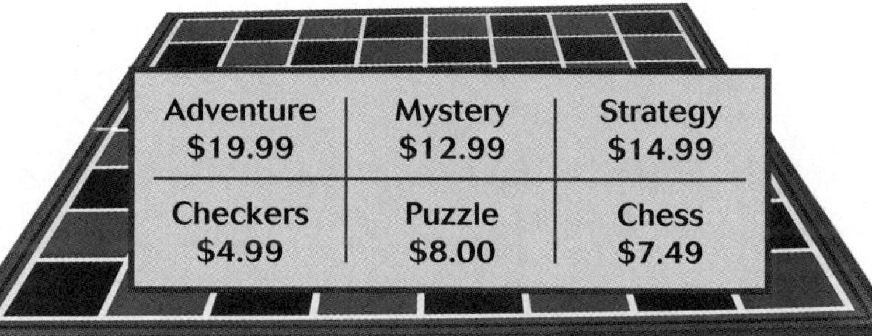

Adventure $19.99
Mystery $12.99
Strategy $14.99
Checkers $4.99
Puzzle $8.00
Chess $7.49

Understand

What do you need to find?

You need to find how much the puzzles cost.

Plan

How can you solve the problem?

Sometimes you can **choose a strategy** to solve a problem.

Solve

Work Backward		Write an Equation
Money paid	$46.48	Puzzle cost = total paid − (tax + cost of games)
Tax	− 2.00	$p = \$46.48 - (\$2 + \$12.48)$
	$44.48	$p = \$46.48 - \$14.48$
Cost of games	− 12.48	$p = \$32$
Cost of puzzles	$32.00	

The puzzles cost $32.

Look Back

How many puzzles did Eric buy?

Additional Standard: Mathematical Reasoning 3.2 (See p. 213.)

Try these or other strategies to solve each problem. Tell which strategy you used.

Problem-Solving Strategies

- *Draw a Diagram*
- *Find a Pattern*
- *Make a Table*
- *Make a List*
- *Write an Equation*
- *Work Backward*

Guided Practice

1. Andrew gave Brent 8 marbles, and he gave Nick twice as many. Now Andrew has 48 marbles left. How many marbles did he have before he gave some to Brent and Nick?

2. Ryan, Gary, Lauren, and Kayla want to play checkers with each other. If each person plays a game with every other person, how many games will they play?

Independent Practice

3. Mr. Lee made a window display of the games his store sells. The games were stacked so that the top row had one game, the next row had 3, the next row had 5, and so on. If there are 9 rows, how many games are in the bottom row?

4. **Math Reasoning** The toy store is offering a special sale on puzzles, as shown in the sign at the right. How much would six puzzles cost?

5. Stan works at the toy store 20 hours a week. He gets paid $5 per hour. When he works more than 20 hours, he earns $3 more for each hour of overtime. How much will he earn if he works 25 hours in one week?

6. There are 35 mystery games and word games on a shelf. There are 15 more word games than mystery games. How many of each game are on the shelf?

7. Bob and Jim played chess on Tuesday, Friday, Monday, and Thursday. If this pattern continues, when will they play next?

Mental Math: Dividing Decimals by 10, 100, or 1,000

Warm-Up Review

1. 1.4 × 10
2. 0.33 × 1,000
3. 450 ÷ 10
4. 3,000 ÷ 100
5. 56,000 ÷ 1,000
6. How many dimes are in $75?

California Content Standard *Number Sense 2.1 (key): . . . [M]ultiply and divide with decimals . . .. Also Number Sense 2.2 (key)* *(See p. 213.)*

Math Link You know how to multiply a decimal by 10, 100, or 1,000 mentally. Now you will use similar methods to divide a decimal by 10, 100, or 1,000.

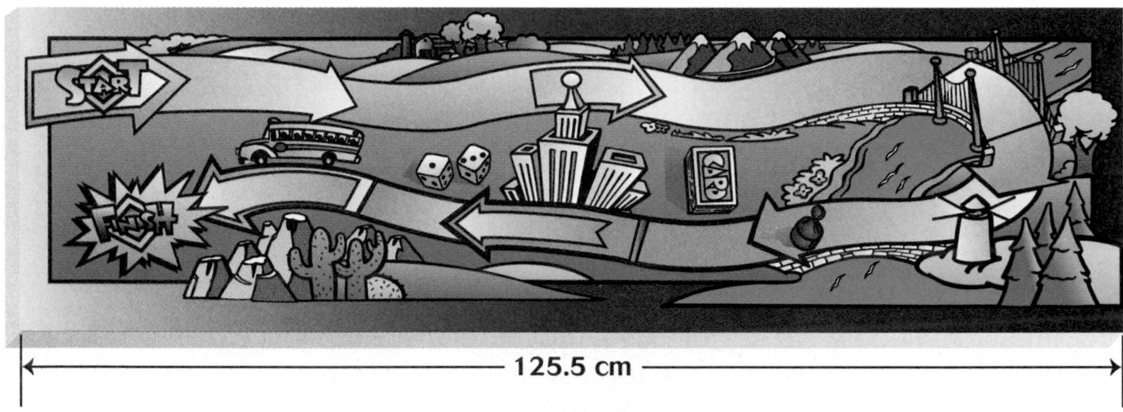

Example

Suppose you want to divide the game board above into 10 sections the same length. How long will each section be?

Find 125.5 ÷ 10.

Study the patterns in the table. What do you notice?

Divide by	Example	Move the decimal point to the left
1	125.5 ÷ 1 = 125.5	0 places
10	125.5 ÷ 10 = 12.55	1 place
100	125.5 ÷ 100 = 1.255	2 places
1,000	125.5 ÷ 1,000 = 0.1255	3 places

Since 125.5 ÷ 10 = 12.55, the length of each section on the game board will be 12.55 centimeters.

Other Examples

A. 64.3 ÷ 1 = 64.3
64.3 ÷ 10 = 6.43 = 6.43
64.3 ÷ 100 = 0.643 = 0.643
64.3 ÷ 1,000 = 0.0643 = 0.0643

B. 56 ÷ 1 = 56
56 ÷ 10 = 5.6 = 5.6
56 ÷ 100 = 0.56 = 0.56
56 ÷ 1,000 = 0.056 = 0.056

Guided Practice *For another example, see Set F on p. 247.*

1. 23.75 ÷ 1 = ■
   23.75 ÷ 10 = ■
   23.75 ÷ 100 = ■
   23.75 ÷ 1,000 = ■

2. 509.3 ÷ 10 = ■
   509.3 ÷ 100 = ■
   509.3 ÷ 1 = ■
   509.3 ÷ 1,000 = ■

3. 98.2 ÷ 100 = ■
   98.2 ÷ 1 = ■
   98.2 ÷ 1,000 = ■
   98.2 ÷ 10 = ■

4. **Math Reasoning** Write a rule that describes how the number of zeros in the divisor relates to the number of places you need to move the decimal point in the quotient when dividing by 10, 100, or 1,000.

Independent Practice *For more practice, see Set F on p. 249.*

5. 21.9 ÷ 100
6. 0.45 ÷ 10
7. 6,394 ÷ 1,000
8. 0.04 ÷ 10
9. 5,050 ÷ 100
10. 2.75 ÷ 100
11. 398 ÷ 100
12. 10.9 ÷ 100
13. 46.7 ÷ 10
14. 51.6 ÷ 1,000
15. 0.282 ÷ 10
16. 73.06 ÷ 100

Algebra Find each *n*.

17. 908 ÷ n = 9.08
18. 1,298 ÷ 10 = n
19. 20.01 ÷ n = 0.2001
20. 19 ÷ 1,000 = n
21. 0.08 ÷ n = 0.0008
22. 3.11 ÷ 10 = n

23. A game board is 65 cm long and 40 cm wide. The length has been divided into 10 sections. How long is each section?

24. **Math Reasoning** A set of 100 number cubes sells for $45 and a set of 1,000 number cubes sells for $380. Which price is the better buy? Explain.

Mixed Review

25. Find the cost of 3.5 pounds of apples at $0.99 per pound. Round your answer to the nearest cent.

26. 0.37 × 4.1
27. 5.6 × 1.1
28. 0.607 × 0.04
29. 0.005 × 1.22

Test Prep **Choose the correct letter for each answer.**

30. (1-6) Which number, when rounded to the nearest 100, is 600?

A 549
B 552
C 654
D 663
E NH

31. (1-6) Which number, when rounded to the nearest tenth, is 4.5?

F 4.409
G 4.448
H 4.502
J 4.551
K NH

Dividing a Decimal by a Whole Number

Warm-Up Review

1. 462 ÷ 7
2. 5,382 ÷ 9
3. 1,035 ÷ 5
4. 868 ÷ 62
5. Beth ordered 24 flower buds at 3 for $2.50. What was the total cost for the buds?

California Content Standard *Number Sense 2.1 (key): . . . [M]ultiply and divide with decimals . . .. Also Number Sense 2.2 (key). (See p. 213.)*

Math Link You know how to divide decimals by 10, 100, or 1,000. In this lesson, you will learn to divide decimals by other whole numbers.

Example 1

Find 4.38 ÷ 2. Estimate first: 4 ÷ 2 = 2

You can use base-ten blocks to show the division.

Step 1 Divide the ones.

$$\begin{array}{r} 2. \\ 2\overline{)4.38} \\ -4 \\ \hline 0 \end{array}$$

← There are 2 ones in each group.

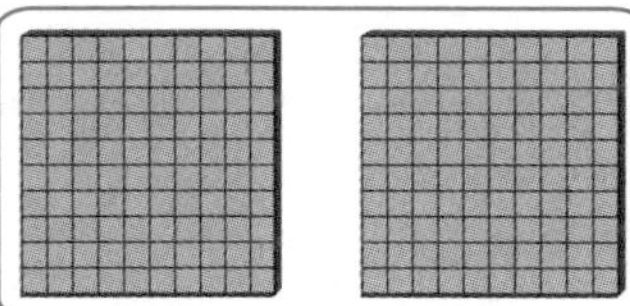
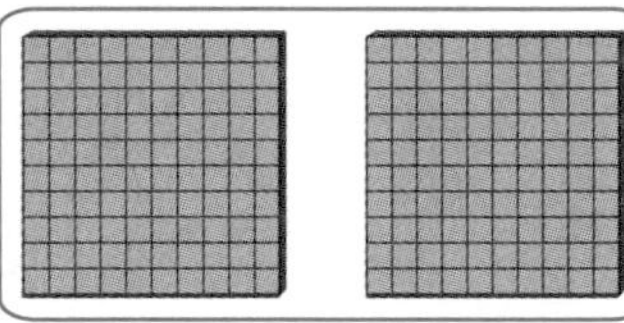
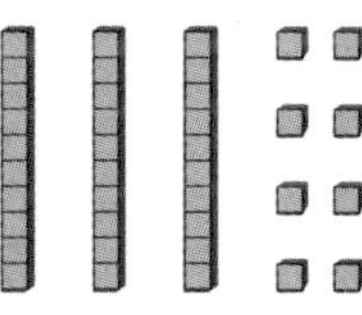

Step 2 Divide the tenths.

$$\begin{array}{r} 2.1 \\ 2\overline{)4.38} \\ -4 \\ \hline 03 \\ -\ 2 \\ \hline 1 \end{array}$$

← There are 2 ones and 1 tenth in each group.

← 1 tenth left over.

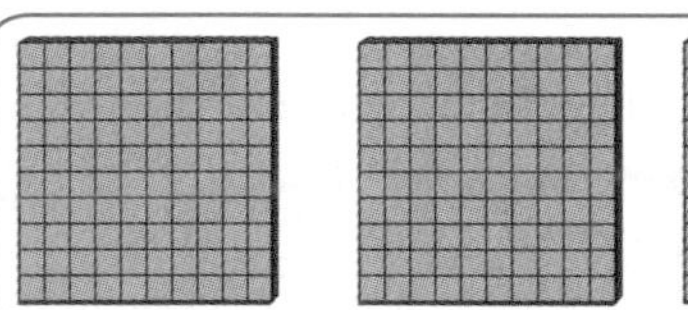
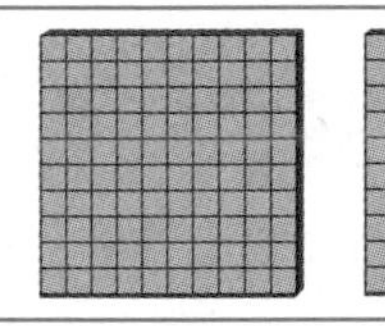

Step 3 Divide the hundredths.

$$\begin{array}{r} 2.19 \\ 2\overline{)4.38} \\ -4 \\ \hline 03 \\ -\ 2 \\ \hline 18 \\ -\ 18 \\ \hline 0 \end{array}$$

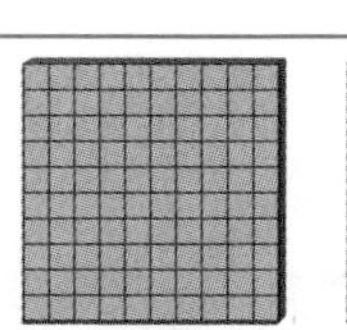

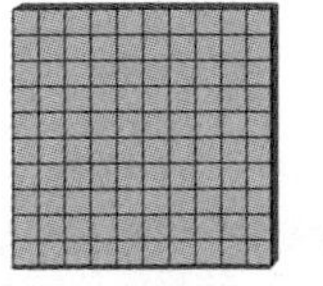

← Regroup 1 tenth as 10 hundredths.
10 hundredths + 8 hundredths = 18 hundredths.

Step 4 Check by multiplying. 2 × 2.19 = 4.38

Example 2

The art teacher is teaching calligraphy after school. She spent $79.60 on 8 calligraphy sets. How much did each set cost?

Find $79.60 ÷ 8.

Estimate first: $80 ÷ 8 = $10
Then find the exact answer.

Step 1 Place the decimal point in the quotient above the decimal point in the dividend.

$$8\overline{)\$79.60}$$ (quotient: .)

Step 2 Divide as you would with whole numbers.

```
     $ 9.95
   8)$79.60
    - 72
       76
     - 72
        40
      - 40
         0
```

Step 3 Check by multiplying.

```
  $9.95
 ×    8
 $79.60
```

The answer $9.95 is reasonable since it is close to the estimate of $10.

Each calligraphy set cost $9.95.

More Examples

A.

```
      0.06
  21)1.26
   - 126
       0
```

When there are not enough ones to divide, write a zero in the ones place.

B.

```
   0.3046
 5)1.5230
  - 15
     023
    - 20
       30
     - 30
        0
```

Write this zero and continue dividing.

Guided Practice *For another example, see Set G on p. 247.*

1. $5\overline{)\$6.85}$ **2.** $12\overline{)2.52}$ **3.** 57.60 ÷ 45 **4.** 71.1 ÷ 5

5. A pack of calligraphy paper costs $38.50. There are 55 sheets in a pack. What is the cost of each sheet?

Independent Practice *For more practice, see Set G on p. 249.*

6. $8\overline{)24.8}$ **7.** $56\overline{)518.00}$ **8.** $34\overline{)2{,}723.4}$

9. $78\overline{)7.02}$ **10.** 6 ÷ 5 **11.** 174.08 ÷ 34

12. 1.136 ÷ 71 **13.** 153.6 ÷ 6 **14.** 48.30 ÷ 5

15. 1.15 ÷ 23 **16.** 0.12 ÷ 8 **17.** 103.53 ÷ 51

18. Calligraphy markers sell in 8-packs for $4.16 and 12-packs for $5.76. In which size pack are the markers less expensive?

19. Alyson works as a waitress. Last week she earned a total of $128.50 in tips in a 5-day period. What was the average amount she earned in tips each day?

20. At one bakery muffins sell for $7.80 a dozen. At another bakery you can buy 8 muffins for $4.80. At which bakery are the muffins less expensive?

The table at the right gives sizes and prices for a variety of dog foods. Find the price per pound for each kind.

	Name	Weight (pounds)	Cost	Price per Pound
21.	Crunchy Chunks	5	$2.50	
22.	Crunchy Chunks	10	$4.80	
23.	Good Doggy	5	$2.95	
24.	Good Doggy	10	$5.50	
25.	Clean Teeth	100	$45.00	

Mixed Review

26. Find the product of 0.037 and 0.12. **27.** Find the product of 0.004 and 8.9.

Mental Math

28. 157 × 100 **29.** 2,700 ÷ 90 **30.** 9.24 ÷ 100 **31.** 3.5 ÷ 10

32. (4-3) **Algebra** Evaluate the expression $24n + 5$, for $n = 2$.

A 53 **D** 31
B 43 **E** NH
C 58

33. (2-10) **Algebra** Which number completes this number sentence?
$4.75 - n = 2.5$

F 7.25 **J** 2
G 2.5 **K** NH
H 2.25

 Use Homework Workbook 6-9.

Dividing a Decimal by a Decimal

California Content Standard *Number Sense 2.1 (🔑): . . . [D]ivide with decimals . . ..*

Warm-Up Review

1. 9.2 ÷ 4
2. 12.96 ÷ 3
3. 3.055 ÷ 5
4. 8.136 ÷ 9
5. 36.38 ÷ 34
6. Yo-yos are sold for $1.79 each. How much would you save if you buy a box of 24 yo-yos for $35.28?

Math Link You know how to divide decimals by whole numbers. Now you will learn to divide by decimals.

Example 1

Find 2.8 ÷ 0.7.

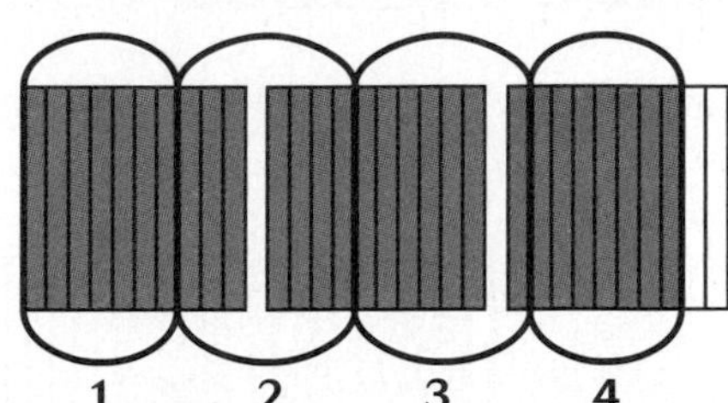

The model at the right shows that 2.8 contains 4 groups of 0.7. So, 2.8 ÷ 0.7 = 4.

It is not always easy to use a model when dividing by a decimal. Another method involves first changing the decimal divisor to a whole-number divisor. To help you learn this method, notice the patterns in the table below.

Dividend	Divisor	Quotient	
8	2	4	
80	20	4	← Dividend and divisor are multiplied by 10.
800	200	4	← Dividend and divisor are multiplied by 100.
8,000	2,000	4	← Dividend and divisor are multiplied by 1,000.

Notice that the quotient stays the same when you multiply the dividend and the divisor by the same number.

Example 2

Find 4.3 ÷ 0.86.

Step 1 Multiply the divisor by a power of 10 to make it a whole number.

Multiply 0.86 by 100.
0.86 × 100 = 86

$0.86\overline{)4.3}$

Step 2 Multiply the dividend by the same power of 10. Sometimes you need to write an extra zero in the dividend.

$0.86.\overline{)4.30.}$

Step 3 Place the decimal point in the quotient and divide as you would with whole numbers.

$$\begin{array}{r} 5. \\ 0.86.\overline{)4.30.} \\ -\,4\,30 \\ \hline 0 \end{array}$$

Step 4 Check by multiplying. 0.86 × 5 = 4.30

Additional Standard: Mathematical Reasoning 2.1 (See p. 213.)

Other Examples

A.

```
        2.14
0.4)0.856
   - 8
     05
    - 4
     16
   - 16
      0
```

Multiply the divisor and the dividend by 10. Place the decimal point in the quotient. Then divide.

B.

```
          41.
0.29)11.89.
   - 1 16
        29
      - 29
         0
```

Multiply the divisor and the dividend by 100. Place the decimal point in the quotient. Then divide.

Guided Practice *For another example, see Set H on p. 247.*

Write the division sentence shown by each model.

1.

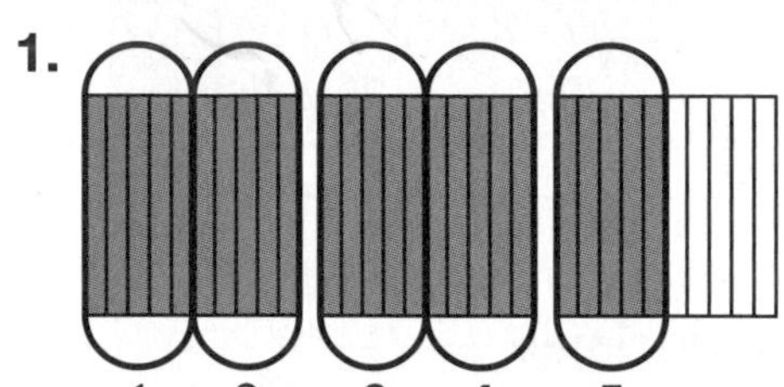

2.

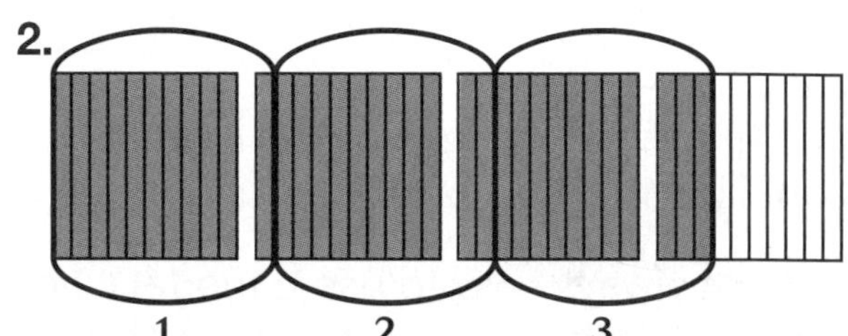

Tell what power of ten you would use to make the divisor a whole number. Then divide.

3. 2.24 ÷ 0.8 **4.** 0.0036 ÷ 0.009 **5.** 5.76 ÷ 1.6 **6.** 10.58 ÷ 2.3

7. Math Reasoning When dividing by a decimal, the estimation rules at the right can help you decide if the decimal point is correctly placed in the quotient. For each division problem, use the rules to decide which quotient is reasonable. Explain your answers.

> **If the dividend is less than the divisor, the quotient is less than 1.**
>
> **If the divident is greater than the divisor, the quotient is greater than 1.**

0.56 ÷ 0.8 = 0.7 *or* 7.0 3.6 ÷ 0.04 = 0.9 *or* 90

Independent Practice *For more practice, see Set H on p. 249.*

8. Write the division sentence shown by the model at the right.

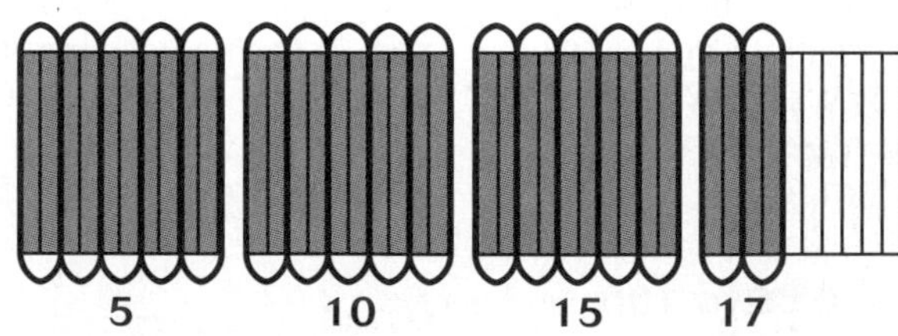

9. 0.104 ÷ 0.08 **10.** 0.804 ÷ 0.4 **11.** 5.49 ÷ 0.9 **12.** 69.09 ÷ 0.7

13. 2.5 ÷ 0.005 **14.** 50.4 ÷ 1.2 **15.** 87.4 ÷ 0.38 **16.** 6.89 ÷ 1.3

17. 0.427 ÷ 6.1 **18.** 3.48 ÷ 5.8 **19.** 0.8449 ÷ 0.71 **20.** 9.483 ÷ 8.7

21. Art boards cost $0.95 each. What is the greatest number you can buy with $15.00? Will there by any money left over? If so, how much?

Math Reasoning Use a divisor of 0.8 and write a division problem.

22. With a quotient less than 1

23. With a quotient greater than 1

The table at the right shows Mrs. Sheng's gasoline purchases during the month of May. Find the missing total costs and prices per gallon. Round the total costs to the nearest cent.

	Date	Amount	Price per Gallon	Total Cost
24.	May 1	7.6 gal	$1.37	
25.	May 9	8.3 gal	$1.40	
26.	May 14	6.8 gal		$9.86
27.	May 22	9.6 gal	$1.45	
28.	May 31	9.5 gal		$14.44

Mixed Review

29. Chris spent half of her money on a poster. Then she spent half of what she had left for a small figurine. She bought lunch for $5.00. When she got home, she had $2.50 left. How much did she have to start? What strategy did you use to find out?

30. **Math Reasoning** Find the next three numbers in the pattern. Then explain what the pattern is.
32, 16, 8, 4, 2, 1, 0.5, . . .

31. **Mental Math** 34.56 ÷ 1,000

32. **Mental Math** 5.7 ÷ 100

33. 9.43 ÷ 23

34. 16.72 ÷ 8

35. **Algebra** Solve $\frac{x}{12} = 3$ for x.

Test Prep **Choose the correct letter for each answer.**

Use the graph at the right for Exercises 36 and 37.

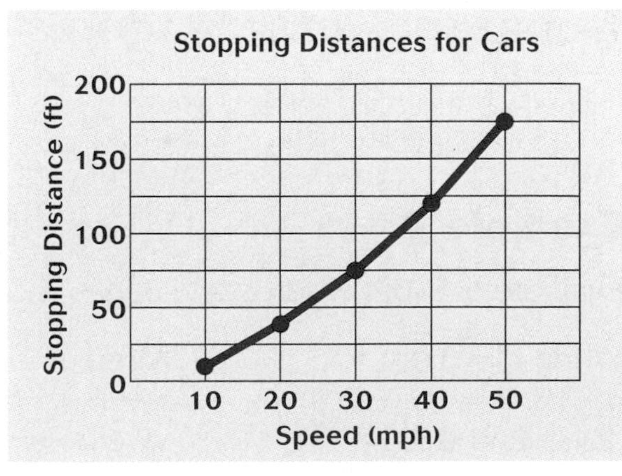

36. At what speed is the stopping distance 175 feet?
(3-5)

A 20 mph **C** 40 mph
B 30 mph **D** 50 mph

37. How many feet does it take for a car traveling 30 mph to stop?
(3-5)

F 30 ft **H** 75 ft
G 50 ft **J** 100 ft

Evaluating Expressions with Decimals

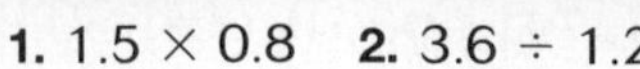

Warm-Up Review

1. 1.5×0.8
2. $3.6 \div 1.2$
3. $0.3 \times (2.5 + 3.5)$
4. $5.1 + 3.85 + 4.9$
5. $12 - (4.2 + 2.9)$
6. Evaluate $\frac{24}{x}$ for $x = 12$, $x = 8$, and $x = 4$.
7. Each lap around the school track is about 0.4 km. What is the total distance for 8 laps around the track?

California Content Standard *Algebra and Functions 1.2 (🔑): Use a letter to represent an unknown number; write and evaluate simple algebraic expressions in one variable by substitution.*

Math Link You have learned to evaluate expressions with whole numbers. Now you will use what you have learned to evaluate expressions with decimals.

Example 1

Evaluate $5n - 3$ when $n = 0.67$, $n = 3.4$, and $n = 22.9$.

When $n = 0.67$:
$$5n - 3 = (5 \times 0.67) - 3 = 3.35 - 3 = 0.35$$

When $n = 3.4$:
$$5n - 3 = (5 \times 3.4) - 3 = 17.0 - 3 = 14.0 \text{ or } 14$$

When $n = 22.9$:
$$5n - 3 = (5 \times 22.9) - 3 = 114.5 - 3 = 111.5$$

Example 2

Evaluate $24 - x$ when $x = 3.49$, $x = 10.6$, and $x = 19.2$.

When $x = 3.49$:
$$24 - x = 24 - 3.49 = 20.51$$

When $x = 10.6$:
$$24 - x = 24 - 10.6 = 13.4$$

When $x = 19.2$:
$$24 - x = 24 - 19.2 = 4.8$$

Example 3

Evaluate $\frac{3.6}{y} + 2.8$ when $y = 3$, $y = 1.8$, and $y = 0.06$.

When $y = 3$:
$$\frac{3.6}{y} + 2.8 = \frac{3.6}{3} + 2.8 = 1.2 + 2.8 = 4.0 \text{ or } 4$$

When $y = 1.8$:
$$\frac{3.6}{y} + 2.8 = \frac{3.6}{1.8} + 2.8 = 2.0 + 2.8 = 4.8$$

When $y = 0.06$:
$$\frac{3.6}{y} + 2.8 = \frac{3.6}{0.06} + 2.8 = 60 + 2.8 = 62.8$$

Example 4

Evaluate $a + 6.4$ when $a = 19$, $a = 7.5$, and $a = 13.88$.

When $a = 19$:
$$a + 6.4 = 19 + 6.4 = 25.4$$

When $a = 7.5$:
$$a + 6.4 = 7.5 + 6.4 = 13.9$$

When $a = 13.88$:
$$a + 6.4 = 13.88 + 6.4 = 20.28$$

Additional Standards: Number Sense 2.1 (🔑), Mathematical Reasoning 3.3 *(See p. 213.)*

Guided Practice *For another example, see Set I on p. 247.*

Evaluate each expression for $x = 8$, $x = 0.72$, and $x = 1.6$.

1. $14.65 + x$ **2.** $x - 0.42$ **3.** $7.8x + 4$ **4.** $\frac{x}{4} - 0.1$

5. Write an expression for Jay's total salary for h hours of work if his hourly pay is \$8.50 per hour. Then find his salary for a 20-hour week, a 37.5-hour week, and a 40-hour week.

Independent Practice *For more practice, see Set I on p. 249.*

Evaluate each expression for $x = 0.08$, $x = 0.24$, and $x = 1.8$.

6. $x + 7.9$ **7.** $8.55 - x$ **8.** $5.2x + 3$ **9.** $\frac{72}{x} - 27.5$

10. $26.78 + x$ **11.** $(x - 0.009) \times 4$ **12.** $1.25x$ **13.** $\frac{x}{2}$

14. Amy earned \$240 last week. Write an expression for her hourly rate for h hours of work. Then find her hourly rate if she worked 40 hours last week. What was her hourly rate if she worked only 37.5 hours last week?

Mixed Review

The table at the right gives hours worked, hourly rates, and total earnings at the J.G. Boat Shop. Find each missing quantity.

	Hours Worked	Hourly Rates	Total Earnings
15.	20	\$7.50	
16.	40	\$8.85	
17.		\$8.00	\$320.00
18.		\$9.00	\$157.50
19.	7.5	\$8.50	
20.		\$9.25	\$370.00

21. Which hourly rate in the table above is the highest? the lowest?

22. $5.68 \div 8$ **23.** $76.8 \div 24$ **24.** $2.88 \div 4.8$ **25.** $1.872 \div 0.9$

Test Prep **Choose the correct letter for each answer.**

26. (2-7) Which expression is the correct translation for "the quotient of a number n divided by 3.5"?

A $3.5n$ **C** $\frac{3.5}{n}$

B $\frac{n}{3.5}$ **D** $n - 3.5$

27. (2-7) Which expression is the correct translation for "6.8 less than a number n"?

F $6.8 - n$ **H** $n - 6.8$

G $6.8 + n$ **J** $n \div 6.8$

Understand
Plan
Solve
Look Back

Problem-Solving Application:

Using Operations

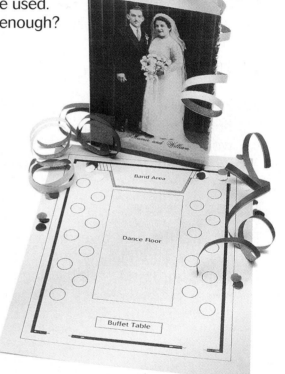

California Content Standard *Mathematical Reasoning 2.6: Make precise calculations and check the validity of the results from the context of the problem.*

Warm-Up Review

1. 5.98×2
2. $13.98 \div 3$
3. \$76.25 + \$32.45
4. \$20.00 − \$4.95
5. $50 - (2 \times 15.5)$
6. Kelli bought 3 sweaters at \$24.95 each. Tax was \$3.76. How much did she spend in all?

Example

Mr. Alvarado is in charge of planning a 50th wedding anniversary party. He expects 172 people to attend. Round tables that can seat a maximum of 10 people will be used. Will the number of tables shown in the diagram be enough?

Understand

What do you need to know?

You need to know the number of people expected and the number of people that can be seated at a table.

Plan

How can you solve the problem?

You can **write an equation** using division to find out how many tables are needed.

Solve

Number of people at party	÷	Number who can sit at a table	=	Number of tables needed
172	÷	10	=	17.2

Since Mr. Alvarado cannot order 0.2 of a table, 18 tables will be needed. The 18 tables shown in the diagram will be enough.

Look Back

How can you check your answer?

$18 \times 10 = 180 \qquad 180 > 172$

There will be more than enough places at 18 tables.

Additional Standard: Number Sense 2.1 (🔑) *(See p. 213.)*

Use the information at the right and on page 240.

Guided Practice

1. Mr. Alvarado is ordering a flower arrangement for each of the 18 tables. Each flower arrangement will cost $37.50. What is the total cost of flowers?

2. Mr. Alvarado wants each party guest to have a 4-ounce serving of turkey. How many pounds of turkey should be prepared if Mr. Alvarado also wants enough for 8 extra guests?

Party Planners
White Dinner Plates
200 or more ... $1.00 ea
100 to 199..... $1.10 ea
50 to 99....... $1.15 ea
1 to 49........ $1.20 ea
Party Favors
Hats........... $2.00 ea
Noisemakers.... $8.00/doz
Balloons....... $10.50/doz
Streamers...... $3.25/pkg
The MusicMakers
Up to 3 h $200/h
From 3 to 4 h... $150/h
More than 4 h.. $125/h

Independent Practice

3. If Mr. Alvarado wants to order one balloon for each of the 172 guests, how many packages of a dozen must he order?

4. Mr. Alvarado wants each guest to have a noisemaker. How many packages must he order? What will be the total cost of the noisemakers?

5. Use the price list to decide how Mr. Alvarado can get the best price for 184 plates.

6. The anniversary party will take place from 8:00 P.M. until 1:30 A.M. The band will play from 8:30 P.M. to 1:00 A.M. The band charges for a whole hour, even if it plays for only part of an hour. If *The MusicMakers* are hired, how much will the band cost for the evening?

Mixed Review

7. Cartons of eggs are packed 8 to a box. How many boxes are needed for 832 cartons of eggs?

8. Mr. Chan's monthly transportation costs are $48.50. What is the total for a year?

Diagnostic Checkpoint

Complete. For Exercises 1–3 choose a word from the Word Bank.

Word Bank
decimal point
dividend
quotient
zero

1. (6-1) When multiplying a decimal by 100, move the ________________ 2 places to the right.

2. (6-6) Sometimes you need to write a ________________ in the product of two decimals in order to place the decimal point correctly.

3. (6-9) When dividing a decimal by a whole number, place the decimal point in the quotient above the decimal point in the ________________.

Find each product.

4. (6-6) 0.04×0.3

5. (6-6) $\$0.03 \times 0.3$

6. (6-6) 0.14×0.6

7. (6-6) 0.009×0.4

8. (6-6) 0.097×0.124

Find each *n*.

9. (6-8) $0.1 \div 10 = n$

10. (6-8) $23.4 \div 100 = n$

Divide.

11. (6-9) $41\overline{)1.435}$

12. (6-9) $11\overline{)22.891}$

13. (6-10) $0.12\overline{)4.5}$

14. (6-10) $0.028\overline{)0.042}$

15. (6-11) Evaluate $12.6n$ when $n = 0.38$, $n = 3.72$, $n = 35$.

16. (6-7) From a catalog, Stephen ordered 3 pounds of oranges at $3.25 per pound, 5 pounds of grapefruit at $2.10 per pound, and some pears at $3.50 per pound. He had to pay a flat rate of $6.25 for shipping. If his order totaled $37.00, how many pounds of pears did he buy?

17. (6-12) Mrs. Nevo wants to buy each of her 215 art students a paintbrush. The brushes come in packages of eight for $2.25. Today the supply store is running a special. Buy two packages of paintbrushes, get one package free. How many packages of paintbrushes does Mrs. Nevo need? How much does she spend?

Chapter 6 Test

Use patterns to multiply or divide.

1. 5.6×100 **2.** $0.079 \times 1{,}000$ **3.** $14.98 \div 10$ **4.** $6.23 \div 1{,}000$

Estimate each product.

5. $\$0.35 \times 12$ **6.** 6.6×23 **7.** $\$1.83 \times 28$

Find each product.

8. 0.785×9 **9.** 1.6×0.05 **10.** 0.0072×0.3

11. 0.36×2.5 **12.** 9.64×15 **13.** 1.76×0.96

Divide.

14. $4\overline{)217.4}$ **15.** $12\overline{)63.72}$ **16.** $5.2\overline{)45.24}$

17. $0.336 \div 1.6$ **18.** $181.2 \div 8$ **19.** $535.05 \div 0.25$

Evaluate each expression for $x = 0.492$, $x = 54.66$, and $x = 7.8$.

20. $0.62x$ **21.** $x \div 6$

Solve.

22. The fitness catalog is advertising hand weights for $14.95 and weight belts for $22.75. If Meg buys 3 weight belts and 2 hand weights, how much will she spend?

23. Hershel gave Alan 9 grapes, and he gave Leslie three times as many. He ate 12 grapes himself. Now he only has 25 grapes left. How many grapes did Hershel have to start with?

24. Jarrod has 63 couples lined up for an egg-tossing contest. Each couple will get one egg. If eggs come in cartons of one dozen, how many cartons of eggs does Jarrod need?

25. Matthew and his sister, Kate, ordered 32 sinkers for their fishing trip. The total bill was $14.40. If the sinkers each cost the same amount, how much did each sinker cost?

Multiple-Choice Chapter 6 Test

Choose the correct letter for each answer.

1. **A local animal shelter houses 100 dogs. If it costs $2.75 a day to feed each dog, how much money does the shelter spend on dog food each day?**

   A $2,750.00
   B $275.00
   C $27.00
   D $0.27

2. **Kate decided to make a fruit salad for dessert for her friends. If she wants 9.5 ounces of fruit for each of her eight friends, how many ounces of fruit should she buy?**

   F 1.2 oz
   G 76 oz
   H 95 oz
   J 115 oz
   K NH

3. **To find the area of a rectangle, you multiply the length by the width. Area is measured in square units. Melissa's room is 13.2 feet long and 8.61 feet wide. What is the area of the floor of her room?**

   A 121.81 square feet
   B 113.652 square feet
   C 43.62 square feet
   D 11.36 square feet

4. **Which is a reasonable estimate for the product of 621×0.39?**

   F 180
   G 210
   H 240
   J 360

5. **Fernando practices the piano for 0.5 hour three times a week. How many hours does he practice in four weeks?**

   A 1.5 hours
   B 3 hours
   C 6 hours
   D 12 hours

6. **How many zeros are to the right of the decimal point in the product of 0.08×0.04?**

   F 4
   G 2
   H 1
   J 0
   K NH

7. **Mr. Ali bought sliced turkey for $3.86, 5 rolls at $0.49 each, and some oranges at $0.25 each. If Mr. Ali spent $9.56, how many oranges did he buy?**

   A 5
   B 7
   C 10
   D 13

8. **Complete the pattern.**
26.8 ÷ 1,000 = ■
26.8 ÷ 100 = ■
26.8 ÷ 10 = ■
26.8 ÷ 1 = ■

F 2,680; 26,800; 26.8; 268
G 0.0268; 0.268; 2.68; 26.8
H 26.8; 2.68; 0.268; 0.0268
J 26.8; 0.268; 2.68; 268.0

9. **Find the quotient of 36.82 ÷ 0.4.**

A 9,205
B 92.05
C 9.205
D 925
E NH

10. **Find the quotient of 729.8 ÷ 41.**

F 17.8
G 1.78
H 0.178
J 0.0178
K NH

11. **If $n = 0.12$, which expression has the least value?**

A $21.6n$
B $11.76 \div n$
C $13.01 - n$
D $10.009 + n$

12. **If $3.01 \div b = 0.0301$, what is b?**

F 1,000
G 100
H 10
J 0.10
K NH

Use the chart for Questions 13–15.

Pens	\$0.75; 5-pack: \$3.25
Pencils	\$0.25; buy 5, get 1 free
Folders	\$0.20; 5-pack: \$0.95

13. **Zech needs 40 pencils to send in care packages. Which is the least amount of money Zech can spend and still get all the pencils he needs?**

A \$12.00
B \$10.00
C \$8.50
D \$6.25

14. **Ariel needs to buy 10 pens and 10 folders. How much will she save if she buys the 5-pack specials instead of buying the items individually?**

F \$9.50
G \$8.40
H \$2.25
J \$1.10

15. **How much does Sue spend if she buys 6 pens, 2 pencils, and 5 folders?**

A \$4.45
B \$4.75
C \$5.45
D \$6.75

16. **Find the product of 32.65 × 0.15.**

F 0.48975
G 4.8975
H 48.975
J 489.75
K NH

Reteaching

Set A (pages 214–215)

Find the product of 62.38 × 1,000.

62.38 × **1,000** = 62.380

1,000 has three zeros. Move the decimal point three places to the right. Write an extra zero when necessary.

62.38 × **1,000** = 62,380

Remember to move the decimal point to the right one place when the other factor is 10, two places when it is 100, and three places when it is 1,000.

1. 3.8 × 10
3.8 × 100
3.8 × 1,000

2. 0.09 × 10
0.09 × 100
0.09 × 1,000

Set B (pages 216–217)

Find the product of 18.33 × 21.

```
  18.33 ←— 2 decimal places
×    21 ←— 0 decimal places
   1833
  36660
 384.93 ←— 2 decimal places
```

Remember, the product of two decimals has the same number of decimal places as the total number of decimal places in the two factors.

1. 17.3 × 2 **2.** 19.2 × 9

Set C (pages 218–219)

Estimate the product of 0.738 × 6.

0.738 × 6
↓ ↓
0.7 × 6 = 4.2 one decimal place

Remember to round when estimating products of whole numbers and decimals.

Estimate each product.

1. 23 × 7.1 **2.** 3.8 × 29

Set D (pages 222–224)

Find the product of 4.34 × 0.28.

```
   4.34 ←— 2 decimal places
×  0.28 ←— 2 decimal places
   3472
   8680
 1.2152 ←— 4 decimal places
```

Remember to count decimal places in the factors to decide where to place the decimal point in the product.

Find each product.

1. 4.81 × 3.93 **2.** 7.29 × 6.38

Set E (pages 226–227)

Find the product of 0.026 × 0.4.

```
 0.026 ←— 3 decimal places
×  0.4 ←— 1 decimal place
0.0104 ←— 4 decimal places
```

Remember, if needed, write a zero in the product before placing the decimal point.

1. 0.38 × 0.2 **2.** 0.05 × 0.5

Set F (pages 230–231)

Use patterns to find each quotient.

602.41 ÷ 10 = 60.241

602.41 ÷ 100 = 6.0241

602.41 ÷ 1,000 = 0.60241

Remember to move the decimal point to the left 1 place when the divisor is 10, 2 places when it is 100, and 3 places when it is 1,000.

1. 24.8 ÷ 1,000 **2.** 79.854 ÷ 10

3. 8.3 ÷ 100 **4.** 45.1 ÷ 1,000

Set G (pages 232–234)

Find the quotient of 15.75 ÷ 21.

```
    0.75
21)15.75
   147
    105
    105
      0
```

Place the decimal point in the quotient above the decimal point in the dividend. Then divide.

Remember when the dividend is a decimal, place the decimal point in the quotient before dividing.

1. 28)1.4 **2.** 12)307.2

3. 7)52.5 **4.** 20)16.2

5. 14)170.8 **6.** 35)10.5

Set H (pages 235–237)

Divide 0.885 ÷ 0.15.

```
       5.9
0.15)0.885
      75
      135
      135
        0
```

Multiply the divisor and the dividend by 100. Place the decimal point in the quotient. Then divide.

Remember to change a decimal divisor to a whole number divisor by multiplying the divisor and the dividend by a power of 10.

1. 0.066 ÷ 0.12 **2.** 43.928 ÷ 2.89

3. 2.664 ÷ 0.36 **4.** 54.36 ÷ 6.04

Set I (pages 238–239)

Evaluate the expression 22.2x for x = 0.008, x = 0.9, x = 10.3.

22.2 × 0.008 = 0.1776

22.2 × 0.9 = 19.98

22.2 × 10.3 = 228.66

Remember to place the decimal point correctly in each answer.

Evaluate each expression for x = 0.04, x = 12.2 and x = 6.132.

1. $x + 2.3$ **2.** $3x - 0.01$

3. $5x$ **4.** $x \div 2$

More Practice

Set A *(pages 214–215)*

Algebra Find each n.

1. $3.21 \times n = 32.1$
2. $0.8 \times 1{,}000 = n$
3. $2.01 \times n = 201$
4. $0.31 \times 10 = n$
5. $n \times 2.16 = 216$
6. $3.75 \times 1 = n$
7. Dave earns $5.50 a week for walking the neighbor's dog every day after school. How much will he have earned after walking the dog for 10 weeks?

Set B *(pages 216–217)*

Multiply.

1. 13.3×4
2. 64.5×8
3. 88.8×3
4. 0.37×9
5. 2.09×7
6. 28.9×5
7. 77.8×9
8. 2.09×58
9. 9.99×18
10. 4.6×27
11. Marco spends $1.25 on a pretzel each day after school. How much will he spend on pretzels if he buys one every day for nine days?

Set C *(pages 218–219)*

Estimate each product.

1. 3.6×9
2. 8.4×3
3. 5.8×6
4. 9.4×22
5. 13.8×19
6. 47×8.5
7. 28.7×25
8. 0.13×27
9. **Using Estimation** Josh buys two posters for $9.96 each and three posters for $5.75 each. About how much change should Josh get back if he gives the salesperson two $20 bills?

Set D *(pages 222–224)*

1. 6.29×3.7
2. 4.7×9.02
3. 28.43×9.1
4. 31.6×2.5
5. 9.33×4.72
6. 6.38×4.59
7. 8.62×3.11
8. 17.1×2.4
9. Audrey works in the school bookstore. If she works 0.75 hour each day, how many minutes each day does she work?

Set E (pages 226–227)

1. 0.6×0.08
2. 0.3×0.04
3. 0.4×0.11
4. 0.05×0.07
5. Tyrone is participating in a walkathon for charity. Twelve people each pledge $1.25 for each mile he walks. How much will he earn for the charity if he walks 2.5 miles?

Set F (pages 230–231)

1. $26.5 \div 10$
2. $3.002 \div 100$
3. $19.5 \div 10$
4. $28.46 \div 100$
5. A total of $2,565.00 was donated by 100 area merchants for the school dance. On average, how much did each merchant donate?

Set G (pages 232–234)

1. $25.92 \div 8$
2. $61.2 \div 9$
3. $80.4 \div 6$
4. $0.56 \div 7$
5. $28\overline{)303.24}$
6. $15\overline{)637.65}$
7. $12\overline{)3.72}$
8. $32\overline{)601.6}$
9. A package of six pens costs $2.94. Individual pens can also be bought for 60 cents each. How much will you save by buying a package rather than six individual pens? Explain.

Set H (pages 235–237)

Tell what power of ten you would use to make the divisor a whole number. Then divide.

1. $2.8548 \div 0.156$
2. $1.092 \div 1.56$
3. $25.2 \div 1.8$
4. $2.26 \div 0.4$
5. Dr. Gonzalez collected 0.005-gram samples of sludge to study under her microscope. The total weight of the samples was 0.3 gram. How many samples did she collect?

Set I (pages 238–239)

Evaluate each expression for $x = 0.05$, $x = 1.3$, $x = 12.46$.

1. $20.2 - x$
2. $x \div 0.2$
3. $9.13x$
4. $0.002x$
5. Kaye's phone bill is calculated using the formula $\$25.43 + \$0.10x$. What is Kaye's bill if $x = 110.5$, $x = 52.5$, and $x = 15$?

TEST PREP

Problem Solving: Preparing for Tests

Choose the correct letter for each answer.

---

1. Eric was numbering the squares on a board for a game he had invented. The first four squares were numbered 1,221; 2,332; 3,443; 4,554. If he used the same pattern to number all the squares on the board, which two numbers might be included?

A 5,665 and 9,889

B 5,665 and 8,998

C 6,556 and 9,889

D 6,556 and 8,998

Tip

Use one of these strategies to solve this problem.

- *Find a Pattern*
- *Make a List*
- *Use Logical Reasoning*

---

2. Kate paid $7.98 for 5 pounds of chicken wings. Which is a reasonable estimate for the cost of 3 pounds of chicken wings?

F About $2

G About $3

H About $5

J About $7

Tip

When solving multiple-choice problems, you can sometimes eliminate one or more answer choices.

---

3. Mandy's computer uses 0.15 kilowatt of electricity per hour. On Sunday she used her computer for 3.2 hours in the morning and 1.85 hours in the afternoon. Which number sentence could be used to find the amount of electricity, *n*, her computer used on Sunday?

A $3.2 \times 1.85 \times 0.15 = n$

B $3.2 + (1.85 \times 0.15) = n$

C $(3.2 \times 1.85) + 0.15 = n$

D $(3.2 + 1.85) \times 0.15 = n$

Tip

When more than one step is needed to solve a problem, you must decide which step to do first.

4. **What is two times 72,000 ÷ 8? Use the pattern to help you.**

$$72 \div 8 = 9$$
$$720 \div 8 = 90$$
$$7{,}200 \div 8 = 900$$

F 900 **H** 9,999
G 1,800 **J** 18,000

5. **Matt needs 560 centimeters of chain to make 8 key chains. It takes him 15 minutes to make one key chain. If 25 centimeters of chain costs 39¢, how much will Matt spend for the chain he needs?**

A $2.18
B $8.58
C $8.74
D $17.47

6. **Diane and 3 friends bought a $48 sweater for Susan. They shared the cost equally. How could you find Diane's share of the cost?**

F Multiply $48 by 3.
G Multiply $48 by 4.
H Divide $48 by 3.
J Divide $48 by 4.

7. **Kim lives 0.7 of the distance that Ari does from the school. Ari lives 3.14 kilometers from the school. Which is the best estimate of how far Kim lives from the school?**

A 21 km **C** 2 km
B 4 km **D** 0.5 km

8. **The graph shows the different animals that came to a clinic in May.**

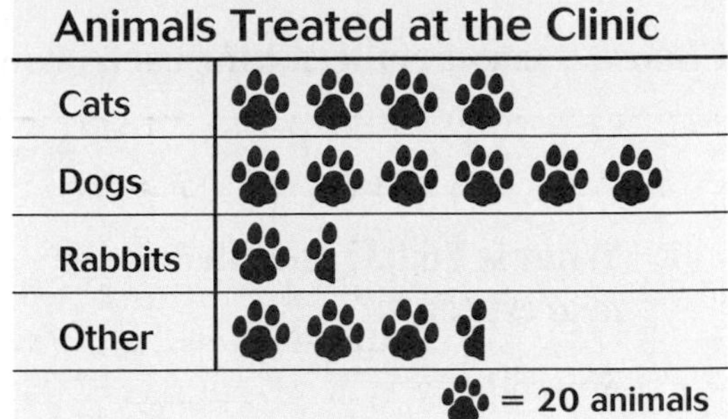

If one-third of all the animals needed medicine, how many animals did NOT need medicine?

F 78 **H** 200
G 155 **J** 310

9. **Jim bicycled 8 miles in 20 minutes. If Suki rides at the same speed as Jim for 50 minutes, which is a reasonable distance for Suki to travel?**

A 10 miles
B 20 miles
C 30 miles
D 50 miles

10. **Pam has a dog-walking service. She walks dogs for several of her customers on Saturdays. She gives each dog a treat and then walks it for 45 minutes. What else do you need to know to find out the total time Pam spends walking dogs on Saturdays?**

F The distance Pam walks each dog
G How much money Pam earns for walking each dog
H The breeds of the dogs
J The number of dogs Pam walks

TEST PREP

Multiple-Choice Cumulative Review

Choose the correct letter for each answer.

Number Sense

1. What is 76.037 rounded to the nearest tenth?

A 80
B 76.4
C 76.04
D 76.0

2. Which of these numbers is 5,890 when rounded to the nearest ten and 5,900 when rounded to the nearest hundred?

F 5,809
G 5,879
H 5,887
J 5,896

3. Which number sentence is NOT true?

A $11.011 < 11.110$
B $9.011 < 9.101$
C $1.289 < 1.199$
D $0.0099 < 0.0988$

4. Which decimal is shown by the shaded part of the grid?

F 4.40
G 0.44
H 0.044
J 0.0044

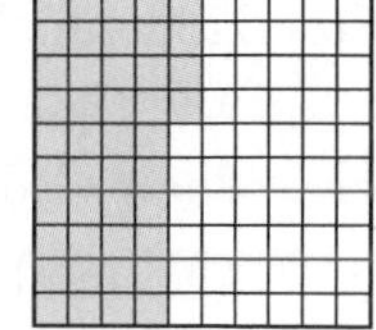

5. What number is the product of 0.473×100?

A 0.0473
B 0.473
C 4.730
D 47.30

6. Jeff runs 14 laps a day in the gym for 20 days. Then he runs 16 laps a day for 10 days. How many laps does he run in the 30 days?

F 160
G 280
H 440
J 520

7. You can buy 10 replacement discs for the Dazer Disc toy for $13.50. How much does each disc cost?

A $135.00
B $1.35
C $0.35
D $0.14

8. Tia rode her bike 2.6 miles on Friday, 4.5 miles on Saturday, and 2.8 miles on Sunday. How many more miles did she ride on Saturday than on Sunday?

F 1.9 mi
G 1.7 mi
H 0.8 mi
J 0.7 mi

Algebra and Functions

9. Which illustrates the identity property of addition?

A $26 + 14 = 14 + 26$

B $45 \times 0 = 0$

C $84 + 0 = 84$

D $9 + (3 + 4) = (9 + 3) + 4$

10. Evaluate $\frac{n}{4} + 6$ when $n = 6.4$.

F 31.6

G 14.0

H 7.6

J 0.64

11. Study the table shown below. Which of the following is the rule?

A Multiply by 10.

B Divide by 10.

C Multiply by 100.

D Divide by 100.

Rule: ?	
12.5	1.25
5.25	0.525
0.55	0.055

12. There are 3.4 grams of fat in a 1-ounce serving of frozen yogurt. Which equation shows how many grams of fat are in a 2.5-ounce serving?

F $3.4 + 2.5 = n$

G $3.4 \times 2.5 = n$

H $3.4 - 2.5 = n$

J $3.4 \div 3.5 = n$

13. Which describes the inverse of dividing by 3?

A Subtracting 3

B Multiplying by 3

C Adding 3

D Dividing by 0.3

14. Which describes the first step to evaluate the following expression?

$$112 - 3 \times 6 - 10$$

F Subtract 3 from 112.

G Add 6 and 10.

H Multiply 3 and 6.

J Subtract 10 from 112.

15. Cal said, " I am thinking of a number. If I add 9 to it, I get 31." What is Cal's number?

A 40

B 39

C 24

D 22

16. If $49x = 352.8$, then $x =$

F 7.2

G 303.8

H 401.8

J 17,287.20

Fraction Concepts

Diagnosing Readiness

In Chapter 7, you will use these skills:

Ⓐ Place Value to Thousandths

(pages 8–9)

Write the short-word form for the value of the underlined digit.

1. $4.2\underline{8}5$ **2.** $8.90\underline{7}$

3. $0.\underline{5}29$ **4.** $0.4\underline{6}$

Write the word name for each decimal.

5. 0.37 **6.** 0.042

7. 3.109 **8.** 5.6

Ⓑ Multiplying Whole Numbers

(pages 140–142)

9. 5×32 **10.** 6×28

11. 3×45 **12.** 4×50

13. 7×17 **14.** 2×31

15. $2 \times 2 \times 3 \times 5 \times 7$

16. $3 \times 3 \times 5 \times 5 \times 11$

17. Kobe read 24 pages a day for 6 days. How many pages did he read?

C Exponents

(pages 148–149)

Write each in standard form.

18. 2^3

19. 5^2

20. 3^4

21. 7^2

22. $2^2 \times 11$

23. $3^2 \times 5$

24. $6^2 \times 2$

25. $3^3 \times 6$

26. A square lawn measures 10 feet on each side. The area of the lawn can be found by multiplying 10 and 10. Write the product using an exponent.

D Dividing Whole Numbers

(pages 172–174)

27. $51 \div 3$

28. $638 \div 2$

29. $435 \div 5$

30. $217 \div 7$

31. $85{,}272 \div 2$

32. $7{,}406 \div 7$

33. $2{,}640 \div 5$

34. $2{,}640 \div 3$

35. $6{,}582 \div 3$

36. $6{,}582 \div 2$

37. $15{,}000 \div 3$

38. $32{,}580 \div 5$

39. A country club used 161 tennis balls in a week. What was the average number of balls used a day?

E Solving Multiplication Equations

(pages 196–197)

Solve each equation.

40. $2x = 48$

41. $5y = 45$

42. $7n = 42$

43. $3m = 48$

44. $5x = 105$

45. $2n = 64$

46. $7z = 56$

47. $3x = 66$

48. $5x = 55$

49. $2m = 84$

50. Tell what you would do to get y in $\frac{y}{9} = 7$ alone.

F Evaluating Expressions with Whole Numbers

(pages 130–131)

Find the value of each expression.

51. $2 \times 3 \times n$ when $n = 5$

52. $3 \times n \times 5 \times 5$ when $n = 3$

53. $n \times 3 \times 7$ when $n = 2$

54. $n \times 4 \times 6$ when $n = 3$

55. $8 \times n \times 2$ when $n = 5$

56. $9 \times 2 \times n \times 3$ when $n = 1$

To the Family and Student

Looking Back	Chapter 7	Looking Ahead
In Grade 4, students learned how to identify parts of a whole and parts of a set. They also learned how to compare and order fractions.	**Fraction Concepts** In this chapter, students will learn how to find and use the greatest common factor (GCF) and least common multiple (LCM) to write equivalent fractions. They will also learn how to compare and order mixed numbers.	In Chapter 8, students will learn how to add, subtract, multiply, and divide fractions and mixed numbers.

Math and Everyday Living

Opportunities to apply the concepts of Chapter 7 abound in everyday situations. During the chapter, think about how fractions can be used to solve a variety of real-world problems. The following examples suggest just a few of the many situations that could launch a discussion about the concepts in this chapter.

Math at the Mall Which store has a bigger discount on the jeans?

Pants and Stuff
Jeans
Regular Price $19.95
SALE! $\frac{1}{3}$ OFF!

Math and Merchandising In a store boxes of two heights are stacked alongside each other. One stack has boxes that are all 12 inches high. The other stack has boxes that are all 15 inches high. What is the shortest height for which both stacks will be exactly the same height?

Math and Gardening You are using a container that holds 16 quarts. You have poured 12 quarts of water into the container. What part of the container has been filled? Give your answer as a fraction in simplest form and as a decimal.

Math and Cooking Matthew is making biscuits. The recipe calls for $1\frac{1}{2}$ cups of flour. He has $1\frac{1}{4}$ cups of flour. Does he have enough?

Math and Nutrition Four servings of cereal has 98 grams of carbohydrates. How many grams are there in one serving? Write your answer as a mixed number.

Math and Food You ate 5 out of 12 pieces of pizza. Did you eat more or less than half of the pizza?

Math and Baby-Sitting Mandy is baby-sitting for the 3 Smith children. She has 50 fish crackers to divide among the 3 children. How many will each child have if she divides the crackers evenly? How many will be left?

California Content Standards in Chapter 7 Lessons*

	Teach and Practice	Practice
Number Sense		
1.0 Students . . . understand the relationship between decimals, fractions	7-6	7-11
1.1 (Gr. 6) (🔑) Compare and order positive . . . fractions . . . and mixed numbers	7-12	
1.3 Understand and compute positive integer powers of nonnegative integers; compute examples as repeated multiplication.		7-2
1.4 (🔑) Determine the prime factors of all numbers through 50 and write the numbers as the product of their prime factors by using exponents to show multiples of a factor (e.g., $24 = 2 \times 2 \times 2 \times 3 = 2^3 \times 3$).	7-2	
1.5 (Gr. 4) . . . [E]xplain equivalents of fractions.	7-7, 7-8	
1.5 (🔑) Identify and represent on a number line . . . fractions, mixed numbers	7-6, 7-7, 7-9, 7-11	
2.4 (Gr. 6) (🔑) Determine the least common multiple and the greatest common divisor of whole numbers	7-3, 7-4	
4.1 (Gr. 4) Understand that many whole numbers break down in different ways (e.g., $12 = 4 \times 3 = 2 \times 6 = 2 \times 2 \times 3$).	7-1	

	Teach and Practice	Practice
Mathematical Reasoning		
1.1 Analyze problems by identifying relationships, distinguishing relevant from irrelevant information, sequencing and prioritizing information, and observing patterns.		7-3, 7-4, 7-7, 7-10
2.1 Use estimation to verify the reasonableness of calculated results.	7-5	
2.3 Use a variety of methods, such as words, numbers, symbols, charts, graphs, tables, diagrams, and models, to explain mathematical reasoning.	7-10	
2.4 Express the solution clearly and logically by using the appropriate mathematical notation and terms and clear language; support solutions with evidence in both verbal and symbolic work.	7-13	
2.6 Make precise calculations and check the validity of the results from the context of the problem.	7-5, 7-13	
3.0 Students move beyond a particular problem by generalizing to other situations.		7-12
3.2 Note the method of deriving the solution and demonstrate a conceptual understanding of the derivation by solving similar problems.		7-10
3.3 Develop generalizations of the results obtained and apply them in other circumstances.		7-1, 7-8, 7-9

* The symbol (🔑) indicates a key standard as designated in the Mathematics Framework for California Public Schools. Full statements of the California Content Standards are found at the beginning of this book following the Table of Contents.

Lesson 7-1 Factors and Divisibility

California Content Standard *Number Sense 4.1 (Grade 4): Understand that many whole numbers break down in different ways . . ..*

Warm-Up Review

Find two numbers whose product is the given number.

1. 12 **2.** 11

3. 15 **4.** 18

5. 37 **6.** 48

7. How many different ways can Lucy arrange 24 chairs in equal rows?

Math Link You know how to multiply and divide whole numbers. Now you will learn about factors and divisibility.

One number is **divisible** by another number when the quotient is a whole number and the remainder is zero.

24 is divisible by 3 because $24 \div 3 = 8$.

3 and 8 are **factors** of 24.

You can use the divisibility rules in the table below to help you find factors of a number.

Word Bank

divisible
factors

Example 1

Is 6 a factor of 288?

If 288 is divisible by 6, then 6 is a factor of 288.

Use the divisibility rule for 6.

288 is even, so it is divisible by 2.

The sum of the digits is $2 + 8 + 8 = 18$. 18 is divisible by 3, so 288 is divisible by 3.

Since 288 is divisible by 2 and by 3, it is divisible by 6.

Divisibility Rules

Divisible by	Rule
2	The number is even.
3	The sum of the digits is divisible by 3.
4	The number formed by the tens and ones digits is divisible by 4.
5	The ones digit is 0 or 5.
6	The number is divisible by 2 and 3.
9	The sum of the digits is divisible by 9.
10	The ones digit is 0.

Example 2

List all of the factors of 28.

Try 1, then 2, then 3, and so on.

Test to see if the number is a factor. If it is, notice that you have also found another factor.

After 6, the factors start repeating.

The factors of 28 are 1, 2, 4, 7, 14, and 28.

Try:	Is it a factor?	Factors:
1	Yes. $1 \times 28 = 28$	1, 28
2	Yes. $2 \times 14 = 28$	2, 14
3	No.	
4	Yes. $4 \times 7 = 28$	4, 7
5	No.	
6	No.	

 Additional Standard: Mathematical Reasoning 3.3 (See p. 257.)

Guided Practice *For another example, see Set A on p. 294.*

Mental Math Tell if each number is divisible by 2, 3, 4, 5, 6, 9, or 10.

1. 37 **2.** 250 **3.** 963 **4.** 1,248

5. List all of the factors of 56. **6.** List all of the factors of 81.

7. Math Reasoning What two numbers are always factors of a number?

Independent Practice *For more practice, see Set A on p. 297.*

Mental Math Tell if each number is divisible by 2, 3, 4, 5, 6, 9, or 10.

8. 84 **9.** 31 **10.** 138 **11.** 800

12. 720 **13.** 615 **14.** 1,920 **15.** 1,000

16. 14,935 **17.** 46,357 **18.** 78,982 **19.** 965,470

List all of the factors of each number.

20. 15 **21.** 50 **22.** 42 **23.** 13

The computer screen shows three digits of a 4-digit code. List all of the ones digits that would make the code number divisible by each given number.

24. 2 **25.** 3 **26.** 4 **27.** 5 **28.** 6 **29.** 10

Mixed Review

30. Brian's test scores are 91, 80, 95, and 88. Find his average score.

31. Evaluate $1.79 + n$ when $n = 1.6$.

32. $43.8 \div 1.5$ **33.** 0.13×0.6 **34.** $4.6 + 23.2 + 0.71$

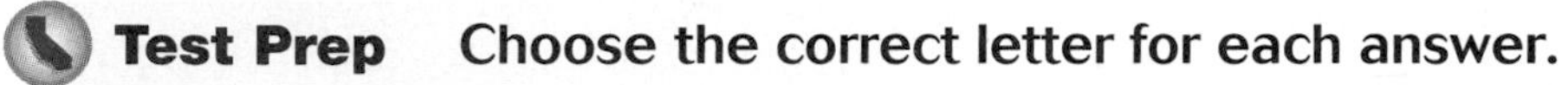

Test Prep **Choose the correct letter for each answer.**

35. $1.6 \times 0.7 =$
(6-5)

A 0.112 **C** 11.2

B 1.12 **D** 0.72

36. Which is the best estimate of $6.39 × 4?
(6-3)

F $6 **H** $18

G $28 **J** $24

LESSON 7-2

Prime Factorization

California Content Standard *Number Sense 1.4 (key): Determine the prime factors of all numbers through 50 and write the numbers as the product of their prime factors by using exponents to show multiples of a factor.*

Warm-Up Review

Write using exponents.

1. $3 \times 3 \times 3 \times 3$
2. $2 \times 2 \times 2 \times 2 \times 2 \times 2$
3. 4×4
4. $10 \times 10 \times 10$
5. It takes Pluto about 3^5 years to orbit the sun. Write this number in standard form.

Math Link You know how to find a factor of a number. Now you will learn how to find all the prime factors of a number.

A whole number greater than 1 is either **prime** or **composite**. A prime number has exactly two factors, 1 and the number itself. A composite number has more than two factors.

3 is an example of a prime number. It has only two factors, 1 and 3.

$3 = 1 \times 3$

6 is an example of a composite number.

Its factors are 1, 2, 3, and 6.

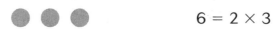

$6 = 2 \times 3$

$6 = 1 \times 6$

Example 1

List the numbers from 1 through 20. Which numbers are prime?

~~1~~ 2 3 ~~4~~ 5 ~~6~~ 7 ~~8~~ ~~9~~ ~~10~~

11 ~~12~~ 13 ~~14~~ ~~15~~ ~~16~~ 17 ~~18~~ 19 ~~20~~

Cross out 1, it is neither prime nor composite.

2 is prime. Cross out every second number after 2. These numbers are divisible by 2. So they are not prime.

3 is prime. Next cross every third number after 3. Notice that some numbers have already been crossed out since they are also divisible by 2.

5 is prime. Continue the process.

The prime numbers from 1 through 20 are 2, 3, 5, 7, 11, 13, 17, and 19.

Here's WHY It Works

Remember, a prime number has exactly 2 factors, itself and 1. Every number greater than 2 that is divisible by 2 will have at least 3 factors: 1, 2, and the number itself, so none of these numbers can be prime. Likewise, every number greater than 3 that is divisible by 3 cannot be prime and so on.

 Additional Standard: Number Sense 1.3

Every composite number greater than one can be written as a product of prime numbers. This product is the **prime factorization** of the number.

$15 = 3 \times 5$ ← 3 and 5 are prime, so 3×5 is the prime factorization of 15.

If a number only has a few factors, it is easy to find the prime factorization.

$4 = 2 \times 2 = 2^2$ $6 = 2 \times 3$ $25 = 5 \times 5 = 5^2$

For numbers with more factors, a factor tree can be helpful.

Word Bank
- prime
- composite
- prime factorization

Example 2

Use a factor tree to find the prime factorization of 380. Then write the product using exponents.

Write 380 as a product of two factors. This can be done in more than one way. Write each factor that is not prime as a product.

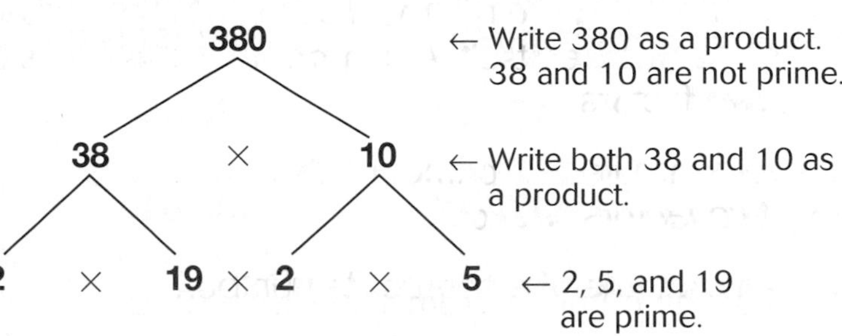

When all the branches end in prime numbers, you can write the prime factorization. The primes are usually written from least to greatest. Whenever factors appear more than once, exponents can be used.

$380 = 2 \times 2 \times 5 \times 19 = 2^2 \times 5 \times 19$

Guided Practice *For another example, see Set B on p. 294.*

Complete each factor tree. Then write the prime factorization using exponents if possible.

1. 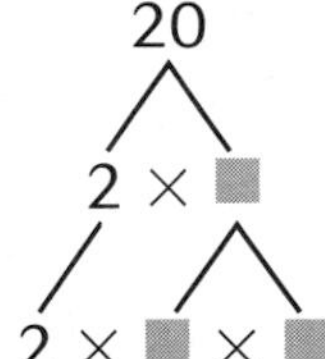

2. 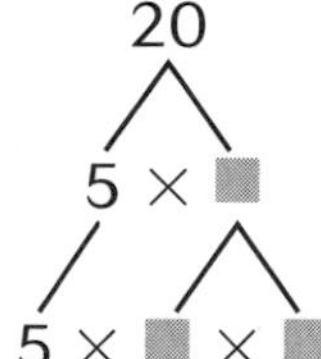

3. Math Reasoning Compare your answers for Exercises 1 and 2. Does the way that you start a factor tree change the final result?

Find the prime factorization of each composite number, using exponents when possible. If the number is prime, write *prime*.

4. 81 **5.** 42 **6.** 43 **7.** 100

Independent Practice *For more practice, see Set B on p. 297.*

Complete each factor tree. Then write the prime factorization using exponents if possible.

8. 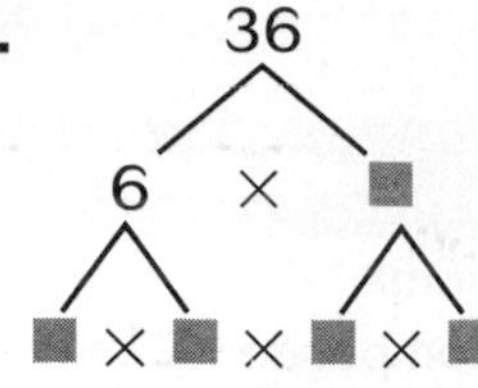

9. 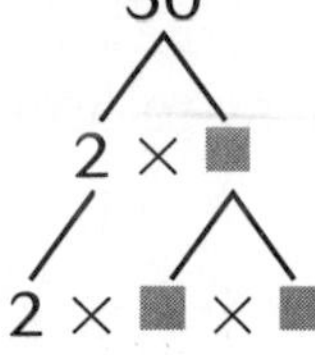

10. 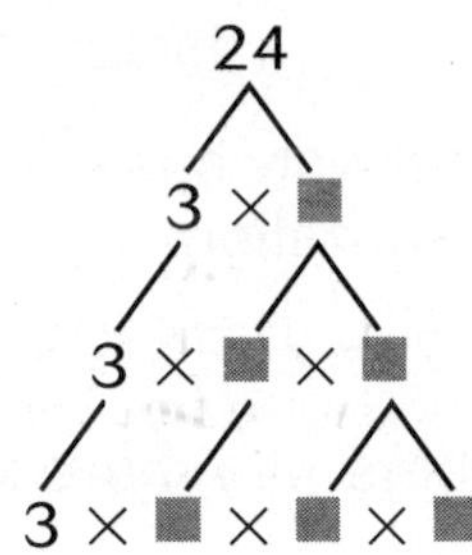

Find the prime factorization of each composite number, using exponents when possible. If the number is prime, write *prime*.

11. 37 **12.** 27 **13.** 65 **14.** 11 **15.** 9

16. 32 **17.** 47 **18.** 84 **19.** 93 **20.** 304

21. List the numbers from 1 through 50. Use the method in Example 1 to find all of the prime numbers through 50.

22. Math Reasoning Which prime numbers are even?

Mixed Review

23. Lori had $45. She bought 5 tapes for $7.95 each. The tax was $2.24. How much did Lori have left?

24. Is 414 divisible by 9? How can you tell?

25. Algebra Evaluate $31.2 \div n$ for $n = 0.6$.

26. $0.46 \times 1{,}000$ **27.** $3.8 \div 100$ **28.** $4.2 \div 8$

 **Test Prep** **Choose the correct letter for each answer.**

29. Which number is less than 0.02?
(1-4)
A 0.0002 **B** 0.2 **C** 0.022 **D** 2.02 **E** NH

30. Algebra Find $n + 6.2$ when $n = 0.8$.
(6-11)
F 7.0 **G** 5.4 **H** 14.2 **J** 2.2 **K** NH

Multiple-Choice Cumulative Review

Choose the correct letter for each answer.

1. Of the 77 entries in the parade, 13 were marching bands. How many entries were not marching bands? Solve the equation $13 + n = 77$ to find out.

A 13
B 60
C 64
D 90

2. Melissa is 5 feet 2 inches tall. Her sister is 5 feet $4\frac{1}{2}$ inches tall. Her mother is 5 feet 7 inches tall. How much shorter is Melissa than her mother?

F $2\frac{1}{2}$ inches
G 3 inches
H 5 inches
J 1 foot 5 inches

3. How many meters are in the *perimeter* of this figure?

12 cm | 7 cm | 7 cm | 15 cm

A 0.56 meters
B 0.85 meters
C 1.05 meters
D 1.80 meters

4. When $n = 15$, $n - 8 =$

F 7
G 8
H 22
J 23
K NH

5. Solve $x + 63 = 150$.

A $x = 87$
B $x = 97$
C $x = 203$
D $x = 213$
E NH

6. $30{,}000 \div 6 =$

F 50
G 500
H 5,000
J 50,000
K NH

7. $11.75 - 7.5 =$

A 3.25
B 4.25
C 11
D 19.25
E NH

8. 2,832 is NOT divisible by which of the following?

F 3
G 4
H 6
J 9

9. $43.2 \div 10 =$

A 0.432
B 4.32
C 43.2
D 432
E NH

Common Factors and GCF

California Content Standard *Number Sense 2.4 (Grade 6) (🔑): Determine . . . the greatest common divisor of whole numbers . . . .*

Math Link You know how to find the factors of a number. Now you will learn how to find common factors of two or more numbers.

Warm-Up Review

List all the factors of each number.

1. 8 **2.** 12

3. 15 **4.** 24

5. 42 **6.** 16

7. Nan has 12 daisies and 32 tulips. How many vases of 3 daisies and 8 tulips can she fill?

Word Bank

common factor

greatest common factor (GCF)

Example

Eighteen fifth graders and twenty-four 6th graders are being separated into equal groups. What is the greatest number that can be in each group if the groups of 5th graders must be the same size as the groups of 6th graders?

List all of the factors of each number. Remember to use divisibility rules.

Factors of 18: 1, 2, 3, 6, 9, 18 ← Possible sizes of equal groups of 5th graders.

Factors of 24: 1, 2, 3, 4, 6, 8, 12, 24 ← Possible sizes of equal groups of 6th graders.

Then list the **common factors,** those numbers that are in both lists of factors.

Common factors: 1, 2, 3, 6

The largest number in this list is 6. The **greatest common factor** (GCF) of 18 and 24 is 6. The greatest common factor is also called the greatest common divisor.

The greatest number that can be in each group is 6.

Guided Practice *For another example, see Set C on p. 294.*

List the factors of each number. Then find the GCF of each set of numbers.

1. 10, 12 **2.** 7, 15 **3.** 15, 20 **4.** 27, 36, 45

5. Math Reasoning Explain how the Venn diagram at the right shows the common factors of 12 and 30.

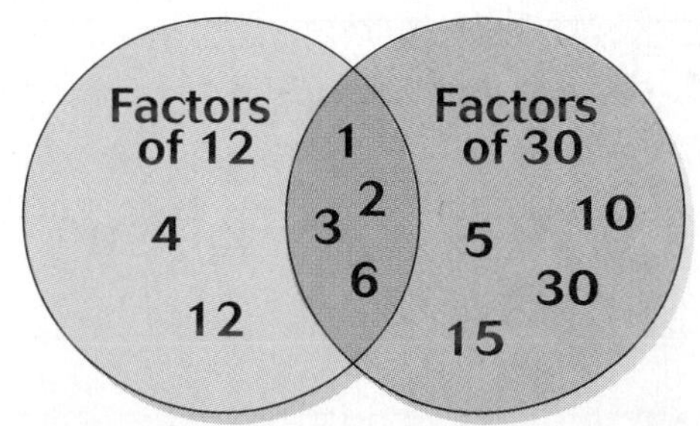

 Additional Standard: Mathematical Reasoning 1.1 (See p. 257.)

Independent Practice *For more practice, see Set C on p. 297.*

List the factors of each number. Then find the GCF of each set of numbers.

6. 14, 26 **7.** 4, 12 **8.** 8, 12 **9.** 7, 21

10. 19, 20 **11.** 25, 40 **12.** 24, 32 **13.** 16, 32

14. 18, 24 **15.** 12, 15, 24 **16.** 18, 24, 36 **17.** 24, 36, 48

18. Math Reasoning Can the GCF of a pair of numbers be equal to one of the numbers? Can it be greater than one of the numbers? Explain.

19. Draw a Venn diagram to show the factors of 16 and 36. What are the common factors? What is the greatest common factor?

20. A florist has 28 roses and 42 fern leaves. What is the greatest number of bouquets he can make with the same number of roses and the same number of leaves in each bouquet? How many roses and how many fern leaves will be in each?

21. Math Reasoning Every pair of numbers has at least one common factor. Why is this true?

Mixed Review

22. Freddy has 346 pennies and he said that he could exchange them for nickels with no pennies left over. Is he correct? Explain.

23. Is 19 prime or composite? How do you know?

24. Algebra Write an expression for 13 more than n.

25. Use the graph in Example 3 on page 99. What is the average high temperature for September 21?

Test Prep Choose the correct letter for each answer.

26. (5-6) If a cable car holds 48 people, how many cars are needed to transport 225 tourists up the mountain?

A 4 cars **C** 177 cars

B 33 cars **D** 5 cars

27. Algebra (5-12) If $n \div 9 = 27$, $n =$

F 3 **H** 243

G 216 **J** 189

Common Multiples and LCM

California Content Standard *Number Sense 2.4 (Grade 6) (key): Determine the least common multiple of whole numbers . . . .*

Warm-Up Review

Give the next five numbers in the pattern.

1. 2, 4, 6, . . .
2. 3, 6, 9, . . .
3. 7, 14, 21, . . .
4. If house numbers follow the pattern 3420, 3424, 3428 . . . , what is the next house number?

Math Link You know how to multiply whole numbers. Now you will find multiples of a number and common multiples of two or more numbers.

A **multiple** of a whole number is the product of that number and any other whole number. 21 is a multiple of 7 because $7 \times 3 = 21$. 21 is also a multiple of 3.

Word Bank

multiple
common multiple
least common multiple (LCM)

Example

After the lighting crew turns on the light panel, the red, blue, and yellow lights will appear according to the timing shown in the table. When is the first time the red and blue lights will appear together?

Color	Appears every:
Red	4 sec
Blue	6 sec
Yellow	10 sec

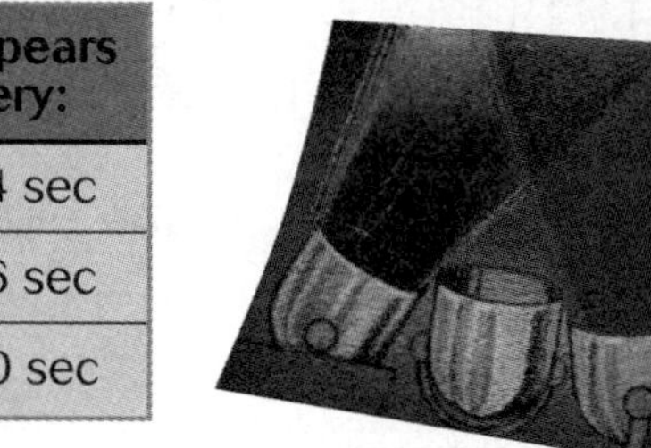

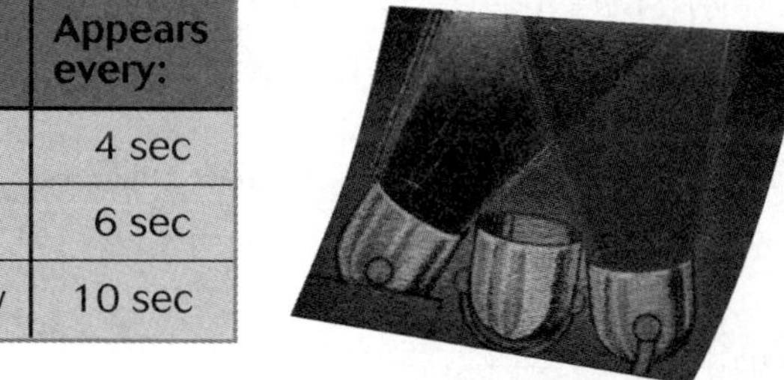

List the first several multiples of each number. Then find **common multiples** and the **least common multiple (LCM).**

Multiples of 4: 4, 8, 12, 16, 20, 24, 28, 32, 36 ← Seconds at which the red light appears.

Multiples of 6: 6, 12, 18, 24, 30, 36 ← Seconds at which the blue light appears.

Common multiples: 12, 24, 36 . . . LCM: 12

The red and blue lights will first appear together after 12 seconds.

Guided Practice *For another example, see Set D on p. 294.*

List the first seven multiples of each number. Then find the LCM of each set of numbers.

1. 12, 10
2. 5, 6
3. 3, 7
4. 9, 15
5. 8, 10, 40

6. **Math Reasoning** When is the LCM one of the numbers in the set?

 Additional Standard: Mathematical Reasoning 1.1

Independent Practice *For more practice, see Set D on p. 298.*

List the first ten multiples of each number. Then find the LCM of each set of numbers.

7. 5, 8 **8.** 6, 4 **9.** 2, 3 **10.** 6, 2

11. 2, 7 **12.** 6, 8 **13.** 4, 9 **14.** 7, 5

15. 18, 24 **16.** 2, 3, 4 **17.** 6, 9, 12 **18.** 8, 10, 16

19. Math Reasoning Look at Exercises 9, 11, and 14. What do you notice about the LCM of a pair of prime numbers?

20. Math Reasoning For any pair of numbers, can the LCM be less than one of the numbers? Can it be equal to one of the numbers?

Use the table on page 266 for Exercises 21-23.

21. When is the first time the red and yellow lights will be on at the same time?

22. When is the first time the blue and yellow lights will be on at the same time?

23. When is the first time the red, blue, and yellow lights will be on at the same time?

Mixed Review

24. The table shows the number of absences one week at Yardley School. Find the mode.

Absences - January 10–14			
	4th	5th	6th
Mon.	3	4	2
Tues.	4	1	2
Wed.	4	1	2
Thurs.	2	0	4
Fri.	0	3	2

25. Find the GCF of 30 and 36.

26. Write the prime factorization of 20.

27. 37×8 **28.** 137×42

 **Test Prep** **Choose the correct letter for each answer.**

29. Mental Math: Find $6 \times 8{,}000$.
(4-5)

A 48 **C** 4,800

B 48,000 **D** 14,000

30. Anne's test scores are 87, 81, and 93. What is her average score?
(5-9)

F 87 **H** 3

G 261 **J** 90

Problem-Solving Skill:

Reasonable Answers

Warm-Up Review

Estimate each answer.

1. 49 × 104 2. 463 ÷ 11
3. 71 × 38 4. 506 ÷ 25
5. The flea market charges from $4.95 to $25 each for old magazines. About how much would it cost to buy 21 magazines at the lowest price?

California Content Standard *Mathematical Reasoning 2.6: Make precise calculations and check the validity of the results from the context of the problem. Also Mathematical Reasoning 2.1 (See p. 257.)*

Read for Understanding

This year the Apollo School play will raise money for playground equipment. The school theater seats 580 people. Student tickets are expected to account for one half of the total ticket sales. The rest will be sold as general admission tickets. There will be two performances, and it is expected that both will sell out.

1. How many people can be seated in the theater?
2. What two types of tickets will be sold?
3. What fractional part of the ticket sales are expected to be student tickets? General admission tickets?

Think and Discuss

Reasonable Answers

It is important to know whether an answer to a problem is reasonable. If you estimate first, you can check to see if the answer is close to the estimate. If it is, then the answer is reasonable.

Reread the paragraph at the top of the page.

4. For each performance, is it reasonable to print about 200 student tickets?
5. Is it reasonable to print 325 general admission tickets for each performance?
6. How can estimation be used to see if your answer is reasonable?

Use the information on page 268 and the newspaper article at the right.

> **School Play Earns More Than $4,000!**
>
> This past weekend our local school staged a successful play! The school held two performances and sold a total of 596 general admission tickets and 528 student tickets! The school plans to donate the money to help build a new playground.

Guided Practice

1. Which sentence tells how to estimate the total amount raised from student ticket sales?
   - **a.** Multiply the approximate total number of student tickets sold by the cost of one student ticket.
   - **b.** Multiply the approximate total number of tickets sold by the number of performances.
   - **c.** Neither of the above.

2. Which expression would you use to estimate the total amount raised from student ticket sales?

   a. 2×500 **b.** $500 \times \$3$ **c.** $2 \times (500 \times \$3)$

3. Is it reasonable to say that $1,584 was made on student ticket sales?
   - **a.** No, about 2 × $1,500, or about $3,000, was made.
   - **b.** Yes, about 500 × $3, or about $1,500, was made.
   - **c.** Yes, about 1,000 tickets were sold.

Independent Practice

The producer said that the sale of general admission tickets brought in about $1,400 more than student ticket sales.

4. How can you decide if $1,400 is reasonable?
   - **a.** Estimate the number of tickets sold at the two performances.
   - **b.** Estimate the amount of money brought in at the two performances.
   - **c.** Estimate the amount of money brought in from the sale of general admission tickets and subtract the amount brought in from the sale of student tickets.

5. How much more money did the sale of general admission tickets bring in than student ticket sales? Tell how you know that your answer is reasonable.

Use Homework Workbook 7-5.

Diagnostic Checkpoint

Mental Math Tell if each number is divisible by 2, 3, 4, 5, 6, 9, or 10.

1. (7-1) 46

2. (7-1) 285

3. (7-1) 548

4. (7-1) 40,545

List all the factors of each number.

5. (7-1) 28

6. (7-1) 42

7. (7-1) 33

8. (7-1) 19

If the number is prime, write *prime.* If the number is composite, write the prime factorization of the number. If the number is *neither* prime nor composite, write *neither.*

9. (7-2) 16

10. (7-2) 37

11. (7-2) 75

12. (7-2) 84

13. (7-2) 1

14. (7-8) 42

15. (7-8) 60

16. (7-8) 48

Find the GCF of each pair of numbers.

17. (7-3) 12, 15

18. (7-3) 7, 14

19. (7-3) 21, 51

20. (7-3) 16, 25

21. (7-3) 20, 35

22. (7-3) 72, 27

23. (7-3) 8, 22

24. (7-3) 12, 30

Find the LCM for each pair of numbers.

25. (7-4) 8, 10

26. (7-4) 10, 5

27. (7-4) 4, 5

28. (7-4) 9, 12

29. (7-4) 3, 7

30. (7-4) 15, 20

31. (7-4) 14, 22

32. (7-4) 4, 28

33. (7-5) Lisa ran 12.3 miles in a charity race. Before the run, she got 5 people each to pledge 30 cents for each mile she ran. After the run, Lisa said she brought in $21 for charity. Is Lisa's number reasonable? Explain your answer.

34. (7-5) Jarod delivers newspapers each morning to 58 customers. He spends about 2 hours delivering all of the papers each morning. He figures that in 1 month he spends about an hour of delivery time on each customer. Is his number reasonable? Explain.

Stop

TEST PREP

Multiple-Choice Cumulative Review

Choose the correct letter for each answer.

1. $4.7 \times 2.1 =$

A 0.987

B 9.87

C 98.7

D 987

E NH

2. Jason needs 14 buns for himself and 6 friends. Buns come in packages of 6. How many packages should Jason buy?

F 2

G 3

H 5

J 6

3. Which sentence illustrates the commutative property of multiplication?

A $2 \times (3 + 5) = 6 + 10$

B $2 \times (3 + 5) = 2 \times (5 + 3)$

C $2 \times (3 + 5) = 2 \times 8$

D $2 \times (3 + 5) = (3 + 5) \times 2$

4. Solve $x - 5 = 7$.

F $x = 12$

G $x = 7$

H $x = 5$

J $x = 2$

5. Tell what you would do to get x alone in $7x$.

A Add 7.

B Subtract 7.

C Multiply by 7.

D Divide by 7.

Use the coordinate grid for Questions 6 and 7.

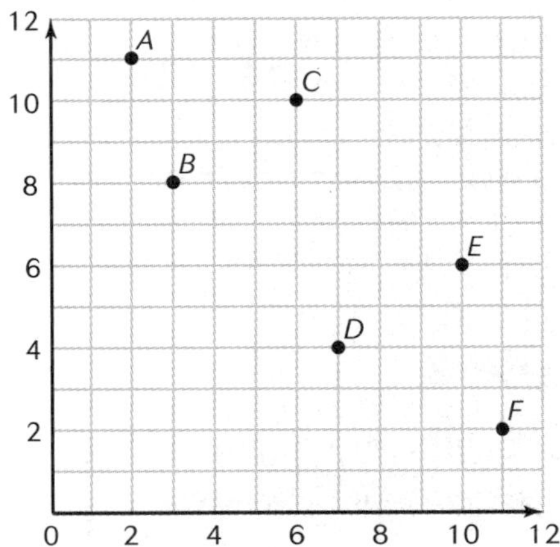

6. Which is the ordered pair for Point A?

F (3, 8)

G (8, 3)

H (2, 11)

J (11, 2)

7. Which point is located at (6, 10)?

A C

B E

C F

D B

Relating Fractions and Decimals

Warm-Up Review

Write as a decimal.

1. seven tenths.
2. one tenth
3. twenty-eight hundredths
4. four hundredths
5. Joseph walked 3 tenths of a mile north, 2 tenths of a mile east, and 3 tenths of a mile south. How far was he from his starting place?

California Content Standard *Number sense 1.0: Students . . . understand the relationship between decimals, fractions, ... Also Number Sense 1.5 (key) (See p. 257.)*

Math Link You have worked with decimals. Now you will see how decimals and fractions are related.

A **fraction** can be used to represent a part of a region or a part of a set.

Word Bank

fraction
numerator
denominator

Example 1

Less than *three tenths* of the earth's surface is land. The circle is divided into tenths. The green part shows three tenths.

Land

Water and Ice

$0.3 = \frac{3}{10}$ ← **Numerator:** number of green parts
← **Denominator:** number of equal parts

Example 2

Write a fraction and decimal for the part of the set that is yellow.

One out of four, or one fourth, of the stars are yellow.

$\frac{1}{4} = 1 \div 4 = 0.25$

Divide 1 by 4: $4\overline{)1.00}$ = 0.25

Example 3

Write a fraction and decimal that names Point D.

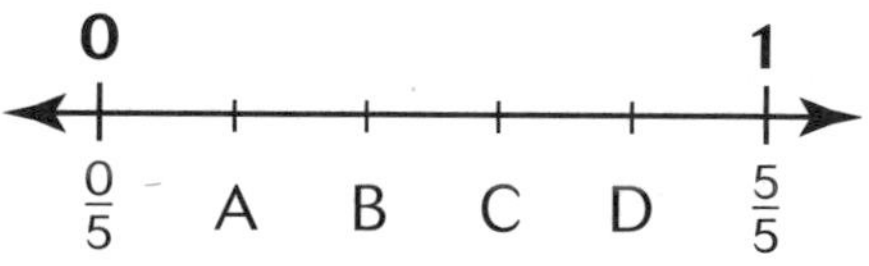

The number line is separated into fifths. Four fifths names Point D.

$\frac{4}{5} = 4 \div 5 = 0.8$

Divide 4 by 5: $5\overline{)4.0}$ = 0.8

Guided Practice

For another example, see Set E on p. 295.

Write a fraction and a decimal for each shaded part.

1.

2. 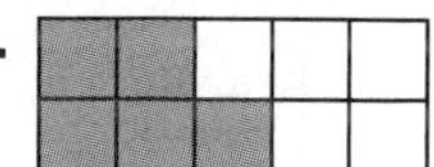

3. 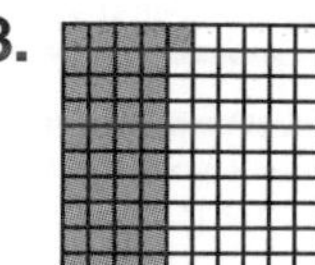

4. 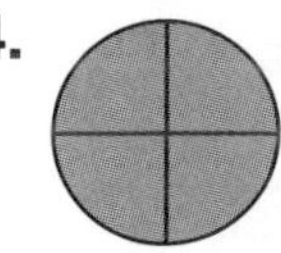

5. Write a fraction and a decimal for 15 hundredths.

Independent Practice *For more practice, see Set E on p. 298.*

Write a fraction and a decimal for each shaded part.

6. 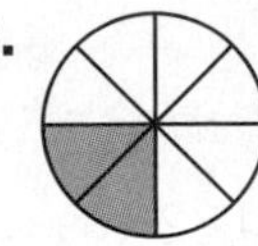

7. 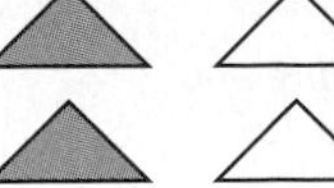

8. 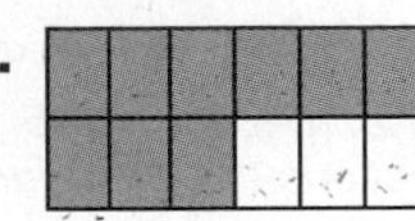

9. 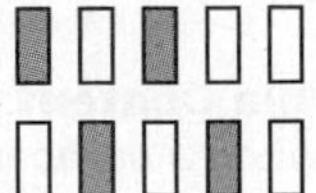

Write a fraction and a decimal to tell how much of the large square is each color.

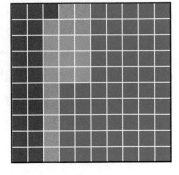

10. Red
11. Blue
12. Green
13. Yellow

Use the number line in Example 3. Write a fraction and a decimal for each of these points.

14. A
15. B
16. C

The approximate area of each continent compared to the earth's total land area is given. Write this number as a fraction and as a decimal.

17. Africa: 2 tenths
18. Asia: 3 tenths
19. Europe: 7 hundredths
20. Antarctica: 9 hundredths
21. North America: 16 hundredths
22. South America: 12 hundredths
23. Australia/Oceania: 6 hundredths

Mixed Review

24. Students are going to the science fair in two cars, each with 4 students, and two vans, each with 7 students. Write an equation that gives the total number of students going to the fair. Then find the total number.

25. Find the LCM of 16 and 24.

26. Find the GCF of 9 and 24.

27. Estimate 192×9.8.

Test Prep **Choose the correct letter for each answer.**

28. (7-2) Which shows the prime factorization of 54?

A 3×2
B 6×9
C $3^2 \times 2$
D 2×3^3
E NH

29. (5-2) The Music Club members are washing cars to raise $150. If they charge $4 to wash each car, which is the best estimate for the number of cars they have to wash?

F 400
G 40
H 100
J 30

Equivalent Fractions

California Content Standard *Number Sense 1.5. (🔑); Identify and represent on a number line . . . fractions . . .. Also Number Sense 1.5 (Grade 4) (See p. 257.)*

Warm-Up Review

Find each missing number.

1. 2 × ■ = 12
2. 4 × ■ = 12
3. 20 ÷ ■ = 5
4. If Phil divided 72 baseball cards equally among 11 friends, how many cards were left.

Math Link You know that a fraction names part of a whole or part of a set. Now you will learn how to find fractions that name the same amount.

Fractions that name the same amount are called **equivalent fractions**.

$\frac{1}{2}$ and $\frac{2}{4}$ are equivalent fractions.

0 $\frac{1}{2}$ 1

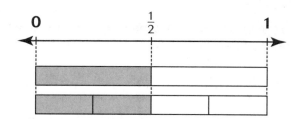

Example 1

Find equivalent fractions for $\frac{3}{4}$.

$\frac{3}{4} = \frac{3 \times \boxed{2}}{4 \times \boxed{2}} = \frac{6}{8}$

$\frac{3}{4} = \frac{3 \times \boxed{3}}{4 \times \boxed{3}} = \frac{9}{12}$

Two fractions equivalent to $\frac{3}{4}$ are $\frac{6}{8}$ and $\frac{9}{12}$.

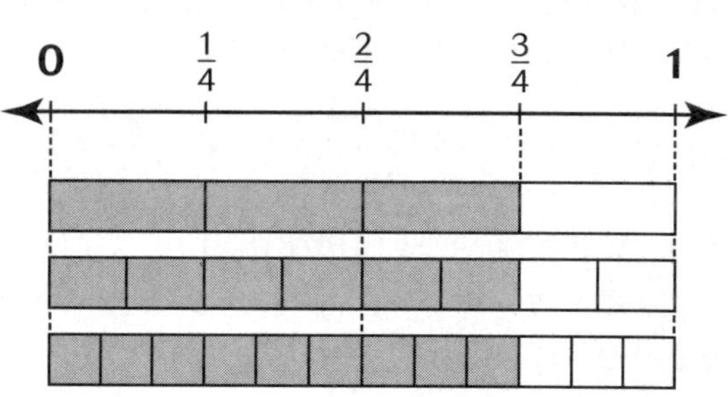

Word Bank

equivalent fractions

Example 2

Find a fraction equivalent to $\frac{5}{6}$ with a denominator of 24.

$\frac{5}{6} = \frac{■}{24}$ ← What do you multiply 6 by to get 24? Multiply 5 by the same number.

$\frac{5}{6} = \frac{5 \times \boxed{4}}{6 \times \boxed{4}} = \frac{20}{24}$, so $\frac{5}{6} = \frac{20}{24}$.

Example 3

Find a fraction equivalent to $\frac{10}{25}$ with a denominator of 5.

$\frac{10}{25} = \frac{■}{5}$ ← What do you divide 25 by to get 5? Divide 10 by the same number.

$\frac{10}{25} = \frac{10 \div \boxed{5}}{25 \div \boxed{5}} = \frac{2}{5}$, so $\frac{10}{25} = \frac{2}{5}$.

Here's WHY It Works

When you multiply or divide the numerator and denominator of a fraction by the same nonzero number, you are multiplying or dividing by 1. Multiplying or dividing by 1 does not change the original fraction.

 Additional Standard: Mathematical Reasoning 1.1 (See p. 257.)

Guided Practice *For another example, see Set F on p. 295.*

Replace each ■ with a number that will make the fractions equivalent.

1. $\frac{3}{4} = \frac{21}{\blacksquare}$ Think: $3 \times ? = 21$

2. $\frac{12}{18} = \frac{2}{\blacksquare}$ Think: $12 \div ? = 2$

3. $\frac{\blacksquare}{4} = \frac{12}{16}$ Think: $16 \div ? = 4$

4. Write the next three fractions in the pattern. $\frac{1}{3}, \frac{2}{6}, \frac{3}{9}, \ldots$

Independent Practice *For more practice, see Set F on p. 298.*

Replace each ■ with a number that will make the fractions equivalent.

5. $\frac{8}{18} = \frac{\blacksquare}{9}$ **6.** $\frac{3}{\blacksquare} = \frac{1}{8}$ **7.** $\frac{10}{12} = \frac{\blacksquare}{6}$ **8.** $\frac{11}{12} = \frac{\blacksquare}{48}$ **9.** $\frac{2}{9} = \frac{\blacksquare}{72}$

10. $\frac{\blacksquare}{21} = \frac{2}{3}$ **11.** $\frac{21}{56} = \frac{3}{\blacksquare}$ **12.** $\frac{1}{12} = \frac{\blacksquare}{60}$ **13.** $\frac{9}{27} = \frac{1}{\blacksquare}$ **14.** $\frac{40}{\blacksquare} = \frac{5}{7}$

15. $\frac{7}{8} = \frac{\blacksquare}{32}$ **16.** $\frac{3}{7} = \frac{21}{\blacksquare}$ **17.** $\frac{17}{51} = \frac{1}{\blacksquare}$ **18.** $\frac{54}{60} = \frac{9}{\blacksquare}$ **19.** $\frac{36}{72} = \frac{1}{\blacksquare}$

Write the next three fractions in each pattern.

20. $\frac{3}{8}, \frac{6}{16}, \frac{9}{24}, \ldots$ **21.** $\frac{5}{100}, \frac{10}{200}, \frac{15}{300}, \ldots$ **22.** $\frac{32}{128}, \frac{16}{64}, \frac{8}{32}, \ldots$

23. Math Reasoning Look back at Exercise 20. Write a rule to find any fraction in the pattern. Then use the rule to find the 11th fraction.

Mixed Review

24. Algebra Write and solve an equation to solve this problem. Jamie is 62 inches tall. She is 8 inches taller than Crystal. How tall is Crystal?

25. Write a fraction and a decimal for two tenths.

26. Find the LCM of 6 and 27.

Test Prep **Choose the correct letter for each answer.**

27. Write 3^3 in standard form.
(4-10)

A 9 **C** 27

B 3 **D** 6

28. Find n: $3 \times (6 + 4) = n$
(4-2)

F 22 **H** 13

G 18 **J** 30

Use Homework Workbook 7-7.

LESSON 7-8

Fractions in Simplest Form

California Content Standard *Number Sense 1.5 (Grade 4) . . . [E]xplain equivalents of fractions.*

Warm-Up Review

Find the GCF of each pair of numbers.

1. 18, 27
2. 6, 16
3. 15, 24
4. 48, 54
5. 27, 54
6. 45, 63
7. What is the least number of pennies that can be exchanged for either dimes or quarters with no pennies left over?

Word Bank

simplest form

Math Link Given a fraction, you know how to find an equivalent fraction. You also know how to find the GCF of two numbers. Now you will use this skill to name a fraction using the least possible numbers as the numerator and denominator.

$$\frac{1}{2} = \frac{2}{4} = \frac{3}{6} = \frac{4}{8} = \frac{5}{10}$$

All of the fractions above are equivalent to $\frac{1}{2}$. But only the fraction $\frac{1}{2}$ is in **simplest form** because the greatest common factor (GCF) of 1 and 2 is 1.

Example

Write $\frac{12}{18}$ in simplest form.

Step 1 Find the greatest common factor (GCF) of the numerator and denominator.

Factors of 12: 1, 2, 3, 4, 6, 12
Factors of 18: 1, 2, 3, 6, 9, 18
GCF: 6

Step 2 Divide both the numerator and the denominator by the GCF.

$$\frac{12 \div 6}{18 \div 6} = \frac{2}{3}$$

A fraction is in simplest form when the GCF of the numerator and the denominator is 1.

$\frac{2}{3}$ is the simplest form of $\frac{12}{18}$ because the GCF of 2 and 3 is 1.

Guided Practice

For another example, see Set G on p. 295.

Write each fraction in simplest form. Some of the fractions may already be in simplest form.

1. $\frac{8}{20}$
2. $\frac{3}{63}$
3. $\frac{4}{7}$
4. $\frac{8}{19}$
5. $\frac{50}{90}$
6. $\frac{5}{11}$

Additional Standard: Mathematical Reasoning 3.3 (See p. 257.)

7. Math Reasoning Dan noticed that both the numerator and the denominator of $\frac{6}{24}$ are even, so he divided by 2 to get $\frac{3}{12}$. Explain why the fraction is not yet in simplest form. What can Dan do now to find the simplest form?

Independent Practice

For more practice, see Set G on p. 298.

Write each fraction in simplest form. Some of the fractions may already be in simplest form.

8. $\frac{9}{12}$ **9.** $\frac{4}{8}$ **10.** $\frac{3}{14}$ **11.** $\frac{8}{18}$ **12.** $\frac{99}{100}$ **13.** $\frac{35}{70}$

14. $\frac{3}{9}$ **15.** $\frac{4}{5}$ **16.** $\frac{2}{3}$ **17.** $\frac{15}{25}$ **18.** $\frac{12}{48}$ **19.** $\frac{18}{20}$

20. $\frac{1}{7}$ **21.** $\frac{3}{12}$ **22.** $\frac{100}{100}$ **23.** $\frac{16}{24}$ **24.** $\frac{30}{50}$ **25.** $\frac{11}{13}$

Math Reasoning **Try different fractions to test each statement. Then write *true* or *false*.**

26. When the numerator is 1, the fraction is in simplest form.

27. When the numerator is not 1, the fraction is not in simplest form.

28. When the denominator is a multiple of the numerator, the fraction is not in simplest form.

29. When the numerator and denominator are different prime numbers, the fraction is in simplest form.

Mixed Review

30. The heights of the starters on the basketball team are 69 in., 70 in., 60 in., 71 in. and 70 in. What is the median height?

31. $\frac{3}{4} = \frac{■}{20}$

32. Write 3 hundredths as a fraction and as a decimal.

Test Prep **Choose the correct letter for each answer.**

33. (2-11) Gil made purchases of $1.19 and 89¢. The tax was 12¢. How much change did he receive from $5?

A $2.20 **C** $2.08

B $2.92 **D** $2.80

34. (5-5) 517 ÷ 32 =

F 16 **J** 16R5

G 17 **K** NH

H 19R9

Relating Fractions to One Half

Warm-Up Review

Divide by 2 to find half of each number.

1. 42 **2.** 26

3. 94 **4.** 136

5. 27 **6.** 81

7. Can 49 students be divided evenly into two groups? Why or why not.

California Content Standard *Number Sense 1.5 (key): Identify and represent on the number line . . . fractions . . . .*

Math Link You know that fractions describe part of a whole or part of a set. Now you will determine if the fractions describe more than $\frac{1}{2}$ or less than $\frac{1}{2}$.

You can use a number line to compare fractions to $\frac{1}{2}$. Look at the fractions for sixths.

- The numerator of a fraction that is equal to $\frac{1}{2}$ is half the denominator.
- The numerator of a fraction that is less than $\frac{1}{2}$ is less than half the denominator.
- The numerator of a fraction that is greater than $\frac{1}{2}$ is greater than half the denominator.

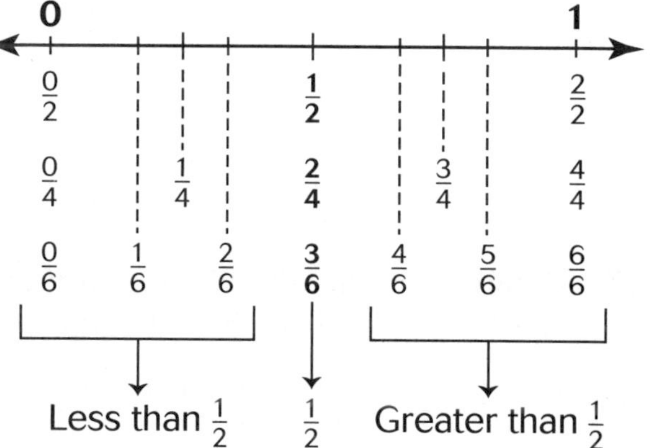

Example 1

Is $\frac{11}{16}$ greater than or less than $\frac{1}{2}$?

$16 \div 2 = 8$, $11 > 8$ so $\frac{11}{16} > \frac{1}{2}$.

Example 2

Is $\frac{23}{50}$ greater than or less than $\frac{1}{2}$?

$50 \div 2 = 25$, $23 < 25$, so $\frac{23}{50} < \frac{1}{2}$.

Guided Practice *For another example, see Set H on p. 296.*

Compare. Write >, <, or = for each ●.

1. $\frac{2}{3}$ ● $\frac{1}{2}$ **2.** $\frac{4}{8}$ ● $\frac{1}{2}$ **3.** $\frac{1}{3}$ ● $\frac{1}{2}$ **4.** $\frac{11}{12}$ ● $\frac{1}{2}$ **5.** $\frac{1}{8}$ ● $\frac{1}{2}$

Write four fractions with a denominator of 10 that are:

6. Greater than $\frac{1}{2}$.

7. Less than $\frac{1}{2}$.

8. Use the number line. Write a fraction equivalent to 1 with a denominator of 6. Write a fraction equivalent to 0 with a denominator of 6.

 Additional Standard: Mathematical Reasoning 3.3 (See p. 257.)

Independent Practice *For more practice, see Set H on p. 299.*

Compare. Write >, <, or = for each ●.

9. $\frac{3}{4}$ ● $\frac{1}{2}$ **10.** $\frac{5}{6}$ ● $\frac{1}{2}$ **11.** $\frac{1}{3}$ ● $\frac{1}{2}$ **12.** $\frac{5}{10}$ ● $\frac{1}{2}$ **13.** $\frac{9}{10}$ ● $\frac{1}{2}$

14. $\frac{3}{7}$ ● $\frac{1}{2}$ **15.** $\frac{2}{8}$ ● $\frac{1}{2}$ **16.** $\frac{2}{9}$ ● $\frac{1}{2}$ **17.** $\frac{7}{14}$ ● $\frac{1}{2}$ **18.** $\frac{4}{11}$ ● $\frac{1}{2}$

19. $\frac{5}{9}$ ● $\frac{1}{2}$ **20.** $\frac{3}{6}$ ● $\frac{1}{2}$ **21.** $\frac{5}{12}$ ● $\frac{1}{2}$ **22.** $\frac{3}{8}$ ● $\frac{1}{2}$ **23.** $\frac{25}{50}$ ● $\frac{1}{2}$

24. Of the 374 students in Grant School, 185 are boys. Do the boys represent more than $\frac{1}{2}$, less than $\frac{1}{2}$, or exactly $\frac{1}{2}$ of the total number of students in the school?

25. Give five fractions that are equivalent to 1.

26. Math Reasoning How can you tell if a fraction is equivalent to 1?

27. Give five fractions that are equivalent to 0.

28. Math Reasoning How can you tell if a fraction is equivalent to 0?

Mixed Review

29. The weights of three different vegetables being weighed were 6.2 ounces, 6.25 ounces, and 6.19 ounces. Order these numbers from least to greatest.

30. Write $\frac{12}{16}$ in simplest form.

31. Find the missing number: $\frac{10}{15} = \frac{■}{3}$

32. 4.6 × 57 **33.** 2.06 − 0.79 **34.** 18.8 ÷ 0.2 **35.** 213.6 + 0.77

Test Prep **Choose the correct letter for each answer.**

36. What digit is in the hundred thousands place of 4,231,805?
(1-1)

A 2 **C** 3
B 4 **D** 1

37. 0.33 × 0.2 =
(6-6)

F 0.66 **J** 0.066
G 6.6 **K** NH
H 0.06

Understand
Plan
Solve
Look Back

Problem-Solving Strategy:
Make a List

 **California Content Standard** *Mathematical Reasoning 2.3: Use a variety of methods, such as words, numbers, symbols, charts, graphs, tables, diagrams, and models to explain mathematical reasoning.*

Warm-Up Review

List all of the factors of each number.

1. 15 **2.** 8 **3.** 21

4. 16 **5.** 3 **6.** 33

7. How many ways can 24 students separate into equal groups of at least 3 but less than 10?

Example

The Drama Club members wrote a play about visiting a tropical island. They made the three props shown. In how many different ways can they line the props up across the back of the stage?

Understand

What do you need to find?

You need to find the different ways the props can be lined up.

Plan

How can you solve the problem?

You can **make a list** of all the possible ways to line up the props.

Solve

sun	boat	tree
sun	tree	boat
boat	sun	tree
boat	tree	sun
tree	sun	boat
tree	boat	sun

Make sure that your arrangements are all different.

There are six different ways the props can be lined up.

Look Back

Is there any other way in which the three props can be arranged in a row?

  *Additional Standards: Mathematical Reasoning 1.1, 3.2*

Guided Practice

Make a list to solve each problem.

1. A trio has three singers: a soprano, tenor, and bass. List the different ways the three singers can stand together in a row. Use S for soprano, T for tenor, and B for bass. How many ways are there?

2. There are twenty-four different ways that Ann, Barbara, Carol, and Denise can stand in the cafeteria line. Use A for Ann, B for Barbara, C for Carol, D for Denise, and list the ways.

3. List the different ways that a 4-digit code can be made using the digits 1, 2, 3, and 4, if the first digit must be 1. A digit cannot be repeated in the code. How many ways are there?

Independent Practice

Make a list to solve each problem.

4. Sue is printing programs on white and yellow paper. The school logo on the program can be black, brown, blue or green. How many different programs can she create?

5. How many different outfits can be made with black, navy, or gray pants and a white, tan, or blue top?

Mixed Review

Try these or other strategies to solve each problem. Tell which strategy you used.

Problem-Solving Strategies

- *Draw a Diagram*
- *Write an Equation*
- *Work Backward*
- *Make a Graph*
- *Make a List*
- *Find a Pattern*

6. Of 35 students in the play, 6 have speaking parts, 4 times that number are extras, and the rest are singers. How many are singers?

7. Gene sold eight student tickets for \$3.50 each and four adult tickets for \$5.75 each. How much money did Gene collect?

8. Six people are sitting at a round table. Mary is at Todd's right. Todd is directly across from Lisa. Beth is not next to Lisa, but she is next to Alan. Don is between Mary and Lisa. Who is at Lisa's right?

Use Homework Workbook 7-10.

LESSON 7-11

Fractions Greater Than One

California Content Standard *Number Sense 1.5 (🔑): Identify and represent on the number line . . . fractions, mixed numbers . . ..*

Math Link You have worked with fractions equal to or less than one. Now you will study fractions greater than one.

Warm-Up Review

Compare. Replace ● with >, <, or =.

1. 6.01 ● 6.1
2. 0.398 ● 0.4
3. 10.5 ● 10.05
4. 0.2 ● 0.20
5. Mr. Lough walks 2.7 miles each day. Does he walk more or less than 20 miles a week?

The picture shows 11 students sitting in the auditorium.

They fill one row of 8 and $\frac{3}{8}$ of another row.

$\frac{11}{8} = \frac{8}{8} + \frac{3}{8} = 1\frac{3}{8}$

A **mixed number** is a number written as a whole number and a fraction. → $1\frac{3}{8}$

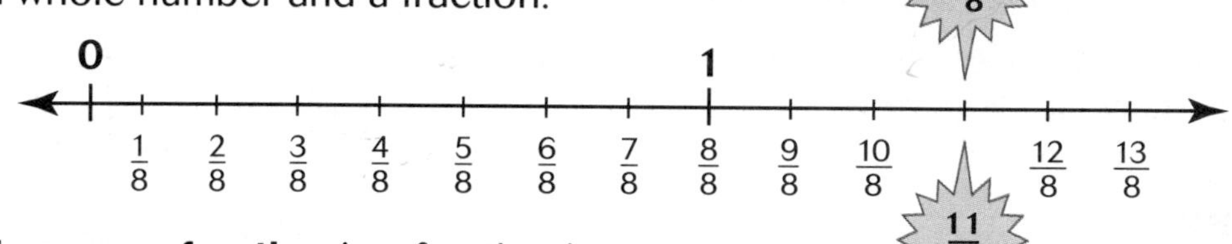

An **improper fraction** is a fraction in which the numerator is greater than or equal to the denominator. → $\frac{11}{8}$

Word Bank

mixed number
improper fraction

Example 1

Write $\frac{16}{6}$ as a mixed number.

Since $\frac{16}{6}$ means $16 \div 6$, use division to change an improper fraction to a mixed number. Express the remainder by using a fraction in simplest form.

$$\frac{16}{6} \rightarrow 6\overline{)16} \text{ quotient } 2,\ -12 = 4 \rightarrow 6\overline{)16} \text{ quotient } 2\tfrac{4}{6},\ -12 = 4;\quad 2\frac{4}{6} = 2\frac{2}{3}$$

Example 2

Write $2\frac{3}{5}$ as an improper fraction.

- Multiply the denominator by the whole number and add the numerator.
- Write the sum over the denominator.

$10 + 3 = 13$

$2\frac{3}{5} \rightarrow 2\frac{3}{5} \rightarrow 2\frac{3}{5} \rightarrow \frac{13}{5}$

$5 \times 2 = 10$

Here's WHY It Works

$2 \times 5 + 3 = 13$

$2\frac{3}{5} = \frac{5}{5} + \frac{5}{5} + \frac{3}{5} = \frac{13}{5}$

Additional Standard: Number Sense 1.0 (See p. 257.)

Guided Practice *For another example, see Set I on p. 296.*

Write each mixed number as an improper fraction.
Write each improper fraction as a mixed number.

1. $\frac{7}{3}$ **2.** $\frac{5}{2}$ **3.** $\frac{23}{5}$ **4.** $5\frac{2}{3}$ **5.** $6\frac{3}{8}$ **6.** $1\frac{15}{16}$

7. Math Reasoning How can you decide if a fraction is less than 1, equal to 1, or greater than 1?

Independent Practice *For more practice, see Set I on p. 299.*

Write each mixed number as an improper fraction.
Write each improper fraction as a mixed number.

8. $1\frac{1}{2}$ **9.** $1\frac{2}{3}$ **10.** $2\frac{3}{8}$ **11.** $2\frac{1}{4}$ **12.** $3\frac{1}{3}$ **13.** $6\frac{2}{7}$

14. $\frac{12}{10}$ **15.** $\frac{25}{8}$ **16.** $\frac{74}{9}$ **17.** $\frac{48}{5}$ **18.** $\frac{29}{2}$ **19.** $\frac{13}{10}$

Compare. Write >, <, or = for each ●.

20. $\frac{3}{8}$ ● 1 **21.** $\frac{4}{4}$ ● 1 **22.** $\frac{7}{2}$ ● 1 **23.** $\frac{8}{6}$ ● 1 **24.** $\frac{13}{5}$ ● 1

25. $\frac{1}{8}$ ● 1 **26.** $\frac{8}{1}$ ● 1 **27.** $\frac{9}{9}$ ● 1 **28.** $\frac{2}{5}$ ● 1 **29.** $\frac{5}{5}$ ● 1

30. You have learned to express a remainder by using a fraction, a decimal, or a whole number. Use 21 ÷ 4 and give an example of each way to express the remainder.

31. Math Reasoning Write 3 as a fraction with a denominator of 5.

Mixed Review

32. Mental Math Two hundred eighty days is how many weeks?

33. Write $\frac{5}{20}$ in simplest form.

34. Replace ● with > or <: $\frac{1}{2}$ ● $\frac{11}{21}$.

Test Prep **Choose the correct letter for each answer.**

35. Solve $n - 89 = 200$.
(2-6)

A $n = 111$ C $n = 211$
B $n = 189$ D $n = 289$

36. 12,261 + 9,187 =
(2-9)

F 21,448 H 11,348
G 21,348 J 3,074

Use Homework Workbook 7-11.

Comparing and Ordering Fractions and Mixed Numbers

California Content Standard *Number Sense 1.1 (Grade 6) (🔑): Compare and order positive . . . fractions . . . and mixed numbers . . . .*

Math Link You know how to compare and order whole numbers and decimals. Now you will compare and order fractions and mixed numbers.

To compare fractions and mixed numbers express the fractions with their **least common denominator (LCD)**. Then compare the numerators.

The distances three joggers covered in 30 minutes are marked on the number line.

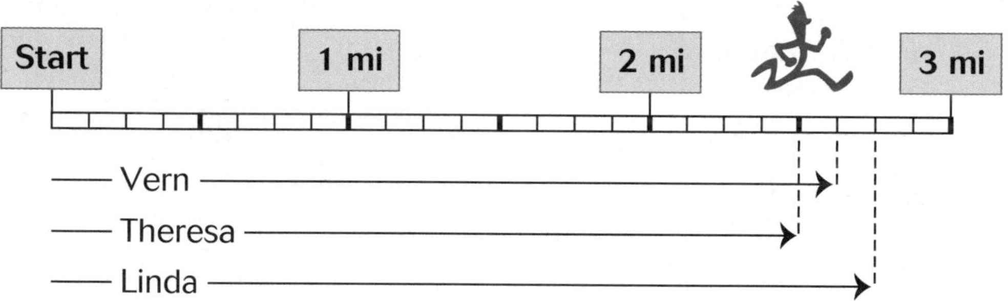

Warm-Up Review

Order the numbers from least to greatest.

1. 0.5, 0.53, 0.05
2. 1.7, 1.07, 1.77
3. 0.12, 0.22, 0.21
4. 2.96, 3, 2.99
5. Which racer had the least time and won the race?
   Gabe: 32.10 seconds
   Raul: 31.84 seconds
   Josh: 31.92 seconds

Word Bank

least common denominator (LCD)

Example 1

Which distance is greater, $2\frac{5}{8}$ miles or $2\frac{3}{4}$ miles?

Since the whole numbers are the same, compare the fractions.

Step 1 Find the LCD of the fractions. The LCD is the least common multiple (LCM) of the denominators.

$\frac{3}{4}$ Multiples of 4: 4, 8, 12, 16 . . .

$\frac{5}{8}$ Multiples of 8: 8, 16, 24 . . .

Step 2 Write each fraction using the LCD as the denominator.

$\frac{3}{4} = \frac{3 \times \mathbf{2}}{4 \times \mathbf{2}} = \frac{6}{8}$

$\frac{5}{8} = \frac{5}{8}$

Step 3 Compare the numerators of the new fractions. Then think back to the original fractions.

Since $6 > 5$, $\frac{6}{8} > \frac{5}{8}$.

Therefore, $\frac{3}{4} > \frac{5}{8}$.

So, $2\frac{3}{4} > 2\frac{5}{8}$.

 Additional Standard: *Mathematical Reasoning 3.0*

Example 2

Order the distances, $2\frac{5}{8}$ miles, $2\frac{1}{2}$ miles, and $2\frac{3}{4}$ miles from least to greatest. Since the whole numbers are the same, order the fractions.

Step 1 Find the LCD of the fractions.

$\frac{5}{8} = \frac{■}{8}$

$\frac{1}{2} = \frac{■}{8}$

$\frac{3}{4} = \frac{■}{8}$

The LCM of 2, 4, and 8 is 8. So, the LCD is 8.

Step 2 Write equivalent fractions using the LCD.

$\frac{5}{8} = \frac{5}{8}$

$\frac{1}{2} = \frac{4}{8}$

$\frac{3}{4} = \frac{6}{8}$

Step 3 Compare the numerators of the new fractions. Put them in order from least to greatest.

$4 < 5 < 6$. So, $\frac{4}{8} < \frac{5}{8} < \frac{6}{8}$.

Think back to the original form of the fractions.

$\frac{1}{2} < \frac{5}{8} < \frac{3}{4}$. So, $2\frac{1}{2} < 2\frac{5}{8} < 2\frac{3}{4}$.

Guided Practice

For another example, see Set J on p. 296.

Compare. Write >, <, or = for each ●.

1. $\frac{1}{4}$ ● $\frac{1}{2}$
2. $\frac{1}{3}$ ● $\frac{1}{6}$
3. $1\frac{11}{12}$ ● $1\frac{7}{8}$
4. $2\frac{3}{4}$ ● $2\frac{5}{8}$

Order the numbers from least to greatest.

5. $\frac{9}{11}, \frac{2}{11}, \frac{7}{11}$
6. $\frac{1}{3}, \frac{1}{2}, \frac{2}{3}$
7. $\frac{5}{6}, \frac{2}{3}, \frac{1}{4}$
8. $1\frac{2}{3}, 1\frac{3}{5}, 2\frac{1}{8}$

Independent Practice

For more practice, see Set J on p. 299.

Compare. Write >, <, or = for each ●.

9. $\frac{2}{3}$ ● $\frac{3}{7}$
10. $\frac{3}{8}$ ● $\frac{3}{4}$
11. $\frac{7}{7}$ ● $\frac{13}{13}$
12. $\frac{16}{15}$ ● $\frac{17}{20}$
13. $6\frac{5}{12}$ ● $6\frac{3}{4}$
14. $4\frac{1}{2}$ ● $3\frac{7}{14}$
15. $5\frac{1}{5}$ ● $5\frac{1}{7}$
16. $3\frac{3}{15}$ ● $3\frac{1}{5}$

Order the numbers from least to greatest.

17. $\frac{2}{3}, \frac{1}{5}, \frac{6}{4}, \frac{3}{4}$
18. $\frac{4}{9}, \frac{4}{5}, \frac{1}{2}, \frac{5}{12}$
19. $2\frac{5}{6}, 2\frac{1}{2}, 3, 2\frac{7}{8}$
20. $1\frac{1}{5}, \frac{3}{10}, \frac{1}{2}, 1\frac{1}{4}$
21. $8\frac{4}{5}, 8\frac{1}{2}, 8\frac{3}{4}, 8\frac{7}{10}$
22. $\frac{3}{10}, \frac{9}{10}, \frac{2}{3}, \frac{1}{5}$

Math Reasoning **Sometimes you can compare fractions without finding common denominators. Give an example of each rule and explain why it works.**

23. **Rule:** If the denominators are the same, compare the numerators. The greater fraction has the greater numerator.

24. **Rule:** If the numerators are the same, compare the denominators. The greater fraction has the smaller denominator.

25. **Rule:** Relate each fraction to $\frac{1}{2}$.

26. **Rule:** Relate each fraction to 1.

27. A pumpkin bread recipe calls for $\frac{3}{4}$ cup of shortening. Martha has $\frac{5}{8}$ of a cup. Does she have enough shortening? How do you know?

28. Martha made two loaves of pumpkin bread the same size. She cut one into 12 equal slices and the other into 16 equal slices. Which slices were larger?

Mixed Review

29. A baker made 250 rolls and is packaging them in bags of 18. How many bags will be completely filled?

Algebra **Solve each equation.**

30. $n + 37 = 51$ 31. $n - 15 = 32$ 32. $9n = 108$ 33. $\frac{n}{3} = 14$

Replace ● with > or <.

34. $\frac{9}{20}$ ● $\frac{1}{2}$ 35. $\frac{3}{12}$ ● 1

Test Prep **Choose the correct letter for each answer.**

36. Which is not a factor of 15?
(7-1)

A 1 **C** 3

B 15 **D** 30

37. $38 \times 75 =$
(4-7)

F 2885 **H** 900

G 2,850 **J** 2,875

Multiple-Choice Cumulative Review

Choose the correct letter for each answer.

1. Find the missing number.

$$\frac{3}{8} = \frac{■}{72}$$

A 9
B 18
C 24
D 27
E NH

2. Which expression shows 48 as a product of prime factors?

F $2^3 \times 3$
G $2^3 \times 3^2$
H $2^4 \times 3$
J $2^4 \times 3^2$
K NH

3. Which number sentence is NOT true?

A $\frac{5}{7} > \frac{1}{2}$
B $\frac{6}{5} > 1$
C $\frac{2}{9} < \frac{1}{2}$
D $\frac{18}{19} > 1$

4. Estimate 4×5.98.

F 16
G 20
H 24
J 36

Use the data in the table for Questions 5–7.

Runs Scored per Game
2, 5, 1, 1, 5, 5, 2

5. Find the median of the number of runs scored per game.

A 1
B 2
C 3
D 5

6. Find the mean of the number of runs scored per game.

F 1
G 2
H 3
J 5

7. Find the mode number of runs scored per game.

A 1
B 2
C 3
D 5

8. $2.6 + 0.74 =$

F 1.01
G 3.34
H 2.34
J 10.1
K NH

Understand
Plan
Solve
Look Back

Problem-Solving Application:

Representing Remainders

Warm-Up Review

1. Find 87 ÷ 4. Express the remainder by using a whole number.
2. Find 73 ÷ 3. Express the remainder by using a fraction.
3. Find 97 ÷ 5. Express the remainder by using a decimal.
4. Betsy is buying as many $0.39 muffins as she can with $5.00. How much money will she have left?

California Content Standard *Mathematical Reasoning 2.6: Make precise calculations and check the validity of the results from the context of the problem. Also Mathematical Reasoning 2.4 (See p. 257.)*

Example

Amber volunteers at a day-care center. She made 50 cups of lemonade and divided the lemonade equally among the 20 children. How many cups of lemonade did each child get?

Understand

What do you need to find?

You need to find the number of cups of lemonade each child got.

Plan

How can you solve the problem?

You can divide 50 by 20. You know you can express the remainder by using a fraction, a decimal, or a whole number. It makes sense to have a fraction of a cup of lemonade, so express the remainder by using a fraction.

Solve

$$\begin{array}{r} 2\frac{10}{20} = 2\frac{1}{2} \\ 20\overline{)50} \\ -\ 40 \\ \hline 10 \end{array}$$

Write the fraction in lowest terms.

Each child got $2\frac{1}{2}$ cups of lemonade.

Look Back

Would it make sense to give the answer as 2.5 cups? As 2 cups? As 10 cups? As 2 R10 cups?

Guided Practice

Give each answer.

1. Amber needs 50 slices of bread for sandwiches. If there are 20 slices in one loaf of bread, how many loaves should she buy?

2. Amber has 50 small boxes of raisins. If she divides them equally among the 20 children, how many boxes of raisins will each child receive?

3. Look at Exercise 2. How many boxes of raisins will be left?

4. It costs $50 a day to feed the 20 children. How much does it cost a day to feed each child?

Independent Practice

Give each answer.

5. Pat volunteered 225 hours over the past 50 weeks. He volunteered an average of how many hours per week?

6. Pat used 450 slices of cheese to make 180 pizzas. If he used the same amount for each pizza, how many slices of cheese did he use for each pizza?

7. Pat packed 128 bag lunches into cartons of 10 bags each. How many cartons did he need?

8. In Exercise 7, how many cartons are completely full? How many cartons are partly full?

9. Thirty-six people collected $81 to buy a gift for Pat. What is the average amount each person contributed?

Mixed Review

Solve each problem.

10. Ben bought a baseball for $2.98, a baseball bat for $9.00, and a mitt for $23.50. He paid for the items, including sales tax, with $40 and he got $2.39 back in change. What was the sales tax?

11. Tina has a black coat and a blue coat. She has scarves that are white, red, yellow, and tan. How many different ways can she choose a coat and a scarf?

Use Homework Workbook 7-13.

Diagnostic Checkpoint

Complete. For Exercises 1–4, use the words from the Word Bank.

Word Bank
prime
composite
multiple
equivalent fractions
simplest form
improper fractions

1. (7-8) A fraction is in ________________ when the GCF of the numerator and denominator is 1.

2. (7-4) A ________________ of a whole number is the product of that number and any other whole number.

3. (7-2) A ________________ number is a whole number greater than 1 that has exactly two factors.

4. (7-7) Fractions that name the same amount are called ________________.

Write a fraction and a decimal for each shaded part.

5. (7-6) 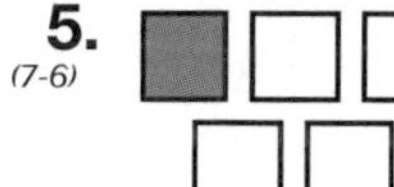

6. (7-6) 

7. (7-6) 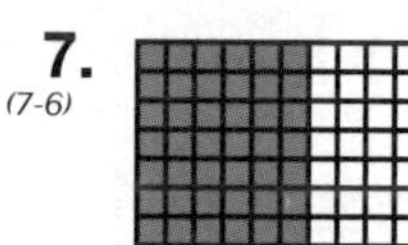

8. (7-6) 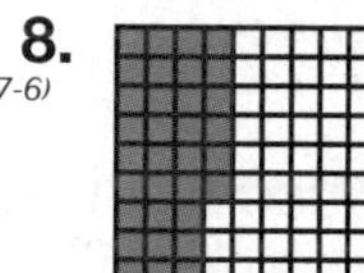

Algebra **Replace each ■ with a number that will make the fractions equivalent.**

9. (7-7) $\frac{3}{4} = \frac{■}{12}$

10. (7-7) $\frac{5}{25} = \frac{1}{■}$

11. (7-7) $\frac{2}{5} = \frac{■}{15}$

12. (7-7) $\frac{■}{6} = \frac{9}{18}$

Mental Math **Write each fraction in simplest form. Some of the fractions may already be in simplest form.**

13. (7-8) $\frac{5}{9}$

14. (7-8) $\frac{15}{18}$

15. (7-8) $\frac{7}{14}$

16. (7-8) $\frac{18}{36}$

Compare. Write >, <, or = for each ●.

17. (7-9) $\frac{5}{8}$ ● $\frac{1}{2}$

18. (7-9) $\frac{1}{2}$ ● $\frac{3}{10}$

19. (7-12) $\frac{8}{9}$ ● $\frac{15}{16}$

20. (7-11) $\frac{4}{3}$ ● 1

21. (7-10) Twenty-four chairs will be set up for the school orchestra in equal rows. How many different ways can the chairs be arranged?

22. (7-13) A baker used 30 cups of flour to make 12 batches of cookies. How many cups of flour did she use for each batch?

Chapter 7 Test

1. Write the prime factorization of 300 using exponents.

Find the GCF and the LCM for each pair of numbers.

2. 9, 15
3. 10, 25
4. 8, 20

5. List all the factors of 40.

6. Is 2,844 divisible by 2, 3, 4, 5, 6, 9, or 10?

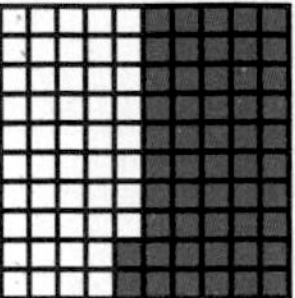

7. Write a fraction and a decimal for the shaded part at the right.

Algebra Replace each ■ with a number that will make the fractions equivalent.

8. $\frac{2}{3} = \frac{■}{6}$
9. $\frac{1}{5} = \frac{■}{15}$
10. $\frac{5}{9} = \frac{20}{■}$

Mental Math Write each fraction in simplest form. Some of the fractions may already be in simplest form.

11. $\frac{4}{12}$
12. $\frac{15}{25}$
13. $\frac{8}{15}$
14. $\frac{18}{27}$

Write each mixed number as an improper fraction. Write each improper fraction as a mixed number.

15. $2\frac{1}{3}$
16. $4\frac{5}{7}$
17. $\frac{21}{6}$
18. $\frac{19}{3}$

Compare. Write $>$, $<$, or $=$ for each ●.

19. $\frac{2}{3}$ ● $\frac{1}{4}$
20. $1\frac{1}{3}$ ● $1\frac{2}{6}$
21. $\frac{8}{11}$ ● $\frac{1}{2}$
22. $\frac{4}{15}$ ● $\frac{1}{2}$

23. A license plate has a letter followed by two numbers. The letters must be A, B, C, or D. The numbers can only be 2 or 3. How many different license plates are possible?

24. Jordan earned \$25 baby-sitting for 4 hours. She said she earned over \$6 an hour. Is this amount reasonable? Explain.

25. Four people share \$19 equally. How much does each get?

TEST PREP

Multiple-Choice Chapter 7 Test

Choose the correct letter for each answer.

1. 2,514 is NOT divisible by which of the following?

A 2

B 3

C 6

D 9

2. Which is the prime factorization of 168?

F $2^2 \times 3 \times 7$

G $2^3 \times 3 \times 7$

H $2^3 \times 3^2$

J $2^2 \times 3^2 \times 7$

3. Which is the GCF of 30 and 42?

A 2

B 3

C 6

D 15

E NH

4. During the months before the school play, the cast uses the stage every third day, the scenery crew uses the stage every sixth day, and the costume crew uses the stage every eighth day. On which day will the cast and the costume crew both be on the stage?

F 3rd day

G 6th day

H 12th day

J 24th day

5. A restaurant served 308 customers one day. About one third bought the daily special for $5.95. Is it reasonable to say about $600 was made on the daily special?

A Yes, about 100 × $6 was made.

B Yes, about 200 daily specials were sold.

C No, about 200 × $6 was made.

D No, about 300 × $6 was made.

6. Which of the following does NOT represent the shaded part?

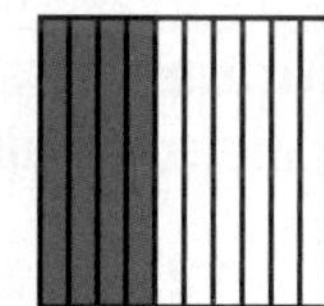

F $\frac{4}{10}$

G $\frac{4}{5}$

H $\frac{2}{5}$

J 0.4

7. If $\frac{24}{64} = \frac{■}{8}$, then ■ =

A 2

B 3

C 4

D 8

E NH

8. **Which fraction is in simplest form?**

F $\frac{8}{10}$

G $\frac{14}{16}$

H $\frac{9}{25}$

J $\frac{15}{63}$

K NH

9. **Which fraction is less than $\frac{1}{2}$?**

A $\frac{3}{4}$

B $\frac{5}{7}$

C $\frac{8}{15}$

D $\frac{7}{16}$

10. **Tina found 5 posters she likes, but she can only buy 2 of them. How many different ways can she choose 2 of the 5 posters?**

F 5 ways

G 10 ways

H 20 ways

J 25 ways

11. **Which equals $9\frac{2}{5}$?**

A $1\frac{4}{5}$

B $\frac{45}{5}$

C $\frac{47}{5}$

D $\frac{92}{5}$

E NH

12. **Which equals $\frac{74}{8}$?**

F $8\frac{1}{8}$

G $8\frac{1}{4}$

H $9\frac{1}{8}$

J $9\frac{1}{4}$

K NH

13. **A group of fifth graders measured their hand spans with a ruler and then put the measurements in order from least to greatest. How did they list these measurements: $5\frac{3}{4}$ in., $6\frac{1}{2}$ in., $5\frac{1}{2}$ in., $6\frac{3}{8}$ in., $5\frac{1}{8}$ in., and $6\frac{3}{4}$ in.?**

A $5\frac{1}{8}, 5\frac{1}{2}, 5\frac{3}{4}, 6\frac{1}{2}, 6\frac{3}{8}, 6\frac{3}{4}$

B $5\frac{1}{8}, 5\frac{1}{2}, 5\frac{3}{4}, 6\frac{3}{8}, 6\frac{1}{2}, 6\frac{3}{4}$

C $5\frac{1}{8}, 5\frac{1}{2}, 5\frac{3}{4}, 6\frac{3}{4}, 6\frac{3}{8}, 6\frac{1}{2}$

D $5\frac{1}{2}, 5\frac{1}{8}, 5\frac{3}{4}, 6\frac{1}{2}, 6\frac{3}{8}, 6\frac{3}{4}$

14. **Which of the following numbers is prime?**

F 8

G 21

H 23

J 46

K NH

15. **Find the average number of students buying school lunch for the five days shown in the table.**

Students in Our Class Buying School Lunch

Day	School Lunch
1	11
2	8
3	14
4	21
5	21

A 14

B 15

C 21

D 75

Reteaching

Set A (pages 258–259)

Is 3,584 divisible by 4?

The number formed by the tens and ones digit is 84.

$84 \div 4 = 21$, so 84 is divisible by 4.

Therefore, 3,584 is divisible by 4.

Remember you can quickly tell if a number is divisible by 2, 3, 4, 5, 6, 9, or 10 by using divisibility rules.

Mental Math Tell if each number is divisible by 2, 3, 4, 5, 6, 9, or 10.

1. 75 **2.** 86 **3.** 147

Set B (pages 260–262)

Use a factor tree to find the prime factorization of 225. Then write the product using exponents.

```
      225
      / \
    9  ×  25
   / \    / \
  3 × 3 × 5 × 5
```

$225 = 3^2 \times 5^2$

Remember a prime number has exactly two factors, 1 and the number itself.

If the number is prime, write *prime*. If the number is composite, write the prime factorization of the number.

1. 25 **2.** 88 **3.** 41

4. 280 **5.** 19 **6.** 320

Set C (pages 264–265)

Find the GCF of 12 and 32.

Factors of 12: **1**, **2**, 3, **4**, 6, 12

Factors of 32: **1**, **2**, **4**, 8, 16, 32

Common factors: 1, 2, 4

GCF is 4.

Remember you can find the GCF of two numbers by finding the largest number that is a factor of both.

Find the GCF of each set of numbers.

1. 14, 7 **2.** 8, 20 **3.** 15, 20

Set D (pages 266–267)

Find the LCM of 8 and 12.

Multiples of 8: 8, 16, **24,** 32, 40, **48**. . .

Multiples of 12: 12, **24,** 36, **48,** 60, 72 . . .

Common multiples: 24, 48, ...

LCM is 24.

Remember you can find the least common multiple of two numbers by finding the smallest number that is a multiple of both.

Find the LCM of each set of numbers.

1. 15, 25 **2.** 8, 10 **3.** 5, 9

Set E (pages 272–273)

Write a fraction and a decimal that names Point F.

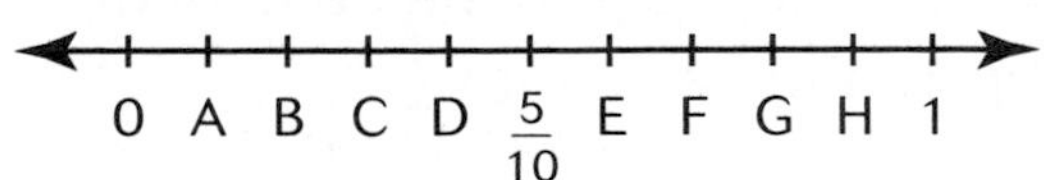

The number line is separated into tenths. Seven tenths names Point F.

$\frac{7}{10} = 7 \div 10 = 0.7$

Remember you can change a fraction to a decimal by dividing the numerator by the denominator.

Write a fraction and a decimal for each point.

1. B **2.** D

3. E **4.** H

Set F (pages 274–275)

Find a fraction equivalent to $\frac{7}{9}$ with a denominator of 36.

$\frac{7}{9} = \frac{■}{36}$ ← What do you multiply by 9 to get 36? Multiply 7 by the same number.

$\frac{7}{9} = \frac{7 \times 4}{9 \times 4} = \frac{28}{36}$

So, $\frac{7}{9} = \frac{28}{36}$

Remember when you multiply the numerator and denominator by the same number, you are multiplying by 1.

Algebra Replace each ■ with a number that will make the fractions equivalent.

1. $\frac{10}{100} = \frac{■}{50}$ **2.** $\frac{9}{36} = \frac{■}{12}$

3. $\frac{16}{36} = \frac{■}{9}$ **4.** $\frac{1}{2} = \frac{■}{70}$

5. $\frac{4}{5} = \frac{■}{25}$ **6.** $\frac{10}{12} = \frac{■}{6}$

Set G (pages 276–277)

Write $\frac{8}{20}$ in simplest form.

Step 1 Find the GCF of 8 and 20.

Factors of 8: **1**, **2**, **4**, 8

Factors of 20: **1**, **2**, **4**, 5, 10, 20

GCF: 4

Step 2 Divide both the numerator and denominator by the GCF.

$\frac{8}{20} = \frac{8 \div 4}{20 \div 4} = \frac{2}{5}$

$\frac{2}{5}$ is the simplest form of $\frac{8}{20}$.

Remember a fraction is in simplest form when the GCF of the numerator and denominator is 1.

Mental Math Write each fraction in simplest form.

1. $\frac{12}{15}$ **2.** $\frac{10}{18}$ **3.** $\frac{10}{25}$

4. $\frac{8}{28}$ **5.** $\frac{14}{42}$ **6.** $\frac{16}{64}$

Reteaching

Set H (pages 278–279)

Is $\frac{4}{9}$ greater or less than $\frac{1}{2}$?

$9 \div 2 = 4 \text{ R}1,\ 4 < 4 \text{ R}1$

So $\frac{4}{9} < \frac{1}{2}$.

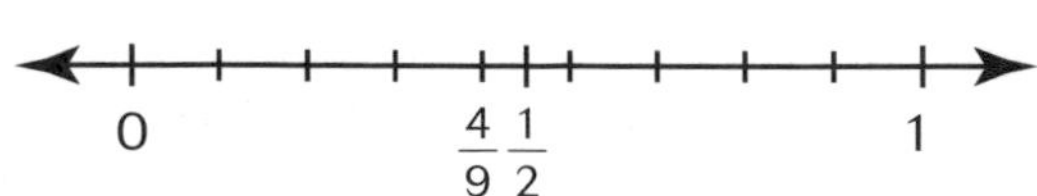

Remember you can divide the denominator of a fraction by 2 and compare the quotient to the numerator to compare the fraction to $\frac{1}{2}$.

Compare. Write >, <, or = for each ●.

1. $\frac{1}{2}$ ● $\frac{5}{8}$
2. $\frac{3}{16}$ ● $\frac{1}{2}$
3. $\frac{5}{10}$ ● $\frac{1}{2}$
4. $\frac{12}{15}$ ● $\frac{1}{2}$
5. $\frac{1}{2}$ ● $\frac{31}{64}$
6. $\frac{1}{2}$ ● $\frac{8}{19}$

Set I (pages 282–283)

Write $\frac{24}{10}$ as a mixed number.

$$\begin{array}{r} 2\,\frac{4}{10} \\ 10\overline{)24} \\ \underline{20} \\ 4 \end{array}$$

$\frac{24}{10} = 2\frac{4}{10} = 2\frac{2}{5}$

Remember you can change a mixed number to an improper fraction by multiplying the whole number by the denominator, adding the numerator, and putting the result over the denominator.

Write each mixed number as an improper fraction. Write each improper fraction as a mixed number.

1. $2\frac{1}{3}$
2. $8\frac{2}{7}$
3. $5\frac{8}{9}$
4. $\frac{11}{8}$
5. $\frac{17}{5}$
6. $\frac{10}{9}$

Set J (pages 284–285)

Compare $1\frac{7}{9}$ and $1\frac{2}{3}$.

The LCM of 9 and 3 is 9, so the LCD of $\frac{7}{9}$ and $\frac{2}{3}$ is 9.

$\frac{2}{3} = \frac{2 \times 3}{3 \times 3} = \frac{6}{9}$

Compare $1\frac{7}{9}$ and $1\frac{6}{9}$.

$1\frac{7}{9} > 1\frac{6}{9}$

So $1\frac{7}{9} > 1\frac{2}{3}$.

Remember you can compare two fractions or mixed numbers by writing them with their LCD.

Compare. Write >, <, or = for each ●.

1. $\frac{4}{15}$ ● $\frac{8}{30}$
2. $\frac{2}{3}$ ● $\frac{5}{8}$
3. $\frac{6}{8}$ ● $\frac{8}{6}$
4. $\frac{1}{2}$ ● $\frac{2}{2}$
5. $\frac{9}{8}$ ● $\frac{17}{26}$
6. $2\frac{1}{5}$ ● $2\frac{1}{3}$

More Practice

Set A *(pages 258–259)*

Mental Math **Tell if each number is divisible by 2, 3, 4, 5, 6, 9, or 10.**

1. 90 **2.** 85 **3.** 68 **4.** 87 **5.** 153 **6.** 204

7. 756 **8.** 920 **9.** 1,341 **10.** 2,634 **11.** 1,260 **12.** 4,678

13. Patrick and Susan need to set up 50 chairs in equal rows. What are all the ways they could do this?

Set B *(pages 260–262)*

If the number is prime, write *prime*. If the number is composite, write the prime factorization of the number. If the number is neither prime nor composite, write *neither*.

1. 54 **2.** 20 **3.** 17 **4.** 1 **5.** 35 **6.** 29

7. 8 **8.** 58 **9.** 400 **10.** 175 **11.** 216 **12.** 441

13. Patti has 11 pencils she wants to give her friends. Can she give the same number of pencils to each friend, with no pencils left over? Explain your answer.

Set C *(pages 264–265)*

Find the GCF of each set of numbers.

1. 7, 21 **2.** 6, 9 **3.** 5, 8 **4.** 9, 21 **5.** 36, 24 **6.** 2, 5, 6

7. There are 16 jazz dancers and 24 tap dancers on the stage at once. Equal groups will be formed, but jazz and tap dancers will not be combined. What is the largest-size group into which both kinds of dancers can be divided? Explain your answer.

8. **Math Reasoning** The greatest common factor of two numbers is 12. One of the numbers is 24. Could the other number be 40?

More Practice

Set D (pages 266–267)

Find the LCM of each set of numbers.

1. 6, 12
2. 3, 4
3. 2, 5
4. 9, 12
5. 5, 15
6. 10, 12
7. One model train travels around a loop every 5 minutes. The other travels on another loop every 4 minutes. If they begin at the same point at the same time, how much time will pass before they meet at that point again?

Set E (pages 272–273)

Write a fraction and a decimal for each shaded part.

1. 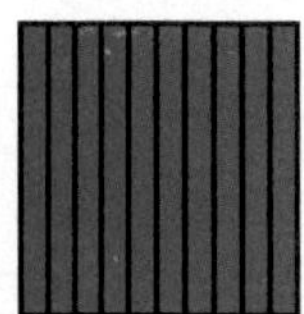
2. 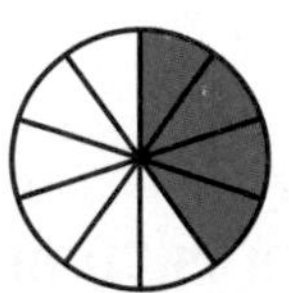
3. 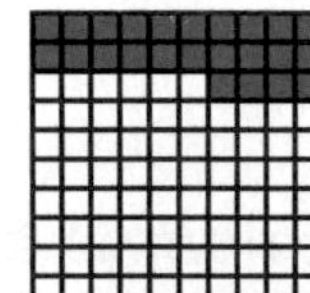
4. 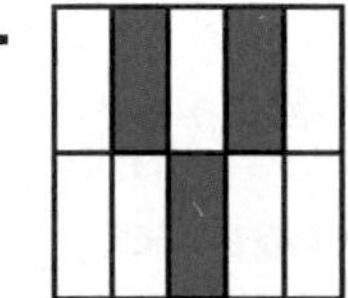

Write a fraction and a decimal for each point.

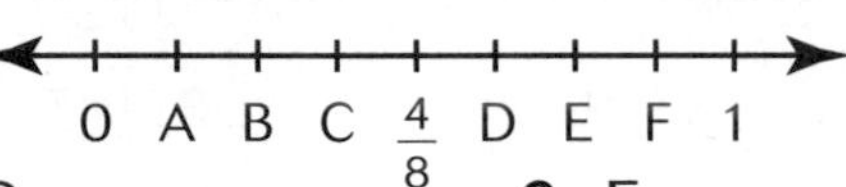

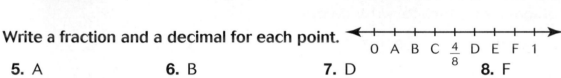

5. A
6. B
7. D
8. F
9. Kendra ate $\frac{3}{4}$ of a pizza. Write $\frac{3}{4}$ as a decimal.

Set F (pages 274–275)

Algebra Replace each ■ with a number that will make the fractions equivalent.

1. $\frac{2}{3} = \frac{■}{6}$
2. $\frac{1}{4} = \frac{■}{16}$
3. $\frac{5}{8} = \frac{■}{40}$
4. $\frac{7}{14} = \frac{■}{2}$
5. $\frac{15}{25} = \frac{■}{5}$
6. On Friday nights, one fifth of the audience at the local theater consists of students who are 12 years old. If 25 people are in the audience, how many are 12 years old?

Set G (pages 276–277)

Mental Math Write each fraction in simplest form. Some of the fractions may already be in simplest form.

1. $\frac{3}{5}$
2. $\frac{9}{18}$
3. $\frac{6}{8}$
4. $\frac{9}{12}$
5. $\frac{7}{11}$
6. $\frac{8}{15}$
7. Does an advertisement that is $\frac{6}{8}$ of a page take up more or less of the page than an advertisement that is $\frac{3}{4}$ of the same page? Why?

More Practice

Set H *(pages 278–279)*

Compare. Write >, <, or = for each ●.

1. $\frac{7}{10}$ ● $\frac{1}{2}$
2. $\frac{12}{24}$ ● $\frac{1}{2}$
3. $\frac{1}{2}$ ● $\frac{3}{16}$
4. $\frac{1}{2}$ ● $\frac{11}{26}$
5. $\frac{1}{2}$ ● $\frac{8}{17}$
6. $\frac{11}{21}$ ● $\frac{1}{2}$
7. $\frac{16}{31}$ ● $\frac{1}{2}$
8. $\frac{1}{2}$ ● $\frac{28}{49}$
9. Five twelfths of the performers in Scene I are ready to go on stage. Is this more or less than one half of the performers?

Set I *(pages 282–283)*

Write each mixed number as an improper fraction. Write each improper fraction as a mixed number.

1. $3\frac{1}{2}$
2. $\frac{34}{8}$
3. $4\frac{6}{7}$
4. $7\frac{2}{3}$
5. $\frac{57}{8}$

Compare. Write >, <, or = for each ●.

6. $\frac{12}{10}$ ● 1
7. $\frac{8}{6}$ ● 1
8. $\frac{5}{5}$ ● 1
9. $\frac{3}{7}$ ● 1
10. Each small pizza is divided into 4 pieces. Tonya ate $\frac{5}{4}$ of a pizza. Did she eat more or less than one pizza?

Set J *(pages 284–285)*

Compare. Write >, <, or = for each ●.

1. $\frac{1}{3}$ ● $\frac{3}{7}$
2. $\frac{3}{6}$ ● $\frac{1}{2}$
3. $\frac{5}{6}$ ● $\frac{7}{18}$
4. $\frac{3}{10}$ ● $\frac{2}{5}$
5. $\frac{10}{90}$ ● $\frac{2}{9}$
6. $\frac{8}{5}$ ● $\frac{9}{10}$
7. $\frac{9}{18}$ ● $\frac{5}{10}$
8. $2\frac{7}{9}$ ● $2\frac{2}{3}$
9. $\frac{18}{3}$ ● $\frac{36}{6}$
10. $3\frac{1}{4}$ ● $3\frac{1}{5}$
11. Students cut ribbon to decorate hats. The pieces are $7\frac{1}{2}$ in., $7\frac{1}{8}$ in., $6\frac{1}{2}$ in., $6\frac{7}{8}$ in., 7 in., $7\frac{3}{8}$ in., and $6\frac{5}{8}$ in. Students placed the pieces in order from shortest to longest. In what order were they placed?

Problem Solving: Preparing for Tests

Choose the correct letter for each answer.

---

1. **Greg planted two rows of rosebushes, with 24 bushes in each row. He planted red (R), white (W), and yellow (Y) rosebushes. For the first row, he used the color pattern RWW, RWW, and so on. For the second row, he used the pattern WYYY, WYYY, and so on. How many times was a white rosebush (W) planted in the row behind a red rosebush (R)?**

A 2 times

B 4 times

C 6 times

D 12 times

> **Tip**
> Use the *Draw a Diagram* strategy to help you solve this problem.

---

2. **Erik estimated that 0.75 of the students in his school think they have too much homework. He took a survey and found that 0.25 of the 240 students disagreed with this opinion. The rest agreed. How many students agreed with his opinion?**

F 100

G 150

H 180

J 200

> **Tip**
> Use *Logical Reasoning* for this problem. Since 0.25 of the 240 students disagreed with Erik's opinion, then 0.75 of the students must have agreed with it.

---

3. **The pictograph shows the number of registered voters in a neighborhood. How many fewer voters live on Pine and Oak than live on Elm and Park?**

A 75

B 100

C 125

D 150

Registered Voters

Street	Number of People
Pine	●●●●●
Oak	●●●●● and $\frac{1}{4}$ ●
Elm	●●●●●●● and $\frac{3}{4}$ ●
Park	●●● and $\frac{1}{4}$ ●
	● = 100 people

> **Tip**
> Start by making sure you understand the key for the graph.

4. **In a three-week period, a pet supply store had weekly sales totals of $7,950; $4,062; and $6,875. Which is the best estimate of the total sales for the period?**

- **F** Less than $16,000
- **G** Between $16,000 and $17,000
- **H** Between $17,000 and $19,000
- **J** More than $19,000

---

5. **What is the area of the shaded triangle in square units?**

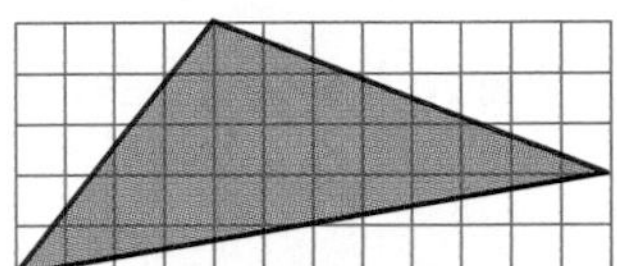

- **A** 20 square units
- **B** 26 square units
- **C** 30 square units
- **D** 36 square units

---

6. **Marge's mother was 26 years old when Marge was born. Marge's father is 4 years younger than her mother. The sum of their ages now is 80. How old is Marge's mother?**

- **F** 34 years
- **G** 38 years
- **H** 42 years
- **J** 46 years

---

7. **José is older than Kara but younger than Luis. Carlos is younger than Amy but older than Luis. Which of these is a reasonable conclusion?**

- **A** José is the oldest.
- **B** Amy is the oldest.
- **C** Luis is the youngest.
- **D** Kara is older than Luis.

In a survey, students at the Jefferson School were asked whether they wanted to go to the zoo or the science museum for their field trip. The graph shows the results of the survey. Use the graph for Questions 8 and 9.

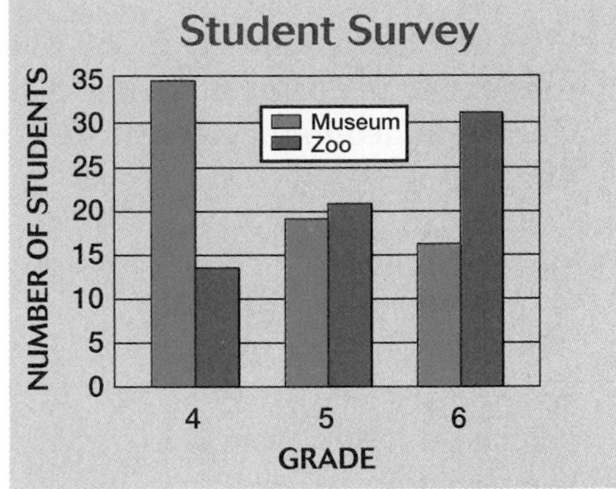

8. **About how many more sixth graders chose the zoo rather than the museum?**

- **F** 10
- **G** 15
- **H** 20
- **J** 25

---

9. **Which are the best estimates of the results of the survey?**

- **A** Museum, 60; Zoo, 70
- **B** Museum, 75; Zoo, 75
- **C** Museum, 70; Zoo, 65
- **D** Museum, 75; Zoo, 60

---

10. **The moon is about 240,000 miles from Earth. About how far would a spacecraft travel if it made 2 trips to the moon and back?**

- **F** 240,000,000 miles
- **G** 480,000 miles
- **H** 720,000 miles
- **J** 960,000 miles

TEST PREP

Multiple-Choice Cumulative Review

Choose the correct letter for each answer.

Number Sense

1. Which of these numbers is 350 when rounded to the nearest ten and 300 when rounded to the nearest hundred?

A 341
B 344
C 347
D 353

2. Which set of numbers is in order from greatest to least?

F 0.788 0.087 0.898 0.888
G 0.898 0.888 0.087 0.788
H 0.087 0.788 0.888 0.898
J 0.898 0.888 0.788 0.087

3. Yesterday, Frank wrote 4 pages of his 10-page report. What fraction of his report did he complete?

A $\frac{4}{5}$
B $\frac{3}{4}$
C $\frac{2}{3}$
D $\frac{2}{5}$

4. Which number sentence represents the models shown?

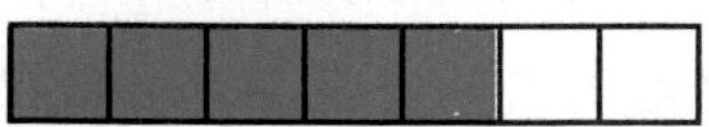

F $\frac{3}{5} = \frac{5}{7}$
G $\frac{2}{5} < \frac{2}{7}$
H $\frac{5}{7} > \frac{3}{5}$
J $\frac{2}{5} = \frac{2}{7}$

5. $10^4 =$

A 100
B 1,000
C 10,000
D 100,000

6. Which of the following is NOT equal to $1\frac{3}{4}$?

F $\frac{7}{4}$
G 1.75
H $1\frac{6}{8}$
J $1\frac{8}{12}$

7. Find the missing number.

$$\frac{2}{3} = \frac{\blacksquare}{60}$$

A 40
B 30
C 20
D 4
E NH

8. $0.6 \times 0.42 =$

F 0.0242
G 0.0252
H 0.242
J 0.252
K NH

Algebra and Functions

9. **Which expression is equivalent to $7 \times (8 + 6)$?**

   A $(7 \times 8) + (7 \times 6)$

   B $15 + 13$

   C $(7 + 8) + (7 + 6)$

   D $56 + 6$

---

10. **Evaluate $7 + 2 \times 3 + 1$.**

   F 14

   G 15

   J 28

   K 36

---

11. **Solve $\frac{n}{3} = 30$.**

   A $n = 10$

   B $n = 27$

   C $n = 33$

   D $n = 90$

---

12. **What would you do to get *n* alone in $n + 10$?**

   F Add 0.

   G Add 10.

   H Subtract 10.

   J Divide by 10.

Statistics, Data Analysis, and Probability

13. **Will's 6 bowling scores were 93, 105, 115, 120, 105, and 98. What was his mean (average) score?**

   A 100

   B 105

   C 106

   D 117

---

14. **There are 4 green marbles, 6 blue marbles, 3 white marbles, and 5 red marbles in a bag. If you choose 1 marble without looking, what is the probability that it will be a green marble?**

   F $\frac{1}{10}$

   G $\frac{2}{9}$

   H $\frac{4}{9}$

   J $\frac{5}{9}$

---

15. **If you spin the spinner 100 times, on which 2 colors is the spinner least likely to stop?**

   A Green or yellow

   B Red or blue

   C Yellow or red

   D Blue or green

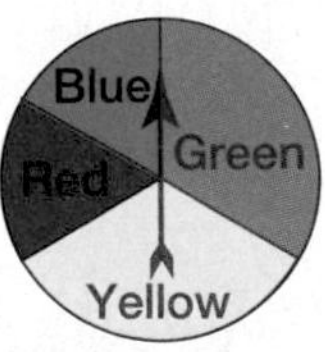

---

16. **Marsha, Ruth, and Ellen are sisters. In how many different ways can they stand in a row for a family picture?**

   F 3

   G 6

   H 12

   J 18

Fraction Computation

Diagnosing Readiness

In Chapter 8, you will use these skills:

Ⓐ Comparing and Ordering

(pages 10–12)

Compare. Write >, <, or = for each ●.

1. 2.85 ● 3.122

2. 0.65 ● 0.065

3. 1.35 ● 1.32

Write each set of numbers in order from least to greatest.

4. 4.18, 4, 3.905, 4.108

5. 12.6, 1.26, 0.126, 1.62

Ⓑ Evaluating Expressions

(pages 55–57, 238–239)

Evaluate $x + 8$ for each value of x.

6. 14 **7.** 0.731

Evaluate $4.2m$ for each value of m.

8. 5 **9.** 0.75

10. The expression $0.75p$ gives the sale price of an item with regular price p. Use the expression to find the sale price of a \$35 pair of jeans.

C Estimating

(pages 52–54, 218–219)

Estimate.

11. 19.8 + 2.8

12. 24.38 − 12.6

13. 0.024 + 0.059

14. 1.05 + 8.732

15. 5 × 2.194

16. 6 × 0.027

17. About how much would you pay for 4 bottles of shampoo that cost $1.79 each?

D Finding GCF and LCM

(pages 264–267)

Find the GCF of each set of numbers.

18. 12, 20 **19.** 25, 35

20. 18, 42 **21.** 28, 63

Find the LCM of each set of numbers.

22. 9, 12 **23.** 8, 11

24. 10, 15 **25.** 14, 21

E Finding Equivalent Fractions

(pages 274–277)

Replace each ■ with a number that will make the fractions equivalent.

26. $\frac{1}{3} = \frac{9}{■}$ **27.** $\frac{18}{27} = \frac{■}{3}$

28. $\frac{8}{■} = \frac{2}{5}$ **29.** $\frac{2}{3} = \frac{■}{33}$

Write each fraction in simplest form.

30. $\frac{8}{12}$ **31.** $\frac{3}{18}$

32. $\frac{10}{25}$ **33.** $\frac{7}{21}$

34. It takes 3 yards of fabric to make two costumes. How many costumes can be made from 12 yards? from 24 yards?

F Finding Patterns

(Grade 4)

Find the next 3 numbers in each pattern.

35. 3, 5, 7, 9, 11, ■, ■, ■

36. 40, 36, 32, 28, ■, ■, ■

37. 3, 6, 12, 24, ■, ■, ■

To the Family and Student

Looking Back	Chapter 8	Looking Ahead
In Chapter 7, students learned how to find the GCF and LCM, how to write fractions in simplest form, and how to compare and order fractions and mixed numbers.	**Fraction Computation** In this chapter, students will learn how to add, subtract, multiply, and divide fractions and mixed numbers.	In Chapter 12, students will learn how to change fractions to decimals and percents and how to write a ratio as a fraction in simplest form.

Math and Everyday Living

Opportunities to apply the concepts of Chapter 8 abound in everyday situations. During the chapter, think about how fraction computations can be used to solve a variety of real-world problems. The following examples suggest just several of the many situations that could launch a discussion about fraction computations.

Math and Food You have to share a pizza with your brother and sister. Your brother ate 5 out of 12 pieces. Your sister ate 4 out of 12, or $\frac{1}{3}$ of the pizza. What fraction of the pizza did they leave for you?

Math at Play You have 7 sections of model railroad track. Each section is straight and is $8\frac{3}{4}$ inches long. How long would the 7 sections be if they were laid end-to-end?

Math and Cooking You are making biscuits. You will need $\frac{1}{2}$ cup milk and $\frac{1}{4}$ cup water. How much liquid do you use altogether?

Math and the Weather How much did it rain in all during the 3 days?

Day	Rainfall
Monday	$1\frac{1}{4}$ in.
Tuesday	$\frac{1}{2}$ in.
Wednesday	$1\frac{1}{2}$ in.

Math and Construction You need a board that is $5\frac{1}{2}$ feet long. You have a board that is $6\frac{3}{4}$ feet long. How much should you cut off?

Math and Physical Fitness You ran $1\frac{3}{8}$ miles on Monday and $1\frac{3}{4}$ miles on Tuesday. How far did you run in the two days? How much farther did you run on Tuesday than on Monday?

On Tuesday you did your running on an outdoor track. How many laps did you run if each lap around the track is $\frac{7}{8}$ mile?

Math and the Grocery Store You need 5 pounds of apples to make apple butter. Each apple weighs about $\frac{3}{8}$ of a pound. How many apples should you buy?

California Content Standards in Chapter 8 Lessons*

	Teach and Practice	Practice
Number Sense		
2.3 (🔑) Solve simple problems, including ones arising in concrete situations, involving the addition and subtraction of fractions and mixed numbers (like and unlike denominators of 20 or less), and express answers in the simplest form.	8-1, 8-2, 8-4, 8-5, 8-6, 8-7, 8-8	8-14
2.4 Understand the concept of multiplication and division of fractions.	8-10, 8-11	8-12
2.5 Compute and perform simple multiplication and division of fractions and apply these procedures to solving problems.	8-10, 8-11, 8-12	8-13, 8-14
Algebra and Functions		
1.2 (🔑) Use a letter to represent an unknown number; . . . evaluate simple algebraic expressions in one variable by substitution.	8-14	8-10

	Teach and Practice	Practice
Mathematical Reasoning		
1.1 Analyze problems by identifying relationships, distinguishing relevant from irrelevant information, sequencing and prioritizing information, and observing patterns.	8-3, 8-13	8-9, 8-10
1.2 Determine when and how to break a problem into simpler parts.		8-9
2.0 Students use strategies, skills, and concepts in finding solutions.		8-3, 8-5, 8-13
2.1 Use estimation to verify the reasonableness of calculated results.	8-7	8-1, 8-4, 8-8
2.2 Apply strategies and results from simpler problems to more complex problems.	8-9	
2.3 Use a variety of methods, such as words, numbers, symbols, charts, graphs, tables, diagrams, and models, to explain mathematical reasoning.		8-1, 8-8
2.4 Express the solution clearly and logically by using the appropriate mathematical notation and terms and clear language; support solutions with evidence in both verbal and symbolic work.		8-2, 8-3
3.1 Evaluate the reasonableness of the solution in the context of the original situation.		8-1
3.2 Note the method of deriving the solution and demonstrate a conceptual understanding of the derivation by solving similar problems.	8-9	8-3
3.3 Develop generalizations of the results obtained and apply them in other circumstances.		8-6, 8-11

* The symbol (🔑) indicates a key standard as designated in the Mathematics Framework for California Public Schools. Full statements of the California Content Standards are found at the beginning of this book following the Table of Contents.

Adding Fractions and Mixed Numbers: Like Denominators

Warm-Up Review

1. 6 + 8.2 **2.** 0.4 + 9

3. 0.7 + 0.3 **4.** 0.51 + 0.3

5. 1.07 + 7.2 +0.9

6. 4.62 + 5.1 + 0.62

7. Tyler walked 3 tenths of a mile to Hank's house and then 5 tenths of a mile to school. How far did he walk?

California Content Standard *Number Sense 2.3 (🔑): Solve simple problems, including ones arising in concrete situations, involving the addition . . . of fractions and mixed numbers (like . . . denominators of 20 or less) and express answers in the simplest form.*

Math Link You know how to add decimals. Now you will add fractions and mixed numbers.

Example 1

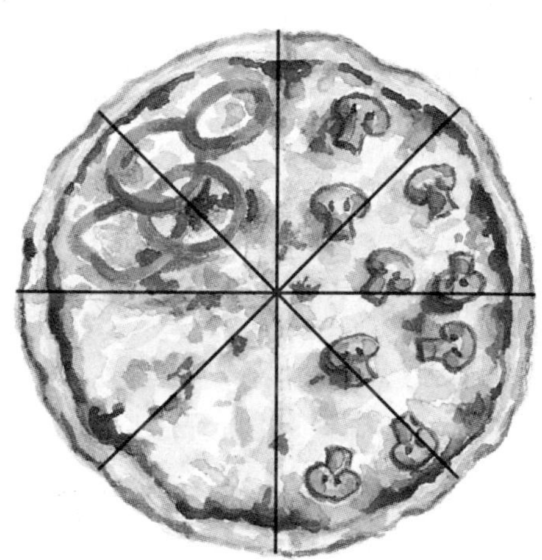

What part of this pizza has extra toppings besides the cheese?

$\frac{2}{8}$ has peppers and $\frac{4}{8}$ has mushrooms, so add $\frac{2}{8} + \frac{4}{8}$.

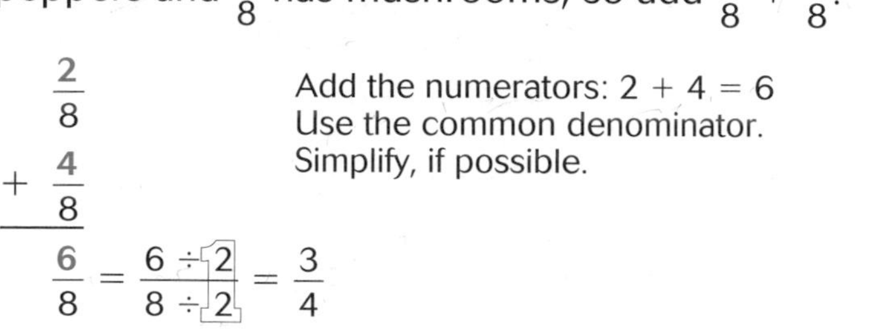

$$\begin{array}{r} \frac{2}{8} \\ + \frac{4}{8} \\ \hline \frac{6}{8} = \frac{6 \div 2}{8 \div 2} = \frac{3}{4} \end{array}$$

Add the numerators: 2 + 4 = 6
Use the common denominator.
Simplify, if possible.

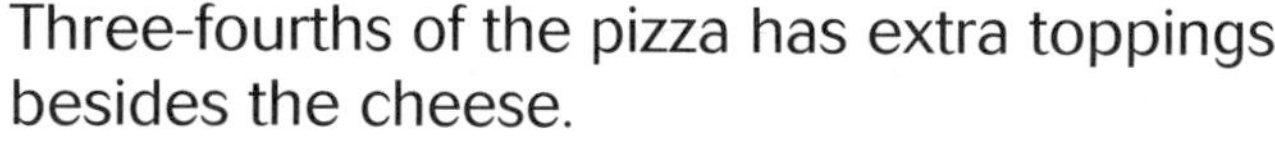

Three-fourths of the pizza has extra toppings besides the cheese.

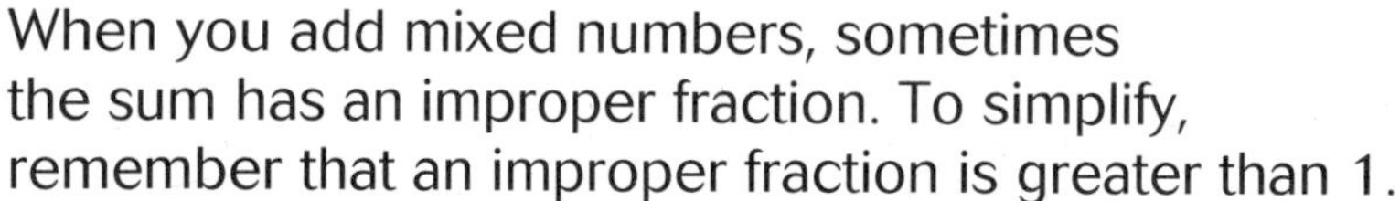

When you add mixed numbers, sometimes the sum has an improper fraction. To simplify, remember that an improper fraction is greater than 1.

Example 2

Simplify $4\frac{5}{3}$.

$$4\frac{5}{3} = 4 + \frac{3}{3} + \frac{2}{3}$$
$$= 4 + 1 + \frac{2}{3}$$
$$= 5 + \frac{2}{3}$$
$$= 5\frac{2}{3}$$

Here's WHY It Works

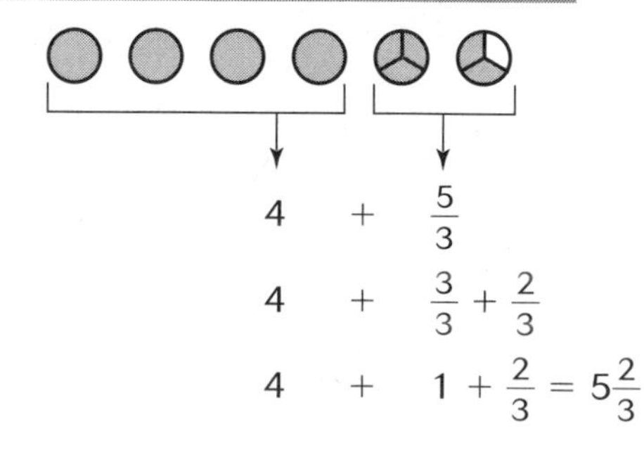

 Additional Standards: Mathematical Reasoning 2.1, 2.3, 3.1 (See p. 307.)

Example 3

Find $1\frac{2}{3} + 2\frac{2}{3}$.

Step 1 Add the fractions.	Step 2 Add the whole numbers.	Step 3 Simplify the sum, if possible.
$\begin{array}{r} 1\frac{2}{3} \\ + 2\frac{2}{3} \\ \hline \frac{4}{3} \end{array}$	$\begin{array}{r} 1\frac{2}{3} \\ + 2\frac{2}{3} \\ \hline 3\frac{4}{3} \end{array}$	$\begin{array}{r} 1\frac{2}{3} \\ + 2\frac{2}{3} \\ \hline 3\frac{4}{3} \end{array} = 3 + 1\frac{1}{3} = 4\frac{1}{3}$

Guided Practice

For another example, see Set A on p. 346.

Simplify.

1. $1\frac{5}{4} = 2\frac{\blacksquare}{4}$
2. $5\frac{3}{2} = 6\frac{\blacksquare}{2}$
3. $8\frac{7}{5}$
4. $1\frac{10}{4}$
5. $\frac{13}{12}$

Add. Write each answer in the simplest form.

6. $\frac{3}{12} + \frac{4}{12} = \frac{\blacksquare}{12}$
7. $4\frac{2}{5} + 3\frac{4}{5} = 7\frac{\blacksquare}{5} = 8\frac{\blacksquare}{5}$
8. $\frac{5}{8} + \frac{2}{8}$
9. $\frac{3}{5} + \frac{2}{5}$
10. $7\frac{2}{5} + 9\frac{4}{5}$
11. $6\frac{2}{3} + 8\frac{1}{3}$
12. $3\frac{5}{8} + 2\frac{7}{8}$

13. **Math Reasoning** Kevin said he ordered a pizza that was $\frac{2}{3}$ onions and $\frac{2}{3}$ mushrooms. Explain why this is possible.

Independent Practice

For more practice, see Set A on p. 349.

Simplify.

14. $5\frac{7}{6}$
15. $2\frac{11}{8}$
16. $1\frac{10}{7}$
17. $3\frac{5}{2}$
18. $12\frac{6}{5}$

Add. Write each answer in the simplest form.

19. $\frac{5}{7} + \frac{1}{7}$
20. $\frac{5}{9} + \frac{4}{9}$
21. $\frac{8}{15} + \frac{2}{15}$
22. $\frac{6}{13} + \frac{4}{13}$
23. $5\frac{4}{8} + 2\frac{3}{8}$
24. $\frac{5}{12} + \frac{11}{12}$
25. $1\frac{3}{4} + 1\frac{3}{4}$
26. $\frac{9}{10} + \frac{3}{10}$

Add. Write each answer in the simplest form.

27. $\frac{9}{10} + \frac{5}{10}$

28. $\frac{3}{8} + \frac{7}{8}$

29. $3\frac{2}{4} + 2\frac{3}{4}$

30. $7\frac{5}{6} + 5\frac{4}{6}$

31. $4\frac{2}{4} + 5\frac{3}{4}$

The table shows the rainfall during 5 rainy days in April.

Day	Mon.	Tue.	Wed.	Thu.	Fri.
Rainfall (inches)	$\frac{3}{8}$	$1\frac{1}{8}$	$\frac{7}{8}$	$\frac{5}{8}$	$\frac{1}{8}$

32. How much rain fell on Monday and Tuesday?

33. How much rain fell on Wednesday and Thursday?

34. How much rain fell during the 5 days?

35. Sam delivers pizza. He traveled $1\frac{1}{10}$ miles to the first stop. From there, he traveled $1\frac{3}{10}$ miles to the second stop. If it was 3 miles back to the pizza parlor, how far did he travel to make the two deliveries and return?

36. Math Reasoning Will the sum of $\frac{5}{8}$ and $\frac{4}{8}$ be greater or less than 1? How do you know without finding the exact sum?

Mixed Review

37. Sally is 8 years older than her sister and 3 years younger than her brother. Her brother is 16 years old. How old is Sally's sister?

Compare. Use > or < for ●.

38. $4\frac{5}{8}$ ● $4\frac{1}{8}$

39. $\frac{15}{10}$ ● 1

40. 1.02 ● 1.022

41. $\frac{1}{2}$ ● $\frac{7}{12}$

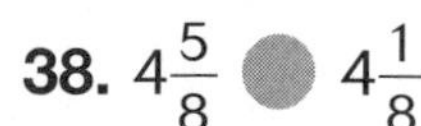

Test Prep Choose the correct letter for each answer.

42. (4-11) Leon bought 5 tennis balls for $0.89 each. How much did he spend?

A $44.50

B $4.45

C $0.94

D $4.05

E NH

43. (7-1) List the prime factors of 15.

F 1, 3, 5, 15

G 3, 5, 15

H 3, 5

J 1, 15

K NH

Subtracting Fractions and Mixed Numbers: Like Denominators

Warm-Up Review

1. 6.7 − 2.3
2. 0.8 − 0.3
3. 3.2 − 1.6
4. 7 − 0.24
5. 5.17 − 3.5
6. 4.87 − 4.271
7. Flo lives 1.3 miles from school. After she walked 0.7 mile, she met Alicia. How much farther did Flo have to walk to get to school?

California Content Standard *Number Sense 2.3 (🔑): Solve simple problems, including ones arising in concrete situations, involving the . . . subtraction of fractions and mixed numbers (like . . . denominators of 20 or less) and express answers in the simplest form.*

Math Link You know how to subtract decimals. Now you will subtract fractions and mixed numbers.

Example 1

According to the diagram, how much closer does Gary live to the mall than Pete?

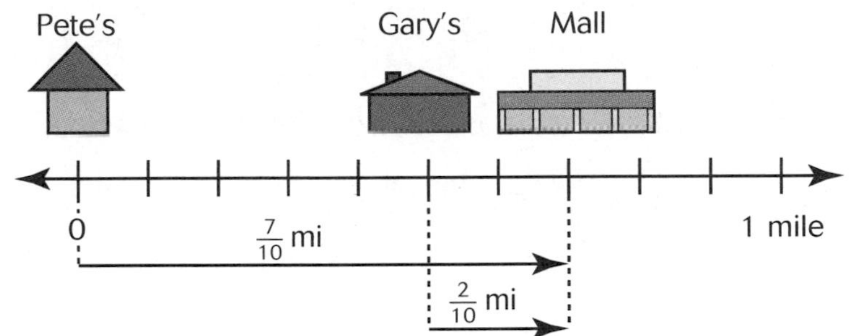

Find $\frac{7}{10} - \frac{2}{10}$.

$$\begin{array}{r} \frac{7}{10} \\ -\ \frac{2}{10} \\ \hline \frac{5}{10} \end{array} = \frac{5 \div 5}{10 \div 5} = \frac{1}{2}$$

Subtract the numerators: 7 − 2 = 5. Use the common denominator. Simplify the answer.

Gary lives $\frac{1}{2}$ mile closer to the mall than Pete.

When you subtract mixed numbers, sometimes you have to rename as shown in Example 2.

Example 2

Rename $3\frac{1}{4}$ to show 4 more fourths.

$$3\frac{1}{4} = 2 + 1 + \frac{1}{4}$$

$$= 2 + \frac{4}{4} + \frac{1}{4}$$

$$= 2 + \frac{5}{4} = 2\frac{5}{4}$$

Here's WHY It Works

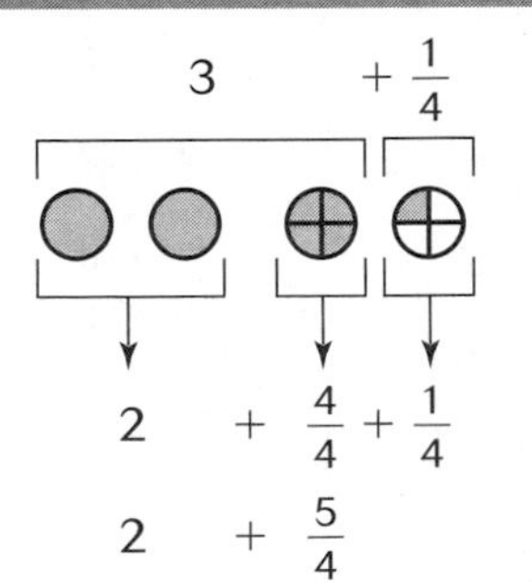

Example 3

Find $4\frac{1}{8} - 1\frac{5}{8}$.

Step 1 $\frac{1}{8} < \frac{5}{8}$, so before you subtract, rename $4\frac{1}{8}$ to show more eighths.

$$4\frac{1}{8} = 3\frac{8}{8} + \frac{1}{8} = 3\frac{9}{8}$$

$$-1\frac{5}{8} = \quad -1\frac{5}{8}$$

Step 2 Subtract the fractions. Then subtract the whole numbers.

$$3\frac{9}{8} - 1\frac{5}{8} = 2\frac{4}{8}$$

Step 3 Simplify, if possible.

$$3\frac{9}{8} - 1\frac{5}{8} = 2\frac{4}{8} = 2\frac{1}{2}$$

Guided Practice *For another example, see Set B on p. 346.*

Find the missing numerator.

1. $4\frac{1}{2} = 3\frac{■}{2}$
2. $7\frac{2}{3} = 6\frac{■}{3}$
3. $12\frac{2}{5} = 11\frac{■}{5}$
4. $2\frac{5}{8} = 1\frac{■}{8}$

Subtract. Write each answer in simplest form.

5. $\frac{7}{12} - \frac{4}{12} = \frac{■}{12} = \frac{■}{■}$
6. $\frac{11}{12} - \frac{5}{12}$
7. $4\frac{3}{8} - 1\frac{5}{8}$
8. $10\frac{1}{3} - 8\frac{2}{3}$

Independent Practice *For more practice, see Set B on p. 349.*

Find each missing numerator.

9. $2\frac{1}{6} = 1\frac{■}{6}$
10. $7\frac{2}{3} = 6\frac{■}{3}$
11. $3\frac{3}{5} = 2\frac{■}{5}$
12. $20\frac{3}{7} = 19\frac{■}{7}$

13. Rename $3\frac{3}{8}$ to show 8 more eighths.

14. Rename $6\frac{3}{4}$ to show 4 more fourths.

Subtract. Write each answer in simplest form.

15. $\frac{5}{8} - \frac{3}{8}$
16. $\frac{3}{5} - \frac{2}{5}$
17. $\frac{9}{10} - \frac{6}{10}$
18. $\frac{6}{7} - \frac{1}{7}$
19. $\frac{8}{9} - \frac{2}{9}$
20. $\frac{11}{12} - \frac{3}{12}$
21. $\frac{7}{10} - \frac{7}{10}$
22. $\frac{5}{5} - \frac{3}{5}$

23. $\frac{8}{11} - \frac{3}{11}$

24. $\frac{13}{15} - \frac{8}{15}$

25. $7\frac{8}{9} - 4\frac{4}{9}$

26. $5\frac{3}{12} - 4\frac{2}{12}$

27. $8\frac{3}{11} - 5\frac{5}{11}$

28. $4\frac{3}{4} - 1\frac{1}{4}$

29. $6\frac{2}{5} - 1\frac{4}{5}$

30. $5\frac{2}{7} - 3\frac{6}{7}$

Math Reasoning Solve each problem and explain your answer.

31. Charlie found seven-twelfths of a dozen muffins on the counter. After he and his friends ate some muffins, one muffin was left. What fraction of a dozen muffins did Charlie and his friends eat?

32. Mr. Wong cut a quiche into equal parts. He and his son each ate two slices. His wife and daughter each ate one slice. If one-fourth of the quiche was left, how many slices had Mr. Wong cut?

Mixed Review

33. The table shows the favorite colors of people buying cars at Wheels Auto Mall. Make a bar graph using the data in the table.

Favorite Car Colors

Color	Number
Green	16
White	15
Light Brown	14
Silver	11
Black	9
Other	35

34. Order $\frac{5}{8}$, $\frac{1}{2}$, and $\frac{3}{4}$ from least to greatest.

35. Round 0.567 to the nearest hundredth.

36. $\frac{5}{13} + \frac{11}{13}$

37. $4\frac{3}{4} + 9\frac{3}{4}$

38. Which is greater, $\frac{2}{8}$ or $\frac{3}{4}$?

Test Prep Choose the correct letter for each answer.

39. (4-10) Write using exponents: $6 \times 6 \times 6$.

A 6^3

B 3×6

C 3^6

D 216

40. (2-7) **Algebra** Which expression is the translation of "x less than 15"?

F $x - 15$

G $15 + x$

H $15 - x$

J $15 \times x$

Problem-Solving Skill:

Too Much or Too Little Information

Warm-Up Review

1. $\frac{5}{6} + \frac{1}{6}$
2. $\frac{7}{8} + \frac{7}{8}$
3. $\frac{5}{9} + \frac{7}{9}$
4. $\frac{11}{12} - \frac{5}{12}$
5. $\frac{2}{3} - \frac{1}{3}$
6. $\frac{9}{10} - \frac{5}{10}$
7. Tony spent \$8.95 on a CD. The sales tax was \$0.45. How much did he spend in all?

California Content Standard *Mathematical Reasoning 1.1 Analyze problems by identifying relationships, distinguishing relevant from irrelevant information, sequencing and prioritizing information, . . .*

Read For Understanding

Mrs. Gleason and her son are planning a picnic with friends. Their picnic basket will be packed with the items listed at the right. They will also put a bottle of juice, a $1\frac{3}{4}$-pound container of potato salad, a $\frac{3}{4}$-pound container of coleslaw, 8 apples, and some sandwiches in their cooler. The picnic grove is $17\frac{1}{2}$ miles away from the Gleasons' home, and they will drive about 35 miles per hour to get there. The grove is part of a 694-acre park.

1. How many sandwiches will be packed?
2. How many miles away is the picnic grove?

Think and Discuss

Too Much or Too Little Information

Sometimes you have more information than you need to solve a problem. At other times you have too little information. You must decide exactly what information you need to solve a problem.

Reread the paragraph at the top of the page. For Problems 3–5, tell what information you need to solve the problem. If the information is not given, write "too little information."

3. Did Mrs. Gleason pack enough glasses, plates, and sandwiches?
4. How long will it take Mrs. Gleason to get from home to the picnic grove?
5. Mrs. Gleason's friends, Patrice and Sarah, are planning to leave their home at 11:00 A.M. At what time will they arrive at the picnic grove?

 Additional Standard: Mathematical Reasoning 2.0 (See p. 307.)

Guided Practice

1. What information is needed to help find the cost of the potato salad?
   a. The size of the container
   b. The cost of one pound of salad
   c. The store at which Mrs. Gleason bought the salad

2. How can you find the total weight of the potato salad and the coleslaw?
   a. Add the two weights.
   b. Subtract $\frac{3}{4}$ from $1\frac{3}{4}$.
   c. Add the cost of the potato salad and the cost of the coleslaw.

Independent Practice

Ken plans to get to the picnic at noon and stay for about two hours. Before leaving, he made a snack using the recipe shown at the right. The raisins, walnuts, and seeds cost $5.76.

Snack Mix
2/3 lb walnuts
2/3 lb raisins
1/3 lb sunflower seeds

3. What information is needed to help find the total weight of the snack?
   a. Ken plans to spend two hours at the park.
   b. Ken used $\frac{2}{3}$ pound of walnuts.
   c. The snack cost $5.76 to make.

4. What information is not needed to find the total weight of the snack?
   a. Ken used $\frac{2}{3}$ pound of raisins.
   b. Ken used $\frac{2}{3}$ pound of walnuts.
   c. The snack cost $5.76 to make.

5. Which of the following tells how to find the total weight of the snack?
   a. Multiply the weight of the walnuts by 2.
   b. Divide the total cost by 3, the number of foods in the snack.
   c. Add the weight of the walnuts, raisins, and sunflower seeds.

6. Which equation can be used to find the total weight of the snack?
   a. $\frac{2}{3} + \frac{2}{3} + \frac{1}{3} = 1\frac{2}{3}$
   b. $5.76 \div 3 = 1.92$
   c. $2 \times \frac{2}{3} = 1\frac{1}{3}$

Solve each problem or tell what information is missing.

Ken is making a salad using a recipe that calls for pasta, 6 cherry tomatoes, and 3 sliced carrots. Ken needs enough salad for two people, so he will only make $\frac{2}{3}$ of the recipe.

7. How much pasta should Ken use?

8. How many people does the whole salad recipe serve?

Estimating Sums and Differences of Mixed Numbers

California Content Standard *Number Sense 2.3 (🔑): Solve simple problems, including ones arising in concrete situations, involving the addition and subtraction of . . . mixed numbers . . ..*

Math Link You have estimated sums and differences with whole numbers and decimals. Now you will estimate sums and differences with fractions.

Warm-Up Review

Estimate each sum or difference. Round to the nearest whole number.

1. 7.8 + 4.5
2. 2.55 + 6.15
3. 5.6 − 3.2
4. 9.86 − 6.99
5. Do three pieces of luggage weighing 24.5 pounds, 31.3 pounds, and 26.7 pounds exceed the weight limit of 75 pounds?

The lengths of N model train cars and HO model train cars are shown.

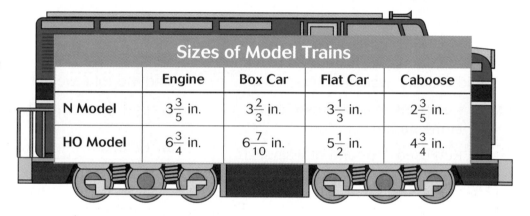

Sizes of Model Trains

	Engine	Box Car	Flat Car	Caboose
N Model	$3\frac{3}{5}$ in.	$3\frac{2}{3}$ in.	$3\frac{1}{3}$ in.	$2\frac{3}{5}$ in.
HO Model	$6\frac{3}{4}$ in.	$6\frac{7}{10}$ in.	$5\frac{1}{2}$ in.	$4\frac{3}{4}$ in.

You can estimate sums and differences of mixed numbers by rounding each to the nearest whole number. If the fraction is greater than or equal to $\frac{1}{2}$, round up to the next whole number. Otherwise round down.

Example 1

Estimate the length of an N model train with an engine and a caboose.

$3\frac{3}{5} \rightarrow 4$ $\quad \frac{3}{5} > \frac{1}{2}$ so round $3\frac{3}{5}$ to 4.

$+\ 2\frac{3}{5} \rightarrow +\ 3$ $\quad$ Round $2\frac{3}{5}$ to 3.

7

Together, the engine and caboose are about 7 inches long.

Example 2

About how much longer is the HO model flat car than the N model flat car?

$5\frac{1}{2} \rightarrow 6$ $\quad \frac{1}{2} = \frac{1}{2}$ so round $5\frac{1}{2}$ to 6.

$-\ 3\frac{1}{3} \rightarrow -\ 3$ $\quad \frac{1}{3} < \frac{1}{2}$ so round $3\frac{1}{3}$ to 3.

3

The HO model flat car is about 3 inches longer than the N model flat car.

Additional Standard: Mathematical Reasoning 2.1 (See p. 307.)

Guided Practice *For another example, see Set C on p. 346.*

Estimate each sum or difference.

1. $2\frac{3}{4} + 5\frac{1}{4}$

2. $6\frac{7}{8} - 2\frac{3}{8}$

3. $2\frac{5}{6} + 5\frac{5}{6}$

4. $8\frac{5}{6} - 2\frac{1}{6}$

5. Estimate the difference in the length of the HO model caboose and the N model caboose.

Independent Practice *For more practice, see Set C on p. 349.*

Estimate each sum or difference.

6. $5\frac{3}{5} - 2\frac{4}{5}$

7. $5\frac{3}{7} + 4\frac{5}{7}$

8. $8\frac{7}{12} - 5\frac{5}{12}$

9. $5 + 3\frac{5}{6}$

10. $9 - 1\frac{1}{5}$

11. $5\frac{3}{10} - 2$

12. $4\frac{6}{7} + 5\frac{4}{7}$

13. $5\frac{4}{5} + 9\frac{2}{5}$

14. $12\frac{3}{7} - 5\frac{6}{7}$

15. $7 - 3\frac{2}{8}$

16. $5\frac{1}{6} - 4\frac{5}{6}$

17. $7\frac{8}{12} - 3\frac{2}{12}$

18. $7\frac{1}{8} - 3\frac{1}{8}$

An HO model train and an N model train each consist of 1 engine, 3 box cars, 2 flat cars, and 1 caboose. Estimate the total length of each train.

19. The N model train

20. The HO model train

21. Math Reasoning Ed calculated that he would need 5 feet of straight track to display 2 N model trains with at least 10 inches of track between them. Is his answer reasonable?

Mixed Review

22. Ms. Hall's company pays her \$0.32 for each mile she drives for work. How much did she receive for a 621-mile trip?

23. $3\frac{7}{8} + 1\frac{5}{8}$

24. $4\frac{3}{4} - 2\frac{1}{4}$

25. 61.5 − 8.72

26. 48.84 ÷ 37

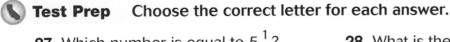

Test Prep **Choose the correct letter for each answer.**

27. Which number is equal to $5\frac{1}{4}$?
(7-6)

A 5.75

B 5.625

C 5.375

D 5.25

28. What is the average of 67, 48, and 51?
(5-9)

F 166

G $55\frac{1}{3}$

H 3

J 55

Adding Fractions: Unlike Denominators

Warm-Up Review

Find the LCM of each pair of numbers.

1. 3, 5 **2.** 6, 12

3. 6, 9 **4.** 6, 8

5. 3, 7 **6.** 4, 10

7. 5, 6 **8.** 9, 12

9. Tony wants to divide 24 oranges evenly among himself and 5 friends. How many oranges can he give to each friend?

California Content Standard *Number Sense 2.3 (key): Solve simple problems, including ones arising in concrete situations, involving the addition . . . of fractions . . . (. . . unlike denominators of 20 or less), and express answers in the simplest form.*

Math Link You have added fractions with like denominators. Now you will add fractions with unlike denominators.

Example 1

Mr. Nochim is building a fence. He wants to bolt together the two boards shown. To decide what length bolt to use, he must find the total thickness of the two boards.

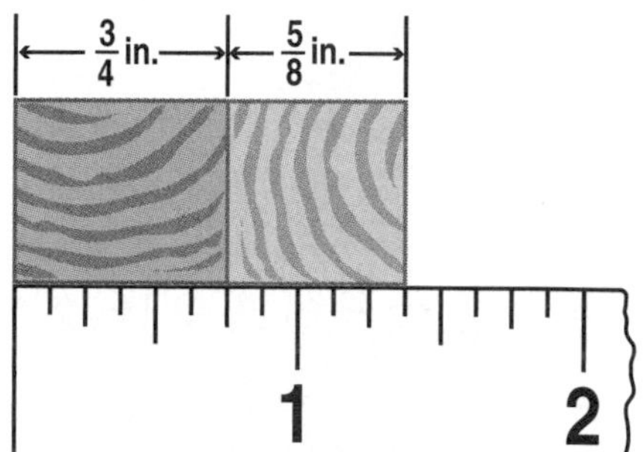

To find the thickness, add $\frac{3}{4} + \frac{5}{8}$.

Step 1 Find the least common denominator. The LCD is the least common multiple of 4 and 8.

$$\frac{3}{4} + \frac{5}{8}$$

Multiples of 4: 4, **8**, 12, . . .

Multiples of 8: **8**, 16, 24, . . .

LCM: **8**

Step 2 Write equivalent fractions using the LCD.

$$\frac{3}{4} = \frac{3 \times 2}{4 \times 2} = \frac{6}{8}$$

$$+\frac{5}{8} = +\frac{5}{8}$$

Step 3 Add. Simplify the sum, if possible.

$$\frac{3}{4} = \frac{6}{8}$$

$$+\frac{5}{8} = +\frac{5}{8}$$

$$\frac{11}{8} = 1\frac{3}{8}$$

The total thickness of the two boards together is $1\frac{3}{8}$ inches.

Example 2

Find $\frac{3}{8} + \frac{5}{6}$.

$$\frac{3}{8} = \frac{3 \times 3}{8 \times 3} = \frac{9}{24}$$

$$+\frac{5}{6} = \frac{5 \times 4}{6 \times 4} = +\frac{20}{24}$$

$$\frac{29}{24} = 1\frac{5}{24}$$

Think: Multiples of 6: 6,12, 18, **24**, 30, . . .
Multiples of 8: 8, 16, **24**, . . .
LCM: **24**

 Additional Standard: Mathematical Reasoning 2.0 *(See p. 307.)*

Guided Practice *For another example, see Set D on p. 346.*

Add. Simplify each sum, if possible.

1. $\frac{2}{5} + \frac{1}{2}$ **2.** $\frac{1}{2} + \frac{3}{10}$ **3.** $\frac{5}{6} + \frac{1}{4}$ **4.** $\frac{3}{8} + \frac{3}{4}$ **5.** $\frac{5}{9} + \frac{3}{4}$

6. Math Reasoning Find $\frac{1}{6} + \frac{1}{4}$ using a common denominator of 12. Then use a common denominator of 24. Compare your answers.

Independent Practice *For more practice, see Set D on p. 349.*

Add. Simplify each sum, if possible.

7. $\frac{7}{10} + \frac{1}{5}$ **8.** $\frac{9}{10} + \frac{1}{4}$ **9.** $\frac{4}{5} + \frac{3}{4}$ **10.** $\frac{4}{5} + \frac{2}{3}$ **11.** $\frac{3}{8} + \frac{1}{2}$

12. $\frac{2}{3} + \frac{1}{9}$ **13.** $\frac{5}{8} + \frac{1}{2}$ **14.** $\frac{5}{6} + \frac{5}{8}$ **15.** $\frac{3}{10} + \frac{1}{4}$ **16.** $\frac{5}{7} + \frac{1}{3}$

17. $\frac{7}{15} + \frac{1}{3}$ **18.** $\frac{1}{8} + \frac{3}{4}$ **19.** $\frac{2}{5} + \frac{2}{3}$ **20.** $\frac{1}{3} + \frac{5}{6}$ **21.** $\frac{1}{3} + \frac{4}{6} + \frac{1}{4}$

22. It took Mr. Nochim $\frac{1}{2}$ hour to attach the gate to the fence and another $\frac{1}{3}$ hour to attach the hand lock. How long did these two tasks take?

23. Will a $1\frac{1}{2}$-inch bolt go through two boards, each $\frac{5}{8}$-inch thick?

Mixed Review

24. For school, Rob can wear blue or black pants and a white shirt, a blue sweater, or a gray sweatshirt. How many different ways can he choose a pair of pants and a top?

25. Estimate: $6\frac{7}{8} - 2\frac{1}{4}$ **26.** Subtract: $3\frac{5}{8} - 1\frac{7}{8}$ **27.** Divide: 3.7 ÷ 1,000

Test Prep **Choose the correct letter for each answer.**

28. $0.06 \times 0.07 =$
(6-6)

A 0.042 **D** 0.42
B 0.00042 **E** NH
C 4.2

29. $15{,}286 - 8{,}195 =$
(2-9)

F 7,091 **J** 6,191
G 23,481 **K** NH
H 7,191

LESSON 8-6

Subtracting Fractions: Unlike Denominators

California Content Standard *Number Sense 2.3 (🔑): Solve simple problems, including ones arising in concrete situations, involving the . . . subtraction of fractions . . . (unlike denominators of 20 or less), and express answers in the simplest form.*

Math Link You have subtracted fractions with like denominators. Now you will subtract fractions with unlike denominators.

Warm-Up Review

Write each fraction in simplest form.

1. $\frac{8}{12}$ 2. $\frac{6}{10}$ 3. $\frac{9}{15}$
4. $\frac{6}{18}$ 5. $\frac{12}{8}$ 6. $\frac{10}{4}$
7. $\frac{6}{5}$ 8. $\frac{8}{3}$ 9. $\frac{7}{7}$
10. Lisa spent one-half hour on reading homework, one-fourth hour on math, and one-third hour on reading. Did she spend more or less than one hour on homework?

Example

At 8:00 A.M. Judy began a long hike with a full bottle of water. At 10:00 A.M. the bottle was $\frac{2}{3}$ full. At noon, it was only $\frac{1}{4}$ full. How much of the water did Judy drink between 10:00 A.M. and noon?

Find $\frac{2}{3} - \frac{1}{4}$.

Step 1 Find the LCD.

$\frac{2}{3}$ Multiples of 3: 3, 6, 9, **12**, 15, . . .

$-\frac{1}{4}$ Multiples of 4: 4, 8, **12**, . . .

Step 2 Write equivalent fractions using the LCD.

$\frac{2}{3} = \frac{2 \times 4}{3 \times 4} = \frac{8}{12}$

$-\frac{1}{4} = \frac{1 \times 3}{4 \times 3} = -\frac{3}{12}$

Step 3 Subtract. Simplify, if possible.

$\frac{2}{3} = \frac{8}{12}$

$-\frac{1}{4} = -\frac{3}{12}$

$\frac{5}{12}$

Judy drank $\frac{5}{12}$ of the water between 10:00 A.M. and noon.

More Examples

A. $\frac{5}{6} - \frac{1}{2} = \frac{5}{6} - \frac{3}{6} = \frac{2}{6} = \frac{1}{3}$

B. $\frac{5}{6} - \frac{1}{4} = \frac{10}{12} - \frac{3}{12} = \frac{7}{12}$

Guided Practice

For another example, see Set E on p. 347.

Subtract. Simplify each difference, if possible.

1. $\frac{3}{8} - \frac{1}{4}$ 2. $\frac{3}{4} - \frac{2}{3}$ 3. $\frac{1}{2} - \frac{1}{8}$ 4. $\frac{5}{9} - \frac{1}{3}$ 5. $\frac{2}{3} - \frac{3}{8}$

6. **Math Reasoning** Can you use a common denominator greater than the least common denominator? If *yes,* give an example.

 Additional Standard: Mathematical Reasoning 3.3 (See p. 307.)

Independent Practice *For more practice, see Set E on p. 350.*

Subtract. Simplify, if possible.

7. $\frac{6}{7} - \frac{1}{2}$ **8.** $\frac{3}{5} - \frac{1}{4}$ **9.** $\frac{3}{6} - \frac{1}{9}$ **10.** $\frac{2}{3} - \frac{5}{9}$

11. $\frac{3}{4} - \frac{1}{2}$ **12.** $\frac{4}{5} - \frac{2}{3}$ **13.** $\frac{7}{8} - \frac{3}{4}$ **14.** $\frac{1}{2} - \frac{3}{10}$

15. $\frac{5}{10} - \frac{1}{4}$ **16.** $\frac{3}{5} - \frac{1}{3}$ **17.** $\frac{6}{8} - \frac{1}{3}$ **18.** $\frac{5}{12} - \frac{1}{3}$

19. $\frac{13}{18} - \frac{2}{9}$ **20.** $\frac{7}{12} - \frac{1}{4}$ **21.** $\frac{11}{12} - \frac{2}{3}$ **22.** $\frac{3}{5} - \frac{2}{5}$

23. How much farther is it from Bear Cave to Silver Creek Crossing than from Fallen Rock to Silver Creek Crossing?

24. Judy is walking from Bear Cave to Lone Tree. She has gone $\frac{1}{2}$ mile. How much farther does she have to go?

25. How far is a walk from the Ranger Station to Lone Tree, to Bear Cave, to Silver Creek Crossing, and back to the Ranger Station?

26. Mental Math How much farther is it from Bear Cave to Lone Tree than from Silver Creek Crossing to the Ranger Station?

Mixed Review

27. If 45 ounces of juice is divided evenly among 6 children, will each child get a cup of juice? One cup is 8 ounces.

28. Is $\frac{6}{7}$ greater than or less than 1?

29. Estimate: $13\frac{8}{9} - 10\frac{1}{3}$

30. $\frac{2}{3} + \frac{3}{5}$ **31.** 12.6×4.7 **32.** $0.7 - 0.14$ **33.** $0.29 + 0.63$

Test Prep **Choose the correct letter for each answer.**

34. Algebra $n + 7 = 16$. Find n.
(2-4)

A $2\frac{2}{7}$ C 9
B 23 D 112

35. Which is the LCM of 18 and 45?
(7-4)

F 9 H 45
G 90 J 3

Adding Mixed Numbers

Warm-Up Review

Write each number in simplest form.

1. $1\frac{10}{7}$
2. $8\frac{4}{3}$
3. $4\frac{9}{5}$
4. $3\frac{8}{3}$
5. $2\frac{7}{4}$
6. $5\frac{11}{10}$
7. Lisa spent \$3.10, \$3.05, and \$0.79 on school supplies. How much did she spend in all?

California Content Standard *Number Sense 2.3. (🔑): Solve simple problems, including ones arising in concrete situations, involving the addition . . . of . . . mixed numbers (. . . unlike denominators of 20 or less), and express answers in the simplest form.*

Math Link You have added fractions. Now you will add mixed numbers.

Example

To make a snack, P.J. bought the raisins, sunflower seeds, and banana chips shown. How many pounds of food did he buy?

$1\frac{2}{3} + 1\frac{1}{4} + 1\frac{1}{6} = n$

Step 1 Find the LCD.

$1\frac{2}{3}$	Multiples of 3: 3, 6, 9, **12**, 15, . . .
$1\frac{1}{4}$	Multiples of 4: 4, 8, **12**, 16, . . .
$+\ 1\frac{1}{6}$	Multiples of 6: 6, **12**, 18, . . .

Step 2 Write equivalent fractions using the LCD.

$$1\frac{2}{3} = 1\frac{8}{12}$$
$$1\frac{1}{4} = 1\frac{3}{12}$$
$$+\ 1\frac{1}{6} = +\ 1\frac{2}{12}$$

Step 3 Add. Simplify, if possible.

$$1\frac{2}{3} = 1\frac{8}{12}$$
$$1\frac{1}{4} = 1\frac{3}{12}$$
$$+\ 1\frac{1}{6} = +\ 1\frac{2}{12}$$
$$3\frac{13}{12} = 4\frac{1}{12}$$

Estimate to check: 2 + 1 +1 = 4.

The food weighed $4\frac{1}{12}$ pounds. The answer is close to the estimate.

Guided Practice *For another example, see Set F on p. 347.*

Find the sum and simplify, if possible. Check by estimating.

1. $3\frac{2}{3} + 5\frac{1}{6}$
2. $2\frac{7}{8} + 1\frac{1}{4}$
3. $9\frac{3}{5} + 5\frac{3}{4}$
4. $8\frac{7}{10} + 5\frac{3}{5}$
5. $2\frac{3}{7} + 5\frac{1}{3}$
6. Give two other numbers you could use as a common denominator in Exercise 1. Is the product of 3 and 6 a common denominator?

 Additional Standard: Mathematical Reasoning 2.1 (See p. 307.)

Independent Practice

For more practice, see Set F on p. 350.

Find each sum and simplify, if possible. Check by estimating.

7. $3\frac{5}{8} + 2\frac{2}{3}$ **8.** $4\frac{6}{7} + 1\frac{1}{2}$ **9.** $8\frac{3}{5} + 2\frac{1}{3}$ **10.** $9\frac{7}{8} + 2\frac{1}{4}$ **11.** $2\frac{3}{8} + 1\frac{5}{6}$

12. $2\frac{3}{4} + 1\frac{3}{5}$ **13.** $6\frac{2}{5} + 1\frac{3}{7}$ **14.** $4\frac{8}{9} + 2\frac{1}{2}$ **15.** $3\frac{6}{7} + 1\frac{2}{3}$ **16.** $5\frac{2}{5} + 3\frac{1}{3}$

17. $5\frac{2}{9} + 3\frac{2}{3}$ **18.** $3\frac{2}{9} + 5\frac{5}{6}$ **19.** $2\frac{4}{5} + 5\frac{3}{8}$ **20.** $8 + 2\frac{3}{4}$ **21.** $9\frac{6}{7} + 3\frac{1}{2}$

Use the table showing train travel times between Orlando and Seattle.

22. Estimate the total travel time on each route.

23. Find the exact time for the shortest route.

24. Find the exact time for the longest route.

Travel Times from Orlando, FL to Seattle, WA

Part of Trip	Route A	Route B	Route C	Route D
1st Segment	$19\frac{1}{3}$ hr	$18\frac{2}{3}$ hr	$63\frac{1}{5}$ hr	$35\frac{2}{3}$ hr
Train Change	$6\frac{1}{3}$ hr	$2\frac{2}{3}$ hr	$3\frac{5}{12}$ hr	$2\frac{5}{12}$ hr
2nd Segment	$19\frac{5}{6}$ hr	19 hr	$34\frac{2}{3}$ hr	$30\frac{1}{2}$ hr
Train Change	$6\frac{1}{6}$ hr	$6\frac{1}{2}$ hr		$2\frac{1}{6}$ hr
3rd Segment	$45\frac{1}{4}$ hr	$45\frac{1}{4}$ hr		$45\frac{1}{4}$ hr

Mixed Review

25. Nanette lives 10 blocks south of Bret. Sis lives 6 blocks north of Bret. Liam lives south of Sis and halfway between Nanette and Sis. How far does Bret live from Liam?

26. $\frac{3}{8} + \frac{4}{10}$ **27.** $\frac{9}{10} - \frac{2}{3}$ **28.** 4.6×0.37 **29.** $62.8 \div 0.4$

Test Prep Choose the correct letter for each answer.

30. (7-5) About 300 adult and student tickets were sold for the play. Student tickets cost $3 and adult tickets cost $5. Which is the most reasonable amount collected from ticket sales?

A $1500 **C** $900
B $300 **D** $1200

31. (7-3) What is the GCF of 28 and 42?

F 7 **J** 84
G 2 **K** NH
H 14

Subtracting Mixed Numbers

Warm-Up Review

Rename:

1. $1\frac{1}{3}$ to show 3 more thirds.
2. $4\frac{2}{5}$ to show 5 more fifths.
3. $3\frac{5}{9}$ to show 9 more ninths.
4. There was a half gallon of milk before lunch and a fourth of a gallon left after lunch. How much milk was used during lunch?

California Content Standard *Number Sense 2.3. (🔑): Solve simple problems, including ones arising in concrete situations, involving the . . . subtraction of . . . mixed numbers (. . . unlike denominators of 20 or less), and express answers in the simplest form.*

Math Link You have subtracted fractions. Now you will subtract mixed numbers.

Example 1

The average rise and fall of the tides in eight cities is shown. For the two cities in Maine, how much higher is the average in Eastport than in Portland?

$19\frac{1}{3} - 9\frac{11}{12} = n$

Average Rise and Fall of the Tides (ft)			
Eastport, ME	$19\frac{1}{3}$	Portland, ME	$9\frac{11}{12}$
Seattle, WA	$11\frac{1}{3}$	Ft. Pulaski, GA	$7\frac{1}{2}$
Vancouver, B.C.	$10\frac{1}{2}$	Philadelphia, PA	$6\frac{3}{4}$
Boston, MA	$10\frac{1}{3}$	San Francisco, CA	$5\frac{5}{6}$

Step 1 Write equivalent fractions with the LCD.

$$19\frac{1}{3} = 19\frac{4}{12}$$
$$-\ 9\frac{11}{12} = -\ 9\frac{11}{12}$$

Step 2 Since $\frac{4}{12} < \frac{11}{12}$, rename $19\frac{4}{12}$ to show more twelfths.

$$19\frac{4}{12} = 18\frac{12}{12} + \frac{4}{12} = 18\frac{16}{12}$$
$$-\ 9\frac{11}{12} \qquad\qquad -\ 9\frac{11}{12}$$

Step 3 Subtract the fractions and the whole numbers. Simplify if possible.

$$18\frac{16}{12} - 9\frac{11}{12} = 9\frac{5}{12}$$

Estimate to check: 19 − 10 = 9.

The average in Eastport is $9\frac{5}{12}$ feet higher. The answer is close to the estimate.

Example 2

$$6 = 5\frac{8}{8}$$
$$-\ 4\frac{2}{8} = -\ 4\frac{2}{8}$$
$$1\frac{6}{8} = 1\frac{3}{4}$$

Example 3

$$12\frac{2}{5} = 12\frac{4}{10} = 11\frac{14}{10}$$
$$-\ 6\frac{1}{2} = -\ 6\frac{5}{10} = -\ 6\frac{5}{10}$$
$$5\frac{9}{10}$$

 Additional Standards: Mathematical Reasoning 2.1 and 2.3 (See p. 307.)

Guided Practice

For another example, see Set G on p. 347.

Find each difference and simplify, if possible. Check by estimating.

1. $\begin{array}{r} 4\frac{1}{4} = 4\frac{3}{12} = 3\frac{■}{12} \\ -\,2\frac{1}{3} = -\,2\frac{4}{12} = -\,2\frac{4}{12} \\ \hline 1\frac{■}{12} \end{array}$

2. $\begin{array}{r} 5 = ■\frac{8}{8} \\ -\,2\frac{3}{8} = -\,2\frac{3}{8} \\ \hline ■\frac{5}{8} \end{array}$

3. $\begin{array}{r} 3\frac{3}{4} = 3\frac{■}{■} \\ -\,2\frac{1}{8} = -\,2\frac{1}{8} \\ \hline 1\frac{■}{■} \end{array}$

4. $\begin{array}{r} 5\frac{1}{2} \\ -\,2\frac{2}{5} \\ \hline \end{array}$

5. $\begin{array}{r} 7\frac{1}{8} \\ -\,4\frac{1}{4} \\ \hline \end{array}$

6. $5\frac{3}{10} - 2\frac{1}{2}$

7. $11 - 5\frac{3}{4}$

8. Use the information in the table in Example 1. How much higher is the average rise and fall of tide in Boston than in Philadelphia?

Independent Practice

For more practice, see Set G on p. 350.

Find each difference and simplify, if possible. Check by estimating.

9. $\begin{array}{r} 8\frac{3}{5} \\ -\,5\frac{3}{10} \\ \hline \end{array}$

10. $\begin{array}{r} 14\frac{2}{3} \\ -\,3\frac{1}{6} \\ \hline \end{array}$

11. $\begin{array}{r} 9\frac{7}{8} \\ -\,2\frac{3}{4} \\ \hline \end{array}$

12. $\begin{array}{r} 5\frac{3}{8} \\ -\,1\frac{1}{2} \\ \hline \end{array}$

13. $\begin{array}{r} 10 \\ -\,4\frac{5}{8} \\ \hline \end{array}$

14. $9 - 5\frac{2}{3}$

15. $18\frac{3}{7} - 3\frac{1}{7}$

16. $6\frac{3}{8} - 2\frac{1}{4}$

17. $2\frac{3}{5} - \frac{7}{10}$

18. $9\frac{1}{4} - 6\frac{3}{4}$

19. $8\frac{2}{7} - 4\frac{3}{14}$

20. $7 - 3\frac{5}{8}$

21. $8\frac{4}{5} - 6$

Use the information in the table in Example 1. Find the difference in the average rise and fall of the tide for each pair of cities.

22. Seattle, WA, and San Francisco, CA

23. Vancouver, B.C., and Portland, ME

24. Boston, MA, and Ft. Pulaski, GA

25. Philadelphia, PA, and Eastport, ME

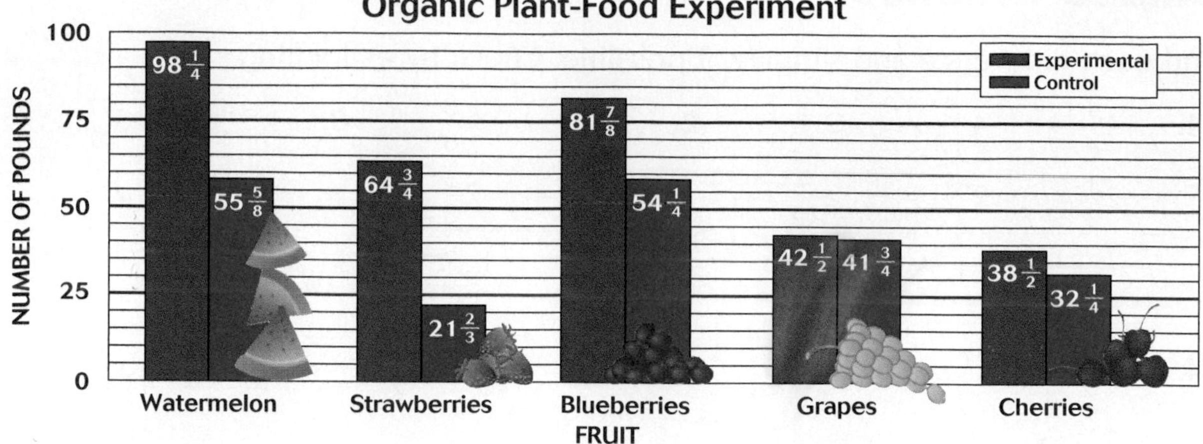

For an agricultural project, some fruit plants were given an experimental plant food. The bar graph above shows the number of pounds of each fruit produced using the plant food (Experimental) and not using the plant food (Control).

26. Which fruit showed the greatest difference in the weight between plants that received the food and those that did not? How much was the difference?

27. Which fruit showed the smallest difference in the weight between plants that received the food and those that did not? How much was the difference?

Mixed Review

28. Mrs. Lillie put 500 bagels in packages with 12 bagels in each package. How many bagels were left over?

29. Is $\frac{5}{8}$ greater than or less than $\frac{1}{2}$?

30. Algebra: Solve $3x = 15$ for x.

31. $3\frac{7}{10} - 2\frac{3}{4}$

32. $\frac{11}{12} - \frac{2}{3}$

33. $\frac{7}{8} + \frac{1}{3}$

34. $1\frac{3}{8} + 1\frac{7}{8}$

 **Test Prep** **Choose the correct letter for each answer.**

35. (3-7) Find the range of these test scores: 72, 86, 100, 90, 85.

A 87

B 82

C 86

D 28

36. (6-4) Amusement park ticket prices are: \$8.75 for adults, \$4.50 for children age 5–15, and free for children under 5. How much would the tickets cost for two adults and three children, ages 13, 8, and 4?

F \$17.75

G \$26.50

H \$28.00

J 23.50

 Use Homework Workbook 8-8.

Diagnostic Checkpoint

Add. Simplify each sum, if possible.

1. (8-1) $\frac{4}{7} + \frac{2}{7}$

2. (8-1) $8\frac{5}{12} + 4\frac{7}{12}$

3. (8-5) $\frac{1}{2} + \frac{1}{3}$

4. (8-5) $\frac{5}{6} + \frac{5}{18}$

5. (8-7) $5\frac{1}{8} + 4\frac{1}{2}$

6. (8-7) $2\frac{3}{10} + 1\frac{1}{5}$

7. (8-7) $3\frac{5}{16} + 1\frac{3}{4}$

8. (8-7) $8\frac{2}{5} + 6\frac{11}{15}$

Estimate each sum or difference.

9. (8-4) $4\frac{3}{5} + 1\frac{1}{5}$

10. (8-4) $7\frac{5}{16} + 8\frac{11}{16}$

11. (8-4) $3\frac{2}{5} - 1\frac{4}{5}$

12. (8-4) $5\frac{3}{7} - 4$

Subtract. Simplify each difference, if possible.

13. (8-2) $\frac{7}{9} - \frac{5}{9}$

14. (8-2) $2\frac{1}{8} - 1\frac{4}{8}$

15. (8-6) $\frac{5}{15} - \frac{1}{3}$

16. (8-6) $\frac{7}{10} - \frac{1}{2}$

17. (8-8) $7\frac{3}{4} - 6\frac{2}{5}$

18. (8-8) $15\frac{3}{8} - 4\frac{9}{16}$

19. (8-8) $9\frac{27}{28} - 5$

20. (8-8) $10 - 4\frac{5}{8}$

21. (8-3) Carole has a bread recipe that requires $3\frac{2}{3}$ cups of flour and $\frac{1}{2}$ cup of water. She wants to double the recipe. How much flour does she need? What information is not needed to solve this problem?

22. (8-4) Ms. Barth needs about $2\frac{1}{2}$ lb of plant food for her corn and about $1\frac{1}{3}$ lb for her green vegetables. About how many pounds of plant food does she need?

23. (8-7) Marcus bought $2\frac{5}{8}$ lb of oats, $1\frac{3}{4}$ lb of hay, and $2\frac{1}{8}$ lb of barley to feed his horse. How many pounds of horse feed did he buy?

Understand
Plan
Solve
Look Back

Problem-Solving Strategy:
Solve a Simpler Problem

California Content Standard *Mathematical Reasoning 2.2: Apply strategies and results from simpler problems to more complex problems. Also Mathematical Reasoning 3.2 (See p. 307.)*

Warm-Up Review

Give the next three numbers in the pattern.

1. 3, 5, 7, 9, . . .

2. 2, 5, 8, 11, . . .

3. 1, 2, 4, 7, 11, . . .

4. In how many different ways can Kelly select a blouse and a skirt from 4 blouses and 2 skirts?

Example

Paul is spending his birthday money on sports video games. The games the store sells are shown. In how many different ways can Paul select two games?

Basketball
Football
Golf
Hockey
Rugby
Lacrosse
Volleyball

Understand

What do you need to find?

You need to find the number of different ways Paul can choose 2 of the 7 games.

Plan

How can you solve the problem?

You can begin by solving a simpler problem. List how many ways Paul can choose 2 games if the store sells only 2 games, then if the store sells only 3 games, and so on.

Solve

Think of the games as B, F, G, H, R, L, and V. Make a table. Look for a pattern.

Number of Games Sold	Ways to Select 2 Games	Number of Ways
2: B and F	BF	1
3: B, F, and G	BF, **BG**, **FG**	3 1 + **2** = 3
4: B, F, G, and H	BF, BG, FG, **BH**, **FH**, **GH**	6 3 + **3** = 6
5: B, F, G, H, and R	BF, BG, FG, BH, FH, GH, **BR**, **FR**, **GR**, **HR**	10 6 + **4** = 10

Follow the pattern: for 2 out of 6 games ⟶ 10 + **5** = 15
Follow the pattern: for 2 out of 7 games ⟶ 15 + **6** = 21

There are 21 ways that Paul can select 2 out of 7 games.

Look Back

List the ways Paul can select 2 out of 7 games. Are there 21?

  *Additional Standards: Mathematical Reasoning 1.1, 1.2 (See p. 307.)*

Guided Practice

Use a simpler problem to help you solve each problem.

1. The students on the baton-twirling team are marching in 6 rows. There is 1 student in the first row, 3 in the second, 5 in the third, and so on. If this pattern continues how many members of the team are marching?

2. A tree grew 3 branches in the first year and 2 new branches each year after that. How many branches did it have after ten years?

Independent Practice

3. Blocks have a letter of the alphabet on each side. How many letters are showing if 18 blocks are lined up side by side?

4. A book has the title on the front cover and the side. How many titles can you see if there are four stacks of six books? The fronts of the books in each stack are facing up.

5. Squares for a quilt are $4\frac{1}{2}$ inches on each side. How many squares can be cut from a piece of material 15 inches wide and 20 inches long?

6. Eight people are buying apples. The first customer buys 1 apple. After the second customer leaves, 4 apples have been sold. After the third customer leaves, 9 apples have been sold. After the fourth customer leaves, 16 apples have been sold. If this pattern continues, how many apples will be sold?

Mixed Review

Try these or other strategies to solve each problem. Tell which strategy you used.

Problem-Solving Strategies

- *Work Backward*
- *Write an Equation*
- *Make a Table*
- *Find a Pattern*

7. A juice recipe contains these juices: $4\frac{5}{8}$ cups orange, $2\frac{1}{4}$ cups lemon, and $\frac{3}{8}$ cups lime. Twice the recipe will make how many cups of juice?

8. Mrs. Kane lives $9\frac{1}{2}$ miles south of Sunset St. and $6\frac{7}{10}$ miles south of Grand St. How much closer is she to Grand than Sunset?

Use Homework Workbook 8-9.

Multiplying by a Fraction

California Content Standard *Number Sense 2.4: Understand the concept of multiplication . . . of fractions. Also Number Sense 2.5.* *(See p. 307.)*

Math Link You know how to multiply by a whole number or a decimal. Now you will learn how to multiply by a fraction.

Warm-Up Review

Write as a mixed number in simplest form.

1. $\frac{34}{10}$ 2. $\frac{27}{6}$ 3. $\frac{48}{9}$

4. $\frac{54}{4}$ 5. $\frac{51}{8}$ 6. $\frac{36}{10}$

7. Bill worked 38 hours in 6 days. What is the average number of hours he worked a day?

Word Bank

reciprocal

Example 1

The Dodd family received a crate of apples as a gift. Three-fourths of the apples were Delicious apples and $\frac{2}{3}$ of the Delicious apples were Golden Delicious. What fraction of the apples in the crate were Golden Delicious apples?

To find $\frac{2}{3}$ of $\frac{3}{4}$, multiply $\frac{2}{3} \times \frac{3}{4}$.

- Multiply the numerators.
- Then multiply the denominators.
- Simplify the product, if possible.

$$\frac{2}{3} \times \frac{3}{4} = \frac{2 \times 3}{3 \times 4} = \frac{6}{12} = \frac{1}{2}$$

One-half of the apples in the crate were Golden Delicious apples.

Here's WHY It Works

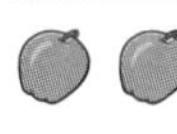

$\frac{3}{4}$ are Delicious

$\frac{2}{3}$ of $\frac{3}{4}$ are Golden

$\frac{6}{12}$, or $\frac{1}{2}$, are Golden Delicious

Example 2

Find $\frac{2}{3}$ of 5.

$\frac{2}{3} \times 5 = \frac{2}{3} \times \frac{5}{1}$ Write 5 as $\frac{5}{1}$.

$= \frac{2 \times 5}{3 \times 1}$ Multiply the numerators. Then multiply the denominators.

$= \frac{10}{3} = 3\frac{1}{3}$ Simplify the product.

Here's WHY It Works

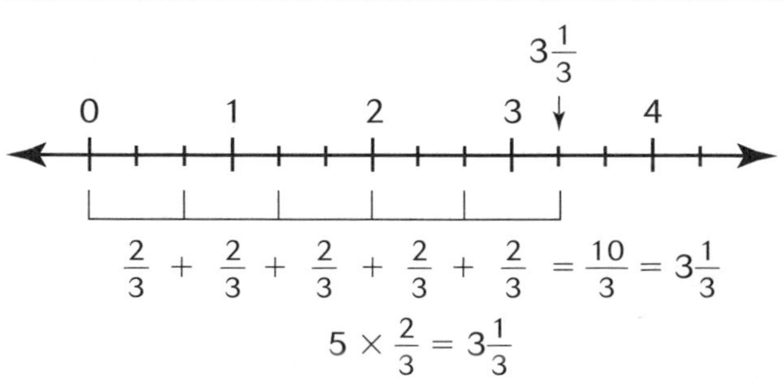

Additional Standards: Algebra and Functions 1.2 (key); Mathematical Reasoning 1.1 *(See p. 307.)*

Two numbers whose product is 1 are **reciprocals** of each other. Recognizing reciprocals can make multiplication easier. The reciprocal of $\frac{5}{6}$ is $\frac{6}{5}$.

Example 3

Find $\frac{5}{6} \times \frac{6}{5}$.

$$\frac{5}{6} \times \frac{6}{5} = \frac{5 \times 6}{6 \times 5} = \frac{30}{30} = 1$$

Here's WHY It Works

For any fraction and its reciprocal, the numerator and denominator are reversed. This means that when a fraction and its reciprocal are multiplied, the numerator and denominator of the product have the same factors, so they are equal. Since its numerator and denominator are equal, the product equals 1.

More Examples

A. $\frac{1}{8} \times 8 = \frac{1}{8} \times \frac{8}{1} = \frac{8}{8} = 1$

B. $4 \times \frac{1}{4} = \frac{4}{1} \times \frac{1}{4} = \frac{4}{4} = 1$

Guided Practice *For another example, see Set H on p. 348.*

Multiply. Simplify the product, if possible.

1. $\frac{2}{3} \times \frac{1}{2} = \frac{2 \times 1}{3 \times 2} = \frac{■}{■}$
2. $\frac{5}{8} \times \frac{8}{5}$
3. $\frac{3}{5} \times 3$
4. Find $\frac{1}{3}$ of 4.
5. Find $\frac{3}{4}$ of $\frac{3}{4}$.
6. Find $\frac{1}{8}$ of $\frac{1}{2}$.
7. Look at Exercise 2. What is the reciprocal of $\frac{5}{8}$? How do you know?
8. **Math Reasoning** If a fraction is less than 1, explain why its reciprocal is greater than 1.

Independent Practice *For more practice, see Set H on p. 351.*

Multiply. Simplify the product, if possible.

9. $\frac{3}{4} \times \frac{1}{6}$
10. $\frac{1}{10} \times \frac{1}{10}$
11. $\frac{3}{4} \times \frac{1}{4}$
12. $\frac{3}{8} \times \frac{2}{3}$
13. $\frac{1}{6} \times \frac{5}{6}$
14. $\frac{1}{8} \times \frac{3}{4}$
15. $\frac{3}{5} \times \frac{7}{8}$
16. $\frac{1}{4} \times \frac{5}{6}$
17. $\frac{1}{2} \times \frac{6}{7}$
18. $\frac{11}{12} \times \frac{3}{4}$
19. Find $\frac{5}{9}$ of 6.
20. Find $\frac{4}{5}$ of 20.
21. Find $\frac{2}{3}$ of 12.

22. Show that $\frac{1}{7}$ is the reciprocal of 7.

23. **Algebra** Find n if $5n = 3$. Show the answer as a fraction.

24. **Math Reasoning** Can you think of two fractions less than 1 with a product greater than 1? Explain.

25. Ben found a recipe that uses $\frac{3}{4}$ cup of chopped apples. If he wants to make half a batch, how many cups of chopped apples should he use?

Last month Pedals sold 80 bicycles in the colors shown in the graph. How many bicycles of each color were sold?

Bicycle Colors

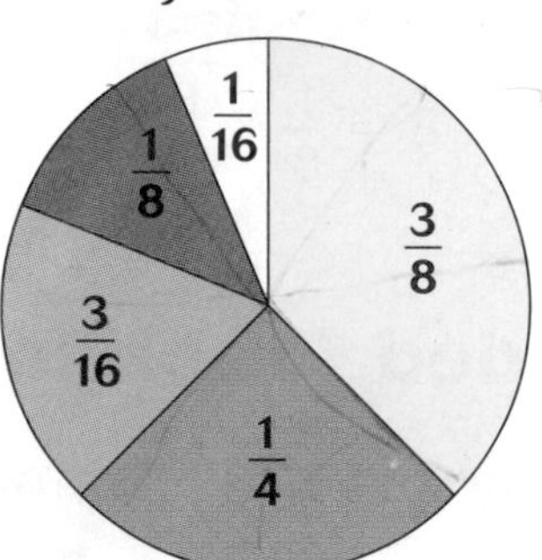

26. Red 27. Blue 28. Yellow

29. Green 30. Other (shown in white)

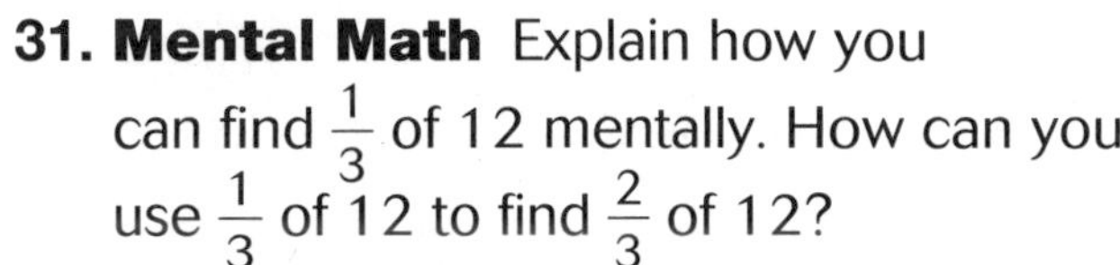

31. **Mental Math** Explain how you can find $\frac{1}{3}$ of 12 mentally. How can you use $\frac{1}{3}$ of 12 to find $\frac{2}{3}$ of 12?

Mixed Review

32. The first hour Greg hiked $2\frac{7}{10}$ miles into Granite Gorge. Then he spent $1\frac{3}{4}$ hours hiking $1\frac{1}{2}$ miles up Granite Mountain. It took him another two hours to hike 4 miles back to his car. How many miles did Greg hike?

33. $4\frac{1}{3} - 1\frac{1}{4}$ 34. $2\frac{3}{8} + 4\frac{1}{6}$ 35. 0.07×0.02 36. $3.862 + 0.45$

Test Prep **Choose the correct letter for each answer.**

37. Which *does not* equal $\frac{8}{20}$?
(7-12)

A $\frac{4}{10}$
B $\frac{2}{5}$
C $\frac{16}{40}$
D $\frac{80}{100}$
E NH

38. Which shows the prime factorization of 24?
(7-2)

F 4×6
G $2^3 \times 3$
H 3×8
J 2×3
K NH

Multiple-Choice Cumulative Review

Choose the correct letter for each answer.

1. **In Maria's science experiment, Frog A weighed 350 grams, and Frog B weighed 425 grams. Frog A then gained 125 grams, while Frog B stayed the same weight. How much more does Frog A now weigh than Frog B?**

A 25 g **C** 475 g
B 50 g **D** 550 g

2. **Evaluate 2^5.**

F 8
G 10
H 16
J 32
K NH

3. **A container holds a dozen eggs. If a transport company needs to ship 835 eggs, how many of these containers does it need?**

A 69 **C** 83
B 70 **D** 84

4. **Which of the following is *not* equal to $\frac{33}{6}$?**

F $5\frac{1}{2}$
G $\frac{11}{2}$
H $5\frac{1}{3}$
J $5\frac{3}{6}$

5. **Amy has 4 beanbag animals to arrange in a row on one shelf. In how many different orders can she arrange the animals?**

A 8 **C** 16
B 12 **D** 24

6. **Find** $\begin{array}{r} 12\frac{5}{8} \\ -\ 6\frac{3}{4} \\ \hline \end{array}$

F $5\frac{1}{8}$ **J** $6\frac{7}{8}$
G $5\frac{7}{8}$ **K** NH
H $6\frac{1}{8}$

7. **Each page of the playbill for the school play can hold eight ads. If $\frac{3}{4}$ of one page is full, what is the greatest number of ads that can still fit on the page?**

A 1 ad **C** 4 ads
B 2 ads **D** 6 ads

8. **Jack and Sue planted seeds in a large seed tray. Jack used $\frac{7}{16}$ of the tray, and Sue used $\frac{5}{16}$ of the same tray. What part of the tray was left unplanted?**

F $\frac{1}{4}$ **H** $\frac{11}{16}$
G $\frac{9}{16}$ **J** $\frac{3}{4}$

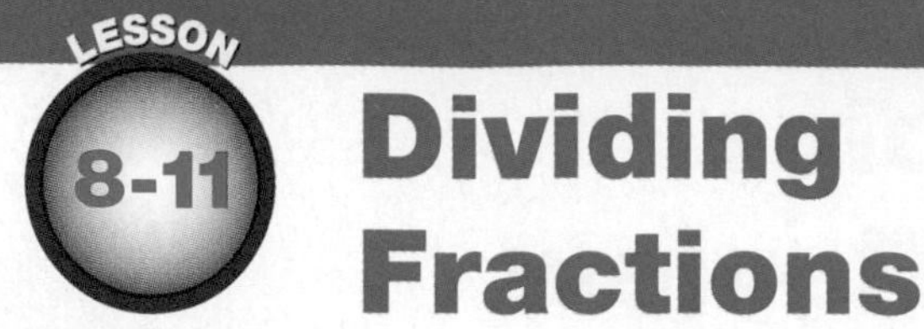

Dividing Fractions

California Content Standard *Number Sense 2.4: Understand the concept of . . . division of fractions. Also Number Sense 2.5. (See p. 307.)*

Math Link You know how to divide by a whole number and by a decimal. Now you will learn to divide by a fraction.

Warm-Up Review

1. $6 \div 2 =$
   $60 \div 20 =$
   $600 \div 200 =$
2. $8 \div 4 =$
   $16 \div 8 =$
   $32 \div 16 =$
3. $2 \div 3 =$
   $4 \div 6 =$
   $6 \div 9 =$
4. How many 4-inch tiles laid end-to-end make 12 feet?

Example 1

Della is making the bracelet shown at the right. How many beads does she need?

Each bead is $\frac{3}{4}$ of an inch long. Divide to find how many $\frac{3}{4}$-inch segments there are in 6 inches.

$$6 \div \frac{3}{4} = \frac{6}{1} \div \frac{3}{4}$$
$$= \frac{6}{1} \times \frac{4}{3}$$
$$= \frac{24}{3} = 8$$

Dividing by $\frac{3}{4}$ is the same as multiplying by the reciprocal of $\frac{3}{4}$. The reciprocal of $\frac{3}{4}$ is $\frac{4}{3}$.

Della needs 8 beads.

Here's WHY It Works

Dividend	Divisor	Quotient
$\left(\frac{6}{1}\right)$	$\div \left(\frac{3}{4}\right)$	$= n$
$\left(\frac{6}{1} \times \frac{4}{3}\right)$	$\div \left(\frac{3}{4} \times \frac{4}{3}\right)$	$= n$
$\left(\frac{6}{1} \times \frac{4}{3}\right)$	$\div (1)$	$= n$
$\left(\frac{6}{1} \times \frac{4}{3}\right)$		$= n$

- You can multiply the dividend and divisor by the same nonzero number without changing the quotient.
- Multiply the dividend and divisor by the reciprocal of the divisor to get a divisor of 1.
- Dividing by 1 does not change the answer.

Example 2

$$\frac{3}{7} \div \frac{1}{2} = \frac{3}{7} \times \frac{2}{1} = \frac{6}{7}$$

Multiply by the reciprocal of the divisor. The reciprocal of $\frac{1}{2}$ is $\frac{2}{1}$.

 Additional Standard: Mathematical Reasoning 3.3 (See p. 307.)

Guided Practice *For another example, see Set I on p. 348.*

Divide. Simplify the quotient if possible

1. $\frac{5}{8} \div \frac{7}{8} = \frac{5}{8} \times \frac{8}{7} = \frac{■}{■}$

2. $\frac{3}{4} \div \frac{1}{8}$

3. $6 \div \frac{2}{3}$

4. Look at Example 1. If Della had used $\frac{1}{2}$-inch beads, how many beads would she need for a 6-inch bracelet?

Independent Practice *For more practice, see Set I on p. 351.*

Divide. Simplify the quotient if possible.

5. $\frac{6}{7} \div \frac{2}{7}$

6. $\frac{1}{4} \div \frac{1}{2}$

7. $\frac{1}{2} \div \frac{1}{4}$

8. $\frac{3}{8} \div \frac{1}{8}$

9. $\frac{2}{3} \div \frac{3}{3}$

10. $2 \div \frac{3}{5}$

11. $\frac{1}{3} \div 6$

12. $5 \div \frac{1}{4}$

13. $\frac{7}{8} \div \frac{3}{8}$

14. $\frac{1}{4} \div \frac{2}{3}$

15. $\frac{1}{5} \div \frac{1}{5}$

16. $\frac{15}{16} \div \frac{3}{4}$

17. Mental Math At the Surf City Sub Shop, each pound of Swiss cheese is divided into $\frac{1}{8}$-lb portions for sandwiches. How many portions does Surf City get from a 5-lb block of cheese?

18. Math Reasoning What fraction of an hour is ten minutes? Explain how you can use division by a fraction to figure out how many ten-minute periods there are in a day.

Mixed Review

19. There are 32 students in Mr. Jackson's class. Three-eighths of them are in the math club. How many of Mr. Jackson's students are in the math club?

20. $\frac{3}{8} \times \frac{4}{5}$

21. $3\frac{1}{4} - 1\frac{1}{2}$

22. $4 - 0.73$

23. $5.4 \div 0.03$

Test Prep Choose the correct letter for each answer.

24. Simplify $\frac{26}{4}$.
(7-11)

A $\frac{13}{2}$

B $6\frac{2}{4}$

C $6\frac{1}{2}$

D $5\frac{6}{4}$

E NH

25. $\frac{5}{12} + \frac{5}{6} =$
(8-5)

F $1\frac{1}{4}$

G $1\frac{5}{12}$

H $\frac{10}{18}$

J $\frac{10}{12}$

K NH

Multiplying and Dividing Mixed Numbers

California Content Standard *Number Sense 2.5: Compute and perform simple multiplication and division of fractions and apply these procedures to solving problems.*

Warm-Up Review

Write as an improper fraction.

1. $2\frac{1}{4}$ **2.** $1\frac{7}{8}$ **3.** $4\frac{2}{5}$

4. 6 **5.** $3\frac{3}{7}$ **6.** $5\frac{2}{3}$

7. For an egg dish, the school chef used 15 dozen eggs. How many eggs is this?

Math Link You have multiplied and divided by fractions. Now you will multiply and divide mixed numbers.

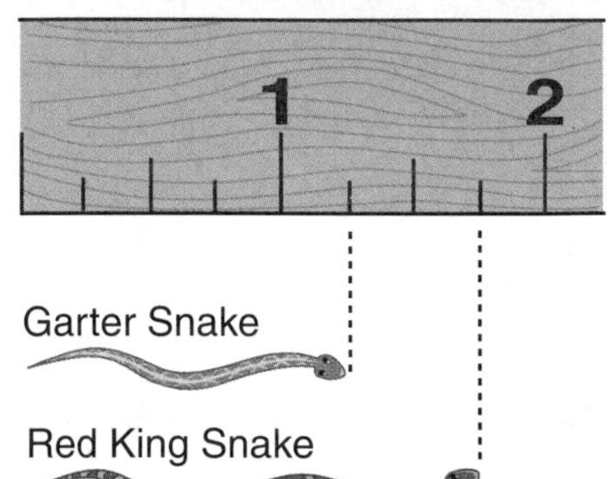

Example 1

The actual length of a garter snake is about 15 times as long as its length in the picture. What is the actual length of the garter snake?

Find $15 \times 1\frac{1}{4}$.

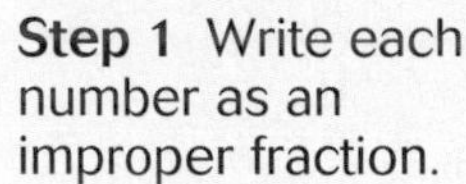

Step 1 Write each number as an improper fraction.

$15 \times 1\frac{1}{4} = \frac{15}{1} \times \frac{5}{4}$

Step 2 Multiply. Write the product in simplest form.

$\frac{15}{1} \times \frac{5}{4} = \frac{15 \times 5}{1 \times 4} = \frac{75}{4} = 18\frac{3}{4}$

Estimate to check: $15 \times 1 = 15$

The answer is reasonable.

The garter snake is about $18\frac{3}{4}$ inches long.

Example 2

$3\frac{1}{2} \times 2\frac{2}{3} = \frac{7}{2} \times \frac{8}{3}$ Write the numbers as improper fractions.

$= \frac{7 \times 8}{2 \times 3}$ Multiply.

$= \frac{56}{6} = 9\frac{2}{6} = 9\frac{1}{3}$ Simplify.

Example 3

$2\frac{1}{4} \div 1\frac{1}{2} = \frac{9}{4} \div \frac{3}{2}$ Write the numbers as improper fractions.

$= \frac{9}{4} \times \frac{2}{3}$ Multiply by the reciprocal of the divisor.

$= \frac{9 \times 2}{4 \times 3}$

$= \frac{18}{12} = 1\frac{6}{12} = 1\frac{1}{2}$ Simplify.

Guided Practice *For another example, see Set J on p. 348.*

Multiply or divide. Simplify, if possible.

1. $2\frac{1}{2} \times 2\frac{1}{2}$ **2.** $2\frac{1}{6} \times 1\frac{1}{3}$ **3.** $9\frac{1}{2} \div 6$ **4.** $4\frac{1}{2} \div 1\frac{1}{4}$

5. The red king snake is 15 times longer than its length in the picture. What is the actual length of the red king snake?

Independent Practice *For more practice, see Set J on p. 351.*

Multiply or divide. Simplify, if possible.

6. $5 \times 1\frac{3}{5}$ **7.** $\frac{3}{5} \times 2\frac{2}{3}$ **8.** $\frac{5}{9} \times 2\frac{1}{2}$ **9.** $6 \times \frac{1}{8}$

10. $1\frac{1}{4} \times 6$ **11.** $9 \times \frac{3}{16}$ **12.** $6 \div 3\frac{1}{2}$ **13.** $2\frac{1}{4} \div \frac{3}{8}$

14. $2\frac{1}{2} \div \frac{15}{16}$ **15.** $7\frac{1}{5} \div 4\frac{1}{2}$ **16.** $5\frac{1}{4} \div 1\frac{3}{4}$ **17.** $8\frac{1}{4} \div 3\frac{2}{3}$

18. If water is coming out of a faucet at a rate of $\frac{1}{5}$ of a gallon per second, how long will it take to fill a $1\frac{1}{2}$-gallon bucket?

19. If a leaky faucet wastes $1\frac{1}{4}$ gallons of water a day. How much water is wasted in a week?

Mixed Review

20. A fifth grade class of 25 students collected bottles to turn in for a $0.05 deposit refund on each bottle. If they received $17.50, how many bottles did they turn in?

21. $\frac{4}{5} \div \frac{1}{5}$ **22.** $\frac{3}{4} \times \frac{2}{3}$ **23.** $\frac{1}{8} + \frac{3}{4}$ **24.** $\frac{9}{10} - \frac{2}{5}$

Test Prep **Choose the correct letter for each answer.**

25. $1\frac{1}{2} - \frac{2}{3} =$ (8-8)

A $\frac{1}{3}$ **D** $\frac{5}{5}$

B $\frac{5}{6}$ **E** NH

C $\frac{1}{6}$

26. $3\frac{5}{8} + 4\frac{3}{4} =$ (8-7)

F $7\frac{3}{8}$ **J** $8\frac{5}{8}$

G 8 **K** NH

H $8\frac{3}{8}$

Problem-Solving Application:

Finding Fraction Patterns

Warm-Up Review

Describe each pattern.

1. 2, 4, 6, 8, . . .
2. 10, 20, 30, 40, . . .
3. 2, 3, 5, 8, 12, . . .
4. Tom is stacking cans. He puts 10 cans in the first row, 9 in the second, 8 in the third, and so on. How many cans are used to make 6 rows?

California Content Standard *Mathematical Reasoning 1.1: Analyze problems by identifying relationships, . . . and observing patterns.*

Example

The drawing shows part of the stepped foundation of a monument. The fraction compares the width of each step to the width of the first step. What fraction of the width of the first step will the tenth step be?

Understand

What do you need to find?

You need to find what fraction of the width of the first step the tenth step will be.

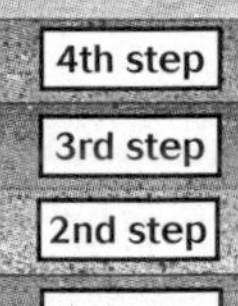

Plan

How can you solve the problem?

You can **look for a pattern** of how the fractions change with each step. Then continue the pattern to the tenth step.

Solve

Look for a pattern.

Step: 1 2 3 4

Fraction: $\frac{1}{1}, \frac{1}{2}, \frac{1}{3}, \frac{1}{4}, \ldots$

Continue the pattern to the 10th step.

5 6 7 8 9 10

$\ldots \frac{1}{5}, \frac{1}{6}, \frac{1}{7}, \frac{1}{8}, \frac{1}{9}, \frac{1}{10}$

The numerator of each fraction is 1. The denominators increase by 1. The tenth step will be $\frac{1}{10}$ the width of the first step.

Look Back

Notice another pattern. The numerators of the fractions are 1 and the denominators are the numbers of the steps. Does the fraction for the tenth step fit this pattern?

Additional Standards: Number Sense 2.5; Mathematical Reasoning 2.0 *(See p. 307.)*

Guided Practice

Look for a pattern to solve these problems.

1. Jenny is knitting a striped scarf by repeating the colors blue, red, white. She is using the pattern $\frac{1}{2}$-inch blue, 1-inch red, $1\frac{1}{2}$-inch white, 2-inch blue, and so on. How wide and what color will the tenth stripe be?

Independent Practice

2. As pieces are cut from a 48-inch submarine sandwich the number of inches remaining follows this pattern: $45\frac{1}{2}$, 43, $40\frac{1}{2}$, 38, and so on. How many inches are left after 8 sandwiches have been cut?

3. To dim the lights on stage, a lighting crew member turns a dial a fraction of a whole turn using this pattern: $\frac{1}{12}$, $\frac{1}{10}$, $\frac{1}{8}$, $\frac{1}{6}$. What are the next two fractions in this pattern?

4. Jason cut a 160-inch long piece of string into fourths. Then he cut each fourth into fourths. He did this two more times. How long was each piece after the fourth cut?

5. A magician has a 160-inch rope. He cut off 80 inches, then 40 inches, then 20 inches, and so on. Following this pattern, what are the next three lengths that will be cut off?

Mixed Review

Solve each problem.

6. Claudia eats one muffin out of every 15 muffins she bakes. How many muffins will she actually have to bake so she has 42 muffins for the bake sale?

7. Four tournament players are sitting at a square table. The champion is on Mai's right. Jeff is across from Mai. Nick is on Jeff's right and across from Sean. Who is the champion?

8. Pedro's car trip took 82 hours. He spent 23 hours in motels and 11 hours eating or taking rest stops. If he was driving the remaining time, how many hours did he drive?

Use Homework Workbook 8-13.

LESSON 8-14

Evaluating Expressions with Fractions

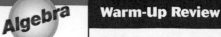

Algebra

Warm-Up Review

Evaluate each expression.

1. $56 + n$ when $n = 27$
2. $6y$ when $y = 1.3$
3. $n - 4.2$ when $n = 10$
4. $\frac{x}{3}$ when $x = 96$
5. Paula has saved \$25.37 towards a radio that costs \$49.95. How much more money does she need?

California Content Standard *Algebra and Functions 1.2: (🔑): Use a letter to represent an unknown number; . . . evaluate simple algebraic expressions in one variable by substitution.*

Math Link You have evaluated expressions with whole numbers and decimals. Now you will evaluate expressions with fractions.

Example 1

The signs at the right show the discounts offered during a sale. How much money would you save if you bought a sweater?

You would save $\frac{1}{4}$ of the original price. Remember, to find a fraction *of* a number, multiply by that fraction. You can use the expression $\frac{1}{4}p$ to find your savings.

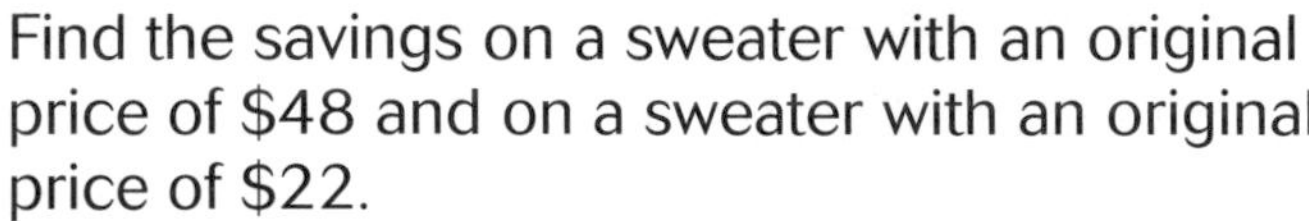

Find the savings on a sweater with an original price of \$48 and on a sweater with an original price of \$22.

Evaluate $\frac{1}{4}p$ when $p = \$48$.

$\frac{1}{4}p = \frac{1}{4} \times 48 = \frac{1}{4} \times \frac{48}{1} = \frac{48}{4} = 12$

The savings on a \$48 sweater would be \$12.

Evaluate $\frac{1}{4}p$ when $p = \$22$.

$\frac{1}{4}p = \frac{1}{4} \times 22 = \frac{1}{4} \times \frac{22}{1} = \frac{22}{4} = 5\frac{1}{2}$

The savings on a \$22 sweater would be $5\frac{1}{2}$ dollars, or \$5.50.

Example 2

Evaluate the expression $\frac{3}{4} - x$ when $x = \frac{2}{3}$.

$\frac{3}{4} - x = \frac{3}{4} - \frac{2}{3}$

$= \frac{9}{12} - \frac{8}{12} = \frac{1}{12}$

Example 3

Evaluate the expression $m + 2\frac{1}{2}$ when $m = 3\frac{3}{8}$.

$m + 2\frac{1}{2} = 3\frac{3}{8} + 2\frac{1}{2}$

$= 3\frac{3}{8} + 2\frac{4}{8} = 5\frac{7}{8}$

Example 4

Evaluate the expression $r \div 2$ when $r = \frac{3}{5}$.

$\frac{3}{5} \div 2 = \frac{3}{5} \div \frac{2}{1}$

$= \frac{3}{5} \times \frac{1}{2} = \frac{3}{10}$

 Additional Standards: Number Sense 2.3 (🔑), 2.5 (See p. 307.)

Guided Practice *For another example, see Set K on p. 348.*

Evaluate.

1. $2\frac{3}{4} - n$, when $n = 1\frac{1}{2}$

2. $\frac{1}{2}x$, when $x = \frac{2}{3}$

3. $\frac{3}{4} \div d$, when $d = \frac{1}{4}$

4. Jeans are on sale for $\frac{1}{3}$ off. Use the expression $\frac{1}{3}p$ to find the savings on a pair of jeans that originally cost $22.50.

Independent Practice *For more practice, see Set K on p. 351.*

Evaluate $x + \frac{2}{3}$ and $2\frac{2}{3} - x$ for each given value of x.

5. $x = \frac{3}{4}$

6. $x = 2\frac{1}{2}$

7. $x = 1\frac{1}{3}$

8. $x = 2$

Evaluate $\frac{2}{3}y$ and $y \div \frac{1}{2}$ for each given value of y.

9. $y = \frac{5}{8}$

10. $y = 1\frac{2}{3}$

11. $y = \frac{7}{8}$

12. $y = 4\frac{2}{3}$

13. Some shoes are on sale for $\frac{2}{3}$ off the original price. Use $\frac{2}{3}p$ to find the savings on shoes with an original price of $36.

14. What is the sale price of the shoes that originally cost $36?

15. **Math Reasoning** With a discount of $\frac{2}{3}$ off the original price, what fraction of the original price would you pay?

Mixed Review

16. The heights of six basketball players in inches are: 76, 80, 78, 86, 89, and 80. What is their average height?

17. $1\frac{1}{8} \times 2\frac{1}{3}$

18. $2\frac{3}{4} \div 1\frac{1}{8}$

19. $\frac{7}{9} \div \frac{2}{3}$

20. $\frac{4}{7} + \frac{3}{4}$

Test Prep **Choose the correct letter for each answer.**

21. $\frac{5}{8} \times \frac{3}{5} =$ (8-10)

A $\frac{3}{8}$

B $1\frac{9}{40}$

C $\frac{8}{13}$

D $\frac{1}{40}$

E NH

22. $\frac{5}{6} \div \frac{2}{3} =$ (8-11)

F $1\frac{1}{2}$

G $\frac{5}{9}$

H $\frac{4}{5}$

J $1\frac{1}{4}$

K NH

Diagnostic Checkpoint

Complete. For Exercises 1–3, use the words from the Word Bank.

Word Bank

- improper fraction
- fraction
- mixed number
- reciprocal
- simplest form
- least common denominator

1. (8-10) The product of a number and its ________________ is 1.

2. (8-1) A(n) ________________ is a number written as a whole number and a fraction.

3. (8-12) A(n) ________________ is a fraction in which the numerator is greater than or equal to the denominator.

Multiply or divide. Simplify, if possible.

4. (8-10) $\frac{3}{4} \times \frac{1}{3}$

5. (8-10) $\frac{1}{2} \times \frac{2}{3}$

6. (8-11) $\frac{2}{3} \div \frac{7}{9}$

7. (8-11) $\frac{1}{2} \div \frac{3}{4}$

8. (8-12) $3\frac{1}{4} \times 1\frac{1}{2}$

9. (8-12) $2\frac{5}{6} \times 8$

10. (8-12) $3\frac{2}{3} \div \frac{3}{10}$

11. (8-12) $7\frac{1}{2} \div 5\frac{1}{4}$

12. (8-10) Find $\frac{2}{3}$ of 42.

13. (8-10) Find $\frac{5}{9}$ of 27.

14. (8-10) Find $\frac{6}{7}$ of 56.

Evaluate.

15. (8-14) $5\frac{1}{2} - x$, when $x = 2\frac{3}{8}$

16. (8-14) $\frac{4}{15}n$, when $n = 4\frac{1}{6}$

17. $x + \frac{3}{4}$, when $x = 2\frac{1}{2}$

18. $\frac{2}{5}a$, when $a = 15$

19. $y - 1\frac{1}{5}$, when $y = 6$

20. $n \div \frac{3}{8}$, when $n = \frac{2}{3}$

21. (8-9) Boxes of fruit are labeled on each of four sides and both ends of each box. The boxes are lined up end-to-end in a single row so that the boxes touch. If there are 10 boxes in one row, how many labels are visible?

22. (8-13) Jill cut a 120-inch long piece of rope into fourths. Then she cut each fourth into fourths. She did this one more time. How long was each piece after the third cut?

Chapter 8 Test

Add or subtract. Simplify, if possible.

1. $1\frac{1}{8} + 1\frac{5}{8}$

2. $\frac{5}{12} + \frac{3}{8}$

3. $6\frac{3}{10} + 4\frac{1}{3}$

4. $7\frac{4}{9} + 6\frac{2}{3}$

5. $4\frac{5}{9} - 2\frac{4}{9}$

6. $\frac{8}{9} - \frac{5}{6}$

7. $8\frac{11}{12} - 4\frac{5}{6}$

8. $9\frac{1}{8} - 3\frac{3}{10}$

Multiply or divide. Simplify, if possible.

9. $\frac{5}{9} \times \frac{18}{25}$

10. $10 \times 4\frac{1}{2}$

11. $\frac{5}{6} \div \frac{1}{3}$

12. $8\frac{2}{3} \div 1\frac{4}{9}$

Estimate each sum or difference.

13. $2\frac{5}{6} + 1\frac{7}{8}$

14. $7\frac{3}{8} + 5\frac{3}{4}$

15. $3\frac{4}{7} - 2\frac{1}{3}$

Evaluate.

16. $x + 4\frac{2}{3}$ when $x = 1\frac{3}{4}$

17. $n \div 2\frac{1}{2}$ when $n = 3\frac{3}{4}$

18. Thomas and Shannon have $8\frac{1}{2}$ yards of red material, $6\frac{2}{3}$ yards of green material, and $5\frac{3}{4}$ yards of yellow material to make costumes for the school play. They need to use the green and yellow material for costumes. How much green and yellow material do they have? What information is *not* needed to solve this problem?

19. Two years ago, Lisa was $4\frac{5}{12}$ feet tall. Last year, she was $4\frac{7}{12}$ feet tall. This year, she is $4\frac{3}{4}$ feet tall. If she continues to grow at the same rate, how tall will she be two years from now?

20. Sheldon is ordering two videos from a list of 5 possible choices. How many different pairs of videos can he pick?

Multiple-Choice Chapter 8 Test

Choose the correct letter for each answer.

1. $2\frac{3}{7} + 3\frac{4}{7} =$

A $1\frac{1}{7}$
B $5\frac{4}{7}$
C 6
D $6\frac{1}{7}$
E NH

2. $3\frac{2}{5} - 1\frac{4}{5} =$

F $1\frac{3}{5}$
G $2\frac{2}{5}$
H $4\frac{2}{5}$
J $5\frac{1}{5}$
K NH

3. **A bag of apples weighs $2\frac{5}{8}$ pounds. A bag of oranges weighs $1\frac{11}{16}$ pounds. Which of the following is the best way to estimate the total weight of the two bags by rounding?**

A $2 + 1 = 3$
B $3 + 1 = 2$
C $2 + 2 = 4$
D $3 + 2 = 5$

4. **How much is $\frac{2}{3}$ cups of yogurt and $\frac{3}{4}$ cups of mayonnaise?**

F $\frac{1}{12}$ cup
G $1\frac{1}{3}$ cups
H $1\frac{5}{12}$ cups
J $1\frac{1}{2}$ cups

Use the following information for Questions 5 and 6.

A basketball gym is $4\frac{2}{3}$ miles from Rahini's home. Rahini and his dad plan to play basketball and then drive on to a restaurant for pizza. The restaurant is $2\frac{3}{4}$ miles from the gym.

5. **What information do you need to find how long Rahini and his dad will spend driving if they do not need to stop on the way?**

A How long they will play basketball.
B What time they leave home.
C The average speed they drive.
D The speed limit near the gym.

6. **How far do Rahini and his dad drive if they come back past the gym on their way home from the restaurant?**

F $5\frac{1}{2}$ mi
G $7\frac{5}{12}$ mi
H $9\frac{1}{3}$ mi
J $14\frac{5}{6}$ mi

7. $\frac{7}{8} - \frac{1}{6} =$

A $\frac{3}{4}$
B $\frac{17}{24}$
C $1\frac{1}{24}$
D 3
E NH

8. **Joanne's cake weighs $7\frac{1}{2}$ ounces more than Larry's cake. If Joanne's cake weighs $18\frac{3}{4}$ ounces, how much does Larry's cake weigh?**

F 11 oz

G $11\frac{1}{4}$ oz

H $11\frac{1}{2}$ oz

J $11\frac{3}{4}$ oz

---

9. **Ralph uses $1\frac{3}{4}$ cup of milk in a muffin recipe. Alicia uses $\frac{1}{2}$ that amount in her muffin recipe. How much milk does Alicia use to make muffins?**

A $\frac{1}{2}$ c

B $\frac{7}{8}$ c

C $\frac{7}{4}$ c

D $3\frac{1}{2}$ c

---

10. $8\frac{1}{2} \div 2\frac{2}{3} =$

F $3\frac{3}{16}$

G $4\frac{3}{4}$

H $16\frac{1}{3}$

J $22\frac{2}{3}$

K NH

---

11. **Paul needs 27 in. of silver braid for a hat band. Which length of braid should Paul buy if he does not want any braid left over?**

A $\frac{7}{8}$ yd

B $\frac{3}{4}$ yd

C $\frac{2}{3}$ yd

D $\frac{1}{2}$ yd

---

12. **Shara has time to take 2 electives from Journalism, Creative Writing, Geometric Art, Painting, Pottery, and Dance. In how many ways can she choose two?**

F 12 ways

G 15 ways

H 30 ways

J 36 ways

---

13. **The students from Jefferson School turned a vacant lot into a vegetable garden. Tomatoes were planted in $\frac{4}{5}$ of the garden space. Cherry tomatoes took up $\frac{1}{6}$ of that space. What part of the garden was planted in cherry tomatoes?**

A $\frac{1}{15}$

B $\frac{2}{15}$

C $6\frac{4}{5}$

D $7\frac{1}{2}$

---

14. **Jake drew squares as part of a pattern for a rug design. The sides of the first four squares, in inches, were $2\frac{1}{4}$, $2\frac{7}{8}$, $3\frac{1}{2}$, and $4\frac{1}{8}$. If Jake continues this pattern, what will be the lengths of the sides for the next three squares?**

F $4\frac{1}{2}$ in., $5\frac{1}{8}$ in., $5\frac{1}{2}$ in.

G $4\frac{5}{8}$ in., 5 in., $5\frac{3}{8}$ in.

H $4\frac{3}{4}$ in., $5\frac{3}{8}$ in., 6 in.

J $4\frac{7}{8}$ in., $5\frac{1}{2}$ in., $5\frac{7}{8}$ in.

---

15. **Find $n + 2\frac{5}{6}$ when $n = 3\frac{4}{9}$.**

A $\frac{1}{2}$

B $1\frac{1}{3}$

C $5\frac{3}{5}$

D $6\frac{5}{18}$

---

16. **Find $x \div \frac{5}{6}$ when $x = 4\frac{3}{8}$.**

F $3\frac{1}{2}$

G $3\frac{3}{4}$

H $3\frac{31}{48}$

J $5\frac{1}{4}$

Reteaching

Set A (pages 308–310)

Find $9\frac{7}{8} + 6\frac{3}{8}$.

$$\begin{array}{r} 9\frac{7}{8} \\ +6\frac{3}{8} \\ \hline 15\frac{10}{8} \end{array}$$

$15\frac{10}{8} = 15 + 1\frac{2}{8} = 16\frac{2}{8} = 16\frac{1}{4}$

Remember, you sometimes have to simplify after you add mixed numbers.

Add. Write each answer in simplest form.

1. $2\frac{1}{8} + 1\frac{5}{8}$
2. $5\frac{3}{8} + 4\frac{5}{8}$
3. $7\frac{11}{12} + 9\frac{3}{12}$
4. $3\frac{4}{5} + 2\frac{3}{5}$

Set B (pages 311–313)

Find $7\frac{3}{9} - 3\frac{4}{9}$.

Think: $7\frac{3}{9} = 6 + 1 + \frac{3}{9}$

$= 6 + \frac{9}{9} + \frac{3}{9}$

$= 6\frac{12}{9}$

$$\begin{array}{r} 6\frac{12}{9} \\ -\ 3\frac{4}{9} \\ \hline 3\frac{8}{9} \end{array}$$

Remember, you sometimes have to rename before you subtract mixed numbers.

Subtract. Write each answer in simplest form.

1. $7\frac{5}{8} - 2\frac{1}{8}$
2. $4\frac{2}{7} - 2\frac{5}{7}$

Set C (pages 316–317)

Estimate $5\frac{7}{12} - 4\frac{5}{12}$.

Think: $\frac{7}{12} > \frac{1}{2}$, so round $5\frac{7}{12}$ to 6.

$\frac{5}{12} < \frac{1}{2}$, so round $4\frac{5}{12}$ to 4.

Then $6 - 4 = 2$.

Remember, you round a mixed number up to the next whole number if the fraction is greater than or equal to $\frac{1}{2}$.

Estimate each sum or difference.

1. $6\frac{3}{4} - 5\frac{7}{8}$
2. $1\frac{2}{3} + 1\frac{1}{3}$
3. $3\frac{1}{2} + 5\frac{5}{14}$
4. $7\frac{1}{9} - 2\frac{5}{8}$

Set D (pages 318–319)

Find $\frac{3}{4} + \frac{2}{10}$.

Multiples of 4: 4, 8, 12, 16, **20**, 24 . . .
Multiples of 10: 10, **20**, 30, 40 . . .
LCM: 20

Think: $\frac{3}{4} = \frac{3 \times 5}{4 \times 5} = \frac{15}{20}$

$\frac{2}{10} = \frac{2 \times 2}{10 \times 2} = \frac{4}{20}$

$$\begin{array}{r} \frac{15}{20} \\ +\ \frac{4}{20} \\ \hline \frac{19}{20} \end{array}$$

Remember, you must change fractions to a common denominator before adding them.

Add. Simplify each sum, if possible.

1. $\frac{3}{4} + \frac{2}{3}$
2. $\frac{7}{10} + \frac{3}{5}$
3. $\frac{5}{6} + \frac{2}{3}$
4. $\frac{5}{8} + \frac{1}{6}$

Set E (pages 320–321)

Find $\frac{5}{6} - \frac{4}{9}$.

Multiples of 6: 6, 12, **18**, 24, 30, **36**, . . .

Multiples of 9: 9, **18**, 27, **36**, 45, . . .

LCM: 18

Think: $\frac{5}{6} = \frac{5 \times 3}{6 \times 3} = \frac{15}{18}$

$\frac{4}{9} = \frac{4 \times 2}{9 \times 2} = \frac{8}{18}$

$$\begin{array}{r} \frac{15}{18} \\ -\ \frac{8}{18} \\ \hline \frac{7}{18} \end{array}$$

Remember, you can find the least common denominator of two fractions by finding the least common multiple of the denominators of the fractions.

Subtract. Simplify each difference, if possible.

1. $\frac{5}{8} - \frac{3}{16}$
2. $\frac{3}{4} - \frac{1}{3}$
3. $\frac{2}{3} - \frac{1}{6}$
4. $\frac{11}{14} - \frac{2}{21}$

Set F (pages 322–323)

Find $5\frac{11}{15} + 2\frac{3}{10}$. Simplify if possible.

Estimate first: 6 + 2 = 8

Multiples of 15: 15, **30**, 45, . . .

Multiples of 10: 10, 20, **30**, 40, . . .

LCM = 30

$$\begin{array}{rcr} 5\frac{11}{15} & = & 5\frac{22}{30} \\ +\ 2\frac{3}{10} & & +\ 2\frac{9}{30} \\ \hline & & 7\frac{31}{30} = 8\frac{1}{30} \end{array}$$

The answer is close to the estimate.

Remember, you can change the fraction parts of mixed numbers to their LCD just as you change fractions to their LCD.

Find each sum and simplify, if possible.

1. $4\frac{7}{8} + 1\frac{1}{4}$
2. $9\frac{1}{10} + 3\frac{1}{5}$
3. $8\frac{2}{9} + 3\frac{1}{6}$
4. $3\frac{5}{6} + 8\frac{1}{24}$
5. $2\frac{1}{8} + 5\frac{3}{10}$

Set G (pages 324–326)

Find $4\frac{2}{9} - 1\frac{5}{6}$. Simplify, if possible.

Estimate first: 4 − 2 = 2.

$$\begin{array}{rcl} 4\frac{2}{9} = & 4\frac{4}{18} = 3\frac{18}{18} + \frac{4}{18} = & 3\frac{22}{18} \\ -1\frac{5}{6} = & -1\frac{15}{18} & = -\ 1\frac{15}{18} \\ \hline & & 2\frac{7}{18} \end{array}$$

The answer is close to the estimate.

Remember, you may need to change to the LCD and rename before you subtract mixed numbers.

Find each difference and simplify, if possible.

1. $7\frac{3}{5} - 2\frac{1}{2}$
2. $11\frac{3}{5} - 6\frac{9}{10}$
3. $14\frac{1}{4} - 3\frac{7}{10}$

Reteaching (continued)

Set H (pages 330–332)

Multiply $\frac{5}{6} \times \frac{2}{7}$. Simplify, if possible.

$\frac{5}{6} \times \frac{2}{7} = \frac{5 \times 2}{6 \times 7} = \frac{10}{42}$

$\frac{10}{42} = \frac{10 \div 2}{42 \div 2} = \frac{5}{21}$

So, $\frac{5}{6} \times \frac{2}{7} = \frac{5}{21}$.

Remember, to multiply fractions, you multiply the numerators and you multiply the denominators.

Multiply. Simplify, if possible.

1. $\frac{1}{2} \times \frac{1}{8}$

2. $\frac{3}{5} \times \frac{2}{3}$

Set I (pages 334–335)

Divide $10 \div \frac{2}{5}$. Simplify, if possible.

$10 \div \frac{2}{5} = \frac{10}{1} \div \frac{2}{5}$

$= \frac{10}{1} \times \frac{5}{2}$

$= \frac{50}{2} = 25$

The reciprocal of $\frac{2}{5}$ is $\frac{5}{2}$.

So, $10 \div \frac{2}{5} = 25$.

Remember, to divide fractions, you can multiply by the reciprocal of the divisor.

Divide. Simplify, if possible.

1. $16 \div \frac{2}{3}$

2. $3 \div \frac{2}{3}$

3. $\frac{4}{5} \div \frac{5}{6}$

4. $\frac{3}{7} \div \frac{3}{4}$

Set J (pages 336–337)

Divide $4\frac{1}{2} \div \frac{2}{5}$. Simplify, if possible.

$4\frac{1}{2} \div \frac{2}{5} = \frac{9}{2} \div \frac{2}{5}$ Write $4\frac{1}{2}$ as $\frac{9}{2}$.

$= \frac{9}{2} \times \frac{5}{2}$ $\frac{5}{2}$ is the reciprocal of $\frac{2}{5}$.

$= \frac{9 \times 5}{2 \times 2}$

$\frac{45}{4} = 11\frac{1}{4}$ Simplify.

Remember to write mixed numbers as improper fractions before you multiply or divide them.

Multiply or divide. Simplify, if possible.

1. $2\frac{3}{5} \times 5$

2. $3\frac{1}{2} \times 2\frac{1}{3}$

3. $1\frac{2}{3} \div \frac{1}{6}$

4. $3\frac{3}{4} \div 1\frac{1}{4}$

Set K (pages 340–341)

Evaluate $n + 2\frac{2}{3}$ when $n = 1\frac{1}{6}$.

$n + 2\frac{2}{3} = 1\frac{1}{6} + 2\frac{2}{3}$

$= 1\frac{1}{6} + 2\frac{4}{6} = 3\frac{5}{6}$

Remember, you can replace the variable in an algebraic expression with a fraction as you did with a whole number or a decimal.

Evaluate.

1. $x - \frac{4}{5}$ when $x = 2$

2. $\frac{5}{9}m$ when $m = 1\frac{1}{2}$

3. $k \div \frac{3}{4}$ when $k = 1\frac{1}{5}$

More Practice

Set A (pages 308–310)

Add. Write each answer in simplest form.

1. $\frac{3}{5} + \frac{1}{5}$
2. $\frac{7}{12} + \frac{5}{12}$
3. $\frac{5}{11} + \frac{3}{11}$
4. $\frac{3}{10} + \frac{2}{10}$
5. $7\frac{3}{8} + 6\frac{1}{8}$
6. $2\frac{1}{5} + 1\frac{4}{5}$
7. $3\frac{7}{9} + 5\frac{4}{9}$
8. $4\frac{5}{6} + 2\frac{5}{6}$
9. Mark emptied $\frac{1}{12}$ of an ice tray, and Jenny emptied $\frac{7}{12}$ of the same tray. What fraction of the tray did they use altogether?

Set B (pages 311–313)

Subtract. Write each answer in simplest form.

1. $\frac{2}{3} - \frac{1}{3}$
2. $\frac{5}{16} - \frac{3}{16}$
3. $\frac{7}{12} - \frac{5}{12}$
4. $\frac{6}{13} - \frac{5}{13}$
5. $5\frac{5}{9} - 1\frac{4}{9}$
6. $2\frac{7}{8} - 1\frac{3}{8}$
7. $4\frac{1}{3} - 1\frac{2}{3}$
8. $8\frac{5}{12} - 4\frac{7}{12}$
9. If there are $2\frac{1}{3}$ boxes of cereal in your cupboard and you eat $\frac{2}{3}$ of a box, how much cereal is left over?

Set C (pages 316–317)

Estimate each sum or difference.

1. $4\frac{3}{5} + 2\frac{1}{5}$
2. $3\frac{2}{11} + 1\frac{7}{11}$
3. $6\frac{1}{8} + 2\frac{5}{8}$
4. $3\frac{5}{12} + 7\frac{1}{12}$
5. $2\frac{2}{3} - 1\frac{2}{3}$
6. $4\frac{8}{10} - 1\frac{7}{10}$
7. $6 - 5\frac{1}{4}$
8. $8\frac{6}{7} - 3\frac{6}{7}$
9. A recipe calls for $2\frac{3}{4}$ teaspoons of garlic powder and $\frac{1}{8}$ teaspoon of salt. About how many teaspoons of seasonings are needed for this recipe?

Set D (pages 318–319)

Add. Simplify each sum, if possible.

1. $\frac{1}{20} + \frac{3}{4}$
2. $\frac{1}{12} + \frac{1}{3}$
3. $\frac{5}{12} + \frac{1}{14}$
4. $\frac{2}{3} + \frac{4}{9}$
5. $\frac{1}{3} + \frac{2}{7}$
6. $\frac{7}{10} + \frac{1}{15}$
7. $\frac{4}{5} + \frac{5}{6}$
8. $\frac{3}{7} + \frac{3}{4}$
9. $\frac{5}{6} + \frac{3}{4}$
10. $\frac{3}{8} + \frac{21}{40}$
11. A recipe for punch for the school dance calls for $\frac{3}{4}$ qt of ginger ale, 1 qt cranberry juice, and $\frac{1}{2}$ qt lemonade. How much punch will the recipe make?

More Practice (continued)

Set E *(pages 320–321)*

Subtract. Simplify each difference, if possible.

1. $\frac{3}{4} - \frac{3}{8}$
2. $\frac{4}{5} - \frac{3}{10}$
3. $\frac{2}{3} - \frac{2}{7}$
4. $\frac{5}{6} - \frac{3}{8}$
5. $\frac{13}{16} - \frac{5}{8}$
6. $\frac{1}{2} - \frac{1}{4}$
7. $\frac{7}{12} - \frac{11}{24}$
8. $\frac{3}{4} - \frac{2}{5}$
9. $\frac{7}{12} - \frac{1}{3}$
10. $\frac{7}{9} - \frac{2}{3}$
11. What is the difference between $\frac{7}{12}$ and $\frac{1}{9}$?
12. One recipe uses $\frac{2}{3}$ cups of flour. A similar recipe uses $\frac{3}{4}$ cups. How much less does the first recipe use than the second?

Set F *(pages 322–323)*

Find each sum and simplify, if possible.

1. $2\frac{7}{10} + 5\frac{3}{15}$
2. $4\frac{2}{5} + 3\frac{1}{4}$
3. $6\frac{2}{7} + 2\frac{1}{3}$
4. $4\frac{4}{9} + 1\frac{5}{6}$
5. $3\frac{1}{3} + 4\frac{3}{4}$
6. Maryanne's mother paid for 6 feet of sub sandwiches at the local sub shop. If the shop gave her a sub $2\frac{1}{3}$ feet long and a sub $2\frac{3}{4}$ feet long, was she charged correctly? Explain your answer.
7. How could you add $4\frac{1}{2} + 1\frac{1}{4} + 2\frac{1}{4}$ mentally?

Set G *(pages 324–326)*

Find each difference and simplify, if possible.

1. $5\frac{5}{9} - 1\frac{1}{3}$
2. $2\frac{4}{5} - 1\frac{1}{2}$
3. $3\frac{7}{8} - 3\frac{1}{16}$
4. $4\frac{2}{3} - 3\frac{1}{7}$
5. $7\frac{7}{12} - 2\frac{2}{3}$
6. $4\frac{5}{18} - 2\frac{5}{6}$
7. $5 - 3\frac{1}{3}$
8. $17\frac{3}{10} - 6\frac{2}{15}$
9. It took Samuel $3\frac{2}{3}$ hours to bake 5 dozen cookies. It took John $1\frac{1}{4}$ hours to bake the same number of cookies. How much longer did it take Samuel to bake the cookies?

Set H (pages 330–332)

Multiply. Simplify, if possible.

1. $\frac{3}{5} \times \frac{1}{2}$
2. $\frac{2}{7} \times \frac{3}{8}$
3. $\frac{2}{3} \times \frac{3}{5}$
4. $\frac{2}{5} \times \frac{1}{3}$
5. Find the reciprocal of $2\frac{1}{2}$.
6. Amy's grandparents sent her family a box of 24 pieces of fruit from Florida. If $\frac{3}{8}$ of the pieces of fruit are grapefruit, how many grapefruit are in the box?

Set I (pages 334–335)

Divide. Simplify, if possible.

1. $2 \div \frac{3}{5}$
2. $4 \div \frac{3}{4}$
3. $8 \div \frac{2}{5}$
4. $12 \div \frac{1}{3}$
5. $\frac{1}{4} \div \frac{2}{3}$
6. $\frac{5}{8} \div \frac{1}{2}$
7. $\frac{3}{5} \div \frac{3}{10}$
8. $\frac{7}{8} \div \frac{4}{7}$
9. How many $\frac{2}{3}$-yard wallpaper border strips can fit end-to-end on a wall that is 4 yards long?

Set J (pages 336–337)

Multiply or divide. Simplify, if possible.

1. $\frac{3}{4} \times 4\frac{1}{2}$
2. $1\frac{1}{4} \times 3\frac{3}{5}$
3. $9\frac{3}{4} \times 4\frac{2}{3}$
4. $3\frac{3}{5} \times 5\frac{1}{2}$
5. $3\frac{1}{4} \div \frac{5}{8}$
6. $6\frac{3}{4} \div 3$
7. $8 \div 2\frac{1}{2}$
8. $3\frac{1}{4} \div 1\frac{1}{6}$
9. Mr. Lee has $10\frac{1}{2}$ bushels of vegetables. He sells $\frac{3}{4}$ of them. How many bushels are left?

Set K (pages 340–341)

Evaluate $y + 1\frac{1}{5}$ for each value of y.

1. $\frac{1}{10}$
2. 8
3. $\frac{7}{8}$
4. $2\frac{9}{10}$
5. $4\frac{3}{4}$

Evaluate $\frac{3}{4}k$ for each value of k.

6. 4
7. 5
8. $\frac{4}{9}$
9. $1\frac{1}{3}$
10. $2\frac{2}{3}$
11. Jack grew $1\frac{1}{2}$ inches last year. Use the expression $h + 1\frac{1}{2}$ to find Jack's height now if he was $48\frac{3}{4}$ inches tall a year ago.

Problem Solving: Preparing for Tests

Choose the correct letter for each answer.

1. Cheryl's company shipped $\frac{5}{8}$ ton of lumber on Saturday and $\frac{3}{4}$ ton on Tuesday. Which number sentence could she use to compare the amounts shipped on the two days?

A $\frac{5}{8} - \frac{3}{4} = n$

B $\frac{3}{4} - \frac{5}{8} = n$

C $\frac{5}{8} \times \frac{3}{4} = n$

D $1 - (\frac{5}{8} \times \frac{3}{4}) = n$

Tip

To choose between choices A and B, you will first need to decide which is greater, $\frac{5}{8}$ or $\frac{3}{4}$.

2. Salmon costs $0.75 cents more per pound than tuna. If $\frac{3}{4}$ lb of salmon costs $8.97, which is a reasonable estimate of the price of salmon per pound?

F $7.50 per lb

G $12.00 per lb

H $14.00 per lb

J $15.00 per lb

Tip

Remember to eliminate information that is not needed to solve the problem.

3. The Parks Department plans to plant a tree every 0.3 mile along certain sections of highway. Each tree will take about 15 minutes to plant. How many trees will they plant along one side of a section that is 2.4 miles long if they plant a tree at each end?

A 8 trees

B 9 trees

C 72 trees

D 80 trees

Tip

The strategy, *Draw a Diagram*, can be used to solve this problem.

4. **For a fruit salad, Wally used about half of a 3-lb bag of nuts. He also used $\frac{3}{4}$ of a 2-lb bag of cherries. In the salad, which weighed more, the nuts or the cherries, and how much more?**

F Nuts; $\frac{1}{4}$ lb

G Nuts; $\frac{1}{8}$ lb

H Cherries; $\frac{1}{4}$ lb

J They weighed the same.

5. **Wendy mailed 3 packages. The heaviest weighed $4\frac{1}{2}$ lb. The lightest weighed $\frac{7}{8}$ lb. Two of the packages weighed the same. Which is reasonable for the total weight of the packages?**

A Between $\frac{7}{8}$ lb and 10 lb

B Between $3\frac{1}{2}$ lb and 12 lb

C Between 4 lb and $12\frac{1}{2}$ lb

D Between 6 lb and 10 lb

6. **Salita had an average of 92 in math. On 3 science tests, she got scores of 90, 75, and 85. What score must she get on the next science test to have an average of at least 85 in science?**

F At least 75 **H** At least 85

G At least 80 **J** At least 90

7. **How many 2-in. pieces can Rose cut from a strip of ribbon $3\frac{2}{3}$ ft long?**

A 20 pieces **C** 22 pieces

B 21 pieces **D** 24 pieces

8. **Hal bought 3 sweaters for \$14 each and 2 hats for \$8 each. Which equation could you use to find *n*, the total amount Hal spent?**

F $(2 + 3) \times (8 + 14) = n$

G $(3 \times 14) \times (2 \times 8) = n$

H $(3 \times 14) + (2 \times 8) = n$

J $(3 \times 14) - (2 \times 8) = n$

9. **The graph shows the results of an election. Who won the election, and by about how many votes?**

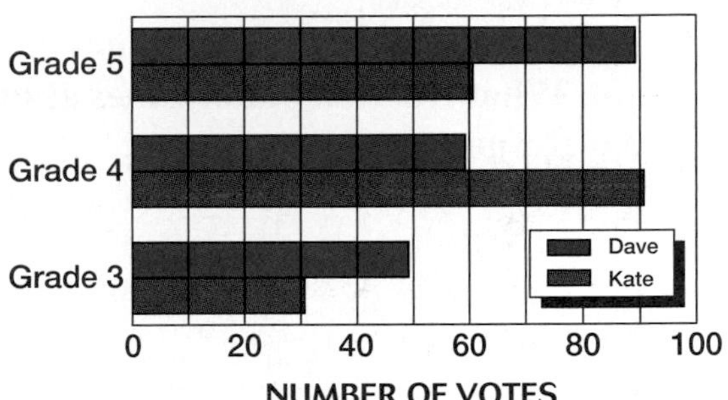

A Dave; by about 10 votes.

B Dave; by about 20 votes.

C Kate; by about 10 votes.

D Kate; by about 20 votes.

10. **Kim drew this design for a brick patio. What is the *area* of the white part of the design?**

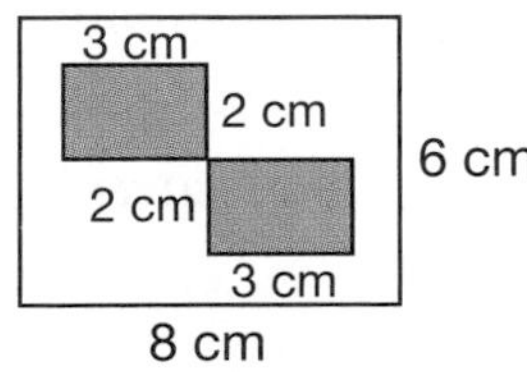

F 12 cm^2

G 36 cm^2

H 42 cm^2

J 48 cm^2

Multiple-Choice Cumulative Review

Choose the correct letter for each answer.

Number Sense

1. Which expression shows 56 as a product of prime factors?

   A 7×8

   B 2×28

   C $2 \times 4 \times 7$

   D $2 \times 2 \times 2 \times 7$

2. Maria got a hit 6 out of 10 times at bat. What fraction of her times at bat did she get a hit?

   F $\frac{1}{4}$

   G $\frac{2}{5}$

   H $\frac{3}{5}$

   J $\frac{5}{6}$

3. Which number sentence is NOT true?

   A $0.567 > 0.0674$

   B $0.45 = 0.450$

   C $0.234 < 0.245$

   D $0.036 < 0.033$

4. A recipe calls for $1\frac{1}{2}$ teaspoons of oil, $\frac{2}{3}$ teaspoon of vanilla, $\frac{3}{8}$ teaspoon of baking soda, and $1\frac{3}{4}$ teaspoons of water. How should these amounts be ordered from *least* to *greatest*?

   F $\frac{3}{8}, \frac{2}{3}, 1\frac{1}{2}, 1\frac{3}{4}$

   G $\frac{3}{8}, \frac{2}{3}, 1\frac{3}{4}, 1\frac{1}{2}$

   H $1\frac{3}{4}, 1\frac{1}{2}, \frac{2}{3}, \frac{3}{8}$

   J $\frac{2}{3}, \frac{3}{8}, 1\frac{1}{2}, 1\frac{3}{4}$

5. Katie sold 45 tickets to the Youth Club car wash. Ryan sold 67 tickets, including 7 tickets to his family. How many more tickets need to be sold to break the club record of 200 tickets?

   A 155 tickets

   B 133 tickets

   C 89 tickets

   D 88 tickets

6. There are 100 chairs set up in the gym. If the first 12 rows have 8 chairs each, how many chairs does the last row have?

   F 10 chairs

   G 8 chairs

   H 6 chairs

   J 4 chairs

7. Bo borrowed \$50 from his brother Ken. He paid half of it back the first month. Then he paid back \$10 more. How much does Bo still owe Ken?

   A \$25

   B \$15

   C \$12.50

   D \$10

8. Jackie and Brenda each bought a bag of 1,500 beads to make bracelets. It takes 50 beads to make a bracelet. If the girls made a total of 23 bracelets, about how many beads did they use?

   F 500 beads

   G 1,000 beads

   H 1,500 beads

   J 2,000 beads

Algebra and Functions

9. Which expression can be used to find the *area* in square units of the section that is *NOT* shaded?

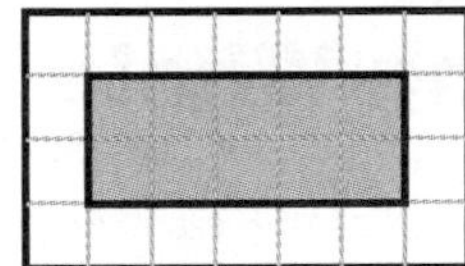

A 7×4
B $(2 \times 7) + (2 \times 4)$
C $(7 \times 4) - (5 \times 2)$
D $2 \times (7 + 2)$

---

10. Which operation should be done first in $1 + 3 \times 5$?

F 3×5 **H** 1×5
G $1 + 3$ **J** $1 + 5$

---

11. Evaluate $4 \times (n + 6)$ when $n = 3$.

A 9 **D** 36
B 18 **E** NH
C 27

---

12. Solve $y + 5 = 15$.

F $y = 3$
G $y = 10$
H $y = 20$
J $y = 75$
K NH

Statistics, Data Analysis, and Probability

13. Dave's baseball team played 15 games this season. Dave struck out 1, 9, 3, 6, and 6 batters in the 5 games he pitched. What was the mean (average) number of batters he struck out per game?

A 5 batters **C** 7 batters
B 6 batters **D** 9 batters

Use the line graph for Questions 14 and 15.

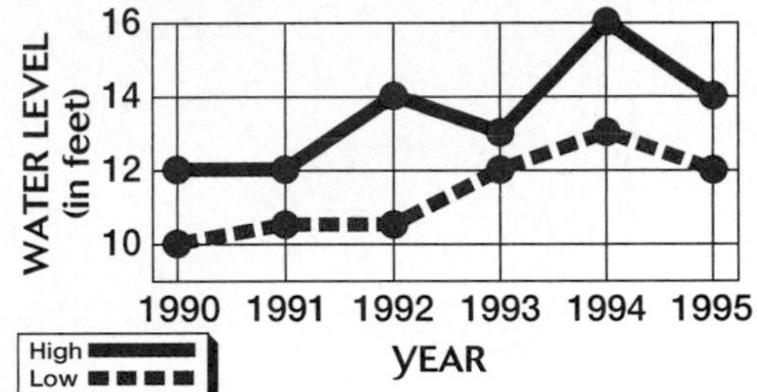

14. What was the low water level in 1994?

F 11 feet **H** 13 feet
G 12 feet **J** 14 feet

---

15. Which is the best estimate of the difference between the high and low water levels in 1992?

A 1 foot
B 2 feet
C $2\frac{1}{2}$ feet
D $3\frac{1}{2}$ feet

Integers, Equations, and Graphs

Diagnosing Readiness

In Chapter 9, you will use these skills:

A Adding and Subtracting Whole Numbers

(pages 60–61)

Find each sum or difference.

1. 376 + 125 + 215

2. 81,365 − 4,013

3. 812 + 677 + 483

4. Alan and his friends planted 78 white pine trees and 51 Japanese maple trees on his uncle's 2,500-acre estate. By the end of the year 17 white pine trees and 6 Japanese maple trees had died. How many total trees remained?

B Locating Numbers on a Number line

(pages 10–12)

Select the value that corresponds to the given point.

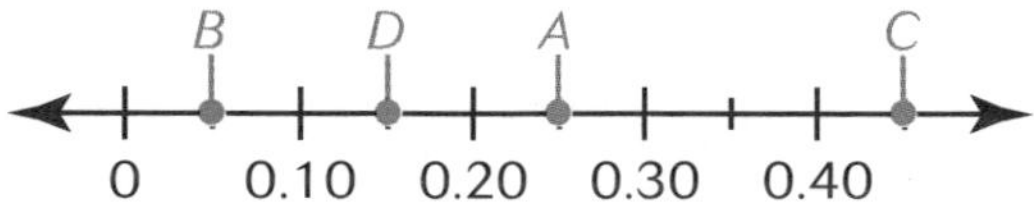

5. *D*

6. *C*

7. *B*

8. *A*

Ⓒ Ordering Whole Numbers

(pages 10–12)

Write the numbers in each set from least to greatest.

9. 84 13 156 1,008

10. 954 967 912 918

11. 32,056 38,004 30,987

Ⓓ Comparing Whole Numbers

(pages 10–12)

Write <, >, or = for each ●.

12. 23,456 ● 23,056

13. 119,000,000 ● 120,000,000

14. 620 + 3,480 ● 2,945 + 787

15. 297 + 16 ● 15 + 298

Ⓔ Evaluating Expressions

(pages 130–131)

Evaluate each expression.

16. $62 - 2x + 12$; when $x = 6$

17. $3 + x + 18$; when $x = 4$

18. The height of Tyler's sculpture, in cm, can be determined by the expression $15a - b$. If $a = 15$ and $b = 10$, what is the height of the sculpture?

Ⓕ Writing Expressions

(pages 55–57)

Write each word phrase as an expression.

19. 8 less than y

20. 44 more than h

21. Sam is n years old. Write an expression for his age 5 years ago.

22. A book costs d dollars. The sales tax is \$1.50. Write an expression for the total cost, including sales tax.

To the Family and Student

Looking Back	Chapter 9	Looking Ahead
In Grade 4, students used number lines to compare and order integers.	**Integers, Equations, and Graphs** In this chapter, students will learn how to add and subtract integers and write and graph equations involving integers.	In Grade 6, students will learn how to multiply and divide integers.

Math and Everyday Living

Opportunities to apply the concepts of Chapter 9 abound in everyday situations. During the chapter, think about how integers, equations, and graphs can be used to solve a variety of real-world problems. The following examples suggest just a few of the many situations that could launch a discussion about integers, equations, and graphs.

Math and Construction Your family decides to hire a contractor to dig a new well in the back of your property. The contractor will hire a crew to dig a hole 62 ft deep by 5 ft wide. Express the depth of the well as an integer.

Math and Elevation The chart below shows the places with the lowest elevations in the world.

Place	Feet Below Sea Level
Caspian Sea, USSR	92
Lake Assai, Djibouti	512
Death Valley, CA	282
Valdes Peninsula, Argentina	131
Dead Sea, Israel	1,312

A hot-air balloon is sailing at an altitude of 2,062 feet above sea level. How many feet is it above Death Valley?

Math and Chemistry Chlorine, a chemical used in swimming pools, has a freezing point of about $^{-}100$°C. Water has a freezing point of 0°C. How much higher is the freezing point of water than the freezing point of chlorine?

Math and Money Last month your family purchased a new computer system, printer, copier, scanner, and CD-ROM writer for a total price of \$2,750. The computer system has a rebate of \$300. Because you bought the scanner and the copier together, you also receive another rebate of \$75. If you decide to use one of the specified Internet companies, you are also entitled to another \$95 rebate. Write an expression, using integers, for the actual price after the rebates.

Math and Maps Use the grid shown below to direct your friend from the post office to the library.

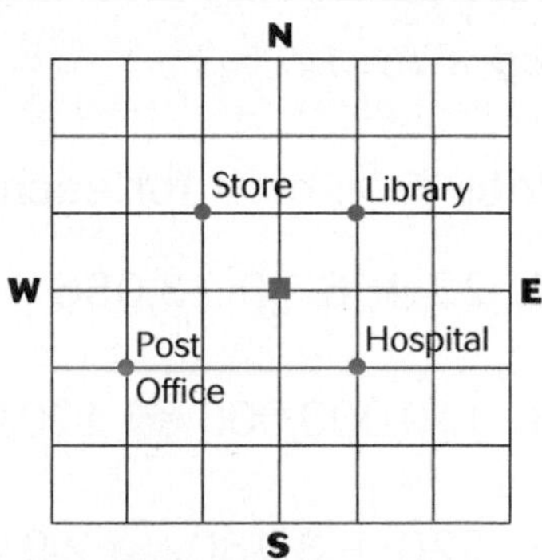

Math on the Job You can get either a newspaper delivery job or a newspaper filler job. The delivery job pays a fee of \$30 plus \$0.25 for every paper you deliver. The filler job pays a fee of \$22 plus \$0.15 for every paper you stuff with advertisements. If you deliver papers, you will probably get a route with 65 subscribers. If you fill papers, you will have the opportunity to stuff over 350 papers. Which job will pay more money?

 California Content Standards in Chapter 9 Lessons*

	Teach and Practice	Practice
Number Sense		
1.5 (🔑) Identify and represent on a number line . . . positive and negative integers.	9-1, 9-2	
2.1 (🔑) Add, subtract, . . . with negative integers; subtract positive integers from negative integers	9-3, 9-4, 9-5	
Algebra and Functions		
1.1 Use information taken from a graph or equation to answer questions about a problem situation.		9-11
1.2 (🔑) Use a letter to represent an unknown number; write and evaluate simple algebraic expressions in one variable by substitution.	9-5	9-2, 9-3, 9-4, 9-6
1.4 (🔑) Identify and graph ordered pairs in the four quadrants of the coordinate plane.	9-7	
1.5 (🔑) Solve problems involving linear functions with integer values; write the equation; and graph the resulting ordered pairs of integers on a grid.	9-8, 9-9, 9-10, 9-11	

	Teach and Practice	Practice
Mathematical Reasoning		
1.1 Analyze problems by identifying relationships		9-3, 9-4
2.3 Use a variety of methods, such as words, numbers, symbols, charts, graphs, tables, diagrams, and models, to explain mathematical reasoning.	9-6, 9-9	9-7, 9-8, 9-10, 9-11
2.4 Express the solution clearly and logically by using the appropriate mathematical notation and terms and clear language; support solutions with evidence in both verbal and symbolic work.		9-6
3.2 Note the method of deriving the solution and demonstrate a conceptual understanding of the derivation by solving similar problems.		9-9

* The symbol (🔑) indicates a key standard as designated in the Mathematics Framework for California Public Schools. Full statements of the California Content Standards are found at the beginning of this book following the Table of Contents.

LESSON
9-1

Meaning of Integers

Algebra

Warm-Up Review

Name the number for each point on the number line.

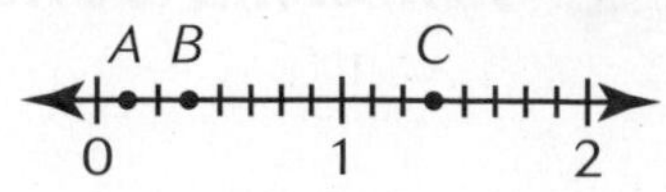

A B C
0
1
2

1. *A* 2. *B* 3. *C*

4. Jane has $579 in her bank account. She makes a withdrawal of $200 and a deposit of $360. How much is in the account now?

California Content Standard *Number Sense 1.5( ): Identify and represent on a number line . . . positive and negative integers.*

Math Link Sometimes temperatures fall below zero. Such temperatures are represented by negative numbers.

The coldest temperature ever recorded in the United States was at Prospect Creek, Alaska, in 1972. The temperature reached $^{-}80$°F. The highest temperature was $^{+}134$°F in Death Valley, California, in 1913.

Numbers such as $^{-}80$ and $^{+}134$ are called **integers**. Integers consist of whole numbers and their opposites.

Word Bank

integers
negative integers
positive integers

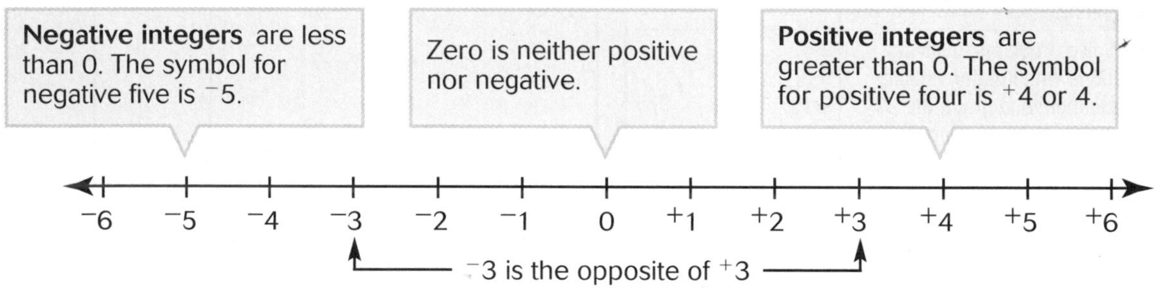

Negative integers are less than 0. The symbol for negative five is $^{-}5$.
Zero is neither positive nor negative.
Positive integers are greater than 0. The symbol for positive four is $^{+}4$ or 4.
$^{-}6$ $^{-}5$ $^{-}4$ $^{-}3$ $^{-}2$ $^{-}1$ 0 $^{+}1$ $^{+}2$ $^{+}3$ $^{+}4$ $^{+}5$ $^{+}6$
$^{-}3$ is the opposite of $^{+}3$

Examples

The table below gives an integer for each word description.

Word Description	Integer
The lowest temperature recorded in South Dakota is $^{-}60$°F.	$^{-}60$
10 steps backward	$^{-}10$
90 feet below sea level	$^{-}90$

Word Description	Integer
The highest temperature recorded in Florida is 109°F.	$^{+}109$
6 steps forward	$^{+}6$
a gain of 20 yards	$^{+}20$

Guided Practice *For another example, see Set A on p. 390.*

Write an integer for each word description.

1. 90 degrees above zero
2. a deposit of $100
3. a loss of 10 yards
4. 10 degrees below zero
5. a withdrawal of $50
6. a gain of 5 yards

Use the number line for Exercises 7–10. What is the coordinate of each point?

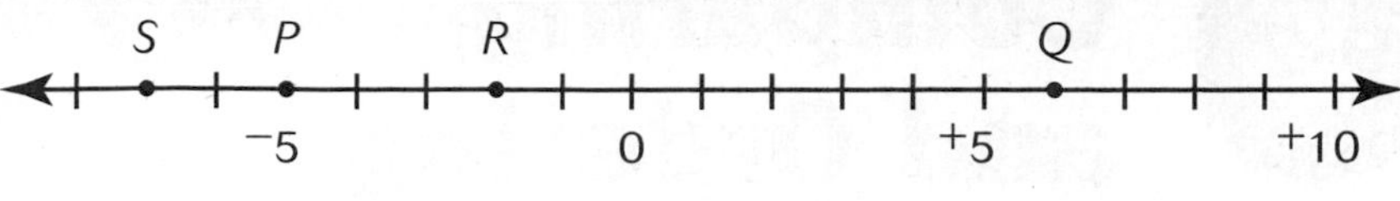

7. *P** **8.** *Q* **9.** *R* **10.** *S*

11. Which integer is neither positive nor negative?

Independent Practice *For more practice, see Set A on p. 392.*

Write an integer for each word description.

12. 20 degrees above zero **13.** a deposit of \$500 **14.** a gain of 30 yards

15. 5 degrees below zero **16.** a withdrawal of \$200 **17.** a loss of 20 yards

Use the number line for Exercises 18–25. What is the coordinate of each point?

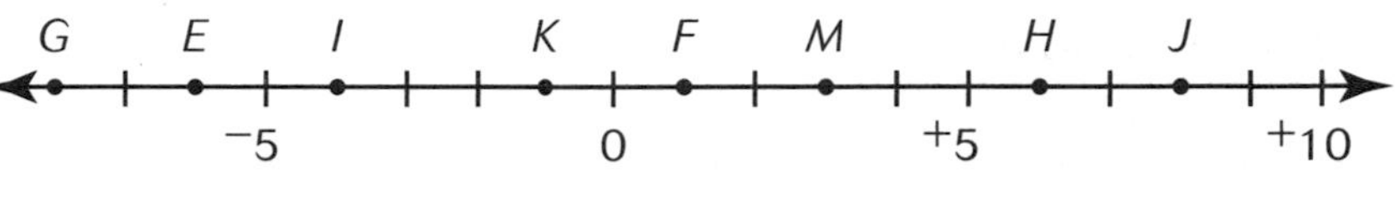

18. *E* **19.** *F* **20.** *G* **21.** *H*

22. *I* **23.** *J* **24.** *K* **25.** *M*

For Exercises 26–32, place each integer on the same number line.

26. $^{-}2$ **27.** $^{+}10$ **28.** $^{-}7$ **29.** $^{+}9$ **30.** $^{-}5$

31. the opposite of $^{+}4$ **32.** the opposite of $^{-}8$

33. At midnight the temperature was 0 degrees. It then went up 5 degrees, dropped 3 degrees, then dropped 4 degrees more. What was the last temperature?

Mixed Review

34. $\frac{1}{2} + \frac{3}{4}$ **35.** $\frac{3}{8} \times \frac{2}{3}$ **36.** $\frac{3}{4} \div \frac{1}{4}$ **37.** $0.5 \div 0.1$

38. Mental Math Evaluate $2 \times (n + \frac{1}{3})$ for $n = \frac{2}{3}$.

39. Susan made scores of 85, 88, and 91 on three tests. What is the mean score for the three tests?

Test Prep Choose the correct letter for the answer.

40. Which shows the prime factorization of 225?
(7-2)

F $3^2 \times 5^2$ **G** $5^2 \times 9$ **H** $3^2 \times 25$ **J** $3^2 \times 5$

Comparing and Ordering Integers

Algebra

California Content Standard *Number Sense 1.5 (🔑): Identify and represent on a number line . . . positive and negative integers.*

Math Link You already know how to compare and order whole numbers, decimals, and fractions. In this lesson you will compare and order integers.

Warm-Up Review

Compare. Use >, <, or = for each ●.

1. 999 ● $10 \times 10 \times 10$
2. 0.1 ● 0.01
3. $\frac{3}{4}$ ● $\frac{3}{8}$
4. $\frac{25}{50}$ ● $\frac{10}{20}$
5. Bart has 198 baseball cards. He displays them on pages that hold 8 cards. How many pages does he need?

Which is less, a temperature of $^{-}5$°F or $^{-}10$°F? Look at the number line below. Integers increase in value as you move from left to right. So $^{-}10 < ^{-}5$. Therefore, $^{-}10$°F < $^{-}5$°F.

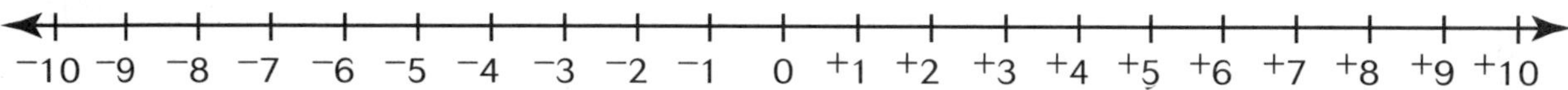

Example 1

Compare. Use >, <, or = for each ●.

a. $^{-}4$ ● $^{+}2$

Since $^{-}4$ is farther to the left on the number line, $^{-}4 < ^{+}2$.

b. $^{-}6$ ● $^{-}8$

Since $^{-}6$ is farther to the right on the number line, $^{-}6 > ^{-}8$.

Example 2

Order $^{-}4$, 0, $^{+}5$, and $^{-}6$ from least to greatest.

To order integers, you can first locate the integers on a number line. Then write the numbers from left to right.

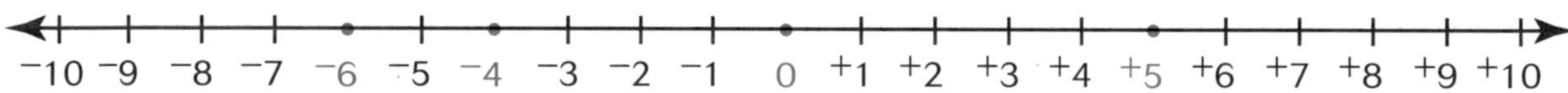

From least to greatest, the integers are $^{-}6$, $^{-}4$, 0, and $^{+}5$.

Guided Practice *For another example, see Set B on p. 390.*

Compare. Use >, <, or = for each ●.

1. $^{-}7$ ● $^{+}2$
2. $^{-}3$ ● $^{+}3$
3. $^{+}4$ ● $^{-}2$
4. $^{-}6$ ● $^{-}9$

Order from least to greatest.

5. $^{-}2$, $^{+}9$, $^{-}5$
6. $^{+}8$, $^{-}8$, $^{+}3$
7. $^{+}9$, $^{-}4$, $^{+}7$, $^{-}6$
8. $^{-}7$, $^{+}6$, 0, $^{-}8$

 Additional Standard: Algebra and Functions 1.2 (🔑) (See p. 359.)

9. Which temperature is higher, $^{-}10$°F or $^{+}2$°F?

Independent Practice

For more practice, see Set B on p. 392.

Compare. Use >, <, or = for each.

10. $^{+}1$ ● $^{-}4$ **11.** $^{-}7$ ● $^{-}2$ **12.** $^{-}3$ ● $^{-}1$

13. $^{-}6$ ● $^{+}7$ **14.** $^{+}5$ ● $^{-}3$ **15.** $^{-}3$ ● $^{+}4$

Write in order from least to greatest.

16. $^{+}4$, $^{-}11$, $^{+}14$ **17.** $^{-}16$, 0, $^{-}18$ **18.** $^{+}11$, $^{+}7$, $^{-}5$

19. $^{-}1$, $^{-}3$, $^{-}4$, $^{-}5$ **20.** $^{+}7$, $^{+}9$, 0, $^{-}4$ **21.** $^{+}4$, $^{-}2$, $^{-}3$, $^{+}6$

22. The high temperature in Chicago one day was $^{-}8$°F and in Des Moines was $^{-}6$°F. Which city had the higher temperature?

23. Algebra If $x > {}^{-}5$, which negative integers could x equal?

24. Math Reasoning How do you know that $^{-}100$ is greater than $^{-}200$?

Mixed Review

25. 9.5×100 **26.** 7.2×1000 **27.** $7.7 \div 10$ **28.** $0.9 \div 100$

29. What integer describes a loss of 8 yards?

30. Algebra Evaluate $3x + 5$ for $x = \frac{5}{6}$.

31. Mental Math What decimal is equivalent to $\frac{3}{25}$?

32. Lou can run around a track in 24 seconds. Ty can run around the same track in 30 seconds. If they leave the starting point at exactly the same time, after how many laps around the track will Lou first pass Ty exactly at the starting point? How many minutes will it take?

Test Prep **Choose the correct letter for each answer.**

33. Which is the same as 3^4?
(4-10)

A 34 **C** 12

B 81 **D** 64

34. Which number is prime?
(7-2)

F 69 **H** 49

G 59 **J** 39

Adding Integers

Algebra

Warm-Up Review

Refer to a number line. Name the integer described.

1. 5 units to the right of 0
2. 5 units to the left of 0
3. 6 units to the right of −3
4. 6 units to the left of −3
5. A hotel costs $59 a night, plus a daily tax of $2.40. What is the cost for 3 nights?

California Content Standard *Number Sense 2.1. (🔑): Add . . . with negative integers . . . .*

Math Link You know how to compare and order integers. In this lesson, you will use a number line to add integers.

Example

In a game contestants use positive and negative numbers to keep score. So far Todd has scores of $^{+}6$ and $^{-}10$. To find Todd's total score, find $^{+}6 + ^{-}10$.

To find $^{+}6 + ^{-}10$, think of walking along the number line. Use the following rule: *Always start at 0 and face the positive integers. Then walk forward for positive numbers, backward for negative numbers.*

Start at 0, facing the positive integers. Walk *forward* 6 steps for positive 6.

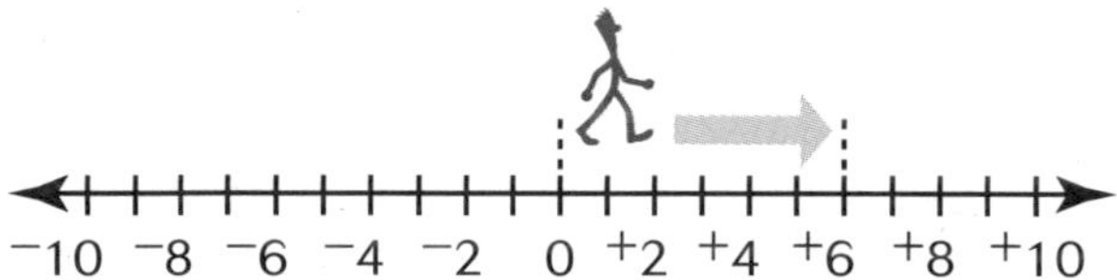

Then walk *backward* 10 steps for negative 10.

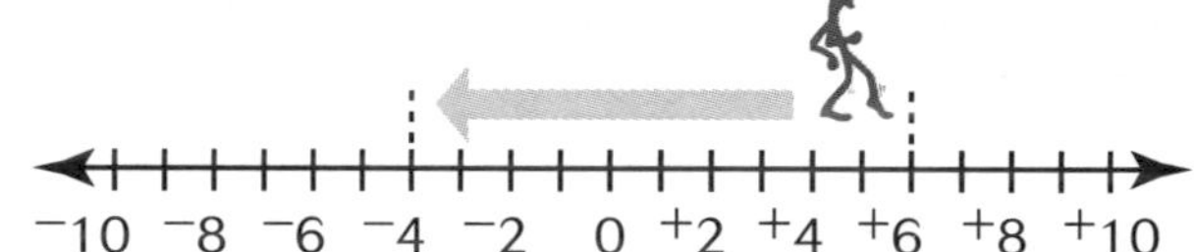

You stop at $^{-}4$. So $^{+}6 + ^{-}10 = ^{-}4$.

More Examples

A. $^{-}2 + ^{+}6$

Start at 0. Move backward 2 units. Then move forward 6 units.

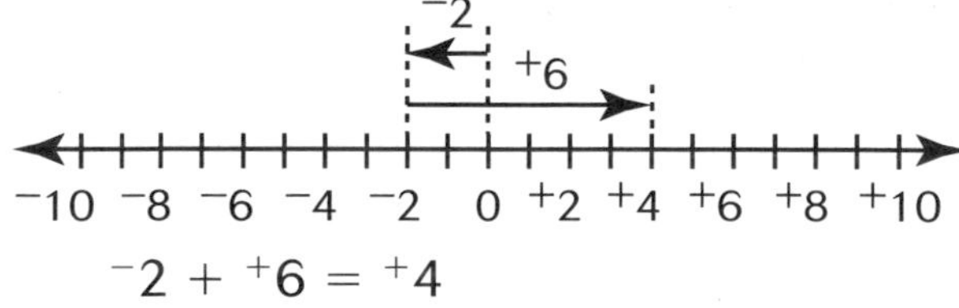

$^{-}2 + ^{+}6 = ^{+}4$

B. $^{-}3 + ^{-}5$

Start at 0. Move backward 3 units. Then move backward 5 more units.

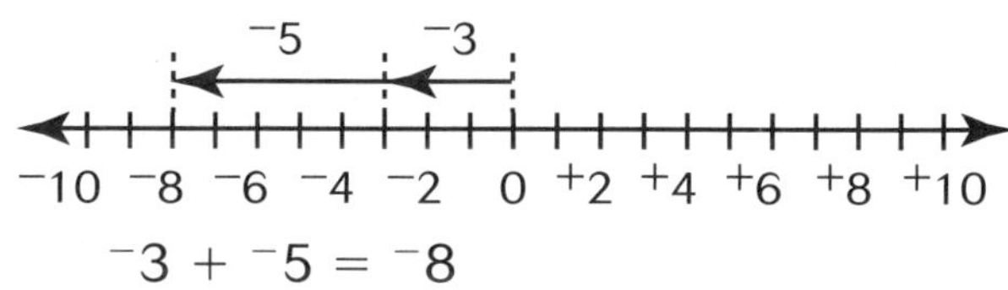

$^{-}3 + ^{-}5 = ^{-}8$

Guided Practice

For another example, see Set C on p. 390.

Add. Use a number line.

1. $^{+}2 + ^{-}7$
2. $^{+}5 + ^{+}3$
3. $^{-}4 + ^{-}8$
4. $^{+}9 + ^{-}5$
5. $^{+}4 + ^{-}8$

6. In a game, Jack's scores were $^{-}6$ and $^{+}2$. What was his final score?

Additional Standards: Algebra and Functions 1.2 (🔑); Mathematical Reasoning 1.1 (See p. 359.)

Independent Practice *For more practice, see Set C on p. 392.*

7. $^{-}12 + ^{+}5$ 8. $^{-}7 + ^{-}5$ 9. $^{+}10 + ^{+}6$ 10. $^{-}15 + ^{+}15$

11. $^{+}11 + ^{-}13$ 12. $^{-}10 + ^{+}2$ 13. $^{+}17 + ^{-}19$ 14. $^{-}20 + ^{+}4$

15. $^{+}10 + ^{-}11$ 16. $^{-}4 + ^{+}16$ 17. $^{+}7 + ^{-}14$ 18. $^{-}14 + ^{+}8$

19. $^{+}10 + ^{-}8$ 20. $^{-}12 + ^{+}2$ 21. $^{+}13 + ^{-}7$ 22. $^{-}13 + ^{+}6$

23. In the morning the temperature was $^{-}5$°F. By noon the temperature had increased 9 degrees. What was the temperature at noon?

24. **Mental Math** What is the sum of $^{-}9$, $^{+}9$, $^{-}8$, $^{+}8$, and $^{+}20$?

25. **Algebra** Solve $x + (^{-}5) = 0$.

26. **Math Reasoning** If the sum of two numbers is 0, what do you know about the numbers?

Mixed Review

27. 3.2×100 28. $980 \div 1000$ 29. $1,287 \div 9$ 30. 7.7×8.99

Compare. Use >, <, or = for each ●.

31. 0.09 ● 0.1 32. $\frac{3}{8}$ ● $\frac{5}{16}$ 33. $5\frac{1}{2}$ ● $5\frac{50}{100}$

34. Write an integer to represent 20 feet below sea level.

35. Order $^{-}8$, $^{+}10$, 0, $^{-}16$, and $^{-}10$ from least to greatest.

36. Sally has $50 to spend. She wants to buy compact discs that sell for $14.99 apiece. How many compact discs can she buy? How much money will she have left over?

37. List all the different 4-digit codes that can be formed by using the numbers 5, 6, 7, or 8. No number can be repeated.

Test Prep **Choose the correct letter for each answer.**

38. (7-3) What is the least common multiple of 48 and 32?

A 16
B 32
C 64
D 96

39. (6-9) $16\overline{)8.96}$

F 56
G 5.6
H 0.56
J 0.056
K NH

Subtracting Integers

Warm-Up Review

1. $^{+}4 + ^{-}1$
2. $^{+}2 + ^{+}1$
3. $^{-}7 + ^{-}1$
4. $^{+}5 + ^{-}8$
5. $^{+}9 + ^{-}3$
6. $^{-}12 + ^{-}2$
7. If the temperature in the morning is $^{-}2$°F, how much would it have to rise to reach 10°F?

California Content Standard *Number Sense 2.1.( ): Add, subtract . . . with negative integers; subtract positive integers from negative integers . . .*

Math Link In the previous lesson you learned to add integers. In this lesson you will subtract integers.

Example 1

Find $^{+}5 - ^{-}3$.

Start at 0. Walk *forward* 5 steps for $^{+}5$. | The subtraction sign, −, means *turn around*. | Then walk *backward* 3 steps for $^{-}3$.

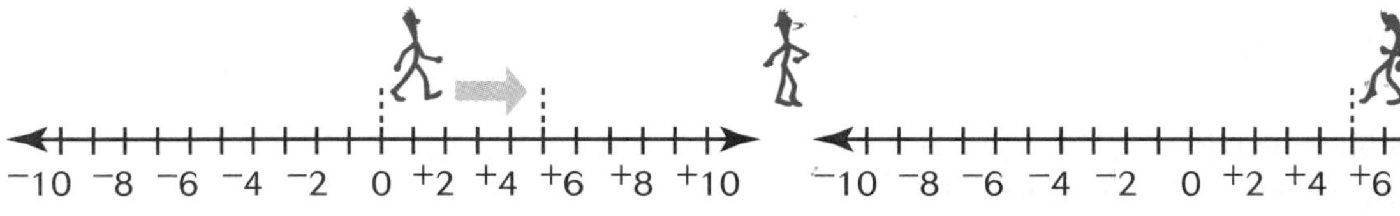

You stop at $^{+}8$. So $^{+}5 - ^{-}3 = ^{+}8$.

Example 2

Find $^{+}6 - ^{+}10$.

Start at 0. Walk forward 6 steps for $^{+}6$. | The subtraction sign, −, means turn around. | Then walk forward 10 steps for $^{+}10$.

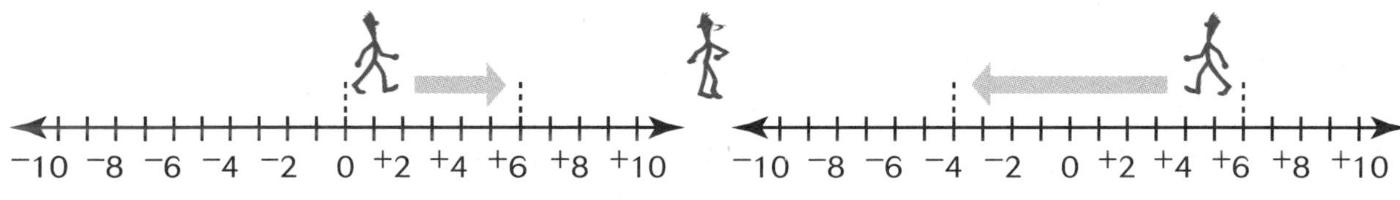

You stop at $^{-}4$. So $^{+}6 - ^{+}10 = ^{-}4$.

Example 3

Find $^{-}7 - ^{-}4$.

Start at 0. Walk backward 7 steps for $^{-}7$. | The subtraction sign, −, means turn around. | Then walk backward 4 steps for $^{-}4$.

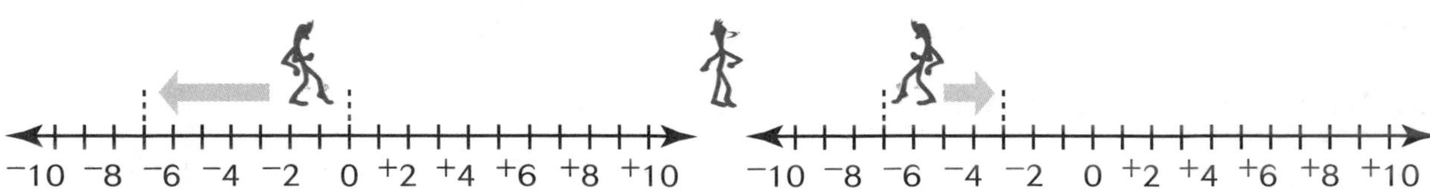

You stop at $^{-}3$. So $^{-}7 - ^{-}4 = ^{-}3$.

Additional Standards: Algebra and Functions 1.2 ( ); Mathematical Reasoning 1.1 *(See p. 359.)*

You saw in Examples 1, 2, and 3 that $^{+}5 - {}^{-}3 = {}^{+}8$, $^{+}6 - {}^{+}10 = {}^{-}4$, and $^{-}7 - {}^{-}4 = {}^{-}3$. By the methods of the preceding lesson, you know that $^{+}5 + {}^{+}3 = {}^{+}8$, $^{+}6 + {}^{-}10 = {}^{-}4$, and $^{-}7 + {}^{+}4 = {}^{-}3$.

Notice the comparisons between the preceding addition and subtraction equations.

$^{+}5 - {}^{-}3 = {}^{+}8$	$^{+}5 + {}^{+}3 = {}^{+}8$
$^{+}6 - {}^{+}10 = {}^{-}4$	$^{+}6 + {}^{-}10 = {}^{-}4$
$^{-}7 - {}^{-}4 = {}^{-}3$	$^{-}7 + {}^{+}4 = {}^{-}3$

The preceding examples illustrate a very important fact.

To subtract an integer, add the opposite.

More Examples

A. $^{+}4 - {}^{-}6 = {}^{+}4 + {}^{+}6$
$= {}^{+}10$

B. $^{+}4 - {}^{+}6 = {}^{+}4 + {}^{-}6$
$= {}^{-}2$

C. $^{-}4 - {}^{+}6 = {}^{-}4 + {}^{-}6$
$= {}^{-}10$

Guided Practice *For another example, see Set D on p. 390.*

Rewrite each subtraction using addition.

1. $^{-}7 - {}^{+}2$ **2.** $^{-}3 - {}^{+}5$ **3.** $^{+}4 - {}^{-}2$ **4.** $^{-}6 - {}^{-}9$

Subtract.

5. $^{-}4 - {}^{+}1$ **6.** $^{-}7 - {}^{+}3$ **7.** $^{+}5 - {}^{-}8$ **8.** $^{-}8 - {}^{-}3$

9. A diver was 20 feet below sea level before coming to the surface and climbing on a raft that was 3 feet above sea level. How much higher was the diver when on the raft than when she was 20 feet below sea level?

Independent Practice *For more practice, see Set D on p. 392.*

Rewrite each subtraction using addition.

10. $^{-}3 - {}^{+}4$ **11.** $^{-}1 - {}^{+}8$ **12.** $^{+}9 - {}^{-}5$ **13.** $^{-}7 - {}^{-}3$

Subtract.

14. $^{-}6 - {}^{+}6$ **15.** $^{-}5 - {}^{+}8$ **16.** $^{+}7 - {}^{-}10$ **17.** $^{-}4 - {}^{-}12$

18. $^{-}8 - {}^{+}12$ **19.** $0 - {}^{-}7$ **20.** $^{+}6 - {}^{-}4$ **21.** $^{-}2 - {}^{-}16$

22. $^-7 - ^-6$ 23. $^-9 - ^+9$ 24. $^+4 - ^-14$ 25. $^-5 - ^-15$

26. $^-13 - ^-4$ 27. $^+12 - ^-7$ 28. $^-5 - ^+6$ 29. $^+5 - ^-3$

30. The temperature rose from $^-10$ degrees to $^+15$ degrees. How much did the temperature rise?

31. **Algebra** If $^+3 + ^-2 = x$ and $^+3 - ^+2 = y$, what do you know about x and y?

32. Mount Everest is 29,028 feet high. Death Valley is 282 feet below sea level. How much higher is Mount Everest than Death Valley?

33. **Math Reasoning** Which is greater, the difference between 2 and 7 or the difference between 2 and $^-7$?

Mixed Review

34. $^-5 + ^-7$ 35. $^+10 + ^-8$ 36. $^-3 + ^-17$

37. Order $^-9$, $^-10$, 0, $^-1$, and $^+15$ from least to greatest.

38. Write $\frac{75}{100}$ as a fraction in simplest form.

Test Prep **Choose the correct letter for each answer.**

39. (3-2) The bar graph shows the number of fiction and nonfiction books checked out of the Glenview Library for the years 1995–2000. In which year were the most nonfiction books checked out?

A 1995 C 1999

B 1998 D 2000

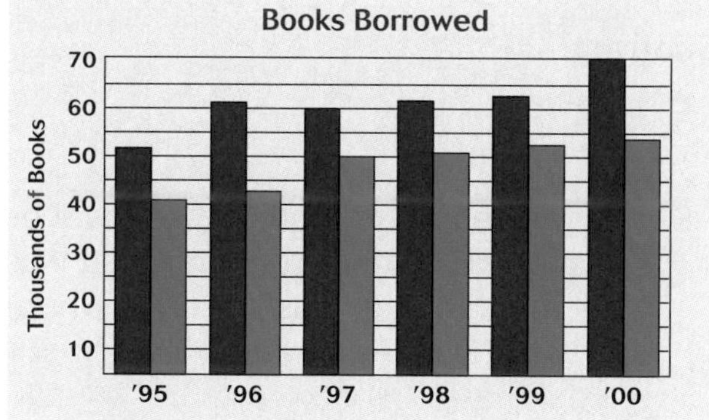

40. (3-5) The graph shows Linda's bicycling distances for a one-week period. How many miles did Linda ride during the week?

F 78 mi H 84 mi

G 80 mi J 96 mi

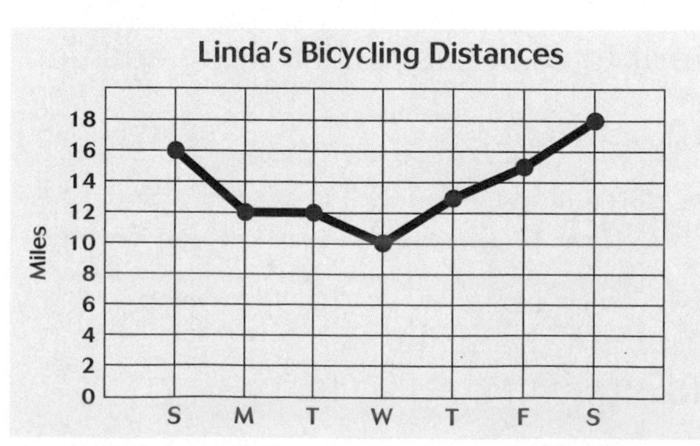

Diagnostic Checkpoint

Write an integer for each word description.

1. (9-1) 60 meters below sea level
2. (9-1) An inventory shortage of 60 shirts
3. (9-1) A loss of 8 yards
4. (9-1) An increase of $11.00
5. (9-1) Temperature decrease of 18°F
6. (9-1) An elevator going up 6 floors

Compare. Use >, <, or = for each ●.

7. (9-2) $^{+}6$ ● $^{-}6$
8. (9-2) $^{-}9$ ● $^{-}4$
9. (9-2) $^{-}4$ ● 0
10. (9-2) $^{+}6$ ● $^{-}12$
11. (9-2) $^{-}9$ ● $^{+}3$
12. (9-2) $^{-}6$ ● $^{-}3$
13. (9-2) $^{-}1$ ● $^{-}2$
14. (9-2) 0 ● $^{+}18$

Write in order from least to greatest.

15. (9-2) $^{-}2, ^{-}4, ^{-}6, ^{-}8$
16. (9-2) $^{-}16, ^{+}8, ^{+}2, ^{+}4$
17. (9-2) $^{+}6, ^{+}8, ^{-}3, ^{+}3$
18. (9-2) $^{+}1, ^{-}1, ^{+}4, ^{-}4$
19. (9-2) $^{+}6, ^{+}2, ^{-}4, ^{-}5$
20. (9-2) $^{-}2, ^{+}10, ^{-}6, ^{-}4$

Add or subtract.

21. (9-4) $^{+}7 - ^{-}6$
22. (9-3) $^{-}5 + 0$
23. (9-3) $^{-}6 + ^{+}13$
24. (9-4) $^{+}15 - ^{-}7$
25. (9-3) $^{-}15 + ^{-}7$
26. (9-4) $^{-}6 - ^{-}3$
27. (9-3) $^{-}20 + ^{+}20$
28. (9-4) $^{+}5 - ^{+}6$
29. (9-3) $^{+}12 + ^{-}3$
30. (9-4) $^{+}15 - ^{-}18$
31. (9-3) $^{-}29 + ^{+}21$
32. (9-4) $^{-}16 - ^{-}14$
33. (9-3) $^{-}13 + ^{+}4$
34. (9-4) $^{+}3 - ^{+}151$
35. (9-4) $^{-}14 - 0$
36. (9-4) $^{-}21 - ^{+}54$

37. (9-2) On Thursday the highest temperature was $^{-}2$°C. On Friday the highest temperature was $^{-}6$°C. Which day was warmer?

38. (9-1) If $^{-}20$ kg represents a downward force of 20 kg, what does $^{+}12$ kg represent?

39. (9-3) If Sally scored 3 under par in the first nine holes of her golf game and 2 over par in the second nine holes, what was her total score, in relation to par, for the 18 holes?

40. (9-1) Sam dug a hole 18 feet deep. He then continued digging another 10 feet. Write an integer to represent the final depth of the hole.

Evaluating Expressions with Integers

California Content Standard *Algebra and Functions 1.2 (🔑): Use a letter to represent an unknown number; write and evaluate simple algebraic expressions in one variable by substitution. Also Number Sense 2.1* *(See p. 359.)*

Warm-Up Review

1. ${}^{+}9 + {}^{-}5$
2. ${}^{-}8 + {}^{+}3$
3. ${}^{-}7 + {}^{-}5$
4. ${}^{-}8 + {}^{+}8$
5. ${}^{+}6 - {}^{-}5$
6. ${}^{-}4 - {}^{+}3$
7. ${}^{+}10 - {}^{-}3$
8. ${}^{-}12 - {}^{+}5$
9. The high temperature on Sunday was ${}^{+}10$°F. The low temperature was ${}^{-}2$°F. What was the difference between the high and low temperatures?

Math Link You have already evaluated expressions with whole numbers and decimals. In this lesson, you will evaluate expressions involving integers.

Remember, when you evaluate an expression with one or more variables, you replace the variables and then do the appropriate calculations.

Example 1

Evaluate $x + {}^{+}9$ for $x = {}^{-}12$.

$x + {}^{+}9 = {}^{-}12 + {}^{+}9$	Replace x with ${}^{-}12$.
$= {}^{-}3$	

Example 2

Evaluate $y - {}^{+}10$ for $y = {}^{-}5$.

$y - {}^{+}10 = {}^{-}5 - {}^{+}10$	Replace y with ${}^{-}5$.
$= {}^{-}5 + {}^{-}10$	Subtracting an integer is the same as adding its opposite.
$= {}^{-}15$	Add ${}^{-}5$ and ${}^{-}10$.

When more than one variable is involved, replace each variable. If only addition and subtraction are involved, proceed from left to right, grouping two numbers at a time.

Example 3

Evaluate $a + b - c$ for $a = {}^{+}4$, $b = {}^{-}10$, and $c = {}^{-}3$.

$a + b - c = {}^{+}4 + {}^{-}10 - {}^{-}3$	Replace a with ${}^{+}4$, b with ${}^{-}10$, and c with ${}^{-}3$.
$= {}^{-}6 - {}^{-}3$	Add ${}^{+}4$ and ${}^{-}10$.
$= {}^{-}6 + {}^{+}3$	Rewrite subtraction as an addition of the opposite.
$= {}^{-}3$	Add ${}^{-}6$ and ${}^{+}3$.

Guided Practice For another example, see Set E on p. 391.

Evaluate each expression for $x = {}^{+}5$ and $x = {}^{-}7$.

1. $x + 9$
2. $x - 7$
3. $8 + x$
4. $12 - x$
5. Evaluate $r + s - t$ for $r = {}^{-}9$, $s = 7$, and $t = {}^{-}6$.

Independent Practice For more practice, see Set E on p. 393.

Evaluate each expression for $x = {}^{-}8$ and $x = {}^{+}2$.

6. $x + 11$
7. $x - 5$
8. $5 + x$
9. ${}^{-}9 - x$
10. $14 + x$
11. $12 - x$
12. ${}^{-}15 + x$
13. $x + x$
14. Evaluate $d - e + f$ for $d = {}^{-}4$, $e = {}^{+}5$, and $f = {}^{-}3$.
15. Evaluate $x - y - z$ for $x = {}^{-}4$, $y = {}^{+}5$, and $z = {}^{-}3$.
16. The range in temperatures between high and low temperatures can be found by evaluating $a - b$, where a is the high and b is the low temperature. Find the range for the three days shown.

Daily Temperatures

	High	Low
Monday	$^{+}13°$	$^{+}1°$
Tuesday	$^{+}5°$	$^{-}6°$
Wednesday	$^{-}1°$	$^{-}8°$

Mixed Review

17. ${}^{+}13 + {}^{-}12$
18. ${}^{+}20 - {}^{-}13$
19. $8{,}000 - 779$
20. $3{,}000 \times 4{,}000$
21. A board is $31\frac{1}{2}$ inches long, but it must be trimmed to a length of $28\frac{3}{4}$ inches. How much must be trimmed from the board?
22. Evaluate $5 + 3 \times 7 - 2$ using the order of operations.

Test Prep Choose the correct letter for each answer.

23. Solve $m - 6 = 18$. (2-4)

    A 3
    B 12
    C 24
    D 108
    E NH

24. If gasoline is priced at $1.39 a gallon, how much would 14.2 gallons cost? (6-5)

    F $10.22
    G $15.59
    H $19.73
    J $19.74
    K NH

Problem-Solving Skill:

Translating and Writing Expressions

Algebra

Warm-Up Review

1. $^{+}3 + {}^{-}8$ 2. $^{+}3 - {}^{-}8$
3. $^{-}16 + {}^{+}5$ 4. $^{-}16 - {}^{+}5$
5. Write an algebraic expression to represent 10 less than a number *n*.
6. Write an algebraic expression to represent the difference between a height of 100 and a height of *y*.

California Content Standard *Mathematical Reasoning 2.3: Use a variety of methods, such as words, numbers, symbols, charts, graphs, tables, diagrams, and models, to explain mathematical reasoning.*

Read for Understanding

Positive and negative numbers can be used to describe locations above and below sea level. A diver is 20 feet below sea level (at $^{-}20$ feet). Then the diver moves 10 feet higher.

1. What number describes the diver's location after moving 10 feet higher?
2. Which expression would describe the situation in question 1, $^{-}20 + {}^{+}10$ or $^{-}20 - {}^{+}10$? (Hint: Evaluate both $^{-}20 + {}^{+}10$ and $^{-}20 - {}^{+}10$.)

Think and Discuss

Translating and Using Expressions

Mathematical expressions use both numbers and variables. Writing and translating expressions can help you solve problems.

3. Suppose the diver is 15 feet below sea level. What integer describes the location?
4. Suppose the diver in question 3 goes 5 feet lower. Which expression describes the new location, $^{-}15 + {}^{+}5$ or $^{-}15 - {}^{+}5$?
5. Suppose the diver is at *p* feet. Write an expression to describe the diver's location after going 8 feet higher.
6. Suppose the diver is at *m* feet. Write an expression to describe the diver's location after going 6 feet lower.

Additional Standards: Algebra and Functions 1.2 (key); Mathematical Reasoning 2.4 (See p. 359.)

For Exercises 1–6, answer each question.

A diver is located 12 feet below sea level. The diver moves either vertically upward or downward. Locations below sea level are represented as negative integers.

Guided Practice

1. Which expression describes the location of the diver after starting at $^-12$ feet and then moving upward 3 feet?

a. $^-12 + {}^-3$

b. $^-12 + {}^+3$

c. $^+3 - {}^-12$

Independent Practice

2. Which expression describes the location of the diver after starting at $^-12$ feet and then moving downward 3 feet?

a. $^-12 + {}^+3$

b. $^-12 + {}^-3$

c. $^+3 - {}^-12$

3. Which expression describes the total number of feet the diver travels in going from 12 feet below sea level to a platform 3 feet above sea level?

a. $^-12 + {}^+3$

b. $^+12 + {}^-3$

c. $^+3 - {}^-12$

When a bank account is overdrawn, the balance is expressed as a negative number. For example, if an account is overdrawn by $50, the balance is $^-50$.

4. An account is overdrawn by $100. Which expression describes the bank balance after a deposit of 150 dollars?

a. $^+100 + {}^-50$

b. $^-100 + {}^-150$

c. $^-100 + {}^+150$

5. A bank account is overdrawn by $50. The bank charges a penalty of $10 for being overdrawn. Which expression describes the final balance in the account?

a. $^-50 + {}^+10$

b. $^+50 + {}^-10$

c. $^-50 + {}^-10$

6. Math Reasoning Write an expression to describe the balance after a deposit of p dollars is made to an account with a balance of $^-50$ dollars.

Use Homework Workbook 9-6.

Graphing Points in the Coordinate Plane

Algebra

California Content Standard *Algebra and Functions 1.4 (🔑): Identify and graph ordered pairs in the four quadrants of the coordinate plane.*

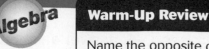

Warm-Up Review

Name the opposite of each of the following.

1. $^{+}3$ **2.** $^{-}10$

3. up 3 feet

4. down 6 feet

5. 3 miles north

6. 6 miles west

Math Link You have already used a coordinate grid in Lesson 3–3. In that lesson all the ordered pairs involved positive numbers.

A coordinate grid can be extended to include both positive and negative numbers. This extended grid is called a **coordinate plane**. An ordered pair is used to describe a location on a coordinate plane. Look at the treasure map at the right.

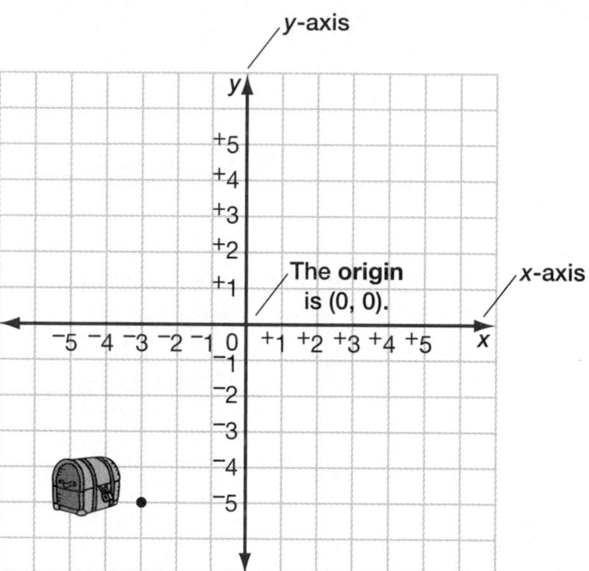

- The first number in an ordered pair is the number of units to the left or right of the origin. The treasure is 3 units to the left of the origin.
- The second number in an ordered pair is the number of units up or down from the origin. The treasure is 5 units down from the origin.

The ordered pair that locates the treasure is $(^{-}3, ^{-}5)$.

Word Bank

coordinate plane

You can also graph or plot a point on a coordinate plane.

Example 1

Graph the ordered pair $(^{-}4, ^{+}2)$.

- Begin at the origin.
- Move left 4 units on the *x*-axis, since $^{-}4$ is a negative integer.
- Then move up 2 units, since $^{+}2$ is a positive integer.

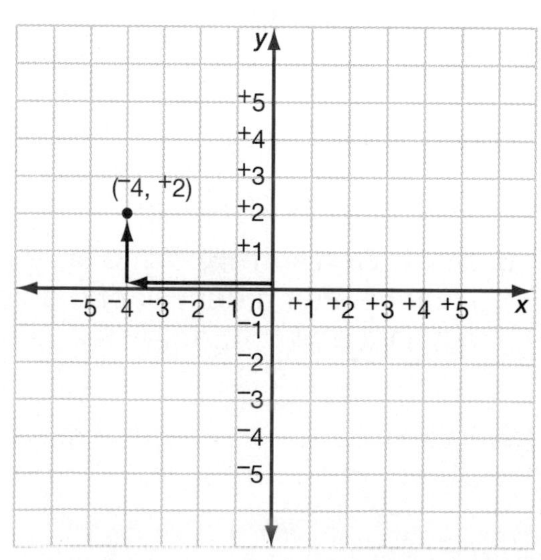

 Additional Standard: Mathematical Reasoning 2.3 (See p. 359.)

Example 2

Look at the grid at the right.

Name the ordered pair for each point shown.

Point *A* $(^{+}3, ^{+}5)$
Point *B* $(^{-}4, ^{+}2)$
Point *C* $(^{-}4, ^{-}5)$
Point *D* $(^{+}5, ^{-}2)$

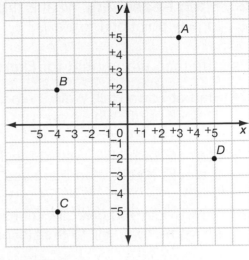

Guided Practice *For another example, see Set F on p. 391.*

Write the ordered pair for each point.

1. *E*
2. *F*
3. *G*
4. *H*

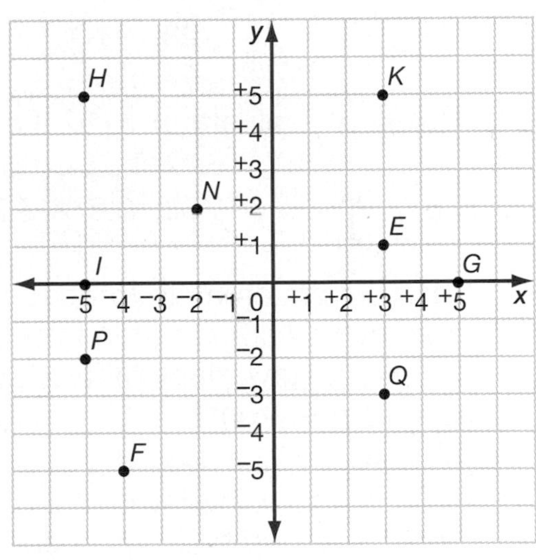

Name the point for each ordered pair.

5. $(^{+}3, ^{+}5)$
6. $(^{-}5, ^{-}2)$
7. $(^{-}2, ^{+}2)$
8. $(^{+}3, ^{-}3)$
9. Which point on the grid is located by starting at the origin and moving 5 units to the left?

Independent Practice *For more practice, see Set F on p. 393.*

Write the ordered pair for each point.

10. *M*
11. *N*
12. *Q*
13. *R*
14. *S*
15. *T*

Name the point for each ordered pair.

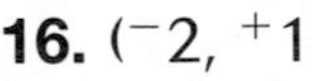

16. $(^{-}2, ^{+}1)$
17. $(^{+}5, ^{+}1)$
18. $(0, ^{+}5)$
19. $(^{+}1, ^{-}3)$
20. $(^{+}4, ^{-}5)$
21. $(^{-}3, ^{-}4)$
22. Which point on the grid is located by starting at the origin and moving 5 units down?

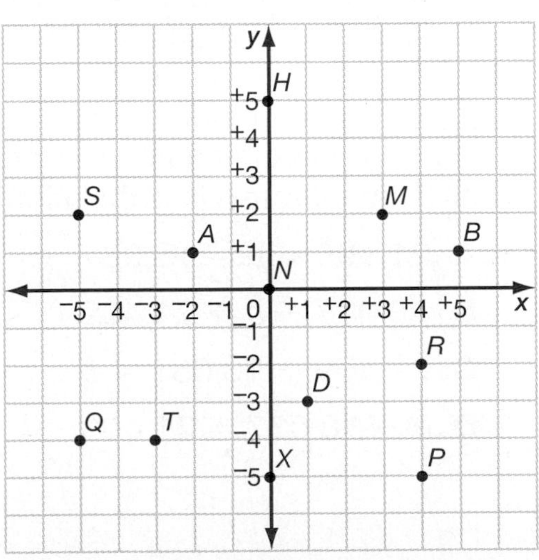

23. **Math Reasoning** What is the *x*-coordinate for any point on the *y*-axis?

Use the map at the right for Exercises 24–26.

24. Start at Town Hall. Walk 3 blocks east and 1 block north. Where are you?

25. Start at Town Hall. Walk 2 blocks west and 3 blocks south. Where are you?

26. How would you give directions to someone to go from Town Hall to the Hospital?

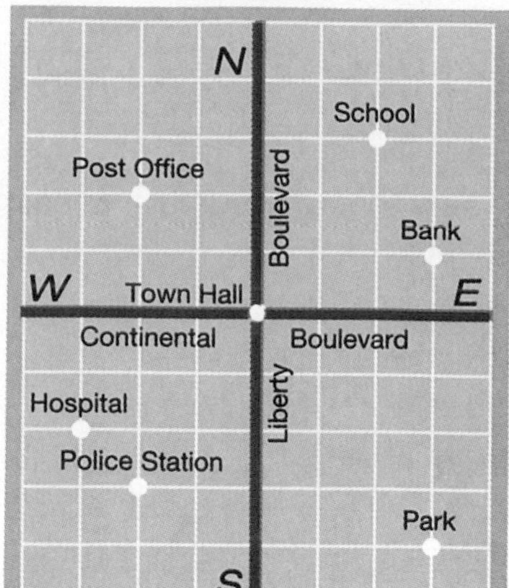

Mixed Review

27. $^{-}8 + {}^{-}7$

28. $^{+}10 + {}^{-}12$

29. $^{-}9 - {}^{+}4$

30. $^{-}8 - {}^{-}9$

31. **Algebra** Evaluate $m - 12$ if $m = {}^{-}9$.

32. $4.6 \div 2.3$

33. 0.8×3.2

34. 129×875

35. $67.2 - 1.289$

36. Chair covers come in three colors: white, black, or tan. The covers can be made from cotton, velvet, wool, or polyester. How many different chair covers does a buyer have to pick from?

37. Adult tickets to a play cost $18.50 and student tickets cost $7.50. A group of 3 adults and 5 students plan to attend the play. They will rent a van costing $35 for the evening. How much is the total cost for the entire group to attend the play?

Test Prep **Choose the correct letter for each answer.**

38. (2-4) In 1990 a town had a population of 18,037. According to town records, the population today is 21,409. Which equation could be used to find the increase in population?

A $21{,}409 + p = 18{,}037$

B $18{,}037 + p = 21{,}409$

C $21{,}409 + 18{,}037 = p$

D $p - 18{,}037 = 21{,}409$

39. (7-9) In which list are $\frac{5}{16}$, $\frac{3}{8}$, and $\frac{1}{4}$ in order from least to greatest?

F $\frac{1}{4}, \frac{3}{8}, \frac{5}{16}$

G $\frac{3}{8}, \frac{5}{16}, \frac{1}{4}$

H $\frac{5}{16}, \frac{1}{4}, \frac{3}{8}$

J $\frac{1}{4}, \frac{5}{16}, \frac{3}{8}$

 Use Homework Workbook 9-7.

Multiple-Choice Cumulative Review

Choose the correct letter for each answer.

1. What is the sum of $^{+}63$ and $^{-}9$?

A $^{+}72$ C $^{-}54$

B $^{+}54$ D $^{-}72$

2. Arrange in order from least to greatest.

$\frac{2}{3}, \frac{3}{4}, \frac{5}{8}, 2\frac{1}{5}, 1\frac{3}{4}, 1\frac{9}{10}$

F $\frac{3}{4}, 1\frac{3}{4}, \frac{5}{8}, 1\frac{9}{10}, \frac{2}{3}, 2\frac{1}{5}$

G $\frac{2}{3}, \frac{5}{8}, 1\frac{3}{4}, \frac{3}{4}, 1\frac{9}{10}, 2\frac{1}{5}$

H $\frac{5}{8}, \frac{2}{3}, \frac{3}{4}, 1\frac{3}{4}, 1\frac{9}{10}, 2\frac{1}{5}$

J $\frac{3}{4}, \frac{5}{8}, \frac{2}{3}, 1\frac{9}{10}, 1\frac{3}{4}, 2\frac{1}{5}$

3. Which number sentence is NOT true?

A $^{-}13 > {}^{-}28$

B $6\frac{1}{2} < 6\frac{11}{12}$

C $^{-}4 < 4$

D $^{-}6 + 2 > 0$

4. The wilderness catalog is advertising corduroy shirts for $17.75. If Mr. Hayes wants to buy one for each of his four children, how much will he have to pay?

F $48.80

G $62.48

H $71.00

J $80.00

5. Altogether, four students have $2\frac{3}{8}$ quarts of juice. If Greg has $\frac{3}{4}$ qt, Frank has $\frac{1}{2}$ qt, Eve has $\frac{5}{8}$ qt, and Jill has $\frac{2}{4}$ qt, who has the *greatest* amount?

A Greg

B Eve

C Frank

D Jill

6. What number is the sum of $^{-}118$ and $^{-}9$?

F $^{-}127$

G $^{-}109$

H $^{+}109$

J $^{+}127$

7. Justine and her family are traveling by car from Chicago to the Grand Canyon. If they use four tanks of gas and travel 1,235 miles, about how many miles do they travel on each tank of gas?

A 250 miles C 390 miles

B 310 miles D 400 miles

8. Gabby photographed 8 out of 28 athletes. What fraction of the athletes did she photograph?

F $\frac{1}{3}$ H $\frac{2}{7}$

G $\frac{4}{6}$ J $\frac{2}{3}$

LESSON 9-8

Graphing Equations

Algebra

California Content Standard *Algebra and Functions 1.5. (🔑): Solve problems involving linear functions with integer values; . . . and graph the resulting ordered pairs of integers on a grid.*

Warm-Up Review

Evaluate each expression if $x = {}^{-}3$.

1. $x + 3$ **2.** $x - 3$

3. $5 - x$ **4.** $7 + x$

5. This morning the temperature was −3°F. Then it rose 8 degrees by noon and dropped 10 degrees by sunset. What was the temperature at sunset?

Math Link You already know how to graph ordered pairs. In this lesson you will apply this skill to graphing equations.

Word Bank

linear equation

For an equation with two variables, such as $y = x + 4$, you can substitute any value for x and then find the corresponding value for y. The two values can be written as an ordered pair (x, y).

Example 1

For the equation $y = x + 4$, find y when $x = {}^{-}5$, when $x = 0$, and when $x = 3$. Name the ordered pairs.

$y = x + {}^{+}4$ is the same as $y = x + 4$.

When $x = {}^{-}5$:	When $x = 0$:	When $x = 3$:
$y = x + 4$	$y = x + 4$	$y = x + 4$
$y = {}^{-}5 + 4$	$y = 0 + 4$	$y = 3 + 4$
$y = {}^{-}1$	$y = 4$	$y = 7$

A positive number can be written with or without the positive sign.

The ordered pairs are $({}^{-}5, {}^{-}1)$, $(0, 4)$, and $(3, 7)$.

Once you know several ordered pairs for an equation, you can graph those ordered pairs on a coordinate plane and draw a line through them.

An equation such as $y = x - 2$ is called a **linear equation**. Its graph is a straight line. In graphing a line, only 2 points are needed to determine the location of the line. But a third point is graphed to serve as a check.

Example 2

Graph the equation $y = x - 2$.

Make a table. Substitute any three convenient values for x and find the corresponding values for y. Plot the ordered pairs and connect the points to graph the equation. Notice that all the points lie on a straight line.

x	y
$^{-}4$	$^{-}6$
0	$^{-}2$
2	0

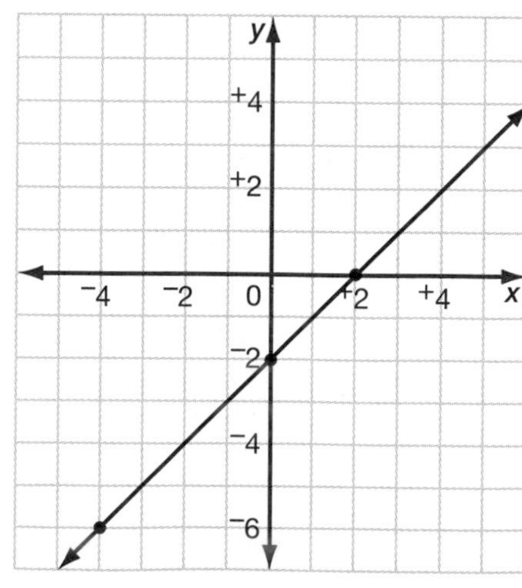

 Additional Standard: Mathematical Reasoning 2.3 (See p. 359.)

Guided Practice *For another example, see Set G on p. 391.*

For each equation, find the value of y when $x = {}^-3$, when $x = 0$, and when $x = 5$. Then name the ordered pairs.

1. $y = x - 4$　　**2.** $y = 3 - x$　　**3.** $y = x + 1$

Graph each equation. First make a table using x-values of $^-3$, 0, and 3.

4. $y = x - 2$　　**5.** $y = 4 - x$　　**6.** $y = x + 5$

Independent Practice *For more practice, see Set G on p. 393.*

For each equation, find the value of y when $x = {}^-4$, when $x = 0$, and when $x = 4$. Then name the ordered pairs.

7. $y = x - 1$　　**8.** $y = 2 - x$　　**9.** $y = x + 4$

Graph each equation. First make a table using x-values of $^-3$, 0, and 3.

10. $y = x - 3$　　**11.** $y = 5 - x$　　**12.** $y = x + 6$

13. Math Reasoning Is the point (2, 20) on the graph of $y = x + 8$? Explain.

Mixed Review

14. Algebra Evaluate $x - 10$ for $x = 20$ and $x = {}^-5$.

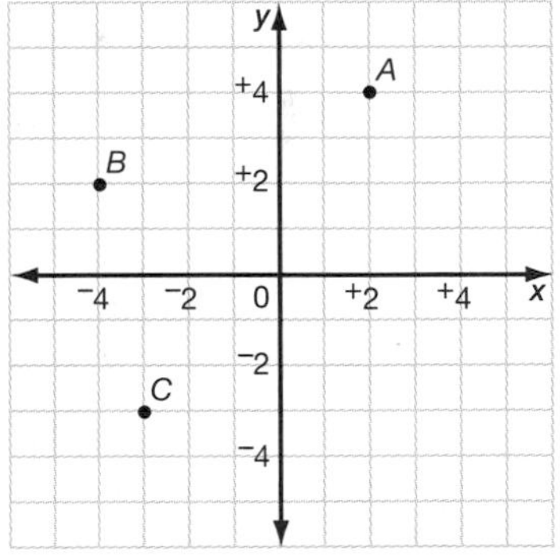

Write the ordered pair for each point.

15. *A*　　**16.** *B*　　**17.** *C*

18. Each can of soup in a box weighs $12\frac{3}{4}$ ounces. There are 12 cans in the box. What is the weight of all the cans?

Test Prep **Choose the correct letter for each answer.**

19. (4-6) Which is the best estimate for 78×42?

A 280　　**C** 2,800
B 320　　**D** 3,200

20. (6-10) Mr. Clark bought 4.8 pounds of chicken for \$9.36. What was the price per pound?

F \$0.513　　**H** \$1.95
G \$0.195　　**J** \$5.13

Understand
Plan
Solve
Look Back

Problem-Solving Strategy:

Make a Graph

California Content Standard *Algebra and Functions 1.5 (🔑): Solve problems involving linear functions with integer values; . . . Also Mathematical Reasoning 2.3* *(See p. 359.)*

Warm-Up Review

Name the ordered pair for each point on the graph.

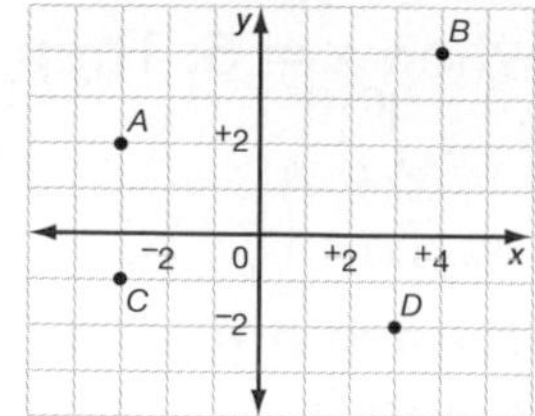

1. *A* **2.** *B*

3. *C* **4.** *D*

5. Name an ordered pair on the *y*-axis with *y*-value of 10.

Example

Kitty saw the following chart giving temperature comparisons for Celsius and Fahrenheit temperatures. She wants to use this information to find what −20°C equals on the Fahrenheit scale.

°C	10°	0°	−5°
°F	50°	32°	23°

Understand

What do you need to find?

You want to find what −20°C equals on the Fahrenheit scale.

Plan

How can you solve the problem?

Make a graph by plotting the three known pairs of temperatures on a coordinate grid. Plot Celsius degrees on the *x*-axis and Fahrenheit degrees on the *y*-axis. Then connect the three points with a line.

Note that every ordered pair on the graph represents a Celsius temperature and its corresponding Fahrenheit temperature. Find an ordered pair on the line where the first number is −20. The second number in the ordered pair is the Fahrenheit temperature.

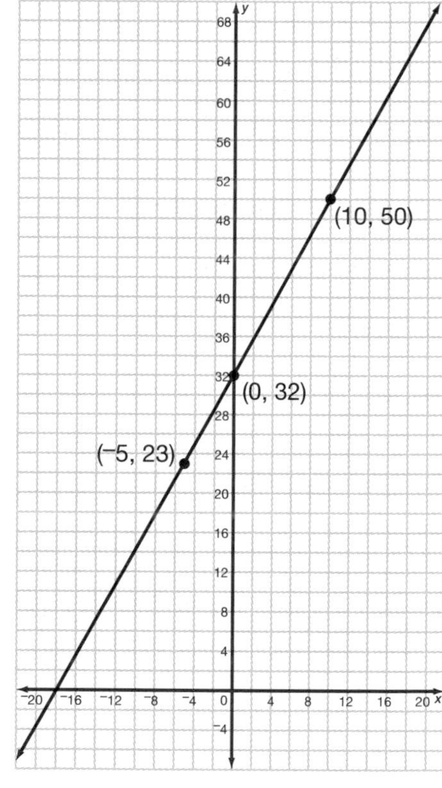

Solve

The point is (−20, −4). A temperature of −20°C is −4°F.

Note that each unit on both the *x*-axis and the *y*-axis equals 2 degrees.

Look Back

Look at the table. A temperature of −20°C is colder than −5°C, so the Fahrenheit reading for −20°C has to be colder than 23°F. The answer is sensible.

Additional Standard: Mathematical Reasoning 3.2

Guided Practice

For questions 1–4, refer to the graph on the preceding page.

1. The point ($^-15$, 5) lies on the graph. What does each number in the ordered pair stand for? What Fahrenheit temperature is equal to $^-15$°C?

2. Does (20, 68) lie on the graph? What Celsius temperature is equal to 68°F?

Independent Practice

3. Does ($^-10$, 14) lie on the graph? What Fahrenheit temperature is equal to $^-10$°C?

4. Does (15, 59) lie on the graph? What Celsius temperature is equal to 59°F?

5. On the same coordinate axes, graph (0, 17), (1, 19), and ($^-2$, 13). Draw a line through the points. What is the value of y when $x = 3$? What is the value of x when $y = 15$?

Mixed Review

Try these or other strategies to solve each problem. Tell which strategy you used.

Problem-Solving Strategies

- *Make a List*
- *Work Backward*
- *Draw a Diagram*
- *Solve a Simpler Problem*

6. The daily attendance figures for four performances of the class play are shown in the table at the right. What is the mean attendance for the four days?

Daily Attendance	
Wednesday	878
Thursday	789
Friday	1,098
Saturday	1,675

7. Bill, Geneva, Chris, and Becky want to play chess with each other. If each person plays a game with every other person, how many games will they play?

8. Paul gave Heather 6 comic books, and he gave Lee Ann twice as many. Now Paul has 24 comic books. How many comic books did he have before he gave away the comic books?

Use Homework Workbook 9-9.

Writing Equations

Algebra

Warm-Up Review

1. $^{+}5 + {}^{-}3$ 2. $^{+}2 + {}^{-}6$
3. $^{-}8 + {}^{+}2$ 4. $^{+}5 - {}^{-}2$
5. $^{-}5 - {}^{-}2$ 6. $^{-}7 - {}^{+}1$
7. What is the difference in heights between a point 12 feet above sea level and a point that is 20 feet below sea level?

California Content Standard *Algebra and Functions 1.5. (🔑): Solve problems involving linear functions with integer values; write the equation; . . .*

Math Link You have made tables of values for equations in two variables and you have graphed equations with two variables. In this lesson you will look at tables of values or at a graph and find the equation that describes the relationships between the variables.

Example 1

Examine the values in the table at the right and write an equation that describes the relationship between x and y.

x	y
$^{-}2$	0
$^{-}1$	1
0	2
1	3
2	4

Notice that each y-value is always 2 more than the corresponding x-value. The relationship can be described by the equation $y = x + 2$.

Example 2

Look at the graph of the line at the right. Find the equation that describes the relationship between x and y.

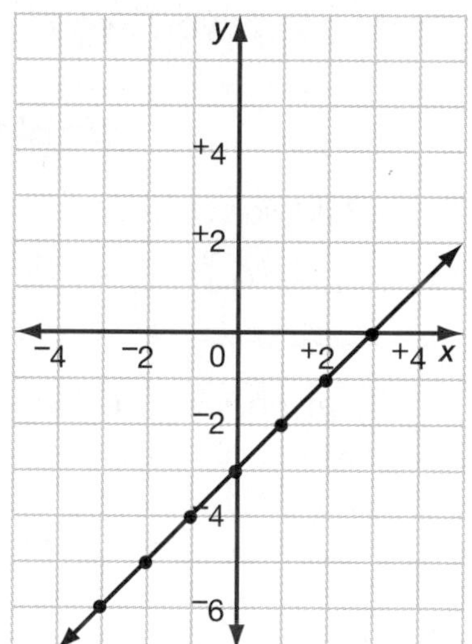

First make a table showing several ordered pairs that describe points on the graph. Look for a pattern. Then write an equation that describes the relationship between x and y.

You can pick any points on the line. The more points you pick, the more obvious the pattern becomes.

The table shows seven ordered pairs on the line.

x	$^{-}3$	$^{-}2$	$^{-}1$	0	1	2	3
y	$^{-}6$	$^{-}5$	$^{-}4$	$^{-}3$	$^{-}2$	$^{-}1$	0

Notice that each y-value is always 3 less than the corresponding x-value. The equation of the line is $y = x - 3$.

 Additional Standard: Mathematical Reasoning 2.3 *(See p. 359.)*

Guided Practice *For another example, see Set H on p. 391.*

Write an equation to describe the relationship between *x* and *y*.

1.

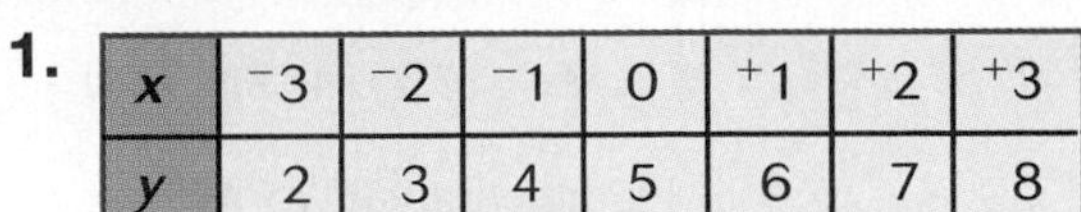

x	−3	−2	−1	0	+1	+2	+3
y	2	3	4	5	6	7	8

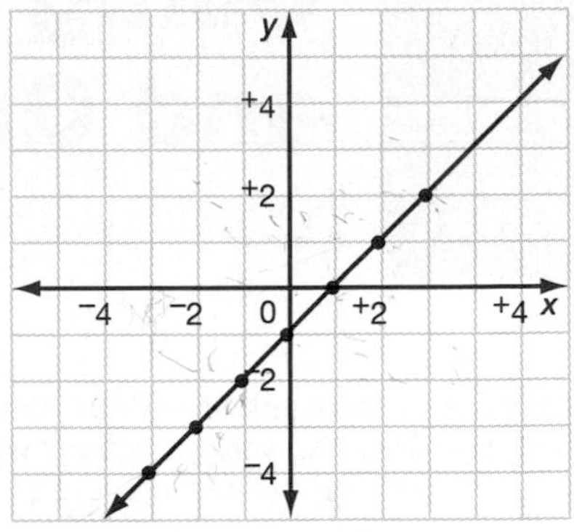

2. Make a table of values to describe the graph at the right. Then write an equation.

Independent Practice *For more practice, see Set H on p. 393.*

Write an equation to describe the relationship between *x* and *y*.

3.

x	*y*
−2	8
−1	9
0	10
1	11
2	12

4.

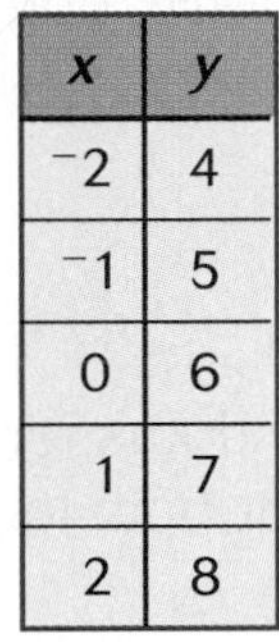

x	*y*
−2	−4
−1	−3
0	−2
1	−1
2	0

5.

x	*y*
−2	4
−1	5
0	6
1	7
2	8

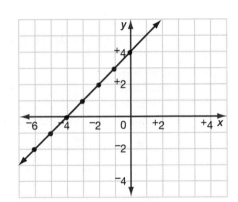

6. Make a table of values to describe the graph above. Then write an equation.

Mixed Review

7. $\frac{2}{3} + \frac{1}{5}$ **8.** $\frac{2}{3} \times \frac{1}{5}$ **9.** $\frac{2}{3} \div \frac{1}{5}$ **10.** $1\frac{1}{5} + 3\frac{9}{10}$

11. On the coordinate plane, why is the point for (−2, 3) different than the point for (3, −2)?

12. Algebra Graph the equation $y = x + 6$. Use *x*-values of −2, 0, and 2.

13. What is the least common multiple of 20 and 30?

Test Prep Choose the correct letter for each answer.

14. $9\overline{)0.81}$ (6-9)

A 0.09 **C** 9

B 0.9 **D** 90

15. 0.04×0.9 (6-5)

F 0.036 **H** 3.6

G 0.36 **J** 36

Problem-Solving Application:

Using Tables and Graphs

Warm-Up Review

Evaluate each expression for $x = 5$, $x = 10$, and $x = 15$.

1. $5x$ **2.** $x + 20$

3. $3x - 15$ **4.** $5(x + 2)$

5. How much would you earn for working 12 hours at $3.50 an hour?

California Content Standard *Algebra and Functions 1.5 (🔑): Solve problems involving linear functions with integer values . . .; and graph the resulting ordered pairs of integers on a grid.*

Example

Sheila was offered two jobs. In Job 1 she would be paid $5 per hour. In Job 2 she would be paid $10 a day plus $3 for each hour she works. Find the number of hours for which her salary would be the same for both jobs.

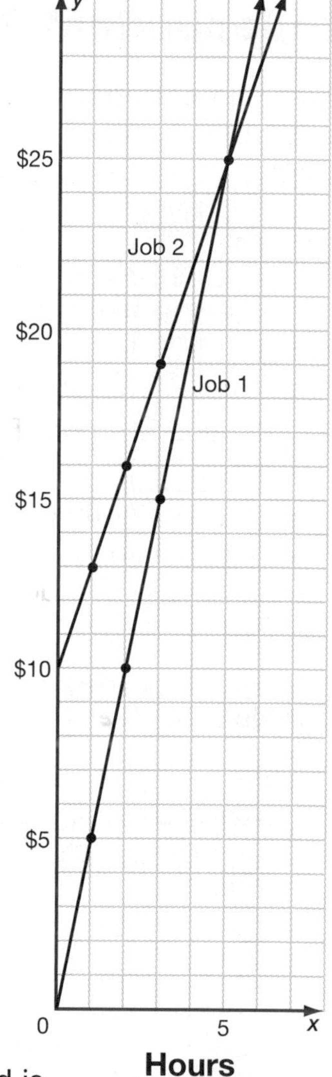

Understand

What do you need to find?

You need to find the number of hours for which her salary would be the same for both jobs.

Plan

Make a table of values for each job. Then graph each table of values on the same set of coordinate axes.

Solve

Let x equal hours she would work. Let y equal her salary.

Job 1

x	1	2	3
y	5	10	15

Job 2

x	1	2	3
y	13	16	19

On each graph, a point (x, y) shows (hours worked, salary earned). The point where the lines cross shows where the number of hours worked and the salary earned is the **same for both jobs**. The point of intersection is (5, 25). For 5 hours of work Sheila would earn $25 for each job.

Look Back

Job 1: 5 hours × $5 per hour = $25
Job 2: $10 plus (5 hours × $3 per hour) = $25

 Additional Standards: Algebra and Functions 1.1; Mathematical Reasoning 2.3 (See p. 359.)

Guided Practice

Refer to the graph on the preceding page.

1. How much would you earn at each job if you work 6 hours?

2. Which job should you choose if you can only work 4 hours or less per day?

3. Which job should you choose if you plan to work more than 5 hours per day?

Independent Practice

Fun Park charges an admission of $10 plus $1 for each ride. Joyland, its competitor, charges an admission of $6 plus $2 for each ride.

4. Make a table of values showing the cost for 1, 2, 3, 4, and 5 rides at Fun Park. Then make a similar table for Joyland. Let x be the number of rides and let y be the total cost.

5. On the same set of coordinate axes draw a graph for each table of values in Exercise 4.

6. For how many rides would the cost be the same at either park?

7. If you plan to ride on 5 rides or more, which park offers the better bargain?

Mixed Review

8. A photograph shows a picture of Heather, Zach, Mackenzie, and Shelby sitting on a bench. Heather is not on either end. Zach is between Heather and Mackenzie. Shelby is not on the left in the photo. In what order are the four people seated from left to right in the photo.

9. Last week Becky swam laps on five different days. The number of laps she swam were 16, 18, 14, 20, and 22. What was the mean number of laps she swam each day?

10. Last week Paul earned $900 for working 40 hours. How much did he earn per hour?

11. Lee Ann has $419.93 in her checking account. She wrote checks for $25.79, $35.95, and $78.90. Then she made a deposit of $250. What is the balance in her checking account now?

Use Homework Workbook 9-11.

Diagnostic Checkpoint

Complete. For Questions 1–3 choose words from the word bank.

Word Bank
coordinate plane
linear equation
negative integer
positive integer

1. (9-1) A ____________________ is less than zero.

2. (9-8) An equation whose graph is a straight line is called a ____________________.

3. (9-7) A coordinate grid that includes both positive and negative numbers is called a ____________________.

Evaluate each expression for $x = {}^-7$ and $x = {}^+10$.

4. (9-5) $x - 11$

5. (9-5) $13 - x$

Write the ordered pair for each point or name the point for each ordered pair. Use the grid at the right.

6. (9-7) S

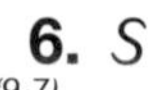

7. (9-7) C

8. (9-7) $({}^+20, {}^-30)$

9. (9-7) $({}^-30, {}^-20)$

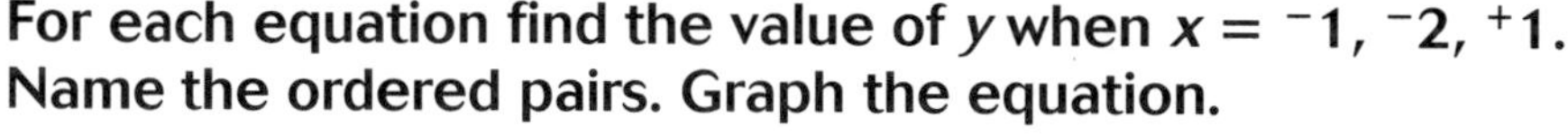

For each equation find the value of y when $x = {}^-1, {}^-2, {}^+1$. Name the ordered pairs. Graph the equation.

10. (9-8) $y = x + 1$

11. (9-8) $x - 8 = y$

12. (9-8) $y = 6 - x$

13. (9-10) Write an equation to describe the relationship between x and y in this table.

x	$^-5$	$^-2$	0	$^+2$	$^+5$
y	$^-15$	$^-12$	$^-10$	$^-8$	$^-5$

14. (9-6) Write an expression showing a loss of 24 yards, a gain of 29 yards, and another loss of 12 yards.

15. (9-9) On the same coordinate axes graph $({}^+2, {}^-13)$, $({}^+8, {}^-7)$, $({}^+10, {}^-5)$, and $({}^-3, {}^-18)$. Draw a line through the points. What is the value of x if $y = {}^-12$?

16. (9-11) Acme Rental charges a flat rate of \$6 plus \$1 per hour. Best Rental charges a flat rate of \$3 plus \$1.50 per hour. For how many hours of rental time would the two companies charge the same amount? Make a table of values showing cost for 2 hours, 4 hours, and 6 hours for each company. Let x be the number of hours and y be the cost. Graph both on the same set of axes.

Chapter 9 Test

Write an integer for each word description.

1. a loss of 25 pounds

2. moving up 8 levels

Write in order from least to greatest.

3. $^{-}101$, $^{-}107$, $^{-}110$, $^{-}111$

4. 0, $^{-}4$, $^{+}3$, $^{-}8$, $^{-}2$

Add or subtract.

5. $^{-}2 + {}^{-}12$

6. $^{+}21 - {}^{-}11$

7. $^{-}20 + {}^{+}10$

8. $^{-}10 - {}^{+}14$

9. $^{+}3 - {}^{-}3$

10. $^{-}16 + {}^{+}4$

Evaluate each expression for $x = {}^{-}6$ and $x = 4$.

11. $6 - x$

12. $x - 2$

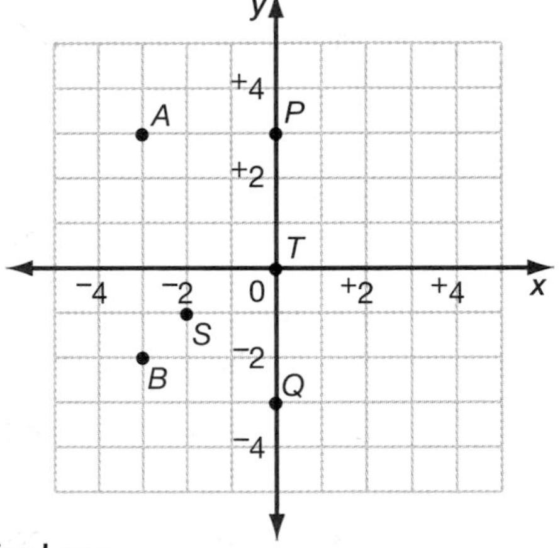

For Questions 13–15, use the grid at the right. Write the ordered pair for each point or name the point for each ordered pair.

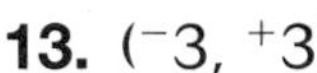

13. ($^{-}3$, $^{+}3$)

14. *B*

15. *Q*

16. Graph the equation $y = 11 + x$. Make a table of values using $x = {}^{-}8, {}^{-}4, {}^{+}1$.

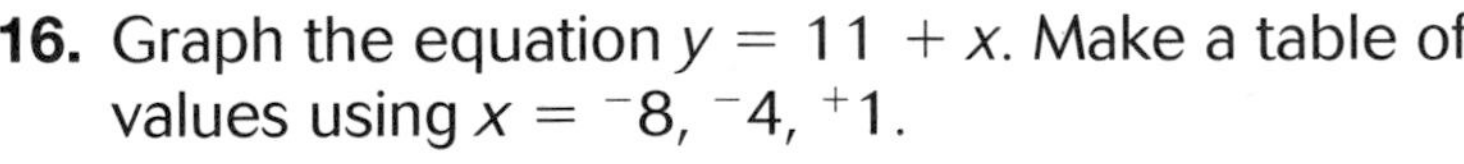

17. Write an expression describing the location of an airplane cruising at an altitude of 28,000 feet and then descending 8,200 feet.

Use the table at the right for Questions 18 and 19.

x	$^{-}3$	$^{-}2$	$^{+}2$
y	$^{-}12$	$^{-}11$	$^{-}7$

18. Write an equation to describe the relationship between *x* and *y*.

19. Graph the points for the values in the table and draw a line through the points. What is the value of *x* when $y = {}^{-}10$?

20. Brad charges a $30 flat fee plus $8 per hour to sew curtains. For the same work, Joann charges a $15 flat fee and $13 per hour. For how many hours would Brad and Joann charge the same? Make a table showing the cost for 1, 2, 3, and 4 hours worth of sewing for each worker. Graph both on the same set of axes.

TEST PREP

Multiple-Choice Chapter 9 Test

Choose the correct letter for each answer.

1. Select the point that best describes $^{-}3 - {}^{-}2$.

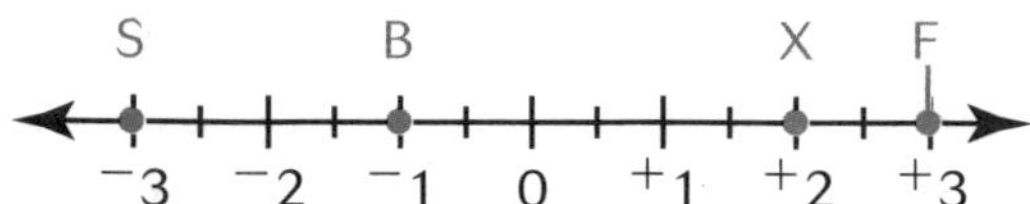

A S **C** X

B B **D** F

2. What is the sum of $^{-}26 + {}^{+}14$?

F $^{+}12$

G $^{-}12$

H $^{-}22$

J $^{-}40$

K NH

3. Which equation describes the relationship between *x* and *y*?

x	0	$^{-}1$	$^{-}2$	$^{-}3$
y	2	$^{+}1$	0	$^{-}1$

A $y = x - 3$

B $y = x + 2$

C $y = x - 8$

D $y = x + 1$

4. The temperature dropped 11 degrees and then rose 14 degrees. What was the total change in temperature?

F $^{+}25$ degrees **J** $^{+}3$ degrees

G $^{+}3$ degrees **K** NH

H $^{-}3$ degrees

5. Which integer describes a decline of 180 feet?

A $^{+}180$

B $^{+}1.8$

C $^{-}18$

D $^{-}180$

6. Which set of integers is in order from least to greatest?

F $^{+}47, {}^{-}22, {}^{+}12, {}^{-}16, {}^{-}2$

G $^{-}9, {}^{-}6, {}^{-}3, {}^{-}2, {}^{+}4$

H $^{-}101, {}^{-}77, {}^{-}93, {}^{+}4, {}^{+}8$

J $^{-}1, {}^{+}2, {}^{-}3, 0, {}^{+}6$

7. Which of the following number sentences is true?

A $^{+}2 - {}^{-}9 = {}^{-}7$

B $^{-}15 + {}^{-}6 = {}^{-}9$

C $^{-}21 - {}^{+}4 = {}^{-}25$

D $^{+}8 + {}^{-}10 = 2$

8. If $x = {}^{-}12$, then $17 - {}^{-}20 + x$ equals

F $^{-}15$

G $^{-}9$

H $^{+}25$

J $^{+}47$

K NH

Use the graph for Questions 9–11.

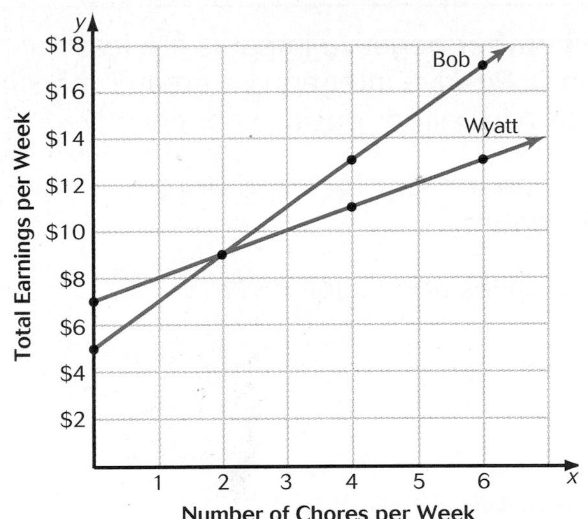

9. **Which describes what the ordered pair (6, 17) means on this graph?**

A For every \$6, Wyatt will have completed 17 chores.

B For 6 chores in one week, Bob will earn \$17.

C Wyatt will earn \$17 for completing 6 chores in one week.

D For every 17 chores, Bob will earn \$6 per week.

---

10. **How much does Wyatt make if he completes 5 chores?**

F \$8

G \$12

H \$14

J \$16

---

11. **For what number of chores will Bob and Wyatt make the same amount of money?**

A 1

B 2

C 4

D 6

---

12. **Which expression shows a loss of \$85 followed a gain of \$110?**

F $^{+}85 + {}^{+}110$

G $^{-}85 + {}^{+}110$

H $^{-}85 + {}^{-}110$

J $^{+}85 - {}^{-}110$

---

13. **Which equation is represented by the graph?**

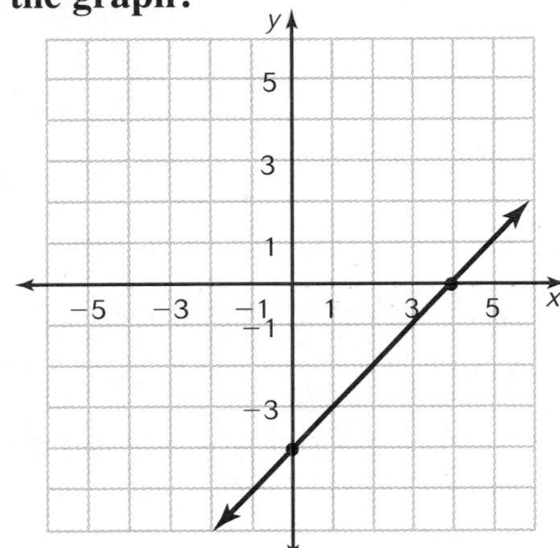

A $y = x - 12$

B $y = x - 4$

C $y = x + 2$

D $y = x + 5$

---

14. **Which ordered pair can be found by moving 6 units left and 8 units down from the origin on a coordinate plane?**

F $(^{-}6, {}^{-}8)$

G $(^{-}8, {}^{-}6)$

H $(^{+}6, {}^{+}8)$

J $(^{-}6, {}^{+}8)$

---

15. **In the equation $y = x - 3$, what is the value of y if $x = {}^{-}4$?**

A $^{-}7$

B $^{-}1$

C $^{+}1$

D $^{+}7$

E NH

Reteaching

Set A (pages 360–361)

Write an integer describing a decrease of $212.

"A decrease" represents a negative integer, so a decrease of $212 is represented by the integer $^{-}212$.

Remember negative integers are less than 0. Positive integers are greater than 0. Zero is neither positive nor negative.

Write an integer for each word description.

1. 7 miles above sea level
2. 24° below zero

Set B (pages 362–363)

Compare. Use >, <, or = for ●.

$^{-}22$ ● $^{-}27$

Use a number line to compare.

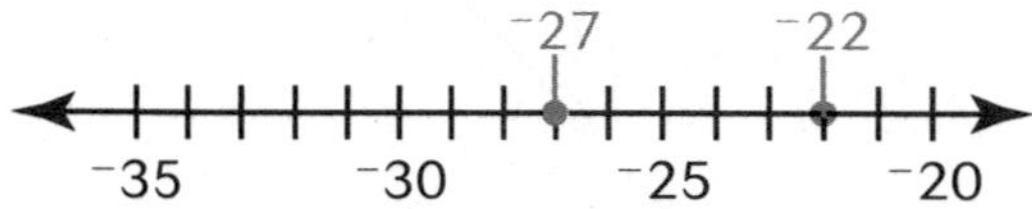

Because $^{-}22$ is farther to the right than $^{-}27$, $^{-}22 > {}^{-}27$.

Remember, to compare integers, you can first locate the integers on a number line.

Compare. Use >, <, or = for each ●.

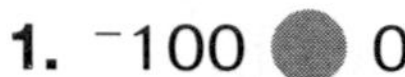

1. $^{-}100$ ● 0
2. $^{+}34$ ● $^{+}14$
3. $^{-}7$ ● $^{-}1$
4. $^{-}4$ ● $^{-}4$
5. 8 ● $^{-}8$
6. 0 ● $^{-}1$

Set C (pages 364–365)

$^{+}4 + {}^{-}3$

Start at zero. Move forward 4 units. Then move backward 3 units.

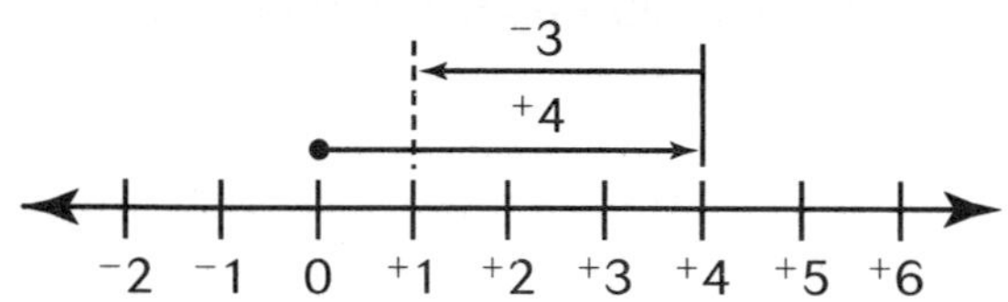

$^{+}4 + {}^{-}3 = {}^{+}1$

Remember, to add integers, think of walking along a number line. Walk forward for positive numbers, backward for negative numbers.

1. $^{+}97 + {}^{-}32$
2. $^{+}2 + {}^{-}64$
3. $^{-}22 + {}^{-}78$
4. $^{-}7 + {}^{+}18$
5. $^{-}56 + {}^{-}6$
6. $^{-}9 + {}^{-}11$

Set D (pages 366–368)

$^{-}21 - {}^{-}8$

$^{-}21 - {}^{-}8 = {}^{-}21 + {}^{+}8$ Add the opposite.

$= {}^{-}13$

Remember, to subtract an integer, add the opposite.

1. $^{-}30 - {}^{-}32$
2. $^{+}64 - {}^{-}6$
3. $^{-}38 - {}^{-}38$
4. $^{+}7 - {}^{-}18$

Set E (pages 370–371)

Evaluate $x - 10$ for $x = {}^{-}7$.

$x - 10 = {}^{-}7 - 10$ Replace x with $^{-}7$.

$= {}^{-}7 + {}^{-}10$ Subtracting an integer is the same as adding its opposite.

$= {}^{-}17$

Remember to replace the variable first. Then do the appropriate calculations.

Evaluate each expression for $x = {}^{+}3$ and $x = {}^{-}6$.

1. $x - {}^{-}1$ **2.** $x - 4$

Set F (pages 374–376)

Write the ordered pair for point *B*.

Start at the origin.

Move 1 unit to the left.

Then move 3 units up.

The ordered pair is $({}^{-}1, {}^{+}3)$.

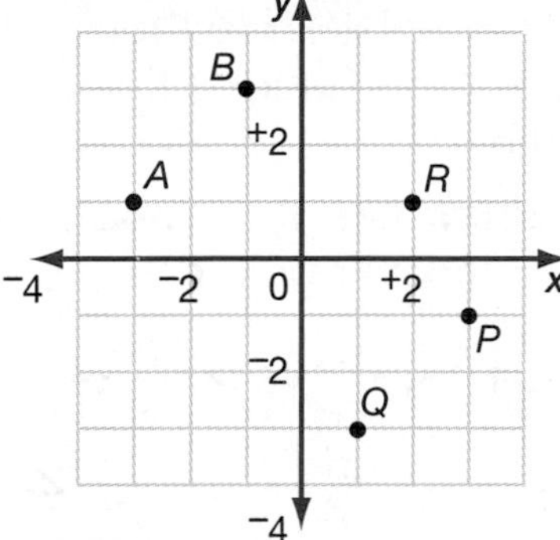

Remember the first number in an ordered pair is the number of units to the left or right of the origin. The second number in an ordered pair is the number of units up or down from the origin.

Write the ordered pair for each point or name the point for each ordered pair.

1. $({}^{+}1, {}^{-}3)$ **2.** *P*

Set G (pages 378–379)

Graph the equation $y = 2 + x$. First make a table using *x*-values of $^{-}3$, 0, 3.

x	y
−3	−1
0	+2
+3	+5

Substitute the values for *x* into the equation. Solve for *y*.

Plot the ordered pairs and connect the points.

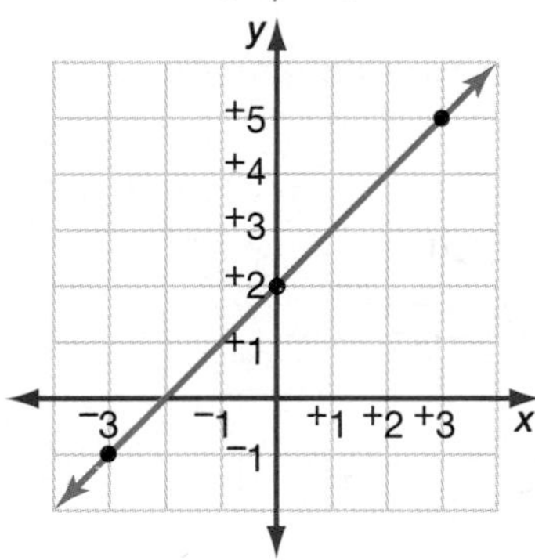

Remember, for an equation with two variables, you can substitute any value for *x* and then find the corresponding value for *y*. Then write the ordered pair (x, y).

Graph each equation. First make a table using *x*-values of 0, $^{-}2$, $^{+}3$.

1. $y = x - 8$ **2.** $y = x + 13$

Set H (pages 382–383)

Write an equation to describe the relationship between *x* and *y*.

x	y
−2	−8
−1	−7
0	−6
+1	−5
+2	−4

Notice that each *y*-value is always 6 less than the corresponding *x* value.

The equation is $y = x - 6$.

Remember to look for a pattern.

Write an equation to describe the relationship between *x* and *y*.

1.

x	y
−2	−3
−1	−2
0	−1
+1	0
+2	+1

2.

x	y
−2	+8
−1	+9
0	+10
+1	+11
+2	+12

More Practice

Set A (pages 360–361)

Write an integer for each word description.

1. 12 floors down **2.** A gain of 7 points **3.** A decrease of 7 inches

Use the number line for Exercises 4–6. What is the coordinate of each point?

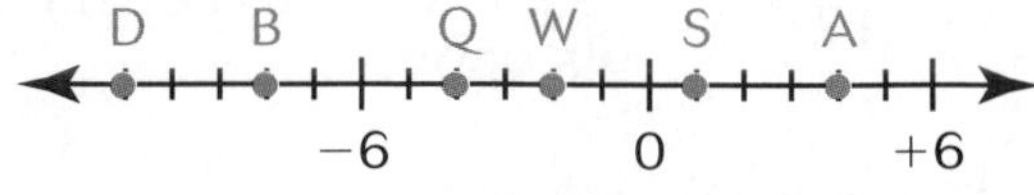

4. *Q* **5.** *W* **6.** *D*

7. Chuck dove 40 meters below the surface of the lake. He then swam up 13 meters. Write an integer to describe Chuck's final location in relation to the surface of the lake.

Set B (pages 362–363)

Compare. Use $>$, $<$, or $=$ for each ●.

1. $^{-}20$ ● $^{-}20$ **2.** $^{+}14$ ● $^{-}1$ **3.** $^{-}28$ ● $^{-}29$ **4.** $^{-}14$ ● $^{-}6$

Order from least to greatest.

5. $^{-}7, ^{-}8, ^{-}13, ^{-}9$ **6.** $0, ^{-}1, ^{+}3, ^{-}7$ **7.** $^{-}6, ^{-}9, ^{-}8, 0$ **8.** $^{+}7, ^{-}3, ^{+}4, ^{-}4$

9. Kate's house is 13 feet below sea level, and Donna's house is 4 feet below sea level. Whose house is at the higher elevation?

Set C (pages 364–365)

Add.

1. $^{+}6 + ^{-}12$ **2.** $^{+}17 + ^{-}34$ **3.** $^{-}55 + ^{-}77$ **4.** $^{-}12 + ^{-}20$

5. At midnight the temperature was $^{-}6$°F. During the next 3 hours it increased 9 degrees. What was the temperature at 3 A.M.?

Set D (pages 366–368)

Subtract.

1. $^{+}15 - ^{-}17$ **2.** $^{-}48 - ^{-}6$ **3.** $^{+}100 - ^{-}100$ **4.** $^{-}13 - ^{-}7$

5. Larson ran for 17 yards on his first down of the football game. On the next down he lost 20 yards. What was Larson's total yardage?

More Practice

Set E (pages 370–371)

Evaluate each expression for $x = {}^{+}4$ and $x = {}^{-}8$.

1. $x - {}^{+}7$
2. $x + {}^{+}16$
3. ${}^{+}13 - x$
4. $15 - x$

5. Evaluate $g - h + j$ for $g = {}^{-}2, h = 0, j = {}^{-}6$.

Set F (pages 374–376)

Write the ordered pair for each point or name the point for each ordered pair.

1. A
2. S
3. Q
4. $({}^{+}4, 0)$
5. $({}^{-}2, {}^{-}5)$
6. C

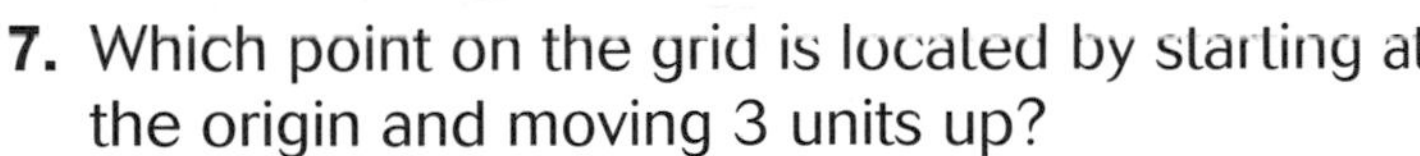
7. Which point on the grid is located by starting at the origin and moving 3 units up?

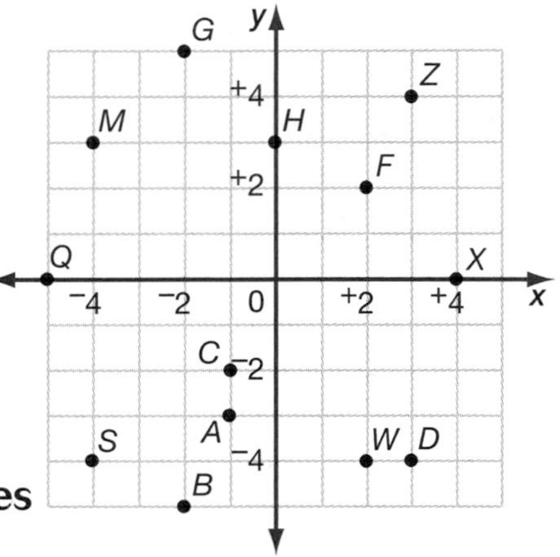

Set G (pages 378–379)

Graph each equation. First make a table using x-values of ${}^{-}2$, 0, ${}^{+}2$.

1. $y = x - 8$
2. $y = x - 5$
3. $y = x + 3$

4. Is the point (0, 0) on the graph of $y = x + 2$? Explain your answer.

Set H (pages 382–383)

Write an equation to describe the relationship between x and y.

1.

x	y
$^{-}2$	$^{-}10$
$^{-}4$	$^{-}12$
$^{-}6$	$^{-}14$
$^{-}8$	$^{-}16$

2.

x	y
$^{-}4$	$^{+}3$
$^{-}2$	$^{+}5$
$^{+}2$	$^{+}9$
$^{+}4$	$^{+}11$

3.

x	y
$^{-}10$	$^{-}30$
$^{-}5$	$^{-}25$
0	$^{-}20$
$^{+}5$	$^{-}15$

4.

x	y
$^{-}3$	$^{+}8$
$^{-}1$	$^{+}10$
$^{+}2$	$^{+}13$
$^{+}4$	$^{+}15$

Problem Solving: Preparing for Tests

Choose the correct letter for each answer.

---

1. If each bus can carry 44 passengers, how many buses are needed to take 188 people to a festival?

A 7

B 6

C 5

D 4

E NH

Tip

Interpret the remainder to solve this problem.

---

2. At a dog kennel, a small cage holds 2 dogs and a large cage holds 5 dogs. If 28 dogs are at the kennel, which combination of cages can they fill so that there are no empty cages and no dogs left over?

F 6 small cages, 3 large cages

G 4 small cages, 4 large cages

H 2 small cages, 8 large cages

J 5 small cages, 2 large cages

Tip

Try the answer choices to see if any fit the situation.

---

3. The masses of 5 fossils range from 1.03 grams to 18.24 grams. Which is reasonable for the total mass of all 5 fossils?

A Between 22 grams and 74 grams

B About 20 grams

C More than 91 grams

D Between 75 grams and 103 grams

Tip

Use *Logical Reasoning* to help eliminate answer choices.

---

4. Jake arranges his model cars on 6 shelves. Each shelf can hold as many as 9 cars, and Jake always puts at least 5 cars on a shelf. Which is a reasonable description of his total number of cars?

F Fewer than 9

G Between 5 and 14

H Between 30 and 54

J More than 54

Tip

Think of the *least* and the *most* to solve this problem.

5. Tricia's grades on 3 tests are 81, 93, and 89. In which number sentence does n represent the grade she needs on the next test to have an average of 90?

A $90 - (81 + 93 + 89) = n$

B $90 = n - 81 + 93 + 89$

C $\frac{90}{4} = n - 81 + 93 + 89$

D $\frac{81 + 93 + 89 + n}{4} = 90$

E NH

---

6. Pete buys 40 kilograms of birdseed. He uses 2.2 kilograms a week. Which is the best estimate of how much seed will be left after 8 weeks?

F About 5 kilograms

G About 10 kilograms

H About 15 kilograms

J About 25 kilograms

K NH

---

7. Last year the population of Berry Middle School increased by 128 students. The year before the population decreased by 38 students. How much did the population change over the 2 years?

A It decreased by 90 students.

B It increased by 90 students.

C It increased by 166 students.

D It decreased by 166 students.

E NH

---

8. The table shows snack bar sales in a 2-week period.

Snack Bar Sales May 1–14

Item	Price Each	Number Sold	Total
Chili	$1.50	162	$243.00
Hot dog	$1.25	490	$612.50
Hot pretzel	$0.75	630	$472.50
Ice pop	$1.00	536	$536.00
Juice	$1.50	1,079	$1,618.50

Estimate the total amount of the snack bar's sales for the 14 days.

F About $2,200.00

G About $2,900.00

H About $3,400.00

J About $4,900.00

---

9. Carson predicts her company will make a little more than a quarter of a million dollars this year. Which of these best describes the amount of money her company may make?

A Less than $150,000

B About $150,000

C Less than $25,000

D More than $250,000

---

10. Shane is older than Paula but younger than Maury. Angie is younger than Paula. Which of these is a reasonable conclusion?

F Shane is younger than Angie.

G Maury is the oldest.

H Angie is older than Paula.

J Paula is older than Maury.

TEST PREP

Multiple-Choice Cumulative Review

Choose the correct letter for each answer.

Number Sense

1. What is the rule of the following table?

Input	Output
15	5
24	8
30	■

A Multiply by 2.
B Divide by 3.
C Subtract 10.
D Add 15.

2. On an 18-day vacation, Eric and his family traveled a total of 3,955 miles. Which is the best estimate for the average distance they traveled each day?

F Less than 150 miles
G More than 200 miles
H About 300 miles
J More than 400 miles

3. What is 134.967 rounded to the nearest hundredth?

A 100
B 134
C 134.97
D 135.0

4. What is the greatest common factor of 6, 70, and 78?

F 2
G 3
H 6
J 12

Use the price list below to answer Questions 5 and 6.

Pizza Special		
Size	Number of Slices	Price
Large	10	\$8.99
Medium	8	\$6.99
Small	6	\$5.99
Personal	4	\$2.99

5. Jim has invited 15 friends for a pizza party. If each person will eat 3 slices, how many large pizzas should he buy?

A 3
B 4
C 5
D 6

6. Which pizza costs the *least* per slice?

F Large
G Medium
H Small
J Personal

7. Which of the following statements is true?

A $0.86 < 0.853$
B $0.70 < 0.68$
C $1.45 > 1.447$
D $0.09 > 0.1$

Algebra and Functions

8. The air temperature at 8:00 A.M. was $^{-}2$°F. By noon the temperature was 17°F. Which change took place in these 4 hours?

F Increase of 17°F

G Increase of 15°F

H Decrease of 15°F

J Increase of 19°F

---

9. Between which two numbers might you plot $^{-}7$ on a number line?

A 0 and $^{+}8$

B $^{-}6$ and $^{+}5$

C $^{-}6$ and $^{-}8$

D $^{-}8$ and $^{-}9$

---

10. If $x \div 9 = 800$, then $x =$

F 8,100

G 7,200

H 720

J 72

---

11. Laura spent 12.5 more minutes on the Internet than Micael. Let *m* equal the amount of time Micael spent on the Internet. What expression shows how much time Laura spent?

A $m - 12.5$

B $12.5m$

C $12.5 + m$

D $12.5 \div m$

Measurement and Geometry

12. Carol's bedroom rug covers 48 square feet of the floor. The rug is 72 inches wide. How many *feet* long is the rug?

F 2 feet

G 4 feet

H 6 feet

J 8 feet

---

13. The sides of triangle *EFG* are equal. What is the perimeter of the triangle?

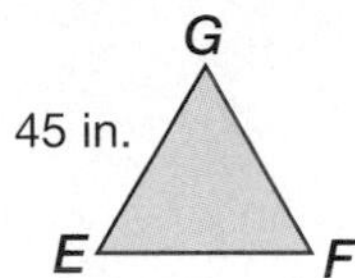

A 135 inches

B 90 inches

C 45 inches

D 20 inches

---

14. A jar holds 5.50 L of water. How many milliliters is this? (1 L = 1,000 mL)

F 0.0055 milliliters

G 0.0550 milliliters

H 550 milliliters

J 5,500 milliliters

---

15. A room is 20 feet long by 10 feet wide. What is the perimeter of the room?

A 30 ft

B 60 ft

C 120 ft

D 200 ft

Geometry

Diagnosing Readiness

In Chapter 10, you will use these skills:

A Adding or Subtracting Whole Numbers

(p. 60–62)

1. 360 − 150 −75 − 25

2. 180 − 66 + 12

3. 22 + 57 + 2

4. 75 + 25 + 126

5. Out of 360 students attending a pep rally, 35 of the students are on the soccer team, 118 are in the band, and 16 are cheerleaders. The remaining students are on the pep team. How many students are on the pep team?

B Drawing Segments

(Grade 4)

Use a ruler to draw segments with the following lengths.

6. 12 centimeters

7. $1\frac{1}{4}$ inches

8. 2.5 centimeters

9. $\frac{1}{2}$ inch

10. 8.2 centimeters

11. 2 inches

C Patterns

(Grade 4)

Find the next two elements in the pattern.

12. 13, 20, 27, 34, . . .

13. ****, III, ***, II, . . .

14. OOO, XX, OOO, X, OOO, XX, . . .

15. 220, 205, 190, 175, . . .

16. Every two weeks Mandy repeats an exercise routine. On the first day she jogs for $\frac{1}{2}$ mile. Every day after that she adds $\frac{3}{4}$ mile to her run from the previous day. How many miles does she run on day ten?

D Solving Equations

(p. 46–47)

Solve for *x*.

17. $x = 180 - 57$

18. $35 + 57 + x = 180$

19. $360 = 98 + x + 16 + 156$

20. $x - (90 + 47) = 43$

21. On a jump-a-thon, Garrett wants to jump 180 times to raise money for charity. In the first two minutes, Garrett jumped 106 times. Write and solve an equation to show how many more times Garrett needs to jump to reach his goal.

E Multiplying Whole Numbers

(p. 146–147, 196–197)

22. 2×185

23. 400×16

24. 72×3

25. 4×96

Solve for *x*.

26. $3x = 216$

27. $\frac{x}{3} = 75$

F Comparing Shapes

(Grade 4)

Are the figures the same shape and same size?

28.

29.

To the Family and Student

Looking Back

In Grade 4, students learned how to model with geometric figures.

Chapter 10

Geometry

In this chapter, students will construct and classify geometric figures.

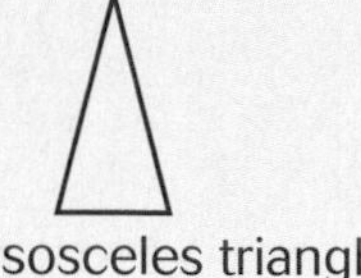

acute, isosceles triangle

Looking Ahead

In Chapter 11, students will learn how to measure and calculate the perimeter and area of geometric figures.

Math and Everyday Living

Opportunities to apply the concepts of Chapter 10 abound in everyday situations. During the chapter, think about how geometry can be used to solve a variety of real-world problems. The following examples suggest just several of the many situations that could launch a discussion about geometry.

Math in Nature On a hike through the woods, you and your family discover some items in nature that are symmetrical. How many lines of symmetry does a ladybug have? How many does a butterfly have?

Math on the Clock On Mondays you typically finish your homework by 5:00 P.M. and go to bed by 9:00 P.M. Classify the angle made by the hands of the clock at 5:00 and at 9:00.

Math and Interior Design Your family wants to tile the floor of the bathroom. The bathroom floor measures 12 feet by 10 feet. Each floor tile measures 1 foot by 1 foot. Approximately how many tiles are needed to cover the floor of the bathroom?

Math on the Road To find directions to your new family dentist, you and your family review a map of the downtown area. The office building is located on 1st Avenue.

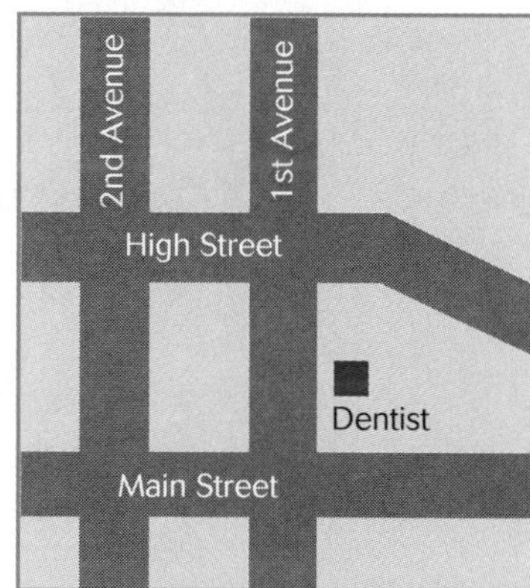

Is 1st Avenue parallel or perpendicular to High Street? What street runs parallel to High Street?

Math and Games You and your family are playing your favorite board game. After answering two questions correctly you get to move your game token four spaces to the right. What type of transformation best describes your move?

Math and Construction Plans are being made to build two new kitchen cabinets with 24-inch by 22-inch rectangular doors. What should be the measure of each door's corner angle?

Math and Leisure Your family decides to purchase an above ground swimming pool. Describe the shape of the swimming pool if the top view is a circle.

 California Content Standards in Chapter 10 Lessons*

	Teach and Practice	Practice
Measurement and Geometry		
2.0 Students identify, describe, and classify the properties of, and the relationships between, plane and solid geometric figures	10-3, 10-5, 10-9, 10-12	
2.1 (🔑) Measure, identify, and draw angles, perpendicular and parallel lines, rectangles, and triangles by using appropriate tools (e.g., straightedge, ruler, compass, protractor, drawing software).	10-1, 10-2, 10-6, 10-7, 10-10	
2.2 (🔑) Know that the sum of the angles of any triangle is 180° and the sum of the angles of any quadrilateral is 360° and use this information to solve problems.	10-3, 10-5	10-6, 10-7
2.3 Visualize and draw two-dimensional views of three-dimensional objects made from rectangular solids.	10-12	
3.4 (Grade 4) Identify figures that have bilateral . . . symmetry.	10-11	
Algebra and Functions		
1.2 (🔑) Use a letter to represent an unknown number; write and evaluate simple algebraic expressions in one variable by substitution.		10-3, 10-6

	Teach and Practice	Practice
Mathematical Reasoning		
1.1 Analyze problems by identifying relationships, distinguishing relevant from irrelevant information, sequencing and prioritizing information, and observing patterns.	10-4, 10-8, 10-11	10-1, 10-3, 10-5, 10-6, 10-7, 10-9
2.0 Students use strategies, skills, and concepts in finding solutions.		10-1, 10-2, 10-4, 10-6, 10-11
2.3 Use a variety of methods, such as words, numbers, symbols, charts, graphs, tables, diagrams, and models to explain mathematical reasoning.		10-10, 10-12
3.2 Note the method of deriving the solution and demonstrate a conceptual understanding of the derivation by solving similar problems.		10-8

* Chapter 10 focuses on the California Content Standards above. The main standard for the lesson is given at the beginning of the lesson. Related standards are given at the bottom of that page. The symbol (🔑) indicates a key standard as designated in the Mathematics Framework for California Public Schools. Full statements of the California Content Standards are found at the beginning of this book following the Table of Contents.

Geometric Ideas

California Content Standard *Measurement and Geometry 2.1 (key): . . . [I]dentify and draw . . . perpendicular and parallel lines.*

Math Link You have used number lines to order numbers and line plots to display data. Now you will study lines and other geometric ideas to see how they are related.

The following chart summarizes some geometric terms and the symbols used to represent them.

Warm-Up Review

Tell which lettered point represents the given number on the number line.

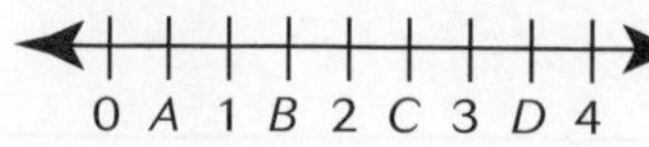

1. 2.5 **2.** 0.5

3. 3.5 **4.** 1.5

5. Paul bought 120 patio blocks at $1.50 each and 32 edging blocks at $1.25 each. Find the total cost of all the blocks.

The Language of Geometry

Term and Description	Example	Symbol and How to Read It
point—an exact location in space	•B	•B point B
line—an endless collection of points along a straight path	A, B	$\overleftrightarrow{AB}$ line AB
line segment—part of a line that has two endpoints	X, Y	$\overline{XY}$ line segment XY
ray—part of a line that has one endpoint and extends endlessly in the other direction	S, T	$\overrightarrow{ST}$ ray ST
plane—an endless, flat surface that is named by any three points not on the same line	L, M, N	▱ LMN plane LMN

 Additional Standards: Mathematical Reasoning 1.1, 2.0 *(See p. 401.)*

The language of geometry helps to define different ways that lines or segments can relate to each other. In the map below, pairs of streets are highlighted to show pairs of lines related in three different ways.

Word Bank

point
line
line segment
ray
plane
intersecting lines
parallel lines
perpendicular lines

Example 1

The two streets highlighted in red represent **intersecting lines.**

Intersecting lines meet at one point. That point is called the *point of intersection.*

Example 2

The two streets highlighted in green represent **parallel lines.**

Parallel lines do not intersect but are in the same plane.

Example 3

The two streets highlighted in blue represent **perpendicular lines.**

Perpendicular lines intersect to form square corners.

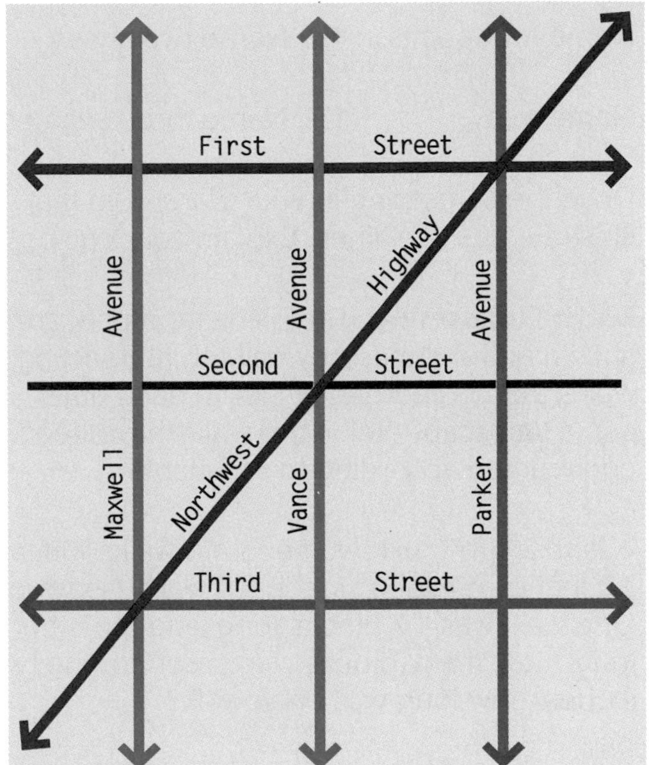

More Examples

Pairs of line segments can also be parallel or perpendicular.

A. $\overline{CD} \parallel \overline{AB}$

The symbol $\parallel$ means "is parallel to."

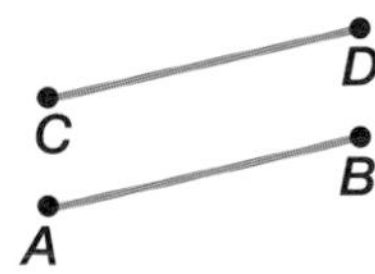

B. $\overline{RS} \perp \overline{TU}$

The symbol $\perp$ means "is perpendicular to."

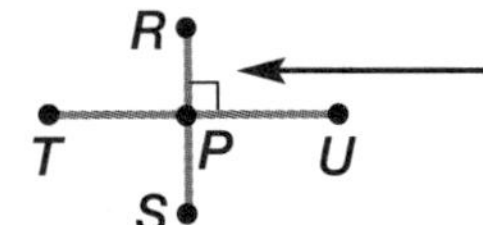

This symbol tells you that this is a square corner, which is also called a right angle. $\overline{RS}$ is perpendicular to $\overline{TU}$.

Guided Practice

For another example, see Set A on p. 442.

Draw and label an example of each.

1. plane *QRS*
2. line segment *TH*
3. ray *JK*
4. $\overleftrightarrow{AB}$ is perpendicular to $\overleftrightarrow{RS}$.
5. $\overleftrightarrow{CD}$ is parallel to $\overleftrightarrow{UV}$.
6. $\overleftrightarrow{EF}$ intersects $\overleftrightarrow{XY}$.
7. Are intersecting lines always perpendicular? Explain.

Independent Practice *For more practice, see Set A on p. 445.*

Draw and label an example of each.

8. Ray *GI* **9.** Plane *ABC* **10.** Two parallel lines

11. Two perpendicular lines **12.** A line with points *M* and *Z* on the line

13. A line segment with endpoints *Q* and *B*

Use the drawing at the right for Exercises 14–17.

A B C D

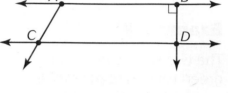

14. Name four points. **15.** Name two lines.

16. Name a ray. **17.** Name three segments.

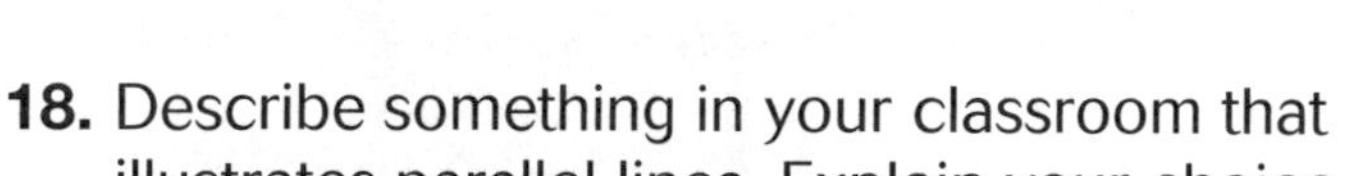

18. Describe something in your classroom that illustrates parallel lines. Explain your choice.

19. Math Reasoning The plans for a park are shown at the right. They call for intersecting walks that are perpendicular to each other. How can a landscaper tell if the walks have been constructed according to the plans?

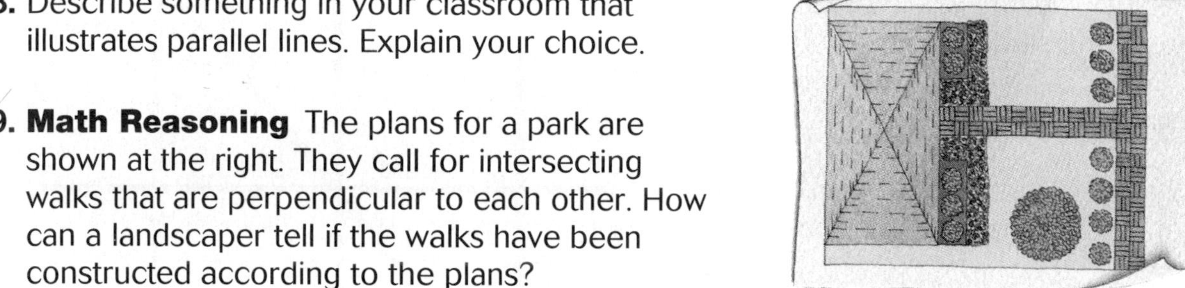

20. A landscaper built two separate walks with square blocks 12 inches on each side. Each walk used two rows of blocks. One walk was 17 blocks long, and the other was 12 blocks long. How many blocks were used for the two walks? In inches, how long was each walk?

Mixed Review

21. Lisa bought $4\frac{1}{2}$ yards of fabric at \$4 a yard. What was the total cost?

22. Algebra Evaluate $x - 9$ for $x = {}^{-}5$.

23. Algebra Graph the equation $y = x - 5$.

Test Prep **Choose the correct letter for each answer.**

24. Algebra Solve $\frac{x}{6} = 12$ for x.
(5-12)

A $x = 2$ **C** $x = 18$

B $x = 6$ **D** $x = 72$

25. Algebra Solve $8n = 40$ for n.
(5-12)

F $n = 32$ **H** $n = 5$

G $n = 48$ **J** $n = 320$

Measuring and Classifying Angles

Warm-Up Review

Draw and label an example of

1. Point *A*
2. Line *BC*
3. Segment *DE*
4. Ray *FG*
5. Describe the difference between a segment and a ray.

California Content Standard *Measurement and Geometry 2.1 (🔑): Measure, identify, and draw angles (and) perpendicular . . . lines . . . by using appropriate tools (e.g., straightedge, . . . protractor . . .).*

Math Link You are familiar with some of the basic geometric ideas. Now you will learn how some of them form geometric figures.

Word Bank

- angle
- vertex (*pl.*, vertices)
- side
- right angle
- straight angle
- acute angle
- obtuse angle

An **angle** is formed when two rays have the same endpoint, called a **vertex.** The two rays that form the *angle* are its **sides.** The symbol for *angle* is ∠. The drawing shows angle *ABC*. It can also be named angle *CBA* or angle *B*.

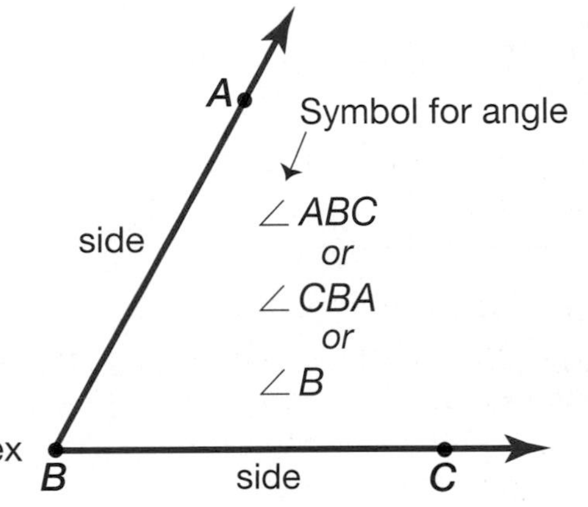

You can use a protractor to find the size, or measure, of an angle. An angle is measured in degrees (°). You can also use a protractor to draw an angle of a certain size.

Example 1

Use a protractor to measure ∠*PQR*.

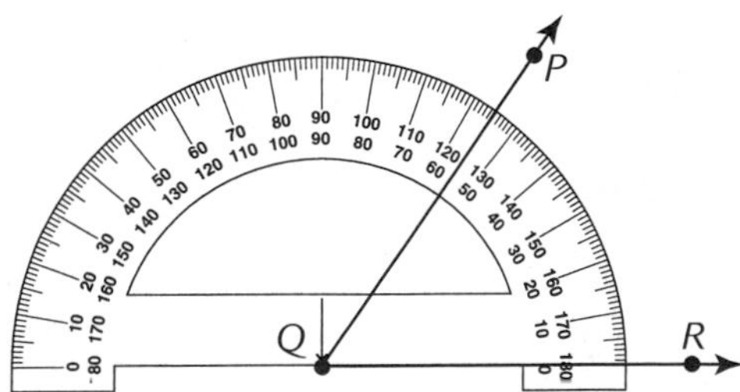

Place the protractor's arrow on the vertex, point *Q*. Place the 0° mark on ray *QR*. Notice that there are two scales on the protractor. Since the zero mark that you placed on ray *QR* is on the inside scale, follow that scale up to ray *QP*. Ray *QP* intersects the protractor at 55°.

∠*PQR* has a measure of 55°.

Example 2

Use a protractor to draw an angle of 140°.

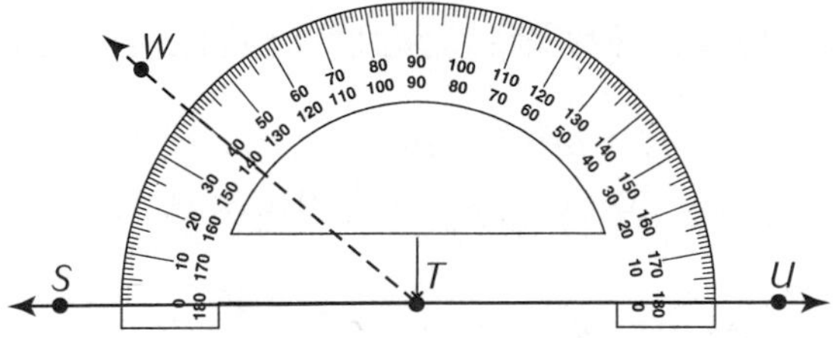

Draw $\overleftrightarrow{SU}$. Place a point on the line. Label it *T*. Place the protractor's arrow on *T* and the 0° marks on $\overleftrightarrow{SU}$. Place a point at 140° on either scale. Use a straightedge to draw $\overrightarrow{TW}$.

∠*WTU* has a measure of 140°.

Additional Standard: Mathematical Reasoning 2.0 (See p. 401.)

Angles can be classified by their measures. An **acute angle** measures less than 90°. A **right angle** measures exactly 90°. An **obtuse angle** measures greater than 90° and less than 180°. A **straight angle** measures 180°.

Example 3

Classify each angle as acute, right, obtuse, or straight.

a. ∠*LMN* is a right angle. Its measure is 90°.

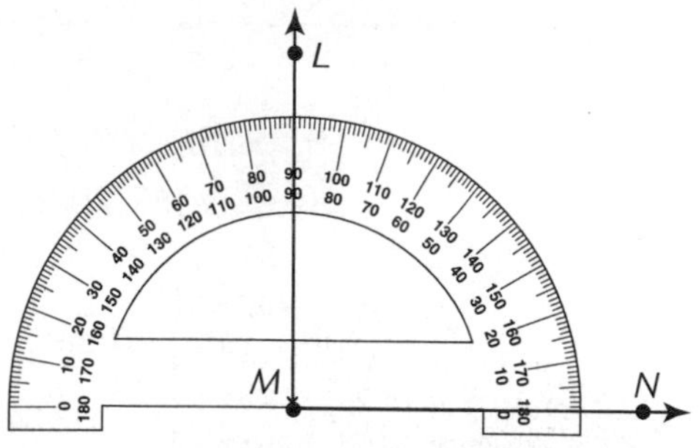

b. ∠*PQR* is an acute angle. Its measure is less than 90°.

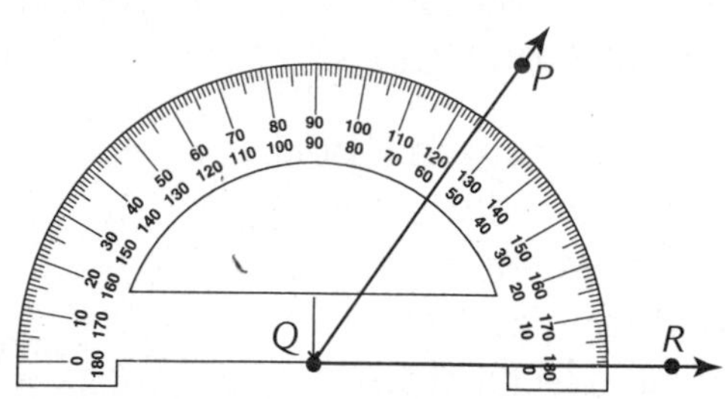

c. ∠*STU* is a straight angle. Its measure is 180°.

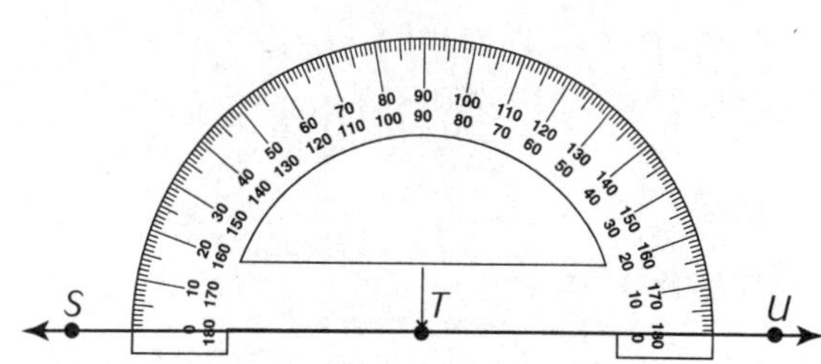

d. ∠*DEF* is an obtuse angle. Its measure is greater than 90° and less than 180°.

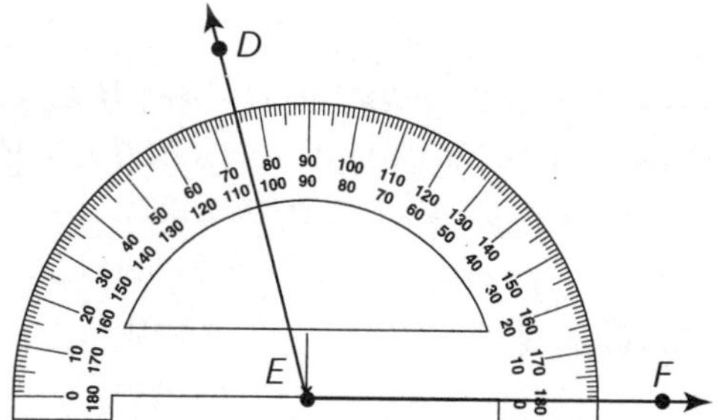

Guided Practice *For another example, see Set B on p. 442.*

Classify each angle as acute, right, or obtuse. Then use a protractor to check each measure.

1.

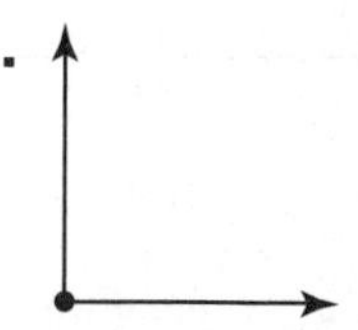

2.

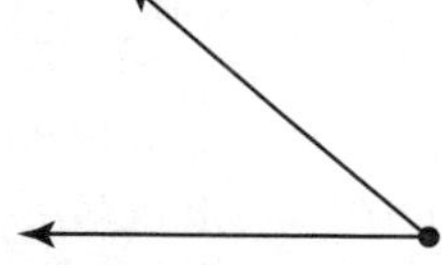

3.

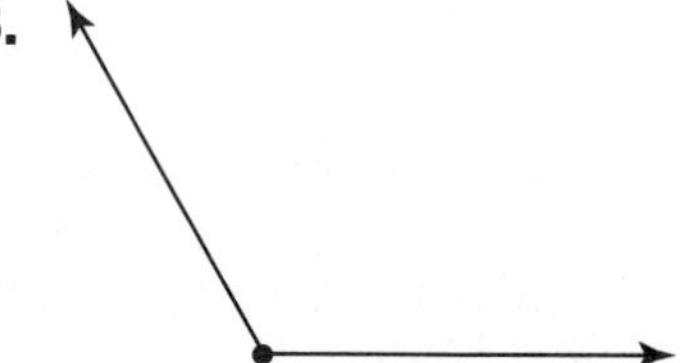

Use a protractor to draw an angle with each measure.

4. 150° **5.** 35° **6.** 180° **7.** 90° **8.** 45°

9. How is a 45° angle related to a 90° angle? How do you know?

Independent Practice *For more practice, see Set B on p. 445.*

Classify each angle as acute, right, obtuse, or straight. Then measure each angle.

10. 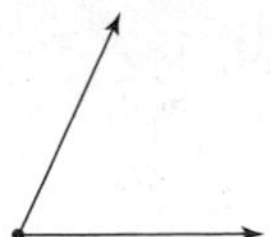

11. 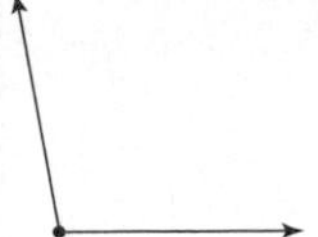

12. 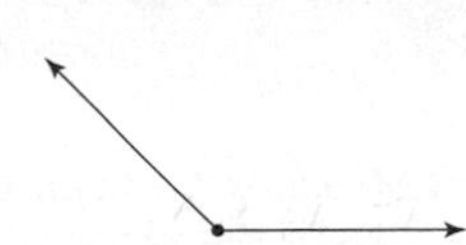

13. 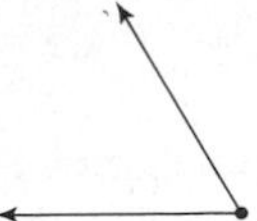

Use a protractor to draw an angle with each measure.

14. 50°

15. 75°

16. 120°

17. 160°

18. The cells in a honeycomb each form a hexagon, as shown. Classify the angles as acute, obtuse, or right. Explain.

19. Describe something in your classroom that illustrates each type of angle defined in this lesson. Explain your choice.

20. Math Reasoning A draftsperson used angles of 45° and 35° in his plans for a new building. If the two angles have the same vertex and one side in common, will the combined angle be acute, right, or obtuse? How do you know?

Mixed Review

21. Math Reasoning Without using a protractor, draw an angle with measure close to 30° and an angle with measure close to 135°. Explain how you made your drawings.

22. Algebra Graph the equation $y = x - 2$.

23. Draw a pair of perpendicular lines.

24. Draw a pair of parallel lines.

 **Test Prep** Choose the correct letter for each answer.

25. Algebra Solve $x - 12 = 24$ for x.
(2-4)

A $x = 12$ **C** $x = 36$

B $x = 0$ **D** $x = 2$

26. Algebra Solve $17 + y = 23$ for y.
(2-4)

F $y = 6$ **H** $y = 30$

G $y = 40$ **J** $y = 16$

LESSON 10-3

Quadrilaterals and Other Polygons

California Content Standard *Measurement and Geometry 2.0: Students identify, describe, and classify the properties of . . . plane . . . geometric figures. Also Measurement and Geometry 2.2 (🔑) (See p. 401.)*

Warm-Up Review

For Exercises 1–4, classify each angle as acute, right, obtuse, or straight.

1. 48° **2.** 90°

3. **4.**

5. $2 \times 60 + 2 \times 80$

6. In a plane, $\overleftrightarrow{AB} \perp \overleftrightarrow{BC}$ and $\overleftrightarrow{BC} \perp \overleftrightarrow{DC}$. Is $\overleftrightarrow{AB} \perp \overleftrightarrow{DC}$? Explain.

Math Link Now that you know about line segments and different types of angles, you will learn about geometric figures formed by them.

A **polygon** is a closed figure made up of three or more line segments. A **regular polygon** is one in which all sides have the same length and all angles have the same measure.

Word Bank

polygon
regular polygon

The table below shows five common polygons.

Triangle	Quadrilateral	Pentagon	Hexagon	Octagon
3 sides 3 angles	4 sides 4 angles	5 sides 5 angles	6 sides 6 angles	8 sides 8 angles

Example 1

Name each polygon. Tell if it is a regular polygon.

a.

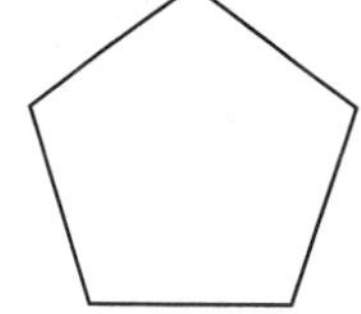

Regular pentagon

The polygon has 5 sides that are the same length and 5 angles that have the same measure.

b.

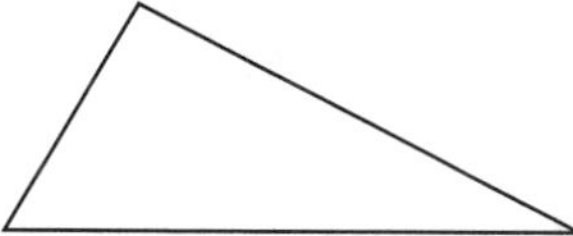

Triangle

The polygon has 3 sides that are not the same length and 3 angles that do not have the same measure.

c.

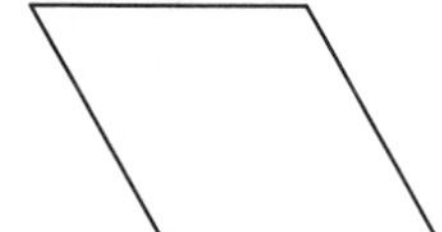

Quadrilateral

The polygon has 4 sides that are the same length, but its 4 angles do not have the same measure.

Additional Standards: Algebra and Functions 1.2 (🔑), Mathematical Reasoning 1.1 (See p. 401.)

Some of the most familiar polygons are quadrilaterals. Quadrilaterals have special names that identify them by their angles or their pairs of sides.

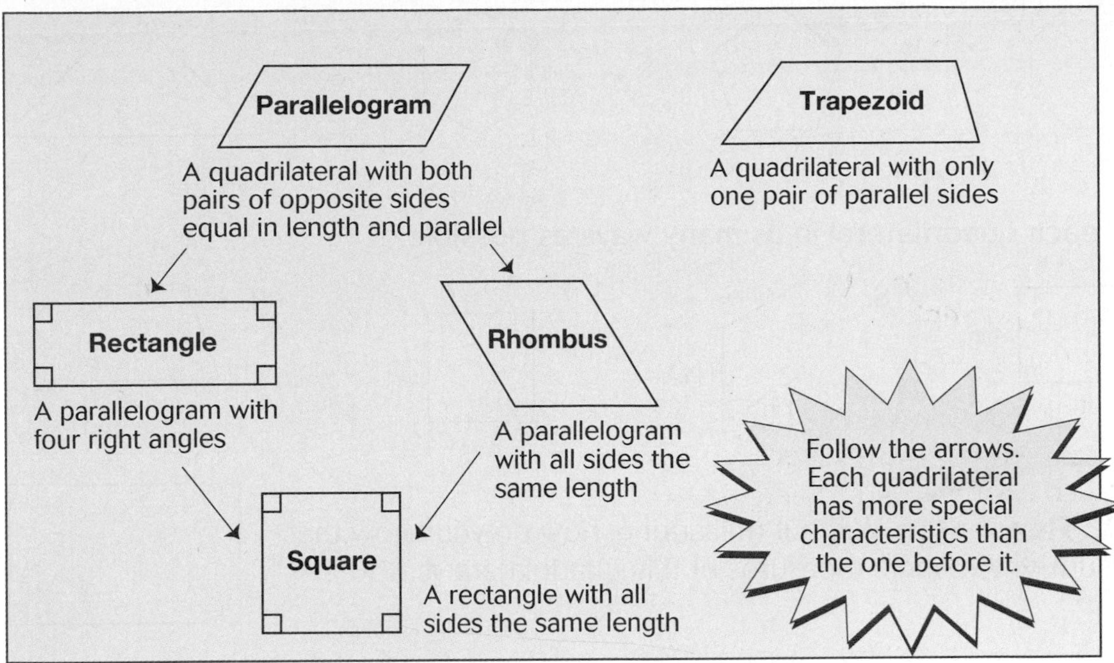

Example 2

Classify each quadrilateral in as many ways as possible.

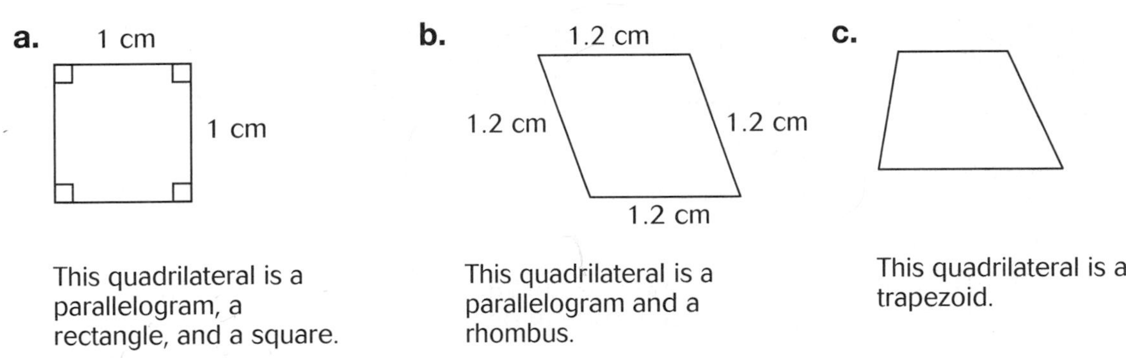

a. This quadrilateral is a parallelogram, a rectangle, and a square.

b. This quadrilateral is a parallelogram and a rhombus.

c. This quadrilateral is a trapezoid.

Example 3

For each quadrilateral, find the sum of the measures of the angles. Compare your answers. What might you conclude?

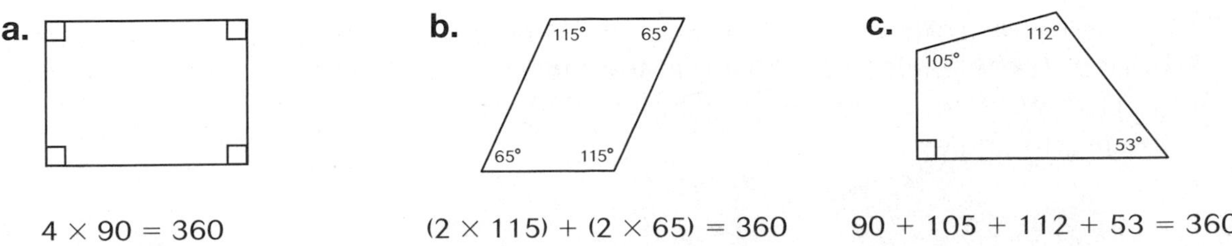

a. $4 \times 90 = 360$

b. $(2 \times 115) + (2 \times 65) = 360$

c. $90 + 105 + 112 + 53 = 360$

The sum of the angle measures of a quadrilateral is 360°.

Guided Practice *For another example, see Set C on p. 442.*

Name each polygon. Tell if it is regular.

1. 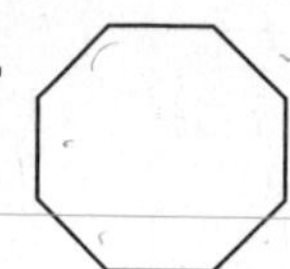

2. 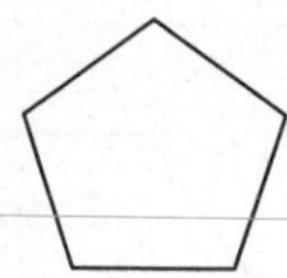

3. 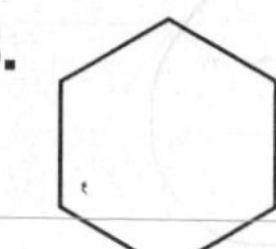

4. 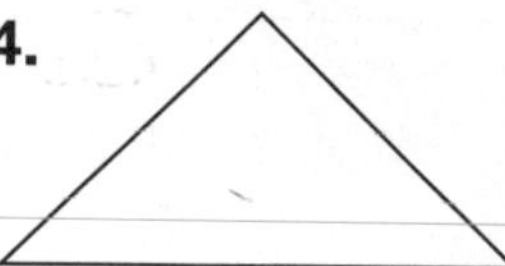

Classify each quadrilateral in as many ways as possible.

5. 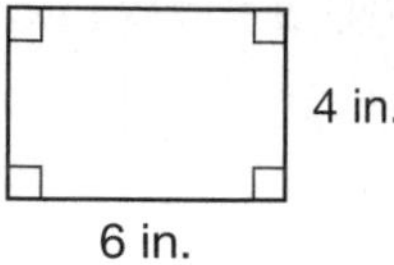

6. 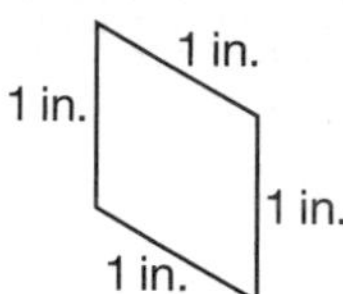

7. 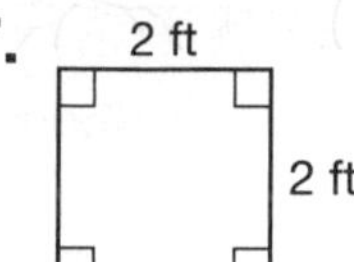

8. 

9. Math Reasoning Without measuring, how do you know that the sum of the angle measures of this quadrilateral is 360°?

Independent Practice *For more practice, see Set C on p. 445.*

Name the polygon each sign represents.
Tell if the polygon is regular.

10. 

11. 

12. 

13. 

Classify each quadrilateral in as many ways as possible.

14. 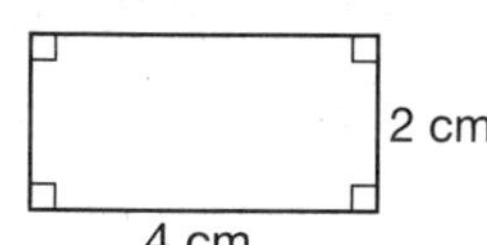

15. 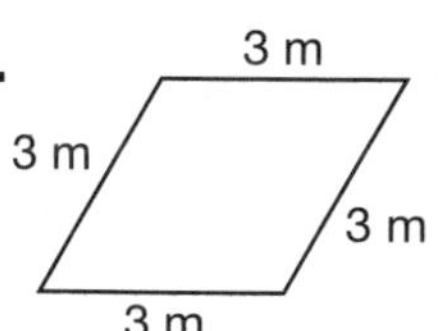

16. 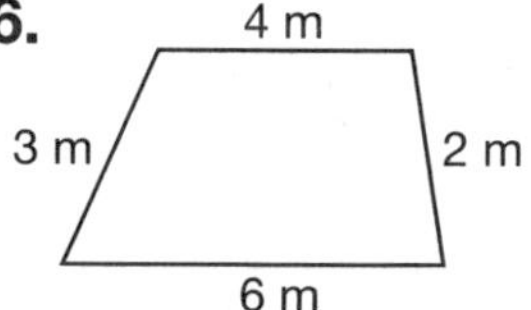

17. 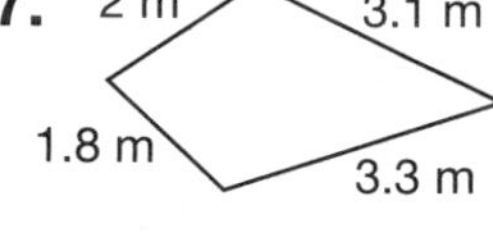

18. Algebra Three angles of a quadrilateral measure 45°, 55°, and 135°. Write and solve an equation to find the measure of the fourth angle.

19. Mental Math Three angles of a parallelogram measure 50°, 50°, and 130°. What is the measure of the fourth angle?

20. Use the photo of Hong Kong at the right. Classify each outlined figure. Be as specific as possible.

Mixed Review

21. Suppose you are asked to tile a floor. Trace the set of tiles at the right and use them to design a pattern for the tiles.

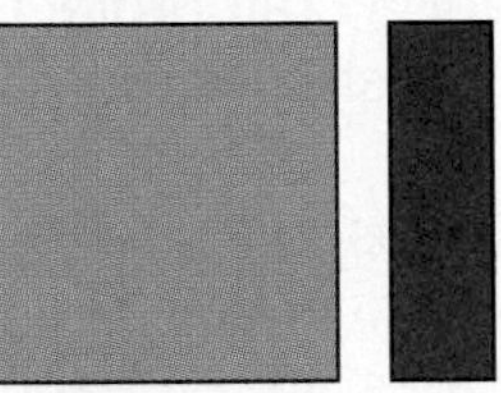

Use the drawing at the right for Exercises 22–25. Give an example of each.

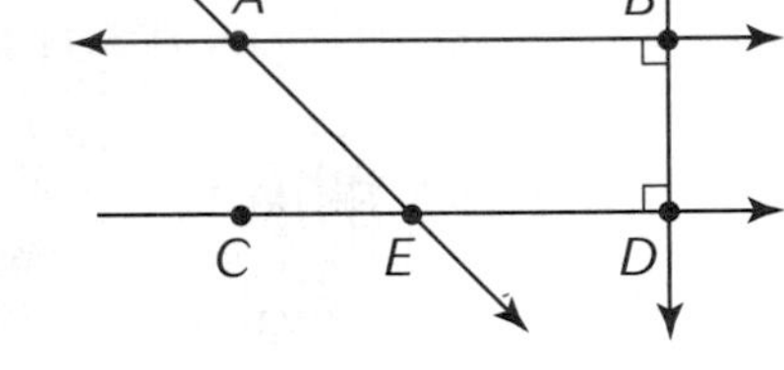

22. Parallel lines

23. Perpendicular lines

24. Acute angle

25. Obtuse angle

26. Write 2^6 in expanded form and in standard form.

27. $\begin{array}{r} 2.83 \\ \times \quad 5 \\ \hline \end{array}$

28. $\begin{array}{r} 27.96 \\ \times \quad 1.7 \\ \hline \end{array}$

29. $4.5 \div 0.3$

Test Prep **Choose the correct letter for each answer.**

30. (8-12) Jody had $3\frac{1}{2}$ pounds of popcorn and wanted to give her mother half. How many pounds of popcorn did her mother get?

A 4 lb

B $1\frac{3}{4}$ lb

C $1\frac{1}{4}$ lb

D 7 lb

31. (8-8) Frank bought 3 pounds of nails and used $1\frac{3}{4}$ pounds of them to build his garage. How many pounds of nails did he have left?

F $1\frac{1}{4}$ lb

G $4\frac{3}{4}$ lb

H $2\frac{3}{4}$ lb

J $1\frac{3}{4}$ lb

Problem-Solving Skill:
Spatial Reasoning

California Content Standard *Mathematical Reasoning 1.1: Analyze problems by identifying relationships . . . and observing patterns.*

Warm-Up Review

Draw the next three figures in each pattern.

1.

2.

3. How are squares and rectangles alike? How are they different?

Read for Understanding

Four tiles like the one shown here are being used to cover a square tabletop for a craft project. Each of the tiles is decorated with 4 small squares.

1. How many tiles will be used?
2. How many small squares are on each tile?
3. In each tile, how many small squares are beige?

Think and Discuss

MATH FOCUS

Spatial Reasoning

Sometimes you can imagine changing the position or shape of objects. This process is called spatial reasoning.

Reread the paragraph and look at the tile above.

4. In how many different ways can the first tile be placed in a corner of the tabletop? Explain.
5. If the corners of the tabletop all have patterned squares, what will the center of the table look like?
6. If the corners of the tabletop all are beige, what will the center of the table look like?
7. How can the tiles be arranged to make a square checkerboard pattern? Explain how you used spatial reasoning to decide.

▲ Two tiles, side by side

Additional Standard: Mathematical Reasoning 2.0 (See p. 401.)

Pete's father made a "Stars and Spots" patchwork quilt. Pete calls it "The Quilt of Many Squares." Each patchwork square is made up of four smaller squares, as shown here.

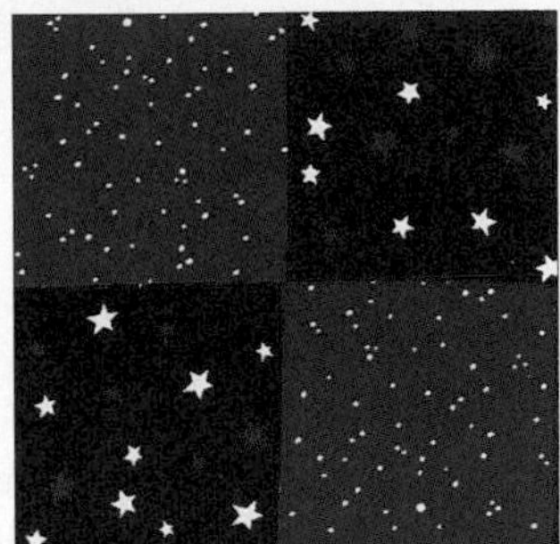

Guided Practice

1. How many squares like the one above were used to make the quilt?

a. 8 **b.** 12 **c.** 24

2. How many small squares are in the quilt?

a. 24 **b.** 38 **c.** 48

Independent Practice

3. The back of the quilt is one color. Pete folds the quilt in half from top to bottom so that the pattern is inside. What are the colors and positions of the two small squares in the top left corner of the folded quilt?

a. A blue square under a blue square

b. A red square under a blue square

c. A blue square under a red square

4. Math Reasoning Pete's father wants to add another row of patchwork squares around the quilt following the same pattern. How many more patchwork squares does he need?

Jen is tossing the color cube below. Each face of the cube has a different color—orange, yellow, green, blue, red, or purple.

5. The pictures at the right show the cube in different positions. Which color is opposite red?

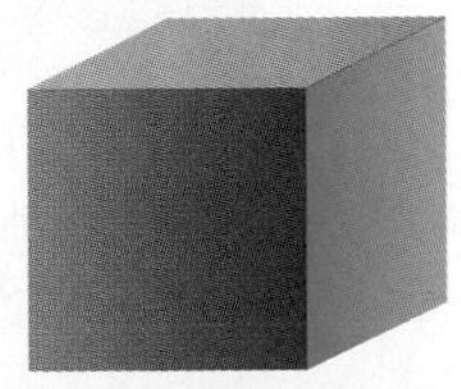

Triangles

California Content Standard *Measurement and Geometry 2.0: Students identify, describe, and classify the properties of . . . plane . . . geometric figures. Also Measurement and Geometry 2.2 (key) (See p. 401.)*

Warm-Up Review

For Exercises 1 and 2, classify each angle as acute, right, or obtuse.

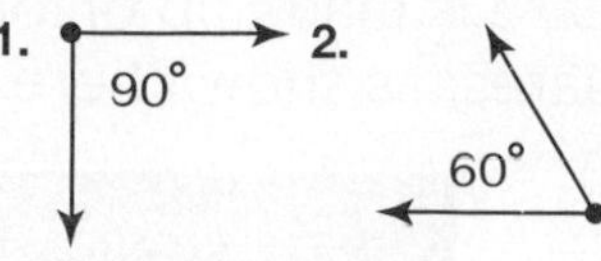

3. 3×40

4. $(2 \times 70) + 20$

5. Three angles of a quadrilateral each measure 100°. What is the measure of the fourth angle?

Math Link You know how to classify quadrilaterals by their angles and their pairs of sides. In this lesson, you will learn to classify triangles by the measures of their angles or by the lengths of their sides.

The table below classifies triangles by the measures of their angles.

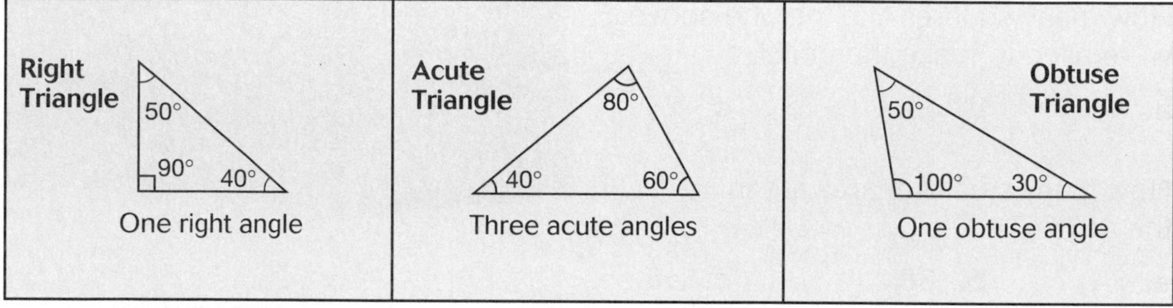

Right Triangle	Acute Triangle	Obtuse Triangle
50°, 90°, 40°	80°, 40°, 60°	50°, 100°, 30°
One right angle	Three acute angles	One obtuse angle

The following table classifies triangles by the lengths of their sides.

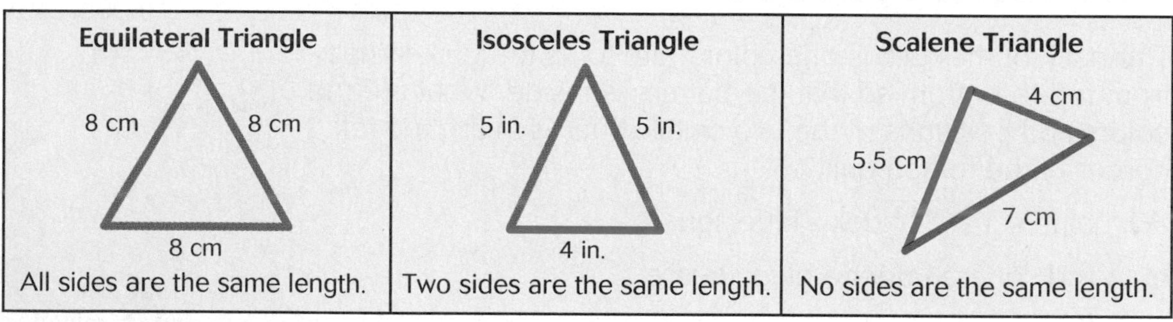

Equilateral Triangle	Isosceles Triangle	Scalene Triangle
8 cm, 8 cm, 8 cm	5 in., 5 in., 4 in.	4 cm, 5.5 cm, 7 cm
All sides are the same length.	Two sides are the same length.	No sides are the same length.

Example 1

Classify each outlined triangle by the measures of its angles.

a.

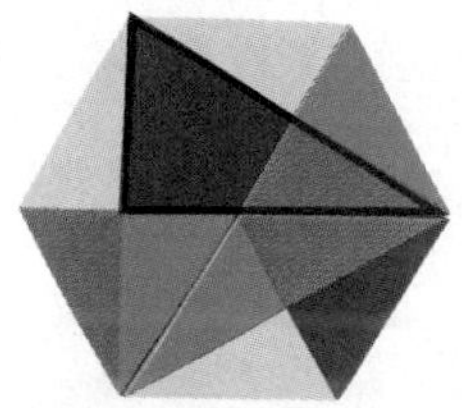

Right triangle
1 right angle

b.

Obtuse triangle
1 obtuse angle

c.

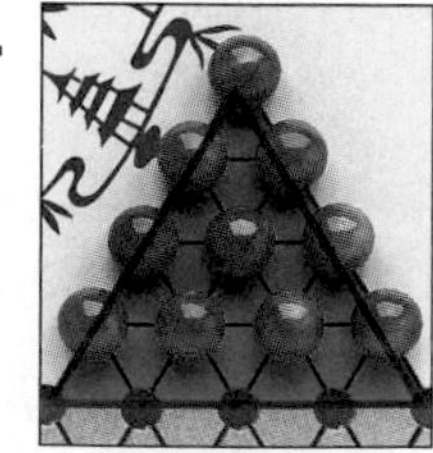

Acute triangle
3 acute angles

 Additional Standard: Mathematical Reasoning 1.1 (See p. 401.)

Example 2

Classify each triangle by the lengths of its sides.

a. $\triangle GHI$

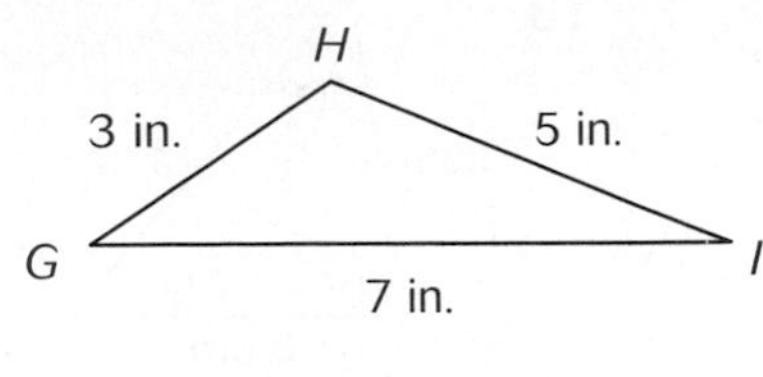

$\triangle GHI$ is read "triangle *GHI*."

Scalene triangle
No sides the same length

b. $\triangle DEF$

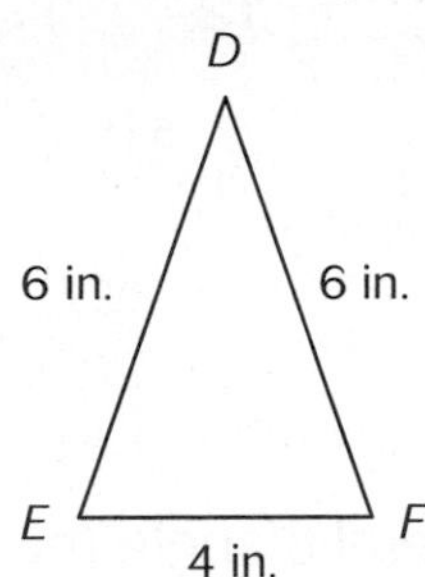

Isosceles triangle
Two sides the same length

c. $\triangle RST$

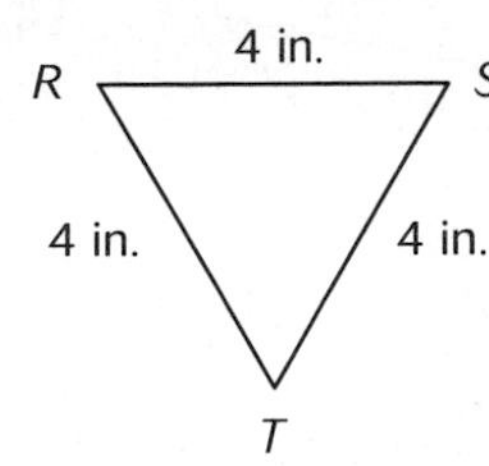

Equilateral triangle
All sides the same length

Example 3

Find the sum of the angle measures in each triangle in the first table on page 414. What conclusion might you make?

a.

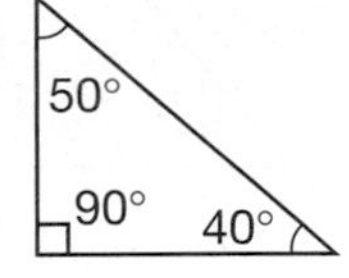

90 + 40 + 50 = 180

b.

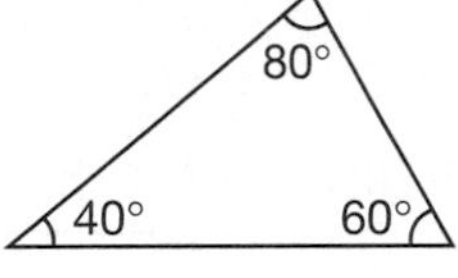

40 + 80 + 60 = 180

c.

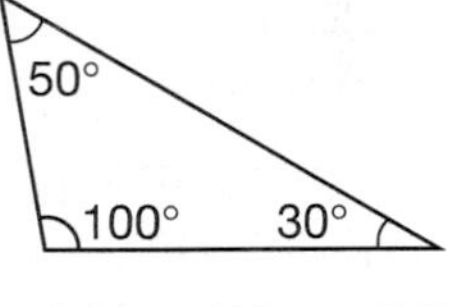

100 + 50 + 30 = 180

The sum of the angle measures of a triangle is 180°.

Guided Practice *For another example, see Set D on p. 443.*

Classify each triangle by the measures of its angles.

1.

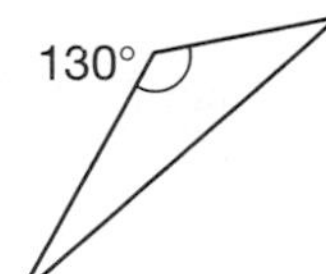

2.

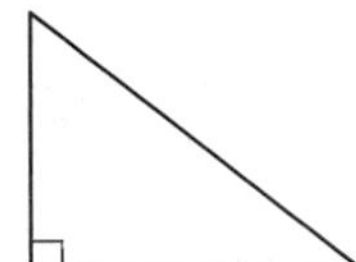

3.

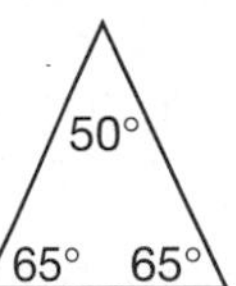

4.

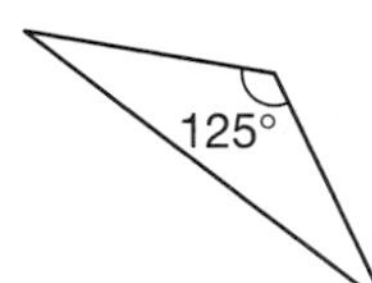

Classify each triangle by the lengths of its sides.

5.

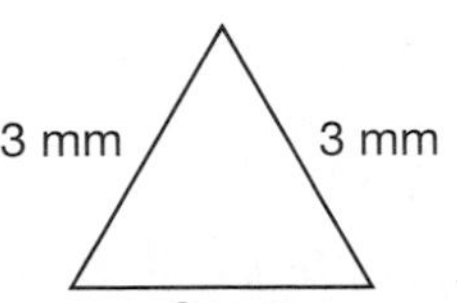

6.

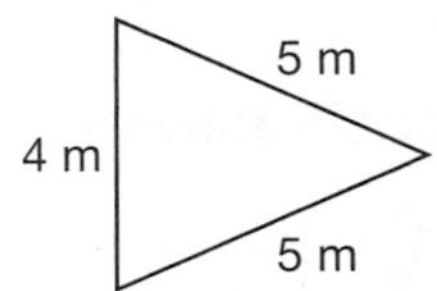

7.

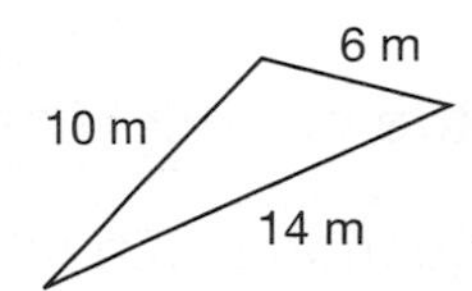

8.

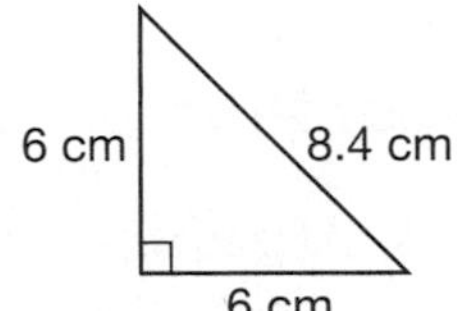

9. The measure of one acute angle of a right triangle is 35°. What is the measure of the other acute angle?

Independent Practice *For more practice, see Set D on p. 446.*

Classify each triangle by the measures of its angles and by the lengths of its sides.

10.

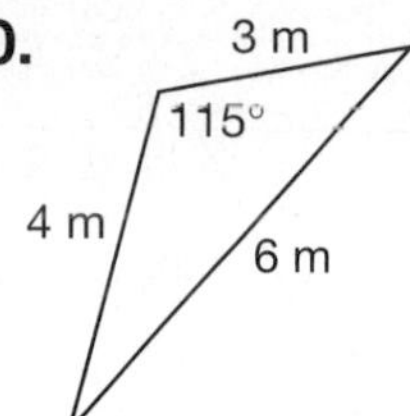

11.

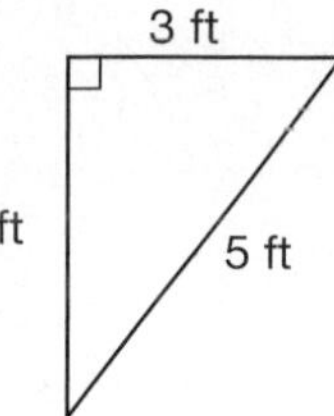

12.

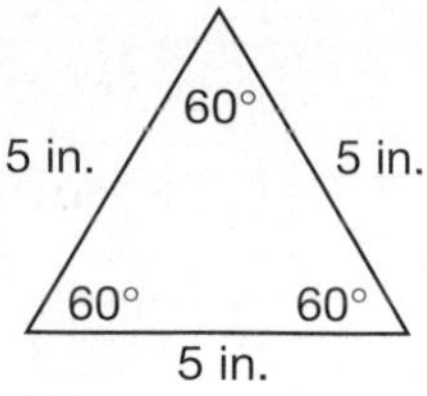

13.

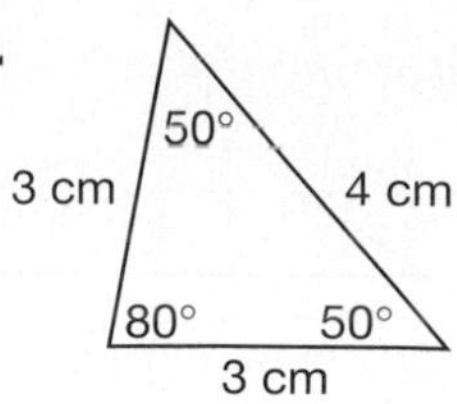

14. A garden in the shape of an equilateral triangle measures 100 feet around the outside edge. How long is each side, in feet?

15. Math Reasoning Study the triangles in Exercises 12 and 13 above. What can you conclude about the lengths of sides that are opposite angles of equal measure in a triangle?

16. Mental Math Use $\triangle ABC$ shown at the right. What is the measure of $\angle B$? Classify the triangle by the measures of its angles.

A
50°
50°
?
C
B

17. Math Reasoning Can a triangle have two right angles? Explain why or why not.

Mixed Review

18. A truck is loaded with 264 cases of games. Each case contains 12 boxes of games. Each box contains 6 dozen small travel games. How many small travel games are in the truck?

Classify an angle that has the given measure.

19. 45°

20. 107°

21. 90°

Name the quadrilaterals that fit the description. There may be more than one answer for each.

22. 4 sides of equal length

23. 2 pairs of parallel sides

Test Prep **Choose the correct letter for each answer.**

24. Algebra Which equation can be used to find the angle measures of a square?
(5-12)

A $4x = 180$ **C** $4x = 360$

B $3x = 180$ **D** $3x = 360$

25. Which of the following sets of angles could form a triangle?
(10-5)

F 30°, 50°, 50° **H** 90°, 45°, 35°

G 100°, 40°, 40° **J** 30°, 30°, 60°

 Use Homework Workbook 10-5.

Diagnostic Checkpoint

Use the drawing at the right for Exercises 1–8.

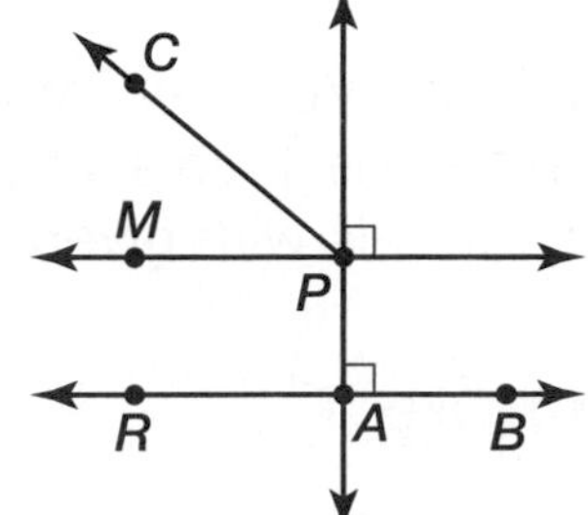

1. (10-1) Name a segment.

2. (10-1) Name a line.

3. (10-1) Name a ray.

4. (10-1) Name a point.

5. (10-1) Name two lines that are parallel.

6. (10-1) Name two lines that are perpendicular.

7. (10-2) Name an acute angle.

8. (10-2) Name a right angle.

Draw an example of each. Use a protractor for Exercises 9 and 11.

9. (10-2) 168° angle

10. (10-1) Point *S* on line *UV*.

11. (10-2) 15° angle

Classify each angle as acute, obtuse, right, or straight. Then use a protractor to measure each angle.

12. (10-2)

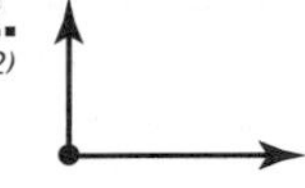

13. (10-2)

14. (10-2)

Classify each triangle by its sides and by its angles.

15. (10-5)

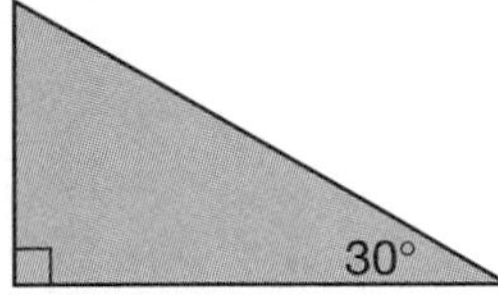

16. (10-5)

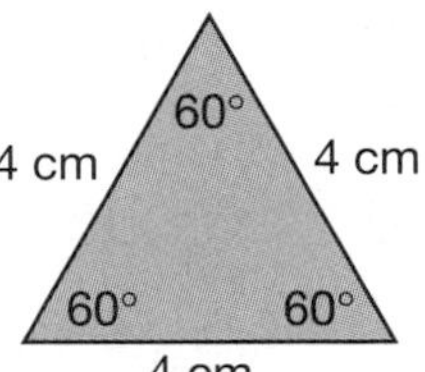

17. (10-5)

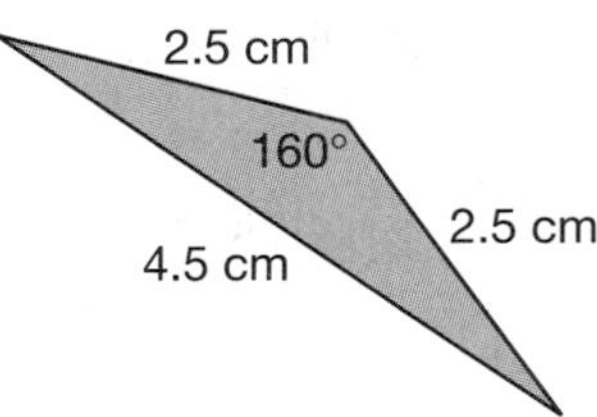

Classify each quadrilateral in as many ways as possible.

18. (10-3)

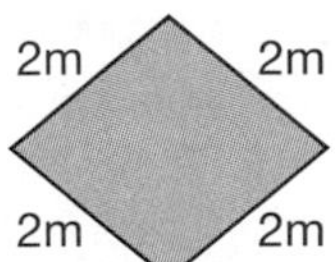

19. (10-3)

20. (10-3)

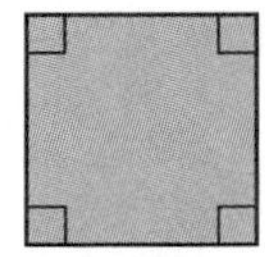

Solve.

21. (10-4) A patchwork square is made up of 4 small squares as shown. Four of these patchwork squares are used to make a small quilt which has red corners. Draw the quilt.

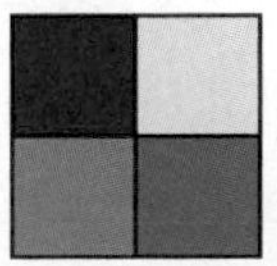

LESSON 10-6 Drawing Parallelograms

California Content Standard *Measurement and Geometry 2.1 (🔑): Measure, . . . and draw angles, perpendicular and parallel lines, [and] rectangles . . . by using appropriate tools (e.g. straightedge, ruler, . . . protractor . . .).*

Math Link You have studied various types of quadrilaterals. In this lesson, you will learn to draw quadrilaterals with given measures.

Warm-Up Review

Give the best name for each quadrilateral.

1. 2.

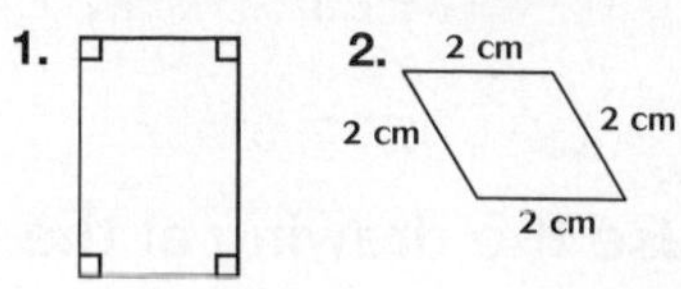

3. 4.

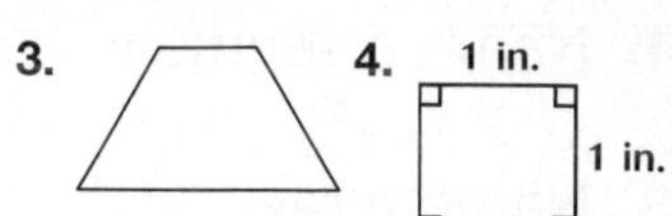

5. A child's play area is in the shape of a regular octagon 10 feet on each side. Find the distance around the play area.

Example 1

Draw a rectangle with sides that measure 4 cm and 2 cm.

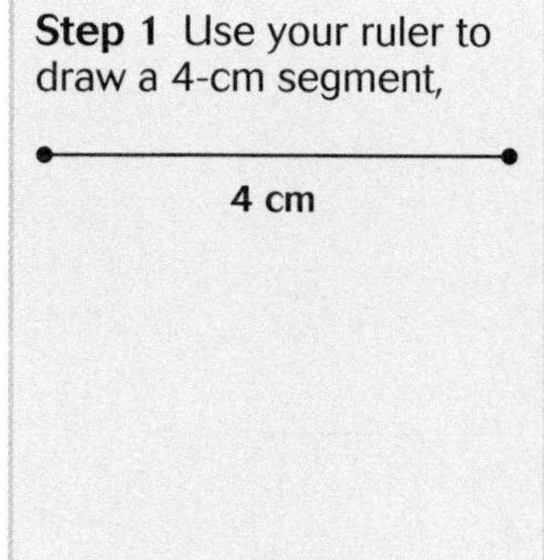

Step 1 Use your ruler to draw a 4-cm segment,

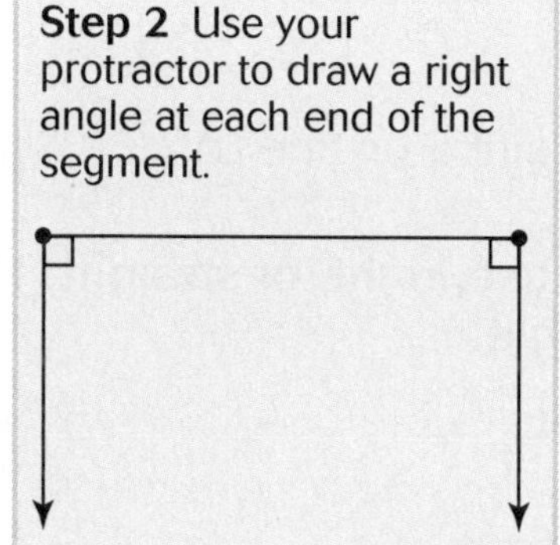

Step 2 Use your protractor to draw a right angle at each end of the segment.

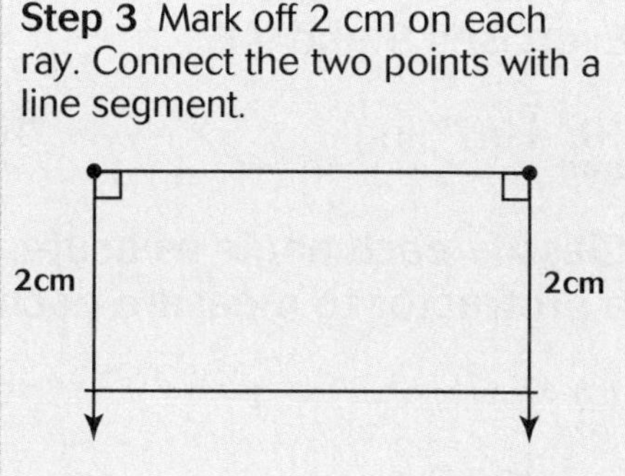

Step 3 Mark off 2 cm on each ray. Connect the two points with a line segment.

Check that the fourth side measures 4 cm and that the lower angles are right angles. Are pairs of opposite sides parallel?

Example 2

Draw a parallelogram with $1\frac{1}{2}$-inch and 1-inch sides and 65° and 115° angles.

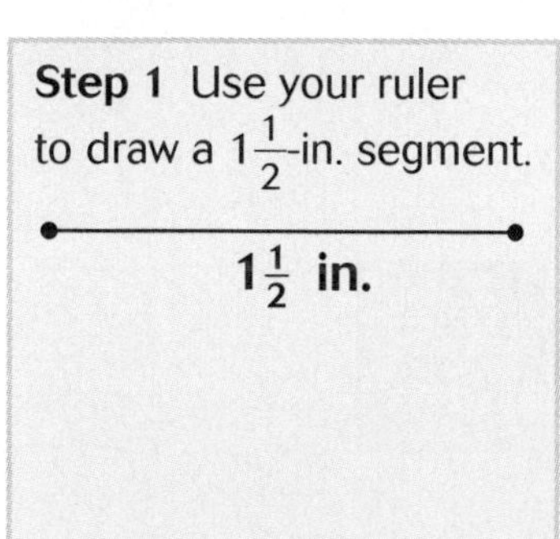

Step 1 Use your ruler to draw a $1\frac{1}{2}$-in. segment.

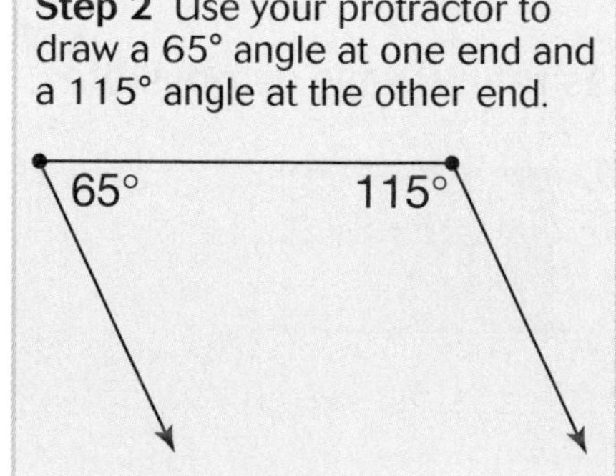

Step 2 Use your protractor to draw a 65° angle at one end and a 115° angle at the other end.

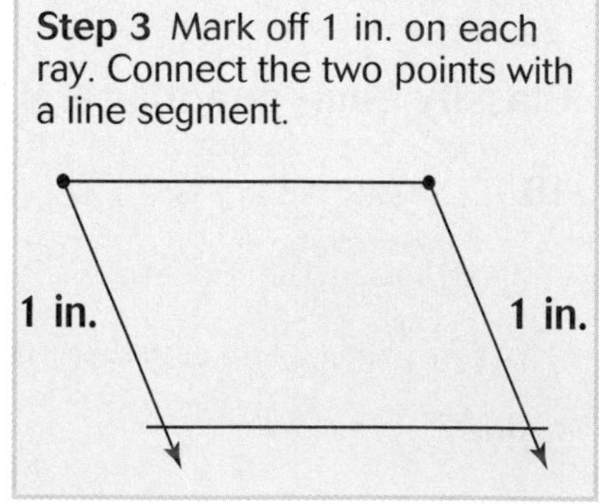

Step 3 Mark off 1 in. on each ray. Connect the two points with a line segment.

Check that the fourth side measures $1\frac{1}{2}$ inches and that the angles measure 65° and 115°. Are pairs of opposite sides parallel?

Additional Standards: Measurement and Geometry 2.2 (🔑); Algebra and Functions 1.2 (🔑), Mathematical Reasoning 1.1, 2.0 *(See p. 401.)*

Guided Practice *For another example, see Set E on p. 443.*

Draw a parallelogram with the given segments and angles.

1. parallelogram

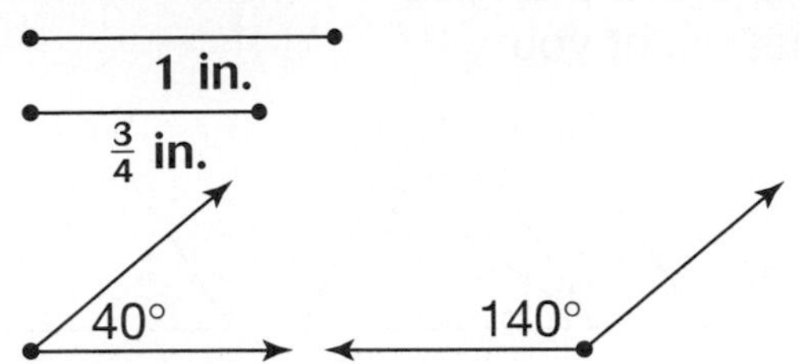

2. rhombus

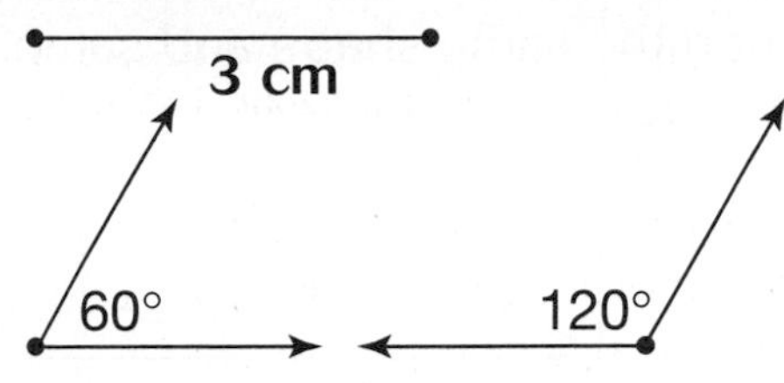

3. What is the sum of the measures of the two angles on any one side of the quadrilaterals in Examples 1 and 2 and Exercises 1 and 2?

Independent Practice *For another example, see Set E on p. 446.*

Draw a parallelogram with the given measures or given segments and angles.

4. Square with 3-inch sides

5. Rhombus with 4-cm sides and 45° and 135° angles

6. Parallelogram with 5-cm and 6-cm sides, 60° and 120° angles

7. Rectangle

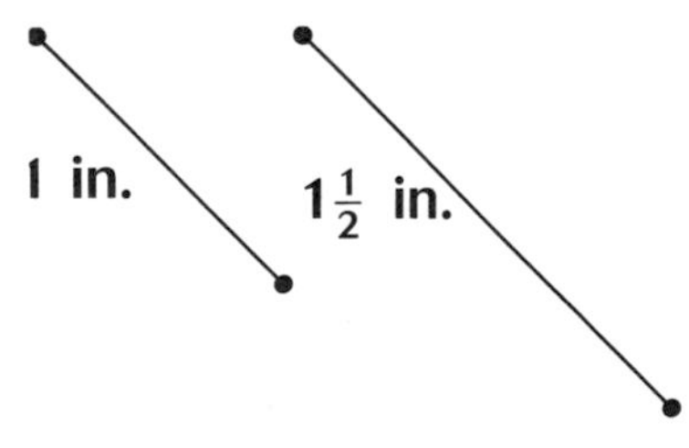

8. Parallelogram

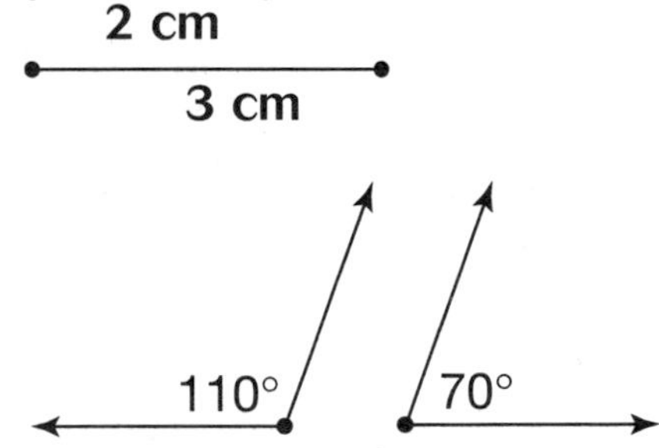

9. Math Reasoning If you have the side lengths and one angle measure, can you draw a parallelogram? Explain.

10. Try to draw two different quadrilaterals with 3-cm and 5-cm sides and a 60° angle. Hint: One is *not* a parallelogram.

11. Draw a square with any length side. Compare it with those of your classmates. What do you notice?

12. Draw a rhombus with a 60° angle and any length side. Compare it with those of your classmates. What do you notice?

13. Copy the quadrilaterals below. Then draw a segment from one vertex to the opposite vertex as shown. Are the two triangles formed the same shape and same size? What might you conclude?

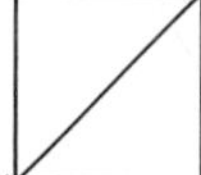
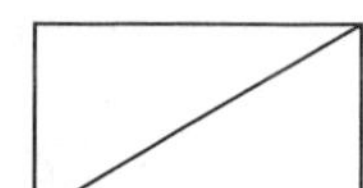

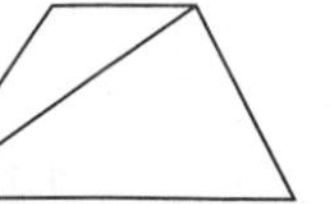
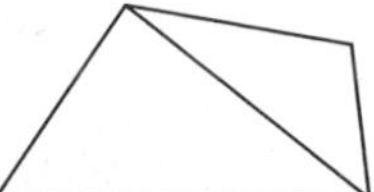

14. Algebra A parallelogram has one angle whose measure is 140°. Write and solve an equation to find the measures of the other three angles.

15. Math Reasoning Study the drawing at the right. How many quadrilaterals can you find? How many triangles? Classify the quadrilaterals and the triangles.

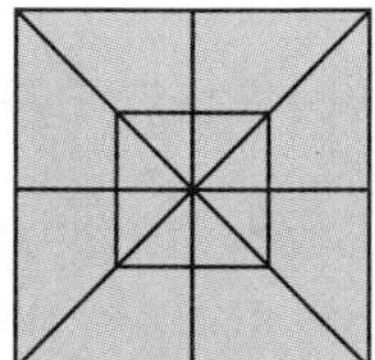

Mixed Review

Write each group of numbers in order from least to greatest.

16. $^{+}7$, $^{-}6$, $^{+}4$, $^{-}1$

17. 4.2, 5.7, 0.2, 1.9

18. $2\frac{1}{4}$, $1\frac{3}{4}$, $1\frac{1}{4}$, $2\frac{1}{8}$

19. Classify this polygon.

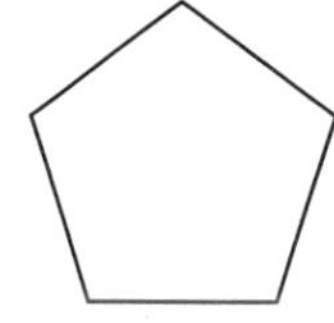

20. Classify this triangle by its sides and by its angles.

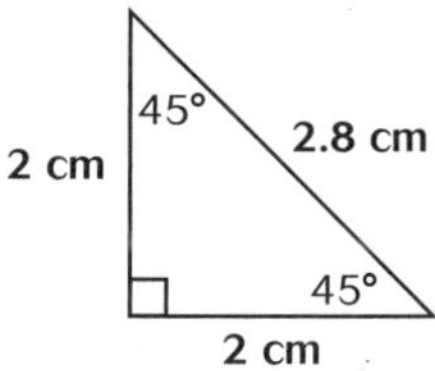

Test Prep **Choose the correct letter for each answer.**

21. (10-5) Every equilateral triangle is also which of the following?

A scalene

B obtuse

C acute

D right

22. (10-3) Every rectangle is also which of the following?

F square

G parallelogram

H rhombus

J pentagon

 Use Homework Workbook 10-6.

Drawing Triangles

California Content Standard *Measurement and Geometry 2.1 (🔑): [I]dentify and draw angles . . . and triangles by using appropriate tools (e.g.straightedge, ruler, . . . protractor . . .).*

Math Link You have studied various types of triangles. In this lesson, you will learn to draw triangles with given measures of angles and sides.

Warm-Up Review

Classify each triangle by its angles and its sides.

1. 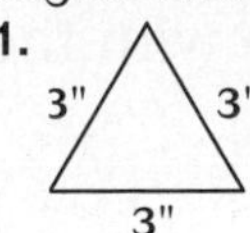

2. 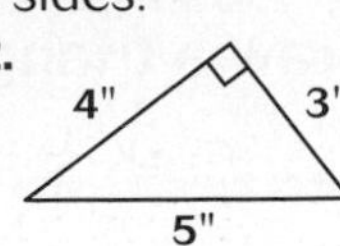

3. What kind of triangles make up this regular octagon?

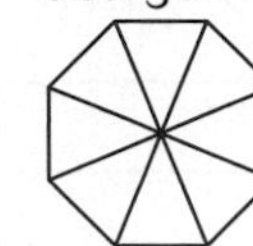

Example 1

Draw a triangle with a 125° angle between sides that measure 2 cm and 3 cm. Classify the triangle by its angles and its sides.

Step 1 Use your protractor to draw a 125° angle.

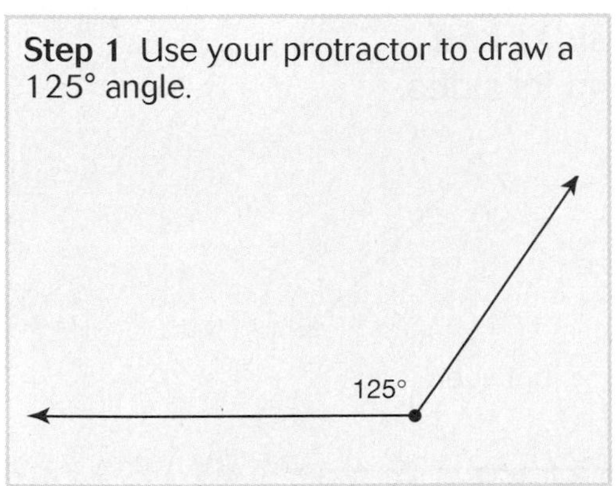

Step 2 Mark off 2 cm on one side of the angle and 3 cm on the other side. Connect the two points.

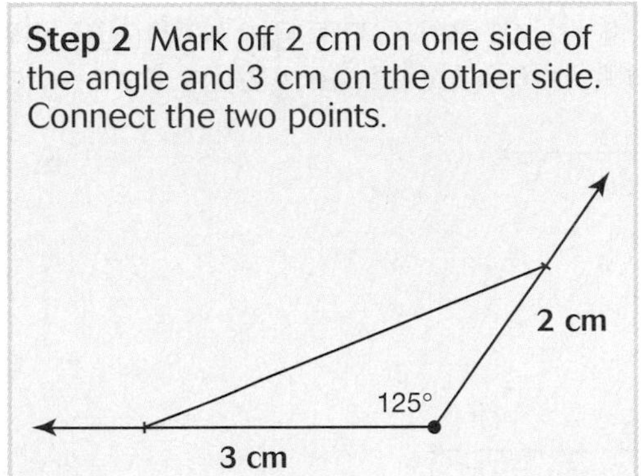

The triangle is an obtuse scalene triangle.

Example 2

Draw a triangle with a 2-inch side between 30° and 70° angles. Classify the triangle by its angles and its sides.

Step 1 Draw a 2-inch segment.

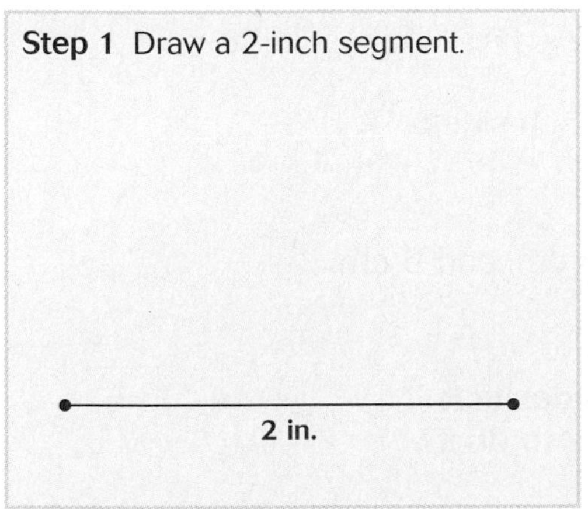

Step 2 Draw a 30° angle on one end of the segment and a 70° angle on the other end. Extend the sides of the angles until they meet.

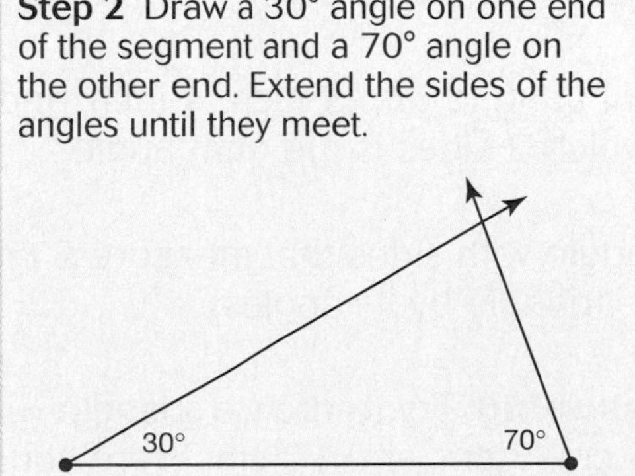

The triangle is an acute scalene triangle.

Additional Standards: Measurement and Geometry 2.2 (🔑); Mathematical Reasoning 1.1 (See p. 401.)

Guided Practice *For another example, see Set F on p. 443.*

Draw a triangle with the given sides and angles.

1.

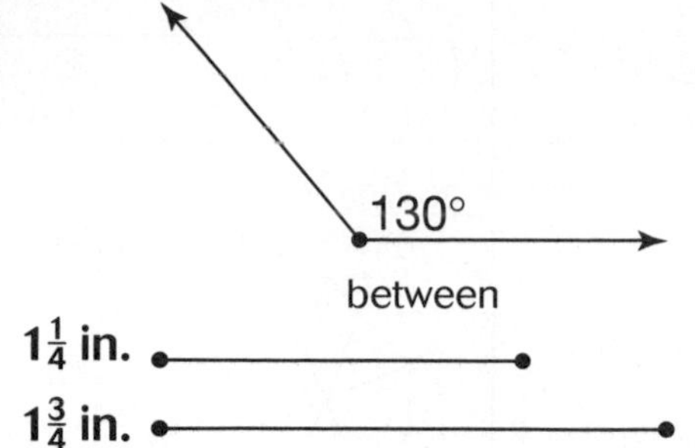

2.

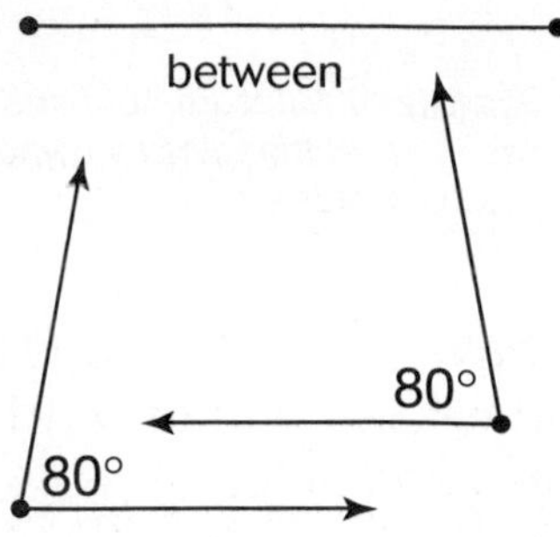

3. Classify each triangle you drew by its angles and its sides.

Independent Practice *For another example, see Set F on p. 446.*

For exercises 4–8, draw a triangle with the given sides and angles. Then classify each triangle by its angles and its sides.

4.

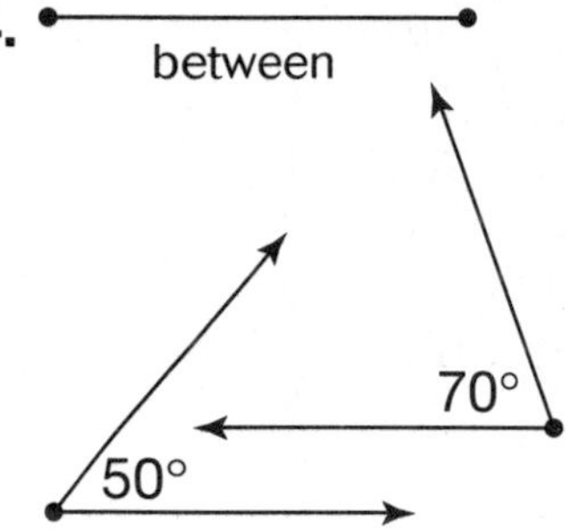

5.

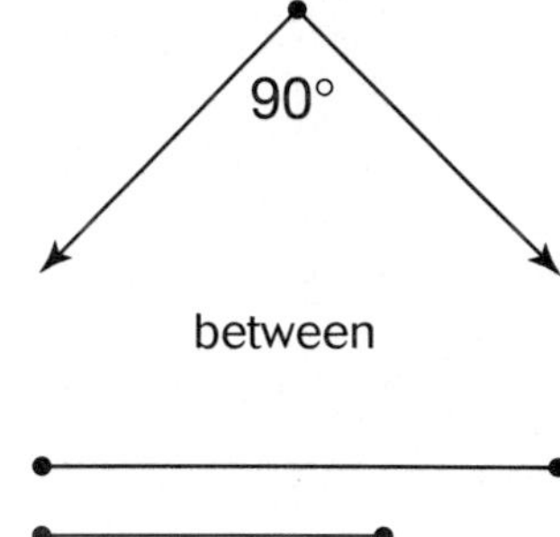

6. 100° angle between two 2-in. sides

7. 6-cm side between two 50° angles

8. 3-cm side between two 60° angles

9. Draw a right triangle with 3-inch, 4-inch, and 5-inch sides. Between which 2 sides is the right angle?

10. Draw a triangle with sides that measure 5 cm, 3 cm, and 6 cm. Classify the triangle by its angles.

11. Math Reasoning Try to draw a triangle with sides that measure 5 cm, 3 cm, and 10 cm. Were you able to do it? Why or why not?

12. Draw a triangle with angles that measure 45°, 60°, and 75° and any length sides. Compare it with those of your classmates. What do you notice?

13. Draw two different triangles with a 50° angle and sides that measure $2\frac{1}{2}$ in. and 3 in. Hint: Do *not* draw the 50° angle between the given sides.

Mixed Review

14. Jenny started a quilt of squares as shown. If she added a row of squares all the way around, how many squares would there be? If she added two rows of squares all the way around, how many squares would there be?

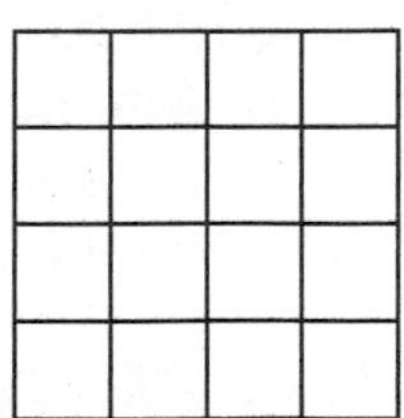

Classify each outlined triangle by its angles and its sides.

15. Backgammon

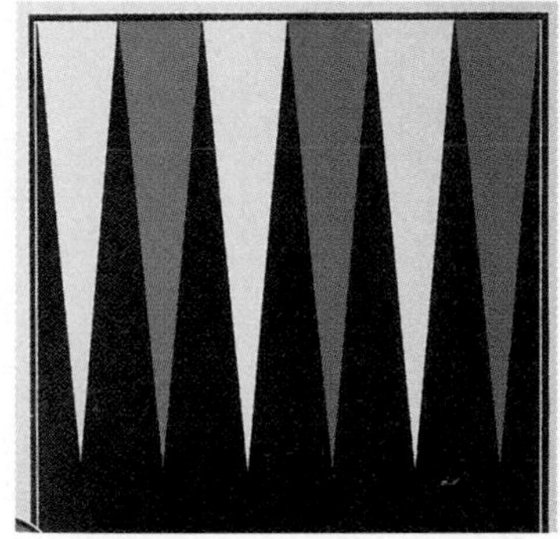

16. Triominoes

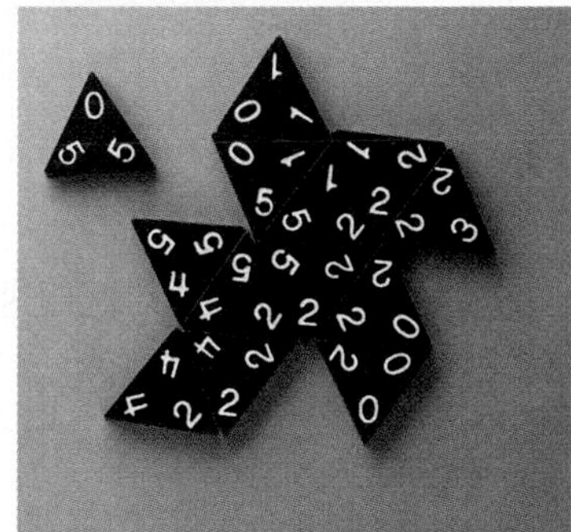

17. Draw a rectangle with the given sides.

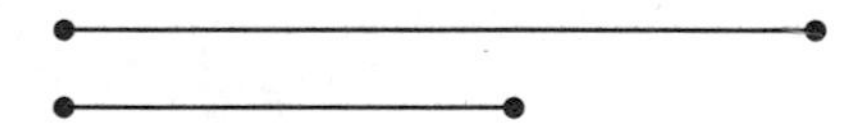

18. Draw a rhombus with 3-inch sides and a 120° angle.

19. 156 ÷ 12

20. 2,459 ÷ 83

21. 6.37 ÷ 0.91

22. 0.456 ÷ 8

Test Prep **Choose the correct letter for each answer.**

Use the graph at the right.

23. Which is the correct ordered pair for Point *A*?
(9-7)

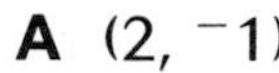

A $(2, {}^-1)$

B $({}^-1, 2)$

C $({}^-1, {}^-2)$

D $({}^-2, 1)$

24. Which lettered point has the coordinates $({}^-2, 2)$?
(9-7)

F *B*

G *C*

H *D*

J *E*

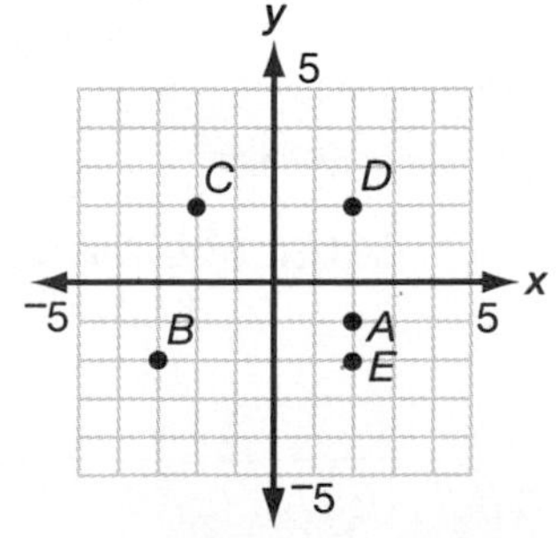

Problem-Solving Strategy:

Find a Pattern

Understand
Plan
Solve
Look Back

California Content Standard *Mathematical Reasoning 1.1: Analyze problems by identifying relationships . . . and observing patterns.*

Warm-Up Review

Draw or describe the next 3 numbers or figures in each pattern.

1. 1, 2, 4, 8, 16
2. ➡ ⬅ ⬇ ➡ ⬅
3. ▲ ▼ ▼ ▲ ▼
4. ◆ ■ ◆ ■ ◆
5. Sid bought 3 rolls of wallpaper at $9.50 each and a brush for $6.50. How much did he spend?

Example

Jen and Kate are painting a border on the walls in their room. Kate painted the section of the border below. Jen wants to continue the border correctly. What shape and color should she paint next?

Understand

What do you need to know?

You need to know the different shapes and colors in the border.

Plan

How can you solve the problem?

You can find a pattern and use it to continue the border.

Solve

The border has two designs that alternate. It also has two colors that alternate. Therefore, Jen should paint a diamond with green on the outside.

Look Back

What should be painted to the left of Kate's border?

Additional Standard: Mathematical Reasoning 3.2 *(See p. 401.)*

Guided Practice

Find each pattern. Then draw or describe the next 3 figures.

1. 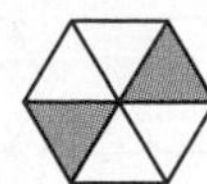 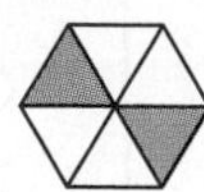

2. 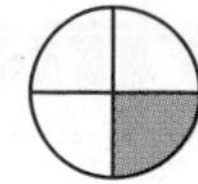   

Independent Practice

Find the pattern. Then draw or describe the next 3 figures.

3.  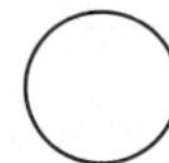     

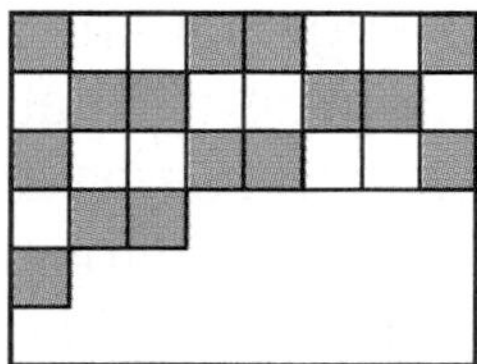

4. Stephen bought a house in which the kitchen floor was only partly tiled. The builders left enough tiles to complete the floor, so Stephen is finishing the tiling. Based on the tile pattern shown at the right, draw a picture to show how he should finish the tiling.

5. If you fold a piece of paper in half 4 times, how many sections will you see when you unfold it? What if you fold it in half 6 times? Then how many sections will you see when you unfold it?

6. Six teams are playing in the first round of a volleyball tournament. Each team will play one match against each of the other teams. How many matches will there be? Use the table at the right to find a pattern.

Number of Teams	Number of Matches
2	1
3	3
4	6
5	10

Mixed Review

Try these or other strategies to solve each problem. Tell which strategy you used.

Problem-Solving Strategies

- *Solve a Simpler Problem*
- *Find a Pattern*
- *Work Backward*
- *Write an Equation*
- *Draw a Diagram*
- *Make a Table*

7. A wallpaper border consists of side-by-side squares. Each square has a segment from the top-left corner to the lower-right corner. How many triangles are in the first four squares? Classify the triangles by their angles and sides.

8. James plans to put a border along the top of each wall in a room that measures 12 ft by 15 ft. How many yards of border does he need?

Use Homework Workbook 10-8.

Congruent Figures and Transformations

California Content Standard *Measurement and Geometry 2.0: Students identify, describe, and classify the . . . relationships between plane . . . geometric figures.*

Math Link You have learned about many individual geometric figures. Now you will learn about pairs of geometric figures.

Warm-Up Review

Tell if the figures in each pair are the same shape and same size.

1. 

2. 

3.

4. Are all squares the same shape? The same size?

Word Bank

congruent
transformation
slide (translation)
flip (reflection)
turn (rotation)

Triangles *A* and *B*, outlined in the plate at the right, are **congruent.** That is, they have the same shape and same size. Notice that the triangles are in different positions, but they are still congruent.

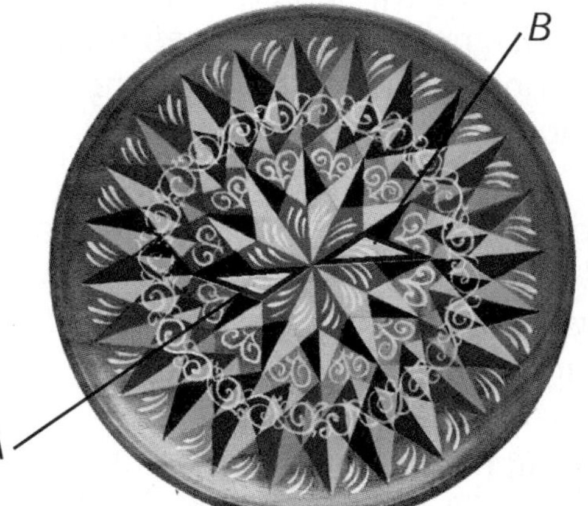
B
A

The change of position of a figure is called a **transformation.**

The symbol for congruence is $\cong$.

In the picture above, $\triangle A \cong \triangle B$.

The following three transformations produce a figure that is congruent to a given figure.

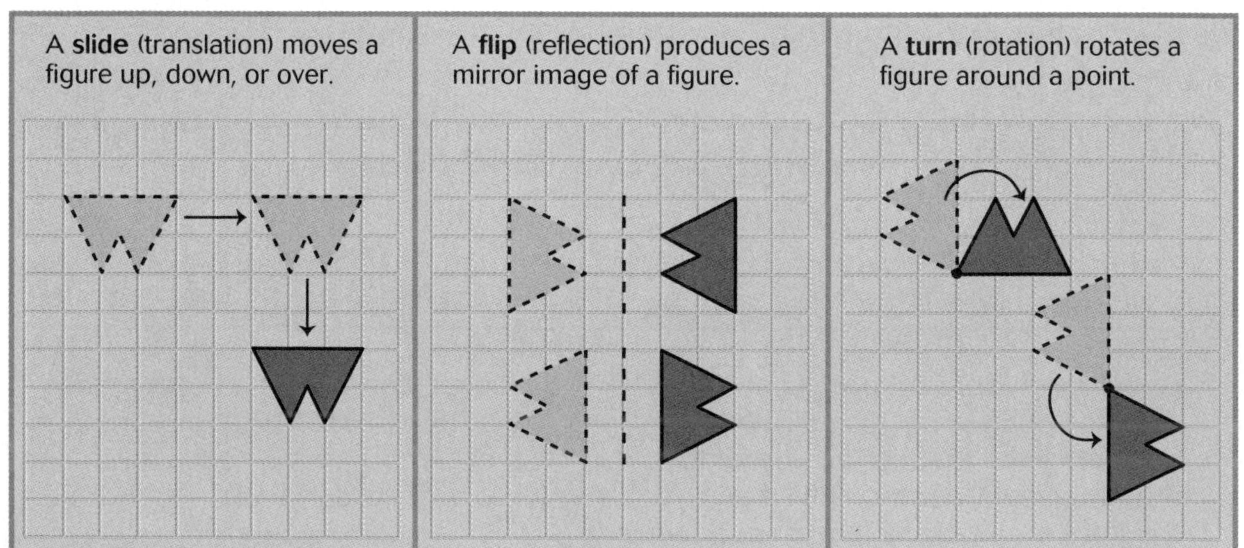
A **slide** (translation) moves a figure up, down, or over.
A **flip** (reflection) produces a mirror image of a figure.
A **turn** (rotation) rotates a figure around a point.

 Additional Standard: Mathematical Reasoning 1.1 (See p. 401.)

Example

Tell how each triangle was moved from position A to position B. Write slide, flip, or turn.

a. 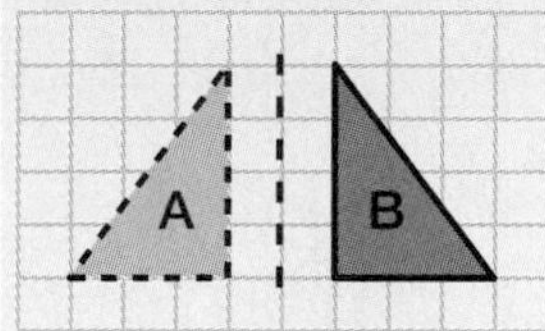

b. 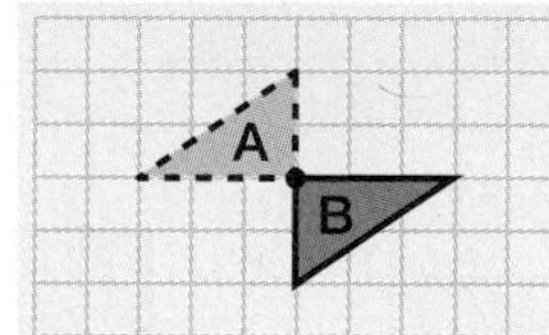

c. 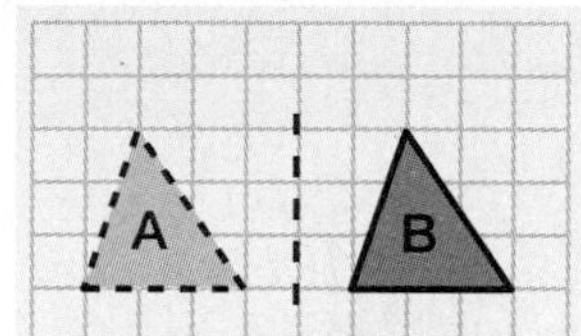

Guided Practice *For another example, see Set G on p. 444.*

Choose the figure that is congruent to the first figure in each row.

1. 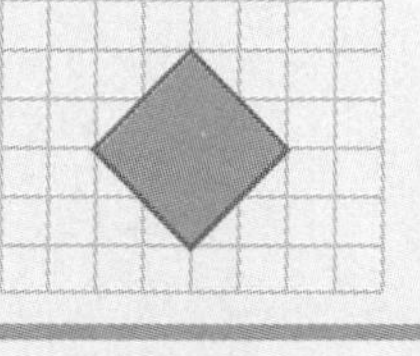 **a.** 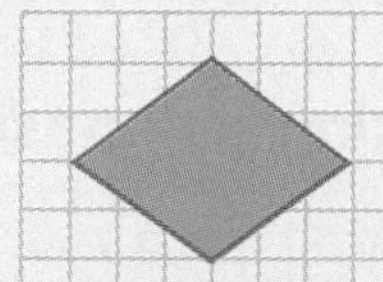 **b.** 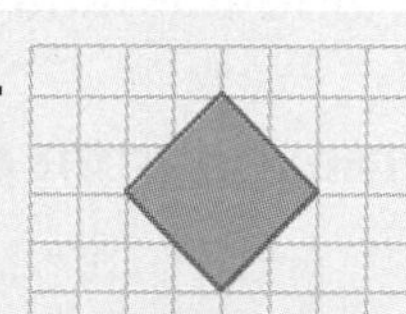 **c.** 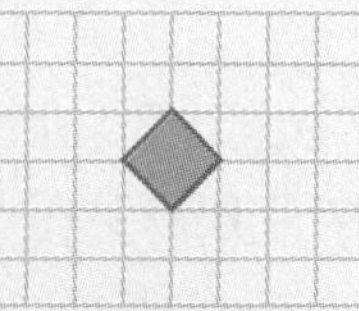

2. 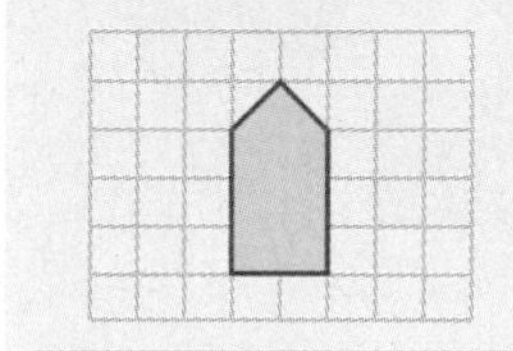 **a.** 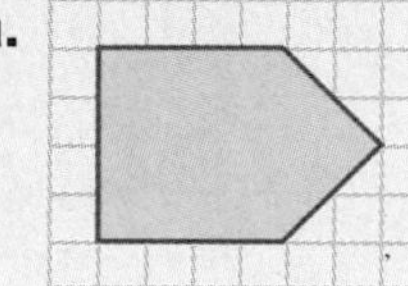 **b.** 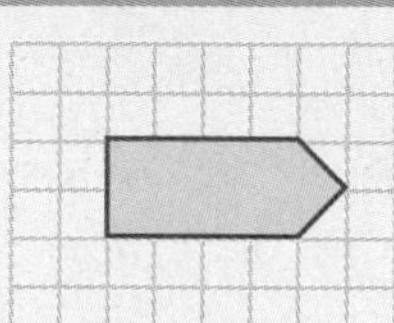 **c.** 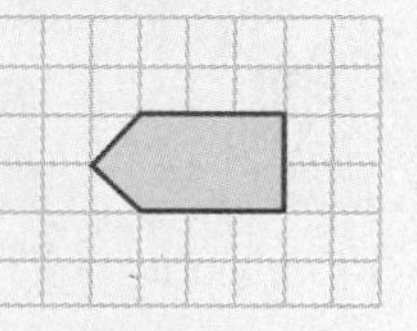

3. In Exercise 2, what transformation is illustrated between the first figure and the figure congruent to it?

Independent Practice *For more practice, see Set G on p. 447.*

Choose the figure that is congruent to the first figure in each row.

4. 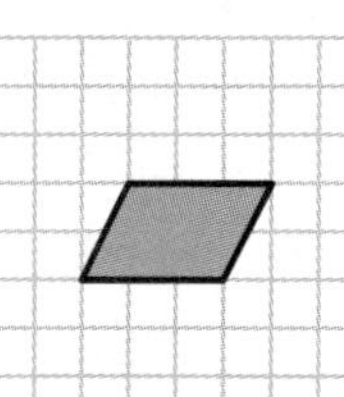 **a.** 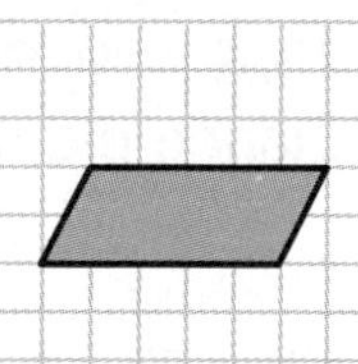 **b.** 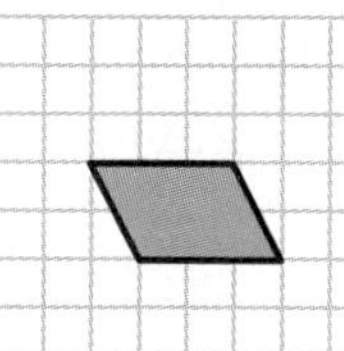 **c.** 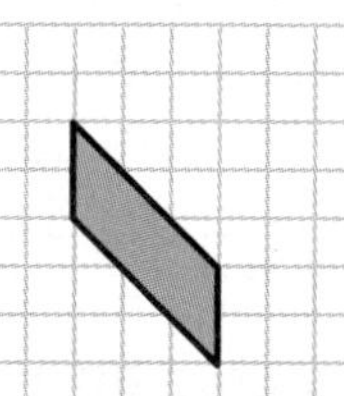

5. 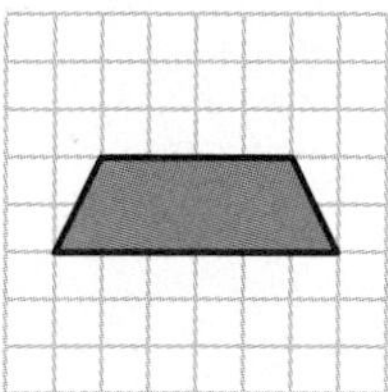 **a.** 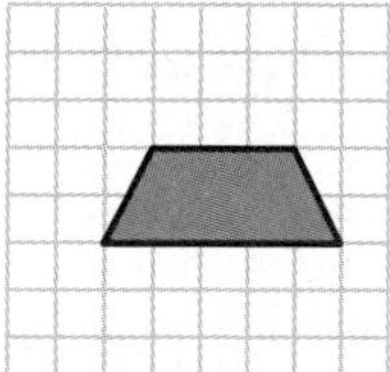 **b.** 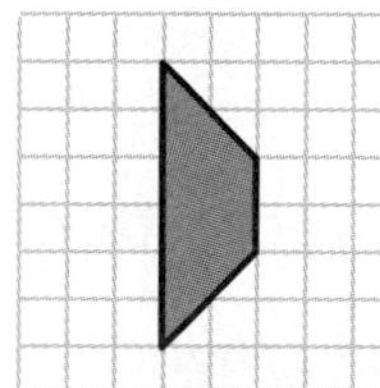 **c.** 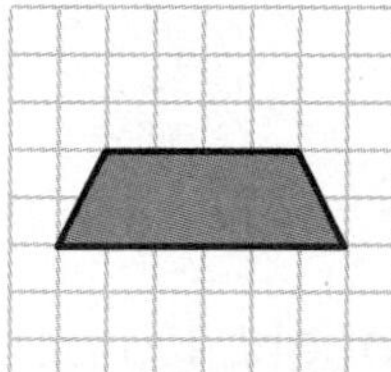

6. 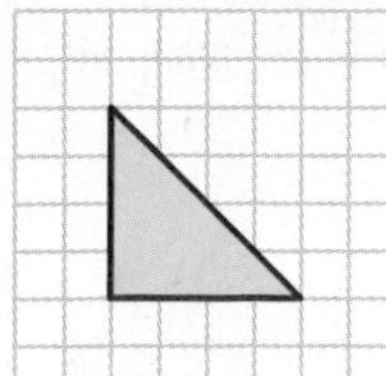

a. 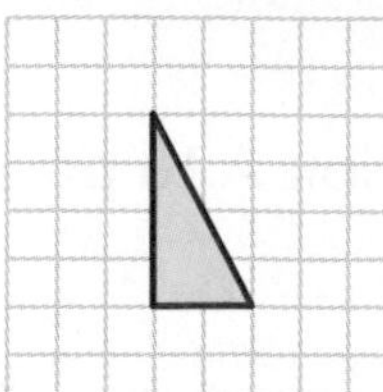

b. 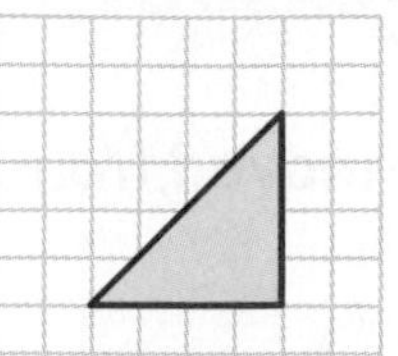

c. 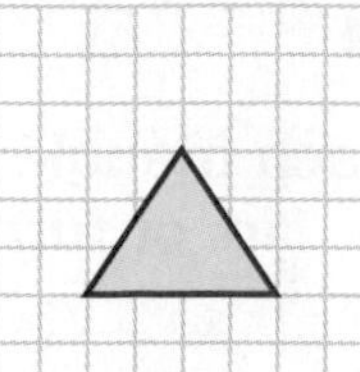

7. 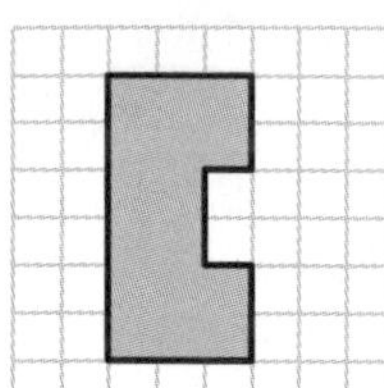

a. 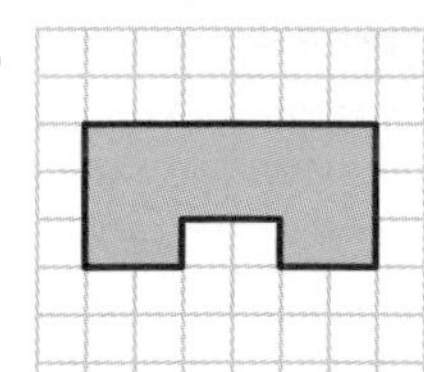

b. 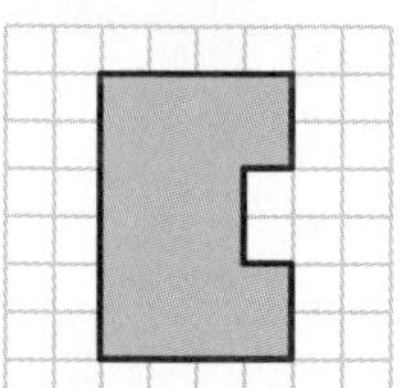

c. 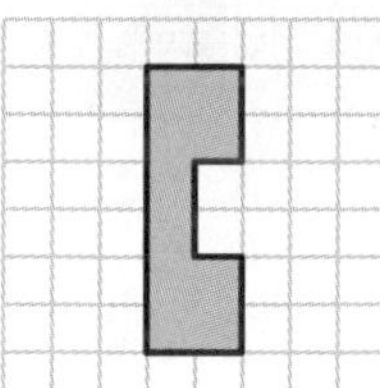

8. In Exercises 6 and 7, what transformation is illustrated between the first figure and the figure congruent to it?

Tell how each figure was moved from position A to position B. Hint: There are two steps.

9. 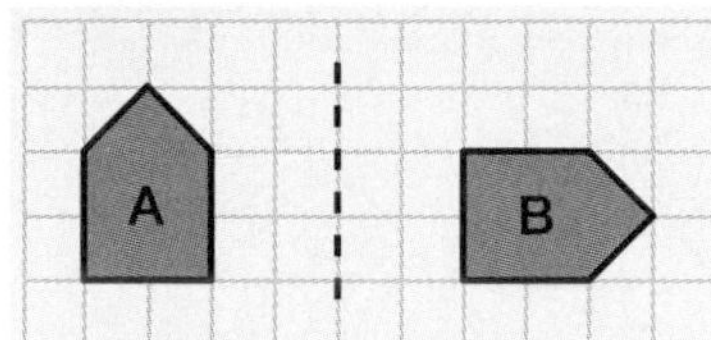

10. 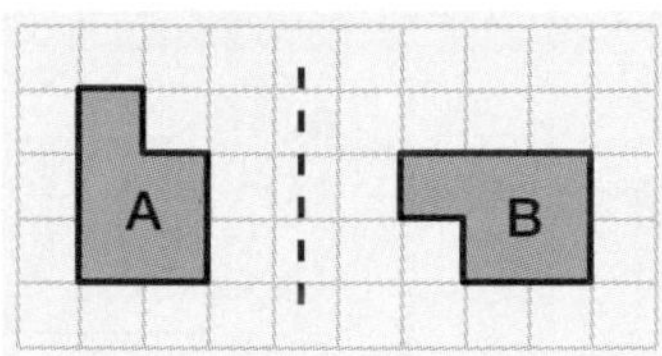

11. **Math Reasoning** Flipping a figure to the right and then flipping it down results in which single transformation?

12. The pattern at the right shows a pattern of transformations. Describe each step.

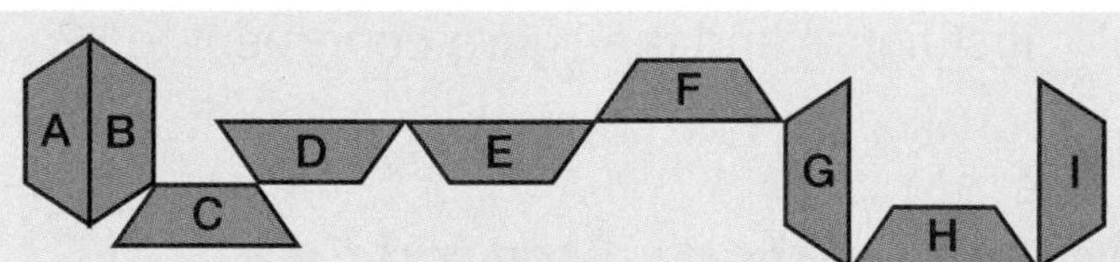

Mixed Review

13. Abby bought four colors of sand to make a sand painting. The sand cost $0.79, $1.19, $0.99, and $2.25. The tax was $0.42. How much change did she receive from a $10 bill?

Use a protractor and a ruler to draw the following figures.

14. Square with 1-inch sides

15. Isosceles triangle with a 50° angle between 2-cm sides

Test Prep **Choose the correct letter for the answer.**

16. C. J. bought 1.5 pounds of ground beef at $1.54 per pound. Find the total cost.
(6-5)

A $1.31 **B** $2.21 **C** $2.31 **D** $9.24 **E** NH

Drawing Congruent Figures

California Content Standard *Measurement and Geometry 2.1 ( ) [D]raw angles, perpendicular and parallel lines, rectangles, and triangles by using appropriate tools (e.g. straightedge . . . compass . . .)*

Warm-Up Review

1. Draw a rectangle with sides that measure 3 in. and 5 in.
2. Draw a parallelogram with sides that measure 5 cm and 7 cm and angles that measure 130° and 50°.
3. Draw a triangle with a 90° angle between two 3-cm sides. Classify that triangle by sides and by angles.

Math Link You have drawn figures of a given size by measuring with a protractor and ruler. Now you will learn to draw figures congruent to given figures using only a compass and a straightedge.

You can use a compass and a straightedge to draw congruent figures. With a compass, you can draw an **arc** to mark off a length. An arc is part of a circle. You can use the straightedge of the compass or another straightedge tool to draw lines, rays, and segments.

Compass

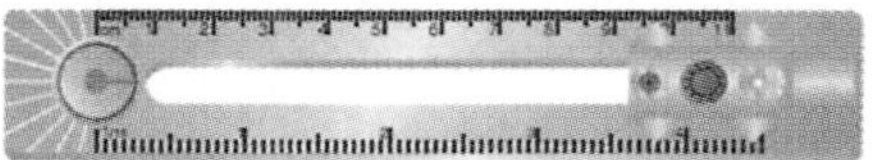

Word Bank

arc

Example 1

Without measuring with a ruler, draw $\overline{CD}$ congruent to $\overline{AB}$.

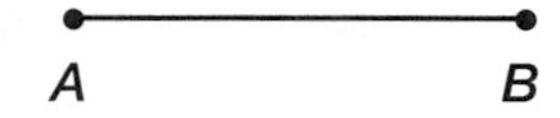

Step 1 Draw a ray. Label the endpoint *C*.	C
Step 2 On $\overline{AB}$, place the compass on point *A* as shown. Move the slider so that it lines up with point *B*. Tighten the knob.	
Step 3 Now place the compass on point *C*. Without changing the slider position, draw an arc that intersects the ray.	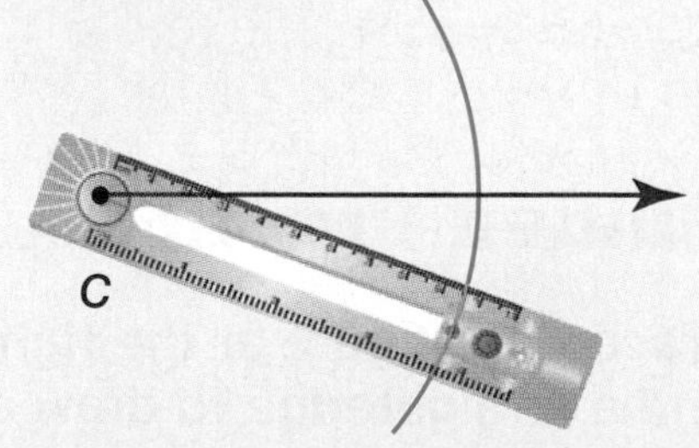
Step 4 Label point *D* where the arc intersects the ray. $\overline{CD} \cong \overline{AB}$	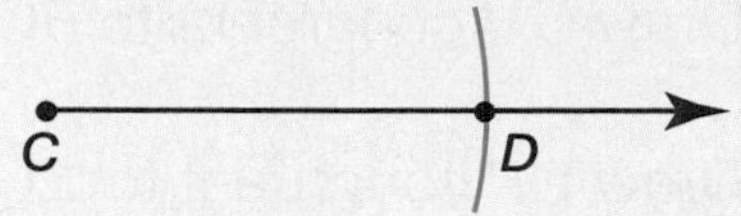

Additional Standard: Mathematical Reasoning 2.3 *(See p. 401.)*

Example 2

Without measuring with a protractor, draw $\angle R$ congruent to $\angle K$.

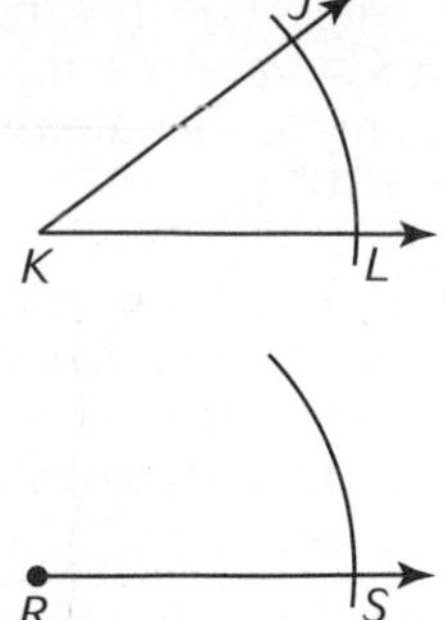

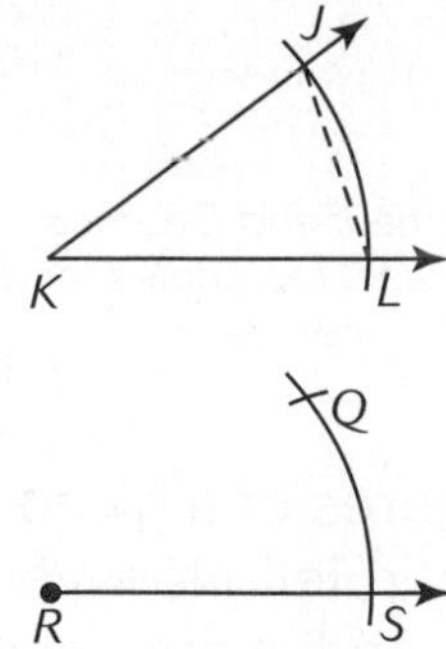

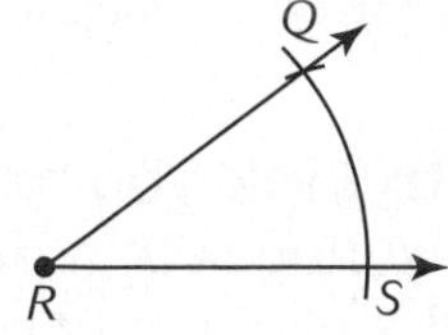

Step 1 Draw a ray with endpoint R. With point K as center, draw an arc that intersects both sides of $\angle K$. Label the points of intersection J and L. With the same compass setting, draw an arc intersecting the ray at point S.

Step 2 Set your compass to the length of $\overline{JL}$. With point S as center, draw an intersecting arc. Label point Q.

Step 3 Draw $\overrightarrow{RQ}$. $\angle K \cong \angle R$

Example 3

Using only a compass and a straightedge, draw $\triangle GHK$ congruent to $\triangle XYZ$.

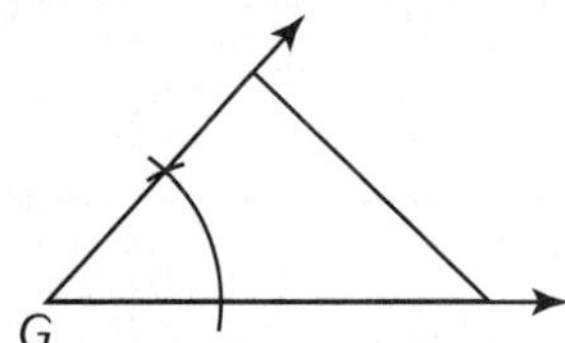

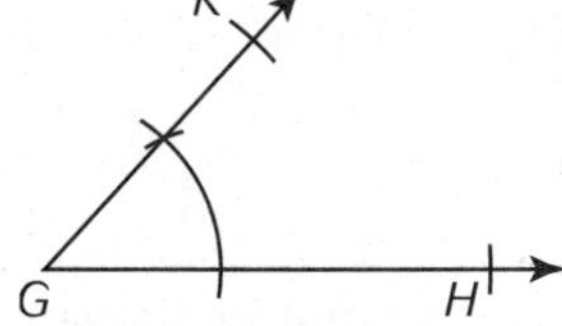

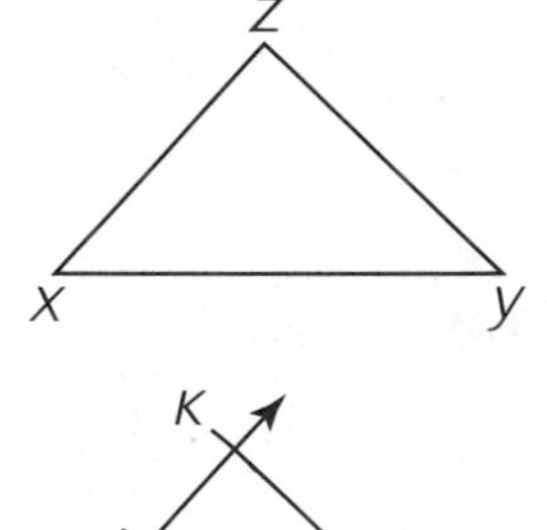

Step 1 Draw $\angle G \cong \angle X$.

Step 2 On one side of $\angle G$, draw $\overline{GH} \cong \overline{XY}$. On the other side of $\angle G$, draw $\overline{GK} \cong \overline{XZ}$.

Step 3 Draw $\overline{HK}$. $\angle G \cong \angle X$, $\overline{GH} \cong \overline{XY}$, $\overline{GK} \cong \overline{XZ}$ $\triangle GHK \cong \triangle XYZ$

Guided Practice For another example, see Set H on p. 444.

Trace each figure at the right. Then use only a compass and a straightedge to draw each congruent figure.

1. Draw $\overline{GH}$ congruent to $\overline{BC}$.

2. Draw $\angle P$ congruent to $\angle Q$.

3. Draw $\triangle LMN$ congruent to $\triangle EDF$.

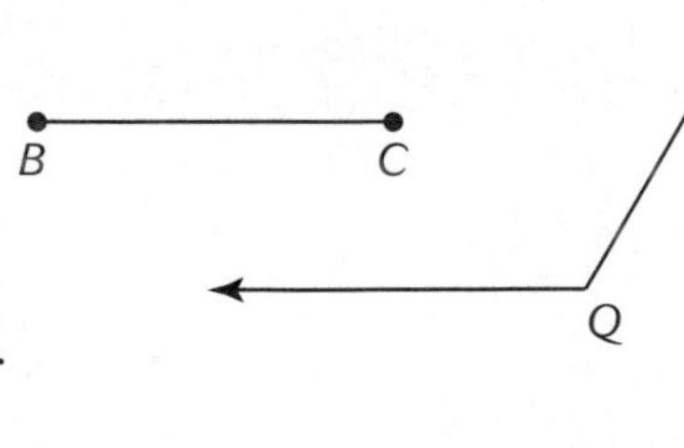

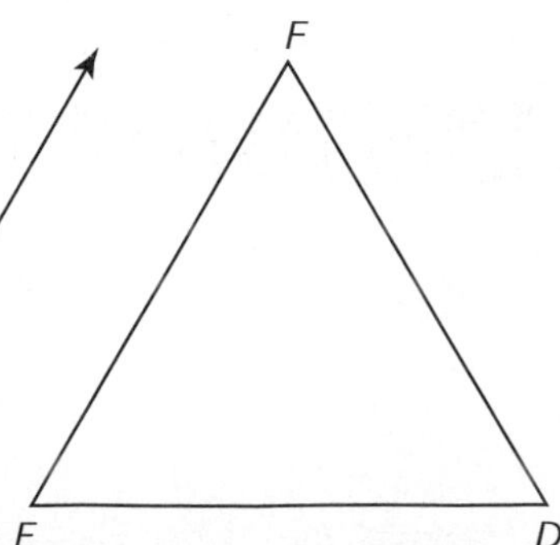

Independent Practice *For more practice, see Set H on p. 447.*

For Exercises 4–9, trace each figure at the right. Then use only a compass and straightedge to draw each congruent figure.

4. Draw $\overline{AB}$ congruent to $\overline{XY}$.

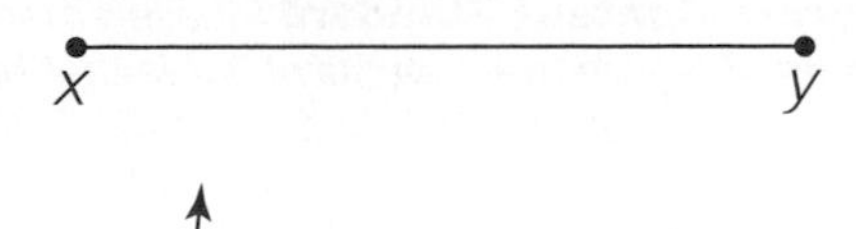

5. Draw $\angle T$ congruent to $\angle S$.

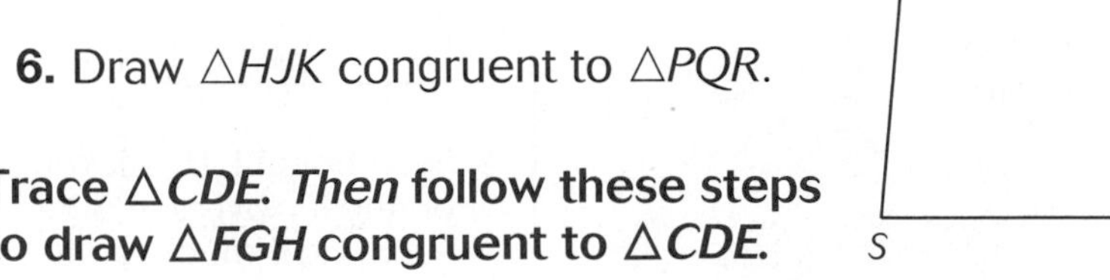

6. Draw $\triangle HJK$ congruent to $\triangle PQR$.

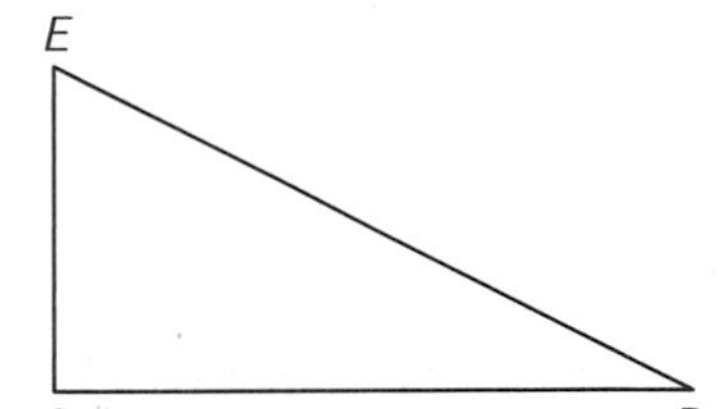

Trace $\triangle CDE$. *Then* follow these steps to draw $\triangle FGH$ congruent to $\triangle CDE$.

7. Draw $\overline{FG}$ congruent to $\overline{CD}$.

8. Set your compass for the length of $\overline{CE}$. With point F as center, make an arc.

9. Set your compass for the length of $\overline{DE}$. With point G as center, make an arc that intersects the first arc. Name the point of intersection H. Draw $\overline{FH}$ and $\overline{GH}$.

10. Trace rectangle $ABCD$ at the right. Follow these steps to draw rectangle $EFGH$ congruent to rectangle $ABCD$, using only a compass and straightedge. **(1)** Draw $\angle E$ congruent to $\angle A$. **(2)** Starting at E, draw $\overline{EF}$ congruent to $\overline{AB}$. **(3)** Draw $\angle F$ congruent to $\angle B$. **(4)** Draw $\overline{EH}$ congruent to $\overline{AD}$ and $\overline{FG}$ congruent to $\overline{BC}$. **(5)** Connect points G and H to make $\overline{GH}$.

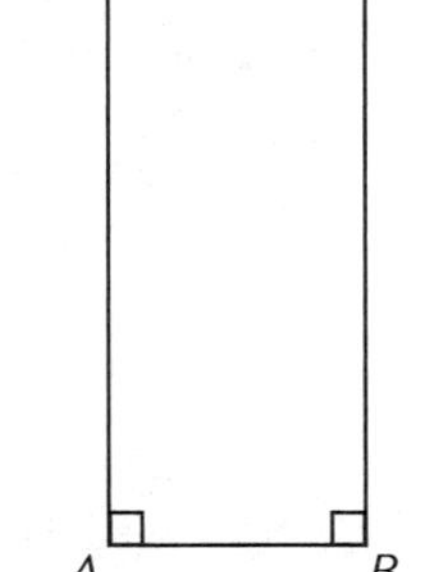

11. **Math Reasoning** Explain how you can use rectangle $ABCD$ to draw two parallel lines, $\overleftrightarrow{PQ}$ and $\overleftrightarrow{RS}$, using only a compass and straightedge. How do you know that the lines are parallel?

Mixed Review

12. Draw a triangle with a 60° angle between two 3-inch sides.

13. **Algebra** Evaluate $n + 1.5$ for $n = 2.3$.

14. Find the quotient $4.5 \div 5$.

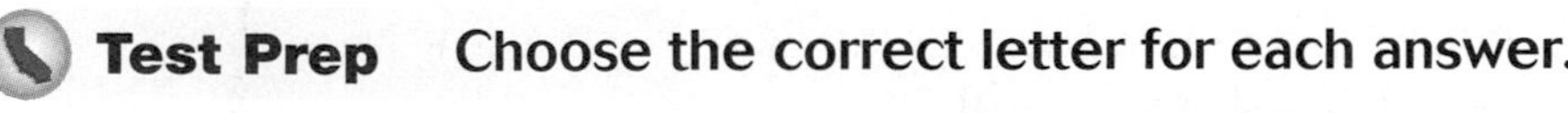

Test Prep **Choose the correct letter for each answer.**

15. Which figure is the result of turning [figure] ?
(10-9)

A 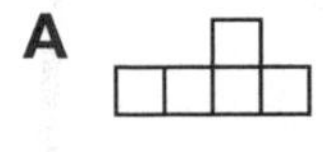

B 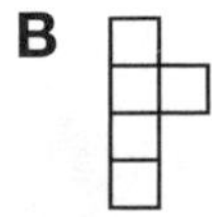

C 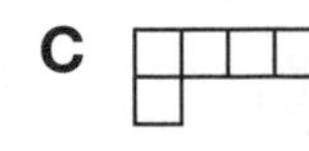

D 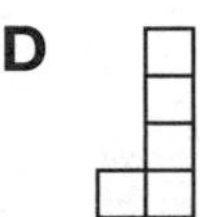

Problem-Solving Application:
Using Symmetry

 **California Content Standard** *Measurement and Geometry 3.4 (Grade 4): Identify figures that have bilateral . . . symmetry. Also Mathematical Reasoning 1.1 (See p. 401)*

Warm-Up Review

Tell if the two parts of each figure would match if you fold along the dashed line.

1. 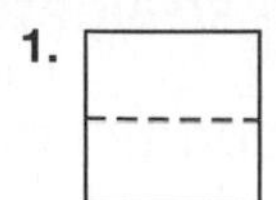
2. 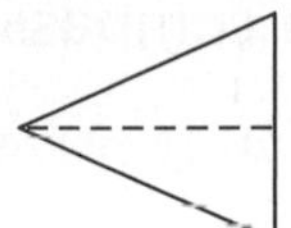
3. 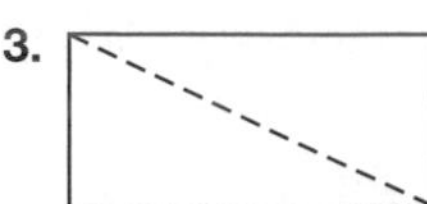
4. Sean bought 10 stickers of 4-leaf clovers at $0.25 each. How much did the stickers cost?

Word Bank

symmetry
line of symmetry

Example

Pam is creating the design for the inside of invitations that are to be folded. The design should look the same on both halves of the folded paper. Will this design work?

Understand

What do you need to find?

You need to find out whether the design can be folded so one half of the design fits exactly on the other half. That is, does the design have **symmetry?**

Plan

How can you solve the problem?

You can trace the design and cut it out. Then fold it to see if one half fits exactly on the other half.

Solve

Trace the design. The design is symmetrical because it can be folded to form two congruent parts. A line that divides a figure into congruent parts is called a **line of symmetry.**

Look Back

Would Pam's design work if the paper were folded along the dashed lines, as shown? Explain.

a. 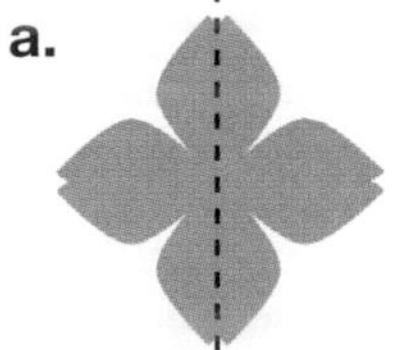

b. 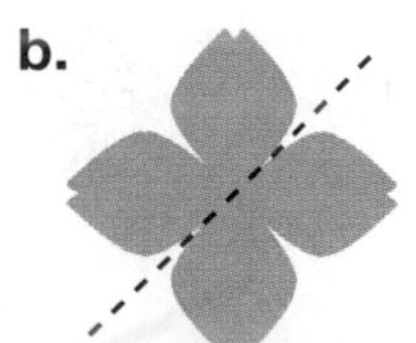

c. 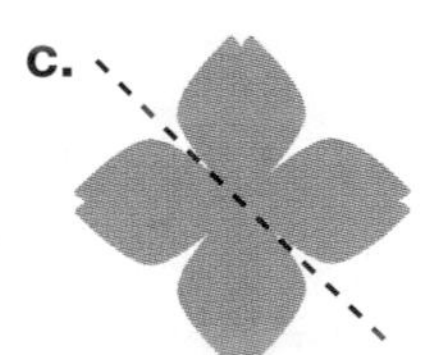

 Additional Standard: Mathematical Reasoning 2.0 (See p. 401.)

Guided Practice

Half of each design for a logo is missing. The dashed line is a line of symmetry. Solve Exercises 1–3 by tracing the design and drawing the other half.

1. 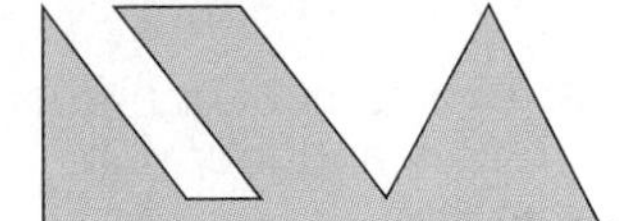

2. 

3. 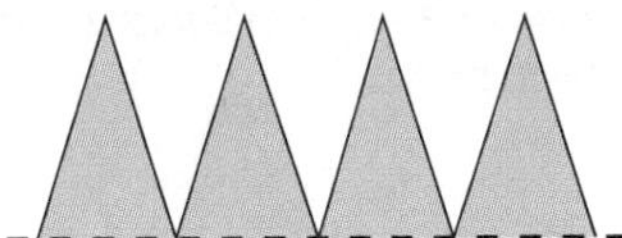

Independent Practice

For Exercises 4–6, use the directions for Exercises 1–3.

4. 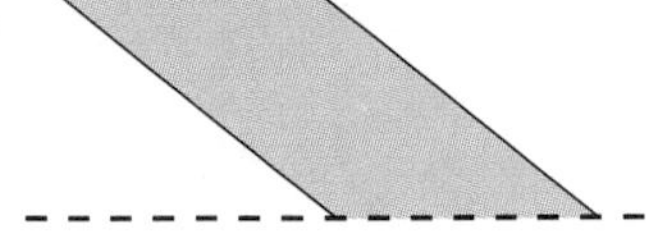

5. 

6. 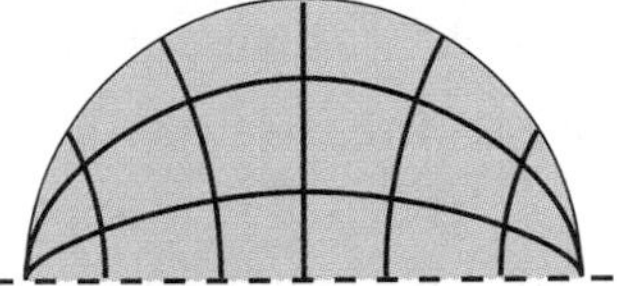

7. Trace each figure. Draw all lines of symmetry.

a. 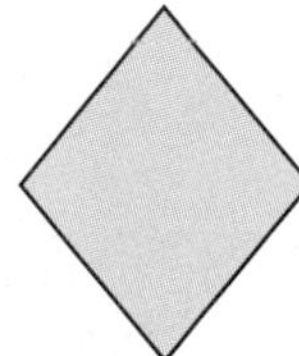

b. 

c. 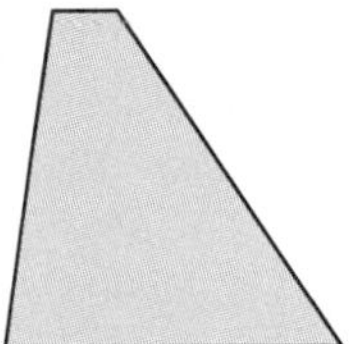

d. 

8. **Math Reasoning** The Gold Key Company uses capital letters on key chains. Which letters have lines of symmetry? Tell how many each has.

How many lines of symmetry does each polygon have?

9. Square
10. Isosceles triangle
11. Equilateral triangle
12. Regular pentagon
13. Regular hexagon
14. Regular octagon

Mixed Review

15. Mr. Chan used $\frac{3}{4}$ of a $2\frac{1}{2}$-pound bag of snow peas in a chicken casserole. How many pounds of snow peas did he use?

16. Elena studied math for $1\frac{1}{2}$ hours, science for $\frac{3}{4}$ hour, and history for $\frac{3}{4}$ hour. How long did she study in all?

Use Homework Workbook 10-11.

Solid Figures

Warm-Up Review

Give the best name for the polygon described.

1. Three congruent sides.
2. Four congruent sides and four right angles.
3. Two pairs of congruent sides and four right angles.
4. Six congruent sides.

California Content Standard *Measurement and Geometry 2.3: Visualize and draw two-dimensional views of three-dimensional objects made from rectangular solids.*

Math Link You have drawn two-dimensional figures. Now you will learn to draw three-dimensional objects as they look from various viewpoints.

You are familiar with the solid figures shown below. Recall that all kinds of prisms and pyramids are made of polygons.

A prism has two congruent bases and is named for the shape of its bases. The other sides, or faces, of a prism are parallelograms.

If you look at a prism from the top or bottom, you will see that polygon that makes up each of the bases. If you look at a prism from any other side, you will see a parallelogram.

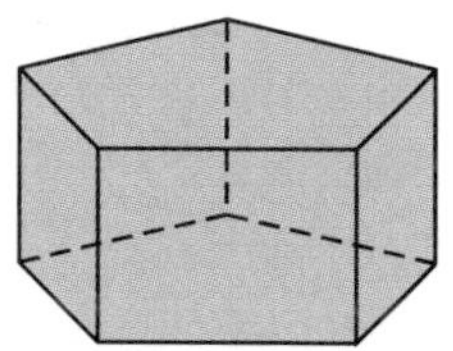
Pentagonal prism

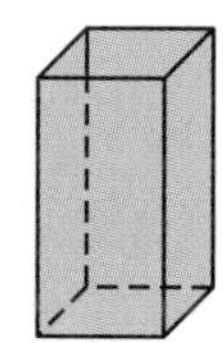
Rectangular prism

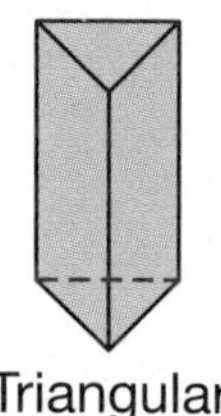
Triangular prism

A pyramid has only one base and is named for the shape of that base. The other sides, or faces, of a pyramid are always triangles.

If you look at the bottom of a pyramid, you will see the polygon that is used as the base. If you look at a pyramid from any other side, you will see a triangle.

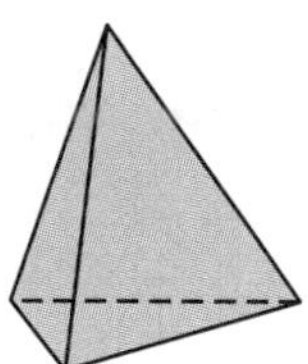
Triangular pyramid

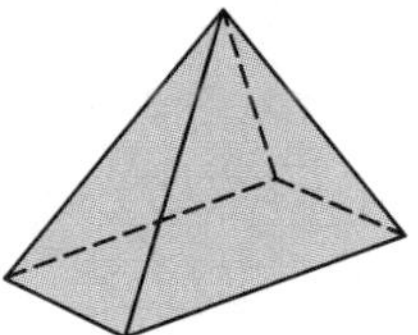
Rectangular pyramid

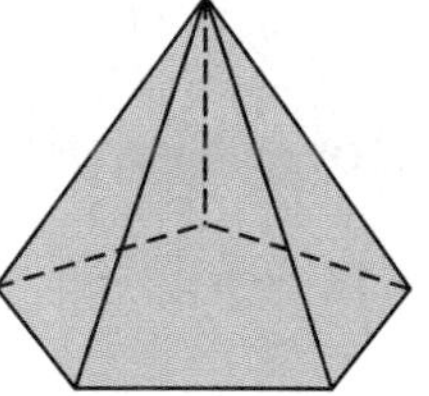
Pentagonal pyramid

Example 1

Name the solid figure and draw its top view.

The figure has two congruent bases that are octagons and its sides are parallelograms, so it is an octagonal prism.

Looking at the solid figure from the top, you would see an octagon.

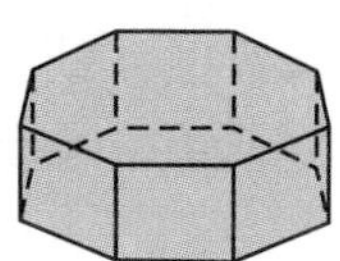

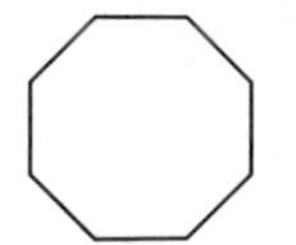

Word Bank

prism
pyramid
sphere
cylinder
cone

 Additional Standard: Mathematical Reasoning 2.3 (See p. 401.)

Some three-dimensional objects that have irregular shapes can be made up of cubes. Recall that a cube is a rectangular prism with six squares as sides.

Example 2

Draw the front, right, and top views of the three-dimensional object shown at the right. There are no hidden cubes.

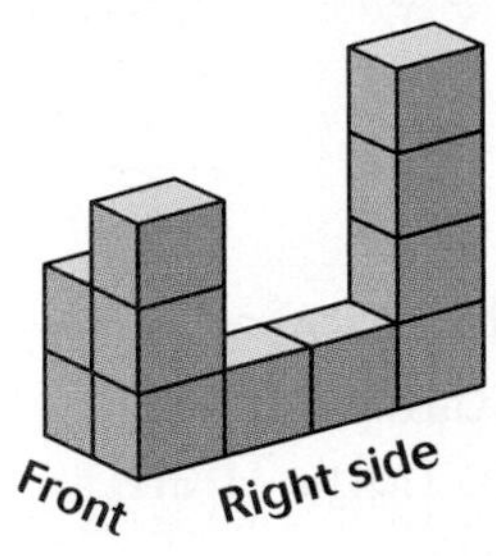

From the front, you would see a stack of 2 cubes and a stack of 4 cubes.

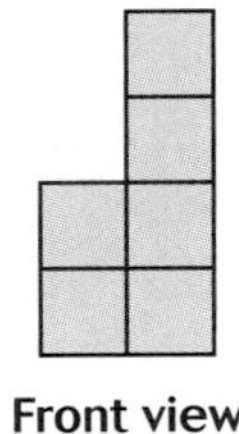

Front view

From the right, you would see a stack of 3 cubes, 2 single cubes and a stack of 4 cubes.

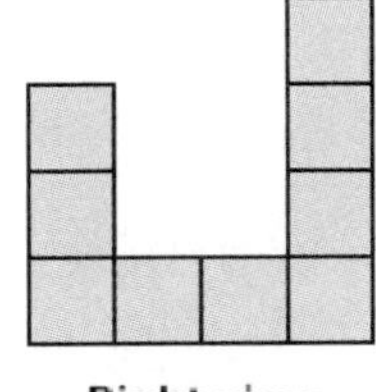

Right view

From the top, you would see only single cubes. The number in each square shows the number of cubes in that stack.

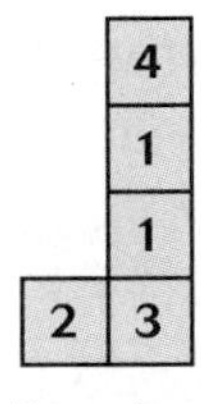

Top view

The solid figures shown below are not made up of polygons. Instead, they have curved surfaces. For all of these solids, a top or bottom view would look like a circle.

Sphere

Cylinder

Cone

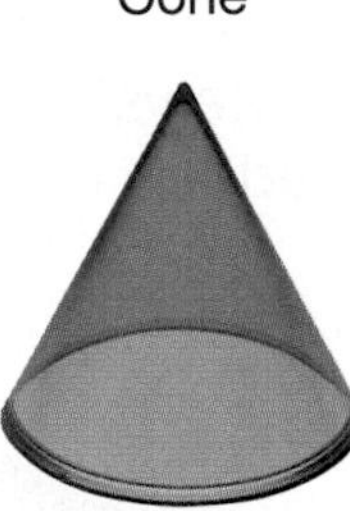

Another way to view solids is by looking at patterns from which they could be made.

Example 3

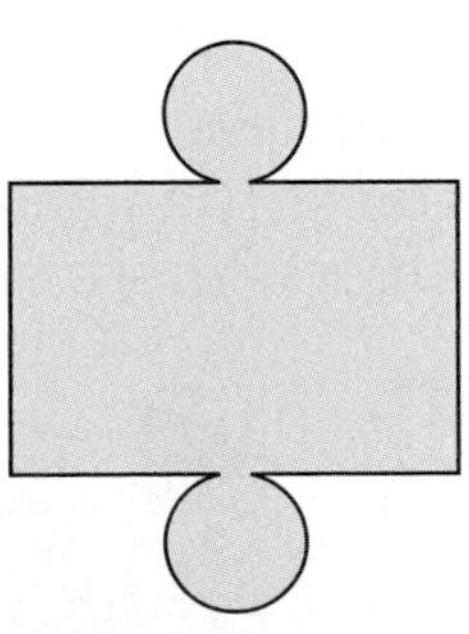

Name the solid figure that can be made from this pattern. Explain your reasoning.

The figure that can be made is a cylinder. The two circles will be the bases. The rectangle will curve around the bases to become the sides of the cylinder.

Guided Practice *For another example, see Set I on p. 444.*

Name each solid figure and draw its top view.

1. 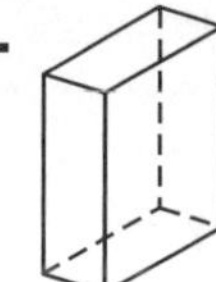

2. 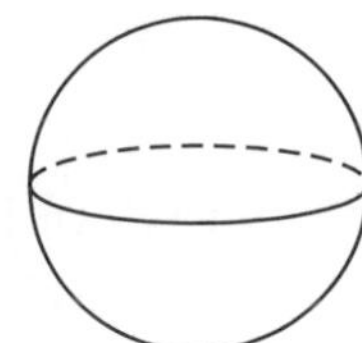

3. Draw the front, right, and top views of the three-dimensional object shown at the right. There are no hidden cubes.

4. Name the solid figure that can be made from the pattern shown at the right.

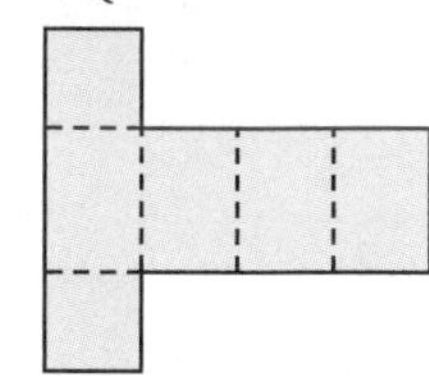

Independent Practice *For more practice, see Set I on p. 447.*

Name each solid figure and draw its top view.

5. 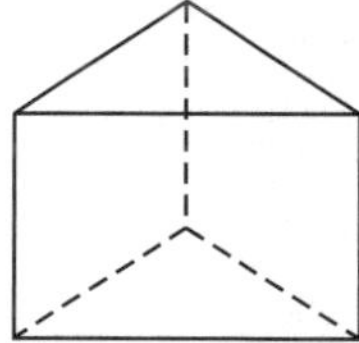

6. 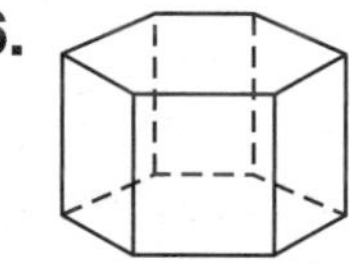

7. 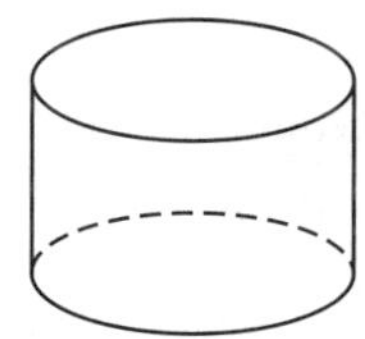

Draw the front, right, and top views of each three-dimensional object shown. There are no hidden cubes.

8. 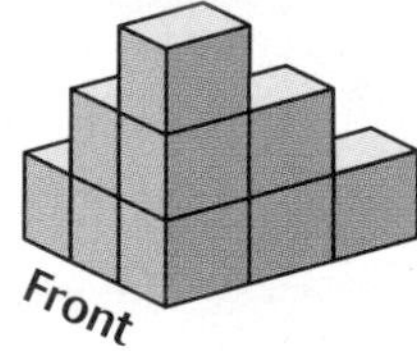

9. 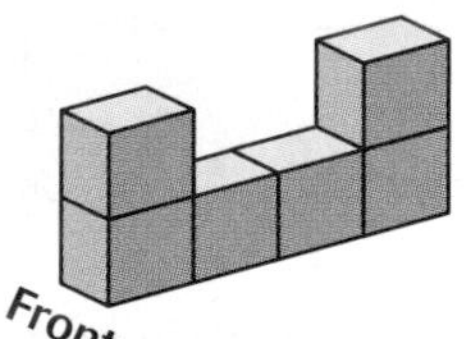

10. 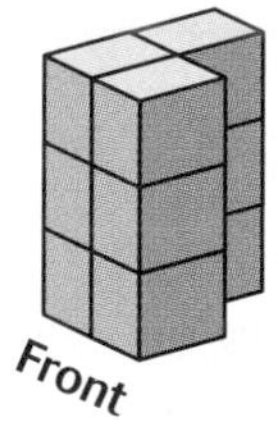

Draw the top view of each three-dimensional object shown. Label each square to indicate the number of cubes in each stack. Then find the total number of cubes used in making the object. There are no hidden cubes.

11. 

12. 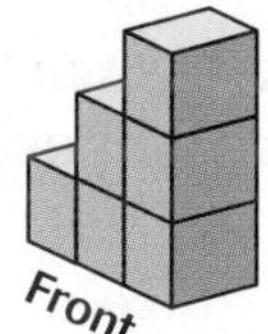

13. 

Name the solid figure that can be made from each pattern. Explain your reasoning.

14.

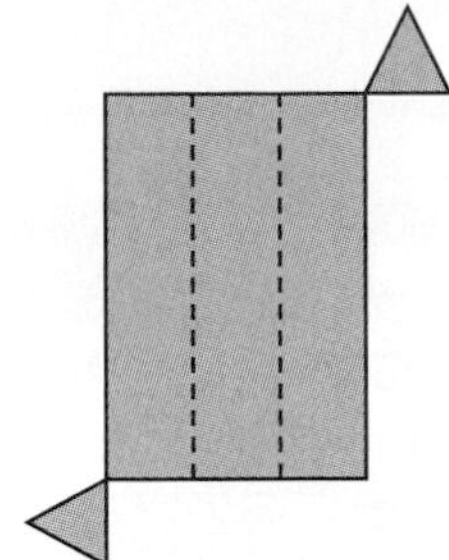

15.

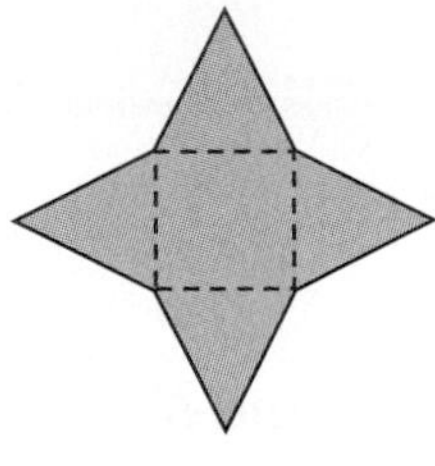

16.

17. Math Reasoning Name the solid figure shown at the right. Then tell how you would describe it to someone over the phone. Include a description of how it would look from the bottom and from any side. Then draw a pattern that could be used to make the figure.

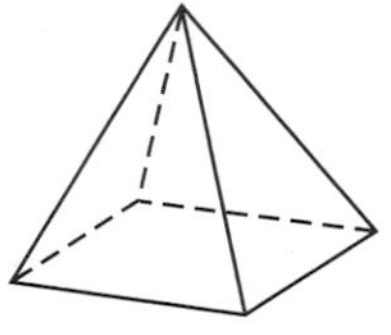

For each building pictured, draw the shape of the view indicated.

18. Top view

19. Front view

20. Side view

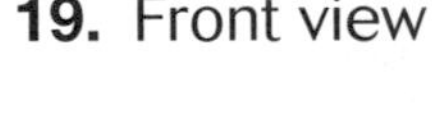

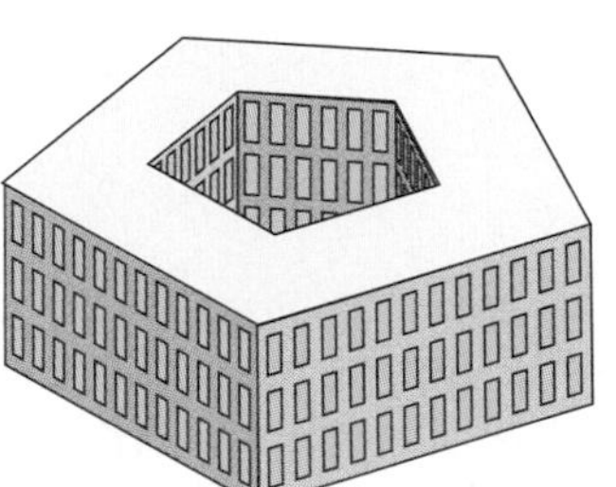

Pentagon, Washington, D.C.

House

Clock Tower

Mixed Review

21. Tell what transformation is illustrated. Write *slide, flip,* or *turn*.

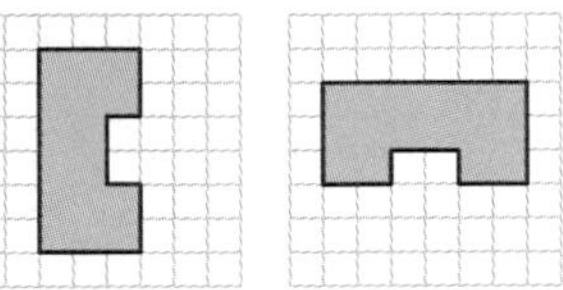

22. At midnight the temperature was 9°F. It then dropped 12° by morning. By noon the temperature rose 10°. What was the temperature at noon?

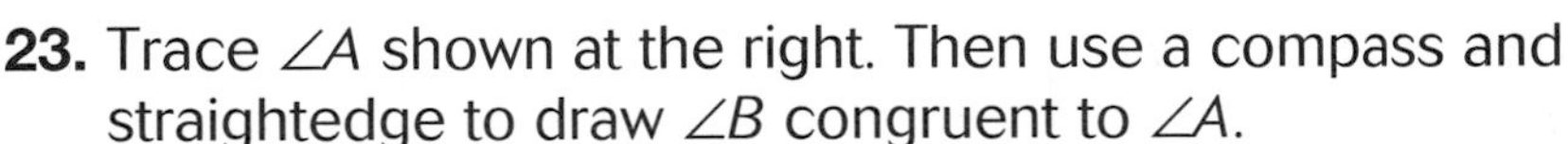

23. Trace $\angle A$ shown at the right. Then use a compass and straightedge to draw $\angle B$ congruent to $\angle A$.

Test Prep **Choose the correct letter for each answer.**

24. Find the GCF of 32 and 48.
(7-3)

A 48 **B** 32 **C** 8 **D** 16

25. Find the LCM of 9 and 12.
(7-4)

A 3 **B** 36 **C** 18 **D** 108

Diagnostic Checkpoint

Complete. For exercises 1–3 choose words from the Word Bank.

Word Bank
congruent figures
line
point
polygon
prism

1. (10-9) Figures that have the same size and same shape are called ____________.

2. (10-3) A ____________ is a closed figure made up of three or more line segments.

3. (10-12) A ____________ has two congruent bases and is named for the shape of its bases.

4. (10-6) Draw a parallelogram with 4-cm and 1-cm sides, and 130° and 50° angles.

5. (10-7) Draw a triangle with a 90° angle between two 1-inch sides.

6. (10-8) Draw the next 3 figures in the pattern.

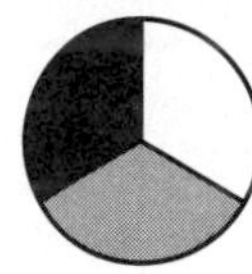 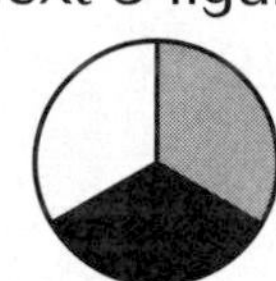 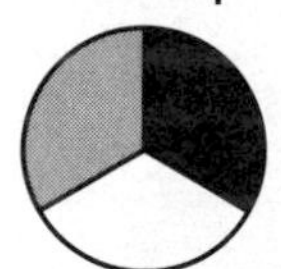 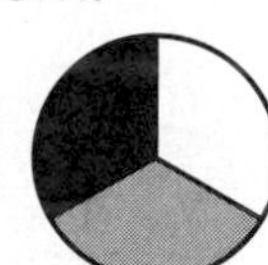

7. (10-9) Write *slide*, *flip*, or *turn* to tell how the figure was moved.

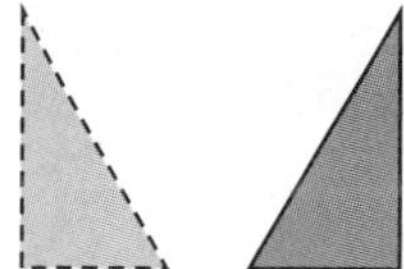

8. (10–12) Name the solid figure that can be drawn from the pattern shown.

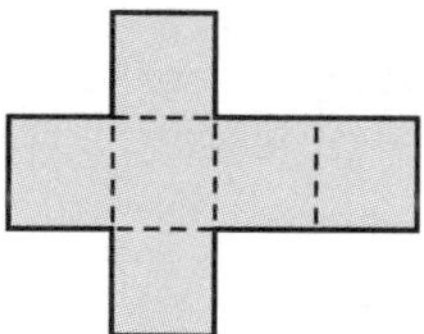

9. (10-11) How many lines of symmetry can be drawn on the figure?

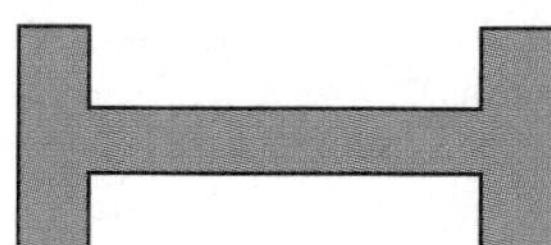

10. (10-10) Trace ∠*M*. Then use only a compass and straightedge to draw ∠*Q* congruent to ∠*M*.

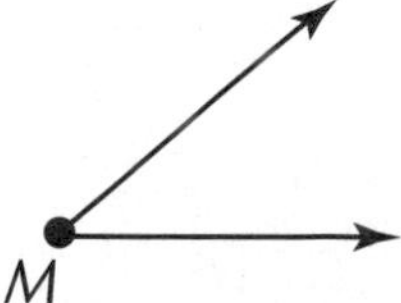

Chapter 10 Test

Use the Figure at the right for Exercises 1-4.

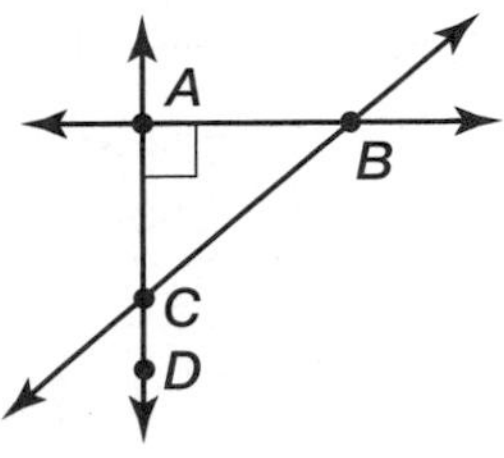

1. Name a line segment.
2. Name a pair of perpendicular lines.
3. Classify and measure $\angle ABC$.
4. Using only a compass and straightedge, draw an angle congruent to $\angle DCB$.

Classify each figure in as many ways as possible.

5. 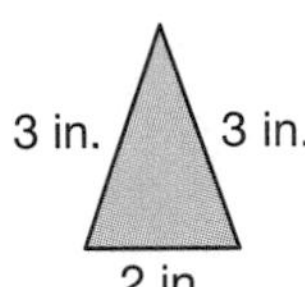

6. 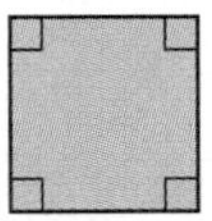

7. If 2 angles of a right triangle have the same measure, what is the measure of each?

Draw each figure with the given measures.

8. Triangle with a 75° angle between two 5-cm sides
9. Rhombus with $\frac{3}{4}$-inch sides, and 25° and 155° angles
10. Trace the figure and then draw the lines of symmetry.

11. Tell how the figure was moved from Position A to Position B.

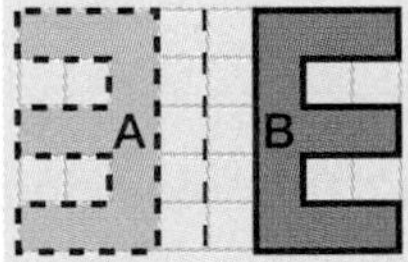

12. Name the solid figure.

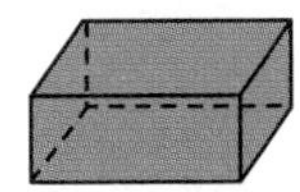

13. Draw the top view of the solid shown. There are no hidden cubes.

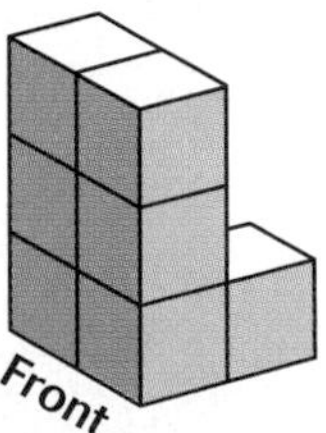

14. Draw the next 3 figures in the pattern.

15. In how many different ways can the tile at the right be positioned so that a star is in the top left corner?

Multiple-Choice Chapter 10 Test

Choose the correct letter for each answer.

1. Choose the correct top view for the solid shown below.

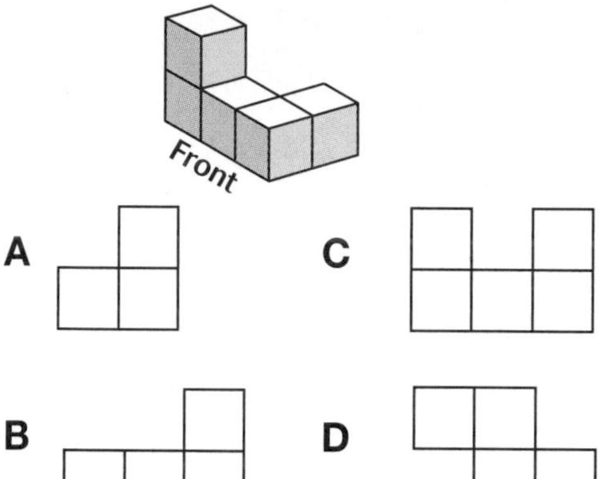

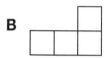

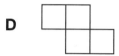

2. Winton drew a triangle with a 4 cm side between 40° and 78° angles. Which classifies the triangle?

F acute and scalene
G right and isosceles
H obtuse and scalene
J equilateral

3. Which comes next in the following pattern?

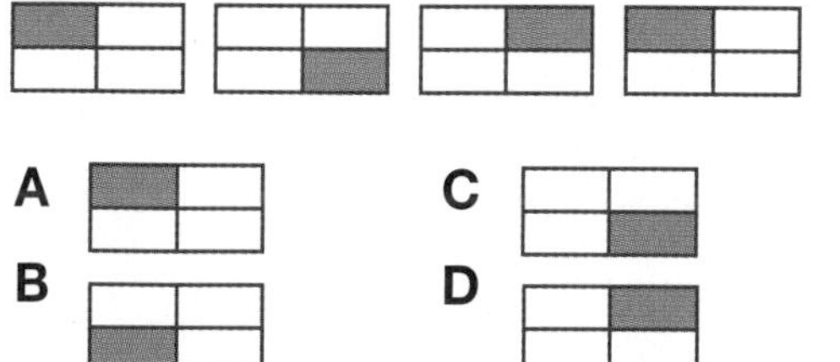

4. How many lines of symmetry does a rhombus have?

F 0
G 1
H 2
J 4

5. Which plane figure forms the base of a rectangular prism?

A Trapezoid
B Rectangle
C Circle
D Triangle

6. Which shape appears to be congruent to Figure 1?

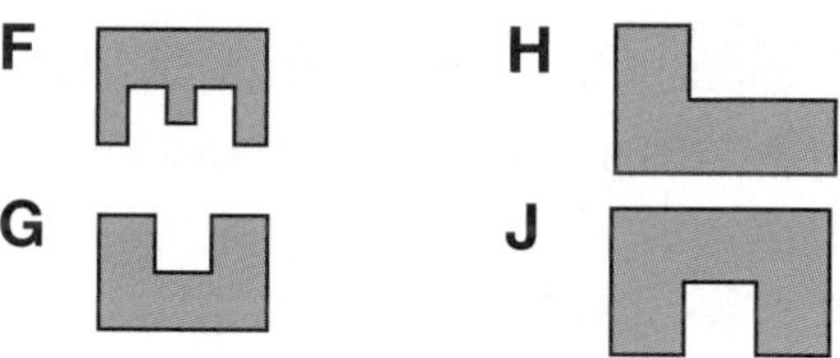

7. Which best describes the figure?

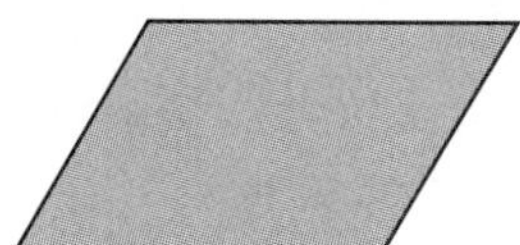

A rhombus
B parallelogram
C trapezoid
D rectangle

8. Three angles of a quadrilateral measure 35°, 65°, and 140°. What is the measure of the 4th angle?

F 60°
G 90°
H 120°
J 240°

Use the diagram below for Questions 9–11.

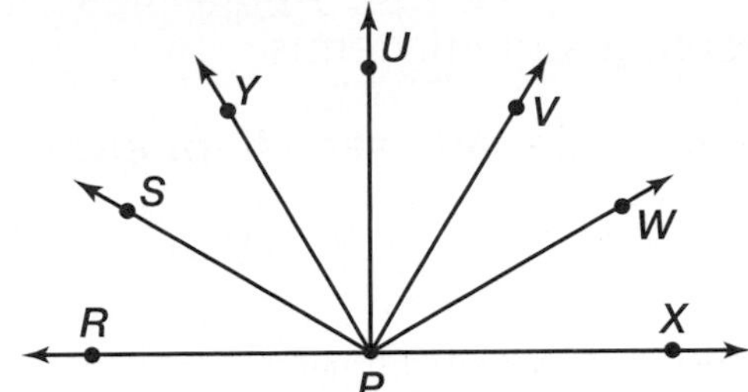

9. Classify $\angle RPU$ and $\angle XPU$.

   A acute angles
   B obtuse angles
   C straight angles
   D right angles

10. Which angle appears to be congruent to $\angle VPW$?

   F $\angle YPW$
   G $\angle RPW$
   H $\angle SPY$
   J $\angle UPW$

11. Which segment is perpendicular to $\overleftrightarrow{XR}$?

   A $\overline{SP}$
   B $\overline{WP}$
   C $\overline{UP}$
   D $\overline{XP}$

12. Flipping a figure to the left and then flipping it up results in which single transformation?

   F flip
   G slide
   H turn
   J reflection

13. Figure $ABCD$ is a rhombus. Which line segment is parallel to line segment AB?

   A $\overline{BC}$
   B $\overline{DC}$
   C $\overline{DA}$
   D $\overline{BD}$

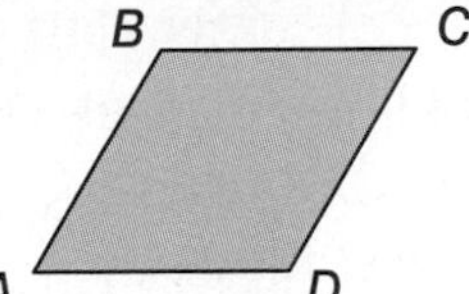

14. Which of the following letters have lines of symmetry?

   A F G W Z

   F only A
   G only W
   H A, F, and Z
   J A and W

15. Two angle measures of a triangle are 90° and 41°. Which describes the third angle?

   A A right angle
   B A 49° acute angle
   C A 41° acute angle
   D A 229° obtuse angle

16. What figure can be drawn given the following segments and angles?

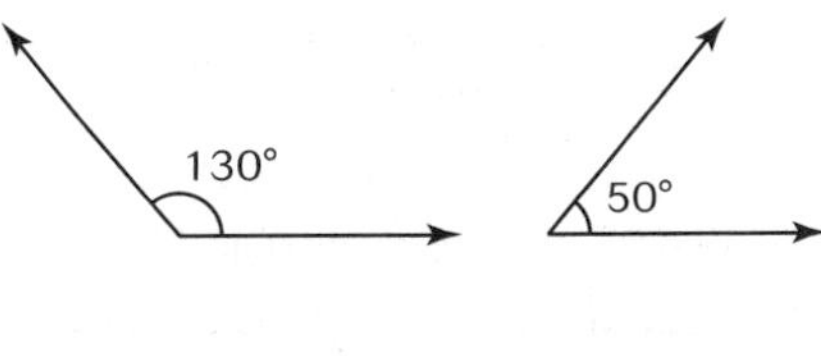

   F parallelogram
   G rhombus
   H rectangle
   J square

Reteaching

Set A (pages 402–404)

Draw and label an example of a line parallel to $\overleftrightarrow{XY}$.

Parallel lines do not intersect but are in the same plane.

$\overleftrightarrow{ST} \parallel \overleftrightarrow{XY}$

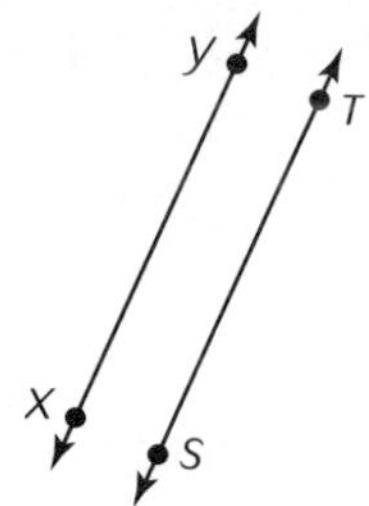

Remember to use the symbols that represent geometric terms.

Draw and label an example of each.

1. line *QR*

2. ray *ST*

3. Two intersecting lines

4. Two perpendicular lines

Set B (pages 405–407)

Classify a 115° angle. Then use a protractor to draw the angle.

A 115° angle is more than 90° and less than 180°, so 115° is an obtuse angle.

Use your protractor to mark off a 115° measure. Use a straightedge to draw the angle.

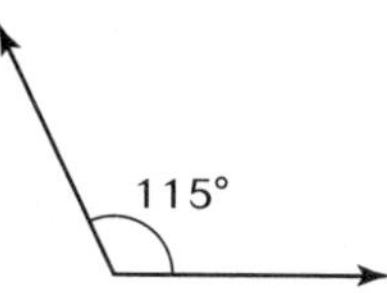

Remember an acute angle measures less than 90°, a right angle measures exactly 90°, an obtuse angle measures greater than 90° and less than 180°. A straight angle measures 180°.

Classify each angle. Then use a protractor to draw each angle.

1. 12°

2. 165°

3. 180°

4. 91°

Set C (pages 408–411)

Name the following polygon. Tell if it is regular.

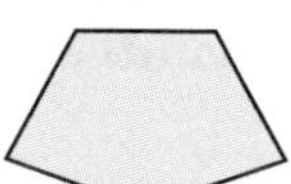

The figure has 5 sides. It is called a pentagon. It is not a regular pentagon because the sides have different lengths and the angles have different measures.

Remember a regular polygon is one in which all sides have the same length and all angles have the same measure.

Name each polygon. Tell if it is regular.

1. 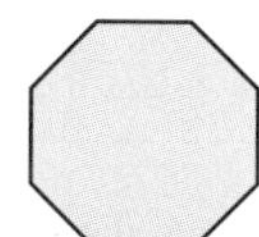

2. 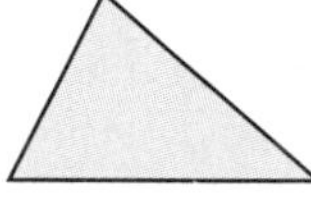

3. 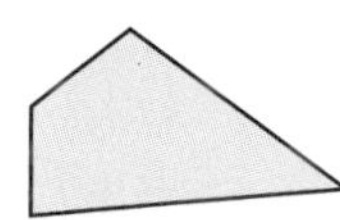

Set D (pages 414–416)

Classify the following triangle by its sides and its angles.

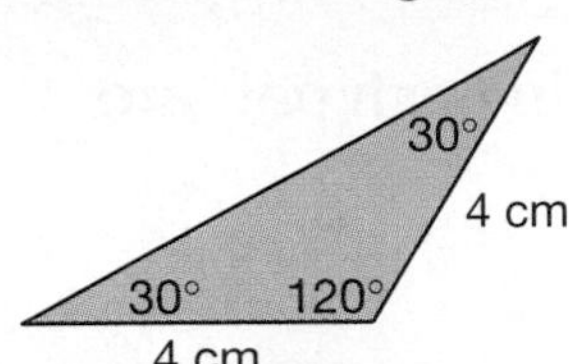

Since two of the side lengths are the same, the triangle is isosceles. Since one of the angles in the triangle is greater than 90°, the triangle is obtuse.

Remember a triangle can be classified by its angle measures as a right, acute, or obtuse triangle, or by the length of its sides as equilateral, isosceles, or scalene.

Classify each triangle by its sides and its angles.

1.

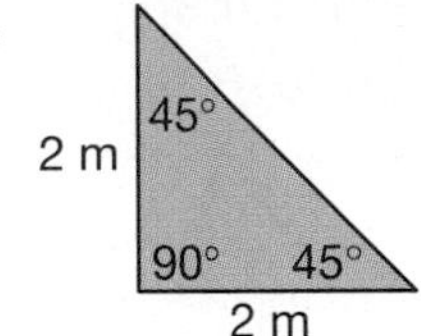

2.

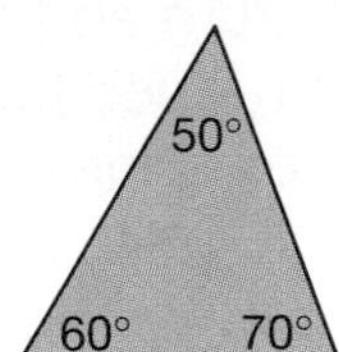

Set E (pages (418–420)

Draw a parallelogram given the following information.

Rhombus with 1.5-cm sides and 110° and 79° angles

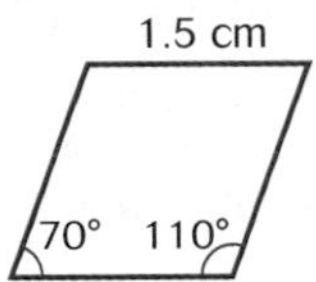

Step 1 Draw a 1.5-cm segment.

Step 2 Draw a 70° angle at one end and a 110° angle at the other end of the segment.

Step 3 Mark off 1.5-cm on each ray. Connect the two points.

Remember to use your ruler and protractor when drawing parallelograms.

Draw a parallelogram given the following information.

1. Rectangle with $1\frac{1}{2}$-inch and 3-inch sides
2. Square with 1-cm sides
3. Parallelogram with 45° and 135° angle

Set F (pages 421–423)

Draw and classify a triangle with a 75° angle between two sides measuring 1.5 cm.

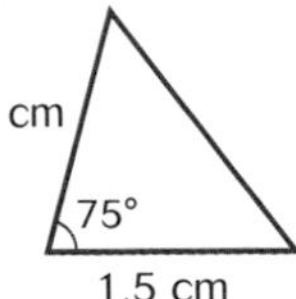

Step 1 Use your protractor to draw a 75° angle.

Step 2 Mark off 1.5 cm on each angle ray. Connect the two points.

The triangle is acute and isosceles.

Remember to classify the triangle by its angles and its sides.

Draw and classify each triangle given the following information.

1. 4.5-cm side between two 80° angles.
2. 135° angle between two $\frac{1}{2}$-inch sides.

Reteaching (continued)

Set G (pages 426–428)

State if the figures in each pair are congruent.

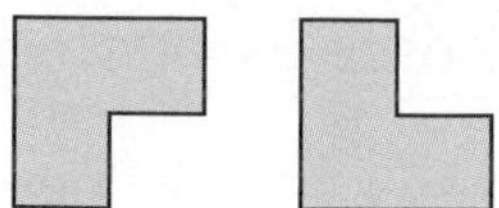

You could turn and then slide the first figure to produce the second figure; so they are congruent.

Remember congruent figures have the same shape and the same size.

State if the figures in each pair are congruent.

1. 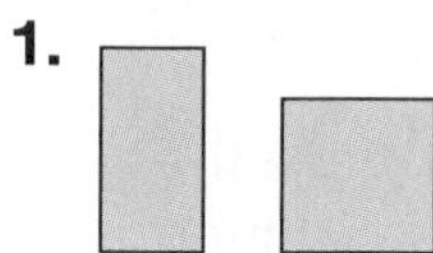

2.

3. Describe how the figure in Question 2 was moved from the first position to the second position.

Set H (pages 429–431)

Use only a compass and a straightedge to draw $\overline{AB}$ congruent to $\overline{CD}$.

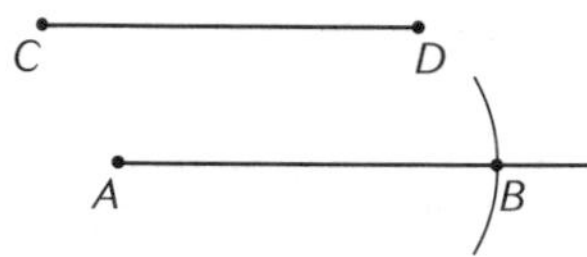

Step 1 Draw a ray. Label the endpoint *A*.

Step 2 Use a compass to mark the position of point *B*. Mark the ray with an arc.

Step 3 Label the point *B*.

Remember you can use a compass and a straightedge to draw congruent figures.

Trace each figure below. Use only a compass and a straightedge to draw the following.

1. $\angle XYZ \cong \angle STU$

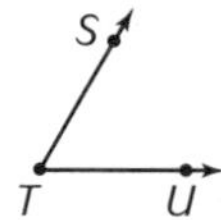

2. $\triangle QRS \cong \triangle ABC$

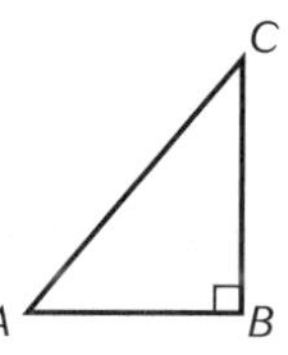

Set I (pages 434–437)

Name the solid figure.

The sides of the figure are parallelograms and the bases are triangles. The figure is a triangular prism.

Remember, the sides or faces of a prism are parallelograms, and the sides or faces of a pyramid are triangles.

Name each solid figure.

1. 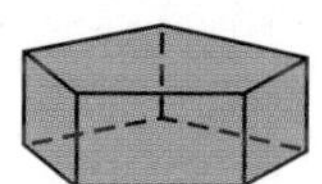

2. 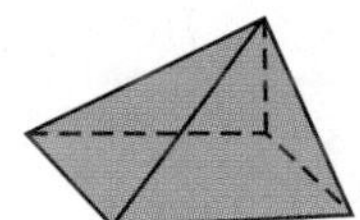

More Practice

Set A (pages 402–404)

Name or describe each figure.

1. A B

2. X Y

3. P Q

Draw and label an example of each.

4. a line segment with end points *X* and *Y*.

5. two parallel lines

6. plane *XYZ*

Set B (pages 405–407)

Classify each angle as acute, obtuse, right, or straight. Then use a protractor to measure each angle.

1. 

2. 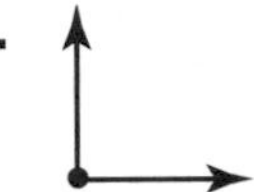

3. 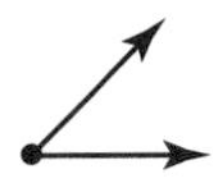

4.

Use a protractor to draw each angle.

5. 75° angle

6. 130° angle

7. 35° angle

8. 90° angle

9. The angle a kite string makes with the ground is 52°. Classify this angle.

Set C (pages 408–411)

Name each polygon. Tell if it is regular.

1. 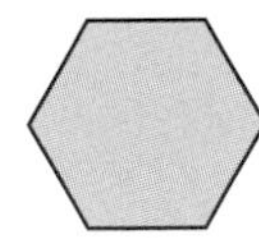

2. 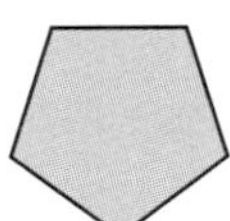

3. 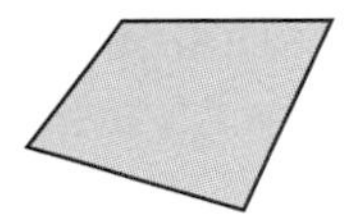

4. 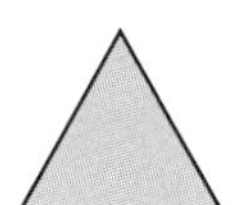

Identify each quadrilateral in the figure at the right.

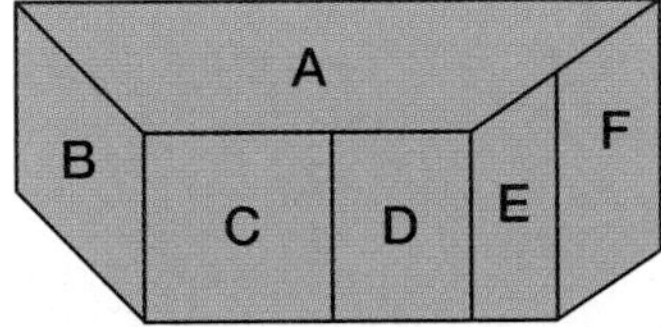

5. A

6. B

7. C

8. D

9. E

10. F

11. Can a hexagon be classified as a pentagon? Explain.

More Practice (continued)

Set D *(pages 414–416)*

Classify each triangle by its sides and by its angles.

1. 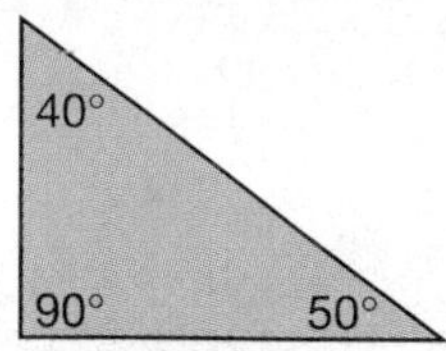

2. 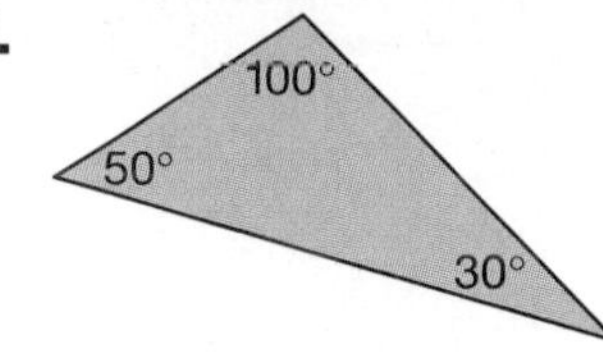

3. 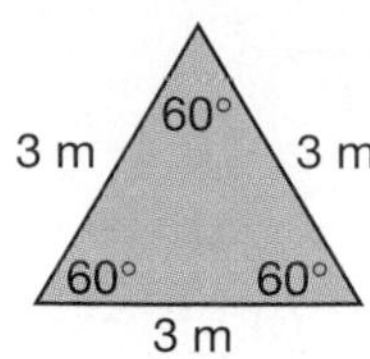

4. An isosceles right triangle has one angle that measures 45°. What is the measure of the other angles?

Set E *(pages 418–420)*

Draw a parallelogram with the given measures or given segments and angles.

1. 3-inch and 5-inch sides and 70° and 110° angles.
2. Rectangle
3. Square with 6-cm sides
4. Rhombus with 2-inch sides and 30° and 150° angles
5. Draw a rectangle with sides measuring 1.5 cm and 3 cm.

Set F *(pages 421–423)*

Draw a triangle with the given sides and angles. Then classify each triangle by its angles and its sides.

1. 110° angle between two 6-cm sides.
2. 4-inch side between two 45° angles.
3. 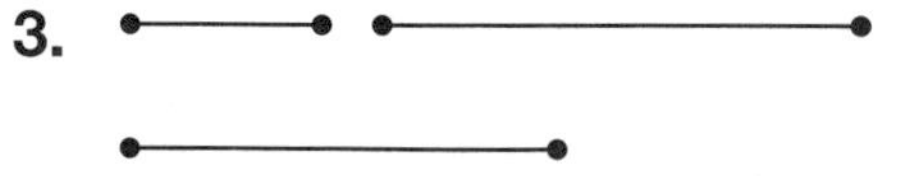
4. 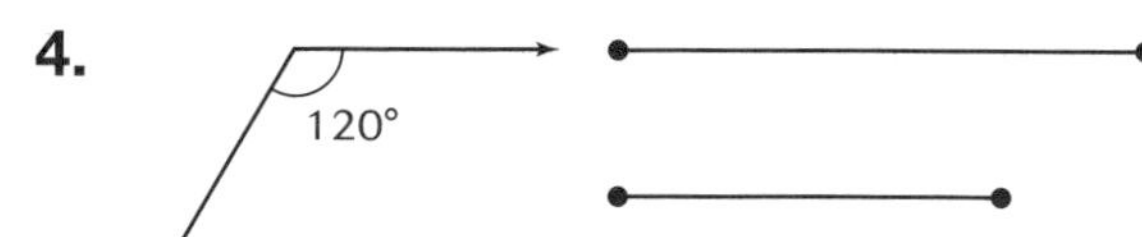

5. Draw a square that measures 6 cm on each side. Then draw 2 segments connecting the opposite corners. What are the angle measures within each of the four isosceles triangles?

Set G (pages 426–428)

Decide if the figures in each pair are congruent. Write *yes* or *no*.

1. 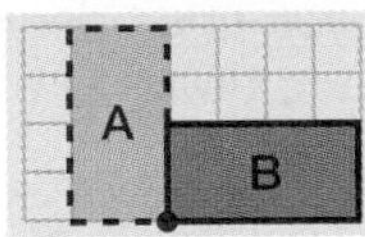

2. 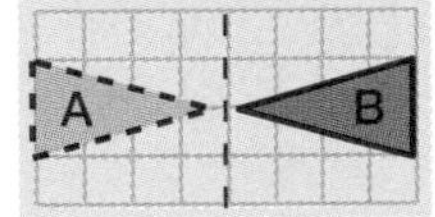

3. 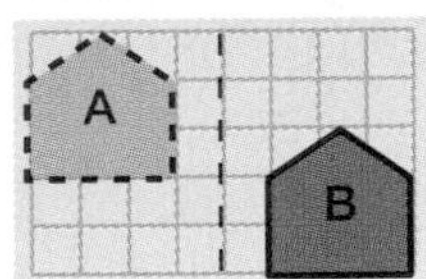

Tell how each figure was moved from position A to position B.

4.

5.

6.

Set H (pages 429–431)

Trace each figure at the right. Then use only a compass and a straight edge to draw each congruent figure.

1. Draw △*QRS* congruent to △*XYZ*.

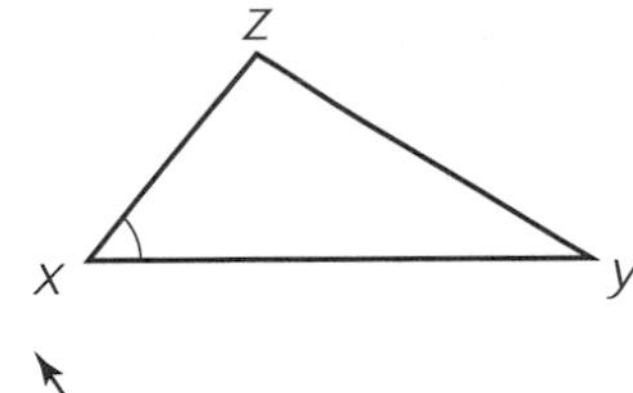

2. Draw ∠*A* congruent to∠*S*.

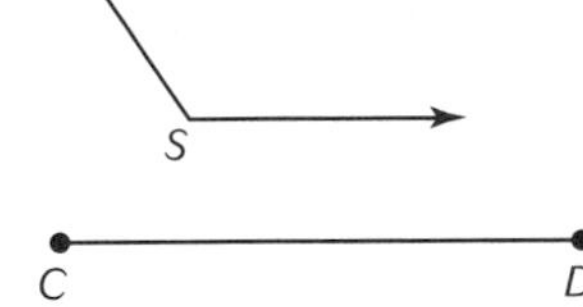

3. Draw $\overline{WY}$ congruent to $\overline{CD}$.

Set I (pages 434–437)

Name each solid figure and draw its top view.

1. 

2. 

Name the solid figure that can be made from each pattern.

3. 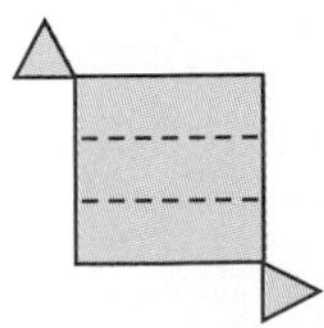

4. 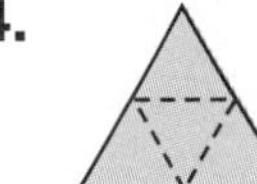

Problem Solving: Preparing for Tests

Choose the correct letter for each answer.

---

1. **Julie started with $78 in her savings account. During the next 3 months, she doubled her savings. Then she spent $23 on a magazine subscription. Which number sentence could be used to find the money she has left?**

   A $(78 \times 2) - 23 = n$

   B $(78 \times 3) - 23 = n$

   C $(78 - 23) \times 2 = n$

   D $2 \times (78 - 23) = n$

Tip

When more than one step is needed to solve a problem, you must decide both what to do and in what order to do it .

---

2. **Herman had an 18-inch by 24-inch sheet of paper. He folded it in thirds the long way so that each fold was 24 inches long. Then he folded the paper in half the short way. What was the length and width of each section of the folded paper?**

   F 6 inches by 9 inches

   G 8 inches by 9 inches

   H 6 inches by 12 inches

   J 9 inches by 12 inches

Tip

You can Draw a Diagram to help you solve this problem.

---

3. **Fred had 10 pieces of scrap lumber. He paid $0.50 for the longest piece, which is 1.3 m. The shortest piece is 0.65 m. Which is reasonable for the total length of the scraps?**

   A Between 0.65 m and 1.3 meters

   B Less than 6.5 meters

   C Between 6.5 m and 13 meters

   D Greater than 13 meters

Tip

Try using one of these strategies.

- *Draw a Diagram*
- *Solve a Simpler Problem*

4. One angle of a triangle measures 42°. The other two angles are congruent. What is the measure of the greatest angle in this triangle?

F 42°

G 48°

H 69°

J 138°

5. Mike used $2\frac{1}{4}$ cups of peppers, $4\frac{3}{4}$ cups of tomatoes, and 3 cups of onions for salsa. How many cups of ingredients did he use altogether?

A 10 cups

B $9\frac{1}{4}$ cups

C $7\frac{3}{4}$ cups

D $5\frac{1}{4}$ cups

6. A bag contains 4 blue, 12 red, 1 green, and 5 yellow counters. Linda picked out 1 counter 20 times, replacing it each time. Which color did Linda probably pick out the greatest number of times?

F Blue

G Green

H Red

J Yellow

7. A shop sells picture frames in these sizes: 2 inches by 3 inches, 4 inches by 6 inches, 6 inches by 9 inches, and 8 inches by 12 inches. What would be the measure of the next largest frame if the pattern continues?

A 8 inches by 14 inches

B 9 inches by 12 inches

C 9 inches by 15 inches

D 10 inches by 15 inches

8. An airplane flight is scheduled to land at 3:30 P.M. Which information do you need to estimate how much time the flight should take?

F The time the plane is scheduled to take off

G How fast the plane will travel

H The distance the plane will fly

J The size and type of the plane

9. A fountain 6 meters high has sides with these lengths: 3.2 m, 5.6 m, 5.6 m, 2.08 m, and 2.08 m. Which is a reasonable measure of the distance around the fountain?

A Less than 15 m

B Between 15 m and 17 m

C Between 17 m and 19 m

D More than 20 m

10. How many right angles are there at the intersection of Pine and Third?

F 0

G 1

H 2

J 4

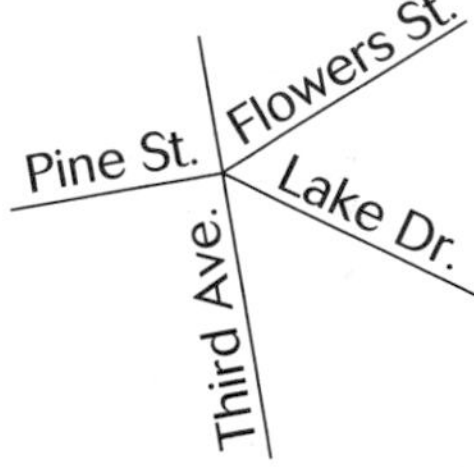

11. As mileage pay, Liam was paid $5\frac{1}{4}$ cents for every mile he traveled over 25 miles. Last week he traveled 33 miles. How much mileage pay did he receive?

A 42 cents

B $4.20

C $42.00

D $173.25

TEST PREP

Multiple-Choice Cumulative Review

Choose the correct letter for each answer.

Number Sense

1. Find 105 ÷ 30.

   A 2 R13
   B 3
   C 3 R15
   D 4

2. Gil sold stationery to help raise money for his school. He sold 2 boxes at $4.50 each, 3 boxes at $5.00 each, and 1 set of cards for $2.25. How much did he raise?

   F $16.25
   G $16.75
   H $24.25
   J $26.25

3. Rawhide dog bones are on sale at 4 for $5.00. How much would 20 bones cost?

   A $20
   B $25
   C $40
   D $100

4. Find 367 + 2,049 + 853 + 4,588.

   F 7,857
   G 7,587
   H 6,857
   J 6,557

Measurement and Geometry

5. A certain polygon has one more side than a pentagon. How many angles does that polygon have?

   A 5 C 7
   B 6 D 8

6. A polygon has three sides and three 60° angles. Which polygon is it?

   F Pentagon
   G Hexagon
   H Equilateral triangle
   J Scalene triangle

7. Which transformation was used to move the figure from Position A to position B?

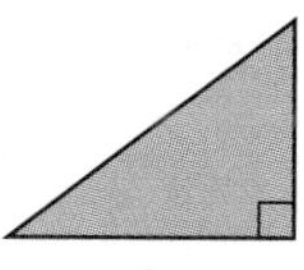

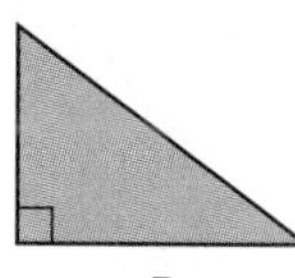

   A Flip C Turn
   B Slide D Graph

8. A piece of lumber is $7\frac{1}{2}$ ft long. How many boards can you cut from the piece of lumber if each board must be $\frac{5}{8}$ ft long?

   F 6 H 12
   G 8 J 15

Measurement and Geometry

9. Andrew is putting a wallpaper border along the top of each wall in his room. The room is 12 ft wide and 18 ft long. How many feet of wallpaper border does he need?

   A 216 feet **C** 60 feet
   B 72 feet **D** 20 feet

10. Grant just built an addition with an area of 300 square feet onto his house. Last year he had a greenhouse with an area of 200 square feet built in the back yard. If the width of the new addition is 20 feet, what is the length? (Area = length × width)

    F 100 feet
    G 60 feet
    H 40 feet
    J 15 feet

11. Lee's sister weighed 6 lb 13 oz when she was born. A year later she weighed 22 lb 10 oz. How much did she gain in one year? (1 lb = 16 oz)

    A 16 lb 13 oz
    B 16 lb 3 oz
    C 15 lb 13 oz
    D 15 lb 3 oz

12. A shoe box is 12 inches long, 5 inches wide, and 4 inches deep. What is the perimeter of the bottom of the box?

    F 240 inches **H** 34 inches
    G 40 inches **J** 21 inches

Statistics, Data Analysis, and Probability

Use the chart for Questions 13-14

Walking Program

Day	Distance
1	$\frac{1}{2}$ mi
2	$\frac{1}{2}$ mi
3	$\frac{3}{4}$ mi
4	1 mi
5	$1\frac{1}{4}$ mi
6	$1\frac{1}{2}$ mi
7	$1\frac{1}{2}$ mi

13. What is the mean, or average, distance walked in the seven days?

    A $\frac{1}{2}$ mile **C** 1 mile
    B $\frac{3}{4}$ mile **D** $1\frac{1}{4}$ miles

14. How many more miles are walked on days 5, 6, and 7 than on days 1, 2, 3, and 4?

    F $1\frac{1}{4}$ **H** 2
    G $1\frac{1}{2}$ **J** $3\frac{3}{4}$

15. There are 3 red pens, 2 blue pens, and 4 purple pens in a box. If 1 pen is chosen without looking, what is the probability that the pen will be green?

    A 1 **C** $\frac{1}{3}$
    B $\frac{4}{9}$ **D** 0

Measurement

Diagnosing Readiness

In Chapter 11, you will use these skills:

A Adding Whole Numbers, Decimals, and Fractions

(pages 60–65, 322–323)

Find each sum or difference.

1. 860 + 250 + 175 + 25
2. 19.3 + 8.48 + 17.3
3. $26\frac{1}{12} + 97 + 4\frac{2}{3}$
4. Many of the students at Rite High attended the baseball game. 114 of the students were seniors, 87 were juniors, and 93 were sophomores. No freshmen attended. How many students attended the game?

B Drawing Segments

(Grade 4)

Use a ruler to draw segments with the following lengths.

5. 12 centimeters
6. $1\frac{1}{2}$ inches
7. 2.5 centimeters
8. $\frac{1}{2}$ inch

C Estimating

(pages 138–139, 170–171)

Estimate each product or quotient.

9. 21×19

10. $103 \div 9$

11. 212×688

12. $1{,}208 \div 60$

13. $3.3 \times 4.78 \times 8.2$

14. Micah buys 3 pounds of pasta for \$0.89 per pound and 8 pounds of tomato sauce for \$2.12 per pound. Micah only has \$22.00. Estimate to see if Micah has enough money.

D Comparing Quantities

(Grade 4)

Determine which is larger.

15. the capacity of a bucket or a pond

16. the height of a tree or a flower

17. the length of a bed or a driveway

18. the weight of a balloon or a brick

19. the capacity of a milk carton or a soup spoon

E Multiplying Whole Numbers, Fractions, and Decimals

(pages 140–141, 222–224, 330–332, 336–337)

20. $2 \times 16.5 \times 3$

21. $42 \times 6 \times \frac{1}{2}$

22. $0.5 \times 15.1 \times 4.8$

23. $10\frac{1}{4} \times 4\frac{6}{8}$

24. $18 \times 19.8 \times 6.24$

25. $\frac{4}{8} \times \frac{3}{5} \times 0.75$

26. Marty hits 200 tennis balls per day. How many does he hit in 9 days?

F Dividing Whole Numbers, Fractions, and Decimals

(pages 172–174, 230–231, 334–335)

27. $87 \div 3$

28. $89.99 \div 10$

29. $1{,}152 \div \frac{1}{2}$

30. Brian paid \$96 for 4 music lessons. What was the cost per lesson?

To the Family and Student

Looking Back	Chapter 11	Looking Ahead
In Grade 4, students learned to measure using customary units of measure and metric units of measure.	**Measurement** In this chapter, students will use customary units of measure for length, capacity, and weight, and metric units of measurement for length, capacity, and mass.	In Grade 6, students will convert between customary and metric units of measures.

Math and Everyday Living

Opportunities to apply the concepts of Chapter 11 abound in everyday situations. During the chapter, think about how measurement can be used to solve a variety of real-world problems. The following examples suggest just a few of the many situations that could launch a discussion about measurement.

Math at the Pool Your family just installed a swimming pool in your backyard. The swimming pool measures 12 feet across, 20 feet long, and 6 feet deep. Your parents only want the pool filled so the depth is 4 feet. You want the pool filled so the depth is 5 feet. What is the difference in volume between a 4-foot-deep swimming pool and a 5-foot-deep swimming pool?

Math and Your Health For health reasons, doctors say it is a good idea to drink 64 fluid ounces of water per day. How many cups of water is this?

Math and the Theater For the school play you are in charge of set decorations. One item needed on the set is a 4-foot cube. Each side is to be painted a different color. What is the surface area of the cube?

Math and Fitness You enter a 10-kilometer race. Every 2,500 meters the race officials hand out water and shout out your race time. How many times will you have a chance to get water?

Math and Taxes Your family owns a home-based business. To deduct a home-office expense you first need to determine the area in your house that is used strictly for the business. Calculate the total area in your house used for the business given the following dimensions:

Closet used to store inventory:
$l = 2$ feet, $w = 4$ feet

Office Area:
$l = 9$ feet, $w = 12$ feet

File Room:
$l = 3$ feet, $w = 4\frac{1}{2}$ feet

Math on the Farm Blanca wants to fence in a rectangular area on her family's farm. She plans to keep horses within the fenced area. How many meters of fencing does Blanca need if the area she wants to fence measures 250 meters wide and 400 meters long?

Math and the Highway Because of road deterioration in your area, trucks weighing over 5 tons are not allowed down Second Avenue and Third Avenue. Police officers patrolling the area pull over 4 different trucks and ask to see the weight verification of the truck.

Truck 1	10,459 pounds
Truck 2	8,677 pounds
Truck 3	14,231 pounds
Truck 4	9,557 pounds

Which of the trucks will get a ticket for exceeding the weight limit?

California Content Standards in Chapter 11 Lessons*

	Teach and Practice	Practice
Number Sense		
2.0 Students perform calculations and solve problems involving addition, subtraction, and simple multiplication and division of fractions and decimals.		11-1, 11-3, 11-4, 11-5, 11-7, 11-8, 11-9, 11-11
2.1 (🔑) Add, subtract, and divide with decimals; add with negative integers; subtract postive integers from negative integers; and verify the reasonableness of the results.		11-2
2.2 (🔑) Demonstrate proficiency with division, including division with positive decimals and long division with multidigit divisors.		11-1, 11-2, 11-4, 11-5, 11-7, 11-8, 11-9
Algebra and Functions		
2.1 (Grade 6) Convert one unit of measurement to another (e.g., from feet to miles, from centimeters to inches).	11-1, 11-2, 11-4, 11-5	
Measurement and Geometry		
1.4 (Grade 4) Understand and use formulas to solve problems involving perimeters . . . of rectangles and squares. . . .	11-7	
1.2 (Grade 6) Know common estimates of π (3.14; $\frac{22}{7}$) and use these values to estimate and calculate the circumference . . . of circles . . .	11-7	

	Teach and Practice	Practice
Measurement and Geometry		
1.1 Derive and use the formula for the area of a triangle and of a parallelogram by comparing it with the formula for the area of a rectangle	11-8	
1.2 (🔑) Construct a cube and rectangular box from two-dimensional patterns and use these patterns to compute the surface area for these objects.	11-10	
1.3 (🔑) Understand the concept of volume and use the appropriate units in common measuring systems (i.e., cubic centimeter [cm^3], cubic meter [m^3], cubic inch [$in.^3$], cubic yard [yd^3]) to compute the volume of rectangular solids.	11-9	
1.4 Differentiate between and use appropriate units of measure for two- and three-dimensional objects (i.e., find the perimeter, area, and volume).	11-11	
Mathematical Reasoning		
2.3 Use a variety of methods, such as words, numbers, symbols, charts, graphs, tables, diagrams, and models, to explain mathematical reasoning.	11-6	
2.5 Indicate the relative advantages of exact and approximate solutions to problems and give answers to a specified degree of accuracy.	11-3	
2.6 Make precise calculations and check the validity of the results from the context of the problem.		11-11
3.2 Note the method of deriving the solution and demonstrate a conceptual understanding of the derivation by solving similar problems.		11-6

* The symbol (🔑) indicates a key standard as designated in the Mathematics Framework for California Public Schools. Full statements of the California Content Standards are found at the beginning of this book following the Table of Contents.

Customary Units of Length

California Content Standard *Algebra and Functions 2.1 (Grade 6): Convert one unit of measurement to another (e.g., from feet to miles, . . .).*

Warm-Up Review

1. 15×12
2. 36×8
3. $3 \times 5{,}280$
4. 162×3
5. $180 \div 36$
6. $60 \div 12$
7. $156 \div 12$
8. $108 \div 3$
9. Bob walked 3 miles each day for 3 weeks. How far did he walk in all?

Math Link You know how to use a ruler to measure length. In this lesson, you will learn to change from one unit of length to another and to add and subtract units of length.

The length of an object can be measured in customary units.

This table tells how some common customary units of length are related.

Customary Units of Length	
12 inches (in.) = 1 foot (ft)	3 feet = 1 yard (yd)
36 inches = 1 yard	5,280 feet = 1 mile (mi)

Example 1

Measure the model car below to the given unit.

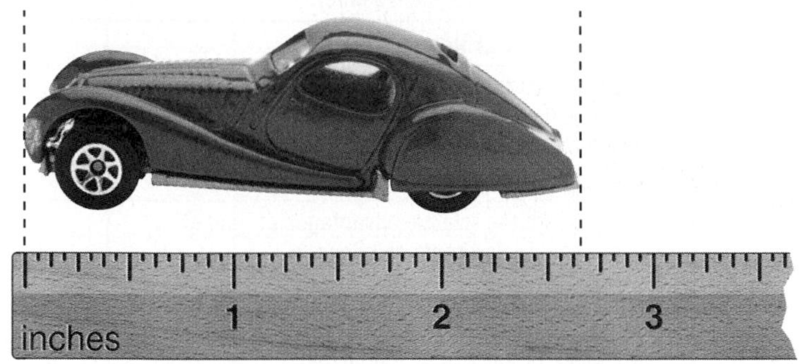

a. nearest inch — 3 in.

b. nearest $\frac{1}{2}$ inch — $2\frac{1}{2}$ in.

c. nearest $\frac{1}{4}$ inch — $2\frac{3}{4}$ in.

d. nearest $\frac{1}{8}$ inch — $2\frac{5}{8}$ in.

Sometimes you need to change from one unit of length to another.

Example 2

To change from a larger unit to a smaller unit, multiply.

2 ft 3 in. = ■ in.   1 ft = 12 in.

$(2 \times 12) + 3 = 24 + 3$

2 ft 3 in. = 27 in.

Example 3

To change from a smaller unit to a larger unit, divide.

27 in. = ■ ft   12 in. = 1 ft

$27 \div 12 = 2$ R3

27 in. = 2 ft 3 in.

Additional Standards: Number Sense 2.0, 2.2 (key) (See p. 455).

You can change units of length to larger or smaller units to add and subtract measurements.

Example 4

Find 1 ft 9 in. + 1 ft 6 in.

$$\begin{array}{r} 1\text{ ft } 9\text{ in.} \\ +\ 1\text{ ft } 6\text{ in.} \\ \hline 2\text{ ft } 15\text{ in.} \end{array} = 2\text{ ft} + 1\text{ ft} + 3\text{ in.} = 3\text{ ft } 3\text{ in.}$$

Rename 15 in. as 1 ft + 3 in.

More Examples

A. 63 in. = ■ yd ■ ft ■ in.
63 ÷ 36 = 1 yd 27 in.
27 ÷ 12 = 2 ft 3 in.
63 in. = 1 yd 2 ft 3 in.

36 in. = 1 yd
12 in. = 1 ft

B.

$$\begin{array}{r} \overset{3}{\not4}\text{ ft }\overset{15}{\not3}\text{ in.} \\ -\ 2\text{ ft } 6\text{ in.} \\ \hline 1\text{ ft } 9\text{ in.} \end{array}$$

Rename 4 ft 3 in. as 3 ft 15 in.

Guided Practice *For another example, see Set A on p. 490.*

Use a ruler to measure each item to the nearest $\frac{1}{4}$ inch, nearest $\frac{1}{8}$ inch, and nearest $\frac{1}{16}$ inch.

1. 
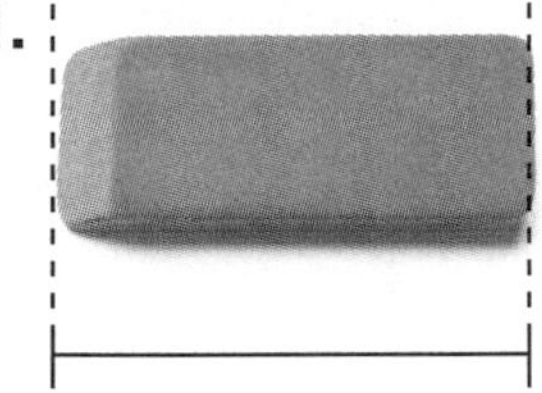

2. 

3. 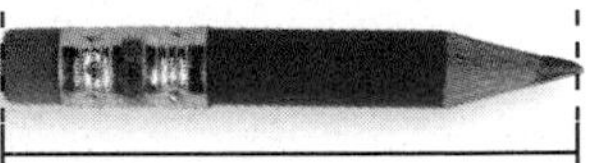

4. 5 yd = ■ ft

5. 84 ft = ■ yd

6. 32 in. = ■ ft ■ in.

7. 10 mi = ■ ft

8. 156 ft = ■ yd

9. 86 in. = ■ ft ■ in.

Add or subtract. Change to a larger unit when possible.

10. $\begin{array}{r} 6\text{ yd } 2\text{ ft} \\ +\ 7\text{ yd } 1\text{ ft} \\ \hline \end{array}$

11. $\begin{array}{r} 5\text{ ft } 1\text{ in.} \\ -\ 2\text{ ft } 10\text{ in.} \\ \hline \end{array}$

12. $\begin{array}{r} 4\text{ mi } 7\text{ ft} \\ +\ 3\text{ mi } 9\text{ ft} \\ \hline \end{array}$

13. $\begin{array}{r} 10\text{ yd } 6\text{ ft } 5\text{ in.} \\ -\ 3\text{ yd } 7\text{ ft } 3\text{ in.} \\ \hline \end{array}$

Independent Practice *For more practice, see Set A on p. 492.*

Use a ruler to measure the length of the box to each unit given.

14. nearest $\frac{1}{2}$ in.

15. nearest $\frac{1}{4}$ in.

16. nearest $\frac{1}{8}$ in.

17. nearest $\frac{1}{16}$ in.

18. 18 yd = ■ in. **19.** 25 ft = ■ yd **20.** 56 in. = ■ ft ■ in.

Add or subtract. Change to a larger unit when possible.

21. 14 yd 1 ft + 8 yd 1 ft

22. 8 ft 10 in. + 9 ft 9 in.

23. 3 mi 150 ft − 2 mi 55 ft

24. 32 yd 2 ft 1 in. − 13 yd 1 ft 7 in.

25. 1 mi 2,000 ft + 1 mi 3,380 ft

26. 2 yd 9 in. + 1 yd 2 in.

27. 21 ft 5 in. − 5 ft 9 in.

28. 15 mi 13 yd 2 ft + 8 mi 12 yd 1 ft

29. Math Reasoning What unit of measure would you use to measure your shoe? a fence around a vegetable garden? the distance to a friend's house in another city?

30. A box is $3\frac{3}{8}$ in. wide. Would five boxes fit side by side in a 20-in.-wide container? Tell how you decided.

31. Could the model car in Example 1 fit in a tunnel 1 in. high? Explain.

32. Math Reasoning Which is more accurate, measuring to the nearest $\frac{1}{4}$ inch or $\frac{1}{8}$ inch?

Mixed Review

33. Tom works $7\frac{1}{2}$ hours a day. How many hours does he work in 5 days? In 20 days?

34. Give the name for each solid figure below.

a.
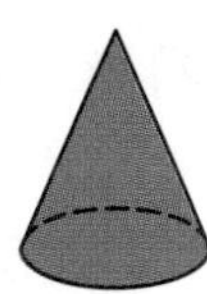
b.
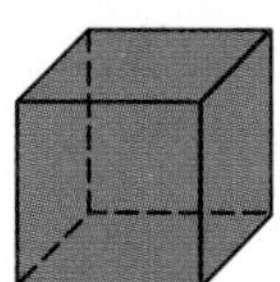

35. Tell whether the figures in each pair are congruent.

a.

b.
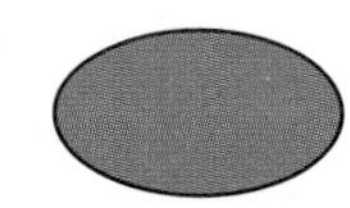

Test Prep Choose the correct letter for each answer.

36. Algebra Evaluate $x - 13$ when $x = {}^-9$. (9-5)

A $^-4$ **C** 22
B 4 **D** $^-22$

37. Algebra Evaluate $25 + y$ when $y = {}^-17$. (9-5)

F 8 **H** 42
G $^-8$ **J** $^-42$

Customary Units of Capacity and Weight

California Content Standard *Algebra and Functions 2.1 (Grade 6): Convert one unit of measurement to another (e.g., from feet to miles, . . .).*

Warm-Up Review

1. 15×8
2. 16×9
3. $4 \times 4 \times 2$
4. $7 \times 2{,}000$
5. $112 \div 6$
6. $40 \div 16$
7. Maria had two boards, one 2 ft long and the other 2 yd long. How many inches long were the boards altogether?

Word Bank

capacity

Math Link In the last lesson, you learned to compute with customary units of length. Now you will use the same ideas to compute with customary units of capacity and weight.

Capacity is the amount of liquid a container can hold. This table shows how customary units of capacity are related.

Customary Units of Capacity	
8 fluid ounces (fl oz) = 1 cup (c)	
2 cups = 1 pint (pt)	2 pints = 1 quart (qt)
4 quarts = 1 gallon (gal)	

The second table shows how customary units of weight are related.

Customary Units of Weight
16 ounces (oz) = 1 pound (lb)
2,000 pounds = 1 ton (T)

Use the relationships in the tables to change units.

Example 1

To change from a larger unit to a smaller unit, multiply.

5 gal = ■ qt 1 gal = 4 qt
$5 \times 4 = 20$
5 gal = 20 qt

Example 2

To change from a smaller unit to a larger unit, divide.

2,500 lb = ■ T ■ lb 2,000 lb = 1 T
$2{,}500 \div 2{,}000 = 1$ R500
2,500 lb = 1 T 500 lb

You can change units of capacity or weight to larger or smaller units to add and subtract measurements.

Example 3

```
   4 gal 2 qt
 + 2 gal 3 qt
   6 gal 5 qt = 6 gal + 1 gal + 1 qt
              = 7 gal 1 qt
```

Rename 5 qt as 1 gal 1 qt

Example 4

```
   2 lb  20 oz
   3̸ lb   4̸ oz
 − 1 lb   8 oz
   1 lb  12 oz
```

Rename 3 lb 4 oz as 2 lb 20 oz.

Additional Standards: Number Sense 2.1, 2.2 (key) *(See p. 455.)*

More Examples

A. 48 fl oz = ■ c   8 fl oz = 1 c
48 ÷ 8 = 6
48 fl oz = 6 c

B. 1 lb 4 oz = ■ oz   1 lb = 16 oz
(1 × 16) + 4 = 20
1 lb 4 oz = 20 oz

C.
```
  7 T 1,200 lb
+     1,200 lb
  7 T 2,400 lb = 7 T + 1 T + 400 lb
               = 8 T 400 lb
```
Rename 2,400 lb as 1 T 400 lb.

D.
```
   1 c  10 fl oz
   2̸ c   2̸ fl oz
 − 1 c   6 fl oz
         4 fl oz
```
Rename 2 c 2 fl oz as 1 c 10 fl oz.

Guided Practice *For another example, see Set B on p. 490.*

1. 6 gal = ■ qt **2.** 14 qt = ■ c **3.** 1,000 lb = ■ T **4.** 3 T = ■ lb

Add or subtract. Change to a larger unit when possible.

5. 9 qt 1 c − 2 qt 3 c **6.** 5 lb 9 oz + 6 lb 11 oz

7. Mental Math How many pounds does an 8-ton truck weigh?

8. Math Reasoning Give an appropriate unit of customary measure for each.

a. water in an aquarium **b.** can of pepper **c.** lemonade in a pitcher

Independent Practice *For more practice, see Set B on p. 492.*

9. 48 oz = ■ lb **10.** 10,000 lb = ■ T **11.** 7 lb 8 oz = ■ oz

12. 36 oz = ■ lb ■ oz **13.** 8 c = ■ fl oz **14.** 11 qt = ■ gal ■ qt

15. $9\frac{1}{2}$ gal = ■ qt **16.** 18 c = ■ pt **17.** $1\frac{1}{2}$ qt = ■ pt

Add or subtract. Change to a larger unit when possible.

18. 5 qt 1 c − 3 qt 3 c **19.** 3 lb 11 oz + 7 lb 5 oz

20. 3 gal 3 qt + 5 gal 1 qt **21.** 3 c − 1 c 6 fl oz

22. 1 T 1,300 lb + 2 T 1,110 lb **23.** 4 lb 2 oz − 3 lb 10 oz

Give an appropriate unit of customary measure for each.

24. flour in a bread recipe **25.** water in a swimming pool

26. 

can of peas

27. 

crate of apples

28. 

packet of sugar

29. 

cement mixer

30. A great shark weighed 1,587 pounds. How many pounds less than 1 ton is this?

31. Math Reasoning You have a gallon jug, several quart containers, and a few pint containers. Give a combination of these containers that equals $1\frac{3}{4}$ gallons.

32. How many 1-oz servings of cereal are in a giant 5 lb 4 oz box?

33. A store ordered 100 backpacks, each weighing 12 oz. The shipping cost is $0.25 per lb, how much will shipping costs be?

34. You have two 5-oz weights and three 4-oz weights. What total weights can you make with 2, 3, 4, and 5 of these weights? Explain your strategy.

Algebra Write an expression for each.

35. The number of pounds in *m* tons

36. The number of pounds in *n* ounces

37. The number of gallons in *s* quarts

38. The number of cups in *x* gallons

Mixed Review

39. A large basket that weighs 2 lb 2 oz holds 85 oz of rice. What is the total weight of the rice and basket?

Give the name for each solid figure.

40. 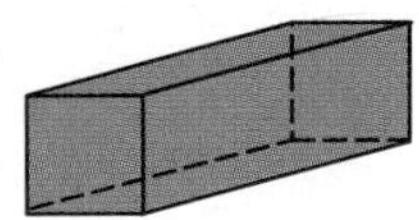

41. 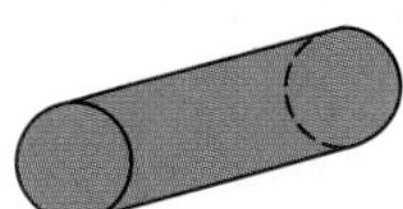

42. 45 in. = ■ ft ■ in.

43. 120 ft = ■ yd

44. 3 mi = ■ ft

Test Prep Choose the correct letter for each answer.

45. Algebra Solve $x - 4 = 9$. (9-4)

A $x = 5$
C $x = 13$
B $x = {}^{-}5$
D $x = {}^{-}13$

46. Algebra Solve $3 = 12 + y$. (9-3)

F $y = {}^{-}9$
H $y = {}^{-}15$
G $y = 9$
J $y = 15$

Use Homework Workbook 11-2.

Problem-Solving Skill:

Is an Estimate Enough?

Warm-Up Review

1. $59.98 + $13.99
2. $18.00 − $14.98
3. $12.95 × 4

For Exercises 4–6, estimate.

4. $17.88 + $14.22
5. $24.15 − $12.99
6. 12 × $3.98
7. Estimate the total cost of 12 CDs at $8.99 and 9 tapes at $4.99.

California Content Standard *Mathematical Reasoning 2.5: Indicate the relative advantages of exact and approximate solutions to problems and give answers to a specific degree of accuracy.*

Read for Understanding

Last summer Anne earned a total of $55 raking leaves. She decided to spend some of her money to buy *The Big Box of Games* from a catalog store. After placing her order, Anne received the confirmation slip shown below.

Totally Games				
Item Number	Description	Cost of Item	Shipping and Handling	Delivery Date
18114	The Big Box of Games	$41.98	$7.35	May 12–May 15

1. What is the cost of *The Big Box of Games*?
2. What is the cost of shipping and handling?

Think and Discuss

Is an Estimate Enough?

Whether or not an estimate or an exact answer is needed depends upon the situation. Some problems can be solved by finding an estimate. Others require an exact answer.

Reread the paragraph at the top of the page.

3. Is an estimate all Anne needs to find if she has enough money to pay for *The Big Box of Games*? Why or why not?
4. How much will Anne have to pay in all for her order? Did you find an exact answer or an estimate? Why?
5. Write a problem that needs to be solved by finding an exact answer and another problem that can be solved by estimating.

 Additional Standard: Number Sense 2.0 *(See p. 455.)*

Totally Games sells more than 700 sets of *The Big Box of Games* each year. This year *The Big Box of Games* costs $41.98. That is a $2.26 increase over last year's price.

Guided Practice

1. Which is true about the number of games sold each year?

a. At least 700 were sold.

b. Less than 700 were sold.

c. Exactly 700 were sold.

2. Which is true about the price increase?

a. It was less than $2.26.

b. It was more than $2.26.

c. It was exactly $2.26.

Independent Practice

3. Which represents the cost of *The Big Box of Games* last year?

a. The sum of the price this year and the increase in price

b. The difference between the price this year and the increase in price

c. The difference between the number sold and the price this year

4. Which number sentence gives the cost of *The Big Box of Games* last year?

a. $41.98 + $2.26 = $44.24

b. $700 − $41.98 = $658.02

c. $41.98 − $2.26 = $39.72

Mr. Cook has $200 to spend on wooden shelves for the classroom. Use the information on the catalog page at the right for Exercises 5 and 6.

5. Mr. Cook would like to buy three shelves. Does he need an exact answer or can he estimate to see if he has enough money? Explain your choice.

6. Mr. Cook decides to buy two wooden shelves. If the cost of shipping and handling is $12.49, what is the total cost? Tell how you found your answer. Is it exact or an estimate?

Metric Units of Length

California Content Standard *Algebra and Functions 2.1 (Grade 6): Convert one unit of measurement to another (e.g., from feet to miles, . . .).*

Warm-Up Review

1. 1.3×100
2. 10×0.29
3. $5.2 \div 10$ 4. $17 \div 1{,}000$
5. Sally bought a large-screen TV priced at $1,000. Tax was $0.07 on every dollar. How much did she pay in all?

Word Bank

metric system
meter

Math Link You have learned about customary units of length. In this lesson, you will learn about metric units of length.

The **metric system** is officially called the International System of Units because it is used around the world. This table shows how the common units of measure are related.

Metric Units of Length
1,000 millimeters (mm) = 1 meter (m)
100 centimeters (cm) = 1 meter
10 decimeters (dm) = 1 meter
1 kilometer (km) = 1,000 meters

Example 1

Measure the width of the CD case below.

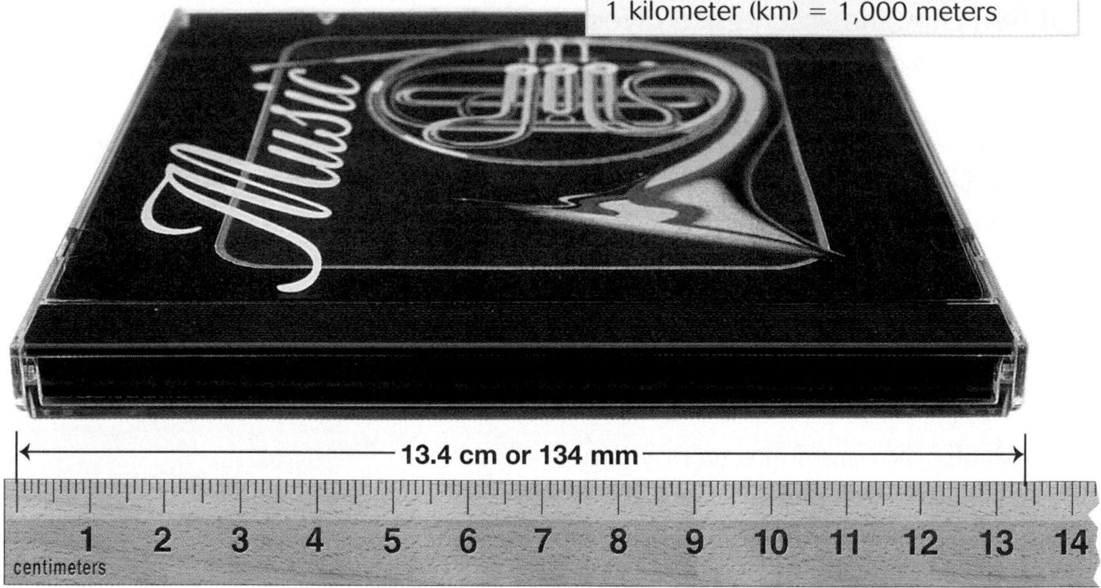

The width of the CD case is 13.4 cm, or 134 mm.

The table below shows the relationships among metric units of length. The **meter** is the basic unit.

1 millimeter	1 centimeter	1 decimeter	1 meter	1 dekameter	1 hectometer	1 kilometer
0.001 m	0.01 m	0.1 m		10.0 m	100.0 m	1,000.0 m

 Additional Standards: Number Sense 2.0, 2.2 (🔑) *(See p. 455.)*

Since the metric system is based on tens, changing from unit one to another is like moving from one place-value position to another.

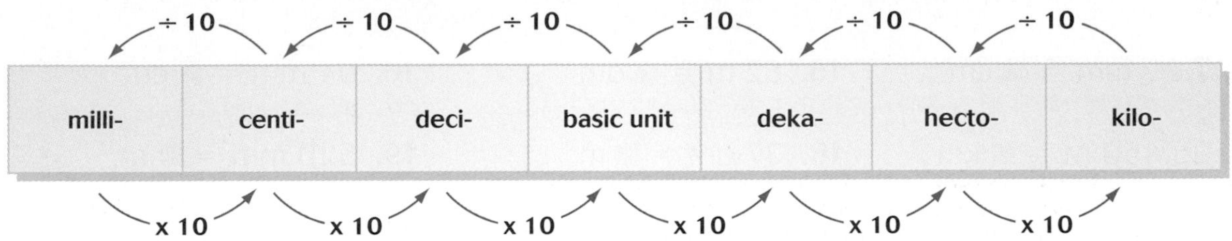

Example 2

To change from a larger unit to a smaller unit, multiply.

1.03 m = ■ cm   1 m = 100 cm
1.03 × 100 = 103
1.03 m = 103 cm

Example 3

To change from a smaller unit to a larger unit, divide.

39 m = ■ km   1 km = 1,000 m
39 ÷ 1,000 = 0.039
39 m = 0.039 km

Guided Practice *For another example, see Set C on p. 490.*

1. Use a ruler to measure the pencil in centimeters and in millimeters.

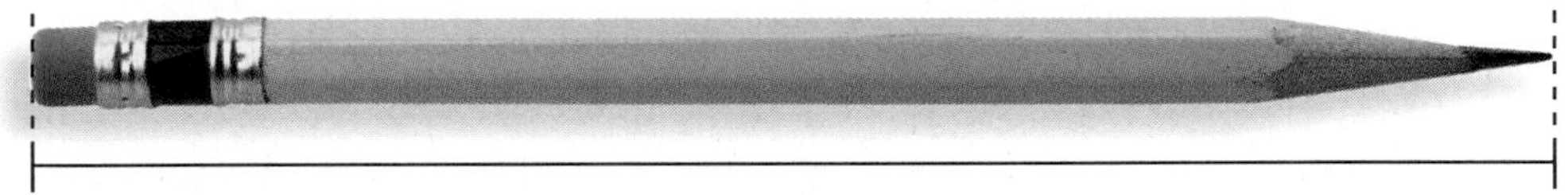

2. 1.8 km = ■ m   3. 750 m = ■ km   4. 95.8 cm = ■ mm   5. 197 cm = ■ m

6. **Math Reasoning** What unit of measure would you use to measure the width of your classroom? the length of a piece of chalk? the distance to a friend's house in another city?

Independent Practice *For more practice, see Set C on p. 492.*

Use a ruler to measure each in centimeters and in millimeters.

7.

8.   9.   10.

Mental Math

11. 8 km = ■ m **12.** 3.8 cm = ■ mm **13.** 9,875 m = ■ km

14. 7.29 mm = ■ cm **15.** 52 m = ■ dm **16.** 94 mm = ■ cm

17. 25,450 m = ■ km **18.** 37 dm = ■ m **19.** 520 mm = ■ m

Complete each sentence with an appropriate metric unit of length.

20. A dime is only 1 ■ thick. **21.** A large paper clip is about 5 ■ long.

22. John's arm is 63 ■ long. **23.** Bob ran 37.195 ■ in a marathon.

24. Three CD storage towers each 14.2-cm wide are placed side by side. What is the total overall width in centimeters?

25. Math Reasoning One CD tower costs $29.95. If you paid $95.25 for 3 towers, how much sales tax did you pay?

26. Tina cut 25 cm off a 2-m piece of ribbon. In meters and in centimeters, how much ribbon was left?

27. Two pieces of chalk measure 95 mm and 9 cm. Which is longer? By how much?

Mixed Review

28. How many feet and inches are in $3\frac{1}{2}$ yd of fabric?

29. 48 ft = ■ yd **30.** 16 lb = ■ oz **31.** 75 in. = ■ ft ■ in.

32. 4 gal 1 qt − 2 gal 2 qt **33.** 3 ft 9 in. + 5 ft 7 in.

Test Prep **Choose the correct letter for each answer.**

A shipping service charges $0.33 for 1 oz or less for regular service and $0.22 for each additional ounce. Express service is $3 for up to 2 lb and $1 for each additional pound. Find each shipping charge.

34. 4-oz letter, regular service
(4-11)

A $0.88 **C** $1.21

B $0.99 **D** $1.32

35. 6-lb package, express service
(4-11)

F $18 **H** $7

G $10 **J** $6

 Use Homework Workbook 11-4.

Diagnostic Checkpoint

Add or subtract. Change to a larger unit when possible.

1. (11-1)
45 yd 7 ft 2 in.
− 16 yd 6 ft 8 in.

2. (11-1)
17 mi 12 yd 2 ft
+ 9 mi 13 yd 3 ft

3. (11-1)
33 ft 4 in.
+ 6 ft 10 in.

4. (11-2)
4 gal 3 qt 1 pt
−3 gal 2 qt 1 pt

5. (11-2)
3 gal 1 qt
+ 1 gal 3 qt

6. (11-2)
8c 6 fl oz
− 3c 7 fl oz

Complete.

7. (11-1) 48 in. = ■ ft

8. (11-1) 20 yd = ■ ft

9. (11-1) 12 ft = ■ in.

10. (11-4) 33 m = ■ cm

11. (11-1) 22 ft = ■ yd

12. (11-1) $1\frac{1}{2}$ ft = ■ in.

13. (11-1) $3\frac{1}{3}$ yd = ■ ft

14. (11-2) 32 oz = ■ lb

15. (11-2) 3 qt = ■ pt

16. (11-2) 3 c = ■ fl oz

17. (11-2) 5 c = ■ pt

18. (11-4) 1,404 cm = ■ m

19. (11-2) 12 c = ■ fl oz

20. (11-2) 16 qt = ■ gal

21. (11-2) 12 gal = ■ qt

22. (11-4) 99 mm = ■ cm

23. (11-2) 108 oz = ■ lb ■ oz

24. (11-2) 15,000 lb = ■ T ■ lb

25. (11-2) $2\frac{1}{2}$ lb = ■ oz

26. (11-4) 400 m = ■ mm

Solve.

27. (11-1) As each runner passes the 3-mile mark, she is handed a cup of water. How many gallons of water are needed for 100 runners at each 3-mile mark?

Amber received $50 as a birthday gift. She hopes to buy a book costing $17.85 and a skirt costing $28.50. Both prices include tax.

28. (11-3) Is an estimate enough or does Amber need an exact answer to find if she has enough money to buy both items? Explain.

29. (11-3) How much change will Amber receive if she buys both items? Do you need to find an exact answer or an estimate?

Metric Units of Capacity and Mass

California Content Standard *Algebra and Functions 2.1 (Grade 6): Convert one unit of measurement to another (e.g., from feet to miles, . . .).*

Warm-Up Review

1. 10×0.9
2. 3.56×100
3. $5.3 \div 10$
4. $4.6 \div 1{,}000$
5. $988 \div 100$
6. One package weighed 2 lb and the other weighed 8 oz. Find the total weight of the two packages in ounces.

Math Link You have learned about customary units of capacity and weight. In this lesson, you will learn about metric units of capacity and mass.

Word Bank

gram

The basic metric units of capacity are given in this table.

Metric Units of Capacity
1 liter (L) = 1,000 milliliters (mL)

In the metric system, the basic unit of mass is the **gram**. This table shows how metric units of mass are related.

Metric Units of Mass
1 kilogram (kg) = 1,000 grams (g)
1 g = 1,000 milligrams (mg)

The examples that follow show how to change metric units of capacity and mass. Just as with metric units of length, you multiply and divide by powers of ten.

Example 1

To change from a larger unit to a smaller unit, multiply.

8 L = ■ mL   1 L = 1,000 mL
$8 \times 1{,}000 = 8{,}000$
8 L = 8,000 mL

Example 2

To change from a smaller unit to a larger unit, divide.

250 mg = ■ g   1,000 mg = 1 g
$250 \div 1{,}000 = 0.25$
250 mg = 0.25 g

More Examples

A. 5,500 mL = ■ L   1,000 mL = 1 L
$5{,}500 \div 1{,}000 = 5.5$
5,500 mL = 5.5 L

B. 45.3 g = ■ kg   1,000 g = 1 kg
$45.3 \div 1{,}000 = 0.0453$
45.3 g = 0.0453 kg

Guided Practice *For another example, see Set D on p. 490.*

1. 5.8 L = ■ mL **2.** 1,500 mL = ■ L **3.** 42 kg = ■ g **4.** 25 g = ■ mg

 Additional Standards: Number Sense 2.0, 2.2 (🔑) (See p. 455.)

5. Give an appropriate metric unit of capacity for each.
   a. a fuel tank **b.** a dose of medicine

6. Give an appropriate metric unit of mass for each.
   a. a pickup truck **b.** a box of tissues

7. A bag of sugar weighs 2.26 kg. How many grams is that?

Independent Practice

For more practice, see Set D on p. 492.

Mental Math

8. 1.55 L = ■ mL **9.** 5,250 mL = ■ L **10.** 500 mL = ■ L **11.** 23 L = ■ mL

12. 250 mL = ■ L **13.** 0.5 L = ■ mL **14.** 15 kg = ■ g **15.** 8,345 g = ■ kg

16. 1.98 g = ■ mg **17.** 20,000 g = ■ kg **18.** 0.8 kg = ■ g **19.** 9,700 mg = ■ g

Give an appropriate metric unit of capacity for each.

20. an aquarium **21.** a teapot **22.** a mug **23.** a blood sample

Give an appropriate metric unit of mass for each.

24. a pen **25.** a toothpick **26.** a box of cereal **27.** a grand piano

Algebra Write an expression for

28. the number of kilograms in m grams.

29. the number of milliliters in n liters.

30. How many 450-gram boxes like the one at the right will you need to have at least 1 kg of pasta?

31. Which has greater mass, one hundred 450-g boxes of macaroni or ten 0.45-kg of boxes?

Mixed Review

32. The Olympic marathon is 42.19 km. How many meters is this?

33. 5.2 km = ■ m **34.** 8 lb 6 oz = ■ oz **35.** 52 gal = ■ qt

Test Prep Choose the correct letter for each answer.

36. Algebra Find $^{-}12 - 5$.
(9-4)

A $^{-}17$ **B** $^{-}7$ **C** 7 **D** 17

37. Algebra Find $17 + {}^{-}33$.
(9-3)

F $^{-}50$ **G** $^{-}16$ **H** 16 **J** 50

Problem-Solving Strategy:

Work Backward

California Content Standard *Mathematical Reasoning 2.3: Use a variety of methods, such as words, numbers, symbols, charts, graphs, tables, diagrams, and models, to explain mathematical reasoning.*

Warm-Up Review

1. $8 - 1\frac{1}{4}$
2. $3 \times \frac{2}{3}$
3. $\frac{1}{2} \times 24$
4. 35 + 25
5. \$45.00 − \$23.75
6. 5 × \$12.50
7. Jay had two pieces of wire, one 10 ft long and the other 18 ft long. How much wire did he have in all? Give your answer in feet, and in yards and feet.

After Kim studied for $2\frac{1}{2}$ hours and practiced the piano for 45 minutes, it was 1:30 P.M. What time did she begin to study?

Understand

What do you need to know?

You need to know what time Kim began to study.

Plan

How can you solve the problem?

You can **work backward** from the ending time to find the beginning time. A time line can help.

Solve

Start at 1:30 P.M. Count back 45 min. and then $2\frac{1}{2}$ h more.

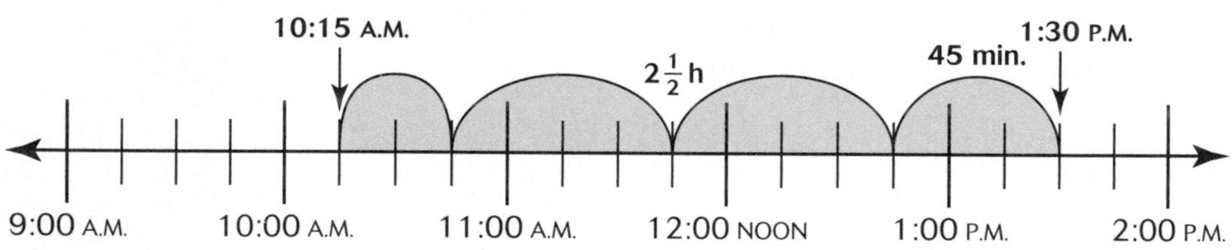

Kim began to study at 10:15 A.M.

Look Back

How can you check the answer? Explain.

Guided Practice

1. Brian was playing a number game with his sisters. He told them to pick a number, multiply it by 3, and add 8. Cindy ended up with 44. What was her number?

Additional Standard: Mathematical Reasoning 3.2 (See p. 455.)

Independent Practice

2. Gary began working in his garden at 9:30 A.M. and finished at 1:15 P.M. How long did he work in his garden?

3. The total cost to rent a car for 7 days is $293.30, including $11.30 in taxes and $79 for insurance. What is the daily rental fee, without taxes and insurance?

4. Lake Erie is half as wide as Lake Michigan and 5 mi wider than Lake Ontario. Lake Superior is 3 times as wide as Lake Ontario. Lake Superior is 159 mi wide. How wide is Lake Michigan?

5. Susan, Yolanda, and Chen did not have any trading cards. Then Brian gave $\frac{1}{3}$ of his trading cards to Susan. Susan then gave $\frac{1}{2}$ of her cards to Yolanda. Yolanda then gave $\frac{1}{4}$ of her cards to Chen. Chen ended up with 3 cards. How many cards did Brian have before he gave any away?

6. The soccer team collected money to clean the park. They bought plastic bags with $\frac{1}{3}$ of the money and rakes with another $\frac{1}{3}$ of the money. After they spent $42.50 for seeds, they had $8 left. How much did they collect?

7. **Math Reasoning** Pam collected stamps. She gave 5 of them to her brother and twice as many to her sister. If Pam has 18 stamps left, how many did she collect?

Mixed Review

Use these or other strategies. Tell which strategy you used.

Problem-Solving Strategies

- *Draw a Diagram*
- *Find a Pattern*
- *Write an Equation*
- *Work Backward*

8. Mr. and Mrs. Thomas left their hotel and drove 15 miles east and 25 miles north. Next, they drove 10 miles west and 25 miles south to Starved Rock State Park. What direction and how far were they from their hotel?

9. Paul had scores of 81, 90, 93, 89, and 92 on five tests. What is his mean score?

Perimeter and Circumference

California Content Standards *Measurement and Geometry 1.4: (Grade 4): Understand and use formulas to solve problems involving perimeters . . . of rectangles and squares . . . . Also, Measurement and Geometry 1.2 (Grade 6) (See p. 455.)*

Warm-Up Review

1. 5×3.14
2. 4×3.68
3. $(2 \times 12) + (2 \times 15)$
4. $2 \times (18 + 14)$
5. $28.8 \div 4$
6. $62.8 \div 3.14$
7. $36 - (2 \times 10)$
8. Find the cost of 3 sweaters at $24 each and 2 blouses at $18 each.

Math Link In Chapter 10, you learned about polygons and circles. Now you will learn to find the distance around these plane figures.

The distance around a polygon is its **perimeter**.

Example 1

Find the perimeter of the swimming pool by adding the lengths of its sides.

Estimate first: $6 + 9 + 5 + 5 + 4 + 8 = 37$ m

$6 + 9.3 + 5.4 + 5.4 + 4 + 7.6 = 37.7$ m

The perimeter of the swimming pool is 37.7 m.

Word Bank

perimeter
formula
diameter
circumference
pi

When polygons have two or more sides the same length, you can use a **formula** to find the perimeter as shown in the examples below.

Example 2

Find the perimeter of the rectangle.

ℓ = length
w = width

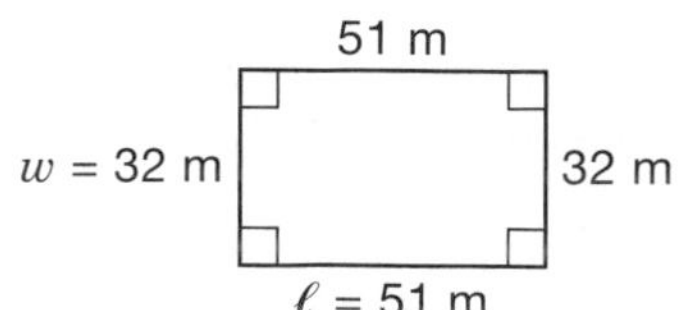

$\mathbf{P = (2 \times \ell) + (2 \times w) = 2\ell + 2w}$

$P = (2 \times 51) + (2 \times 32)$

$P = 102 + 64 = 166$ m

Example 3

Find the perimeter of the square.

s = side

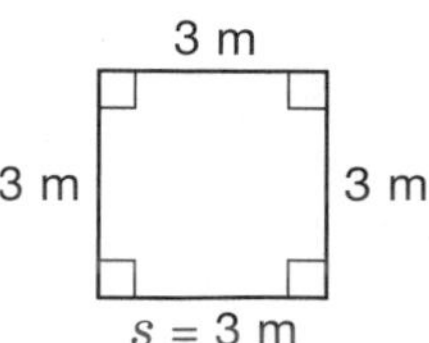

$\mathbf{P = 4 \times s = 4s}$

$P = 4 \times 3 = 12$ m

Additional Standards: Number Sense 2.0, 2.2 (key) (See p. 455.)

The distance across a circle is its **diameter**, and the distance around is its **circumference**. The table at the right shows the result of dividing the circumference by the diameter for three different circular objects.

Circumference	Diameter	$\frac{C}{d}$
188.52 cm	60 cm	3.142
78.575 ft	25 ft	3.143
125.64 mm	40 mm	3.141

Notice that in each case the ratio *is approximately equal to* ($\approx$) 3.14. The ratio of the circumference to the diameter of a circle is always the same. The Greek letter **pi** (π) represents this ratio. The value of π is approximately 3.14 or $\frac{22}{7}$. This relationship can be stated as follows:

Circumference divided by diameter equals pi, or $\frac{C}{d} = \pi$.

Another way to state the relationship is $C = \pi \times d$.

Example 4

Find the circumference of the circle at the right. Use 3.14 for π.

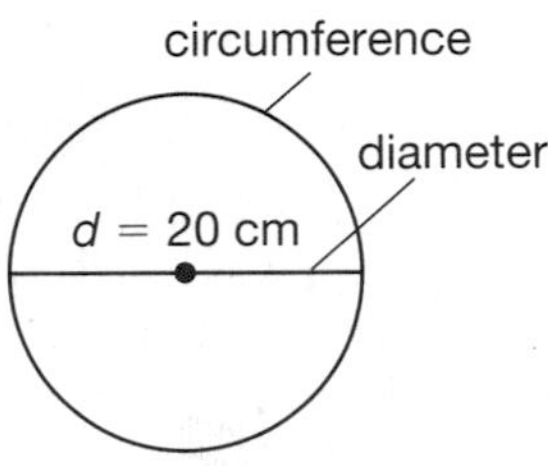

$C = \pi \times d$

$\approx 3.14 \times 20$ — Remember that π is approximately equal to 3.14.

≈ 62.8 cm

Guided Practice *For another example, see Set E on p. 491.*

Find the perimeter or the circumference of each figure.

1. 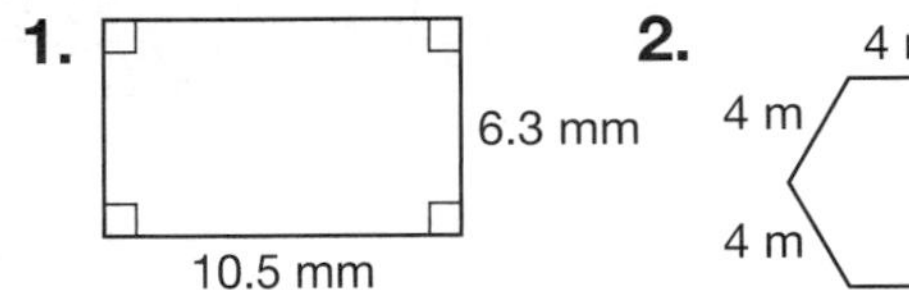

2. 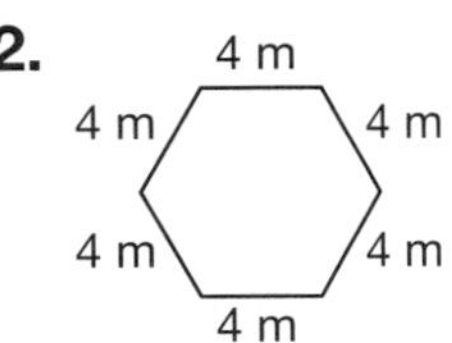

3. 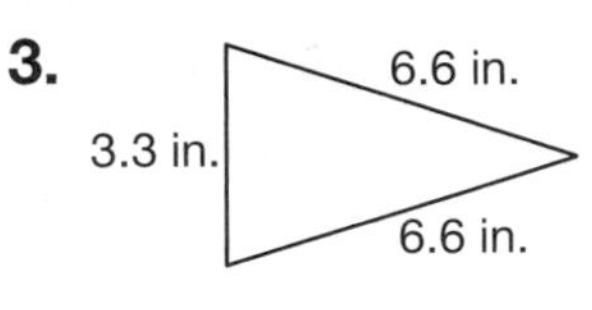

4. 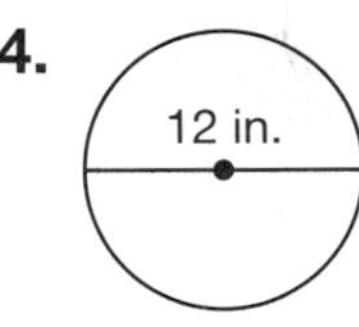

5. Find the circumference of a pizza with a diameter of 14 in.

Independent Practice *For more practice, see Set E on p. 493.*

Find the perimeter or the circumference of each figure.

6. 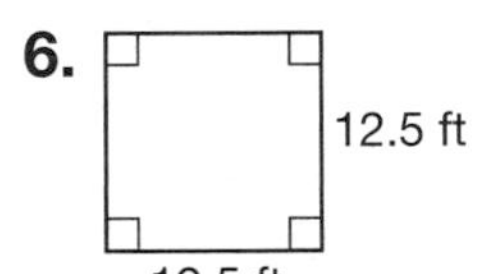

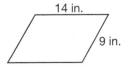

7.

8. 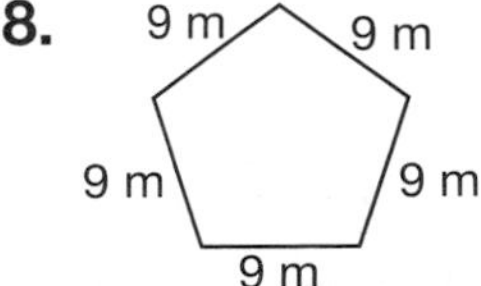

9. 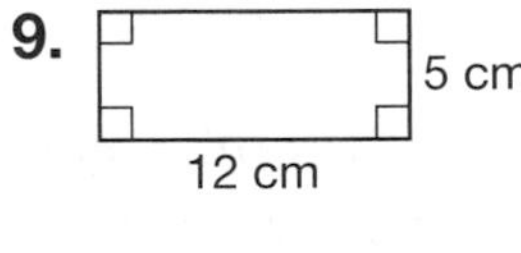

10. 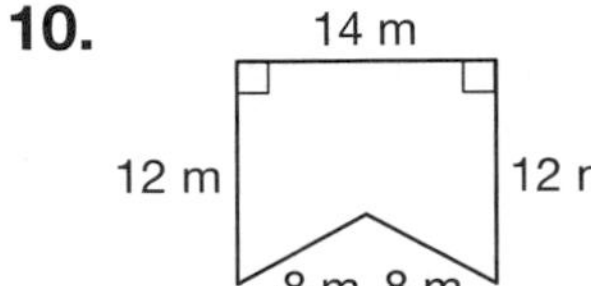

11. 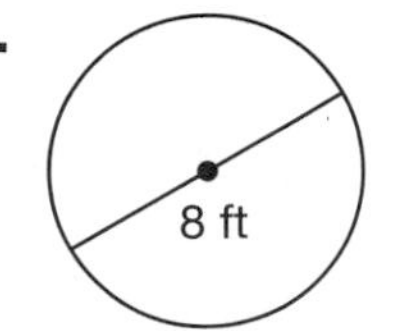

12. 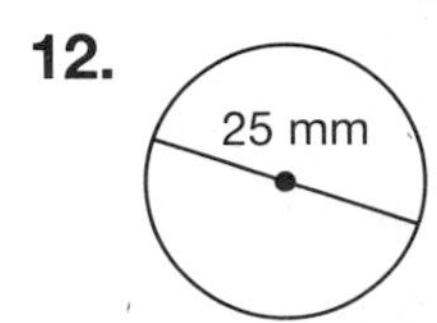

13. 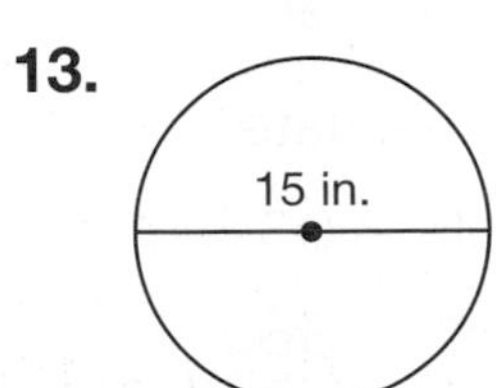

Find each missing measurement.

14. 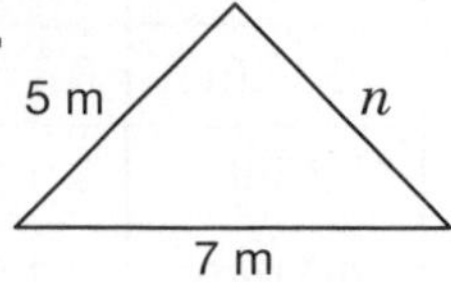

$P = 17$ m
$n = \blacksquare$

15. 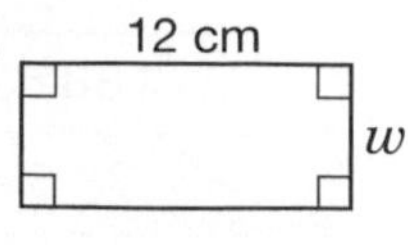

$P = 38$ cm
$w = \blacksquare$

16. 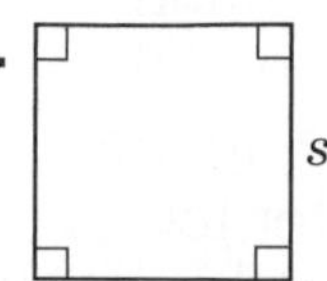

$P = 80$ cm
$s = \blacksquare$

17. 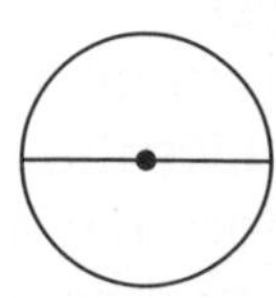

$C = 78.5$ in.
$d = \blacksquare$

18. Math Reasoning Use r for radius to write a formula for the circumference of a circle.

19. Math Reasoning Write a formula for the perimeter of an equilateral triangle. Use P for perimeter and s for each side length. Explain why your formula works.

20. How much fencing is needed to enclose a rectangle 75 ft by 40 ft? Explain whether you would need more or less fencing to enclose a square with 60-ft sides.

21. Complete the table at the right for rectangles with the measurements given. What happens to the perimeter when both the length and the width are doubled?

ℓ	w	p
2 cm	3 cm	
4 cm	6 cm	
8 cm	12 cm	
16 cm	24 cm	

22. Van wants to frame a painting 80 cm by 50 cm. It costs $0.25 for each centimeter of framing. How much will it cost to frame the painting?

23. Deanna cut out a cardboard circle with a diameter of 12 in. She will display earrings around the edge of the circle. Each pair takes 2 in. on the circumference of the circle. About how many pairs of earrings will fit?

Mixed Review

24. There are flags on every post of a 300-ft fence. There are posts at each end and every 6 ft apart. How many flags are there?

25. 320 cm = ■ m **26.** 8.9 km = ■ m **27.** 95 g = ■ kg **28.** 5 L = ■ mL

Test Prep Choose the correct letter for each answer.

29. Evaluate $3.14d$ for $d = 9.5$
(6-11)

A 3.03 **C** 12.64

B 6.36 **D** 29.83

30. Evaluate $0.5s$ for $s = 7.2$.
(6-11)

F 3.6 **H** 36

G 12.2 **J** 360

LESSON 11-8

Area

Warm-Up Review

1. 12×9 2. 4×16
3. 11×11 4. 15×15
5. $\frac{1}{2} \times 6 \times 8$
6. $\frac{1}{2} \times 10 \times 20$
7. At $3 a foot for fencing, how much will it cost to enclose a square garden with 20-ft sides?

California Content Standard *Measurement and Geometry 1.1 (Key): Derive and use the formulas for the area of a triangle and of a parallelogram by comparing it with the formula for the area of a rectangle.*

Math Link You have used a formula to find the distance around a polygon. In this lesson, you will learn formulas to find the amount of space covered by polygons.

Word Bank

area
base
height

Area is the number of square units (units^2) a figure covers. The area of this figure is 3×5, or 15, square units.

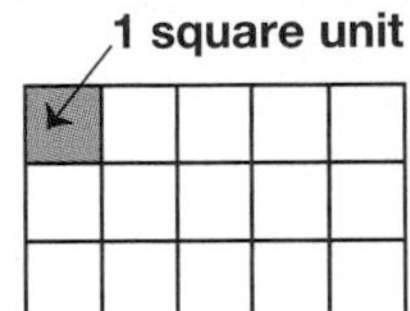

Example 1

Find the area of the rectangle.

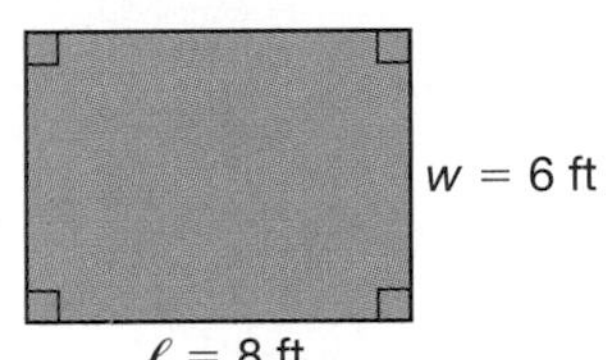

$\boldsymbol{A = \ell \times w = \ell w}$

$A = 8 \times 6$

$A = 48$ square feet (ft^2)

Example 2

Find the area of the square.

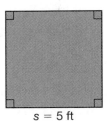

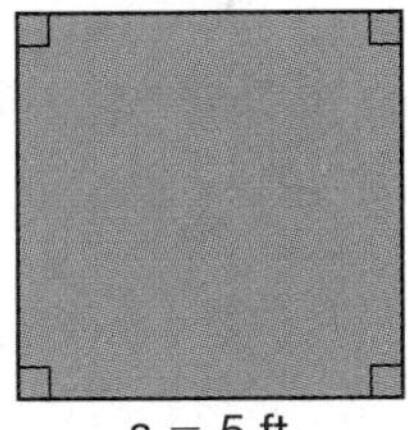

$\boldsymbol{A = s \times s = s^2}$

$A = 5 \times 5$

$A = 25 \text{ ft}^2$

Example 3

Find the area of the parallelogram.

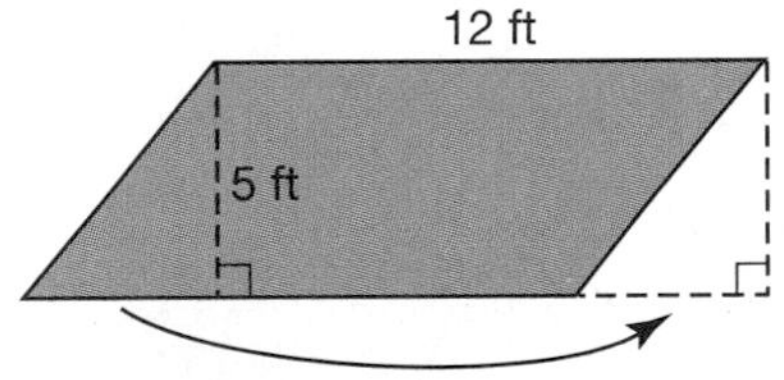

If you slide the triangle to the other side, you have a rectangle.

$A = 12 \times 5$

$A = 60 \text{ ft}^2$

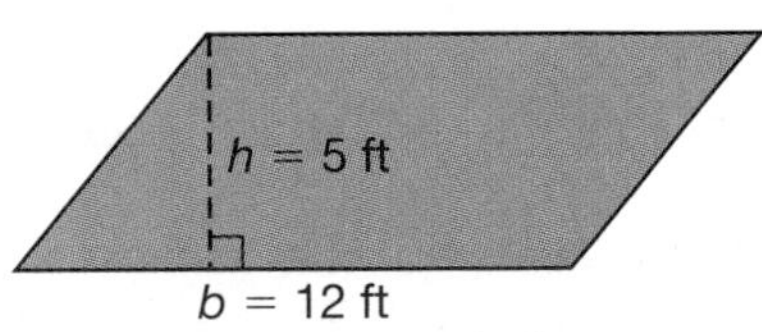

The **base** (b) and the **height** (h) correspond to the dimensions of the rectangle.

$\boldsymbol{A = b \times h = bh}$

$A = 12 \times 5$

$A = 60 \text{ ft}^2$

Additional Standards: Number Sense 2.0, 2.2 (Key) *(See p. 455.)*

Example 4

Find the area of the triangle.

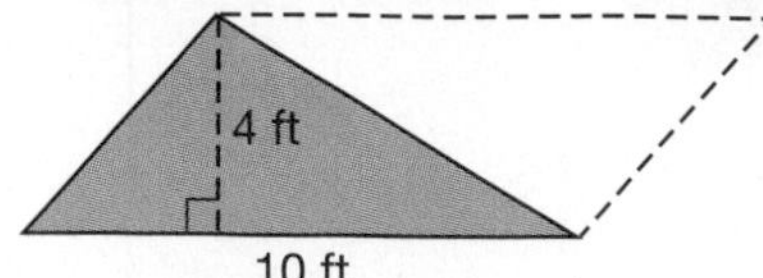

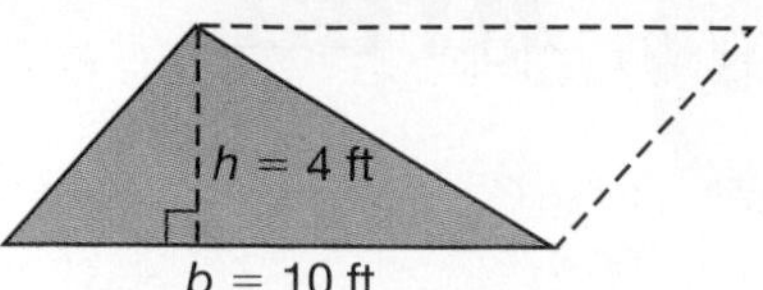

If you position a congruent triangle as shown, you have a parallelogram.

$A = 10 \times 4$

$A = 40 \text{ ft}^2$

The area of each triangle is half the area of the parallelogram.

$$\mathbf{A = \frac{1}{2} \times b \times h = \frac{1}{2}bh}$$

$A = \frac{1}{2} \times 10 \times 4$

$A = \frac{1}{2} \times 40$

$A = 20 \text{ ft}^2$

More Examples

A. $A = 9 \times 6$

$A = 54 \text{ ft}^2$

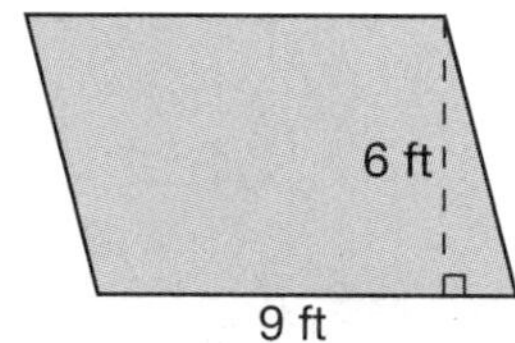

B. $A = \frac{1}{2} \times 5 \times 6$

$A = \frac{1}{2} \times 30$

$A = 15 \text{ m}^2$

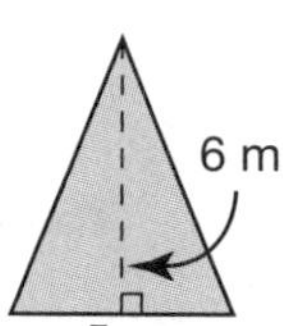

Guided Practice *For another example, see Set F on p. 491.*

Find the area of each figure.

1. 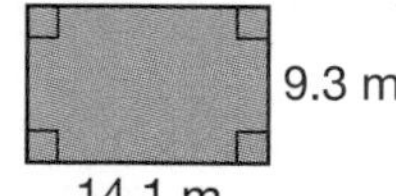

2. 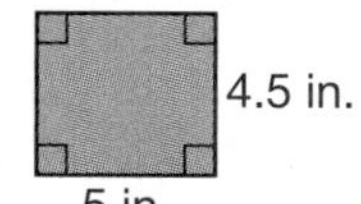

3. 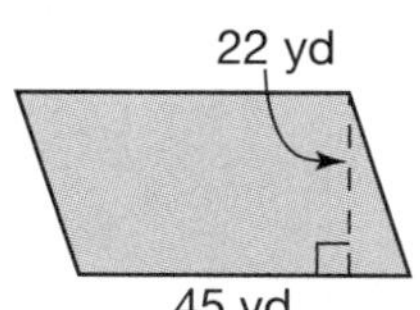

4. 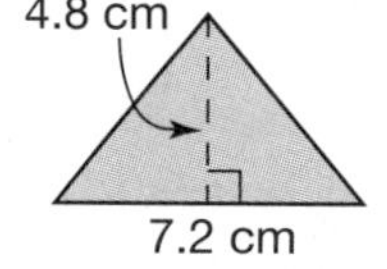

5. Find the cost of crushed stone for a rectangular area 30 ft long and 20 ft wide if the stone is $2 a square foot.

Independent Practice *For more practice, see Set F on p. 493.*

Find the area of each figure.

6. 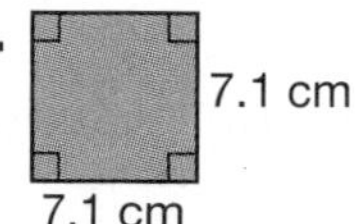

7. 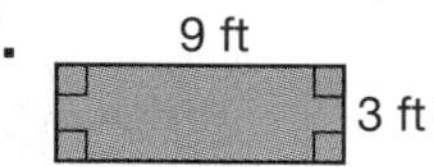

8. 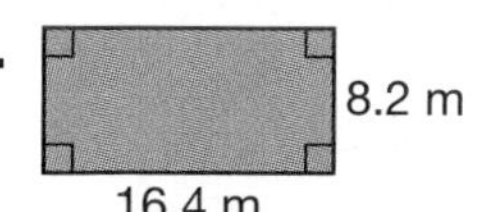

9. 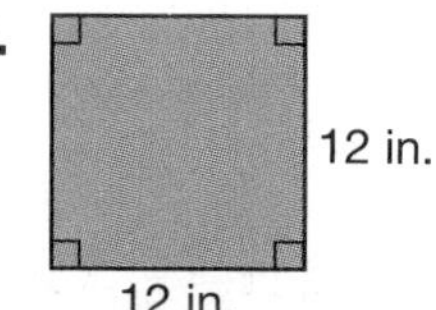

10. 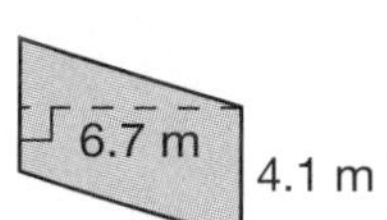

11. 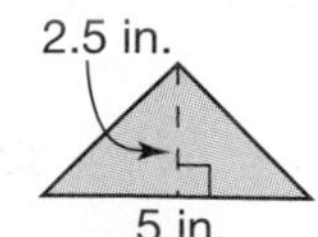

12. 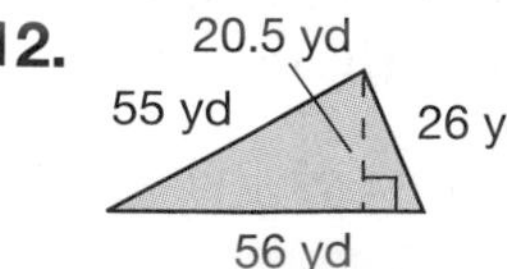

13. 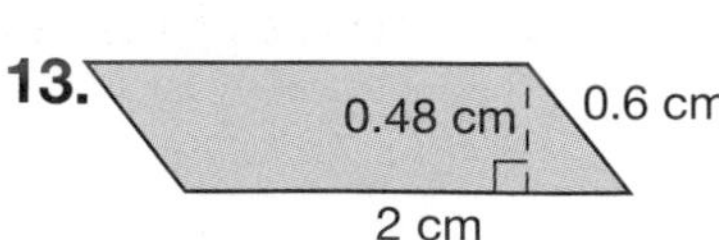

Find each missing measurement.

14. $\ell = 1.6$ m
$w = 3$ m
$A = ■$

15. $A = 420$ in^2
$\ell = 30$ in.
$w = ■$

16. $s = 12\frac{1}{2}$ yd
$A = ■$

17. $A = 25$ cm^2
$s = ■$

18. triangle
$b = 7$ yd
$h = 10$ yd
$A = ■$

19. parallelogram
$b = 12$ ft
$h = 20$ ft
$A = ■$

20. triangle
$b = ■$
$h = 20$ m
$A = 90$ m^2

21. parallelogram
$b = 16$ cm
$h = ■$
$A = 224$ cm^2

22. Math Reasoning How many square feet are in a square yard? Draw a diagram to show how you know.

23. Students are painting a mural 14 ft by 19 ft. If one can of paint covers 75 square feet, how many cans are needed?

24. Complete the table at the right for rectangles with the measurements given. What happens to the area when both the length and the width are doubled?

ℓ	w	A
2 cm	3 cm	
4 cm	6 cm	
8 cm	12 cm	
16 cm	24 cm	

25. Math Reasoning A triangular sign has a base of 3 ft and a height of 2 ft. What is its area? How could the manufacturer change the dimensions to double the area of the sign? Explain.

26. Math Reasoning Without computing, tell whether it would take more fencing to surround a square with 30-ft sides or a circle with a 30-ft diameter. Explain how you know.

Mixed Review

27. How many milligrams are in 0.5 kilogram?

28. 3.7 kg = ■ g

29. 460 mL = ■ L

Find the perimeter of each figure.

30. a square with 8.5-in. sides

31. a rectangle with sides 12 cm and 15 cm

Test Prep **Choose the correct letter for the answer.**

32. The height of a triangle is twice its base. If the base is 8 m, what is the area of the triangle?
(11-8)

A 32 m^2 **B** 64 m^2 **C** 128 m^2 **D** 256 m^2

Volume

California Content Standard *Measurement and Geometry 1.3 (🔑): Understand the concept of volume and use the appropriate units in common measuring systems (i.e., cubic centimeter [cm³], cubic meter [m³], cubic inch [in³], cubic yard [yd³]) to compute the volume of rectangular solids.*

Math Link You have used a formula to find perimeter and area. In this lesson, you will learn formulas to find the amount of space contained in rectangular prisms.

Warm-Up Review

1. $7 \times 9 \times 5$
2. $6 \times 6 \times 6$
3. $8 \times 5 \times 4$
4. $10 \times 20 \times 3$
5. $0.5 \times 6 \times 12$
6. A triangular flag has a base of 8 in. and height of 24 in. What is the area of the flag?

Volume is the number of cubic units (units^3) contained in a solid figure. The volume of the figure at the right is 5 cubic units.

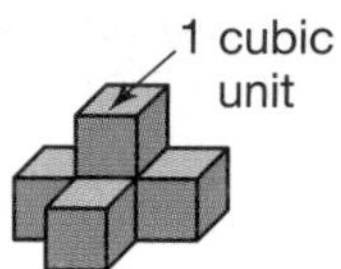

Word Bank

volume

Example 1

Find the volume of the rectangular solid.

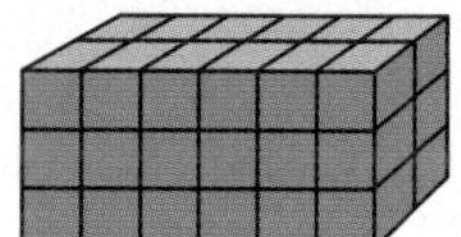

There are 12 cubes in the bottom layer and 3 layers.

$V = 12 \times 3 = 36$ cubic units (units^3)

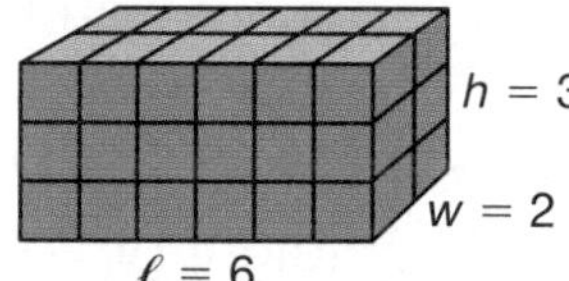

Use a formula to find the volume.

$\mathbf{V = \ell \times w \times h} = 6 \times 2 \times 3 = 36$ units^3

Example 2

Find the volume of the time capsule.

Use the formula.

$V = \ell \times w \times h$

$V = 35 \times 10 \times 20$

$V = 7{,}000$ cm^3

The volume of the time capsule is 7,000 cm^3.

Additional Standards: Number Sense 2.0, 2.2 (🔑) (See p. 455.)

More Examples

A.

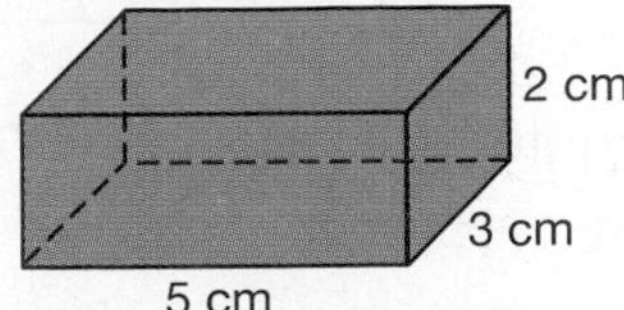

$V = 5 \times 3 \times 2$

$V = 30$ cubic centimeters (cm^3)

B.

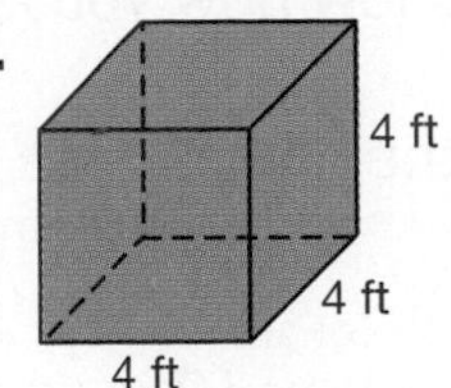

$V = 4 \times 4 \times 4$

$V = 64\ ft^3$

Guided Practice *For another example, see Set G on p. 491.*

Find the volume of each rectangular prism.

1.

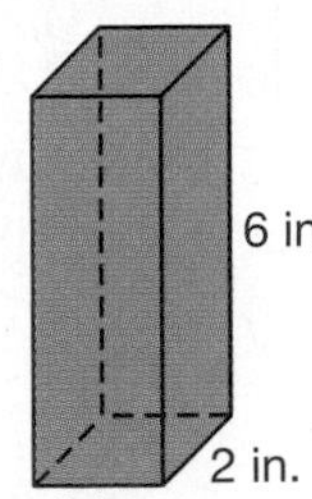

2.

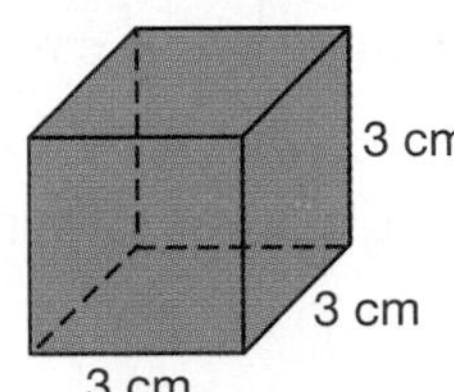

3. $\ell = 8$ m
$w = 4$ m
$h = 5$ m

4. $\ell = 12$ in.
$w = 12$ in.
$h = 12$ in.

5. The price of sand is $3.95 a cubic foot. Find the cost to fill a square sandbox 6 ft by 6 ft and 6 in. deep.

Independent Practice *For more practice, see Set G on p. 493.*

Find the volume of each rectangular prism.

6.

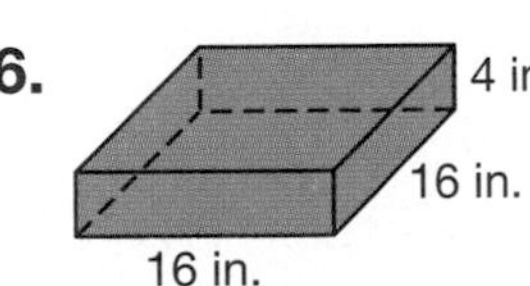

7.

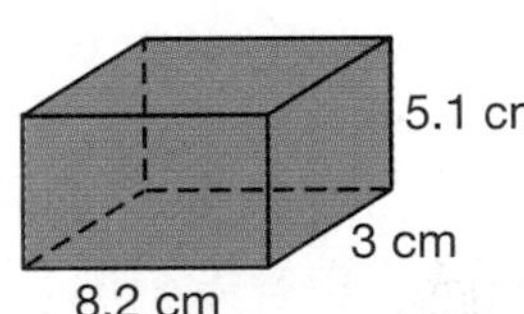
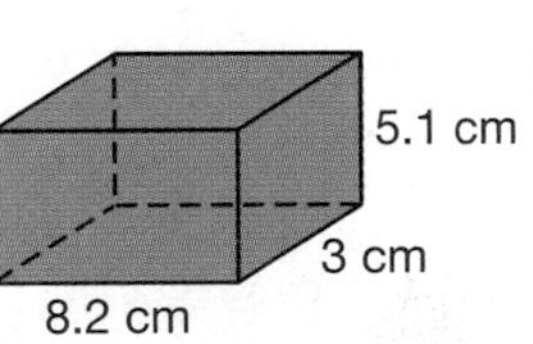

8.

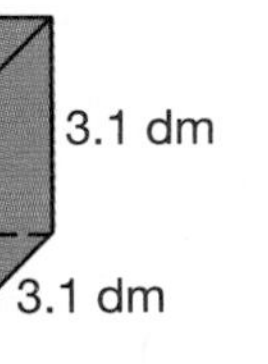

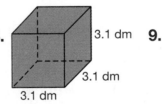

9.

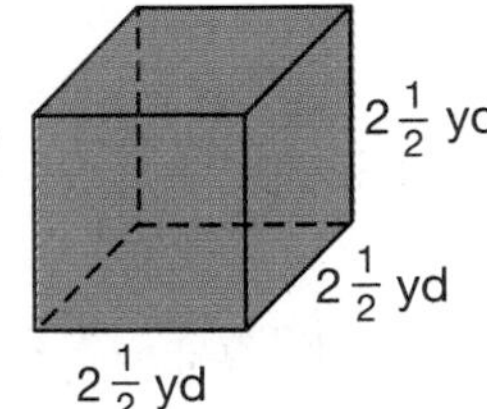

10. $\ell = 6$ ft
$w = 4$ ft
$h = 2$ ft

11. $\ell = 10$ in.
$w = 10$ in.
$h = 10$ in.

12. $\ell = 4.5$ cm
$w = 3.2$ cm
$h = 6$ cm

13. $\ell = 1.4$ m
$w = 1.7$ m
$h = 0.5$ m

Find each missing measurement. Figures are rectangular prisms.

14. $\ell = 10$ mm
$w = 5$ mm
$h = 2$ mm
$V = $ ■

15. $\ell = $ ■
$w = 9$ dm
$h = 3$ dm
$V = 135\ dm^3$

16. $\ell = 9$ cm
$w = $ ■
$h = 9$ cm
$V = 729\ cm^3$

17. $\ell = 11$ ft
$w = 8$ ft
$h = $ ■
$V = 440\ ft^3$

18. **Math Reasoning** How many cubic feet are in a cubic yard? Draw a diagram to show how you know.

19. Write a formula for the volume of a cube. Use s for the length of an edge.

20. **Math Reasoning** A box 12 in. long and 2 in. high has a volume of 288 in^3. Will it fit in a space 13 in. wide? Explain.

21. Complete the table at the right for rectangular solids with the measurements given. What happens to the volume when the length, the width, and the height are doubled?

ℓ	w	h	V
3 cm	2 cm	1 cm	
6 cm	4 cm	2 cm	
12 cm	8 cm	4 cm	
24 cm	16 cm	8 cm	

22. **Mental Math** Find the volume of a rectangular swimming pool 20 ft wide, 30 ft long, and 10 ft deep.

Mixed Review

23. **Mental Math** How many centimeter cubes will fit in a box with edges that measure 1 meter?

Find the perimeter and the area of each figure.

24. square with 4.2-in. sides

25. rectangle with sides 18 cm and 12 cm

26. The diameter of a circle is 20 ft. Find its circumference. Use 3.14 for π.

Test Prep **Choose the correct letter for each answer.**

27. (9-4) Yesterday's low temperature was $^-4$°F. Tomorrow's predicted high temperature is 24°F. Find the difference between yesterday's low temperature and tomorrow's predicted high temperature.

A $^-6$°F **B** 6°F **C** 20°F **D** 28°F

28. (8-8) (11-1) Last year Patti was $5\frac{1}{6}$ ft tall. This year she is $5\frac{1}{3}$ ft tall. How many inches has she grown?

F $\frac{1}{6}$ in. **G** $\frac{1}{6}$ ft **H** 2 in. **J** 2 ft **K** NH

Use Homework Workbook 11-9.

Multiple-Choice Cumulative Review

Choose the correct letter for each answer.

1. Which number is the least common multiple of 50 and 75?

A 25 **C** 150
B 125 **D** 300

2. If you cut a sphere in half, what shape would you see on the cut surface?

F Circle
G Square
H Rectangle
J Triangle

3. A fountain 2 meters high has sides with these lengths: 3.2 meters, 5.6 meters, 5.6 meters, 2.08 meters, and 2.08 meters. Which is a reasonable measure of the distance around the fountain?

A Less than 15 meters
B Between 15 meters and 17 meters
C Between 17 meters and 19 meters
D More than 20 meters

4. 5,000 pounds = ■ tons

F 2
G 2.5
H 2,000
J 2,500

5. Tasha sold 31 sketches at a flea market. She sold half as many car sketches as van sketches. She sold 16 truck sketches. How many of each kind did she sell?

A 16 truck, 10 van, 5 car
B 16 truck, 8 van, 4 car
C 16 truck, 6 van, 3 car
D 16 truck, 15 van, 7 car

6. Which of these space figures has only one base?

F Rectangular prism
G Triangular prism
H Cube
J Pyramid

7. One angle of a triangle measures 62°. The other two angles are congruent. What is the measure of one of the congruent angles in this triangle?

A 42°
B 48
C 59°
D 138°

8. Which figure has only 1 line of symmetry?

F 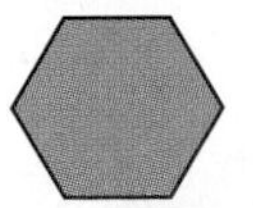
H 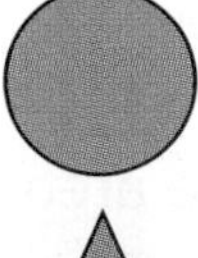
G 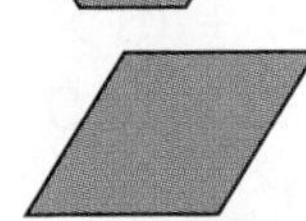
J

Surface Area

California Content Standard *Measurement and Geometry 1.2 (🔑): Construct a cube and rectangular box from two-dimensional patterns and use these patterns to compute the surface area for these objects.*

Warm-Up Review

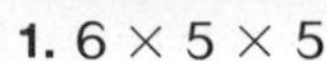

1. $6 \times 5 \times 5$
2. $10 \times 10 \times 6$
3. $3 \times 4 + 4 \times 2 + 2 \times 3$
4. $8 \times 5 + 5 \times 4 + 4 \times 8$
5. Erik has two rectangular flower beds. One is 10 ft by 20 ft, and the other is 20 ft by 30 ft. What is the total area of the beds?

Math Link You know how to find the area of a rectangle or square. In this lesson, you will learn to find the surface area of a rectangular prism.

Surface area is the sum of the areas of all the faces of a solid figure.

Word Bank

surface area

Example 1

The figure at the right could be cut out and folded to form a cube. The length of each edge is 1 cm. What is surface area of the cube?

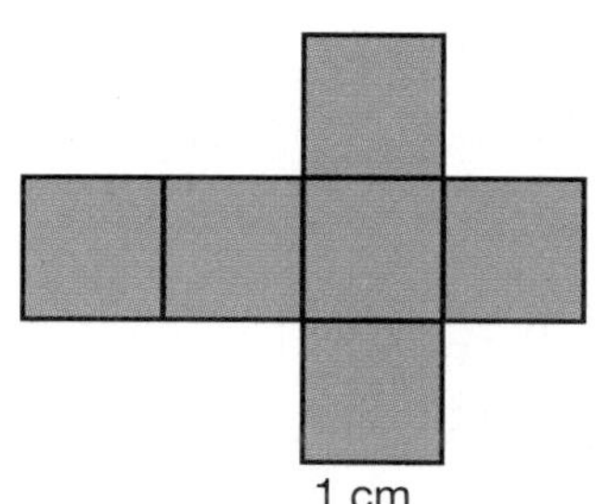

For each square,

$A = s \times s$

$= 1 \times 1$

$= 1 \text{ cm}^2$

Since there are 6 squares, the total surface area is 6 cm^2.

Example 2

A figure having the dimensions shown below could be cut out and folded to form the rectangular prism shown at the right. What is the surface area of the rectangular prism?

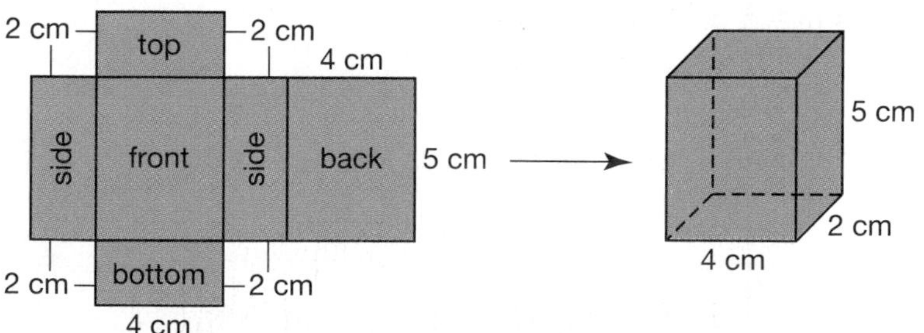

Add the areas of all the faces to find the surface area.

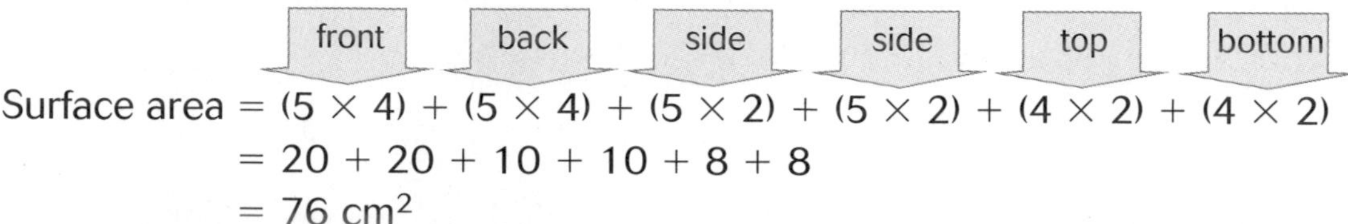

Surface area $= (5 \times 4) + (5 \times 4) + (5 \times 2) + (5 \times 2) + (4 \times 2) + (4 \times 2)$

$= 20 + 20 + 10 + 10 + 8 + 8$

$= 76 \text{ cm}^2$

Guided Practice *For another example, see Set H on p. 491.*

1. On a separate sheet of paper, draw a figure similar to the pattern shown in Example 1 on page 482. Make each square 3 cm on a side. Then cut out the figure and fold it to form a cube. Find the surface area of the cube.

Find the surface area of each figure.

2. 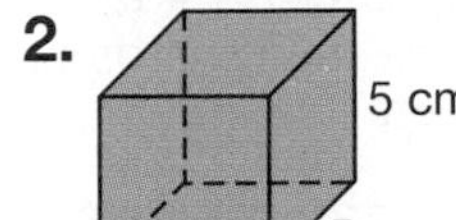

3. 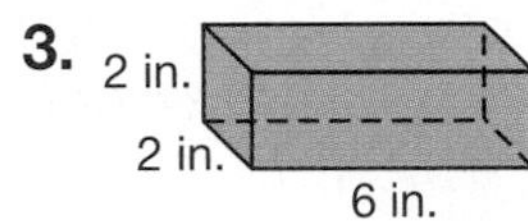

4. 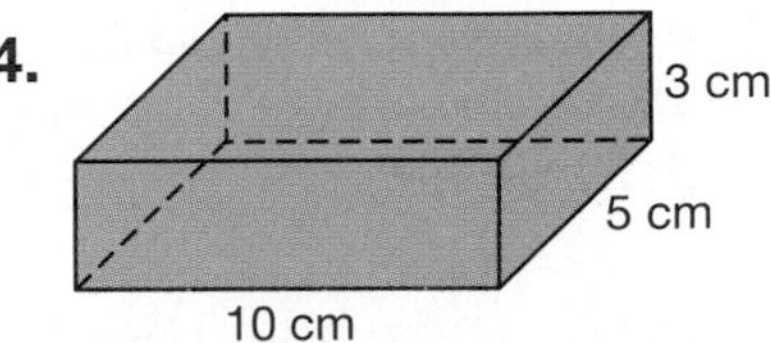

Independent Practice *For more practice, see Set H on p. 493.*

5. On a separate sheet of paper, draw a figure having the dimensions shown in the first figure for Example 2 on page 482. Cut out the figure and fold it to form a rectangular prism.

Find the surface area of each figure.

6. 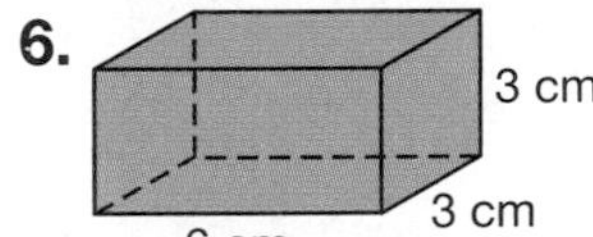

7. 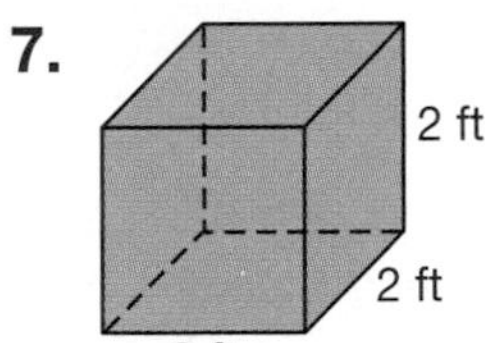

8. 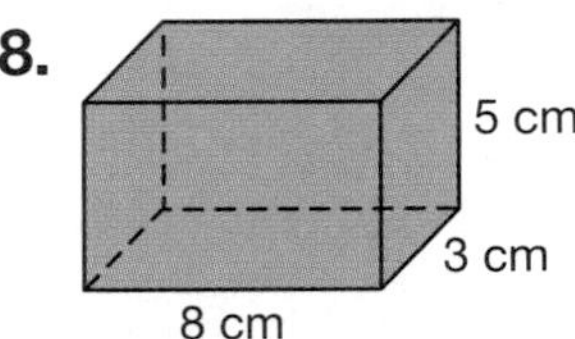

9. What is the surface area of a toy box that is 4 ft long, $2\frac{1}{2}$ ft wide, and 2 ft high?

Mixed Review

10. A gift box is 10 in. high and has a volume of 240 in^3. What are possible whole-number measurements for the length and width?

Find the area of each figure.

11. 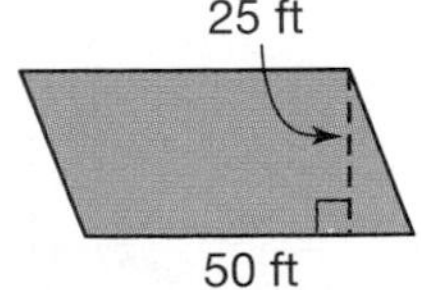

12. 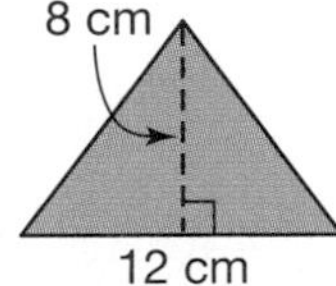

Find the volume of each figure.

13. 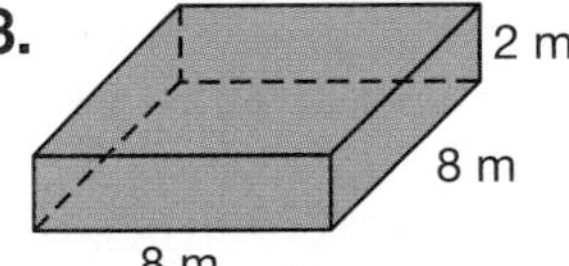

14. 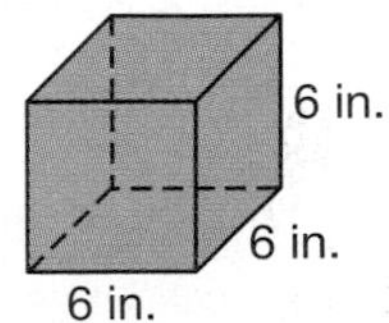

Test Prep **Choose the correct letter for the answer.**

15. Find $2\frac{1}{2} \times 7\frac{1}{2}$.
(8-12)

F 3 **G** 5 **H** 10 **J** $18\frac{3}{4}$

Use Homework Workbook 11-10.

Problem-Solving Application:

Using Appropriate Units of Measure

California Content Standard *Measurement and Geometry 1.4: Differentiate between, and use appropriate units of measures for, two- and three-dimensional objects (i.e., find the perimeter, area, volume).*

Warm-Up Review

1. $\frac{1}{2} \times 3 \times 4$
2. 15×10
3. $40 - 5 \times 3$
4. 25×8
5. $4 \times 5 + 8 \times 3$
6. $12 \times \$6.50$
7. Tony has two pieces of wire. One is 16 ft long and the other is 14 ft long. How many yards of wire does Tony have?

Andy's Landscaping Service has been hired to install a play lot for the Taubner children. A diagram of the play lot is at the right.

How much edging should Andy's Landscaping Service order to surround the play lot?

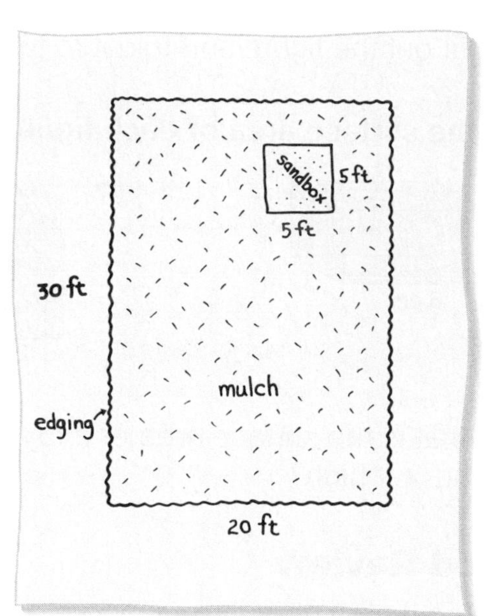

Understand

What do you need to find?

You need to find the distance around the play lot.

Plan

How can you solve the problem?

You can find the perimeter of the play lot.

Solve

Use the formula $P = 2\ell + 2w$.

$2 \times 30 + 2 \times 20 = 60 + 40 = 100$ ft

Andy's Landscaping Service should order 100 ft of edging.

Look Back

Would it make sense to use ft^2 or ft^3 to label your answer? Explain.

Additional Standards: Number Sense 2.0; Mathematical Reasoning 2.6 *(See p. 455.)*

For Exercises 1-6, tell if you need to find perimeter, area, or volume. Then solve the problem and give your answer using appropriate units. Refer to the diagram on the preceding page.

Guided Practice

1. Before putting the mulch down on the play lot, Andy's Landscaping Service will install a layer of plastic to cover the play area. How much plastic will be needed?

2. The mulch is to be 6 in. deep. How much mulch should be ordered?

Independent Practice

3. The sandbox will have a plastic edging. How much edging will it take for the sides of the sandbox?

4. The Taubners want at least 8 in. of sand in the sandbox. How much sand will they need?

5. If there is no mulch under the sandbox, how much of the play lot will be covered by mulch?

6. A gravel walk 3 ft wide and 3 in. deep is to surround the play lot. How much gravel will be in the walk?

Mixed Review

7. Supports for the edging around the play lot are to be placed at each corner and every 5 feet. How many supports will be needed?

8. What is the greatest rectangular area that can be enclosed by 12 m of edging? 16 m of edging?

9. **Math Reasoning** Think about your solutions to Exercise 8. If you have a given perimeter, what shape of quadrilateral encloses the greatest area?

10. Mrs. Taubner wants a flower garden to be planted as in the diagram at the right. What will be the area of the garden?

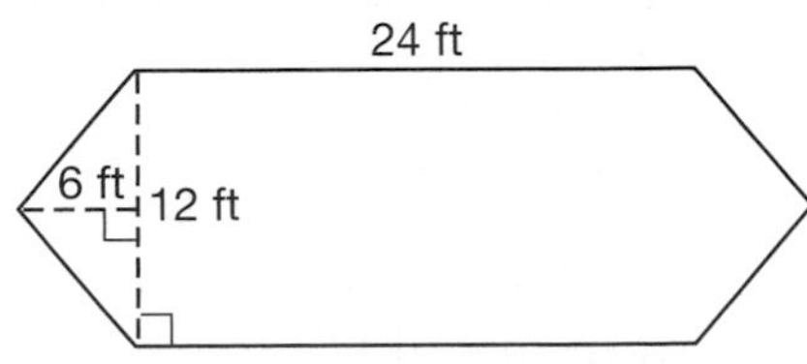

11. Mulch comes in 4-cubic-foot bags at \$4.50 per bag. How much would it cost to cover the entire play lot with 4 in. of mulch?

Diagnostic Checkpoint

Complete. For Exercises 1–3 choose a word from the Word Bank.

Word Bank
capacity
gram
perimeter
pi
volume

1. (11-5) In the metric system, the basic unit of mass is called the ____________.

2. (11-7) The distance around a polygon is its ____________.

3. (11-2) A customary unit of ____________ is a fluid ounce.

4. (11-5) 66 g = ■ mg

5. (11-5) ■ kg = 2,500 g

6. (11-5) 220 mL = ■ L

7. (11-5) 760 L = ■ mL

Find the perimeter or circumference of each figure. Use 3.14 for π.

8. (11-7)

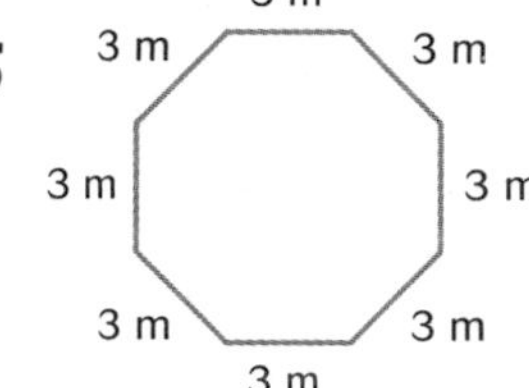

9. (11-7)

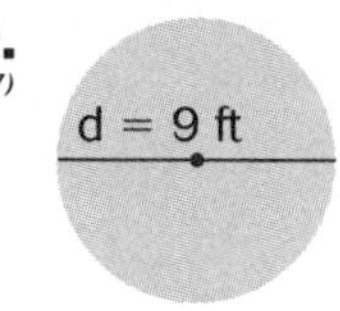

10. (11-7)

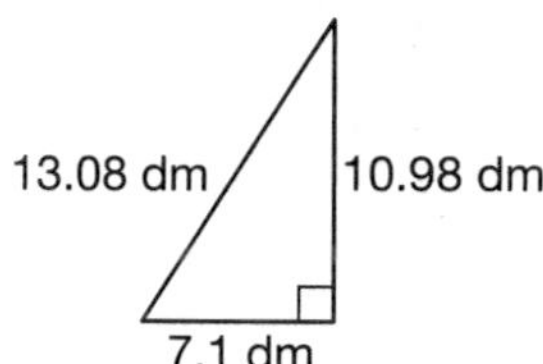

Find the area of each figure.

11. (11-8)

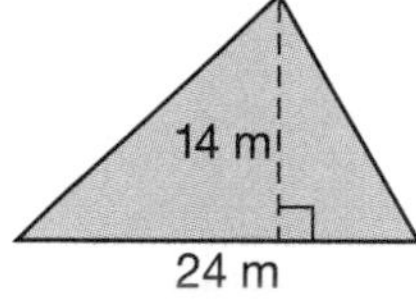

12. (11-8)

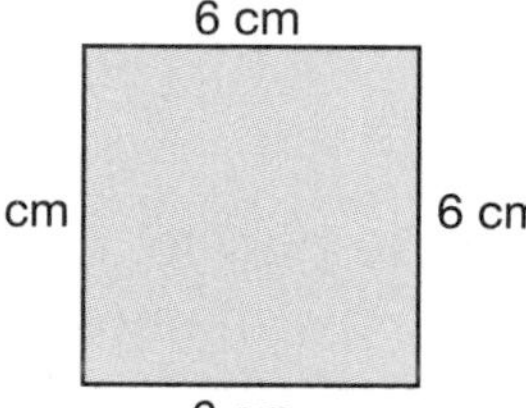

13. (11-8)

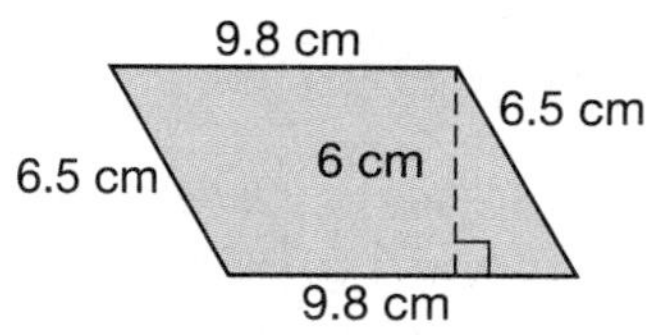

Find the volume and surface area of each rectangular prism.

14. (11-9 & 11-10)

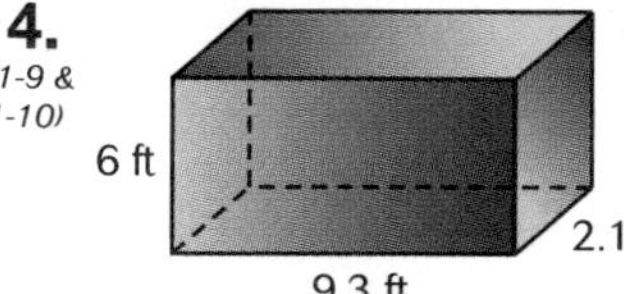

15. (11-9 & 11-10)

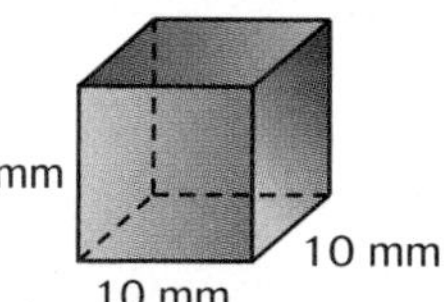

16. (11-9 & 11-10)

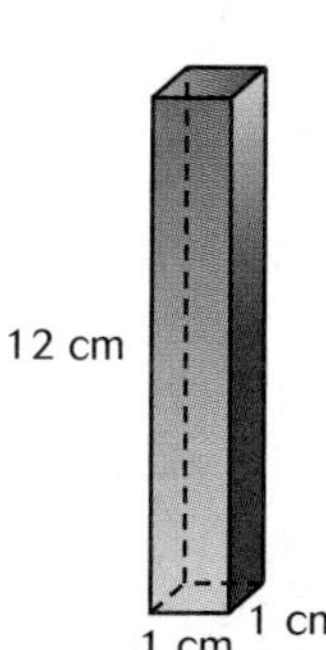

17. (11-6) Angie needs to be at school by 8:15 A.M. It takes her 45 minutes to get ready, 10 minutes to eat, and she has a 25-minute bus ride to school. What time should Angie wake up to make it to school on time?

18. (11-11) Samuel wants to fill a 2 feet × 6 feet × 6 feet container with potting soil. Should Samuel calculate a perimeter, area, or volume to determine how much soil he needs?

Chapter 11 Test

Add or subtract. Change to a larger unit when possible.

1. 8 yd 2 in. + 5 yd 2 in.

2. 3 yd 1 ft − 2 yd 2 ft

3. 5 gal 3 qt + 2 gal 2 qt

Complete.

4. 5 cm = ■ mm

5. 5,000 g = ■ kg

6. 1,100 mL = ■ L

7. 5.5 m = ■ cm

8. 9 qt = ■ gal ■ qt

9. 2 mi = ■ ft

Find the perimeter and area of each polygon.

10.

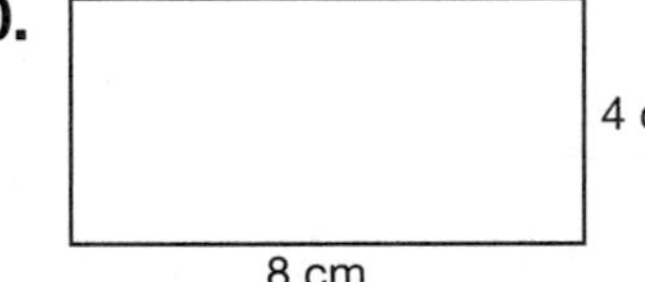

11.

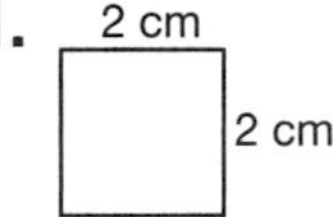

12.

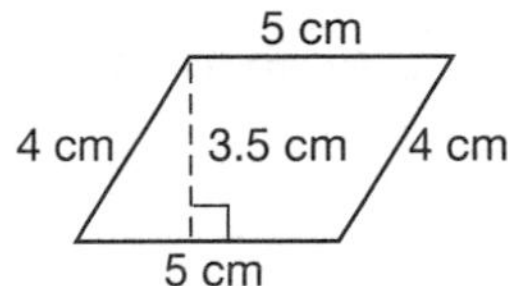

13.

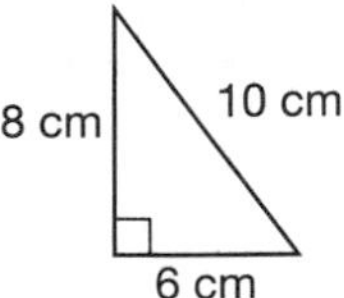

14. Use the picture at the right. About how far will a marble roll if it rolls once around the green track? Use 3.14 for π.

10 cm

Find the volume and surface area of each rectangular prism.

15. $l = 8$ m
$w = 4$ m
$h = 3$ m

16. $l = 2.3$ cm
$w = 2.0$ cm
$h = 6.2$ cm

17. $l = 5$ in.
$w = 3$ in.
$h = 4\frac{1}{4}$ in.

18. A swimming pool is 50 feet long by 30 feet wide by 6 feet deep. To find how much water the pool will hold, do you need to calculate area, perimeter, or volume? Solve the problem and give your answer with appropriate units.

19. Bianca makes flower arrangements and sells them for $9.95 apiece. She sold 8 arrangements this weekend. Her goal was to earn $100. Is an estimate enough or does she need an exact answer to find if she met her goal? Explain.

20. The total cost to rent a bicycle is $24.90 for 3 days. This includes a $3.00 per day fee for a bike helmet. How much is it to rent a bike for one day with no helmet?

Multiple-Choice Chapter 11 Test

Choose the correct letter for each answer.

1. **1 ft 3 in.**
+ 2 ft 9 in.

- **A** 3 feet 6 inches
- **B** 3 feet 8 inches
- **C** 3 feet 10 inches
- **D** 4 feet
- **E** NH

2. **What is the missing measurement?**

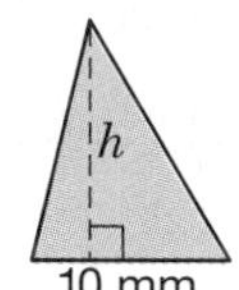

$A = 60 \text{ mm}^2$

$h = $ ■

- **F** 8 mm
- **G** 10 mm
- **H** 12 mm
- **J** 30 mm
- **K** NH

3. **How many grams is 0.732 kilogram?**

- **A** 0.00732 gram
- **B** 73.2 grams
- **C** 732 grams
- **D** 7,320 grams
- **E** NH

4. **Which measure would you use to measure the distance between two towns?**

- **F** millimeters
- **G** centimeters
- **H** meters
- **J** kilometers

A basketball weighs from 20 to 22 ounces. Use this fact to answer Questions 5 and 6.

5. **What is true about the weight of the basketball?**

- **A** It weighs at least 22 ounces.
- **B** It never weighs more than 20 ounces.
- **C** 3 balls weigh at least 60 ounces.
- **D** 5 balls weigh less than 100 ounces.

6. **What is the least that 12 basketballs could weigh in pounds?**

- **F** 15 pounds
- **G** 16.5 pounds
- **H** 240 pounds
- **J** 264 pounds

7. **A cereal company wants to pack 10 boxes in one carton for shipping. Each cereal box is 6 inches × 9 inches × 12 inches. What size carton, by volume, does the company need?**

- **A** 648 in^3
- **B** 6,480 in^3
- **C** 3,240 in^3
- **D** 7,625 in^3

8. **A container with a circular opening has a diameter of 8 centimeters. Find the circumference of the lid that fits on top of this container.**

- **F** 251.2 millimeters
- **G** 252.2 millimeters
- **H** 2,512 millimeters
- **J** 25,122 millimeters
- **K** NH

9. Trent gave $\frac{1}{4}$ of his flowers to Kelly. Then Kelly gave $\frac{1}{2}$ of her flowers to Lark. Lark then gave $\frac{1}{4}$ of her flowers to Tiko. Tiko ended up with 6 flowers. How many flowers did Trent have before he gave them away?

A 24
B 48
C 192
D 260

10. Find the measurement n and P in the figure. P = perimeter

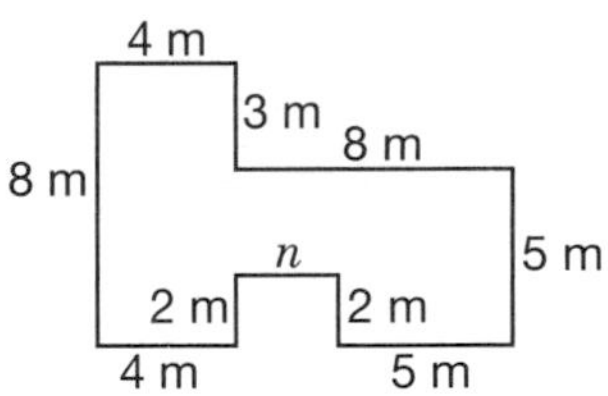

F $n = 1$; $P = 42$ meters
G $n = 4$; $P = 45$ meters
H $n = 3$; $P = 44$ meters
J $n = 2$; $P = 43$ meters

11. What is the surface area of a cube with sides of length 1.8 millimeters?

A 10.80 mm^2
B 19.44 mm^2
C 19.44 mm^3
D 34.99 mm^3

12. 50 oz = ▒ lb ▒ oz

F 3 pounds 2 ounces
G 3 pounds 6 ounces
H 4 pounds 2 ounces
J 4 pounds 6 ounces

13. You want to cover the bottom of your fish tank with a 2-inch layer of stones. The tank is 18 inches long and 12 inches wide. What do you need to calculate to find out how many cubic inches of stones you need?

A perimeter
B area
C volume
D surface area

Use the diagram for Question 14.

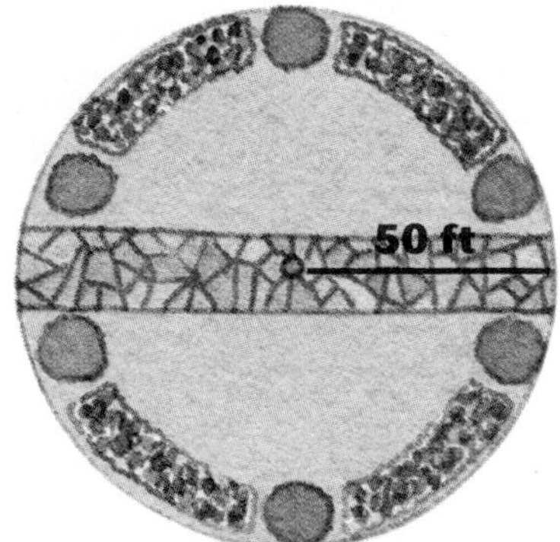

14. The mayor of Troydale wants to place bricks around the outside edge of the garden. What is the circumference of the garden?

F About 157 feet
G About 314 feet
H About 1,266 feet
J About 7,850 feet

15. Mr. O'Hara ran 21,222 meters last week. How many kilometers did he run?

A 2.1222 kilometers
B 21.222 kilometers
C 212.22 kilometers
D 2122.2 kilometers

Reteaching

Set A (pages 456–458)

Complete 16 yd = ■ in.

16 yd = ■ in.

Think: 1 yd = 36 in. Then multiply.

16 × 36 = 576

16 yd = 576 in.

Remember when changing from a smaller unit to a larger unit, divide. When changing from a larger unit to a smaller unit, multiply.

1. 6 mi = ■ ft

2. 94 yd = ■ ft

3.
```
  4 yd 1 ft
+ 6 yd 2 ft
```

4.
```
  3 yd 2 ft 4 in.
- 1 yd 1 ft 9 in.
```

Set B (pages 459–461)

Complete 16 qt = ■ gal.

16 qt = ■ gal

Think: 4 qt = 1 gal. Then divide.

16 ÷ 4 = 4

16 qt = 4 gal

Remember you can change units of capacity or weight to a larger or smaller unit when adding or subtracting measurements.

1. 6 pt = ■ cups

2. 19 lb = ■ oz

3.
```
  5 c 3 fl oz
- 2 c 5 fl oz
```

4.
```
  3 lb  5 oz
+      12 oz
```

Set C (pages 464–466)

Complete 20.3 km = ■ m.

20.3 km = ■ m

Think: 1 km = 1,000 m. Then multiply.

20.3 × 1,000 = 20,300

20.3 km = 20,300 m

Remember the metric system is based on tens. Changing from unit to unit is like moving from one place-value position to another.

1. 3 m = ■ cm

2. 12 cm = ■ mm

3. 3,000 m = ■ km

4. 24 mm = ■ m

Set D (pages 468–469)

Complete 0.90 mg = ■ g.

0.90 mg = ■ g

Think: 1,000 mg = 1g. Then divide.

0.90 ÷ 1,000 = 0.0009

0.90 mg = 0.0009 g

Remember in the metric system the basic unit of mass is the gram and the basic unit of capacity is the liter.

1. 687 g = ■ kg

2. 0.34 kg = ■ g

3. 4,000 mL = ■ L

4. 87 kg = ■ g

Set E (pages 472–474)

Find the perimeter of the figure.

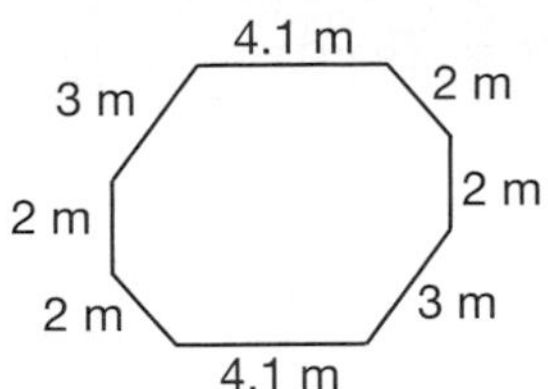

$P = 4.1 + 2 + 2 + 3 + 4.1 + 2 + 2 + 3$

$P = 22.2$ m

Remember the distance around a polygon is its perimeter. The distance around a circle is its circumference. The circumference C equals $\pi \times d$, where $d =$ the diameter of the circle.

Find the perimeter or circumference of each figure. Use 3.14 for π.

1. **2.**

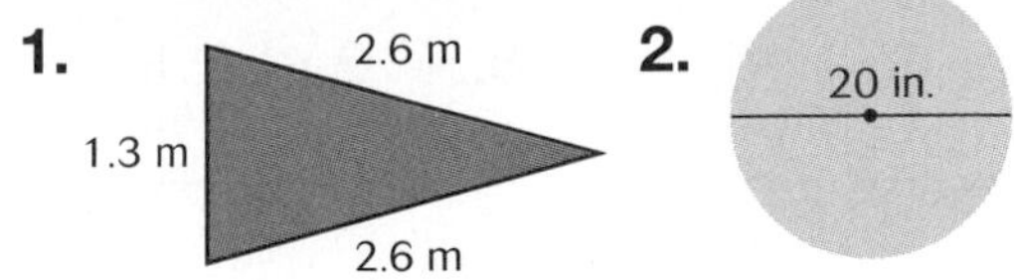

Set F (pages 475–477)

Find the area of the figure.

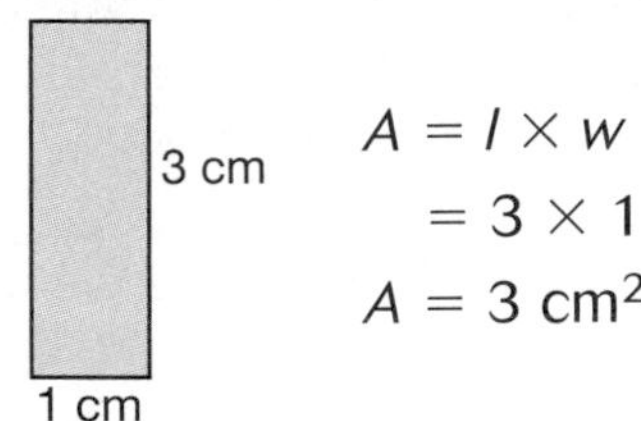

$A = l \times w$

$= 3 \times 1$

$A = 3 \text{ cm}^2$

Remember the formulas for area:
rectangle: $A = l \times w$;
parallelogram: $A = b \times h$
square: $A = s^2$; triangle $A = \frac{1}{2} b \times h$

Find the area of each figure.

1. triangle
$b = 3$ ft, $h = 8$ ft

2. square
$s = 6$ m

Set G (pages 478–480)

Find the volume of the rectangular prism.

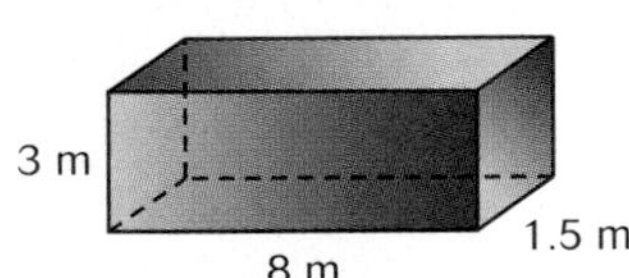

$V = l \times w \times h$

$V = 8 \text{ m} \times 1.5 \text{ m} \times 3 \text{ m}$

$V = 36 \text{ m}^3$

Remember the formula for the volume of a rectangular prism: $V = l \times w \times h$

Find the volume of each rectangular prism.

1.

8 ft
3 ft
2 ft

2.

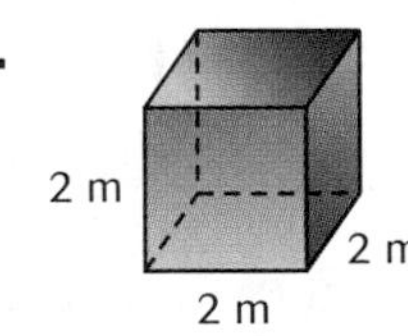

Set H (pages 482–483)

Find the surface area of the figure.

front = $20 \times 10 = 200$
back = $20 \times 10 = 200$
side = $15 \times 20 = 300$
side = $15 \times 20 = 300$
top = $10 \times 15 = 150$
bottom = $10 \times 15 = 150$

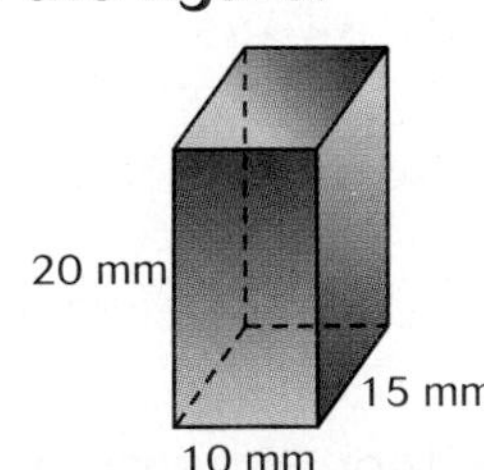

Surface Area
$= 200 + 200 + 300 + 300 + 150 + 150$
$= 1{,}300 \text{ mm}^2$

Remember the surface area is the sum of the areas of all the faces of a solid figure.

Find the surface area of each figure.

1. **2.**

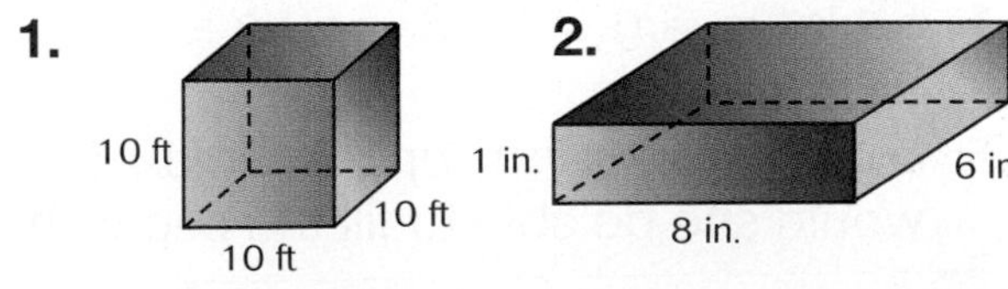

More Practice

Set A (pages 456–458)

Complete each statement.

1. 5 yd = ■ in.
2. 108 in. = ■ yd
3. 42 ft = ■ yd
4. 3 mi = ■ ft
5. 19 ft = ■ in.
6. 17 yd = ■ ft

Add or subtract. Change to a larger unit when possible.

7. 3 mi 1 yd + 2 mi 1 yd
8. 2 yd 2 ft − 1 yd 1 ft
9. 4 ft 1 in. − 1 ft 2 in.
10. 2 yd 2 ft 8 in. + 2 yd 2 ft 8 in.

11. A football player ran 11 yards on the first play and 13 yards on the second. How many feet did he run altogether?

Set B (pages 459–461)

Complete each statement.

1. 7 qt = ■ pt
2. 2 gal = ■ qt
3. 16 c = ■ pt
4. 3 lb 4 oz = ■ oz
5. 5 T = ■ lb
6. 10 lb 6 oz = ■ oz
7. A truck weighing over 3 tons cannot cross the Tallyho Bridge. Joann's truck weighs 5,600 pounds. Can she cross the bridge in her truck? Explain.

Set C (pages 464–466)

Complete each statement.

1. 30 m = ■ km
2. 4.5 m = ■ cm
3. 4,569 m = ■ km
4. Susan is entering a 5-kilometer race. How many meters will she run?

Set D (pages 468–469)

Complete each statement.

1. 50 kg = ■ g
2. 650 g = ■ kg
3. 7 L = ■ mL
4. 11,000 mL = ■ L
5. Joan's measuring cup can hold 250 milliliters. How many times would she be able to fill the cup with a 2-liter bottle of juice?

Set E (pages 472–474)

Find the perimeter or the circumference of each figure. Use 3.14 for π.

1. 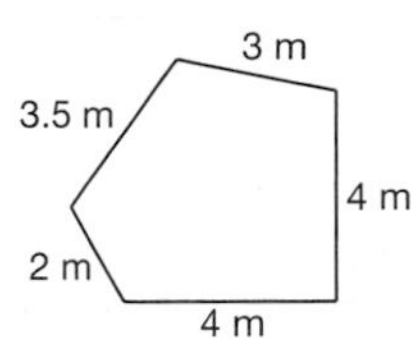

2. 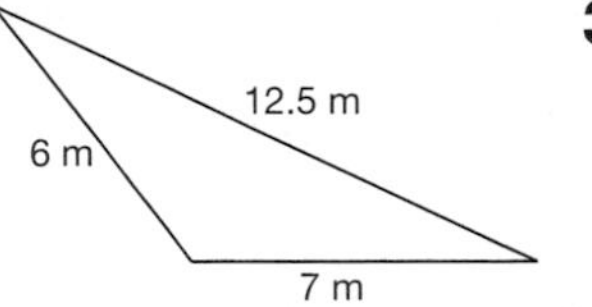

3. 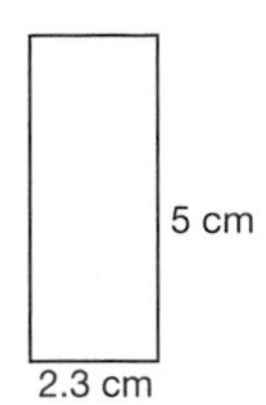

4. 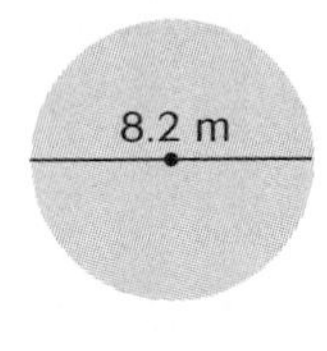

5. A water fountain in Paisley Park has a radius of 12 feet. What is the circumference of the fountain? Use 3.14 for π.

Set F (pages 475–477)

Find the area of each figure.

1. 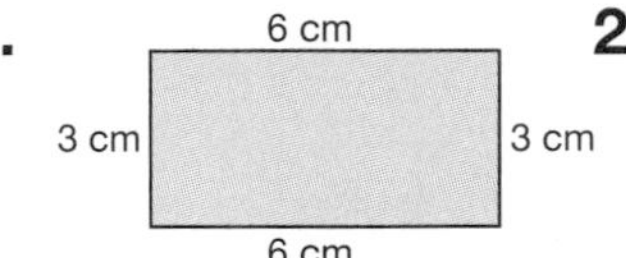

2. 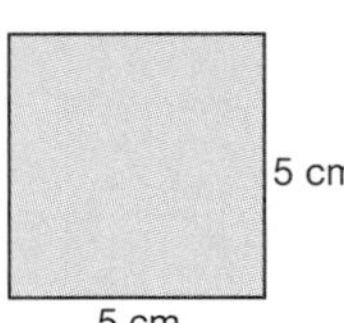

3. 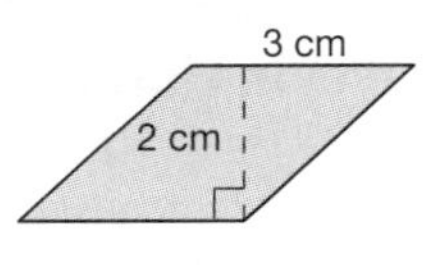

4. 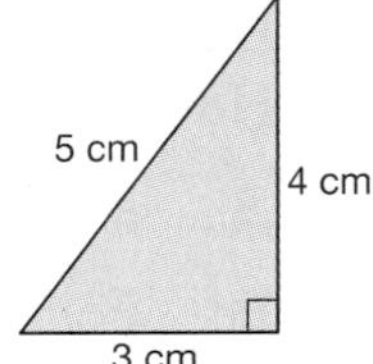

5. Bill needs to carry brownies to school for a class party. If each brownie is 6 centimeters on a side, how many brownies can he fit in one layer in a box that is 30 centimeters by 48 centimeters?

Set G (pages 478–480)

Find the volume of each rectangular prism.

1. $l = 8$ m
$w = 4$ m
$h = 3$ m

2. $l = 1.0$ m
$w = 6.3$ m
$h = 2.1$ m

3. $l = 10$ ft
$w = 11$ ft
$h = 9$ ft

4. $l = 2.1$ m
$w = 2.1$ m
$h = 0.6$ m

5. What is the volume of a storage trunk with the dimensions 4 feet by 2 feet by 5 feet?

Set H (pages 482–483)

Find the surface area of each figure.

1. 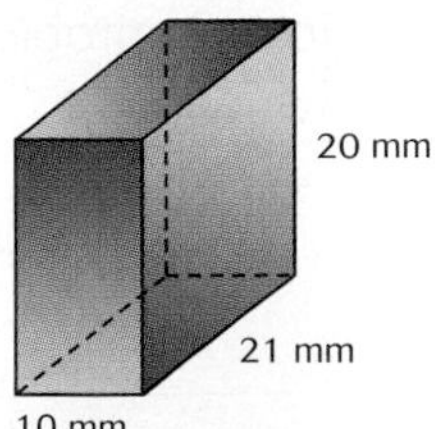

2. 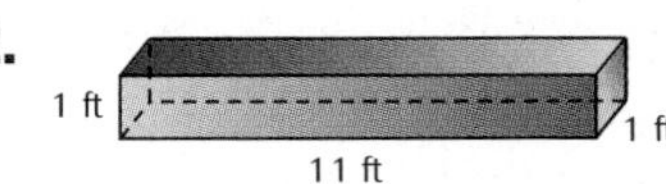

3. 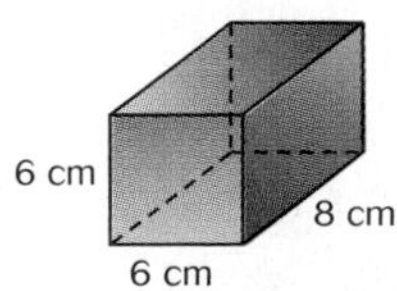

TEST PREP

Problem Solving: Preparing for Tests

Choose the correct letter for each answer.

1. Laura drew a graph of her 6-hour bicycle trip.

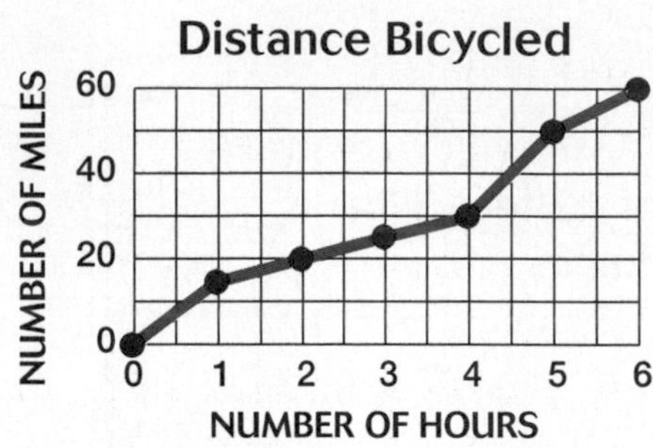

During which hour did she ride the farthest? How far did she travel in that hour?

A Fourth hour, 20 miles
B Fourth hour, 30 miles
C Fifth hour, 20 miles
D Fifth hour, 50 miles

> **Tip**
> For this problem, you might start by making a table or list showing how many miles she rode each hour.

2. Dan bought 4.3 kilograms of cheese and 3 kilograms of tomatoes for his deli. He used 350 grams of the cheese for sandwiches. He grated another 120 grams and used it for salads. What is a reasonable amount of cheese to be left?

F 3.83 grams
G 38.3 grams
H 383 grams
J 3,830 grams

> **Tip**
> *Use Logical Reasoning* to help you solve the problem. Remember, 1 kg = 1,000 g.

3. Paula has a red skirt and a black skirt. She also has 2 pairs of blue jeans and 3 different sweaters. How many outfits of skirts and sweaters can Paula make with these pieces of clothing?

A 5 outfits
B 6 outfits
C 9 outfits
D 12 outfits

> **Tip**
> Try the strategy *Draw a Diagram* for this problem.

4. Which two triangles are congruent?

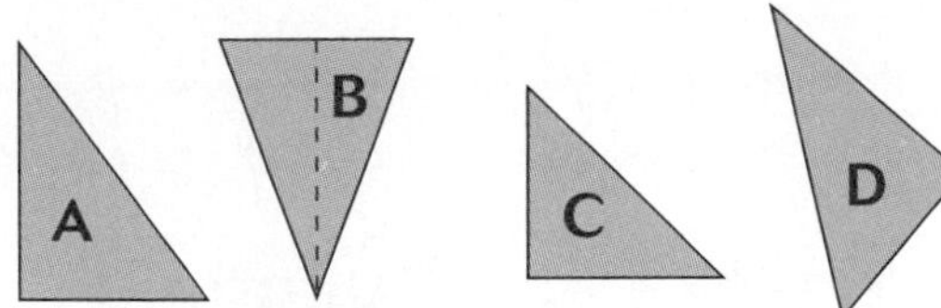

F Triangles *A* and *B*

G Triangles *A* and *C*

H Triangles *A* and *D*

J Triangles *C* and *D*

---

5. Harriet needs $1\frac{1}{2}$ yards of fabric to make a pillow. She finds remnants on sale at a fabric store. Which of these remnants should she buy?

A 50 inches

B 4 feet

C $4\frac{1}{2}$ feet

D $1\frac{3}{8}$ yards

---

6. Jai has 64 baseball cards and some football cards. He wants to share the baseball cards equally among himself and his friends. What information do you need to find out how many cards each person will get?

F How much the cards cost

G How many football cards Jai has

H How many friends Jai has

J How many cards Jai has altogether

---

7. Martin folded a piece of paper in half 4 times. How many sections were made by the fold lines?

A 10

B 12

C 16

D 32

8. For a family party, George formed an L-shaped table by putting a 30-inch square table against the long side of a 30-inch by 72-inch table. He plans to put a paper border around the sides of the L-shaped table. About what length of paper will he need?

F 190 inches

G 260 inches

H 350 inches

J 440 inches

---

9. Ben drew a rectangle with a length of 40 centimeters and a width of 30 centimeters. What was the area of the rectangle?

A 70 cm^2

B 120 cm^2

C 140 cm^2

D 1,200 cm^2

---

10. The graph shows the time spent by 4 students who worked as a team on a science project.

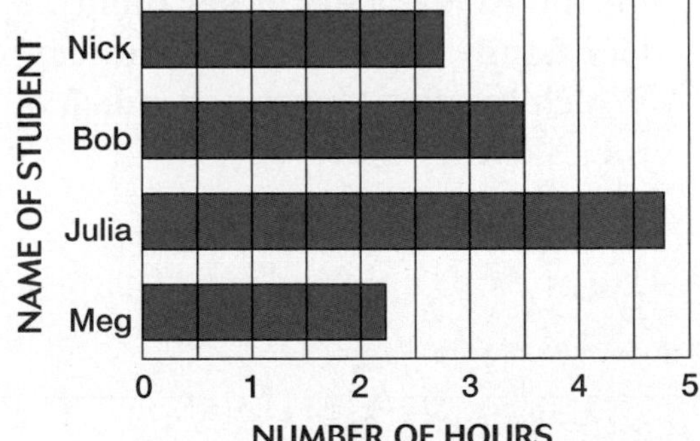

What was the approximate range of the times spent by the 4 students?

F $13\frac{1}{4}$ hours

G $7\frac{1}{2}$ hours

H $4\frac{3}{4}$ hours

J $2\frac{1}{2}$ hours

TEST PREP

Multiple-Choice Cumulative Review

Choose the correct letter for each answer.

Number Sense

1. Which of these numbers is 50 when rounded to the nearest ten and 53 when rounded to the nearest one?

   A 50.1
   B 52.4
   C 53.1
   D 53.5

2. Which shaded region does NOT represent $\frac{1}{3}$ of the figure?

   F 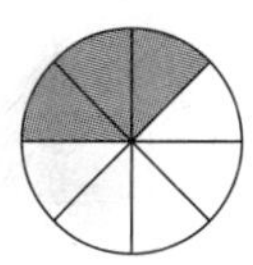
   H 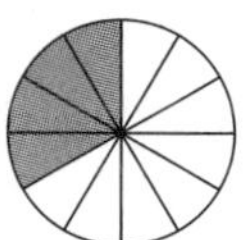
   G 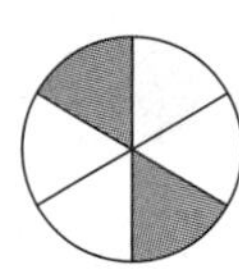
   J 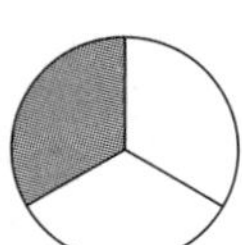

3. Minnie cut a sheet cake into 24 pieces for the 12 members of her family. Her family ate 8 pieces for dessert. Which fraction shows how much of the cake they ate?

   A $\frac{1}{6}$ C $\frac{2}{5}$
   B $\frac{1}{3}$ D $\frac{3}{4}$

4. Which product is equal to 75?

   F $3 \times 3 \times 5$
   G $15 \times 2 \times 2$
   H $5 \times 2 \times 3$
   J $3 \times 5 \times 5$

Algebra and Functions

5. Which expression is equivalent to $(4 \times 3) + (4 \times 6)$?

   A $4 + (3 \times 6)$ C 12×10
   B $7 + 10$ D $4 \times (3 + 6)$

6. What is the value of $n + {}^{-}8$ if $n = {}^{-}10$?

   F $^{-}18$ H 2
   G $^{-}2$ J 18

Use the graph below to answer Questions 7 and 8.

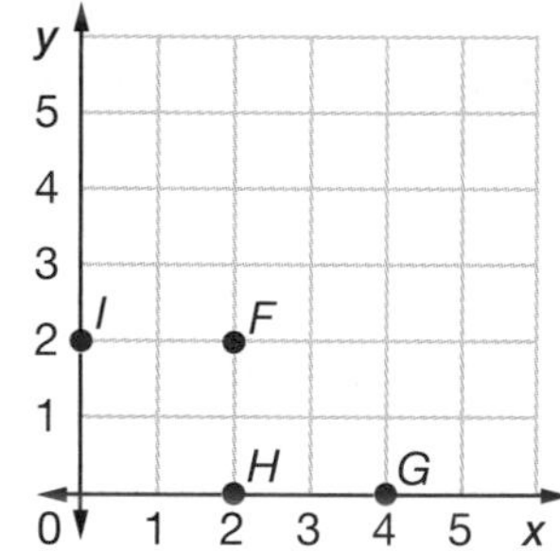

7. Which point best represents the ordered pair (2, 2)?

   A *F* C *H*
   B *G* D *I*

8. Which ordered pair names the point you would reach if you moved two units vertically down from point *I*?

   F (1, 1) H (1, 2)
   G (0, 1) J (0, 0)

Measurement and Geometry

9. ***EFGH*** **is a parallelogram. Which statement is true?**

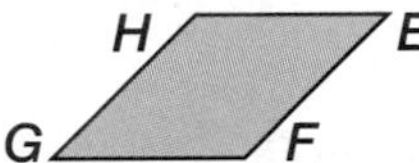

A $\angle E$ is congruent to $\angle F$
B $\angle E$ is congruent to $\angle G$
C $\angle F$ is congruent to $\angle G$
D $\angle G$ is congruent to $\angle H$

---

10. Which figures appear to be congruent?

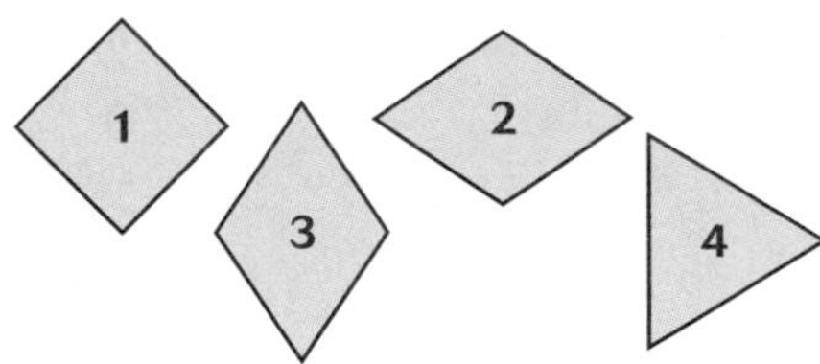

F 3 and 4
G 1 and 2
H 2 and 3
J 1 and 4

---

11. If you dipped the shape shown below in paint and rolled it in a straight line along a piece of paper, what shape would you make?

A Rectangle
B Circle
C Triangle
D Square

---

12. How many lines of symmetry does a square have?

F 1 **H** 3
G 2 **J** 4

---

13. A tree in Henry's yard is 33.4 meters tall and 2.2 meters in diameter. The top of Henry's house is 16 meters high. How much taller is the tree than the house?

A 21.2 meters **C** 17.4 meters
B 18.2 meters **D** 13.8 meters

---

14. What is the *area* of the triangle?

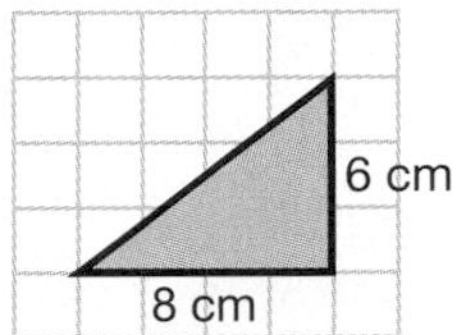

F 48 cm^2 **H** 14 cm^2
G 24 cm^2 **J** 7 cm^2

---

15. This is a diagram of a new pool being built. What is its *perimeter*?

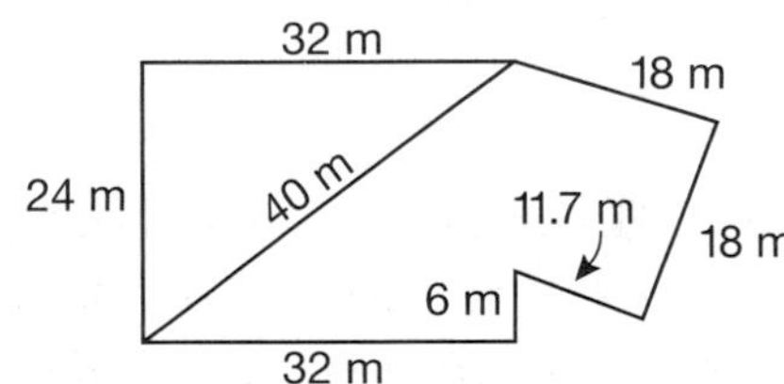

A 141.7 meters **C** 171.7 meters
B 161.7 meters **D** 181.7 meters

---

16. Jim bought 6 liters of a sports drink for $1.09 per liter. His glass holds about 120 milliliters. Which is reasonable for the number of glasses he can fill with the sports drink? (1 L = 1,000 mL)

F 500 **H** 40
G 50 **J** 30

Ratio, Percent, and Probability

Diagnosing Readiness

In Chapter 12, you will use these skills:

A Finding Equivalent Fractions

(pages 274–275)

Write two equivalent fractions for each fraction.

1. $\frac{4}{3}$ **2.** $\frac{5}{10}$

3. $\frac{18}{5}$ **4.** $\frac{1}{12}$

5. $\frac{11}{22}$ **6.** $\frac{2}{3}$

7. $\frac{20}{48}$ **8.** $\frac{9}{18}$

B Writing Fractions in Simplest Form

(pages 276–277)

Simplify each fraction. Write *yes* if the fraction is already in simplest form.

9. $\frac{12}{18}$ **10.** $\frac{49}{70}$

11. $\frac{18}{45}$ **12.** $\frac{10}{15}$

13. $\frac{32}{64}$ **14.** $\frac{18}{42}$

15. $\frac{2}{72}$ **16.** $\frac{7}{20}$

17. Sylvia has 20 postcards, and 12 of them are from Guam. Write the fraction of postcards from Guam in simplest form.

C Writing Fractions as Decimals

(pages 272–273)

Write each fraction as a decimal.

18. $\frac{6}{8}$

19. $\frac{3}{4}$

20. $\frac{1}{8}$

21. $\frac{25}{100}$

22. $\frac{47}{100}$

23. $\frac{2}{50}$

24. A "penny stock" is priced at $\frac{3}{4}$ of a dollar. Write the price as a decimal.

D Writing Decimals as Fractions

(pages 272–273)

Write each decimal as a fraction in lowest terms.

25. 0.25

26. 0.125

27. 0.65

28. 0.86

29. 0.01

30. 0.41

31. Liz lives 0.625 mile from school. Write this distance as a fraction in simplest form.

E Writing Expressions

(pages 55–57)

Write an expression using math symbols to describe the following.

32. 12 divided by y

33. 44 times h

34. the product of 8 and 3

35. 11 more than y

36. 16 multiplied by 2

F Solving Equations Involving Multiplication and Division

(pages 196–197)

Solve for x.

37. $10x = 200$

38. $\frac{x}{24} = 3$

39. $\frac{x}{22} = 45$

40. $2x = 48$

41. $\frac{x}{5} = 25$

To the Family and Student

Looking Back	Chapter 12	Looking Ahead
In Chapter 7, students learned how to find equivalent fractions and common multiples.	**Ratio, Percent, and Probability** In this chapter, students will learn how to find equivalent ratios, relate ratios and percents, and determine the outcome of an event.	In Grade 6, students will learn how to use ratios and proportions to solve percentage and probability problems.

Math and Everyday Living

Opportunities to apply the concepts of Chapter 12 abound in everyday situations. During the chapter, think about how ratio, percent, and probability can be used to solve a variety of real-world problems. The following examples suggest just several of many situations that could launch a discussion about ratio, percent, and probability.

Math and Design In designing a new deck to build onto the back of your house, you and your family make a scale drawing. You use a scale of $\frac{1 \text{ inch}}{5 \text{ feet}}$. Use the dimensions from your drawing to calculate the actual dimensions of the deck.

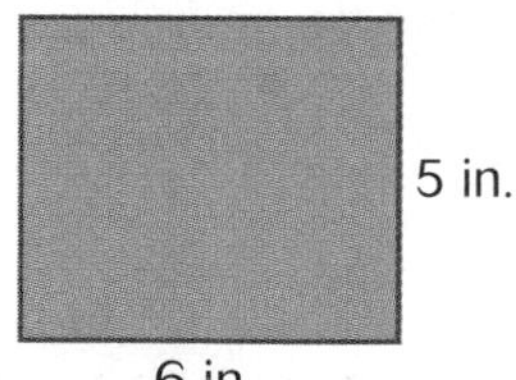

Math and Technology You scan a graph measuring 8 inches (width) by 10 inches (length) into your computer. You want to reduce the graph so you can use it in the sidebar of your science report. If you reduce the width of the graph to 2 in., what will the length be?

Math at a Party At a family gathering a variety of vegetables and dips are served. You decide to try every combination of one vegetable and dip at least once. The following chart shows the vegetables and dips you have to choose from. How many combinations can you try?

Vegetable	Dip
Celery	Salsa
Cauliflower	Cheese
Broccoli	Green-onion
Carrot	
Radish	

Math and Real Estate Last month your family sold your house for $150,000. Your family's real estate agent charged a fee of $9,000. Your neighbors plan to use the same agent to sell their house. If their house sells for $200,000, how much money can they expect to pay to the agent?

Math and the Government Your aunt is self-employed as an independent make-up consultant. Because she is self-employed, she must pay a self-employment tax equal to 15% of her earnings. How much self-employment tax will she have to pay the government if she made $14,785 last year?

Math and Education The local college graduates about 900 students each year. Typically 80 of the graduates are art majors, 450 students are business majors, 300 are education majors, and 70 are music majors. What is the probability that a graduate from your local college is a business major?

California Content Standards in Chapter 12 Lessons*

	Teach and Practice	Practice
Number Sense		
1.2 (🔑) Interpret percents as a part of a hundred; find decimal and percent equivalents for common fractions and explain why they represent the same value; compute a given percent of a whole number.	12-6, 12-7, 12-8	
1.2 (Gr. 6) (🔑) Interpret and use ratios in different contexts (e.g., batting averages, miles per hour) to show the relative sizes of two quantities, using appropriate notations (*a*/*b*, *a* to *b*, *a*:*b*).	12-1, 12-2	
Algebra and Functions		
2.2 (Gr. 6) (🔑) Demonstrate an understanding that *rate* is a measure of one quantity per unit value of another quantity.	12-4	
2.3 (Gr. 6) Solve problems involving rates, average speed, distance, and time.		12-4, 12-6, 12-7
Statistics, Data Analysis, and Probability		
1.2 Organize and display single-variable data . . . (e.g., . . . circle graphs)	12-13	
1.3 Use fractions and percentages to compare data sets of different sizes.	12-10, 12-11	12-13
2.0 (Gr. 4) Students make predictions for simple probability situations.		12-10, 12-11
3.1 (Gr. 6) (🔑) Represent all possible outcomes for compound events in an organized way (e.g., tables, grids, tree diagrams) and express the theoretical probability of each outcome.	12-12	

	Teach and Practice	Practice
Mathematical Reasoning		
2.0 Students use strategies, skills, and concepts in finding solutions	12-5	
2.3 Use a variety of methods, such as words, numbers, symbols, charts, graphs, tables, diagrams, and models, to explain mathematical reasoning.	12-3, 12-9, 12-11	12-13
2.4 Express the solution clearly and logically by using the appropriate mathematical notation and terms and clear language; support solutions with evidence in both verbal and symbolic work.		12-5
3.2 Note the method of deriving the solution and demonstrate a conceptual understanding of the derivation by solving similar problems.		12-9

* The symbol (🔑) indicates a key standard as designated in the Mathematics Framework for California Public Schools. Full statements of the California Content Standards are found at the beginning of this book following the Table of Contents.

Understanding Ratios

California Content Standard *Number Sense 1.2 (Grade 6) (key): Interpret and use ratios . . . using appropriate notations (a/b, a to b, a:b).*

Warm-Up Review

Write each fraction in simplest form.

1. $\frac{10}{12}$
2. $\frac{6}{8}$
3. $\frac{10}{15}$
4. $\frac{20}{30}$
5. Out of 25 people surveyed, 10 people named blue as their favorite color. What fraction named blue?

Math Link Often you need to describe the relationship between two quantities. In this lesson you will learn how ratios can be used to compare two quantities.

Word Bank

ratio

The necklace at the right uses three round beads for every seven long beads. The **ratio** of round beads to long beads is 3 to 7. There are four different ways to write the ratio.

three to seven **3 to 7** **3:7** $\frac{3}{7}$

Example

On the entire necklace there are 18 round beads and 42 long beads. What are four ways to write this ratio?

eighteen to forty-two 18 to 42

18:42 $\frac{18}{42}$

Guided Practice *For another example, see Set A on p. 534.*

Write each ratio in two different ways.

1. 4:7
2. $\frac{10}{3}$
3. 2 to 3
4. one to nine
5. 8 to 4
6. 2:5
7. $\frac{16}{5}$
8. 3 to 5
9. two to seven
10. 10 to 5

Use the jewelry pin at the right to write a ratio for Exercises 11–13.

11. turquoise stones to red stones
12. red stones to teardrop-shaped stones
13. turquoise stones to total stones

Independent Practice *For more practice, see Set A on p. 537.*

Write two different ratios for each string of beads. Tell what your ratios represent.

14. 

15. 

Make a drawing for each ratio in Exercises 16–25.
Hint: Use color, shape, or size to show the ratio.

16. $\frac{4}{3}$ **17.** $\frac{3}{4}$ **18.** 1:2 **19.** 3 to 8 **20.** $\frac{4}{5}$

21. 5:2 **22.** 12:8 **23.** 6:3 **24.** 1 to 7 **25.** 5:3

26. Math Reasoning Karen and Kate looked at a collection of stones. Karen said the ratio was 2:3. Kate said the ratio was 2:5. They were both right. Explain why.

27. Use the table at the right to choose beads for your own string of beads. Label the colors and sizes of the beads. Then exchange drawings with a classmate and write as many ratios as you can for the string of beads.

Number and Kinds of Beads

	Red	Yellow	Blue
Small	20	30	25
Medium	10	15	20
Large	4	5	6

Mixed Review

28. Each box in a crate weighs 1.2 pounds. The cost of shipping each box is $3.50. There are 24 boxes. What is the total weight of all the boxes?

29. $\frac{2}{3} \times \frac{1}{3}$ **30.** $\frac{2}{5} + \frac{1}{10}$ **31.** $^{-}5 + (^{-}7)$ **32.** $3 - (^{-}5)$

33. Find the volume of the figure shown at the right.

34. Find the surface area of the figure shown at the right.

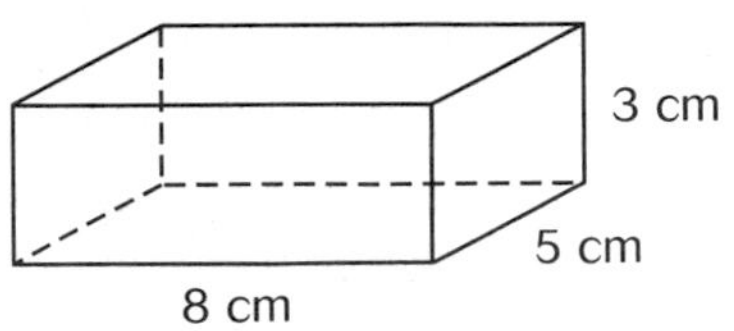

Test Prep Choose the correct letter for each answer.

35. (8-8) One cat weighs $8\frac{3}{4}$ pounds. Another weighs $9\frac{1}{2}$ pounds. How much more does the larger cat weigh?

A 1 pound **C** $1\frac{3}{4}$ pounds

B $1\frac{1}{4}$ pounds **D** $\frac{3}{4}$ pound

36. (6-8) It costs a manufacturer $4,830 to make 1,000 T-shirts. What does it cost to make one T-shirt?

F $0.48 **J** $483.00

G $4.83 **K** NH

H $48.30

Equivalent Ratios

 **California Content Standard** *Number Sense 1.2 (🔑) (Grade 6): Interpret and use ratios in different contexts (e.g., batting averages, miles per hour) to show the relative sizes of two quantities, using appropriate notations (a/b, a to b, a:b).*

Warm-Up Review

Write two equivalent fractions for each fraction.

1. $\frac{1}{2}$
2. $\frac{1}{3}$
3. $\frac{1}{5}$
4. $\frac{3}{8}$
5. A board is $5\frac{1}{2}$ feet long. It must be trimmed to a length of 50 inches. How many inches must be trimmed?

Word Bank

ratio table
equivalent ratios

Math Link You know that a fraction can be named by many equivalent fractions. Likewise, a relationship between two quantities can be named by many equivalent ratios.

A quilt pattern calls for 2 triangles and 5 squares in each panel. It takes 10 triangles for five quilt panels. How many squares are needed for five panels?

$$\frac{2 \text{ triangles}}{5 \text{ squares}} = \frac{10 \text{ triangles}}{? \text{ squares}}$$

Example 1

Use a **ratio table** to find how many triangles are needed for 5 panels.

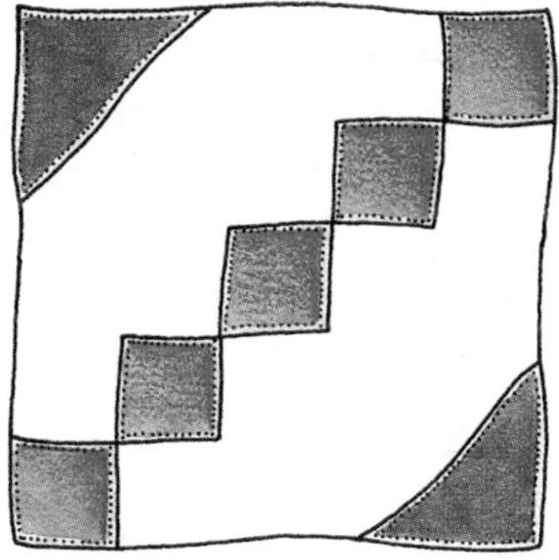

Panels	×1	×2	×3	×4	×5
Number of squares	5	10	15	20	25
Number of triangles	2	4	6	8	10

The table shows that 25 squares are needed for 5 quilt panels.

The ratios 5:2, 10:4, 15:6, 20:8, and 25:10 express the same relationship. They are **equivalent ratios.**

You can multiply or divide each number in a ratio by the same nonzero number. The resulting ratio is equivalent to the original ratio.

Example 2

Write three other ratios equivalent to $\frac{3}{4}$. Multiply the numerator and denominator in $\frac{3}{4}$ by 2, 5, and 10.

$\frac{3 \times 2}{4 \times 2} = \frac{6}{8}$ $\frac{3 \times 5}{4 \times 5} = \frac{15}{20}$ $\frac{3 \times 10}{4 \times 10} = \frac{30}{40}$

Guided Practice *For another example, see Set B on p. 534.*

Copy and complete each ratio table.

1.

	×2	×3	×4	×5	×6
3					
5					

2.

	×2	×3	×4	×5	×6
3					
7					

Write three other equivalent ratios for each given ratio.

3. $\frac{1}{4}$ **4.** $\frac{2}{3}$ **5.** 1 to 5 **6.** $\frac{2}{7}$ **7.** 1:10

8. Each vase needs 3 roses and 8 lilies. There are 80 lilies for 10 vases. How many roses are needed?

Independent Practice *For more practice, see Set B on p. 537.*

Copy and complete each ratio table.

9.

	×2	×3	×4	×5	×6
4					
9					

10.

	×2	×3	×4	×5	×6
5					
8					

Write three other equivalent ratios for each given ratio.

11. $\frac{1}{8}$ **12.** $\frac{7}{16}$ **13.** $\frac{4}{5}$ **14.** $\frac{7}{8}$ **15.** $\frac{7}{12}$

16. 8 to 12 **17.** 20:30 **18.** 16 to 24 **19.** 3 to 9 **20.** 28:140

21. Each bag needs 6 apples and 4 oranges. There are 30 apples for 5 bags. How many oranges are needed?

Mixed Review

22. What is the surface area of a box that is 3 feet by 2 feet by 1 foot?

23. 0.8×20 **24.** $1.2 \div 8$ **25.** 0.08×100 **26.** $8.7 \div 100$

27. Write the ratio 3:10 in two other ways.

Test Prep **Choose the correct letter for each answer.**

28. Which is a prime number?
(7-2)

A 10 **C** 50
B 11 **D** 88

29. How many cups equal 3 quarts?
(11-2)

F 3 cups **H** 9 cups
G 6 cups **J** 12 cups

Use Homework Workbook 12-2.

Scale Drawings

California Content Standard *Mathematical Reasoning 2.3: Use a variety of methods, such as words, numbers, symbols, charts, graphs, tables, diagrams, and models, to explain mathematical reasoning.*

Warm-Up Review

1. $6 \times 3\frac{1}{2}$ **2.** $70 \div 20$

3. 30×5 **4.** $100 \div 50$

5. In a photograph, a building is 5 inches tall. Each inch in the photograph represents $3\frac{1}{2}$ feet. How tall is the actual building?

Math Link The dimensions of an object drawn on paper usually are not the same size as the actual object. Ratios are helpful in showing the relationship between lengths in a drawing and actual lengths.

Scale is a ratio that compares the size of an object in a photo or drawing to the size of an actual object. This ratio can be expressed as $\frac{\text{scale length}}{\text{actual length}}$.

Word Bank

scale

Example 1

The rectangle at the right represents a room. The scale is $\frac{1 \text{ inch}}{12 \text{ feet}}$. This means that 1 inch on the drawing represents 12 feet. What is the actual length of the room?

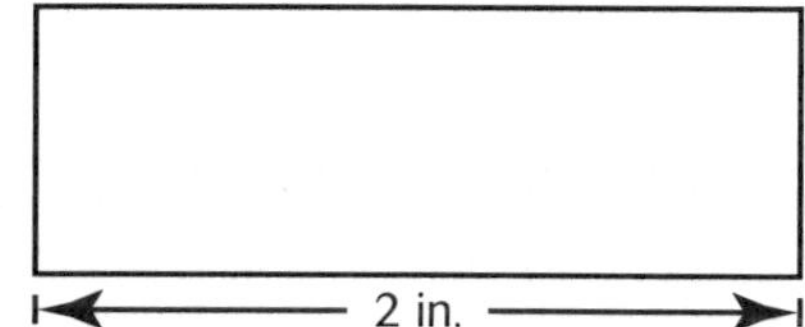

The scale length is 2 inches. Find an equivalent ratio for $\frac{1 \text{ inch}}{12 \text{ feet}}$ in which the scale length is 2 inches. That is, find x if $\frac{1 \text{ inch}}{12 \text{ feet}} = \frac{2 \text{ inches}}{x \text{ feet}}$. Since $1 \times 2 = 2$, multiply each term of the scale by 2.

$$\frac{1 \text{ inch} \times 2}{12 \text{ feet} \times 2} = \frac{2 \text{ inches}}{24 \text{ feet}} \begin{array}{l} \leftarrow \text{ scale length} \\ \leftarrow \text{ actual length} \end{array}$$

The actual length of the room is 24 feet.

Example 2

An artist is drawing a tree that has an actual height of 18 feet. If the scale is $\frac{1 \text{ inch}}{12 \text{ feet}}$, how tall should the drawing be?

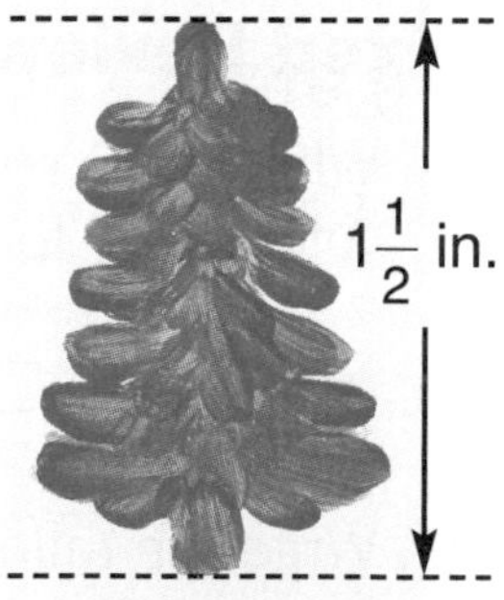

Find an equivalent ratio to $\frac{1 \text{ inch}}{12 \text{ feet}}$ in which the actual height is 18 feet. That is, find x if $\frac{1 \text{ inch}}{12 \text{ feet}} = \frac{x \text{ inches}}{18 \text{ feet}}$. Since $12 \times \frac{18}{12}$ is 18, multiply each term of the scale by $\frac{18}{12}$ or $1\frac{1}{2}$.

$$\frac{1 \text{ inch} \times 1\frac{1}{2}}{12 \text{ feet} \times 1\frac{1}{2}} = \frac{1\frac{1}{2} \text{ inches}}{18 \text{ feet}} \begin{array}{l} \leftarrow \text{ scale length} \\ \leftarrow \text{ actual length.} \end{array}$$

The tree should be $1\frac{1}{2}$ inches tall in the drawing.

Guided Practice

For another example, see Set C on p. 534.

If the scale is $\frac{\text{1 inch}}{\text{6 feet}}$, what is the actual length for each scale length?

1. 3 inches

2. $1\frac{1}{2}$ inches

3. 18 inches

If the scale is $\frac{\text{1 inch}}{\text{10 feet}}$, what is the scale length for each actual length?

4. 20 ft

5. 35 ft

6. 60 ft

Independent Practice

For another example, see Set C on p. 537.

If the scale is $\frac{\text{1 inch}}{\text{8 feet}}$, what is the actual length for each scale length?

7. 4 inches

8. $3\frac{1}{2}$ inches

9. 10 inches

If the scale is $\frac{\text{1 inch}}{\text{20 feet}}$, what is the scale length for each actual length?

10. 60 feet

11. 50 feet

12. 100 feet

13. For the drawing at the right, the scale is $\frac{\text{1 inch}}{\text{12 feet}}$. What is the actual length of the boat?

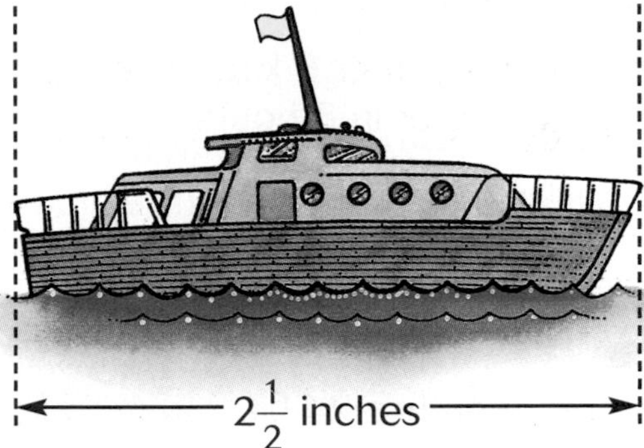

Mixed Review

14. Write $\frac{3}{50}$ as a decimal.

15. Algebra Evaluate $a - b$ for $a = 5$ and $b = {}^-7$.

16. Write three equivalent ratios for $\frac{2}{3}$.

17. Write the ratio 3 to 8 in two other ways.

Test Prep **Choose the correct letter for each answer.**

18. Which best describes the triangle?
(10-5)

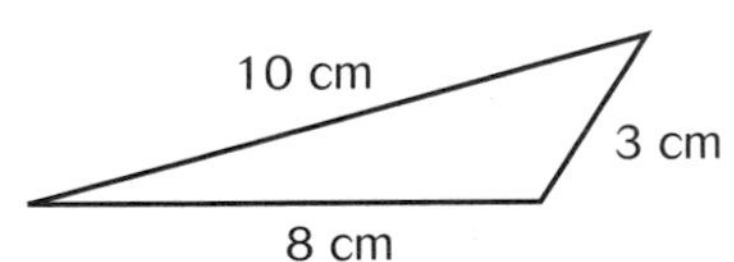

A isosceles
B right
C equilateral
D scalene

19. Which best describes the solid?
(10-12)

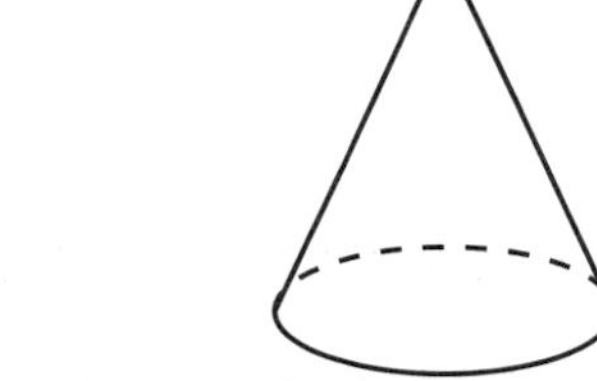

F cube
G cone
H cylinder
J sphere

Understanding Rates

California Content Standard *Algebra and Functions 2.2. (🔑) (Grade 6): Demonstrate an understanding that rate is a measure of one quantity per unit value of another quantity.*

Warm-Up Review

Give two other equivalent ratios for each given ratio.

1. $\frac{2}{5}$ **2.** $\frac{40}{50}$

3. 5:8 **4.** 6 to 10

5. If 12 geraniums cost $18, what is the cost for 1 geranium?

Math Link You already know that a ratio compares two quantities. A rate is a special kind of ratio.

As a hobby, Dan puts kites together. He can put together 6 kites in 2 hours.

A **rate** such as *6 kites in 2 hours* is a ratio that compares different units. The rate *6 kites in 2 hours* compares the number of kites made to the number of hours worked.

Word Bank

rate

unit price

Example 1

If Dan can put together 6 kites in 2 hours, how many kites can he put together in 8 hours?

To find out, you can find an equivalent ratio.

$$\frac{\text{number of kites}}{\text{number of hours}} = \frac{6 \text{ kites}}{2 \text{ hours}} = \frac{24 \text{ kites}}{8 \text{ hours}}$$

Remember that you can multiply both terms of a ratio by the same number to find an equivalent ratio. In this case, multiply both terms in $\frac{6 \text{ kites}}{2 \text{ hours}}$ by 4 since 8 hours is 2×4 hours.

Dan can put together 24 kites in 8 hours.

A special kind of rate is **unit price,** the price for one part or one unit.

Example 2

If 12 jars of paint sell for $24, find the unit price.

Since 12 jars sell for $24, divide $24 by 12 to find the unit price, that is, the cost for 1 jar.

$24 ÷ 12 = $2

The unit price is $2.

Guided Practice

For another example, see Set D on p. 535.

Use equivalent ratios or division to complete.

1. 3 miles in 40 minutes

6 miles in _____ minutes

2. 6 tickets for $18

2 tickets for _____

3. 12 bagels for $4.20

1 bagel for _____

 Additional Standards: Algebra and Functions 2.3 (Grade 6)

4. If 12 rolls cost \$4.80, what is the unit price?

Independent Practice *For another example, see Set D on p. 538.*

Use equivalent ratios or division to complete.

5. \$15 in 3 hours

 _____ in 18 hours

6. 50 feet in 10 seconds

 10 feet in _____ seconds

7. 15 slices for \$22.50

 1 slice for _____

8. 12 miles in 30 minutes

 2 miles in _____ minutes

9. 80 feet in 10 minutes

 400 feet in _____ minutes

10. 18 buns for \$2.70

 1 bun for _____

11. If Sue can assemble 8 kits in 3 hours, how many kits can she assemble in 12 hours?

12. If 25 feet of fencing costs \$125, what is the unit price?

Use the signs to answer Exercises 13–14.

Carol's Crafts
Beads—18 for \$7.20
Ben's Hobbies
Beads—12 for \$4.32

13. Which shop has the better buy on beads? Justify your answer by giving the unit price for beads at each shop.

14. What is the cost of 27 beads at Carol's Crafts?

15. **Math Reasoning** A rate is always a ratio but is a ratio always a rate? Give an example to justify your answer.

Mixed Review

16. What is the area of a rectangle having a length of 12 feet and a width of 9 feet?

17. Write three equivalent ratios for $\frac{3}{8}$.

18. If the scale in a drawing is $\frac{1 \text{ inch}}{12 \text{ feet}}$, how long should the drawing be for an item that is 36 feet long?

19. Find $\frac{3}{8} \div \frac{1}{4}$.

Test Prep **Choose the correct letter for each answer.**

20. What is the volume of a cube if the length of one edge is 4 inches? (11-9)

 A 12 in^3 C 64 in^3

 B 16 in^3 D 96 in^3

21. Evaluate $5 - x$ if $x = {}^-9$. (9-5)

 F ${}^-4$ H 14

 G 4 J ${}^-14$

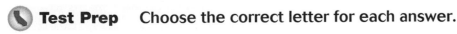

Problem-Solving Skill:
Choose the Operation

Warm-Up Review

1. $5.60 ÷ 4
2. $25 − $4.75
3. $1.45 × 5
4. $0.75 + $5 + $12.85
5. If $\frac{1}{4}$ of the students in a class of 32 walk to school, how many students walk to school?

California Content Standard *Mathematical Reasoning 2.0: Students use strategies, skills, and concepts in finding solutions.*

Read For Understanding

Denise wants to make six wall decorations and nine jigsaw puzzles to sell at the school's arts-and-crafts fair. She made the list at the right of all the materials and their prices. She has $35 to spend for materials.

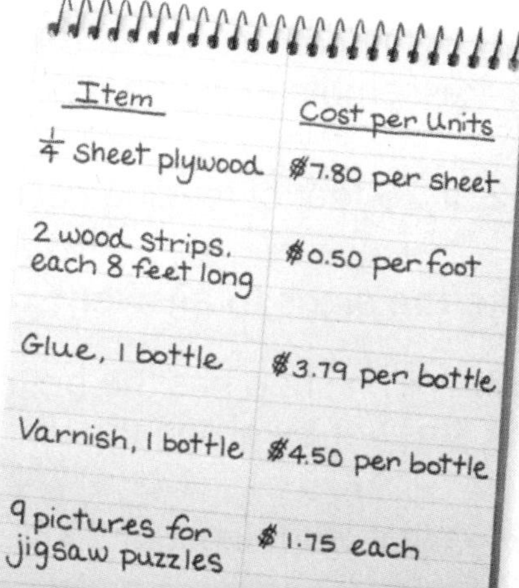

Item	Cost per Units
$\frac{1}{4}$ sheet plywood	$7.80 per sheet
2 wood strips, each 8 feet long	$0.50 per foot
Glue, 1 bottle	$3.79 per bottle
Varnish, 1 bottle	$4.50 per bottle
9 pictures for jigsaw puzzles	$1.75 each

1. How much money does Denise have to spend?
2. What is the cost of one sheet of plywood? one foot of wood strip? one picture for a jigsaw puzzle?

Think and Discuss

Choose the Operation

Clues in a problem can help you decide what operation to use. You add to combine groups, subtract to compare groups, multiply to combine equal groups, and divide to separate into equal groups.

Reread the paragraph at the top of the page.

3. Which operation would you use to find the total cost of the plywood? Why?
4. Which operation would you use to find the total cost of the wood strips? the nine puzzle pictures? Why?
5. Does Denise have enough money to buy all the materials? Which operations did you use to find out?
6. Why might it be difficult to know which operation to use?

 Additional Standard: Mathematical Reasoning 2.4 (See p. 501.)

Guided Practice

Marta made 20 potholders to sell for the price shown at the right. She bought 5 bags of loops at \$1.59 each to make the potholders. She sold 17 potholders at the fair.

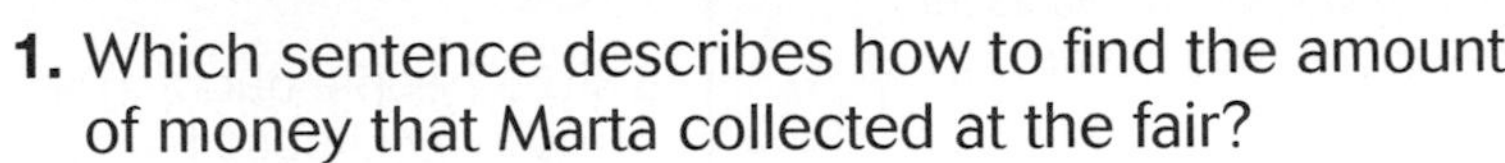

1. Which sentence describes how to find the amount of money that Marta collected at the fair?

- **a.** Multiply the price of the potholders by the number sold.
- **b.** Divide the price of the potholders by the number sold.
- **c.** Add the cost of a potholder and the cost of a bag of loops.

2. Which expression describes the amount of money Marta collected?

a. \$1.25 × 17 **b.** \$1.25 + \$1.59 **c.** \$1.25 ÷ 17

Independent Practice

3. Which sentence describes how to find the amount that Marta spent on loops?

- **a.** Multiply the cost per bag by 20.
- **b.** Multiply the cost per bag by the number of bags she bought.
- **c.** Multiply the cost per bag by the number of potholders Marta made.

4. Which expression describes the amount that Marta spent on loops?

- **a.** \$1.59 × 4
- **b.** \$1.59 × 20
- **c.** \$1.59 × 5

5. Profit is the amount of money collected less the expenses. Which sentence describes how to find Marta's profit?

- **a.** Subtract the money collected from the money spent on materials.
- **b.** Add the cost of materials and the price of potholders.
- **c.** Subtract the money spent on materials from the money collected.

6. Which expression describes the amount of profit Marta made?

- **a.** (\$1.25 ×17) − (\$1.59 × 5)
- **b.** (\$1.59 × 5) − (\$1.25 × 17)
- **c.** (\$1.59 × 5) + (\$1.25 × 5)

Tabitha is making 4 pillows like the one at the right. She is using 2 kinds of fabric. For the front of each pillow, she makes a patchwork pattern, using 20 squares.

7. How would she find the number of squares of each fabric needed for 4 pillows? Explain.

Use Homework Workbook 12-5.

Understanding Percent

California Content Standard *Number Sense 1.2 (key): Interpret percents as part of a hundred; find decimal and percent equivalents for common fractions and explain why they represent the same value . . ..*

Math Link You have already learned about ratios. A special kind of ratio is called a percent.

The quilt block shown at the right has 100 squares. Four of the squares are red, 44 are blue, and 52 are yellow.

A ratio that shows the relationship between a number and 100 is called **percent.** *Percent* means "per hundred." The percent symbol is %.

The ratio $\frac{44}{100}$ tells how many of the total squares are blue.

So the ratio $\frac{44}{100}$ can be written as 44%.

44% is read "44 percent."

$44\% = \frac{44}{100} = \frac{44 \div 4}{100 \div 4} = \frac{11}{25} \leftarrow$ fraction in simplest form

Warm-Up Review

Write each fraction in simplest form.

1. $\frac{50}{100}$
2. $\frac{20}{50}$
3. $\frac{4}{8}$
4. $\frac{20}{30}$
5. If 25 people out of 100 in a survey choose blue as their favorite color, what fraction chose blue?

Word Bank

percent

Example 1

In the quilt pattern, what percent of the squares are yellow?

Since 52 out of 100 squares are yellow, the ratio is $\frac{52}{100}$ or 52%.

Example 2

In the quilt pattern, what percent of the squares are red? Write the percent as a fraction in simplest form.

Since 4 out of 100 squares are red, the percent is 4%.

Then $4\% = \frac{4}{100} = \frac{4 \div 4}{100 \div 4} = \frac{1}{25}$

Guided Practice *For another example, see Set E on p. 535.*

Write each ratio as a percent.

1. $\frac{27}{100}$
2. 45 out of 100
3. $\frac{9}{10}$

 Additional Standards: Algebra and Functions 2.3 (Grade 6)

Tell what percent of each grid is shaded. Then write the ratio in simplest form.

4. 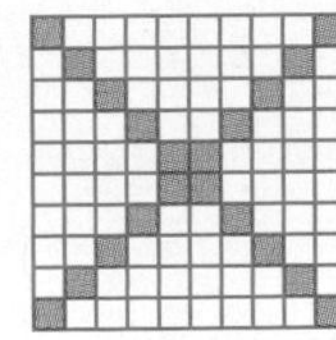

5. 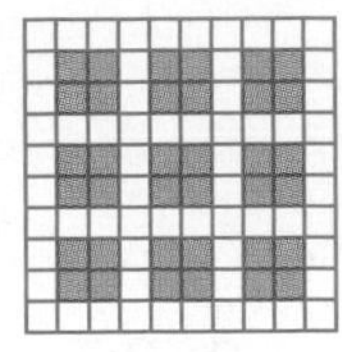

6. 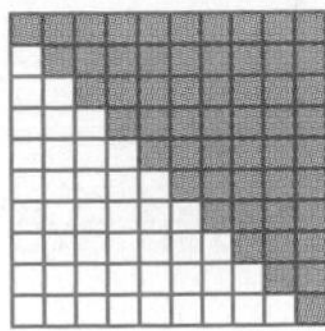

Independent Practice

For more practice, see Set E on p. 538.

Write each ratio as a percent.

7. 47 out of 100 **8.** $\frac{35}{100}$ **9.** 3 out of 4 **10.** $\frac{35}{50}$

Tell what percent of each grid is shaded. Then write the ratio in simplest form.

11. 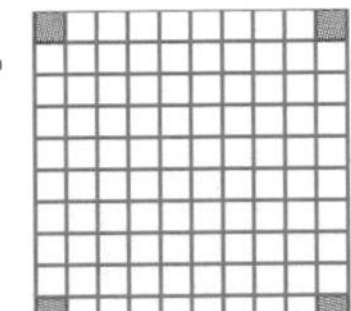

12. 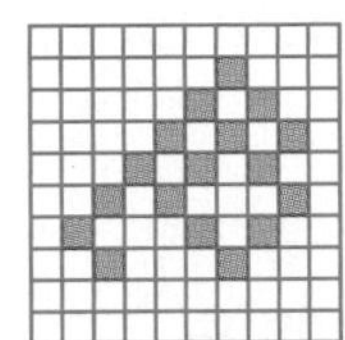

13. 

Write each percent as a ratio. Write the ratio in simplest form.

14. 60% **15.** 40% **16.** 50% **17.** 6% **18.** 32%

19. In a group of 100 people, 17 people have blue eyes. What percent of the people in the group have blue eyes?

Mixed Review

20. $1\frac{3}{4} + 2\frac{7}{8}$ **21.** $3\frac{1}{4} - 1\frac{7}{16}$ **22.** $1\frac{3}{4} \times 4$

23. If 20 tennis balls sell for $18.60, what is the unit price?

24. If the scale is $\frac{1 \text{ inch}}{10 \text{ feet}}$, how long should the scale drawing be for a lap pool that is 25 feet long?

25. Algebra Evaluate $x \div y$ if $x = \frac{2}{3}$ and $y = \frac{1}{2}$.

 **Test Prep** **Choose the correct letter for each answer.**

26. Which decimal equals $\frac{3}{1,000}$?
(7-6)

A 0.3 **C** 0.003

B 0.03 **D** 3.0

27. Which equals 3 yards?
(11-1)

F 36 inches **H** 90 inches

G 36 feet **J** 108 inches

Diagnostic Checkpoint

Write each ratio in two different ways.

1. (12-1) 4 to 5 **2.** (12-1) 9:8 **3.** (12-1) 3:7 **4.** (12-1) 8 to 4

Write three other equivalent ratios for each given ratio.

5. (12-2) $\frac{10}{12}$ **6.** (12-2) $\frac{8}{15}$ **7.** (12-2) $\frac{1}{2}$ **8.** (12-2) $\frac{5}{6}$

If the scale is $\frac{\text{1 inch}}{\text{6 feet}}$, what is the actual length for each scale length?

9. (12-3) 4 inches **10.** (12-3) 9 inches **11.** (12-3) 17 inches

If the scale is $\frac{\text{1 inch}}{\text{25 feet}}$, what is the scale length for each actual length?

12. (12-3) 75 feet **13.** (12-3) 350 feet **14.** (12-3) 150 feet

Use equivalent ratios or division to complete.

15. (12-4) 3 silk flowers for $15
1 flower for ______

16. (12-4) 48 cans in 8 boxes
______ cans in 1 box

17. (12-4) 18 ounces in 3 cans
24 ounces in ______ cans

18. (12-4) 14 invitations written in 1 hour
28 invitations written in ______ hours

Write each percent as a ratio. Write the ratio in simplest form.

19. (12-6) 50% **20.** (12-6) 18% **21.** (12-6) 76% **22.** (12-6) 16%

Write each ratio as a percent.

23. (12-6) 2:5 **24.** (12-6) 7:10 **25.** (12-6) $\frac{89}{100}$ **26.** (12-6) 12 to 50

27. (12-5) Alison is buying five sets of markers for each of her 12 art students. Each set of markers costs $5.75. Which operation would you use to find how much the markers cost? What is the total cost?

28. (12-3) What is the actual wingspan of the airplane shown at the right?

29. (12-3) If the actual length of the tail section is 75 ft, how long is the tail section on the model?

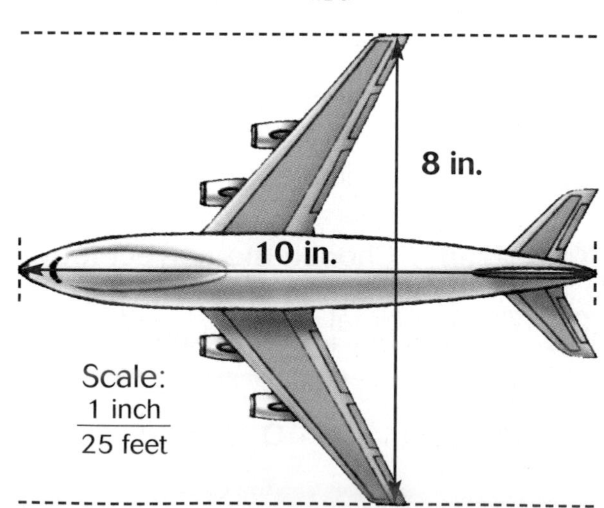

Multiple-Choice Cumulative Review

Choose the correct letter for each answer.

1. What is the volume of the prism shown?

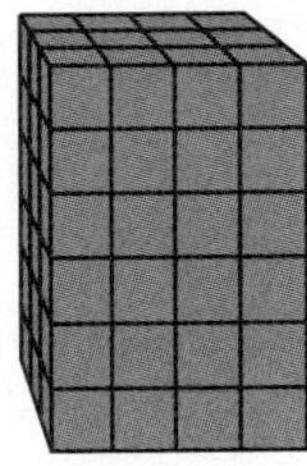

A 12 cubic units
B 18 cubic units
C 24 cubic units
D 72 cubic units

2. A jar holds 350 mL of water. How many liters is this?

(1 L = 1,000 mL)

F 0.035 L
G 0.35 L
H 3.5 L
J 35 L

3. Which is the correct rule?

A	B
0.05	0.5
0.50	5.0
5.00	50.0

A Multiply by 1.
B Multiply by 10.
C Divide by 10.
D Add 100.

4. The first thermometer shows the temperature at 6 A.M., and the second shows the temperature at noon. Which change took place in the 6 hours between 6 A.M. and noon?

F $^{-}23°F$
G $^{-}13°F$
H $^{+}13°F$
J $^{+}23°F$

60, 55, 50 — 6 A.M.
70, 65, 60 — Noon

5. Two sides of a cube are green, 1 is blue, 2 are red, and 1 is pink. If you toss the cube once, what is the probability that you will get green?

A $\frac{1}{3}$
B $\frac{1}{2}$
C $\frac{2}{3}$
D $\frac{3}{4}$

6. A circle has a circumference of 310 meters. Which measure is the best estimate of the *radius* of the circle?

F 40 meters
G 50 meters
H 60 meters
J 100 meters

7. Robert has bales of hay in his barn. He used $3\frac{3}{4}$ bales of hay in the morning and $2\frac{1}{2}$ bales in the afternoon. If he used 1 more bale in the evening, how many bales did he use altogether?

A $5\frac{3}{4}$
B $7\frac{1}{4}$
C $6\frac{1}{2}$
D 8

Relating Percents, Decimals, and Fractions

California Content Standard *Number Sense 1.2. (Key): Interpret percents as part of a hundred; find decimal and percent equivalents for common fractions . . ..*

Warm-Up Review

Write each fraction as a decimal.

1. $\frac{7}{10}$
2. $\frac{9}{100}$

Write each fraction as a percent.

3. $\frac{3}{100}$
4. $\frac{9}{10}$
5. If 30 out of 100 people dislike a movie, what fraction disliked the movie?

Math Link You know that a fraction can also be named by a decimal. Now that you have learned about percents, you can relate percents, decimals, and fractions.

The wrapping-paper design was made with rubber stamps. A piece with 100 stamp prints will be cut off. Twenty out of 100 prints are red. What part of the 100 prints is red?

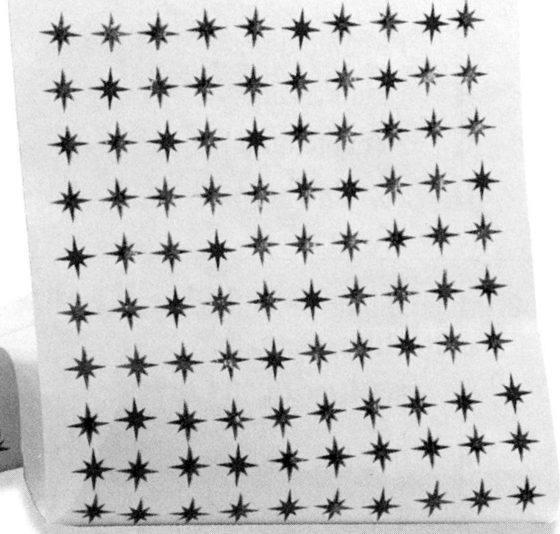

- **As a fraction** $\frac{20}{100}$ In simplest form, $\frac{20}{100} = \frac{1}{5}$
- **As a percent** 20% Remember: percent means "per hundred"
- **As a decimal** 0.20 or 0.2

Example

Express 75 out of 100 as a fraction in simplest form, as a percent, and as a decimal.

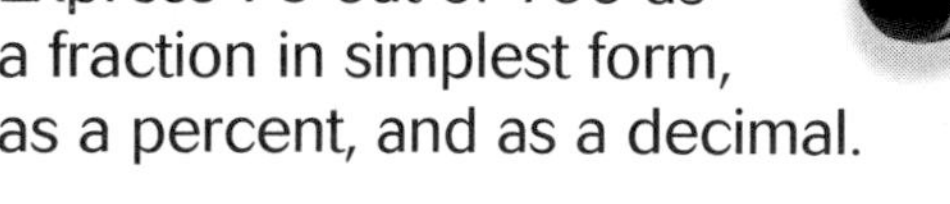

- As a fraction $\frac{75}{100} = \frac{3}{4}$
- As a percent 75%
- As a decimal 0.75

Guided Practice

For another example, see Set F on p. 535.

Write each expression in two other ways.

1. 3%
2. $\frac{17}{100}$
3. $\frac{9}{10}$
4. 0.6
5. 51%

Write each percent as a decimal and as a fraction in simplest form.

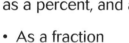

6. 40%
7. 9%
8. 72%
9. 64%
10. 55%

Additional Standard: Algebra and Functions 2.3 (Grade 6) (See p. 501.)

Independent Practice *For more practice, see Set F on p. 538.*

Write each percent as a decimal and as a fraction in simplest form.

11. 5% **12.** 88% **13.** 65% **14.** 78% **15.** 1%

16. 2% **17.** 125% **18.** 15% **19.** 33% **20.** 200%

Express each shaded part as a decimal, as a percent, and as a fraction in simplest form.

21. 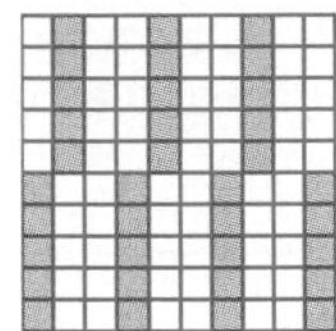

22. 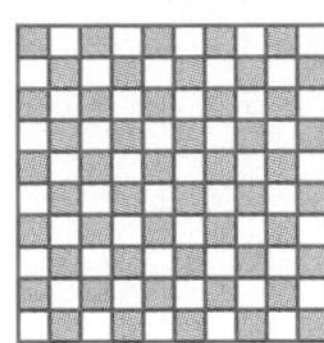

23. 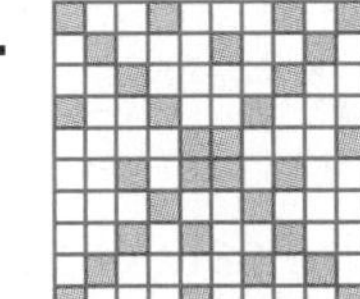

24. Math Reasoning The pattern at the right continues downward for a total of ten rows. How many dark tiles are in the tenth row? What percent of all the tiles in the ten-row pattern are dark?

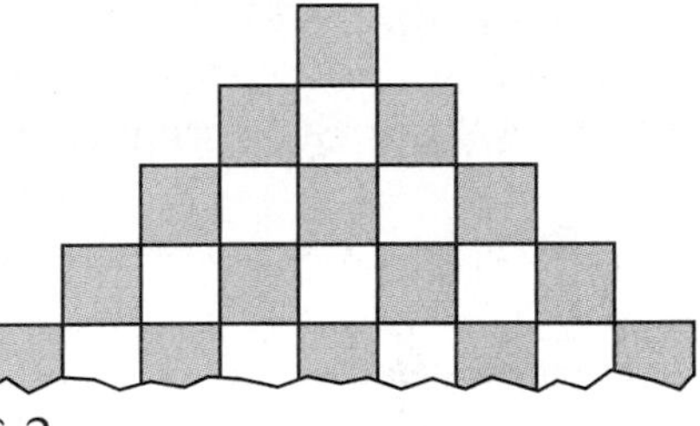

25. Refer to the wrapping-paper design on page 516. What part of the 100 prints is green? Write the part as a fraction, as a percent, and as a decimal.

Mixed Review

26. $^{-}6 + {}^{+}8$ **27.** $^{-}9 + {}^{-}2$ **28.** $^{-}4 - {}^{-}1$ **29.** $^{+}8 - {}^{-}5$

30. If 8 markers sell for $4.80, what is the unit price?

31. If a door is 2 meters tall, what is the height in centimeters?

32. What is the surface area of the box at the right?

33. What is the volume of the box?

34. Write 40% as a fraction in simplest form.

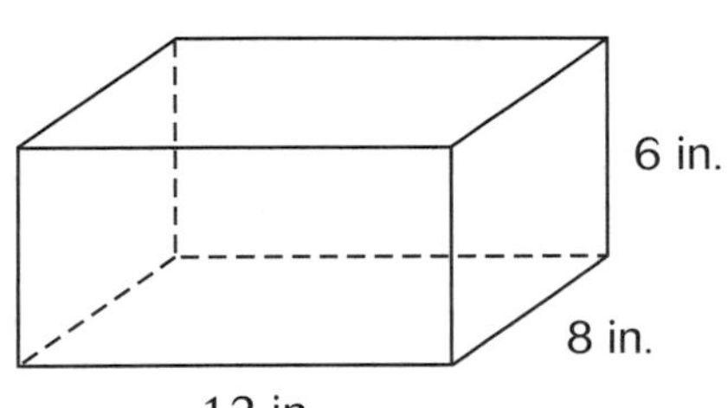

Test Prep Choose the correct letter for each answer.

35. (10-3) Which name best describes the figure?

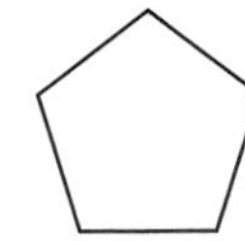

A triangle **C** pentagon
B quadrilateral **D** hexagon

36. (10-1) What figure is illustrated?

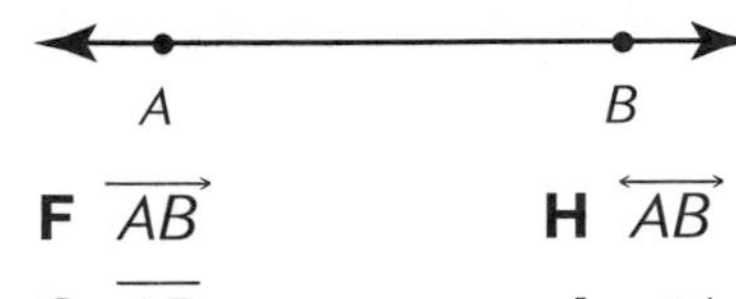

F $\overrightarrow{AB}$ **H** $\overleftrightarrow{AB}$
G $\overline{AB}$ **J** $\angle A$

Use Homework Workbook 12-7.

Finding Percent of a Number

California Content Standard *Number Sense 1.2. (🔑): . . . compute a given percent of a whole number.*

Warm-Up Review

1. 56×0.05
2. 400×0.09
3. 126×0.59
4. 360×0.95

Round to the nearest hundredth.

5. 0.987
6. 24.783
7. 12.4789
8. 7.9999
9. In one town 25% of the people live in apartments. Write 25% as a fraction in simplest form and as a decimal.

Math Link In many states you must pay a sales tax on all purchases. In order to find out how much sales tax you owe, you need to find a percent of a number.

Example 1

In one state the sales tax is 6%. If you buy the sweater shown at the right, how much sales tax must you pay?

You know that 6% means $\frac{6}{100}$ or 0.06.

To find 6% of 50, multiply 50 by 0.06.

$$\begin{array}{r} 50 \\ \times\ 0.06 \\ \hline 3.00 \end{array}$$

The sales tax is $3.

Example 2

A. Find 25% of 78.

Multiply 78 by 0.25.

$$\begin{array}{r} 78 \\ \times\ 0.25 \\ \hline 390 \\ 156 \\ \hline 19.50 \end{array}$$

B. Find 98% of 500.

Multiply 500 by 0.98.

$$\begin{array}{r} 0.98 \\ \times\ \ 500 \\ \hline 490.000 \end{array}$$

Remember that $500 \times 0.98 = 0.98 \times 500$.

Guided Practice *For another example, see Set G on p. 535.*

Find each amount.

1. 3% of 20
2. 30% of 12
3. 32% of 800
4. 75% of 80
5. If the sales tax is 5%, how much sales tax would you pay on an item costing $86?

Independent Practice *For more practice, see Set G on p. 538.*

Find each amount.

6. 5% of 40 **7.** 88% of 59 **8.** 65% of 250 **9.** 78% of 850

10. 2% of 76 **11.** 25% of 48 **12.** 15% of 500 **13.** 33% of 65

14. If the sales tax is 9%, how much sales tax would you pay on an item costing $350?

15. Math Reasoning What is a shortcut for finding 50% of a number? 25% of a number?

16. Mental Math What is 10% of 250?

Mixed Review

17. 24.5×0.08 **18.** 0.9×0.08 **19.** $1.25 \div 25$ **20.** $0.36 \div 0.4$

21. What is the least common multiple of 12 and 8?

22. Estimate the sum of $13\frac{3}{4}$ and $5\frac{1}{8}$.

23. What is the perimeter of the rectangle shown at the right?

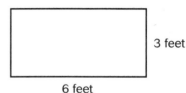

3 feet

6 feet

24. Write $\frac{55}{100}$ as a percent.

25. Write 30% as a fraction in simplest form and as a decimal.

Test Prep **Choose the correct letter for each answer.**

26. Which angle is obtuse?
(10-2)

A **B** **C** **D**

27. Which ordered pair represents point *A*?
(9-7)

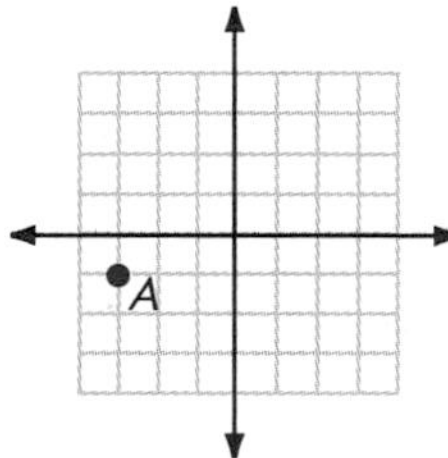

F (3, 1) **G** $(^-1, 3)$ **H** $(3, ^-1)$ **J** $(^-3, ^-1)$

LESSON 12-9

Understand
Plan
Solve
Look Back

Problem-Solving Strategy: Make a Table

California Content Standard *Mathematical Reasoning 2.3: Use a variety of methods, such as words, numbers, symbols, charts, graphs, tables, diagrams, and models, to explain mathematical reasoning.*

Warm-Up Review

1. $14 × 30
2. $25 × 50
3. $365 + $480 + $1,000
4. $0.85 × 9
5. If Sue buys 2 books for $12.95 apiece and 3 pens for $1.95 apiece, how much change will she receive from a $50 bill?

Example

The town council is planning a fireworks display for the Fourth of July. The council wants to buy 5 Wagon Wheels, 20 Ring Shells, and 40 Gold Spider fireworks. Wagon Wheels cost $35 each. Ring Shells cost $12 each. Gold Spiders cost $25 each. What will be the total cost of the display?

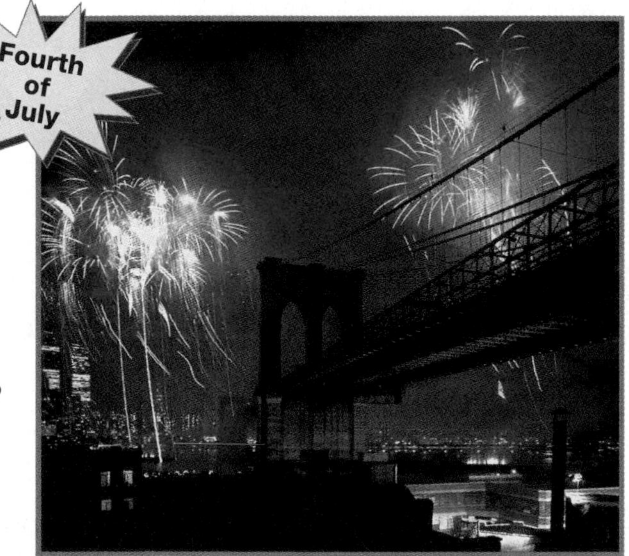

Understand

What do you need to find?

You need to find the total cost of the display.

Plan

How can you solve the problem?

You can **make a table** to help you solve the problem. Then use the information in the table to find the total cost.

Solve

Fireworks Displays

Fireworks	Number	Cost of One	Total Cost of Each
Wagon Wheel	5	$35	$35 × 5 = $175
Ring Shell	20	$12	$12 × 20 = $240
Gold Spider	40	$25	$25 × 40 = $1,000

To find the total cost of the display, add.

$175 + $240 + $1,000 = $1,415.

The fireworks will cost $1,415.

Look Back

How does making a table help solve the problem? Explain.

 Additional Standard: Mathematical Reasoning 3.2 (See p. 501.)

Guided Practice

Make a table to solve Exercises 1–3. Use the information from the preceding page for Exercise 1.

1. Each year the council has a different display. Suppose that the council wants 15 Wagon Wheels, 25 Ring Shells, and 16 Gold Spiders. How much will these fireworks cost?

Independent Practice

2. A vendor sold 125 glow sticks for $3.00 each, 105 glow rings for $4.25 each, and 213 boxes of popcorn for $3.25 each. How much money did the vendor take in?

3. Wagon Wheels last 8 seconds, Ring Shells last 6 seconds, and Gold Spiders last 5 seconds. How long would a display of 12 Wagon Wheels, 13 Ring Shells, and 15 Gold Spiders last if the fireworks were set off one right after the other? How do you know if your answer is reasonable?

Mixed Review

Try these or other strategies to solve each problem. Tell which strategy you used.

Problem-Solving Strategies

- *Make a List*
- *Work Backward*
- *Draw a Diagram*
- *Make A Table*

4. Craig bought some crushed ice for $1.75. Then he spent twice as much on snacks. If Craig had $5.62 left, how much money did he have before buying the ice and snacks?

5. June leaves the playground and walks 120 yards west. Then she walks 40 yards north. After that, she walks 50 yards east and then 40 yards south. Where is she now?

6. Two vendors are selling the T-shirts advertised at the right. Vendor A sold 25 small shirts and 10 large shirts. Vendor B sold 12 medium shirts and 16 large shirts.
   a. How much money did each vendor take in?
   b. What is the difference in the total number of T-shirts sold by Vendor A and Vendor B?

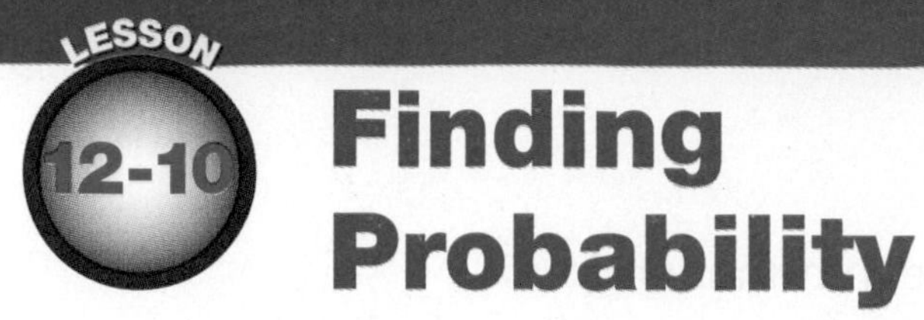

Lesson 12-10 Finding Probability

California Content Standard *Statistics, Data Analysis, and Probability 1.3: Use fractions and percentages to compare data sets of different sizes.*

Warm-Up Review

Write two equivalent fractions for each ratio.

1. 6 out of 18 **2.** 12:20

3. $\frac{30}{40}$ **4.** $\frac{50}{100}$

5. If 7 out of 10 students in a class walk to school, what percent walk to school?

Math Link Words such as "possibly" or "rarely" can be used to describe the chances of an event occurring in the future. In this lesson you will learn a more exact way to describe chance.

In an **experiment,** such as tossing a coin, each possible result is an **outcome.** If each outcome is as likely to occur as every other, they are **equally likely** outcomes.

Word Bank

- experiment
- outcome
- equally likely
- event
- probability

Example 1

Name the possible outcomes for each event.

a. tossing a coin

Possible outcomes: head, tails

b. tossing a standard number cube

Possible outcomes: 1, 2, 3, 4, 5, 6

An **event** can consist of one or more outcomes. When all outcomes are equally likely, you can describe the **probability** of an event by using a ratio.

$$\text{Probability of an event} = \frac{\text{number of ways an event can happen}}{\text{total number of possible outcomes}}$$

The probability of an event is always 0, 1, or any number between 0 and 1. An impossible event has a probability of 0. A certain event has a probability of 1.

Example 2

Find the probability of rolling a 5 when rolling a standard number cube.

One out of 6 outcomes is "5."
There are 6 possible outcomes when rolling a number cube.

$$\text{Probability of rolling a 5} = \frac{\text{number of ways an event can happen}}{\text{total number of possible outcomes}} = \frac{1}{6}$$

Guided Practice

For another example, see Set H on p. 536.

Name the possible outcomes for each event.

1. dialing the first digit of a 3-digit number between 100 and 999

2. picking one letter from the word MATH.

Additional Standard: Statistics, Data Analysis, and Probability 2.0 (Grade 4) (See p. 501.)

Refer to the art at the right. What is the probability of each of the following?

3. selecting a triangle
4. selecting a square
5. selecting a triangle or a square
6. selecting a circle

Independent Practice *For more practice, see Set H on p. 539.*

Name the possible outcomes for each event.

7. picking one letter from the word SQUARE.

8. choosing a month at random

Refer to the spinner at the right. What is the probability that the pointer will stop on each of the following?

9. blue
10. section 4
11. not yellow
12. not blue
13. not 4 or 5
14. an even number

A bag holds 26 cards, one with each letter of the alphabet. You pick a card out of the bag without looking. After you pick a card, you return it to the bag. Find each probability.

15. z
16. a vowel
17. a 6
18. p, q, r, s, t
19. a letter after m
20. a consonant

Mixed Review

21. $\frac{3}{8} - \frac{1}{4}$
22. $2\frac{2}{3} - 1\frac{5}{6}$
23. $2\frac{3}{4} \times 1\frac{1}{2}$
24. $\frac{2}{5} \div 5$

25. Write 45% as a decimal and as a fraction in simplest form.

26. Find 33% of 250.

Test Prep Choose the correct letter for each answer.

27. Find $^-3 - {}^-8$.
(9-4)
A $^-11$
B $^-5$
C 5
D 11

28. If the scale is $\frac{1 \text{ inch}}{10 \text{ feet}}$, what is the actual height of a segment that is 2 inches long in a scale drawing?
(12-3)
F 20 inches
G 20 feet
H $\frac{1}{5}$ inch
J 5 feet

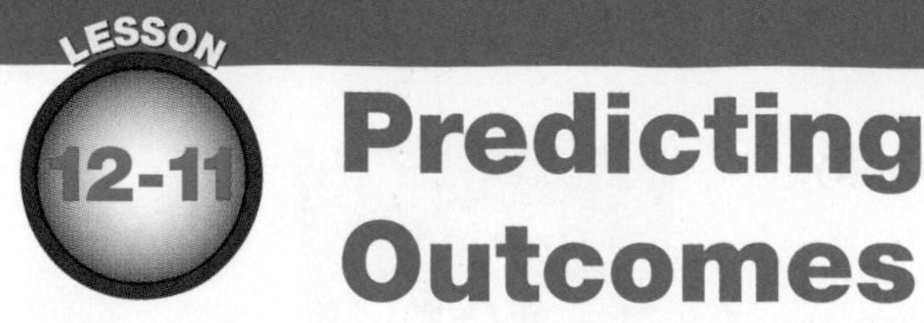

Predicting Outcomes

California Content Standard *Statistics, Data Analysis, and Probability 1.3: Use fractions and percentages to compare data sets of different sizes. Also, Mathematical Reasoning 2.3 (See p. 501.)*

Warm-Up Review

Write each of the following as a fraction in lowest terms.

1. 15 out of 25
2. 60 out of 100
3. 28 out of 50
4. If 68 people of 100 voted in a election, what percent voted?

Word Bank

sample

Math Link You have already determined probability by counting from data based on real-world situations.

A **sample** is a set of data that can be used to predict how a particular situation might happen. You can use sample data to determine probability.

Example 1

The owner of a pizza parlor collected the following data during one lunch shift. Based on this data, what is the probability that a lunch customer will order a cheese slice?

Pizza	Slices ordered
Sausage	23
Cheese	10
Vegetable	5
Combination	12

There were 50 slices ordered. Of these 50 slices, 10 were cheese. The owner can predict that $\frac{10}{50}$ or $\frac{1}{5}$ of the customers will order cheese. So the probability of a customer ordering cheese is $\frac{10}{50}$ or 20%.

Example 2

At a second pizza parlor owned by the same person as in Example 1, the owner found that 6 people out of 25 ordered cheese pizza. Since only 6 people chose cheese pizza at this parlor, he concluded that cheese was not as popular at this location. Was he correct?

No, 6 people of 25 means that $\frac{6}{25}$ or 24% of the people ordered cheese. At the first pizza parlor, 10 out of 50 or 20% ordered cheese.

Additional Standard: Statistics, Data Analysis, and Probability 2.0 (Grade 4) (See p. 501.)

Guided Practice *For another example, see Set I on p. 536.*

Refer to the chart in Example 1 on the preceding page. Use it to find the probability that a customer would choose the following.

1. sausage **2.** vegetable **3.** combination

4. Millie conducted a survey in which she asked 25 people to name their favorite dessert. Out of 25 people, 12 chose pie. Based on this survey, what is the probability that pie would be chosen as the favorite dessert?

Independent Practice *For more practice, see Set I on p. 539.*

Use the chart at the right to find the probability that a customer would buy each T-shirt size.

T-shirt Sales	
size	**number sold**
small	10
medium	27
large	13

5. small **6.** medium **7.** large

The chart at the right shows the results of a survey in which people were asked to name their favorite color. Find the probability that a person would name a particular color.

Favorite Color Survey	
Color	**Number**
red	4
blue	9
yellow	3
green	2
other	7

8. red **9.** blue **10.** yellow

11. green **12.** red or blue **13.** not blue

Mixed Review

14. $0.9 + 0.05$ **15.** 0.9×0.05 **16.** $0.9 \div 0.05$ **17.** $0.9 - 0.05$

18. List $^{-}4$, $^{-}10$, 1, 0 in order from least to greatest.

19. Algebra Graph the equation $y = x + 2$. First make a table of ordered pairs using x-values of $^{-}3$, 0, and 3.

20. Find 26% of 450.

21. If a standard number cube is tossed, what is the probability that the result will be 2 or 5?

Test Prep **Choose the correct letter for each answer.**

22. Which ratio is equivalent to $\frac{3}{5}$?
(12-2)

A 6 to 9 **C** 6 to 10

B 3:10 **D** 18:25

23. Which equals 1 meter?
(11-4)

F 10 cm **H** 10 km

G 100 cm **J** 100 km

LESSON 12-12

Tree Diagrams

California Content Standard *Statistics, Data Analysis, and Probability 3.1 (🔑) (Grade 6): Represent all possible outcomes for compound events in an organized way (e.g., tables, grids, tree diagrams) and express the theoretical probability of each outcome.*

Math Link You know that making a list can be helpful in finding all possible outcomes in a probability situation. However, it is important that your list includes all possible outcomes. In this lesson, you will learn a method that will help you to be sure your list is complete.

Warm-Up Review

A standard number cube is tossed. Find the probability for each result.

1. 3 **2.** 5 or 6

3. an even number

4. a prime number

5. If 7 out of 50 in a survey like a television program, what is the probability that any person chosen at random will like the program?

Word Bank

tree diagram

Example 1

Heather is making party favors, using one bow and one flower. The pictures show the colors of the flowers and bows. How many different kinds of favors can she make?

Make a **tree diagram.**

Bow Color Choices **Flower Color Choices** **Possible Outcomes**

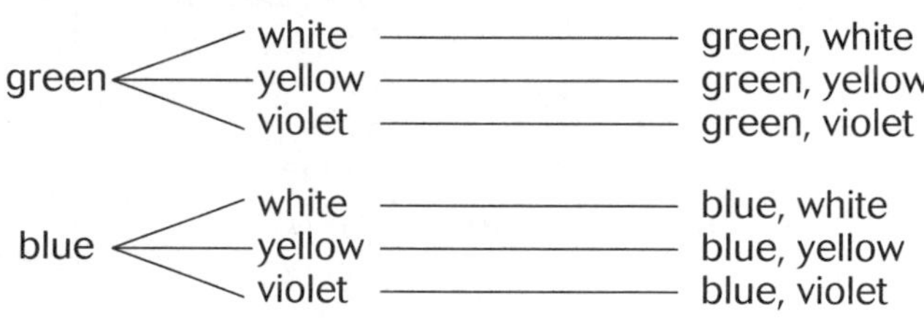

Heather can make 6 different kinds of favors.

Example 2

There is an equal number of the 6 possible kinds of favors. What is the probability that a guest at Heather's party will receive a party favor that has a blue bow and a yellow flower?

Only 1 out of the 6 possible outcomes has a blue bow and a yellow flower. So the probability is $\frac{1}{6}$.

Guided Practice

For another example, see Set J on p. 536.

Refer to the tree diagram in Example 1. Find the probability for each kind of favor.

1. green bow with a violet flower

2. blue bow with any color flower

3. white flower with any color bow

4. white flower or yellow flower, any bow

Independent Practice *For another example, see Set J on p. 539.*

Use the tree diagram of earring beads below for Exercises 5–6.

Gold Bead Choices	Colored Bead Choices	Possible Outcomes
large gold	black	large gold, black
	red	large gold, red
small gold	black	small gold, black
	red	small gold, red

5. What is the probability that an earring will have a small gold bead and a red bead?

6. Find the probability of choosing a large gold bead and a blue bead.

Use the pictures at the right for Exercises 7–9.

7. Make a tree diagram to show the possible outcomes of picking a bow and a flower.

8. What is the probability of choosing a gold bow and a pink flower?

9. What is the probability of choosing a gold bow and not a pink flower?

Mixed Review

10. If a letter is picked at random from the word HAPPY, what is the probability that the letter is P?

11. If 12 people out of 50 in a survey listen to a certain radio station, what is the probability that a person chosen at random will listen to the same station?

Compare. Write $>$, $<$, or $=$ for each ●.

12. 0.5 ● 0.05. **13.** $\frac{3}{5}$ ● $\frac{3}{4}$ **14.** $^{-}10$ ● $^{-}12$

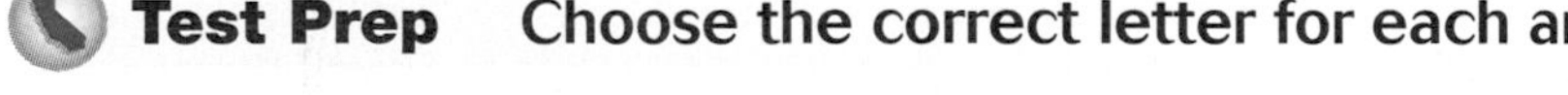

Test Prep Choose the correct letter for each answer.

15. Which mass equals 1 kilogram? (11-5)

A 10 grams C 1,000 grams
B 100 grams D 0.1 gram

16. Algebra If $y = x + 4$, find y when $x = {}^{-}3$. (9-8)

F $^{-}1$ H 7
G 1 J $^{-}7$

Problem-Solving Application:

Using Circle Graphs

Warm-Up Review

What fraction represents each section of the entire circle?

1. Section 1
2. Section 2
3. Section 3
4. Which two sections together represent half of the total?

California Content Standard *Statistics, Data Analysis, and Probability 1.2: Organize and display single-variable data . . . (e.g., . . . circle graphs)*

Example

Magda makes and sells pottery. She found a circle graph in a craft magazine showing the annual sales for a pottery factory. Magda will use this information to choose 3 kinds of items to make. She wants to sell as many items as possible. Which three items should she make?

Understand

What do you need to find?

You need to find the three best selling items shown by the circle graph.

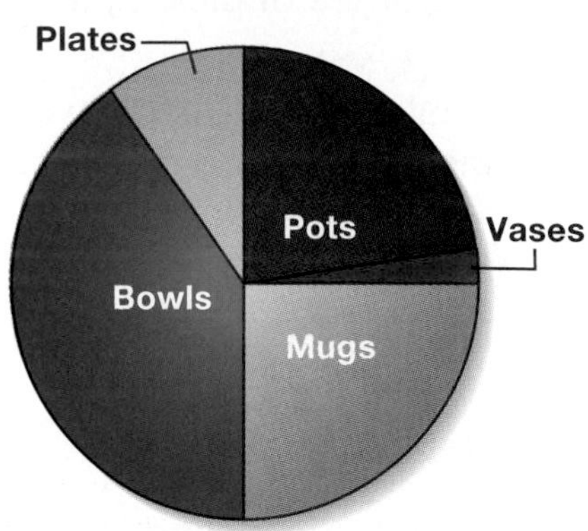

A circle graph represents 100%.

Plan

How can you solve the problem?

A circle graph is divided into sections, one for each item. The whole circle represents 100% of the items. The size of each section depends on what part of the total amount it represents.

Solve

The largest section is for bowls. Sales for bowls make up more than 25%, but less than 50% of the entire amount. The next largest section is mugs. This section is about 25% of the circle graph. The section for pots is slightly less than 25%, but greater than the section for plates.

Magda should make bowls, mugs, and pots.

Look Back

Use logical reasoning. Since the sections for vases and plates are less than those for bowls, mugs, and pots, the answer is reasonable.

 Additional Standards: Statistics, Data Analysis, and Probability 1.3; Mathematical Reasoning 2.3 (See p. 501.)

Guided Practice

Refer to the circle graph on page 528.

1. Which two items together make up exactly half the sales?

2. Which two items together make up slightly less than 50% of the sales?

3. Which two items together make up exactly 25% of the sales?

Independent Practice

Use the circle graph at the right to answer Exercises 4–7.

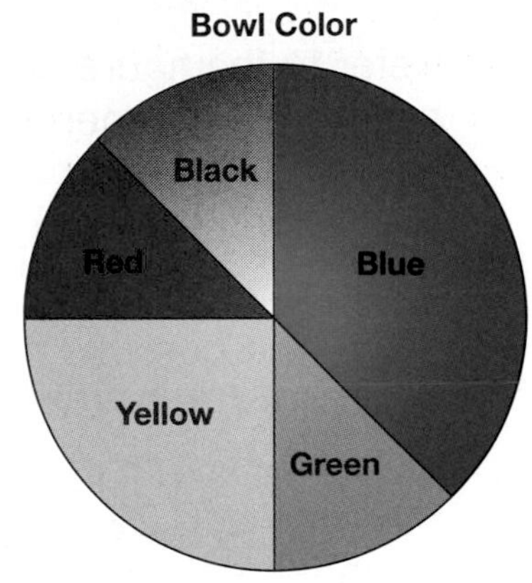

4. Which color bowl was the most popular?

5. Compare the combined number of yellow and green bowls sold to the number of blue bowls sold. Tell how the numbers sold compare.

6. Which color accounts for 25% of the sales?

7. Which color accounts for more than 25% but less than 50% of the sales?

Mixed Review

8. Each bus holds 30 people. If 140 people are going on a field trip, how many buses are needed?

9. As bricks are laid end to end to form a walk, the total length follows this pattern: $\frac{1}{2}$ foot, 1 foot, $1\frac{1}{2}$ feet, 2 feet, and so on. What is the total length of the walk after 9 bricks are laid?

10. A group of 3 students, 5 adults, and 2 senior citizens are visiting a museum. How much was the total admission for the group? Use the chart at the right.

Museum Admission	
Students	$3.50
Adults	$6.00
Senior Citizens	$4.25

11. Todd was playing a number game with his brothers. He told them to pick a number, multiply it by 4, and add 8. Chris ended with 48. What was his number?

Use Homework Workbook 12-13.

Diagnostic Checkpoint

Complete. For Exercises 1–3, choose a word from the Word Bank.

Word Bank
outcome
percent
rate
ratio
tree diagram

1. (12-12) A(n) ____________ can be used to organize outcomes of an experiment.

2. (12-1) The comparison of two quantities is a(n) ____________.

3. (12-10) The result of a probability experiment is a(n) ____________.

4. (12-7) Refer to the figure at the right. Express the shaded part as a decimal, as a percent, and as a fraction in simplest form.

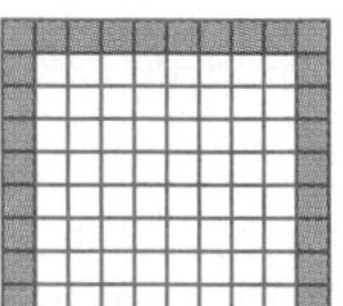

5. (12-8) Find 13% of 110. **6.** (12-8) Find 4% of 12. **7.** (12-8) Find 60% of 80.

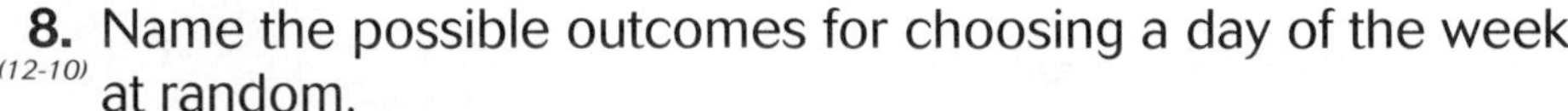

8. (12-10) Name the possible outcomes for choosing a day of the week at random.

9. (12-9) Margie made 22 swags,16 wreaths, and 12 vase arrangements. She sold each swag for \$10.25, each wreath for \$25.50, and each vase arrangement for \$8.15. Make a table to find the amount of money Margie made.

10. (12-11) Out of 80 people surveyed, 22 chose grapes as their favorite fruit. On the basis of this survey, what is the probability that grapes would be someone's favorite fruit?

11. (12-12) Jamie is making decorations with pictures of an instrument (drum, piano, or guitar) and a musical note (eighth note or quarter note). Draw a tree diagram to show all the possible outcomes of picking an instrument and a musical note. What is the probability of picking a guitar and a quarter note?

Use the circle graph for Exercises 12 and 13.

12. (12-13) What percent of students prefer baseball?

13. (12-13) Which sport was the least popular?

Favorite Sport

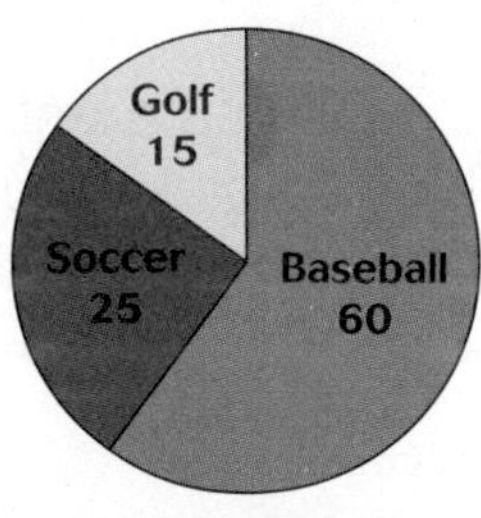

Chapter 12 Test

Write each ratio in two different ways.

1. $\frac{1}{2}$

2. 2:3

Write three other equivalent ratios for each given ratio.

3. $\frac{3}{4}$

4. $\frac{5}{7}$

5. If the scale is $\frac{1 \text{ inch}}{15 \text{ feet}}$, what is the scale length for an actual length of 75 feet?

6. If 9 stickers cost $0.63, what is the unit cost?

7. If 15 tickets cost $45, how many tickets will you get for $9?

8. Find 15% of 85.

9. Find 60% of 40.

Write each ratio as a decimal and then as a percent.

10. 37:100

11. 9 to 10

12. 4:25

Write each percent as a decimal and as a simplified fraction.

13. 16%

14. 75%

Use the bag of 16 chips. Find the probability of picking each color if you replace the chip after each pick.

15. Red

16. Orange

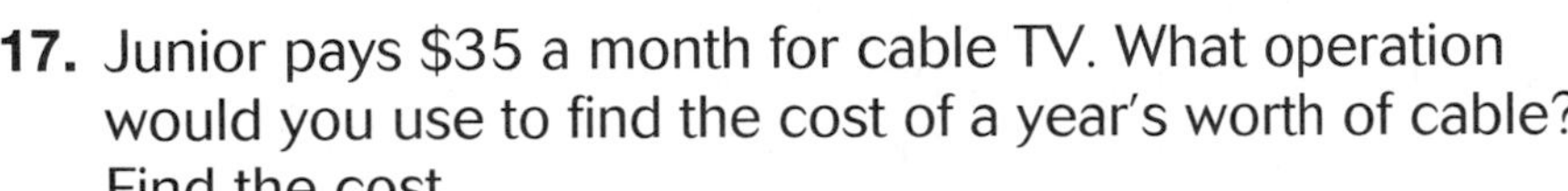

17. Junior pays $35 a month for cable TV. What operation would you use to find the cost of a year's worth of cable? Find the cost.

18. Payton buys 30 toothbrushes for $2.15 each, 12 tubes of toothpaste for $1.97 each, and 10 boxes of dental floss for $0.87 each. Make a table to find how much he pays.

19. How many kinds of sandwiches are possible if you can choose white or wheat bread and one type of meat—turkey, ham, or chicken? Use a tree diagram to help.

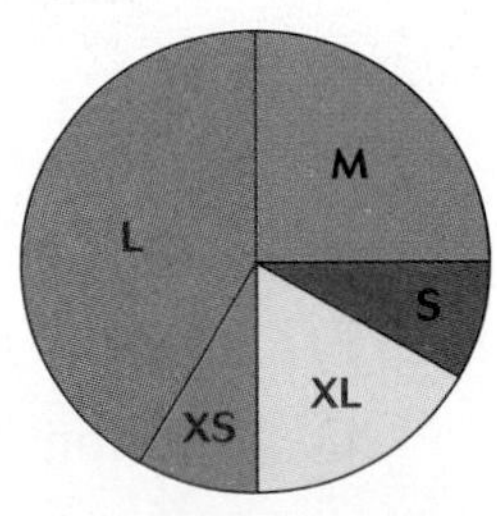

20. Use the circle graph to find which size accounts for more than 25% but less than 50% of popular shirt sizes.

Multiple-Choice Chapter 12 Test

Choose the correct letter for each answer.

1. A box contains 4 white tickets and 5 black tickets. What is the probability that Kit will draw a black ticket?

A $\frac{5}{9}$ **C** $\frac{1}{4}$

B $\frac{4}{9}$ **D** $\frac{1}{5}$

2. Jen stopped for yogurt. There were 4 flavors and 3 choices of toppings. What is the number of possible choices for yogurt with a topping?

F 6 **H** 12

G 8 **J** 15

3. Which completes the following statement?

19 marbles for $5.51

___?___ for 1 marble

A $0.29 **C** $1.51

B $0.43 **D** $2.10

4. Which part of the circle graph represents more than $\frac{1}{4}$ but less than $\frac{1}{2}$ of the total?

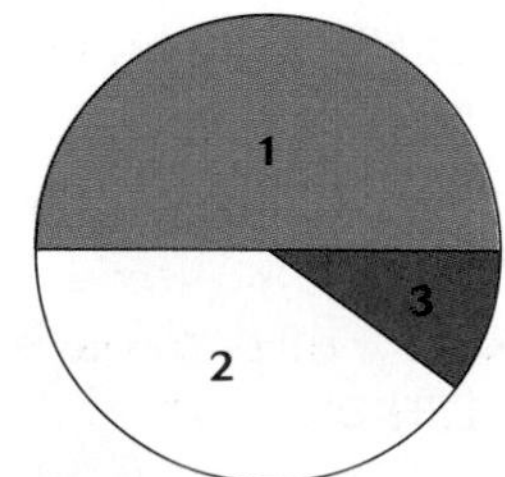

F Section 1 **H** Section 3

G Section 2 **J** Sections 1 & 2

Use the blueprint for Question 5.

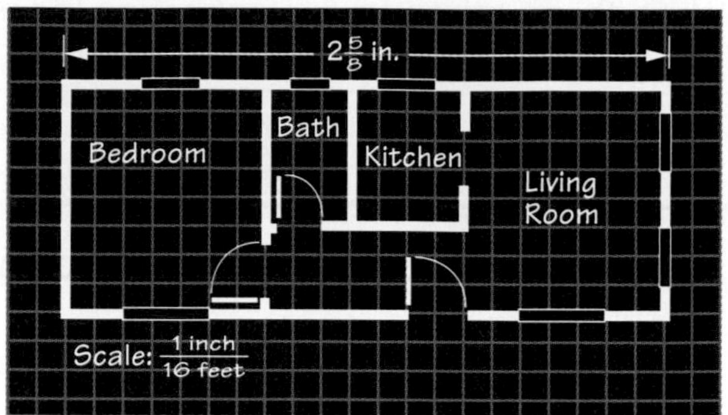

5. What is the actual length of the house?

A $2\frac{5}{8}$ inches

B 16 feet

C 32 feet

D 42 feet

6. Which equation can be used to find 57% of 987?

F $0.57 \times 987 = n$

G $987 \div 5.7 = n$

H $57 \times 987 = n$

J $987 \div 0.57 = n$

K NH

7. Which of the following ratios is not equivalent to 18:6?

A 6 to 2

B 3:1

C 36:18

D $\frac{72}{24}$

Use the bag of cards for Questions 8–9.

8. Which describes the possible outcomes if you pick one card at a time?

F circle, square, circle, triangle

G hexagon, triangle, triangle, triangle

H triangle, square, circle, square

J square, triangle, hexagon, circle

---

9. What is the probability that the card you choose is not a triangle?

A $\frac{4}{7}$ C $\frac{3}{7}$

B $\frac{2}{7}$ D $\frac{4}{3}$

---

10. Which is not a way to state the ratio 14 to 32?

F $\frac{32}{14}$

G 14:32

H fourteen to thirty-two

J $\frac{14}{32}$

---

11. Write the ratio 1:5 as a percent.

A 0.2%

B 10%

C 20%

D 200%

E NH

12. Express the shaded part of the grid as a decimal, a percent, and a fraction.

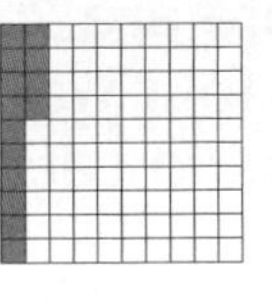

F 0.20; 20%; $\frac{1}{5}$

G 0.14; 14%; $\frac{7}{50}$

H 0.10; 10%; $\frac{1}{10}$

J 0.28; 28%; $\frac{28}{100}$

Use the following description for Questions 13 and 14.

Gabe made 11 candles to sell for $22.50 each at the craft mall. He purchased 20 pounds of wax for $0.85 per pound. Gabe sold 8 candles at the craft mall.

13. Which expression describes the amount of money Gabe collected?

A $(11 \times 22.50) + (0.85 \times 20)$

B 20 × $22.50

C $22.50 × 11

D 8 × $22.50

---

14. If Gabe also purchased 24 inches of wick for $0.10 per inch and 11 trays for $3.25 each, how much money did Gabe spend on supplies?

F $43.20 H $55.15

G $46.20 J $115.62

---

15. Bob wants to take an art class (pottery, painting, sketching, or sculpting) and join an athletic team (soccer, lacrosse, basketball, or softball). Which shows the number of possible outcomes for an art and a sport?

A 8 C 16

B 12 D 24

Reteaching

Set A (pages 502–503)

There are 7 dogs and 8 cats. What are four ways to write the ratio of dogs to cats?

seven to eight   7 to 8

7:8 $\frac{7}{8}$

Remember ratios are used to compare two quantities. There are four different ways to write ratios.

Write each ratio in two different ways.

1. six to ten
2. 18:20
3. $\frac{6}{11}$
4. 9 to 12

Set B (pages 504–505)

Use a ratio table to write ratios that are equivalent to $\frac{6}{11}$.

	×2	×3	×4	×5	×6
6	12	18	24	30	36
11	22	33	44	55	66

The equivalent ratios are:

$\frac{12}{22}$, $\frac{18}{33}$, $\frac{24}{44}$, $\frac{30}{55}$, and $\frac{36}{66}$.

Remember you can multiply or divide each number in a ratio by the same nonzero number. The resulting ratio is equivalent to the original ratio.

Copy and complete each ratio table.

1.

	×2	×3	×4	×5	×6
6					
10					

2.

	×2	×3	×4	×5	×6
2					
15					

Set C (pages 506–507)

Delilah made a scale drawing of a mural with an actual length of 28 feet. If the scale is $\frac{\text{1 inch}}{\text{7 feet}}$, how long is the drawing?

Find an equivalent ratio to $\frac{\text{1 inch}}{\text{7 feet}}$ in which the actual length is 28 feet.

$\frac{\text{1 inch} \times 4}{\text{7 feet} \times 4} = \frac{\text{4 inches}}{\text{28 feet}}$ ← scale length / ← actual length

The drawing is 4 inches long.

Remember the scale ratios can be expressed as $\frac{\text{scale length}}{\text{actual length}}$.

1. If the scale is $\frac{\text{1 inch}}{\text{5 feet}}$, what is the actual size for a scale size of 7 inches?
2. If the scale is $\frac{\text{1 inch}}{\text{40 feet}}$, what is the scale size for an actual size of 110 feet?

Set D (pages 508–509)

Complete.

7 brushes for \$29.33
_____ for 1 brush

Since 7 brushes sell for \$29.33, divide \$29.33 by 7 to find the cost for 1 brush.

$\$29.33 \div 7 = \$4.19$

The unit price is \$4.19 for 1 brush.

Remember a rate is a type of ratio.

Complete.

1. 240 miles in 4 hours
   _____ miles in 8 hours
2. 54 muffins in 18 bags
   _____ muffins in 3 bags

Set E (pages 512–513)

Write the ratio 44:50 as a percent.

Write an equivalent ratio to show the relationship of a number to 100.

$\frac{44}{50} = \frac{44 \times 2}{50 \times 2} = \frac{88}{100} = 88\%$

So, the ratio 44:50 can be written as 88%.

Remember percent means "per hundred."

Write each ratio as a percent.

1. 16 out of 50
2. $\frac{72}{100}$
3. 12:100
4. 92:100

Set F (pages 516–517)

Express 22 out of 100 as a fraction in simplest form, as a percent, and as a decimal.

As a fraction: $\frac{22}{100} = \frac{11}{50}$

As a percent: 22%

As a decimal: 0.22

Remember when writing a percent as a decimal or fraction, divide by 100.

Write each percent as a decimal and as a fraction in simplest from.

1. 81%
2. 50%
3. 27%
4. 94%

Set G (pages 518–519)

Find 70% of 22.

You know that 70% means $\frac{70}{100}$ or 0.7.

To find 70% of 22, multiply 22 by 0.7.

$$\begin{array}{r} 22 \\ \times 0.7 \\ \hline 15.4 \end{array}$$

So, 70% of 22 is 15.4.

Remember to find the percent of a number, multiply the number by the decimal equivalent of the percent.

Find each amount.

1. 12% of 113
2. 9% of 90
3. 60% of 106
4. 45% of 360

Reteaching (continued)

Set H *(pages 522–523)*

A bag holds 10 cards, labeled 1 through 10. You pick a card at random. Find the probability of picking a prime number.

There are 4 prime numbers from 1 through 10:
2, 3, 5, 7.

There are 10 possible outcomes:
1, 2, 3, 4, 5, 6, 7, 8, 9, 10.

Probability of a prime number

$$= \frac{\text{number of ways an event can happen}}{\text{number of possible outcomes}}$$

$$= \frac{4}{10} = \frac{2}{5}$$

Remember probability is the ratio of the number of ways an event can happen to the number of possible outcomes.

Using the bag of 10 cards described to the left, find each probability.

1. The card is a 2.
2. The card is an even number.
3. The card is divisible by 3.
4. The card is not an 8.

Set I *(pages 524–525)*

Use the chart to find the probability that a person has blue eyes.

Color of eyes	brown	blue	green	gray
Number of people	68	29	2	1

Since 68 + 29 + 2 + 1 = 100, there were 100 people in the sample. Of these, 29 had blue eyes.

So, the probability is $\frac{29}{100}$ or 29%.

Remember a sample is a set of data that can be used to predict probability.

Use the chart at the left to find the probability that a person has the following.

1. brown eyes
2. gray eyes
3. blue eyes or green eyes
4. not blue eyes

Set J *(pages 526–527)*

A penny and a dime are tossed. Make a tree diagram to determine the number of possible outcomes.

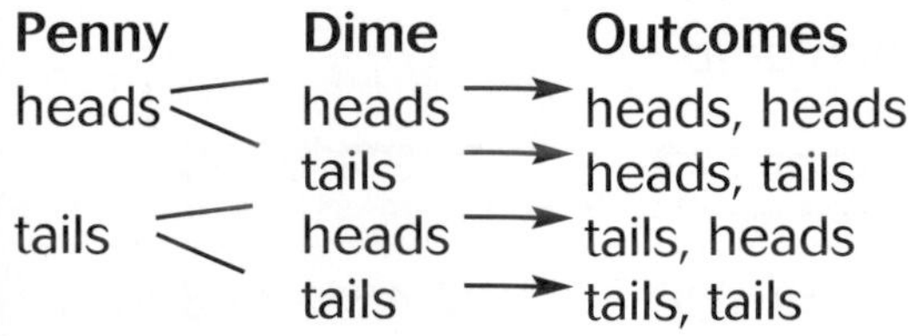

There are four possible outcomes.

Remember a tree diagram is a method you can use to determine possible outcomes.

Refer to the tree diagram at the left.

1. Find the probability that the coins both land on tails or both land on heads.
2. Find the probability that the penny lands on heads and the dime lands on tails.

More Practice

Set A (pages 502–503)

Write each ratio in two different ways.

1. 4 to 5 **2.** $\frac{3}{7}$ **3.** 7:9 **4.** 6:5 **5.** 9 to 13

Use the bead chain at the right to answer each question.

6. What is the ratio of red beads to blue-green beads?

7. What is the ratio of yellow beads to red beads?

Set B (pages 504–505)

Copy and complete each ratio table.

1.

	×2	×3	×4	×5	×6
4					
9					

2.

	×2	×3	×4	×5	×6
8					
15					

Write three ratios equivalent to each ratio given.

3. 8 to 9 **4.** 30:40 **5.** 4:9 **6.** $\frac{6}{12}$ **7.** $\frac{2}{3}$ **8.** $\frac{7}{14}$

9. In the time it takes Minna to make two origami pinwheels, Jen can make seven. If Minna makes 50 pinwheels, how many can Jen make?

Set C (pages 506–507)

If the scale is $\frac{\text{1 inch}}{\text{4 feet}}$, what is the actual length for each scale length?

1. 4 inches **2.** 17 inches **3.** 32 inches **4.** 6 inches

If the scale is $\frac{\text{1 inch}}{\text{9 feet}}$, what is the scale length for each actual length?

5. 81 feet **6.** 36 feet **7.** $22\frac{1}{2}$ feet **8.** 12 feet

9. Maggie made a 5-inch model car using a scale of $\frac{\text{1 inch}}{\text{3 feet}}$. What is the actual length of the car?

10. Laurence made a scale drawing of a tower using a scale of $\frac{\text{1 inch}}{\text{20 feet}}$. The actual building is 150 feet tall. How tall is the building in the drawing?

More Practice (continued)

Set D *(pages 508–509)*

Use equivalent ratios or division to complete.

1. 55 labels in 5 hours
   ______ labels in 1 hour
2. 25 push-ups in 25 seconds
   ______ push-ups in 5 seconds
3. 72 jars in 6 boxes
   ______ jars in 1 box
4. 45 yards of ribbon on 3 rolls
   ______ yards in 1 roll
5. If 7 pens sell for $3.64, what is the unit price?

Set E *(pages 512–513)*

Write each ratio as a percent.

1. 7 out of 10
2. $\frac{18}{100}$
3. 1 out of 5
4. $\frac{8}{50}$

Write each percent as a ratio. Write the ratio in simplest form.

5. 62%
6. 45%
7. 10%
8. 5%
9. Forty-three squares in a grid with 100 squares are not shaded. What percent of the grid is shaded?

Set F *(pages 516–517)*

Write each expression in two other ways.

1. 21%
2. $\frac{8}{10}$
3. 25%
4. $\frac{51}{100}$
5. 0.40

Write each percent as a decimal and as a fraction in simplest form.

6. 48%
7. 26%
8. 15%
9. 61%
10. 49%
11. A magazine ad says that 31 out of every 50 fifth graders like to drink apple juice. What percent is this?

Set G *(pages 518–519)*

Find each amount.

1. 10% of 210
2. 25% of 16
3. 40% of 50
4. 12% of 18
5. A new calculator is on sale for $78.00. If sales tax is 6%, how much sales tax would you pay when you buy the calculator?

Set H (pages 522–523)

Name the possible outcomes for each event.

1. tossing a coin
2. rolling a number cube numbered 1–6
3. picking one letter from the word BANANA

Use the spinner. Find the probability that the pointer will stop on each section.

4. K
5. J
6. M
7. not L
8. not M
9. not L or M

Set I (pages 524–525)

The chart at the right shows the results of a survey in which people were asked to name their favorite pet. Find the probability that a person would name each pet.

Type of Pet	
Pet	**Number**
Dog	25
Cat	30
Rabbit	5
Turtle	2
Fish	18

1. Turtle
2. Fish
3. Not a cat
4. Dog
5. Rabbit or turtle
6. Dog or cat
7. Out of 130 people surveyed, 20 people chose tomato soup as their favorite type of soup. What is the probability that someone would prefer tomato soup?

Set J (pages 526–527)

Beth is making paper decorations for each classroom door. Her first pick is from an apple or a pear. Her second pick is from a carrot, a radish, a tomato, or a cucumber.

1. Make a tree diagram showing the possible combinations of paper decorations for each door.
2. What is the probability of picking an apple and a cucumber?
3. What is the probability of not picking a pear and a carrot?
4. What is the probability of picking an apple and not a tomato?

TEST PREP

Problem Solving: Preparing for Tests

Choose the correct letter for each answer.

---

1. Jenny spent \$1.50 on lemons and sugar to make lemonade. Then she used a gallon pitcher to fill $\frac{1}{4}$-pint glasses. Which equation could you use to find the number, *n*, of $\frac{1}{4}$-pint glasses she could fill? (1 gal = 8 pt)

A $4 \times \frac{1}{4} = n$

B $4 \div \frac{1}{4} = n$

C $8 \times \frac{1}{4} = n$

D $8 \div \frac{1}{4} = n$

Tip

First change 1 gallon into pints. Then be sure to think about what would be a reasonable answer.

---

2. Fred likes tacos more than he likes chicken but not as much as he likes lasagna. He likes shrimp more than he likes tacos. Which is a reasonable conclusion?

F He prefers shrimp over lasagna.

G He prefers tacos over lasagna.

H He prefers shrimp over chicken.

J He prefers chicken over shrimp.

Tip

Try the *Use a Simulation* strategy for this problem. Start by writing the name of a different food on each of 4 slips of paper.

---

3. Yoko arranged the plants in her garden in a series of 3 squares around a single plant in the middle. Each square had a plant at each corner. The innermost square had only the corner plants. Besides the corner plants, the middle square had 1 plant on each side, and the outer square had 2 plants on each side. How many plants did she use?

Tip

Use one of these strategies to solve this problem.

- *Draw a Diagram*
- *Find a Pattern*
- *Make a Table*

A 25

B 30

C 37

D 40

4. **The PTA sold 9,894 tickets for a drawing. If the PTA gives one prize for every 2,000 tickets sold, what is a reasonable number of prizes?**

F 5 prizes
G 10 prizes
H 20 prizes
J 200 prizes

5. **On the basis of the information in the graph, how many fewer students are in the math and science clubs than are in the other 3 clubs?**

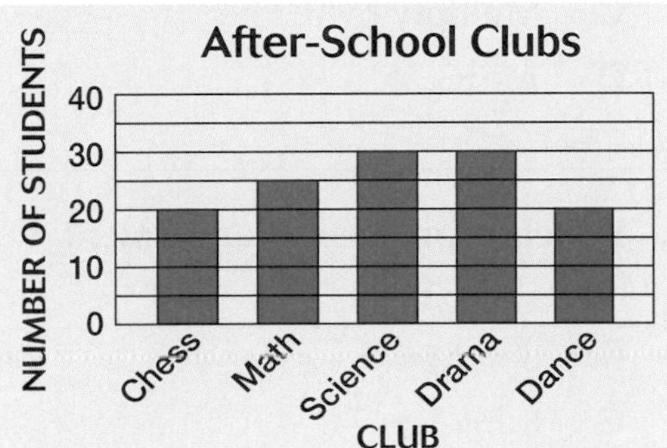

A 15
B 20
C 55
D 70

6. **Amanda practiced the piano for $1\frac{1}{4}$ hours on Monday, $2\frac{1}{4}$ hours on Tuesday, and $\frac{3}{4}$ hour on Wednesday. If she plans to practice $7\frac{1}{2}$ hours this week, how many more hours does she need to practice?**

F $3\frac{1}{4}$ hours
G $3\frac{1}{2}$ hours
H $4\frac{1}{4}$ hours
J $4\frac{1}{2}$ hours

7. **In March, Ann sold $2,400 worth of merchandise. Her sales then increased 50% in April. How much did Ann sell in April?**

A $1,200
B $3,000
C $3,600
D $4,800

8. **On the basis of the information in the graph, how many more artificial plants than live plants were sold in January and February?**

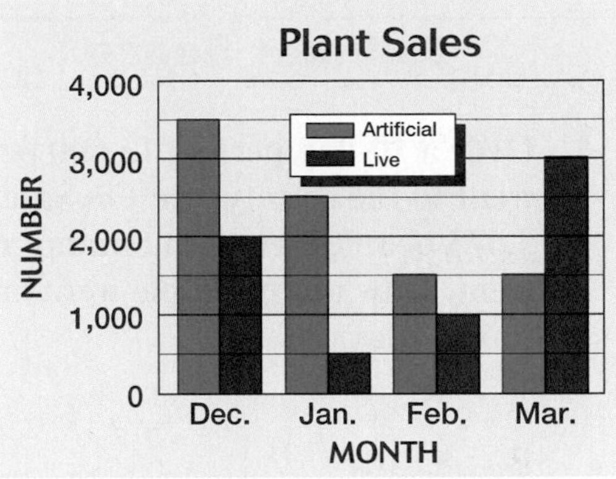

F 1,500
G 2,500
H 3,500
J 4,000

9. **There are 1,597 students in a school, with about the same number of girls as boys. About 50% of the girls and 25% of the boys walk or bike to school. The rest of the students take the bus. How many students take the bus?**

A About 400
B About 600
C About 1,000
D About 1,600

10. **Jill can write up 14 orders in 2 hours. Sam can do 18 orders in 3 hours. Jill usually works 6 more hours than Sam does each week. How many more orders will Jill have completed than Sam after 8 hours?**

F 1
G 8
H 10
J 12

TEST PREP

Multiple-Choice Cumulative Review

Choose the correct letter for each answer.

Number Sense

1. **Over a 10-day period, 15,000 people went to the county fair. On Saturday, 5,673 people went. On Sunday, 6,190 went. How many people went on those 2 days?**

A 3,137
B 8,810
C 9,327
D 11,863

2. **Forty-seven skaters each rented skates for $4.50 per pair. There were 105 skaters at Skate World. How much did Skate World make in skate rentals?**

F $211.50
G $222.50
H $472.50
J $493.50

3. **Sid had $50. He bought 2 video games that cost $14 each. He also bought a poster for $5.69. How much money did he have left after his purchases?**

A $33.69
B $28.69
C $19.69
D $16.31

4. **A restaurant has 242 plates and 484 glasses. There is an equal number of plates on each of 11 tables. How many plates are there per table?**

F 44
G 40
H 22
J 11

Algebra and Functions

5. **What would you do to get n alone in $n - 2.75$?**

A Add 2.75.
B Subtract 2.25.
C Multiply by 0.25.
D Add 3.25.

6. **Which expression is equivalent to $(8 + 5) + 7$?**

F $8 + 5 \times 7$
G $8 + (5 + 7)$
H $13 + 6$
J $(8 \times 7) + (5 \times 7)$

7. **Solve $n - 2 = 107$.**

A 105
B 109
C 123
D 133

8. **Evaluate $4x$ when $x = 24$.**

F 96
G 28
H 20
J 6

Measurement and Geometry

9. This lampshade is shaped most like which space figure?

A Triangular prism

B Cube

C Cylinder

D Cone

10. Which of the polygons listed has 6 sides and 6 angles?

F Quadrilateral

G Pentagon

H Hexagon

J Octagon

11. Which of the following shows an example of a reflection?

A 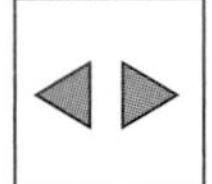

C 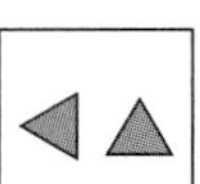

B 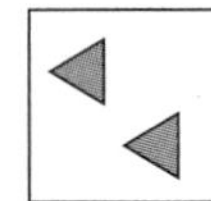

D 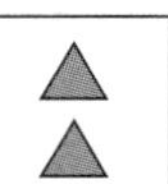

12. Which does NOT show a figure with a line of symmetry?

F

G

H

J

13. Jeff's fish tank is 2.5 feet long by 1.5 feet wide by 2 feet deep. The fish tank is on a stand that is 3 feet high. What is the volume of the tank?

A 6.0 ft^3

C 7.5 ft^3

B 6.75 ft^3

D 11.25 ft^3

14. Gary went on a 4-day fishing trip with his family. He was proud of all the fish he caught, especially the one fish that was 5 feet long. How many inches long was this fish?

F 60 inches

G 30 inches

H 20 inches

J 12.5 inches

15. The radius of a flying disc is 12 inches. What is the circumference of the flying disc? (Use 3.14 for π.)

A 31.40 inches

B 37.68 inches

C 62.80 inches

D 75.36 inches

16. An empty van weighs 2 T 450 lb. After 9 football players get into the van, it weighs 3 T 400 lb. How much do the football players weigh?

F 1 T

G 1 T 50 lb

H 1,950 lb

J 900 lb

Credits

Photographs

All photographs owned by Scott Foresman unless listed here.

Front Cover and Back Inset: Carr Clifton; Front and Back Cover Background: PhotoDisc

60: Allen Prier/Panoramic Images

176: Kelly O'Neil Photography

184: Robert Holmes/Corbis

220(T): Lee Foster/Bruce Coleman Inc.

220(B): Michael Ma Po Shum/Stone

407: Cesar Lucas/Image Bank

411: Dallas & John Heaton/Corbis-Westlight

472: J.B. Grant/Leo de Wys Photo Agency

520: SuperStock

Illustrations

10, 22: Reggie Holladay

38: George Hamblin

43, 52: Dennis Dzielak

57: Chris Pappas

145, 256, 284: George Hamblin

308: Burgandy Beam

311: Chris Pappas

316, 318: George Hamblin

321: Burgandy Beam

330: George Hamblin

336: Carla Kiwior

364, 366, 372, 374, 403, 437, 484: George Hamblin

504, 507: Chris Pappas

Additional Resources

Tables

Measures—*Customary*

Length

1 foot (ft) = 12 inches (in.)
1 yard (yd) = 3 feet, or 36 inches
1 mile = 5,280 feet, or 1,760 yards

Weight

1 pound (lb) = 16 ounces (oz)
1 ton (T) = 2,000 pounds

Capacity

1 cup (c) = 8 fluid ounces (fl oz)
1 pint (pt) = 2 cups
1 quart (qt) = 2 pints
1 gallon (gal) = 4 quarts

Time

1 minute (min) = 60 seconds (s)
1 hour (h) = 60 minutes
1 day (d) = 24 hours
1 week (wk) = 7 days
1 month (mo) = 28 to 31 days, or about 4 weeks
1 year (yr) = 12 months (mo), or 52 weeks, or 365 days

Measures—*Metric*

Length

1 meter (m) = 1,000 millimeters (mm)
1 meter = 100 centimeters (cm)
1 meter = 10 decimeters (dm)
1 centimeter (cm) = 10 millimeters
1 decimeter = 10 centimeters
1 kilometer (km) = 1,000 meters

Mass/Weight

1 gram (g) = 1,000 milligrams (mg)
1 kilogram (kg) = 1,000 grams

Capacity

1 liter (L) = 1,000 milliliters (mL)

Symbols

=	is equal to
>	is greater than
<	is less than
≈	is approximately equal to
≅	is congruent to
2:5	ratio of 2 to 5
%	percent
π	pi (approximately 3.14)
°	degree
°C	degree Celsius
°F	degree Fahrenheit
10^2	ten to the second power
∥	is parallel to
⊥	is perpendicular to
$\overleftrightarrow{AB}$	line *AB*
$\overline{AB}$	line segment *AB*
$\overrightarrow{AB}$	ray *AB*
$\angle ABC$	angle *ABC*
$\triangle ABC$	triangle *ABC*
(3, 4)	ordered pair 3, 4

Formulas

P = *sum of all sides*	Perimeter (general formula)
$P = (2 \times l) + (2 \times w)$	Perimeter of a rectangle
$P = 4 \times s$	Perimeter of a square
$A = l \times w$	Area of a rectangle
$A = s \times s$	Area of a square
$A = b \times h$	Area of a parallelogram
$A = \frac{1}{2} \times b \times h$	Area of a triangle
$C = \pi \times d$	Circumference of a circle
$V = l \times w \times h$	Volume of a rectangular prism

Test-Taking Tips

Follow Instructions

- Listen carefully as your teacher explains the test.

Budget Your Time

- Do the questions in order if you can.
- If a question seems very hard, skip it and go back to it later.

Read Carefully

- Watch for extra information in a problem.
- Watch for words like *not.*
- Be sure to answer the question asked.

Make Smart Choices

- **Estimate** when you can so that you have a better idea what the answer might be.
- **Eliminate** answer choices that are not reasonable or are clearly wrong.
- **Check** an answer that you *think* is correct by working backward.

Mark Answers Correctly

- If you are using a "bubble" answer sheet or a gridded response form, be careful to match each question number with the correct number of the answer row.
- If you skip a question, be sure to leave that question's answer space blank.

Glossary

acute angle An angle that measures less than 90°. (p. 406)
Example:

acute triangle A triangle with three acute angles. (p. 414)

angle Two rays with a common endpoint called the vertex. (p. 405)
Example:

arc A part of a circle connecting two points on a circle. (p. 429)

area The number of square units needed to cover a region. (p. 475)

associative property of addition The way that addends are grouped does not change the sum. (p. 40) *Example:* $(2 + 3) + 4 = 2 + (3 + 4)$

associative property of multiplication The way that factors are grouped does not change the product. (p. 126)

average (mean) The sum of the addends divided by the number of addends. (p. 104)

axis Either the horizontal line (called *x*) or the vertical line (called *y*) that form the base lines of a graph. (p. 88)
Example:

bar graph A graph with bars of different lengths. (p. 85)

base (in arithmetic) The number that is multiplied by itself when raised to a power. (p. 148) *Example:* In 5^3, 5 is the base.

base (in geometry) The length of a side in a plane figure (rectangle, parallelogram, or triangle). (p. 475) Also see *base* for a solid figure. (p. 434)

capacity The amount a container can hold. (p. 459)

circle A closed plane figure. All the points of a circle are the same distance from a point called the center. (p. 472)
Example:

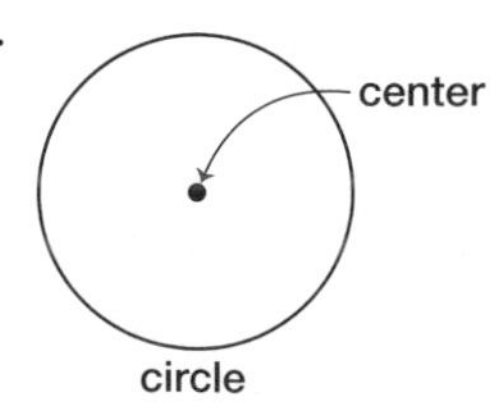

circle graph A graph that shows how a total amount has been divided into parts. (p. 108)

circumference The distance around a circle. (p. 473)

clustering An estimation method used when numbers are close to the same number. (p. 53)

common factor A number that is a factor of two or more given numbers. (p. 264) *Example:* 1, 2, and 4 are common factors of 4 and 8.

common multiple A number that is a multiple of two or more given numbers. (p. 266) *Example:* 6, is a common multiple of 2 and 3.

commutative (order) property of addition The order of the addends does not change the sum. (p. 40) *Example:* $9 + 7 = 7 + 9$

commutative (order) property of multiplication The order of the factors does not change the product. (p. 126)

compatible numbers Numbers that are easy to compute mentally. (p. 42)

compensation A mental math method in which numbers are adjusted up or down to make addition and subtraction easier. (p. 42)

composite number A whole number greater than one that has more than two factors. (p. 260)

cone A space figure with one circular base and one vertex. (p. 435)
Example:

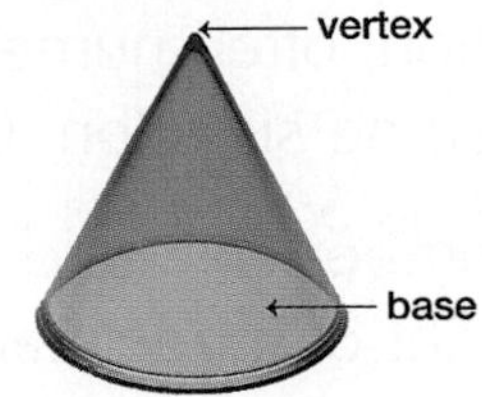

congruent figures Figures that have the same size and shape. (p. 426)

coordinate plane A coordinate grid that is extended to include both positive and negative numbers. (p. 374)

coordinates Numbers used to locate a point on a line, on a surface, or in space. (p. 91)

cube A rectangular prism with six squares as sides. (p. 435)

cubed A special name for a number to the third power. (p. 148)

cubic unit Unit used to measure volume. (p. 478) *Example:* a cubic meter, m^3

customary system A system of weights and measures that measures length in inches, feet, yards, and miles; capacity in cups, pints, quarts, and gallons; weight in ounces, pounds, and tons; and temperature in degrees Fahrenheit. (p. 456, 459)

cylinder A space figure with two parallel circular bases. (p. 435)
Example:

Glossary

D

data Information, often numerical, that describes some situation. (p. 84)

decimal A number with one or more digits to the right of a decimal point. (p. 8)

degree (°) A unit for measuring angles. (p. 405)

denominator The number below the fraction bar in a fraction. (p. 272)
Example: $\frac{2}{5}$ The denominator is 5.

diameter A line segment that passes through the center of the circle and has both endpoints on the circle. (p. 473)
Example:

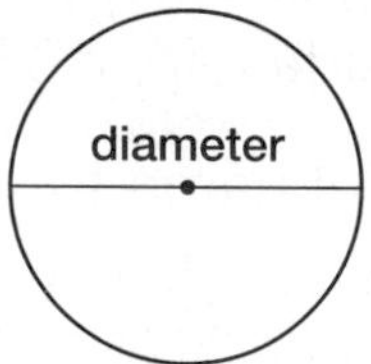

digit Any of the symbols used to write numbers: 0, 1, 2, 3, 4, 5, 6, 7, 8, and 9. (p. 4)

distributive property Multiplying a sum by a number is the same as multiplying each addend by the number and adding the products. (p. 126) *Example:*
$2 \times (3 + 4) = (2 \times 3) + (2 \times 4)$

divisible A number is divisible by another number if the remainder is 0 after dividing. (p. 258)

double bar graph A graph that uses pairs of bars to compare information. (p. 88)

E

endpoint A point at the end of a line segment or ray. (p. 402)
Example:

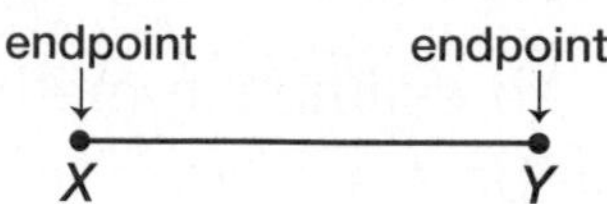

equally likely outcomes Outcomes that have the same chance of occurring. (p. 522)

equation A number sentence with an equal sign. (p. 46)

equilateral triangle A triangle with all sides congruent. (p. 414)
Example:

equivalent fractions Fractions that name the same number. (p. 274)

equivalent ratios Ratios that represent the same rate or make the same comparison. (p. 504)

estimate An approximate rather than an exact answer. (p. 48)

evaluate an expression Substitute values for each variable and simplify. (p. 55)

event One or more outcomes of an experiment. (p. 522)

expanded form A number written as the sum of the values of its digits. (p. 4) *Example:* 500 + 50 + 5 is the expanded form for 555.

expanded form (numbers with exponents) A number involving exponents written as a product. (p. 148)

experiment A plan to find possible outcomes or test a prediction. (p. 522)

exponent A number that tells how many times the base is used as a factor. (p. 148) *Example:* $10^3 = 10 \times 10 \times 10$ The exponent is 3 and the base is 10.

exponential form A number written in the form with a base and an exponent. (p. 148)

expression A mathematical phrase made up of a variable or combination of variables and/or numbers and operations. (p. 55) *Example:* $5n$, $4x - 7$, $(5 \times 2) - \frac{6}{3}$

face In a solid figure, a flat surface that is shaped like a polygon. (p. 434)

factor One of the numbers that is multiplied to give a product. (p. 148) *Example:* $3 \times 5 = 15$ The factors are 3 and 5.

factor tree A diagram used to show the prime factors of a number. (p. 261) *Example:*

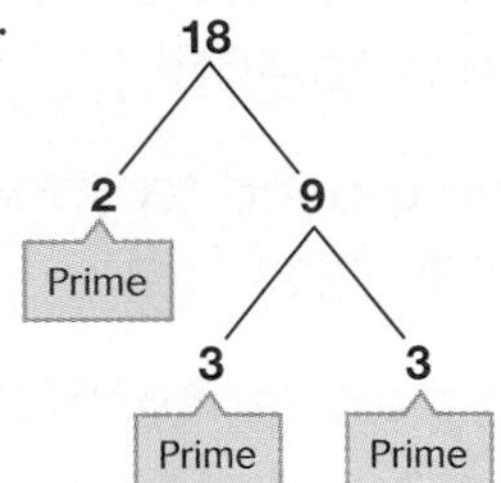

flip (reflection) A change of position that produces a mirror image of a figure. (p. 426) *Example:*

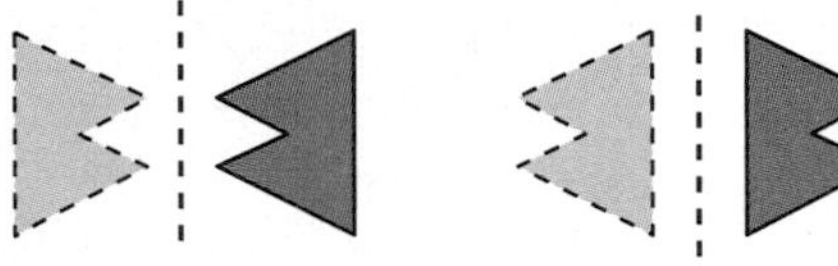

formula An equation that states a rule. (p. 472)

fraction A number that names part of a whole. (p. 272) *Examples:* $\frac{1}{2}$, $\frac{2}{3}$, $\frac{6}{6}$

frequency table A table used to record and summarize the number of times something occurs. (p. 84)

front digit The digit in the place with the greatest value, used in front-end estimation. (p. 52)

front-end estimation A method of estimating sums, differences, products, and quotients using front digits. (p. 52)

Glossary

G

gram (g) The basic unit of mass in the metric system. (p.468)

graph A drawing used to show numerical information. (p. 22)

greatest common factor (GCF) The greatest number that is a factor of each of two or more numbers. (p. 264)
Example: The greatest common factor of 36 and 48 is 12.

grouping property See associative property of addition; associative property of multiplication. (pp. 40, 126)

height (of a geometric figure) The length of a perpendicular segment drawn from a vertex to the base in a figure (rectangle, parallelogram, or triangle). (p. 475)
Example:

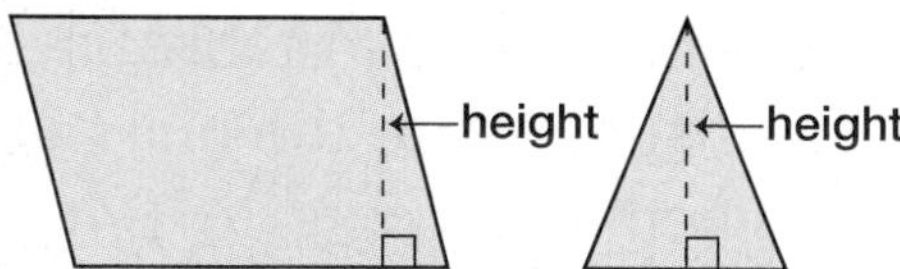

hexagon A polygon with six sides. (p. 408)

histogram A bar graph where there is no space between the bars and the horizontal axis is separated into equal intervals. (p. 107)

identity property of addition The sum of any number and zero is that number. (p. 40)

identity property of multiplication The product of any number and one is that number. (p. 126)

improper fraction A fraction in which the numerator is greater than or equal to the denominator. (p. 282)

integers The numbers in the set $\{\ldots\ {}^{-}3, {}^{-}2, {}^{-}1, 0, {}^{+}1, {}^{+}2, {}^{+}3, \ldots\}$. (p. 360)

intersecting lines Lines that have exactly one point in common. (p. 403)

inverse operations Two operations that have the opposite effect. Addition and subtraction are inverse operations. Multiplication and division are inverse operations (except that you cannot divide by 0). (pp. 44, 194)

isosceles triangle A triangle with two congruent sides. (p. 414)
Example:

least common denominator (LCD) The least common multiple of the denominators of two or more fractions. (p. 284)

least common multiple (LCM) The least number, other than zero, that is a multiple of each of two or more numbers. (p. 266)

line An endless collection of points along a straight path. A line has no endpoints. (p. 402)

line graph A graph used to show changes over a period of time. (p. 94)

line of symmetry A line that divides a figure, when folded along the lines into two congruent parts. (p. 432)

line plot A graphing method that shows each item of data on a number line. (p. 84)

line segment Part of a line that has two endpoints. (p. 402)

linear equation An equation with two variables whose graph is a straight line. (p. 378)

liter The basic unit of capacity in the metric system. (p. 468)

lowest terms See *simplest form*. (p. 276)

M

mass The amount of matter an object contains that causes it to have weight. (p. 468)

mean The average of the numbers in a set of data. (p. 104)

median The middle number or average of the two middle numbers in a collection of data when the data are arranged in order. (p. 104)

mental math Performing a computation without the use of paper and pencil or a calculator. (p. 42)

meter (m) The basic unit of length in the metric system. (p. 464)

metric system A system of weights and measures that is based on the decimal system. The gram is the basic unit of mass; the meter is the basic unit of length; and the liter is the basic unit of capacity. (p. 464)

mixed number A number written as a whole number and a fraction. (p. 282)
Example: $2\frac{5}{6}$

mode The number or numbers that occur most often in a set of data. (p. 104)

multiple The product of a whole number and any other whole number. (p. 266)
Example: 0, 2, 4, 6, are multiples of 2.

multiplication An operation on two or more numbers, called factors, to find a product. (p. 126)

N

negative integer The numbers in the set {. . . $^-4$, $^-3$, $^-2$, $^-1$}. (p. 360)

Glossary

number line A line that shows numbers in order. (p. 11)

number sentence An equation written in horizontal form. (p. 46)

numerator The number above the fraction bar in a fraction. (p. 272)
Example: $\frac{3}{4}$ The numerator is 3.

obtuse angle An angle that measures greater than 90° but less than 180°. (p. 406)
Example:

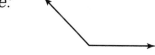

obtuse triangle A triangle with one obtuse angle. (p. 414)

octagon A polygon with eight sides. (p. 408)
Example:

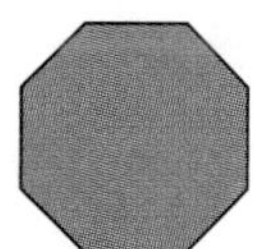

order of operations The order in which operations are done in calculations. Work inside parentheses is done first. Then multiplication and division are done from left to right, and finally addition and subtraction are done from left to right. (p. 128)

ordered pair A pair of numbers often used to locate a point in a plane. (p. 91)

outcome Possible results of an experiment. (p. 522)

outlier A data value that is very different from the rest of the data. (p. 105)

parallel lines Lines in the same plane that never intersect. (p. 403)
Example:

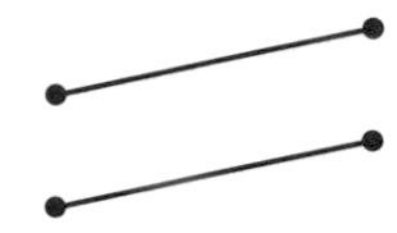

parallelogram A quadrilateral with each pair of opposite sides parallel and congruent. (p. 409)
Example:

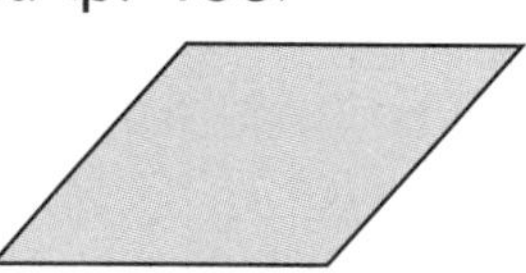

pentagon A polygon with five sides. (p. 408)
Example:

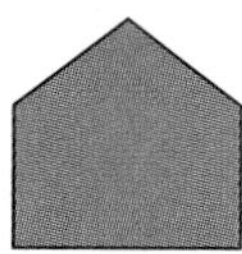

percent A ratio that show the relationship between a number and one hundred. (p. 512) *Example:* 75% means 75 parts per hundred.

perimeter The distance around a polygon. (p. 472)

perpendicular lines Two lines that intersect at right angles. (p. 403)
Example:

pi (π) A number representing the ratio of the circumference to the diameter of a circle. (p. 473)

pictograph A graph that represents numerical data using pictures. (p. 85)

place value chart A chart indicating the value of each digit in a number determined by the position of the digit in a number. (p. 4)

plane An endless, flat surface that is named by any three points not on the same line. (p. 402)

point An exact location in space. (p. 402)

polygon A closed plane figure made up of three or more line segments. (p. 408)

positive integer The numbers in the set $\{^+1, ^+2, ^+3, ^+4, \ldots\}$. (p. 360)

prime factorization Writing a number as the product of prime factors. (p. 261)
Example: $24 = 2 \times 2 \times 2 \times 3 = 2^3 \times 3$

prime number A whole number greater than one with only two factors—itself and one. (p. 260)

prism A space figure with two parallel and congruent bases that are polygons. (p. 434)

probability (of an event) A ratio of the number of favorable outcomes to the number of all possible outcomes of an experiment. (p. 522)

product The answer in multiplication. (p. 126)

proper fraction A fraction in which the numerator is less than the denominator. (p. 282)

protractor An instrument used to measure or draw angles. (p. 405)

pyramid A space figure whose base is a polygon and whose faces are triangles with a common vertex. (p. 434)
Example:

quadrilateral A polygon with four sides. (p. 408)

range The difference between the greatest and least numbers in a set of data. (p. 104)

rate A ratio that compares different units. (p. 508)

ratio A comparison of two quantities. (p. 502) *Example:* 3 to 5, 3:5, $\frac{3}{5}$

Glossary

ray Part of a line that has one endpoint and extends endlessly in the other direction. (p. 402)
Example:

reciprocal A given number is a reciprocal to another number when the product of the two equals 1. (p. 331)

rectangle A parallelogram with four right angles. (p. 409)

regular polygon A polygon in which all sides have the same length and all angles have the same measure. (p. 408)
Example:

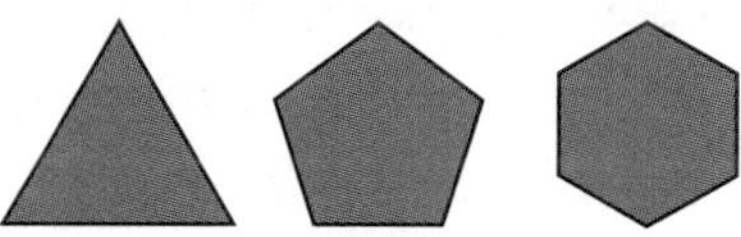

rhombus A parallelogram with all sides congruent. (p. 409)

right angle An angle that measures 90°. (p. 406)
Example:

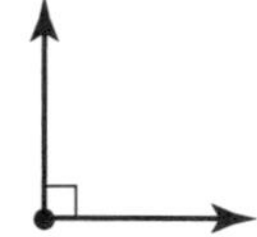

right triangle A triangle with one right angle. (p. 414)
Example:

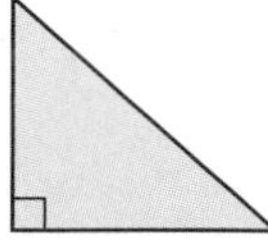

rounding Replacing a number by expressing it to the nearest ten, hundred, thousand, and so on. (p. 16)
Example: 23 rounded to the nearest ten is 20.

S

sample A set of data that can be used to predict the results of a particular situation. (p. 524)

scale The ratio of the measurements in a drawing, or model, to the measurements of the actual objects. (p. 85)

scalene triangle A triangle that has no congruent sides. (p. 414)
Example:

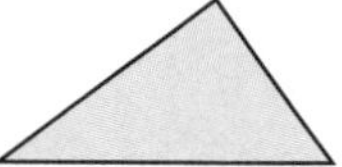

side The two rays that form an angle. (p. 405)

simplest form A fraction is in simplest form when the greatest common factor of the numerator and denominator is one. (p. 276)

slide (translation) A change of position that moves a figure up, down, or over. (p. 426)
Example:

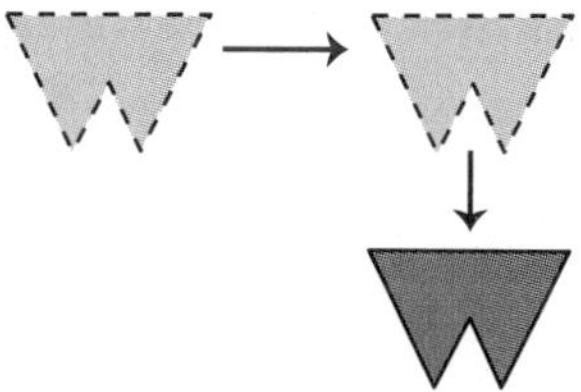

sphere A space figure with all points an equal distance from the center. (p. 435)

square A rectangle with all sides congruent. (p. 409)

square unit A unit used to measure area. (p. 475) *Example:* a square centimeter, cm^2

squared A special name for a number to the second power. (p. 148)

standard form A number written with commas separating groups of three digits. (p. 4) *Example:* 1,255,362

standard form (numbers with exponents) A number written without any exponents or operations. (p. 148)

stem-and-leaf plot A diagram used to organize numerical data. (p. 84)

straight angle An angle that measures 180°. (p. 406)

sum The answer in addition. (p. 40)

surface area The sum of the areas of all the faces of a space figure. (p. 482)

survey To collect data to analyze some characteristic of a group. (p. 84)

symmetry A figure is symmetric if it can be folded along a line so that the two resulting parts match exactly. (p. 432)
Example:

thousandths A place in a number where a digit is three places to the right of the decimal point. (p. 8)

transformation A change of position (turning, sliding, or flipping) of a plane figure. (p. 426)

trapezoid A quadrilateral with only one pair of parallel sides. (p. 409)
Example:

tree diagram A diagram used to show and organize all outcomes of an experiment. (p. 526)

trends Patterns that occur in data over a period of time, helps to make predictions about data. (p. 98)

triangle A polygon with three sides. (p. 408)
Example:

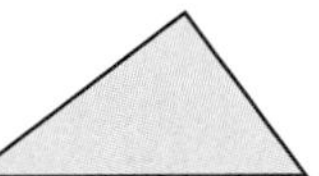

turn (rotation) A change of position that rotates a figure around a point. (p. 426)

unit price A rate, the price for one part or one unit. (p. 508)

Glossary

variable A letter, such as *n*, that stands for a number in an expression or equation. (p. 19)

vertex The common endpoint of the two sides of an angle. The point of intersection of two sides of a polygon. The point of intersection of three edges of a space figure. (p. 405

volume The number of cubic units contained in a space figure. (p. 478)

whole numbers The numbers in the set {0, 1, 2, 3, . . .}. (p. 4)

zero property of multiplication The product of any number and zero is zero. (p. 126)

Index

A

B

C

Index

Index

Index

Index

Index

N

Index

Index

Index

Index

Index